PRESIDENT LEX

J.M. DEMATTEIS
JOE KELLY
JEPH LOEB
GREG RUCKA
MARK SCHULTZ
KARL KESEL
• • • • • • • • • • •
Writers

ED MCGUINNESS
DUNCAN ROULEAU
PACO MEDINA
DOUG MAHNKE
DALE EAGLESHAM
CARLO BARBERI
TONY HARRIS
MATTHEW CLARK
DWAYNE TURNER
MIKE MILLER
TODD NAUCK
MIKE WIERINGO
PAUL PELLETIER
HUMBERTO RAMOS
ROB LIEFELD
ART ADAMS
IAN CHURCHILL
JOE MADUREIRA
• • • • • • • • • • •
Pencillers

CAM SMITH
MARLO ALQUIZA
RAY KRYSSING
RAY SNYDER
JUAN VLASCO
TOM NGUYEN
JAIME MENDOZA
DANNY MIKI
ARMANDO DURRUTHY
WALDEN WONG
KLAUS JANSON
WAYNE FAUCHER
NORM RAPMUND
ART ADAMS
TIM TOWNSEND
• • • • • • • • • • •
Inkers

COMICRAFT
KEN LOPEZ
BILL OAKLEY
• • • • • • • • • • •
Letterers

RICHARD & TANYA HORIE
WILDSTORM FX
TOM MCCRAW
ROB SCHWAGER
• • • • • • • • • • •
Colorists

SUPERMAN **created by** JERRY SIEGEL & JOE SHUSTER

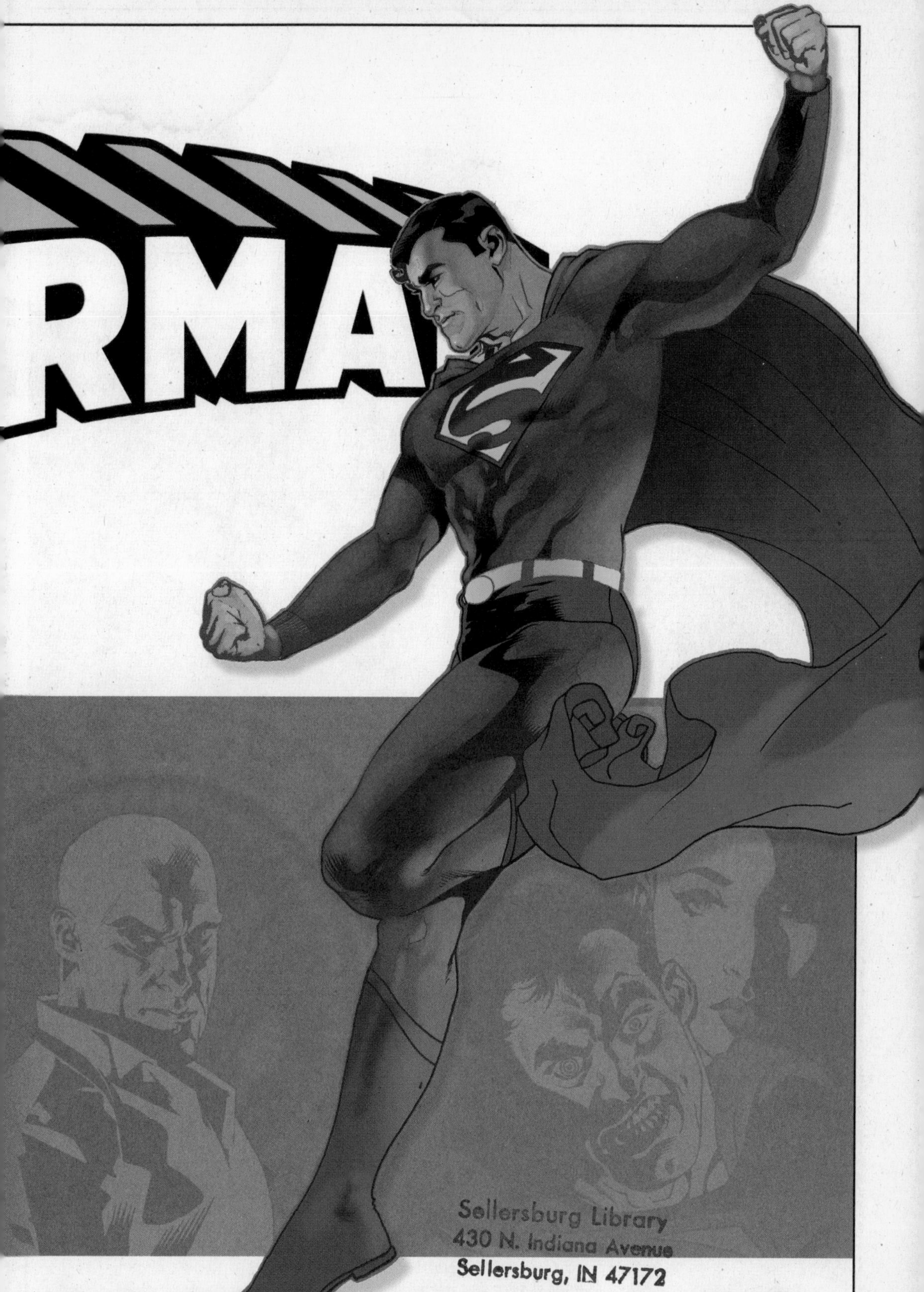

PRESIDENT LEX

SUPERMAN: PRESIDENT LEX

Published by DC Comics.
Cover and compilation copyright © 2003 DC Comics.
All Rights Reserved.

Originally published in single magazine form in PRESIDENT LUTHOR SECRET FILES 1,
ACTION COMICS 773, THE ADVENTURES OF SUPERMAN 581, 586, SUPERMAN 162-166,
SUPERMAN: THE MAN OF STEEL 108-110, and SUPERMAN: LEX 2000 1.
Copyright © 2000, 2001 DC Comics.
All Rights Reserved.
DC Comics, 1700 Broadway, New York, NY 10019
A division of Warner Bros. — An AOL Time Warner Company
Printed in Canada. First Printing.
ISBN: 1-56389-974-4
Cover illustration by Tony Harris.

CAST OF CHARACTERS

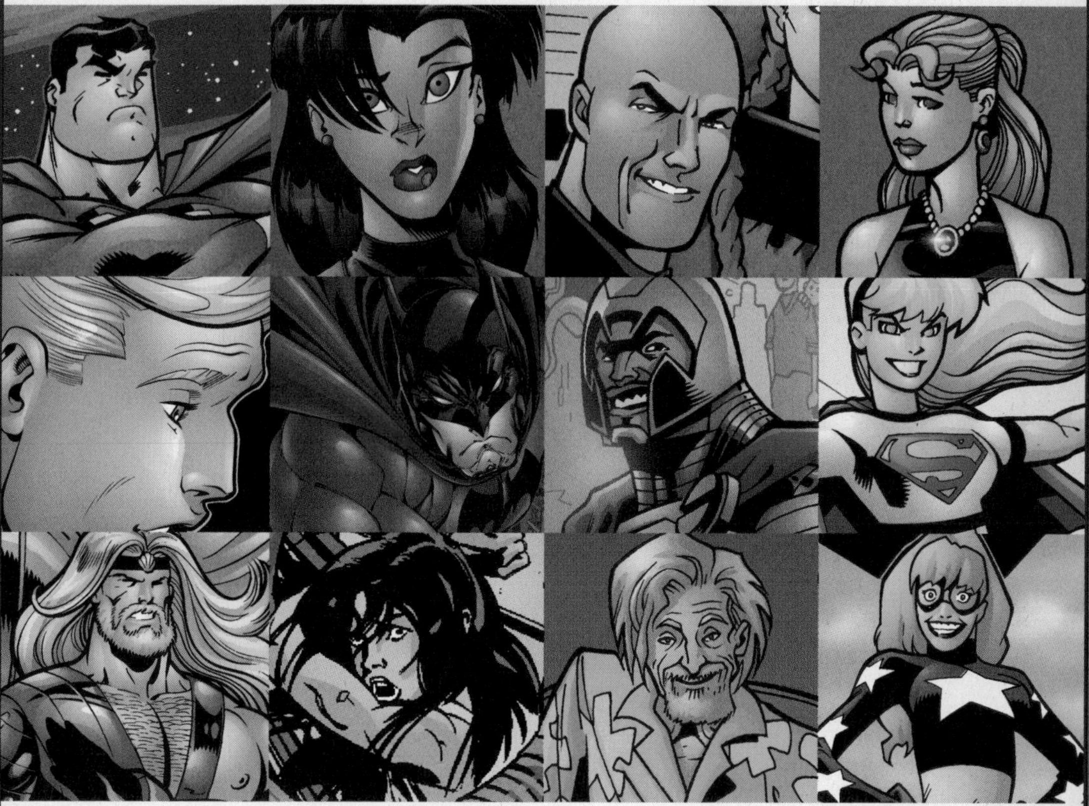

THE MAN OF STEEL, HIS FRIENDS AND FOES, AT THE TIME DEPICTED IN THIS VOLUME:

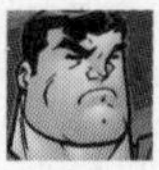

SUPERMAN

Kal-El, the Last Son of Krypton: Faster than a speeding bullet, more powerful than a locomotive, able to leap the tallest buildings with a single bound — with all this and the love of his wife, Lois Lane, Kal-El believed he had it all. Their relationship has already endured a great deal, including Superman's near-death from Kryptonite radiation poisoning and Lois's abduction and replacement by the malicious Parasite, but their love continues to see them through the best and worst of times.

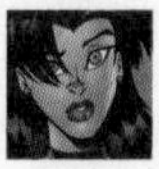

LOIS LANE

Ace reporter for the great Metropolis paper *The Daily Planet*, Lois is also married to fellow reporter Clark Kent, whom she knows to be Superman. Lois has endured Lex Luthor in her life for years, and she currently suffers under a bargain with him — in exchange for Luthor's selling *The Planet* to Perry White, she will kill any one story of Luthor's choosing.

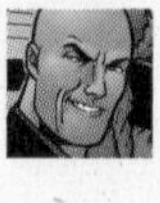

LEX LUTHOR

Before there was Superman, Metropolis and Lex Luthor were synonymous. One of the world's wealthiest men, Luthor made certain that he owned the best of everything, including corporations, technology, and people. The mere presence of the Man of Steel continues to infuriate him, and Luthor means to do something to negate Superman's influence — and to dilute the people's affection for him.

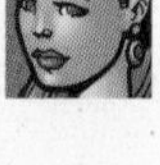

LANA LANG

Clark Kent and Lana were childhood friends, growing up in Smallville with everyone thinking they would be together forever. All that changed as high school ended and Clark revealed he was more than he seemed. He left to pursue his destiny while she remained in Smallville. Their paths next crossed when Luthor had Lana tortured in hopes of finding the secret of the alien super-hero. Frustrated over Clark's declaration of love for Lois Lane, she sold her family's farm and moved to Washington, D.C. where she began a romance with Pete Ross, now working for a Kansas senator. They married and had a child — named Clark — whom Superman rescued from Brainiac and saved from Doomsday. Things have settled down for the family, and Lana continues to tell herself she is happy.

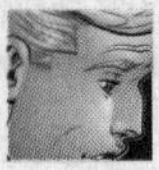

PETE ROSS

Pete, Lana, and Clark were all childhood friends, and while Lana loved Clark, Pete loved Lana. Pete and Lana stayed in touch after he left Smallville to obtain his law degree, and their friendship resumed when he returned home as a county agent. Eventually he was offered a job in Washington, D.C. working for a Kansas senator. After seeing how happy Clark was with Lois Lane, Lana finally put her feelings for him aside and entered into a long-awaited romance with Pete. They married and had a child, and to this day Pete remains unaware of the secrets Lana has kept and pain she has endured.

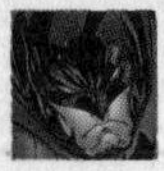

BATMAN

Gotham City's Dark Knight Detective has trained himself to the peak of physical and mental perfection. Considered the world's greatest detective, Batman prefers to concentrate his efforts on the crime and corruption in Gotham City. He has his own methods, and Superman often doesn't agree with them. When Luthor used LexCorp to oversee the rebuilding of Gotham City after a devastating earthquake, he came into direct opposition with the Dark Knight.

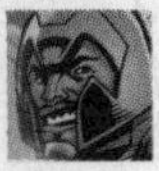

STEEL

John Henry Irons uses a suit of armor he has built to live up to the ideals and standards of Superman. A brilliant engineer, Irons and his niece Natasha (an Advanced Studies intern) work in a huge Metropolis-based lab called Steelworks. He's ably supported by a Kryptonian-made robot, Kelex. Steel proudly calls Superman a friend.

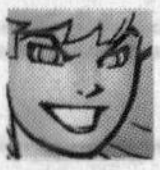

SUPERGIRL

Matrix was cloned from a parallel universe's version of Lana Lang, but imbued with powers and abilities resembling Superman's. She came to his world to seek his help and, inspired by him, relocated to Earth. Later, her essence was merged with that of troubled teenager Linda Danvers. Now that combined essence is truly an Earth-born Angel, dealing with occult problems while still struggling to find her way in the world.

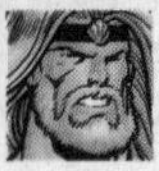

AQUAMAN

A founding member of the Justice League, Arthur is the royal ruler of a kingdom that covers over two-thirds of the planet. His abilities to withstand the awesome pressure of the deep and to communicate with all the ocean's inhabitants help to make him the undersea world's greatest protector. He is usually aided by Tempest, an Atlantean boy Arthur rescued from near death and raised as his own son.

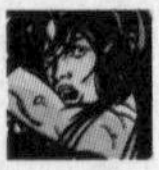

TALIA

Her father is the enigmatic Ra's al Ghul, a near-immortal who seeks ways to return the Earth to its original natural glory — *sans* humankind. Knowing he could not live forever, Ra's wanted to turn his vast organization over to an heir — the husband of his beautiful daughter, Talia. After Talia fell in love with Batman, Ra's al Ghul studied the Detective and concluded he was the appropriate man. Batman's rejection of the plan put the two men at odds, and they have opposed each other over the years with Talia caught in between. While remaining loyal to her father, she has come into her own as a woman and has been carving out a destiny of her own choosing. Given her extensive training in the arts, sciences, and combat techniques, she can be a formidable businesswoman or deadly opponent.

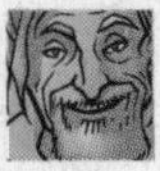

PROFESSOR EMIL HAMILTON

Luthor usurped the brilliant Hamilton's weapons research, nearly driving the old professor insane. Only after fighting Superman and losing was Hamilton able to tame his madness. Since then, working out of his small lab, he has remained the Man of Steel's staunch supporter. Whenever Superman needed scientific help, Hamilton was his first choice. He lost an arm when Luthor, his schemes exposed by Lois Lane, tried to destroy all Metropolis. The limb was replaced with a cybernetic prosthetic. When the Brainiac 13 computer virus remade Metropolis, Hamilton got caught up in the change. Studying the new technology, he disappeared from sight for a time.

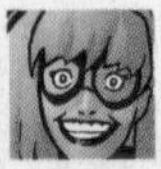

STAR-SPANGLED KID

When Courtney Whitmore first discovered the cosmic converter belt once worn by the Justice Society of America's original Star-Spangled Kid, she saw it as an opportunity to cut class and kick some butt. Now, she is slowly — very slowly — beginning to learn about the awesome legacy she has become a part of. Her stepfather, Pat Dugan, worked with the original Kid and is now an inventor.

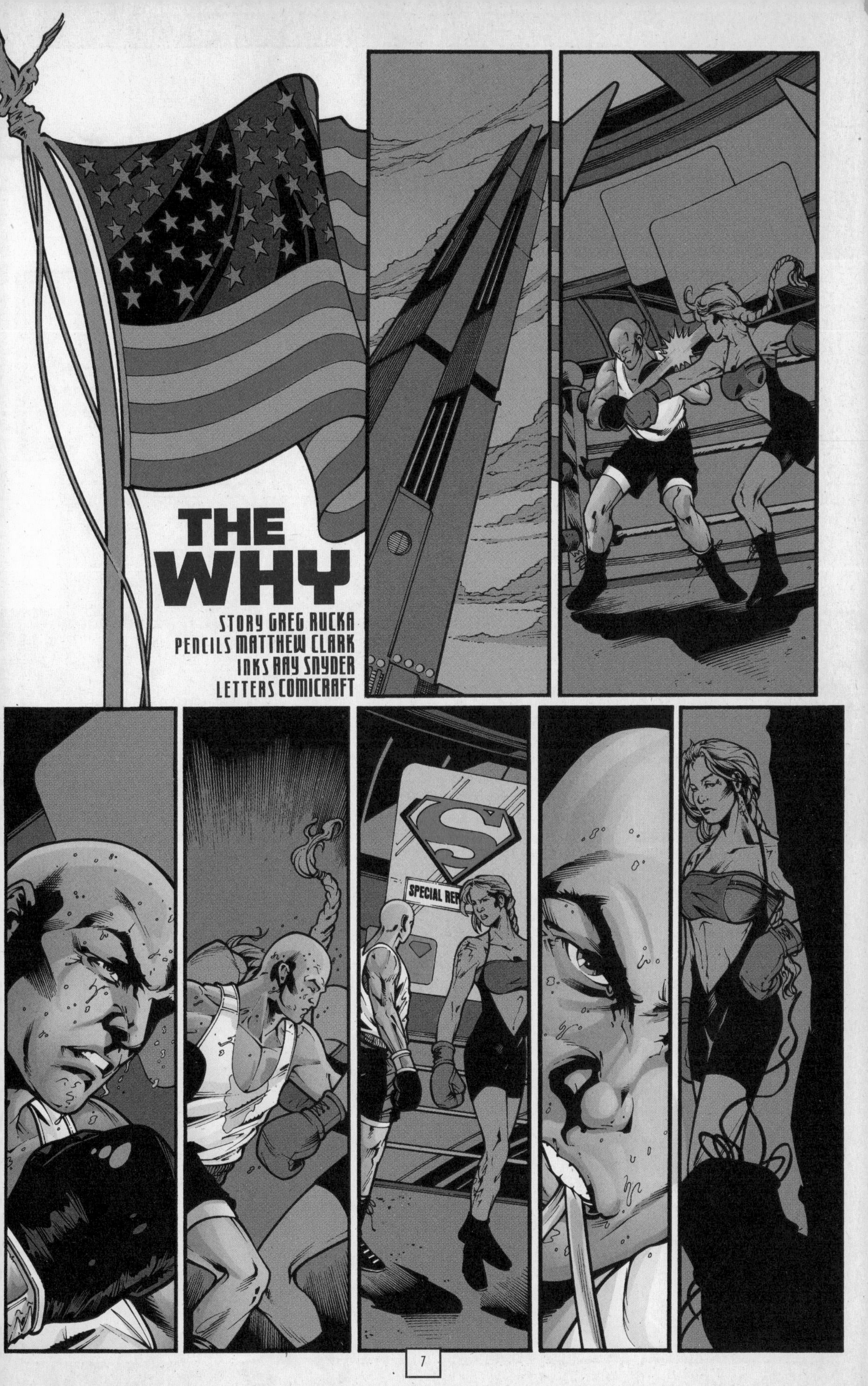
THE WHY
STORY GREG RUCKA
PENCILS MATTHEW CLARK
INKS RAY SNYDER
LETTERS COMICRAFT
SPECIAL REP

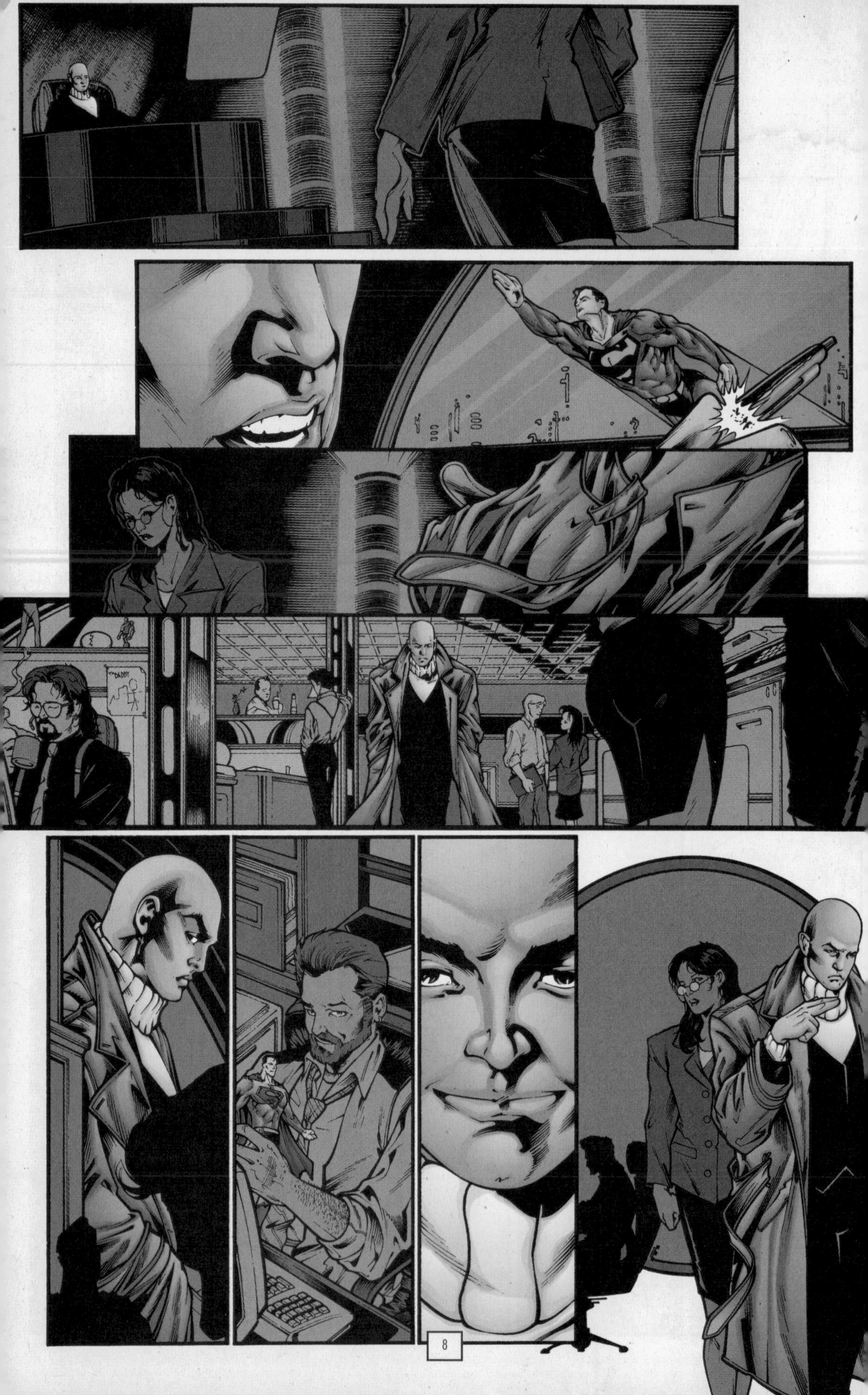

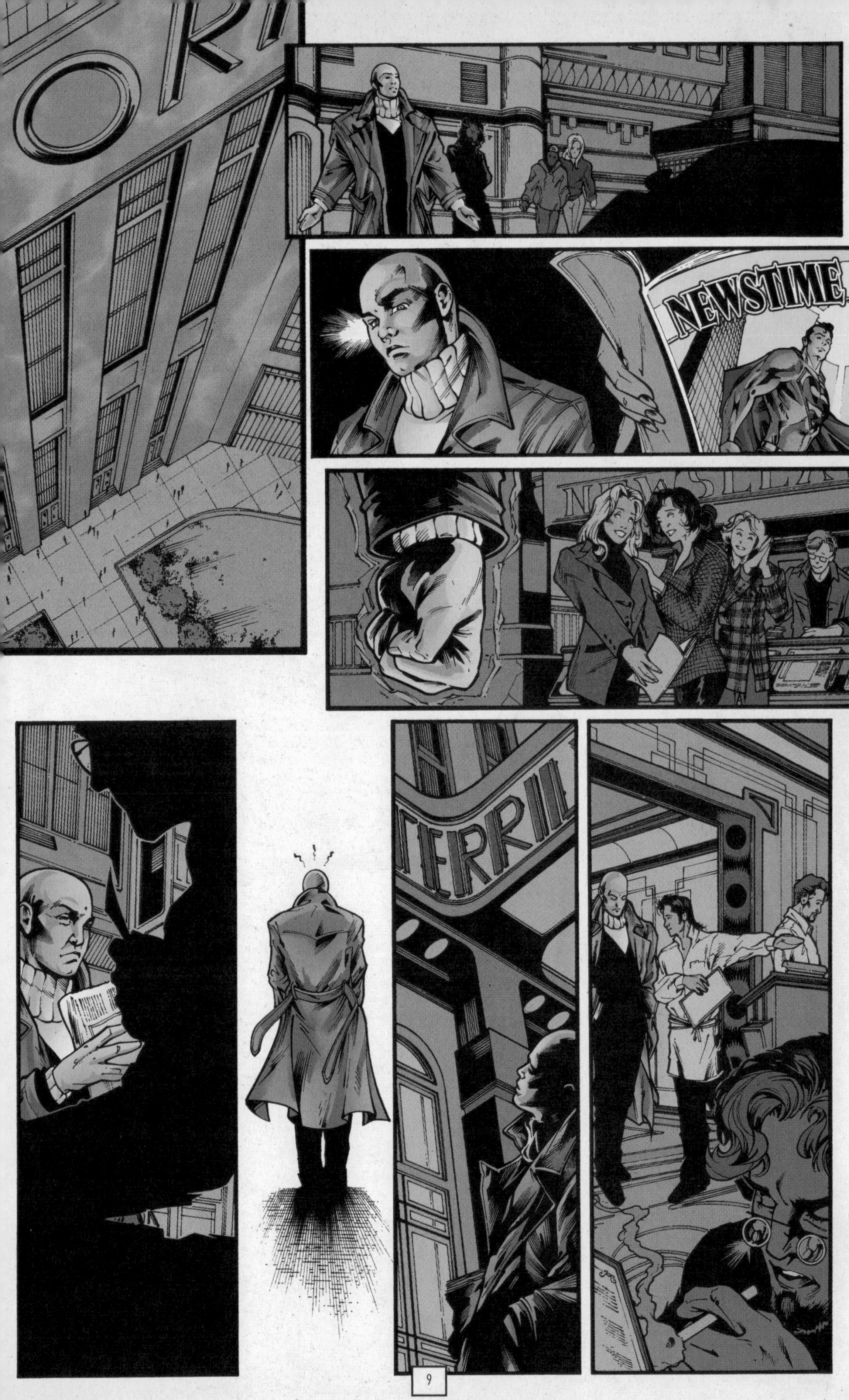
NEWSTIME

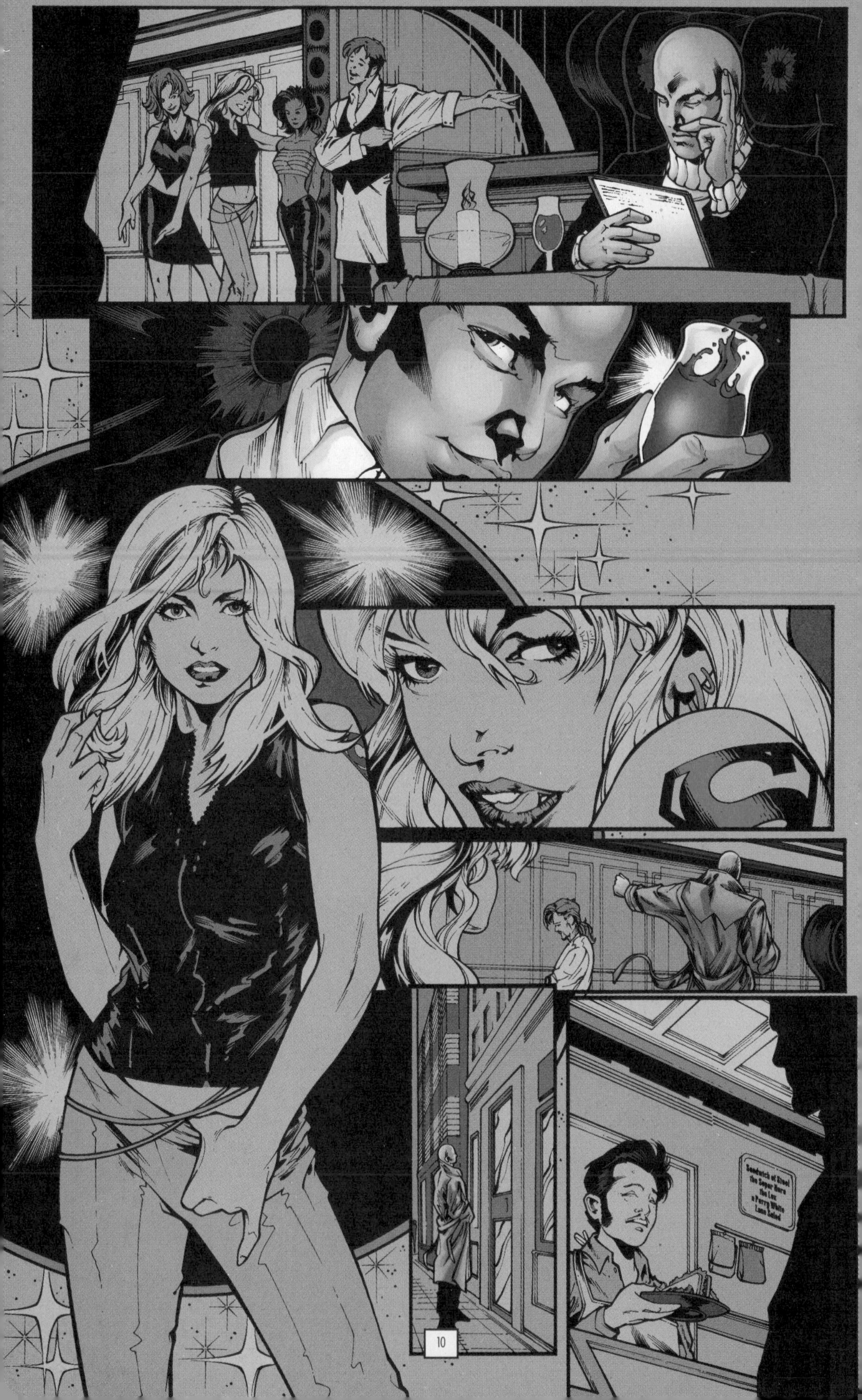
Sandwich of Steel
The Super Hero
The Lex
Perry White

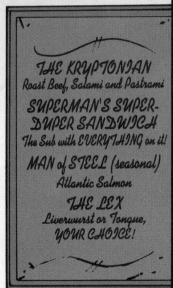

THE KRYPTONIAN
Roast Beef, Salami and Pastrami

SUPERMAN'S SUPER-
DUPER SANDWICH
The Sub with EVERYTHING on it!

MAN of STEEL *(seasonal)*
Atlantic Salmon

THE LEX
Liverwurst or Tongue,
YOUR CHOICE!

PRESIDENTIAL RACE HEATING UP

IT'S LUTHOR...

...CALL *LEGAL* AND TELL THEM I WANT TO RUN FOR *PRESIDENT*...

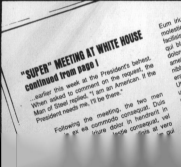

"SUPER" MEETING AT WHITE HOUSE
continued from page 1

...earlier this week at the President's behest. When asked to comment on the request, the Man of Steel replied, "I am an American. If the President needs me, I'll be there."

Following the meeting, the two men

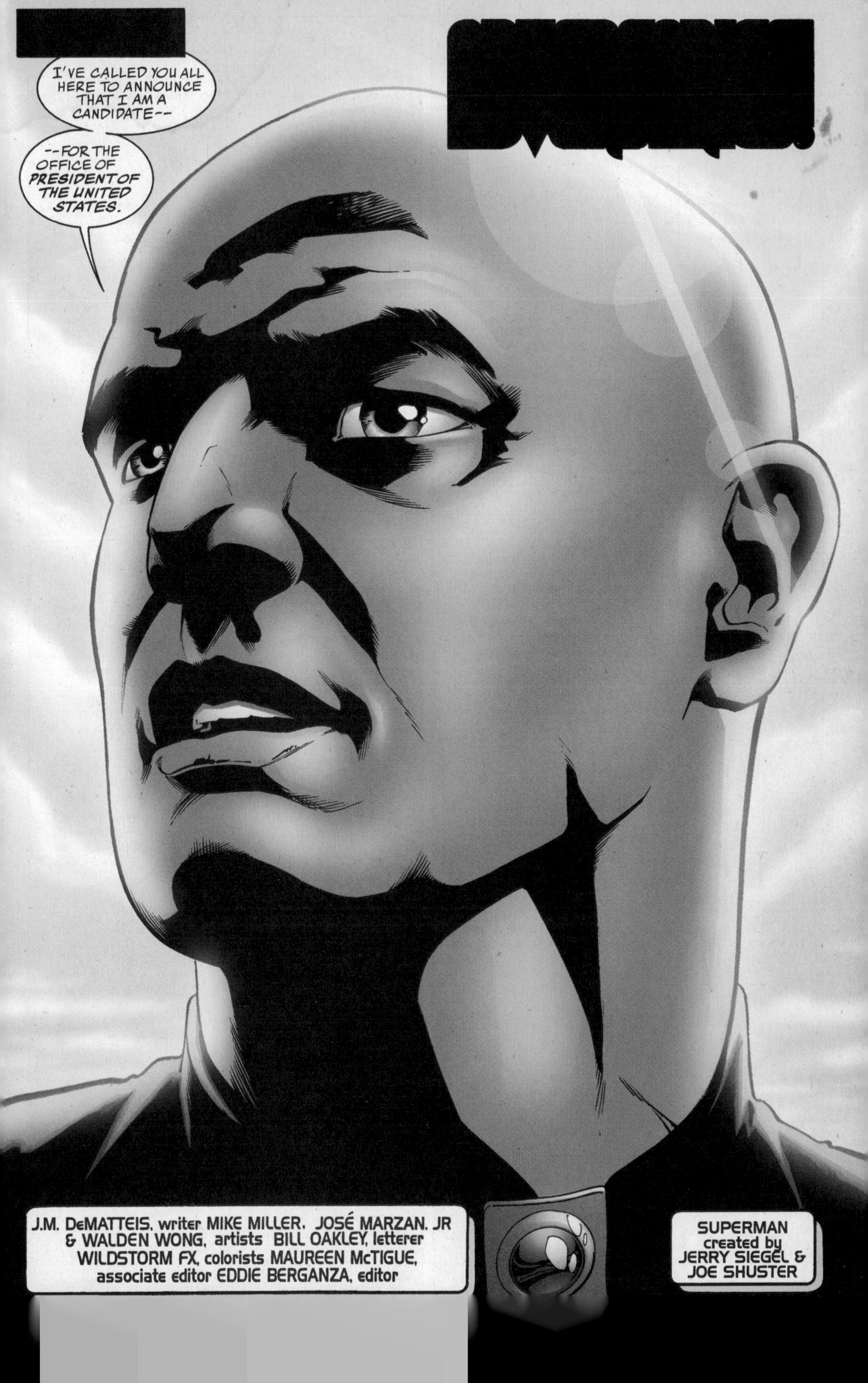
[redacted]
I'VE CALLED YOU ALL HERE TO ANNOUNCE THAT I AM A CANDIDATE--
--FOR THE OFFICE OF PRESIDENT OF THE UNITED STATES.
[redacted]
J.M. DeMATTEIS, writer MIKE MILLER, JOSÉ MARZAN, JR & WALDEN WONG, artists BILL OAKLEY, letterer WILDSTORM FX, colorists MAUREEN McTIGUE, associate editor EDDIE BERGANZA, editor
SUPERMAN created by JERRY SIEGEL & JOE SHUSTER

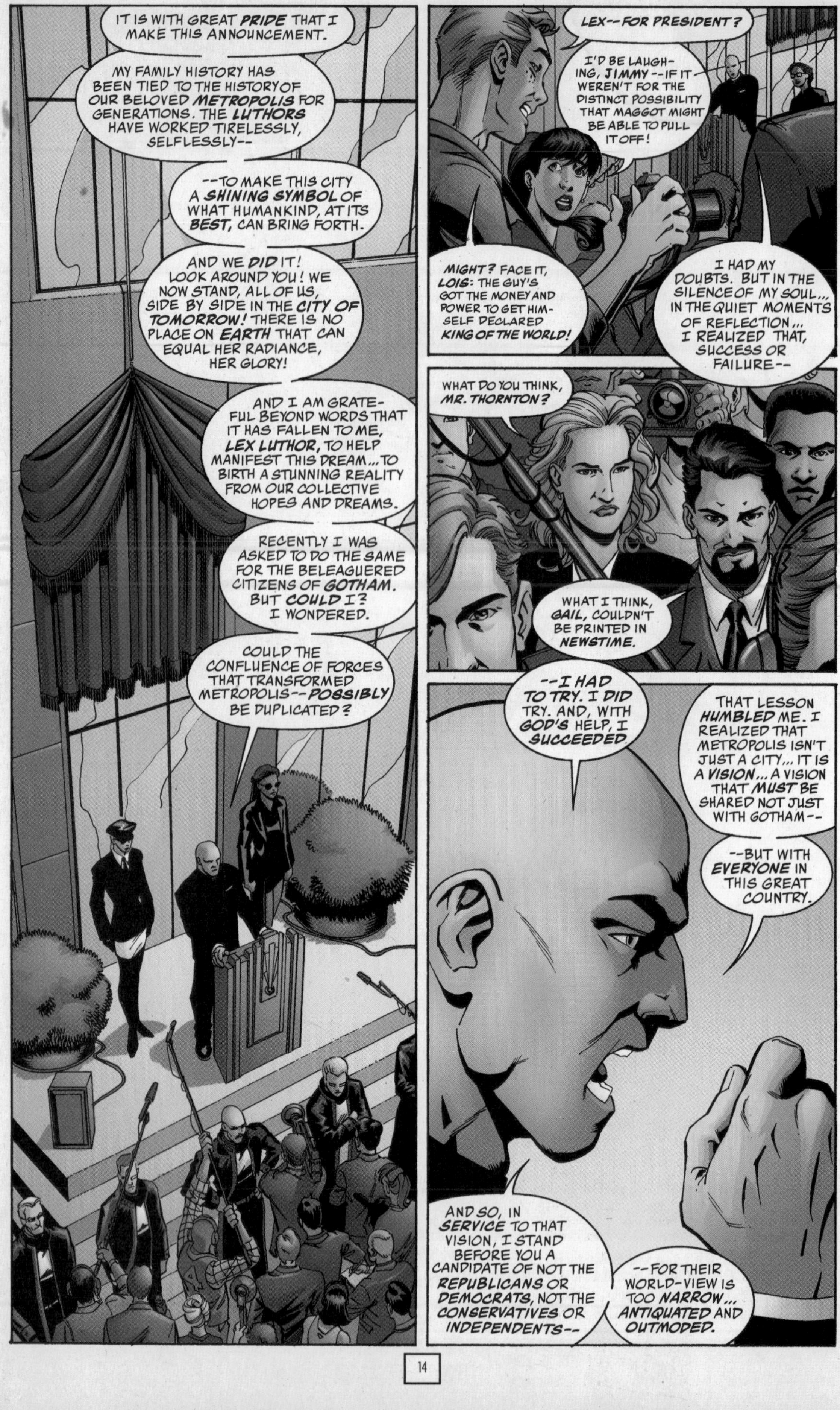
IT IS WITH GREAT PRIDE THAT I MAKE THIS ANNOUNCEMENT.
MY FAMILY HISTORY HAS BEEN TIED TO THE HISTORY OF OUR BELOVED METROPOLIS FOR GENERATIONS. THE LUTHORS HAVE WORKED TIRELESSLY, SELFLESSLY--
--TO MAKE THIS CITY A SHINING SYMBOL OF WHAT HUMANKIND, AT ITS BEST, CAN BRING FORTH.
AND WE DID IT! LOOK AROUND YOU! WE NOW STAND, ALL OF US, SIDE BY SIDE IN THE CITY OF TOMORROW! THERE IS NO PLACE ON EARTH THAT CAN EQUAL HER RADIANCE, HER GLORY!
AND I AM GRATEFUL BEYOND WORDS THAT IT HAS FALLEN TO ME, LEX LUTHOR, TO HELP MANIFEST THIS DREAM... TO BIRTH A STUNNING REALITY FROM OUR COLLECTIVE HOPES AND DREAMS.
RECENTLY I WAS ASKED TO DO THE SAME FOR THE BELEAGUERED CITIZENS OF GOTHAM. BUT COULD I? I WONDERED.
COULD THE CONFLUENCE OF FORCES THAT TRANSFORMED METROPOLIS--POSSIBLY BE DUPLICATED?
LEX--FOR PRESIDENT?
I'D BE LAUGHING, JIMMY--IF IT WEREN'T FOR THE DISTINCT POSSIBILITY THAT MAGGOT MIGHT BE ABLE TO PULL IT OFF!
MIGHT? FACE IT, LOIS: THE GUY'S GOT THE MONEY AND POWER TO GET HIMSELF DECLARED KING OF THE WORLD!
I HAD MY DOUBTS. BUT IN THE SILENCE OF MY SOUL... IN THE QUIET MOMENTS OF REFLECTION... I REALIZED THAT, SUCCESS OR FAILURE--
WHAT DO YOU THINK, MR. THORNTON?
WHAT I THINK, GAIL, COULDN'T BE PRINTED IN NEWSTIME.
--I HAD TO TRY. I DID TRY. AND, WITH GOD'S HELP, I SUCCEEDED.
THAT LESSON HUMBLED ME. I REALIZED THAT METROPOLIS ISN'T JUST A CITY... IT IS A VISION... A VISION THAT MUST BE SHARED NOT JUST WITH GOTHAM--
--BUT WITH EVERYONE IN THIS GREAT COUNTRY.
AND SO, IN SERVICE TO THAT VISION, I STAND BEFORE YOU A CANDIDATE OF NOT THE REPUBLICANS OR DEMOCRATS, NOT THE CONSERVATIVES OR INDEPENDENTS--
--FOR THEIR WORLD-VIEW IS TOO NARROW... ANTIQUATED AND OUTMODED.

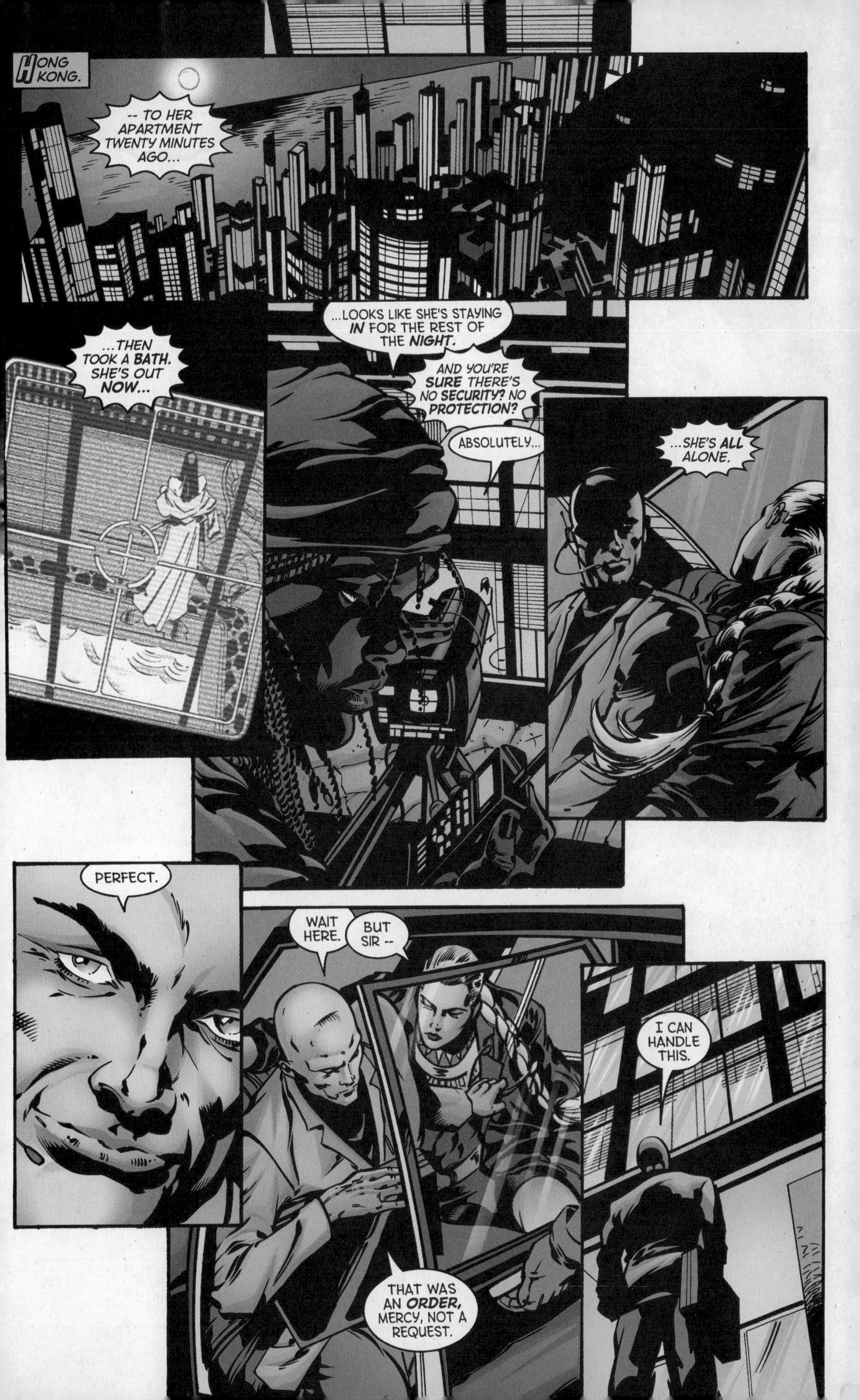
HONG KONG.
-- TO HER APARTMENT TWENTY MINUTES AGO...
...THEN TOOK A BATH. SHE'S OUT NOW...
...LOOKS LIKE SHE'S STAYING IN FOR THE REST OF THE NIGHT.
AND YOU'RE SURE THERE'S NO SECURITY? NO PROTECTION?
ABSOLUTELY...
...SHE'S ALL ALONE.
PERFECT.
WAIT HERE.
BUT SIR --
THAT WAS AN ORDER, MERCY, NOT A REQUEST.
I CAN HANDLE THIS.

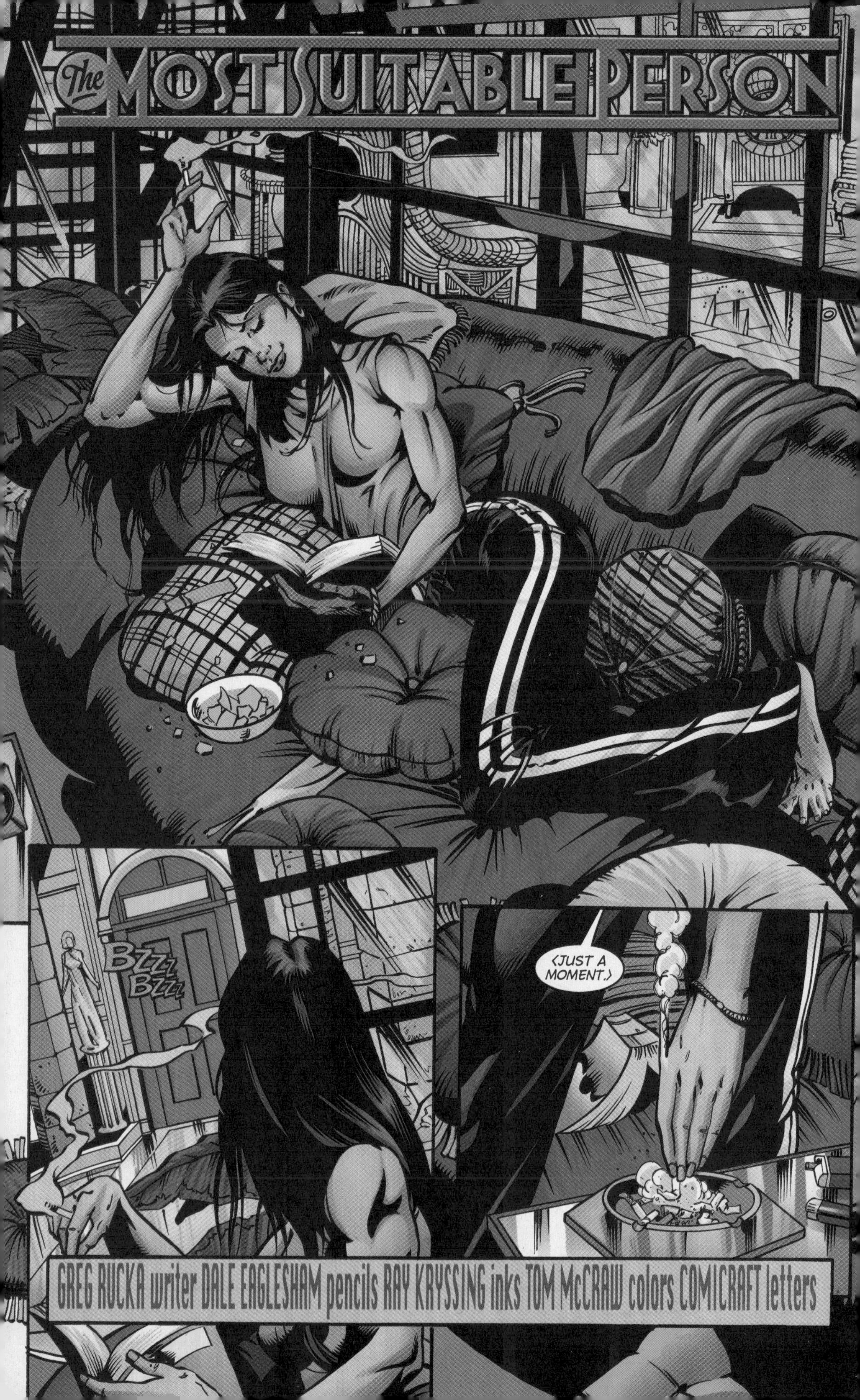
The Most Suitable Person
BZZZ BZZZ
<JUST A MOMENT.>
GREG RUCKA writer DALE EAGLESHAM pencils RAY KRYSSING inks TOM McCRAW colors COMICRAFT letters

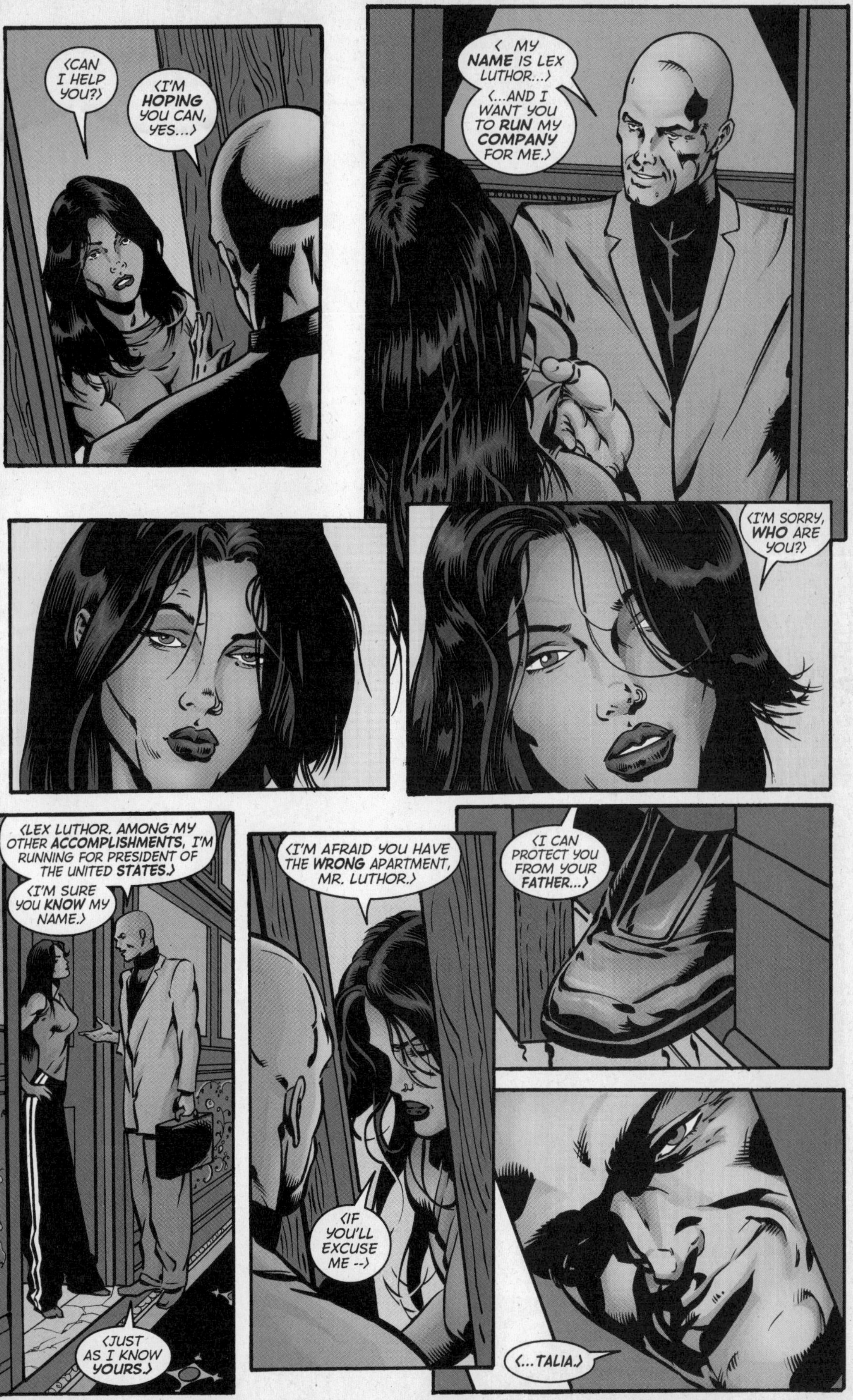

<CAN I HELP YOU?>
<I'M HOPING YOU CAN, YES...>
< MY NAME IS LEX LUTHOR...>
<...AND I WANT YOU TO RUN MY COMPANY FOR ME.>
<I'M SORRY, WHO ARE YOU?>
<LEX LUTHOR. AMONG MY OTHER ACCOMPLISHMENTS, I'M RUNNING FOR PRESIDENT OF THE UNITED STATES.>
<I'M SURE YOU KNOW MY NAME.>
<JUST AS I KNOW YOURS.>
<I'M AFRAID YOU HAVE THE WRONG APARTMENT, MR. LUTHOR.>
<IF YOU'LL EXCUSE ME -->
<I CAN PROTECT YOU FROM YOUR FATHER...>
<...TALIA.>

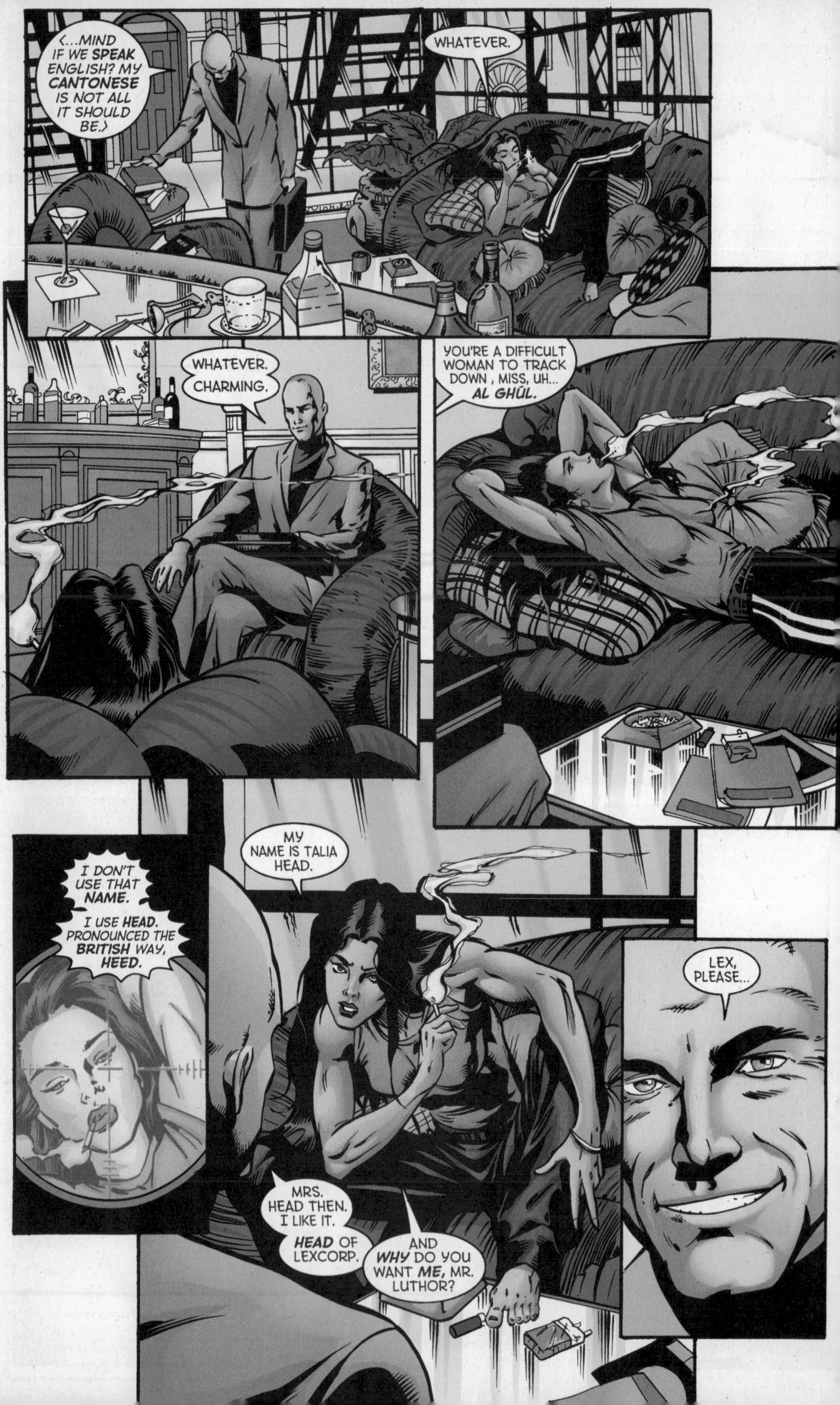
<...MIND IF WE SPEAK ENGLISH? MY CANTONESE IS NOT ALL IT SHOULD BE.>
WHATEVER.
WHATEVER. CHARMING.
YOU'RE A DIFFICULT WOMAN TO TRACK DOWN , MISS, UH... AL GHÛL.
I DON'T USE THAT NAME.
I USE HEAD. PRONOUNCED THE BRITISH WAY, HEED.
MY NAME IS TALIA HEAD.
MRS. HEAD THEN. I LIKE IT. HEAD OF LEXCORP.
AND WHY DO YOU WANT ME, MR. LUTHOR?
LEX, PLEASE...

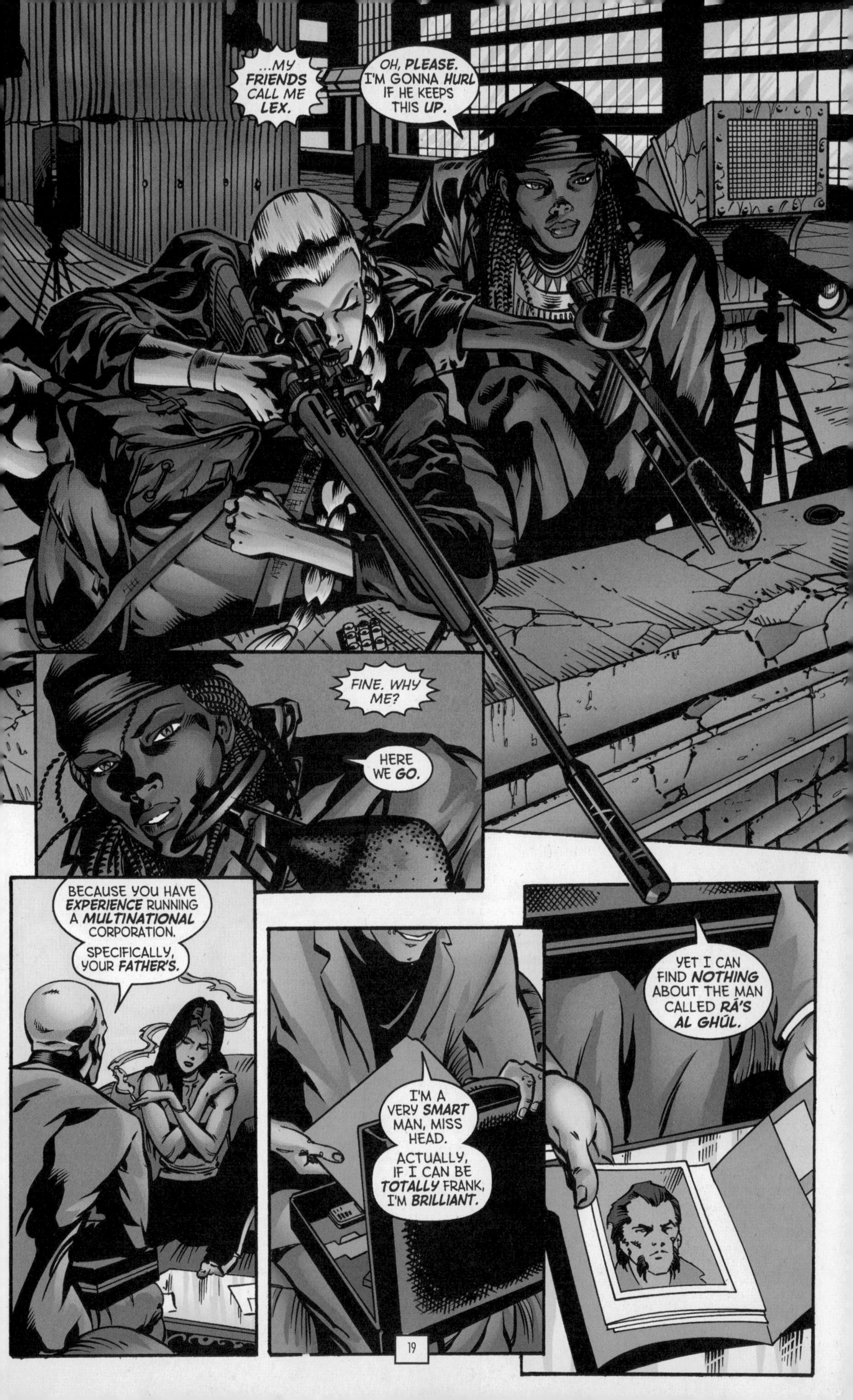
...MY FRIENDS CALL ME LEX.
OH, PLEASE. I'M GONNA HURL IF HE KEEPS THIS UP.
FINE. WHY ME?
HERE WE GO.
BECAUSE YOU HAVE EXPERIENCE RUNNING A MULTINATIONAL CORPORATION.
SPECIFICALLY, YOUR FATHER'S.
I'M A VERY SMART MAN, MISS HEAD.
ACTUALLY, IF I CAN BE TOTALLY FRANK, I'M BRILLIANT.
YET I CAN FIND NOTHING ABOUT THE MAN CALLED RĀ'S AL GHŪL.

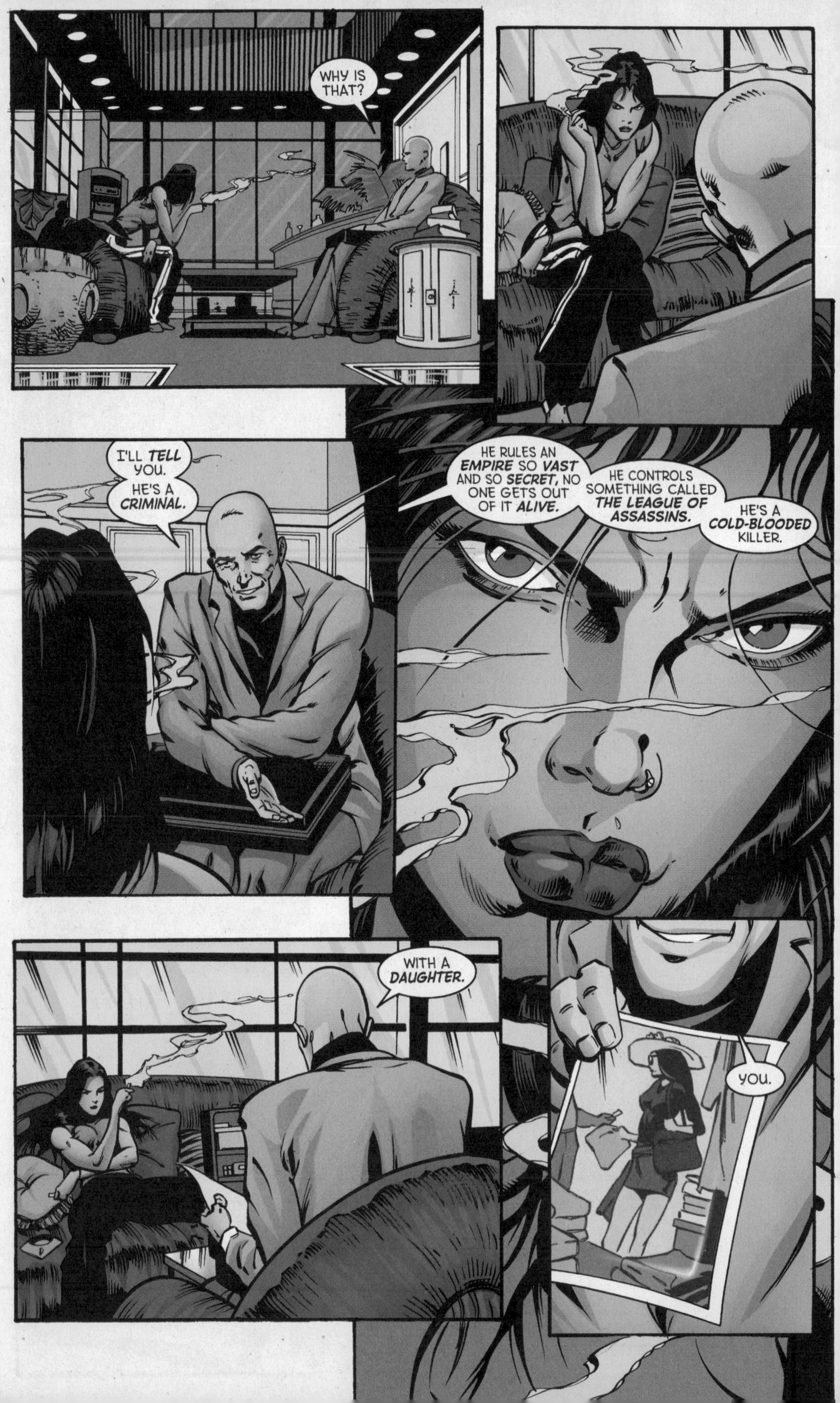
WHY IS THAT?
I'LL TELL YOU.
HE'S A CRIMINAL.
HE RULES AN EMPIRE SO VAST AND SO SECRET, NO ONE GETS OUT OF IT ALIVE.
HE CONTROLS SOMETHING CALLED THE LEAGUE OF ASSASSINS.
HE'S A COLD-BLOODED KILLER.
WITH A DAUGHTER.
YOU.

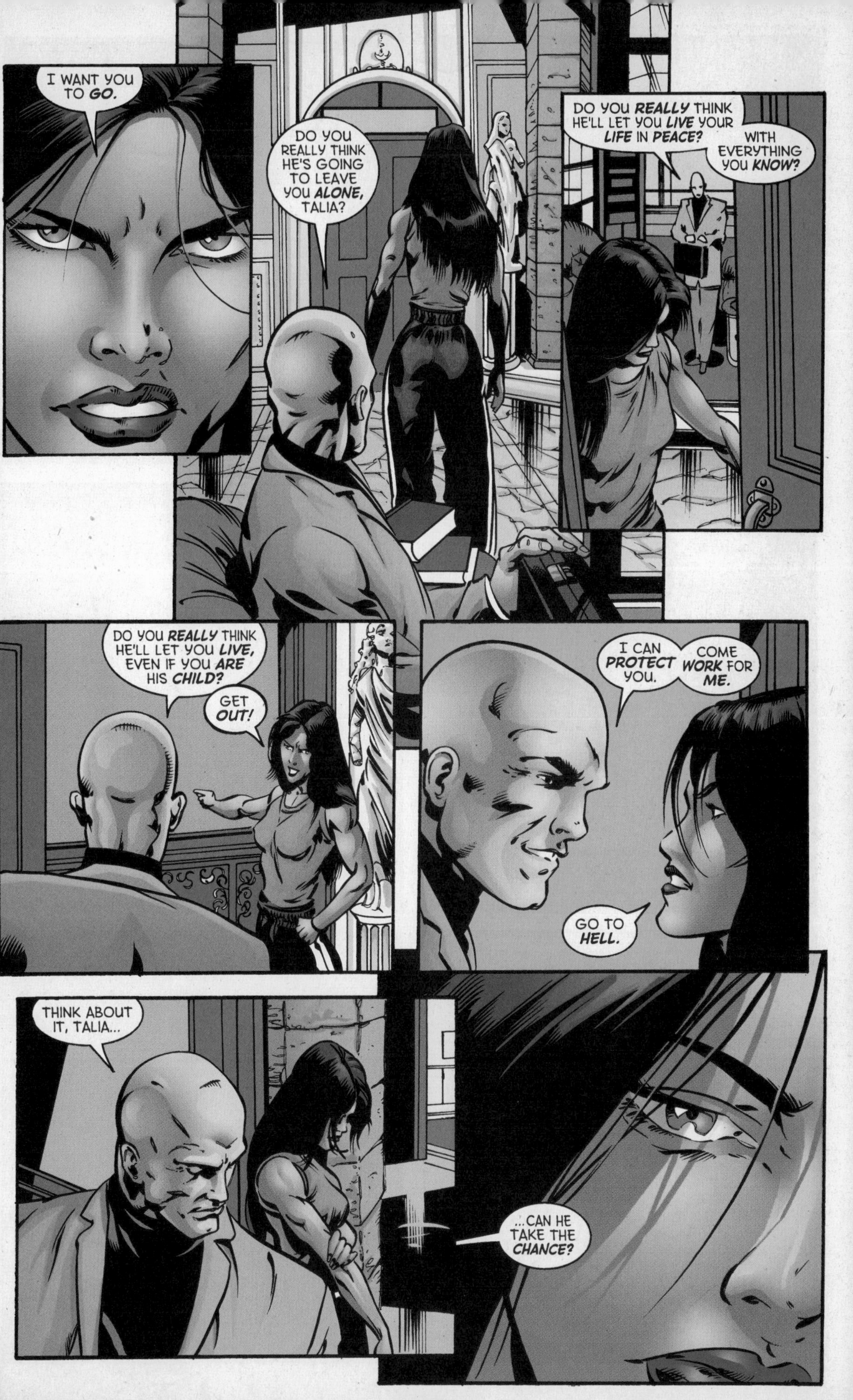

I WANT YOU TO GO.
DO YOU REALLY THINK HE'S GOING TO LEAVE YOU ALONE, TALIA?
DO YOU REALLY THINK HE'LL LET YOU LIVE YOUR LIFE IN PEACE?
WITH EVERYTHING YOU KNOW?
DO YOU REALLY THINK HE'LL LET YOU LIVE, EVEN IF YOU ARE HIS CHILD?
GET OUT!
I CAN PROTECT YOU.
COME WORK FOR ME.
GO TO HELL.
THINK ABOUT IT, TALIA...
...CAN HE TAKE THE CHANCE?

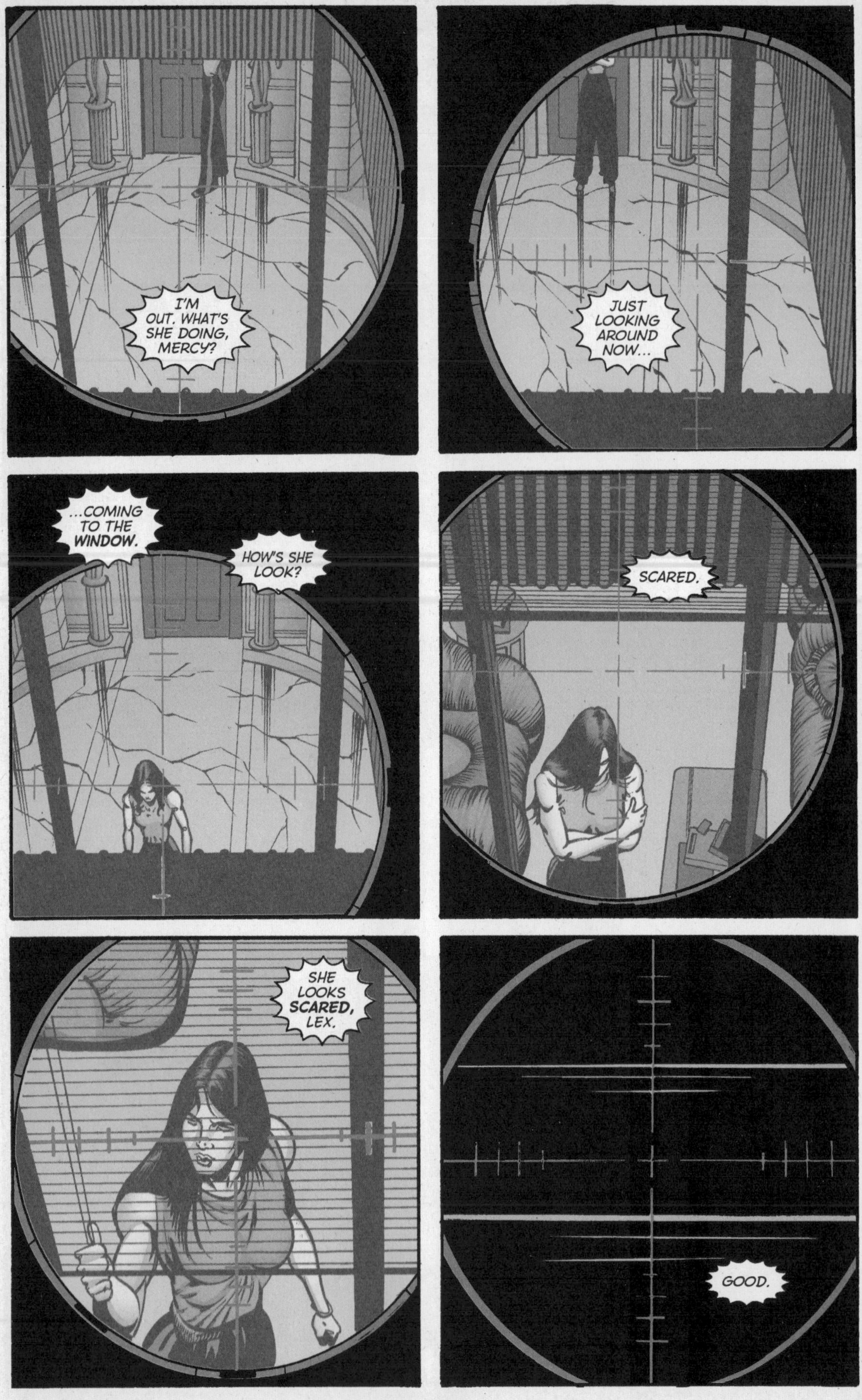
I'M OUT. WHAT'S SHE DOING, MERCY?
JUST LOOKING AROUND NOW...
...COMING TO THE WINDOW.
HOW'S SHE LOOK?
SCARED.
SHE LOOKS SCARED, LEX.
GOOD.

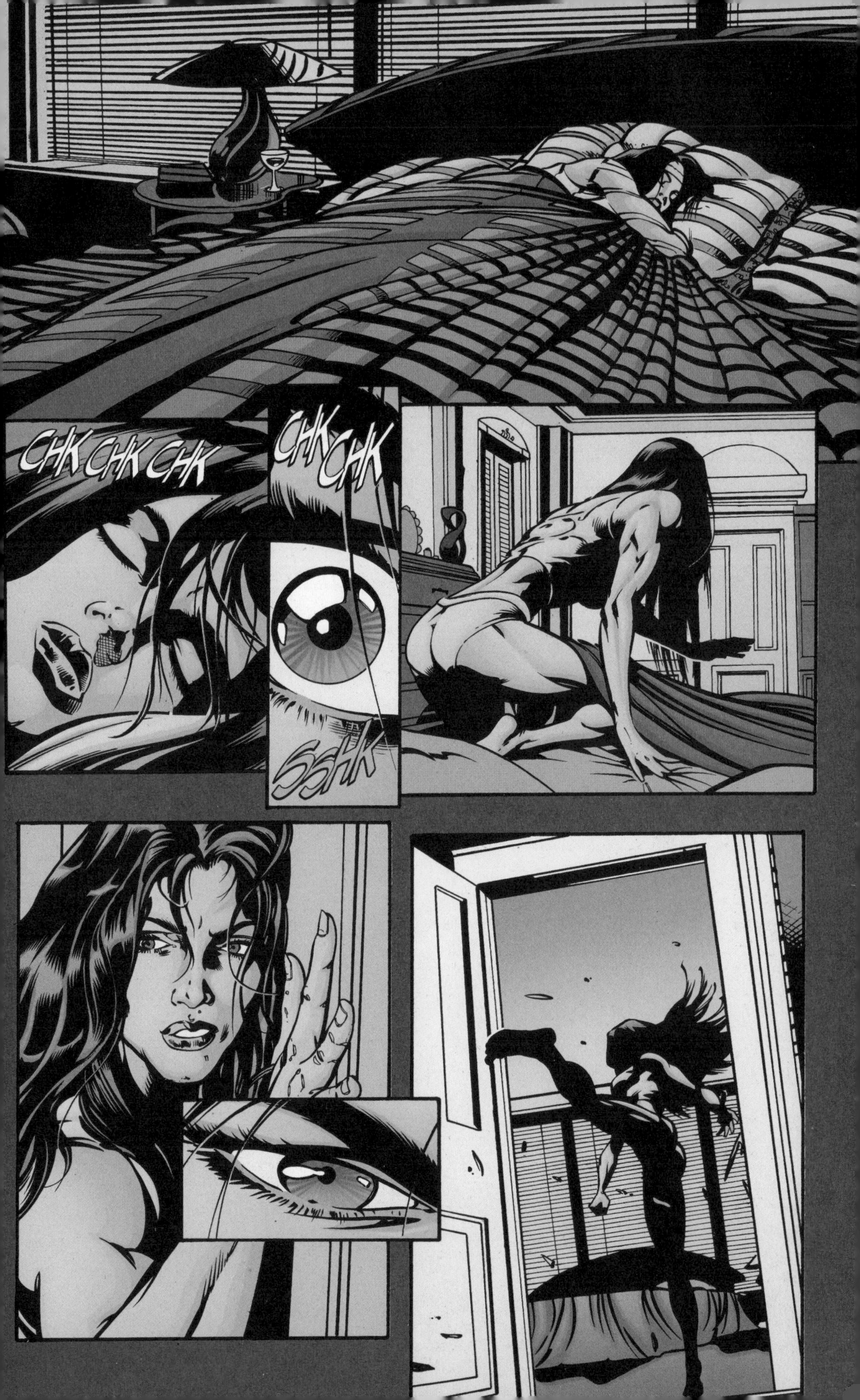
CHK CHK CHK
CHK CHK
SSHK

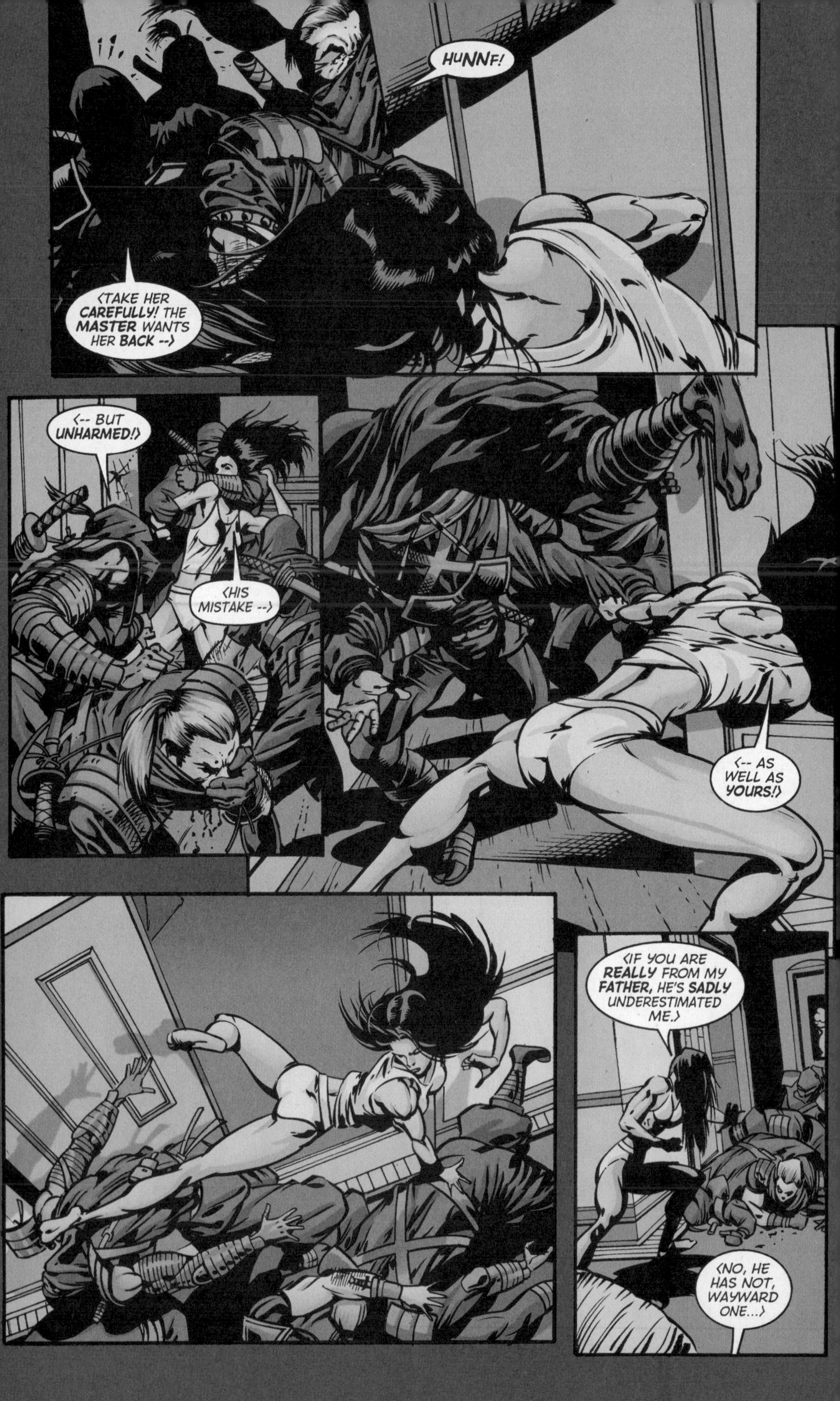
HUNNF!
‹TAKE HER CAREFULLY! THE MASTER WANTS HER BACK --›
‹-- BUT UNHARMED!›
‹HIS MISTAKE --›
‹-- AS WELL AS YOURS!›
‹IF YOU ARE REALLY FROM MY FATHER, HE'S SADLY UNDERESTIMATED ME.›
‹NO, HE HAS NOT, WAYWARD ONE...›

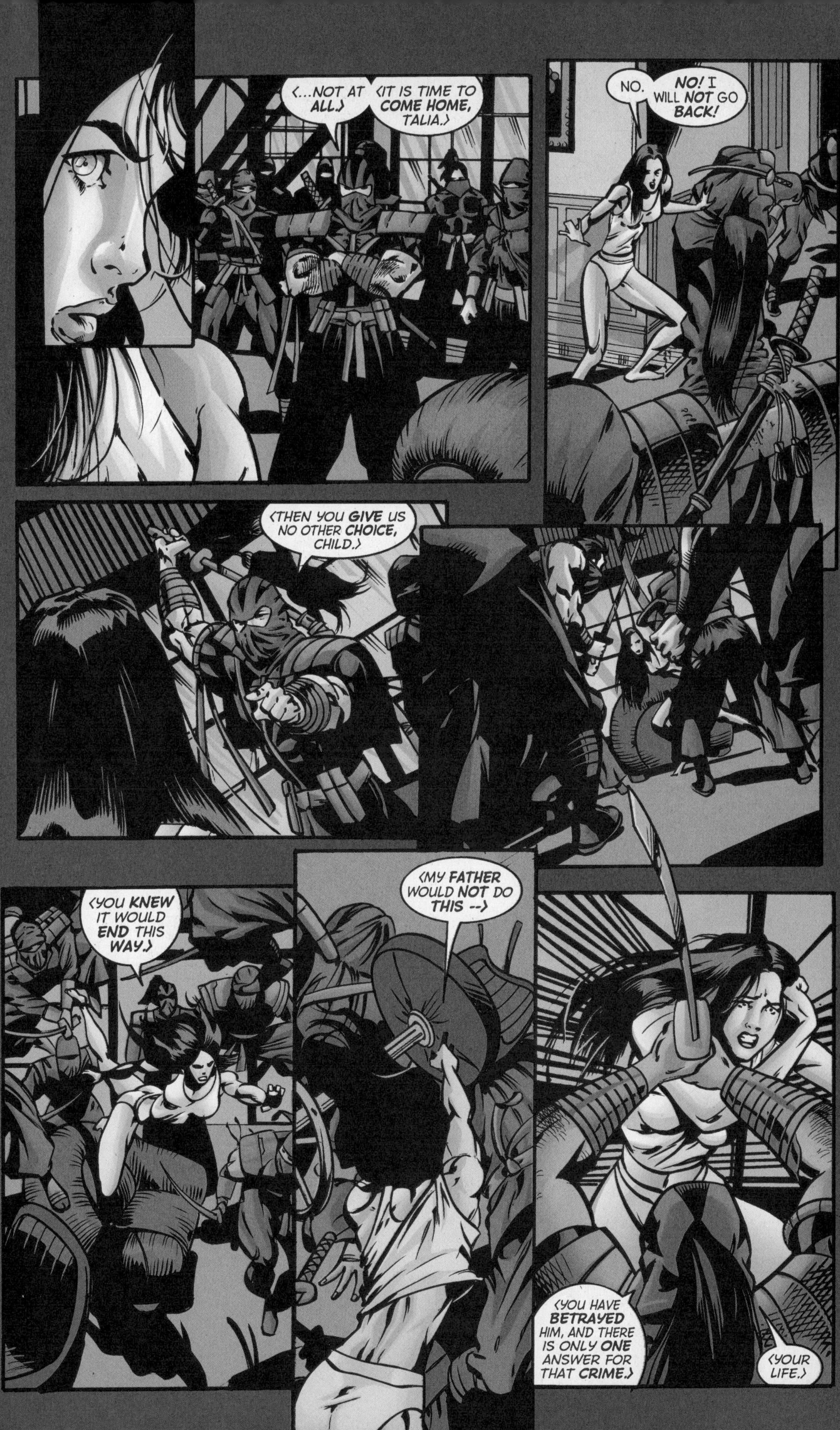

⟨...NOT AT ALL.⟩
⟨IT IS TIME TO COME HOME, TALIA.⟩
NO.
NO! I WILL NOT GO BACK!
⟨THEN YOU GIVE US NO OTHER CHOICE, CHILD.⟩
⟨YOU KNEW IT WOULD END THIS WAY.⟩
⟨MY FATHER WOULD NOT DO THIS --⟩
⟨YOU HAVE BETRAYED HIM, AND THERE IS ONLY ONE ANSWER FOR THAT CRIME.⟩
⟨YOUR LIFE.⟩

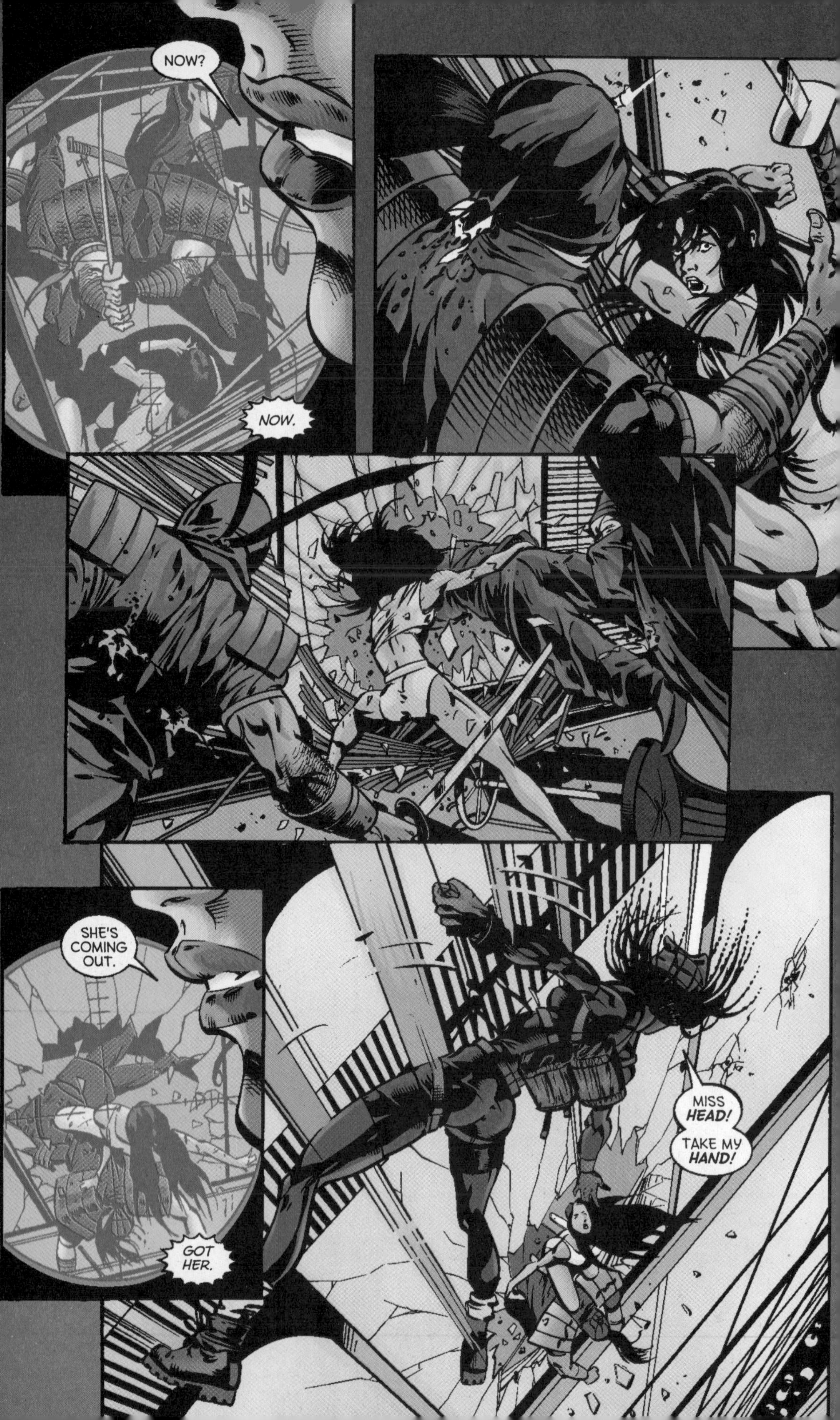
NOW?
NOW.
SHE'S COMING OUT.
GOT HER.
MISS HEAD!
TAKE MY HAND!

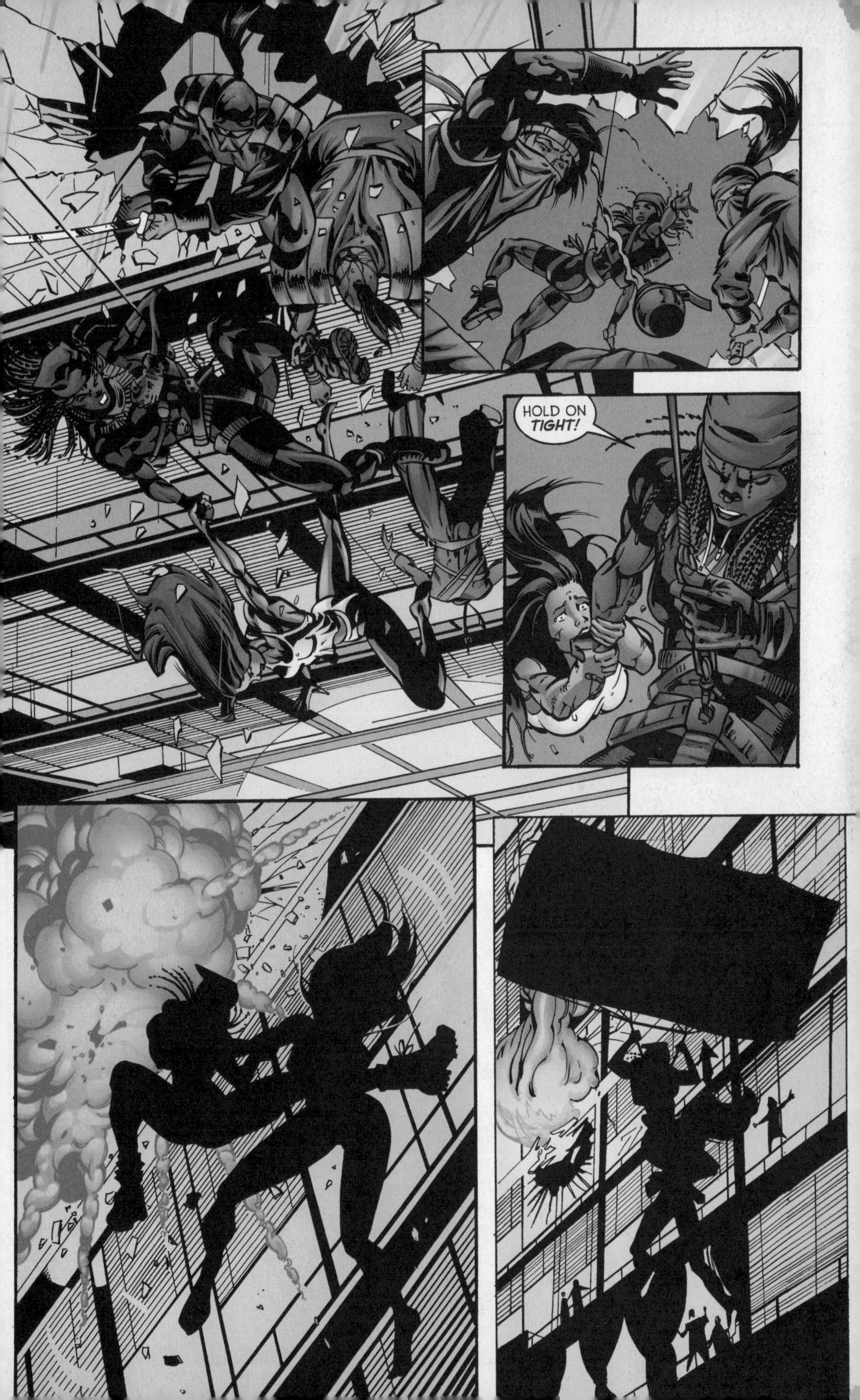
HOLD ON *TIGHT!*

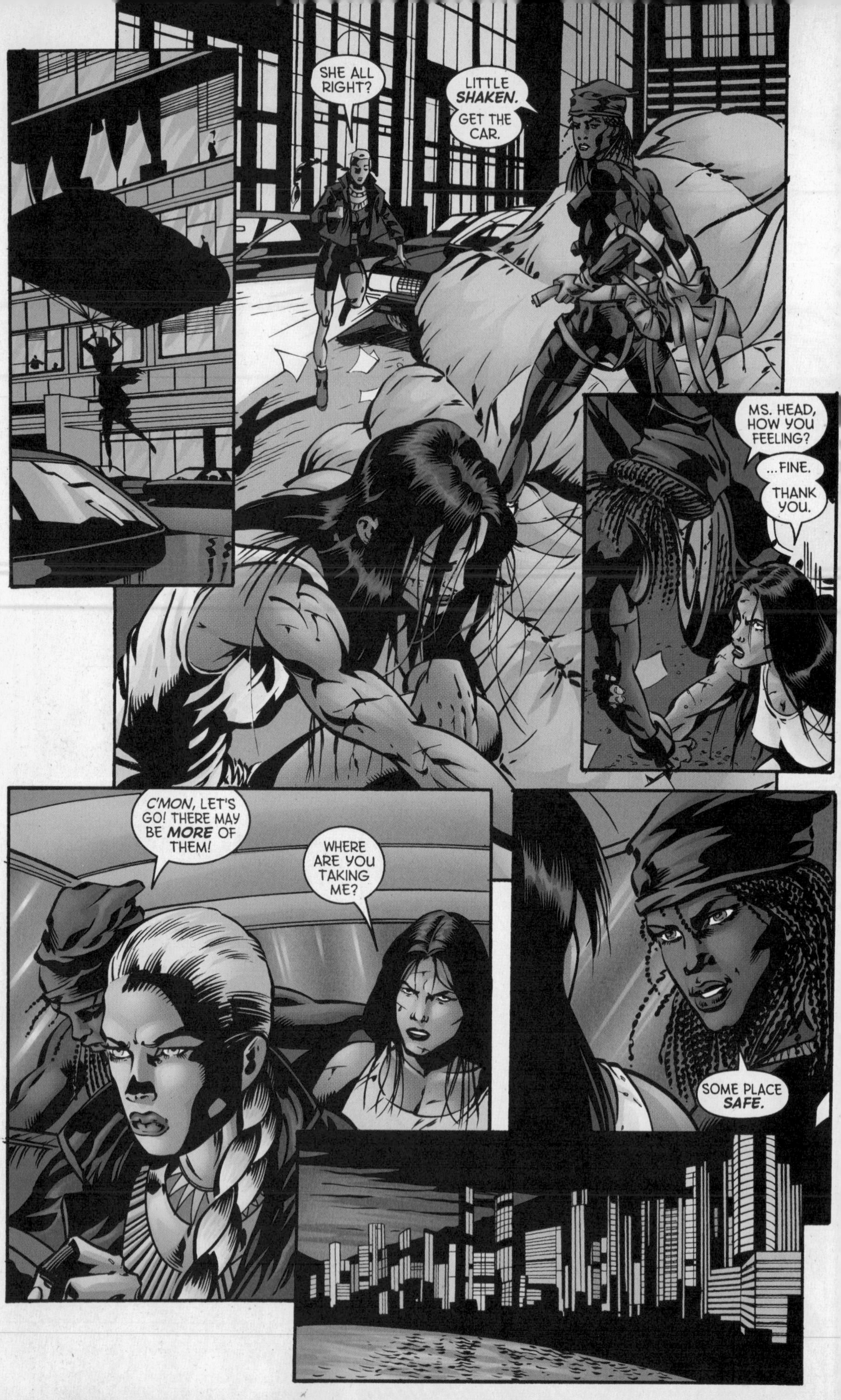
SHE ALL RIGHT?
LITTLE SHAKEN.
GET THE CAR.
MS. HEAD, HOW YOU FEELING?
...FINE.
THANK YOU.
C'MON, LET'S GO! THERE MAY BE MORE OF THEM!
WHERE ARE YOU TAKING ME?
SOME PLACE SAFE.

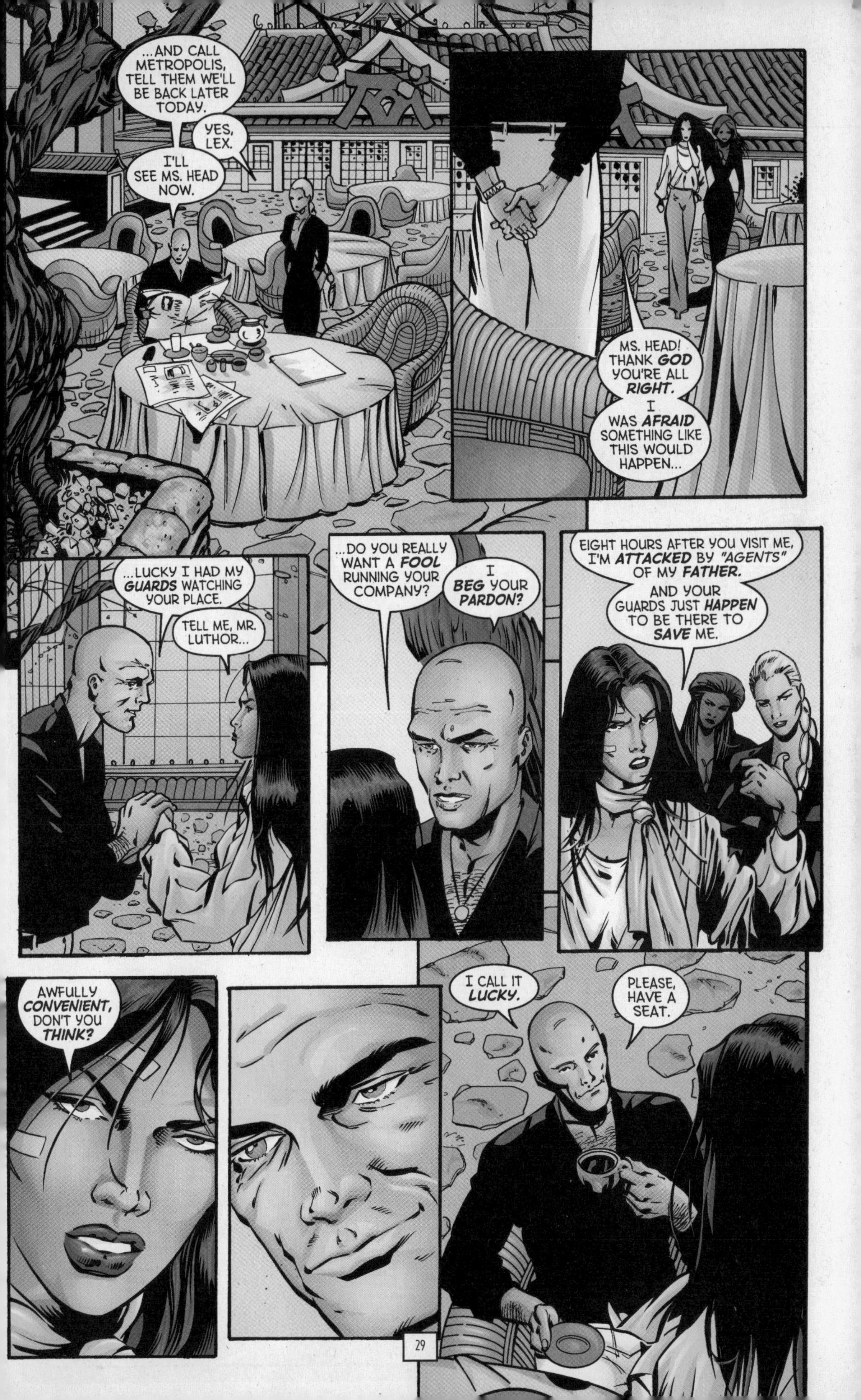

...AND CALL METROPOLIS, TELL THEM WE'LL BE BACK LATER TODAY.
YES, LEX.
I'LL SEE MS. HEAD NOW.
MS. HEAD! THANK **GOD** YOU'RE ALL **RIGHT.**
I WAS **AFRAID** SOMETHING LIKE THIS WOULD HAPPEN...
...LUCKY I HAD MY **GUARDS** WATCHING YOUR PLACE.
TELL ME, MR. LUTHOR...
...DO YOU REALLY WANT A **FOOL** RUNNING YOUR COMPANY?
I **BEG** YOUR **PARDON?**
EIGHT HOURS AFTER YOU VISIT ME, I'M **ATTACKED** BY *"AGENTS"* OF MY **FATHER.**
AND YOUR GUARDS JUST **HAPPEN** TO BE THERE TO **SAVE** ME.
AWFULLY **CONVENIENT,** DON'T YOU **THINK?**
I CALL IT **LUCKY.**
PLEASE, HAVE A SEAT.

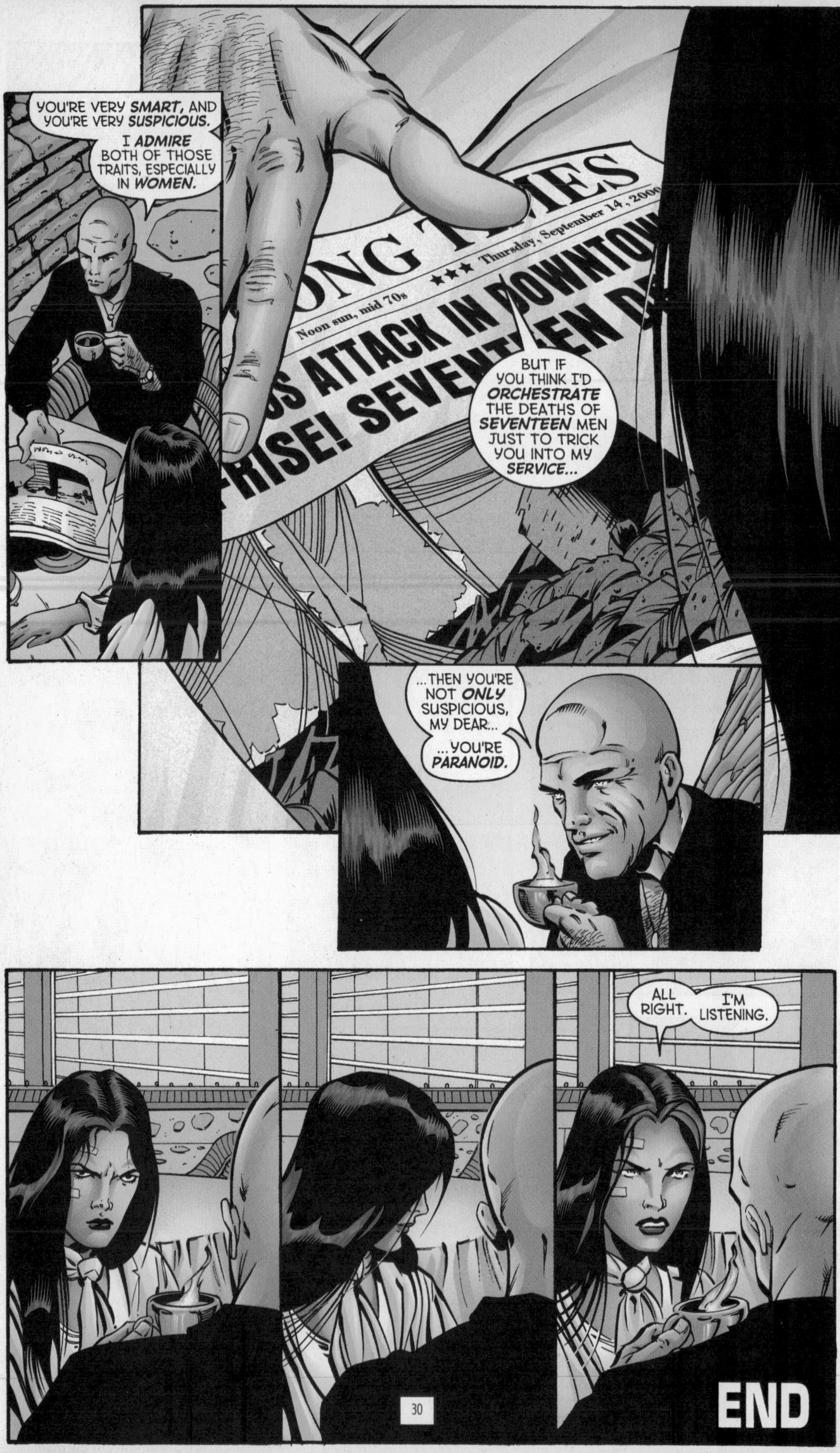
YOU'RE VERY SMART, AND YOU'RE VERY SUSPICIOUS.
I ADMIRE BOTH OF THOSE TRAITS, ESPECIALLY IN WOMEN.
Thursday, September 14, 2000
Noon sun, mid 70s
BUT IF YOU THINK I'D ORCHESTRATE THE DEATHS OF SEVENTEEN MEN JUST TO TRICK YOU INTO MY SERVICE...
...THEN YOU'RE NOT ONLY SUSPICIOUS, MY DEAR...
...YOU'RE PARANOID.
ALL RIGHT.
I'M LISTENING.
END

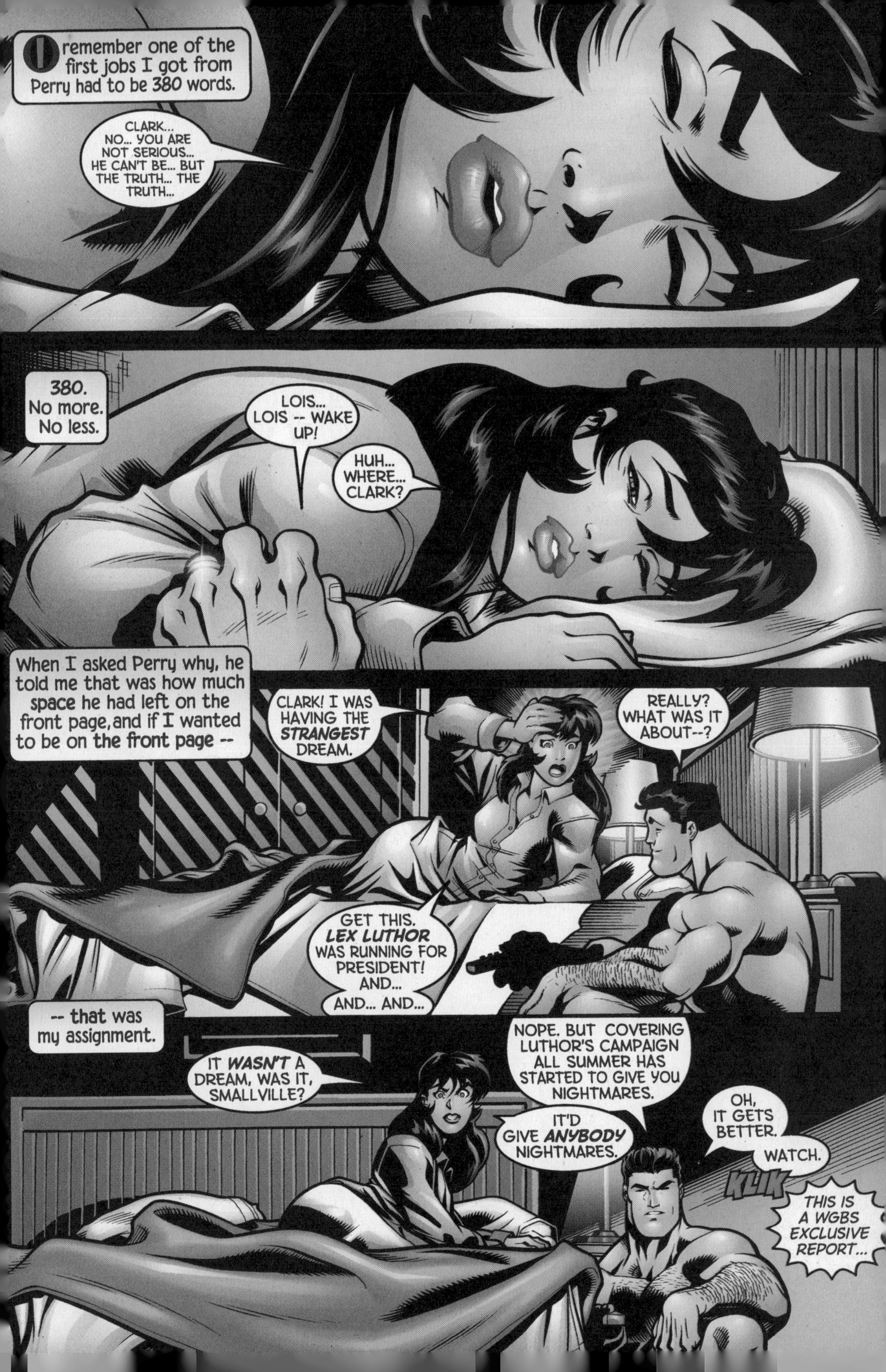
I remember one of the first jobs I got from Perry had to be 380 words.
CLARK... NO... YOU ARE NOT SERIOUS... HE CAN'T BE... BUT THE TRUTH... THE TRUTH...
380. No more. No less.
LOIS... LOIS -- WAKE UP!
HUH... WHERE... CLARK?
When I asked Perry why, he told me that was how much space he had left on the front page, and if I wanted to be on the front page --
CLARK! I WAS HAVING THE STRANGEST DREAM.
REALLY? WHAT WAS IT ABOUT--?
GET THIS. LEX LUTHOR WAS RUNNING FOR PRESIDENT! AND... AND... AND...
-- that was my assignment.
IT WASN'T A DREAM, WAS IT, SMALLVILLE?
NOPE. BUT COVERING LUTHOR'S CAMPAIGN ALL SUMMER HAS STARTED TO GIVE YOU NIGHTMARES.
IT'D GIVE ANYBODY NIGHTMARES.
OH, IT GETS BETTER.
WATCH.
KLIK
THIS IS A WGBS EXCLUSIVE REPORT...

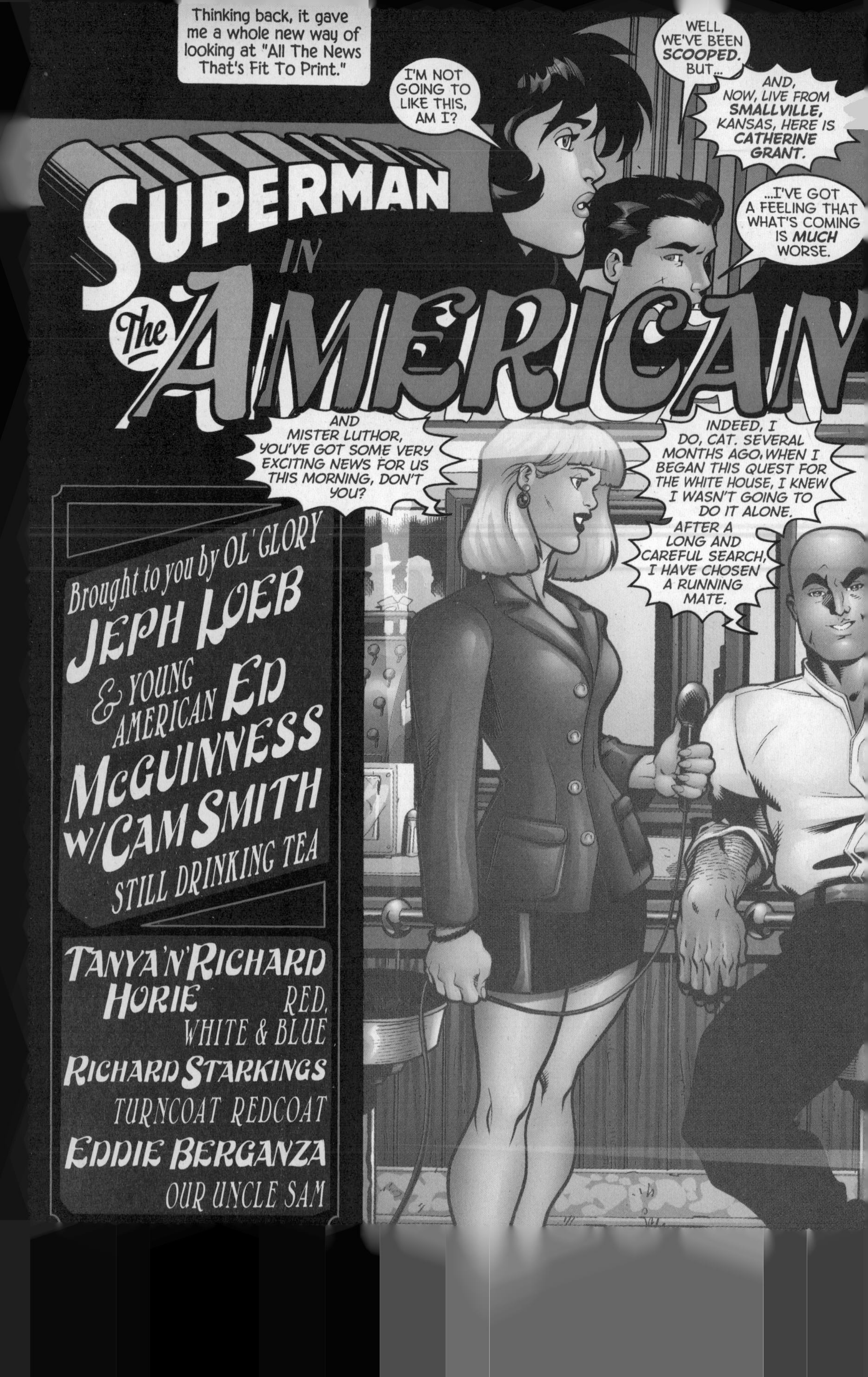
Thinking back, it gave me a whole new way of looking at "All The News That's Fit To Print."
I'M NOT GOING TO LIKE THIS, AM I?
WELL, WE'VE BEEN SCOOPED. BUT...
AND, NOW, LIVE FROM SMALLVILLE, KANSAS, HERE IS CATHERINE GRANT.
...I'VE GOT A FEELING THAT WHAT'S COMING IS MUCH WORSE.
SUPERMAN IN The AMERICAN
AND MISTER LUTHOR, YOU'VE GOT SOME VERY EXCITING NEWS FOR US THIS MORNING, DON'T YOU?
INDEED, I DO, CAT. SEVERAL MONTHS AGO, WHEN I BEGAN THIS QUEST FOR THE WHITE HOUSE, I KNEW I WASN'T GOING TO DO IT ALONE.
AFTER A LONG AND CAREFUL SEARCH, I HAVE CHOSEN A RUNNING MATE.
Brought to you by OL' GLORY
JEPH LOEB
& YOUNG AMERICAN ED McGUINNESS
w/CAM SMITH
STILL DRINKING TEA
TANYA 'N' RICHARD HORIE RED, WHITE & BLUE
RICHARD STARKINGS TURNCOAT REDCOAT
EDDIE BERGANZA OUR UNCLE SAM

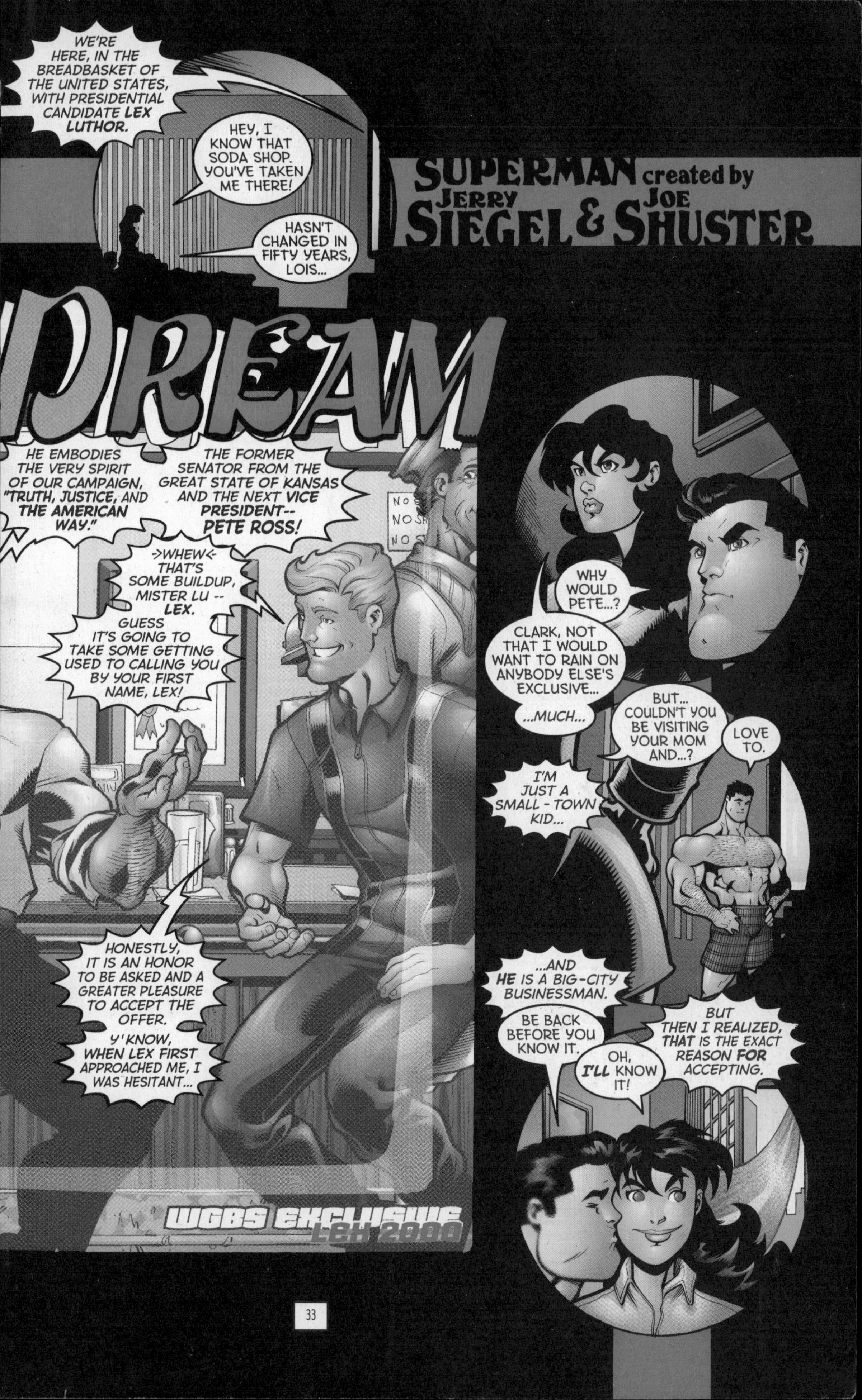
WE'RE HERE, IN THE BREADBASKET OF THE UNITED STATES, WITH PRESIDENTIAL CANDIDATE LEX LUTHOR.
HEY, I KNOW THAT SODA SHOP. YOU'VE TAKEN ME THERE!
HASN'T CHANGED IN FIFTY YEARS, LOIS...
SUPERMAN created by JERRY SIEGEL & JOE SHUSTER
DREAM
HE EMBODIES THE VERY SPIRIT OF OUR CAMPAIGN, "TRUTH, JUSTICE, AND THE AMERICAN WAY."
THE FORMER SENATOR FROM THE GREAT STATE OF KANSAS AND THE NEXT VICE PRESIDENT-- PETE ROSS!
->WHEW<- THAT'S SOME BUILDUP, MISTER LU -- LEX.
GUESS IT'S GOING TO TAKE SOME GETTING USED TO CALLING YOU BY YOUR FIRST NAME, LEX!
HONESTLY, IT IS AN HONOR TO BE ASKED AND A GREATER PLEASURE TO ACCEPT THE OFFER.
Y'KNOW, WHEN LEX FIRST APPROACHED ME, I WAS HESITANT...
WGBS EXCLUSIVE
LEX 2000
WHY WOULD PETE...?
CLARK, NOT THAT I WOULD WANT TO RAIN ON ANYBODY ELSE'S EXCLUSIVE...
...MUCH...
BUT... COULDN'T YOU BE VISITING YOUR MOM AND...?
LOVE TO.
I'M JUST A SMALL - TOWN KID...
...AND HE IS A BIG-CITY BUSINESSMAN.
BE BACK BEFORE YOU KNOW IT.
OH, I'LL KNOW IT!
BUT THEN I REALIZED, THAT IS THE EXACT REASON FOR ACCEPTING.

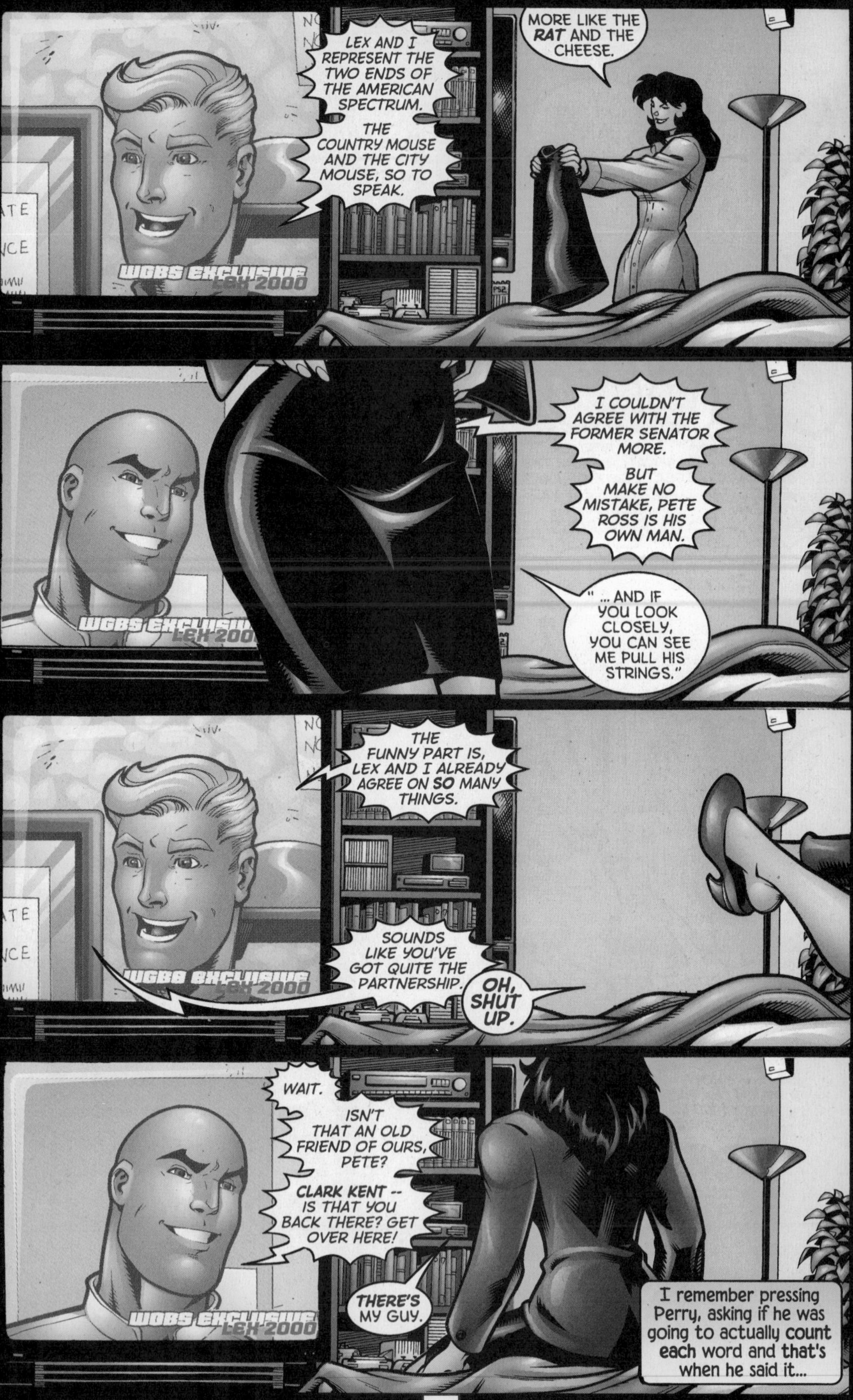
WGBS EXCLUSIVE
LEX 2000
LEX AND I REPRESENT THE TWO ENDS OF THE AMERICAN SPECTRUM.
THE COUNTRY MOUSE AND THE CITY MOUSE, SO TO SPEAK.
MORE LIKE THE RAT AND THE CHEESE.
WGBS EXCLUSIVE
LEX 2000
I COULDN'T AGREE WITH THE FORMER SENATOR MORE.
BUT MAKE NO MISTAKE, PETE ROSS IS HIS OWN MAN.
" ... AND IF YOU LOOK CLOSELY, YOU CAN SEE ME PULL HIS STRINGS."
THE FUNNY PART IS, LEX AND I ALREADY AGREE ON SO MANY THINGS.
WGBS EXCLUSIVE
LEX 2000
SOUNDS LIKE YOU'VE GOT QUITE THE PARTNERSHIP.
OH, SHUT UP.
WAIT.
ISN'T THAT AN OLD FRIEND OF OURS, PETE?
CLARK KENT -- IS THAT YOU BACK THERE? GET OVER HERE!
THERE'S MY GUY.
WGBS EXCLUSIVE
LEX 2000
I remember pressing Perry, asking if he was going to actually count each word and that's when he said it...

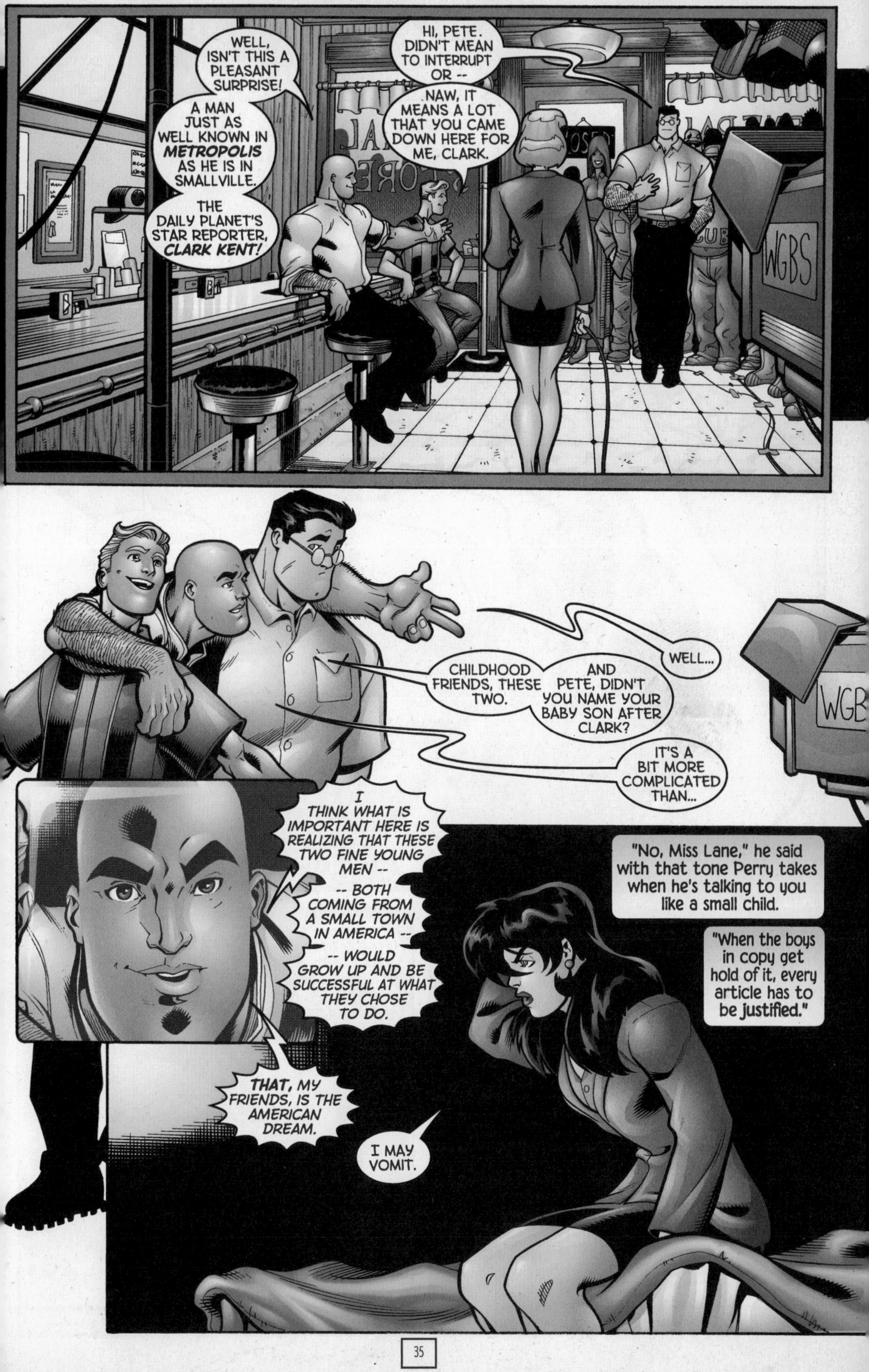
WELL, ISN'T THIS A PLEASANT SURPRISE!
A MAN JUST AS WELL KNOWN IN METROPOLIS AS HE IS IN SMALLVILLE.
THE DAILY PLANET'S STAR REPORTER, CLARK KENT!
HI, PETE. DIDN'T MEAN TO INTERRUPT OR --
NAW, IT MEANS A LOT THAT YOU CAME DOWN HERE FOR ME, CLARK.
WGBS
WELL...
CHILDHOOD FRIENDS, THESE TWO.
AND PETE, DIDN'T YOU NAME YOUR BABY SON AFTER CLARK?
IT'S A BIT MORE COMPLICATED THAN...
WGB
I THINK WHAT IS IMPORTANT HERE IS REALIZING THAT THESE TWO FINE YOUNG MEN --
-- BOTH COMING FROM A SMALL TOWN IN AMERICA --
-- WOULD GROW UP AND BE SUCCESSFUL AT WHAT THEY CHOSE TO DO.
THAT, MY FRIENDS, IS THE AMERICAN DREAM.
I MAY VOMIT.
"No, Miss Lane," he said with that tone Perry takes when he's talking to you like a small child.
"When the boys in copy get hold of it, every article has to be justified."

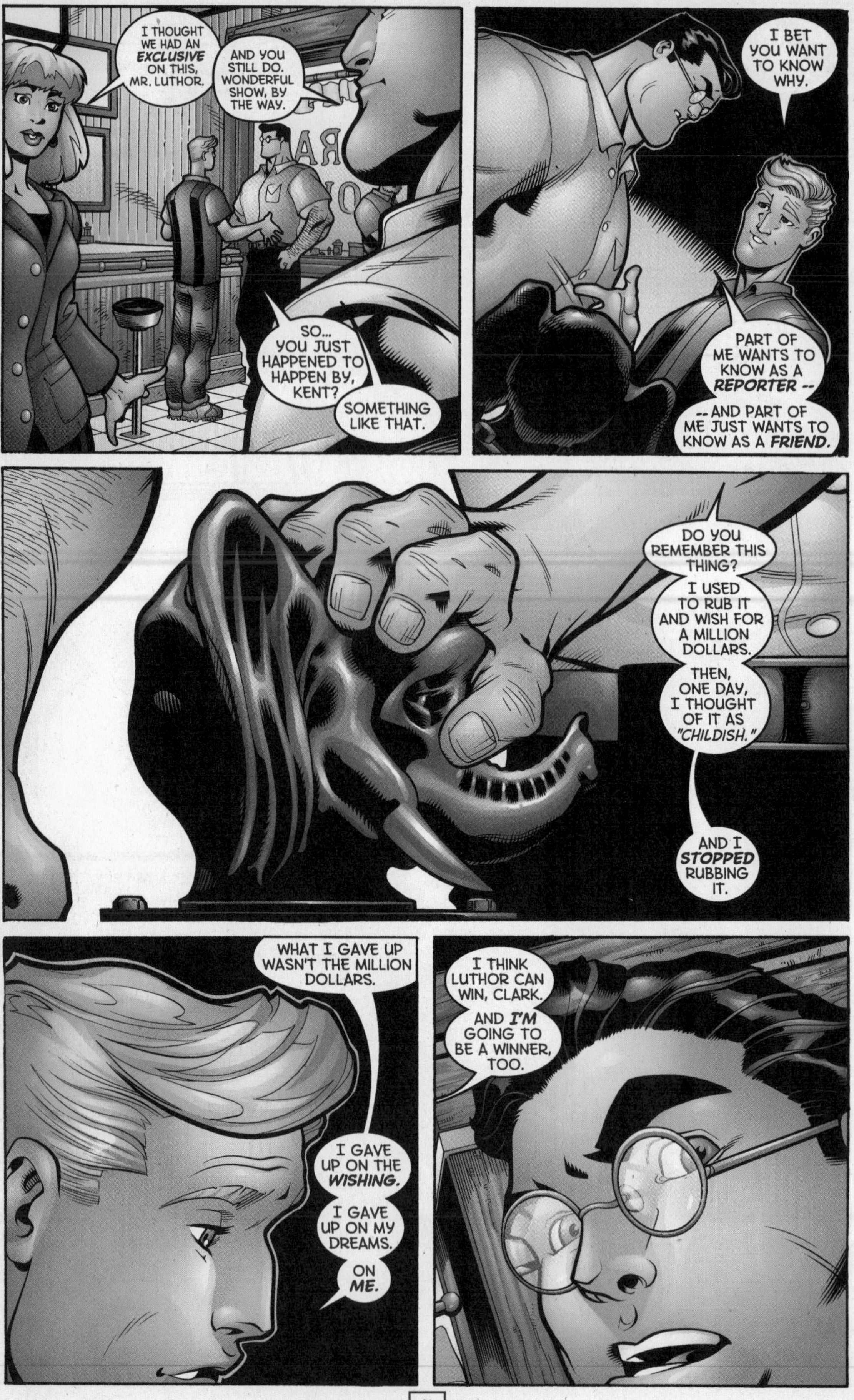
I THOUGHT WE HAD AN EXCLUSIVE ON THIS, MR. LUTHOR.
AND YOU STILL DO. WONDERFUL SHOW, BY THE WAY.
SO... YOU JUST HAPPENED TO HAPPEN BY, KENT?
SOMETHING LIKE THAT.
I BET YOU WANT TO KNOW WHY.
PART OF ME WANTS TO KNOW AS A REPORTER --
-- AND PART OF ME JUST WANTS TO KNOW AS A FRIEND.
DO YOU REMEMBER THIS THING?
I USED TO RUB IT AND WISH FOR A MILLION DOLLARS.
THEN, ONE DAY, I THOUGHT OF IT AS "CHILDISH."
AND I STOPPED RUBBING IT.
WHAT I GAVE UP WASN'T THE MILLION DOLLARS.
I GAVE UP ON THE WISHING.
I GAVE UP ON MY DREAMS.
ON ME.
I THINK LUTHOR CAN WIN, CLARK.
AND I'M GOING TO BE A WINNER, TOO.

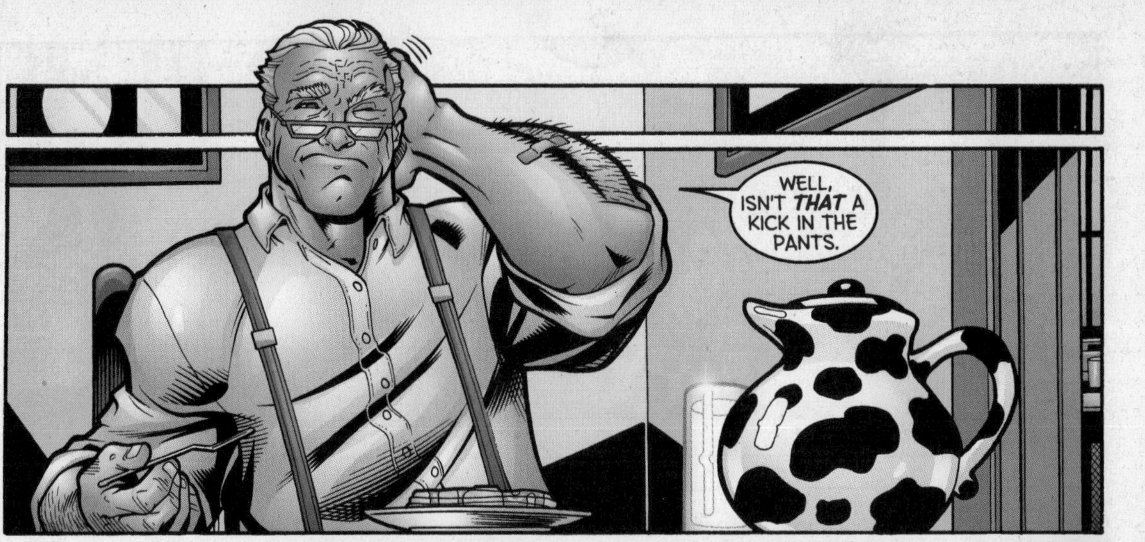
WELL, ISN'T *THAT* A KICK IN THE PANTS.

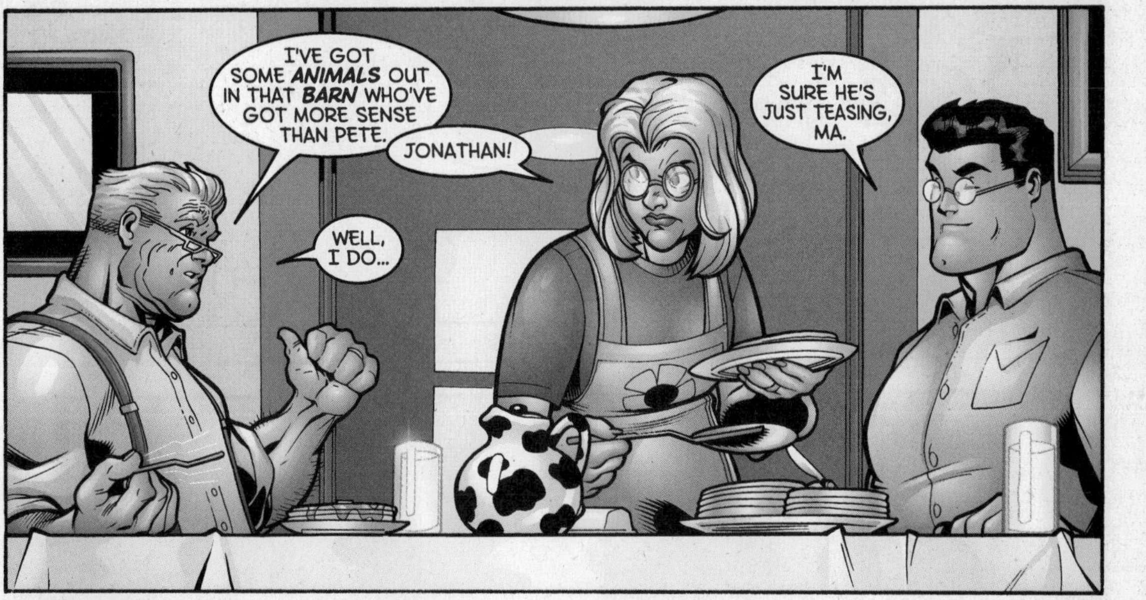
I'VE GOT SOME *ANIMALS* OUT IN THAT *BARN* WHO'VE GOT MORE SENSE THAN PETE.
JONATHAN!
I'M SURE HE'S JUST TEASING, MA.
WELL, I DO...

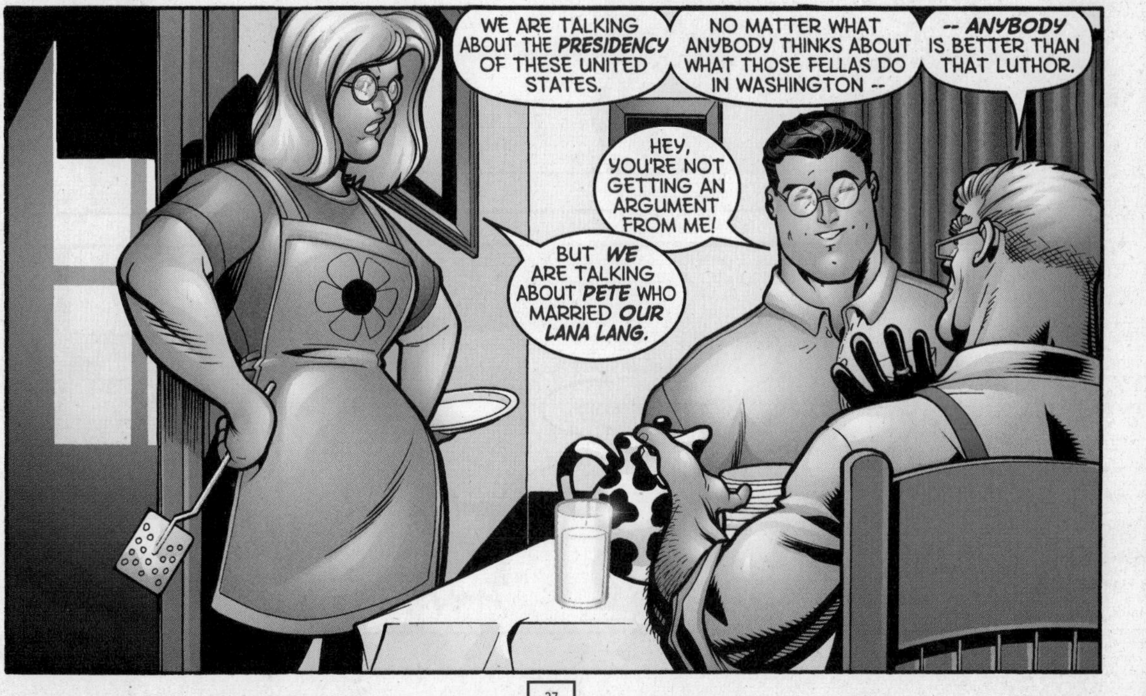
WE ARE TALKING ABOUT THE *PRESIDENCY* OF THESE UNITED STATES.
NO MATTER WHAT ANYBODY THINKS ABOUT WHAT THOSE FELLAS DO IN WASHINGTON --
-- *ANYBODY* IS BETTER THAN THAT LUTHOR.
HEY, YOU'RE NOT GETTING AN ARGUMENT FROM ME!
BUT *WE* ARE TALKING ABOUT *PETE* WHO MARRIED *OUR LANA LANG.*

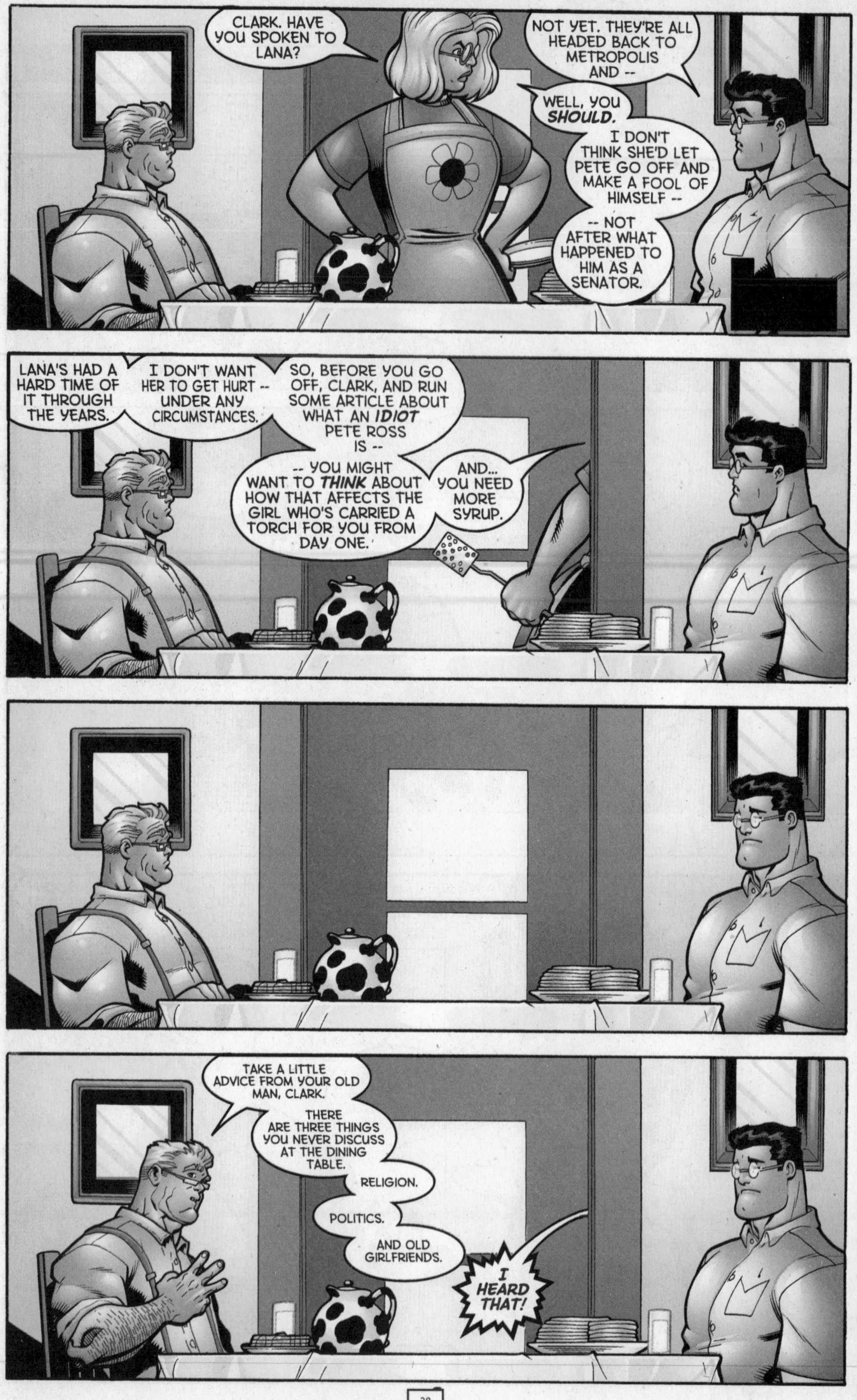
CLARK. HAVE YOU SPOKEN TO LANA?
NOT YET. THEY'RE ALL HEADED BACK TO METROPOLIS AND --
WELL, YOU SHOULD.
I DON'T THINK SHE'D LET PETE GO OFF AND MAKE A FOOL OF HIMSELF --
-- NOT AFTER WHAT HAPPENED TO HIM AS A SENATOR.
LANA'S HAD A HARD TIME OF IT THROUGH THE YEARS.
I DON'T WANT HER TO GET HURT -- UNDER ANY CIRCUMSTANCES.
SO, BEFORE YOU GO OFF, CLARK, AND RUN SOME ARTICLE ABOUT WHAT AN IDIOT PETE ROSS IS --
-- YOU MIGHT WANT TO THINK ABOUT HOW THAT AFFECTS THE GIRL WHO'S CARRIED A TORCH FOR YOU FROM DAY ONE.
AND... YOU NEED MORE SYRUP.
TAKE A LITTLE ADVICE FROM YOUR OLD MAN, CLARK.
THERE ARE THREE THINGS YOU NEVER DISCUSS AT THE DINING TABLE.
RELIGION.
POLITICS.
AND OLD GIRLFRIENDS.
I HEARD THAT!

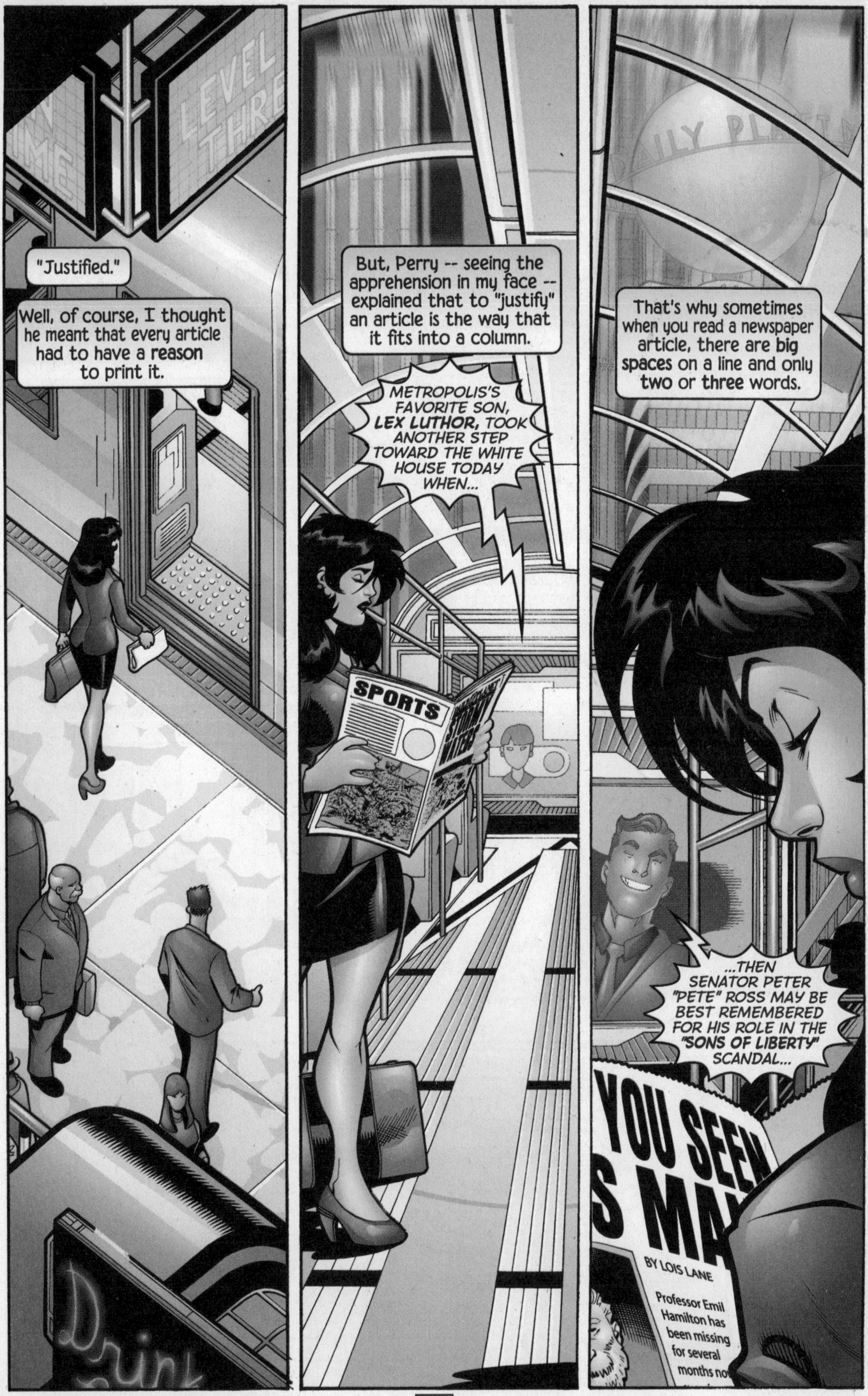
LEVEL
THRE
"Justified."
Well, of course, I thought he meant that every article had to have a reason to print it.
But, Perry -- seeing the apprehension in my face -- explained that to "justify" an article is the way that it fits into a column.
METROPOLIS'S FAVORITE SON, LEX LUTHOR, TOOK ANOTHER STEP TOWARD THE WHITE HOUSE TODAY WHEN...
SPORTS
STORMY WATERS
That's why sometimes when you read a newspaper article, there are big spaces on a line and only two or three words.
...THEN SENATOR PETER "PETE" ROSS MAY BE BEST REMEMBERED FOR HIS ROLE IN THE "SONS OF LIBERTY" SCANDAL...
YOU SEEN
S MA
BY LOIS LANE
Professor Emil Hamilton has been missing for several

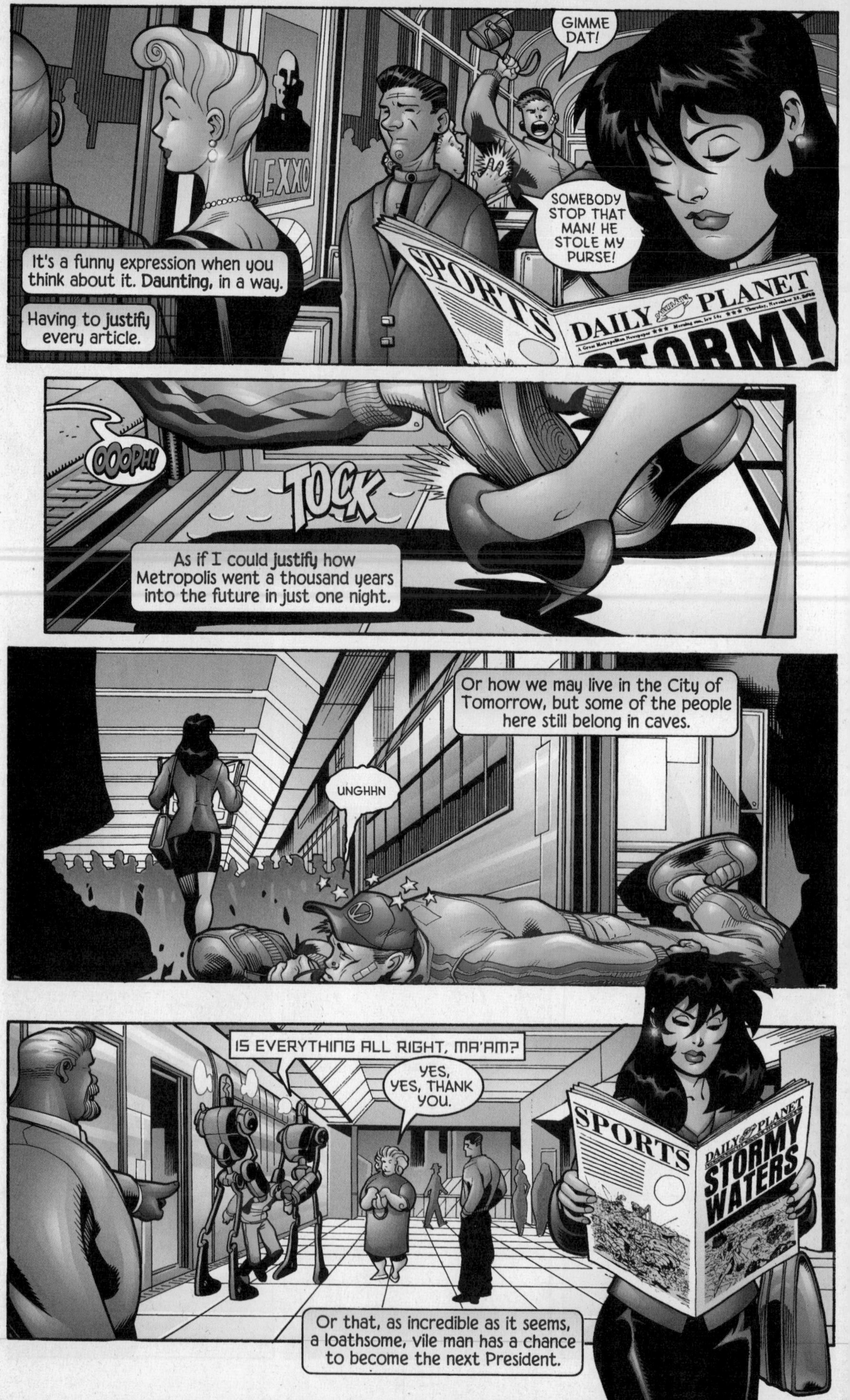
GIMME DAT!
It's a funny expression when you think about it. Daunting, in a way.
Having to justify every article.
SOMEBODY STOP THAT MAN! HE STOLE MY PURSE!
LEXXO
SPORTS
DAILY PLANET
STORMY
OOOPH!
TOCK
As if I could justify how Metropolis went a thousand years into the future in just one night.
Or how we may live in the City of Tomorrow, but some of the people here still belong in caves.
UNGHHN
IS EVERYTHING ALL RIGHT, MA'AM?
YES, YES, THANK YOU.
SPORTS
DAILY PLANET
STORMY WATERS
Or that, as incredible as it seems, a loathsome, vile man has a chance to become the next President.

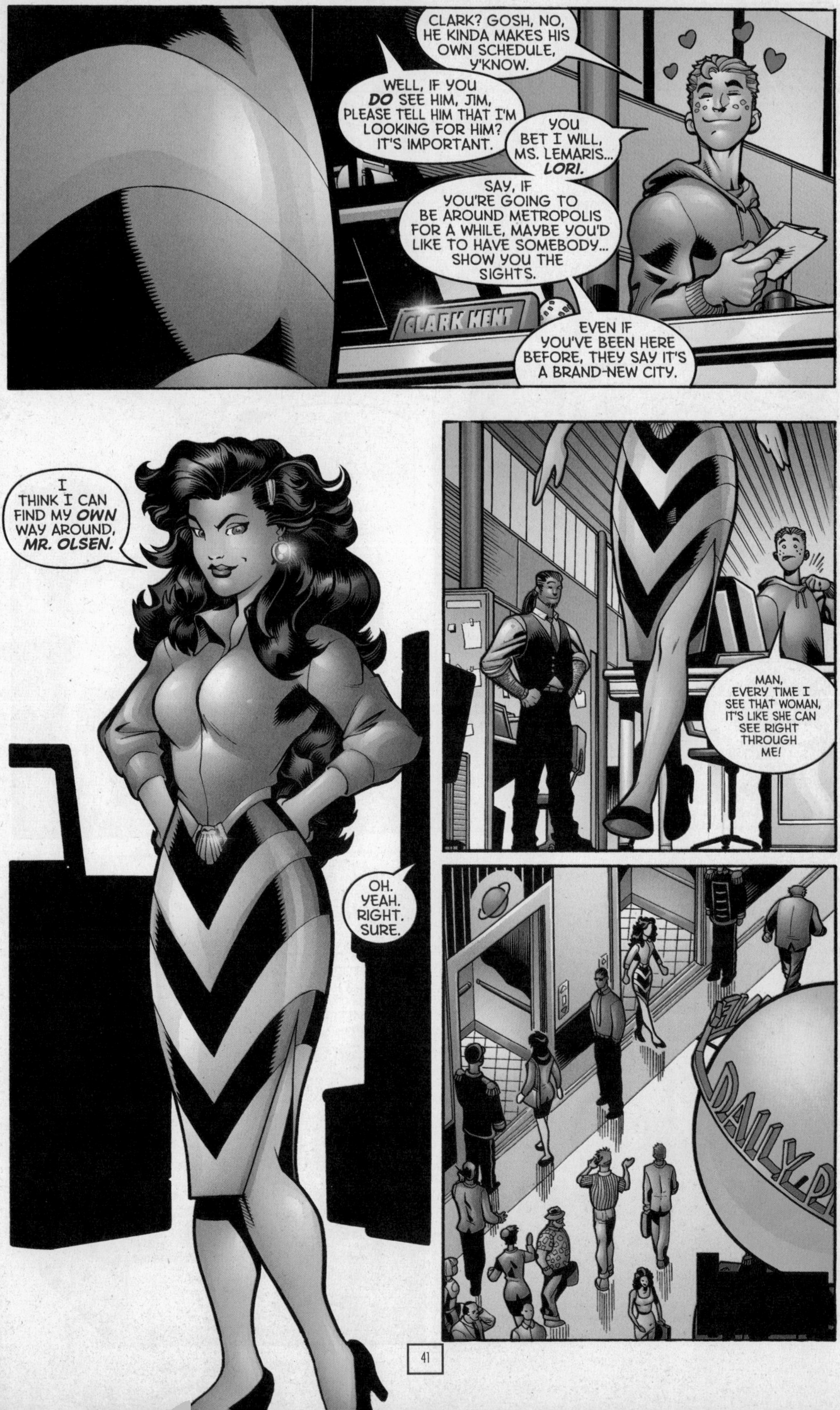
CLARK? GOSH, NO, HE KINDA MAKES HIS OWN SCHEDULE, Y'KNOW.
WELL, IF YOU DO SEE HIM, JIM, PLEASE TELL HIM THAT I'M LOOKING FOR HIM? IT'S IMPORTANT.
YOU BET I WILL, MS. LEMARIS... LORI.
SAY, IF YOU'RE GOING TO BE AROUND METROPOLIS FOR A WHILE, MAYBE YOU'D LIKE TO HAVE SOMEBODY... SHOW YOU THE SIGHTS.
CLARK KENT
EVEN IF YOU'VE BEEN HERE BEFORE, THEY SAY IT'S A BRAND-NEW CITY.
I THINK I CAN FIND MY OWN WAY AROUND, MR. OLSEN.
OH. YEAH. RIGHT. SURE.
MAN, EVERY TIME I SEE THAT WOMAN, IT'S LIKE SHE CAN SEE RIGHT THROUGH ME!
DAILY PL

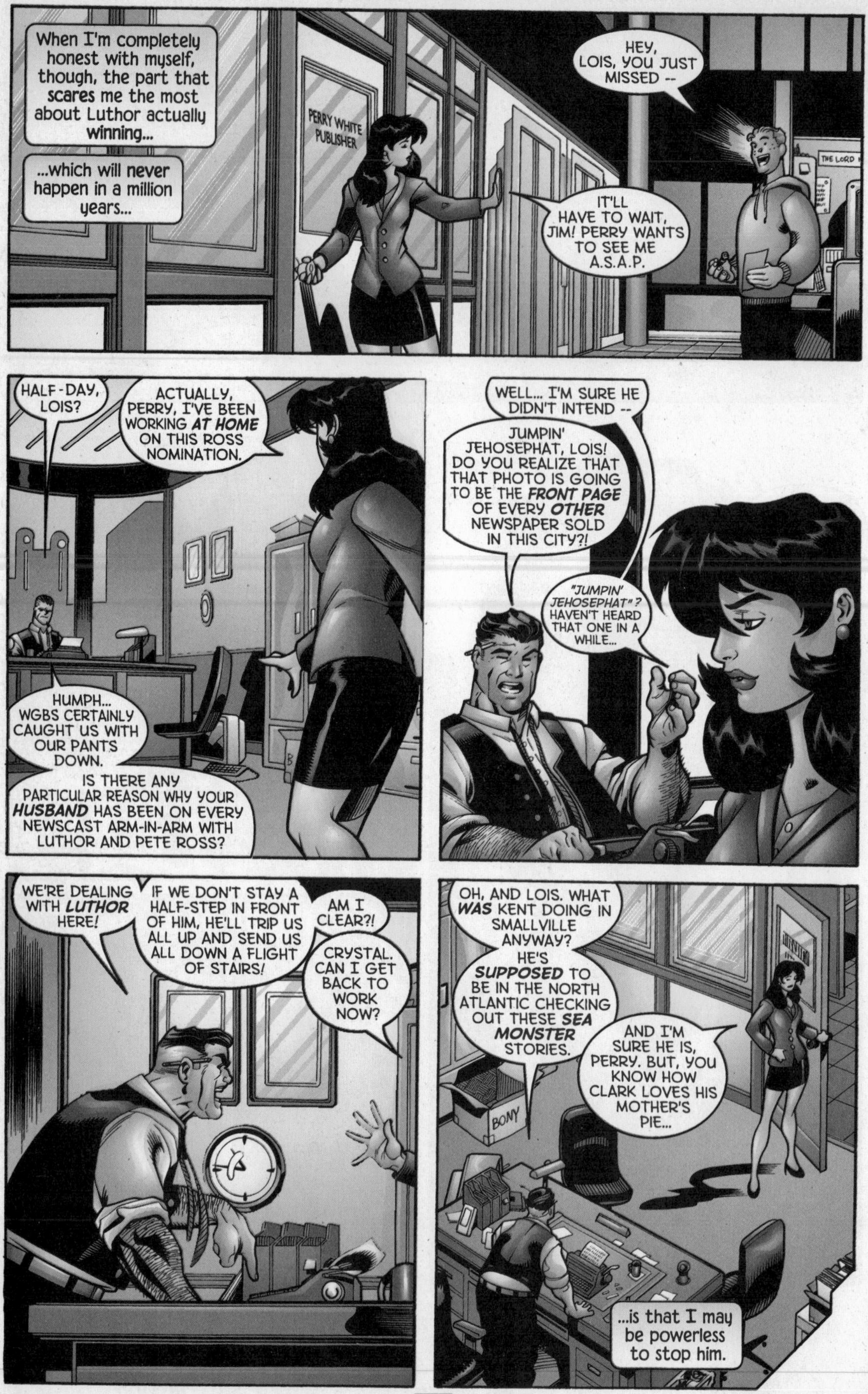
When I'm completely honest with myself, though, the part that scares me the most about Luthor actually winning...
...which will never happen in a million years...
PERRY WHITE PUBLISHER
HEY, LOIS, YOU JUST MISSED --
IT'LL HAVE TO WAIT, JIM! PERRY WANTS TO SEE ME A.S.A.P.
HALF-DAY, LOIS?
ACTUALLY, PERRY, I'VE BEEN WORKING AT HOME ON THIS ROSS NOMINATION.
HUMPH... WGBS CERTAINLY CAUGHT US WITH OUR PANTS DOWN.
IS THERE ANY PARTICULAR REASON WHY YOUR HUSBAND HAS BEEN ON EVERY NEWSCAST ARM-IN-ARM WITH LUTHOR AND PETE ROSS?
WELL... I'M SURE HE DIDN'T INTEND --
JUMPIN' JEHOSEPHAT, LOIS! DO YOU REALIZE THAT THAT PHOTO IS GOING TO BE THE FRONT PAGE OF EVERY OTHER NEWSPAPER SOLD IN THIS CITY?!
"JUMPIN' JEHOSEPHAT"? HAVEN'T HEARD THAT ONE IN A WHILE...
WE'RE DEALING WITH LUTHOR HERE!
IF WE DON'T STAY A HALF-STEP IN FRONT OF HIM, HE'LL TRIP US ALL UP AND SEND US ALL DOWN A FLIGHT OF STAIRS!
AM I CLEAR?!
CRYSTAL. CAN I GET BACK TO WORK NOW?
OH, AND LOIS. WHAT WAS KENT DOING IN SMALLVILLE ANYWAY?
HE'S SUPPOSED TO BE IN THE NORTH ATLANTIC CHECKING OUT THESE SEA MONSTER STORIES.
AND I'M SURE HE IS, PERRY. BUT, YOU KNOW HOW CLARK LOVES HIS MOTHER'S PIE...
BONY
...is that I may be powerless to stop him.

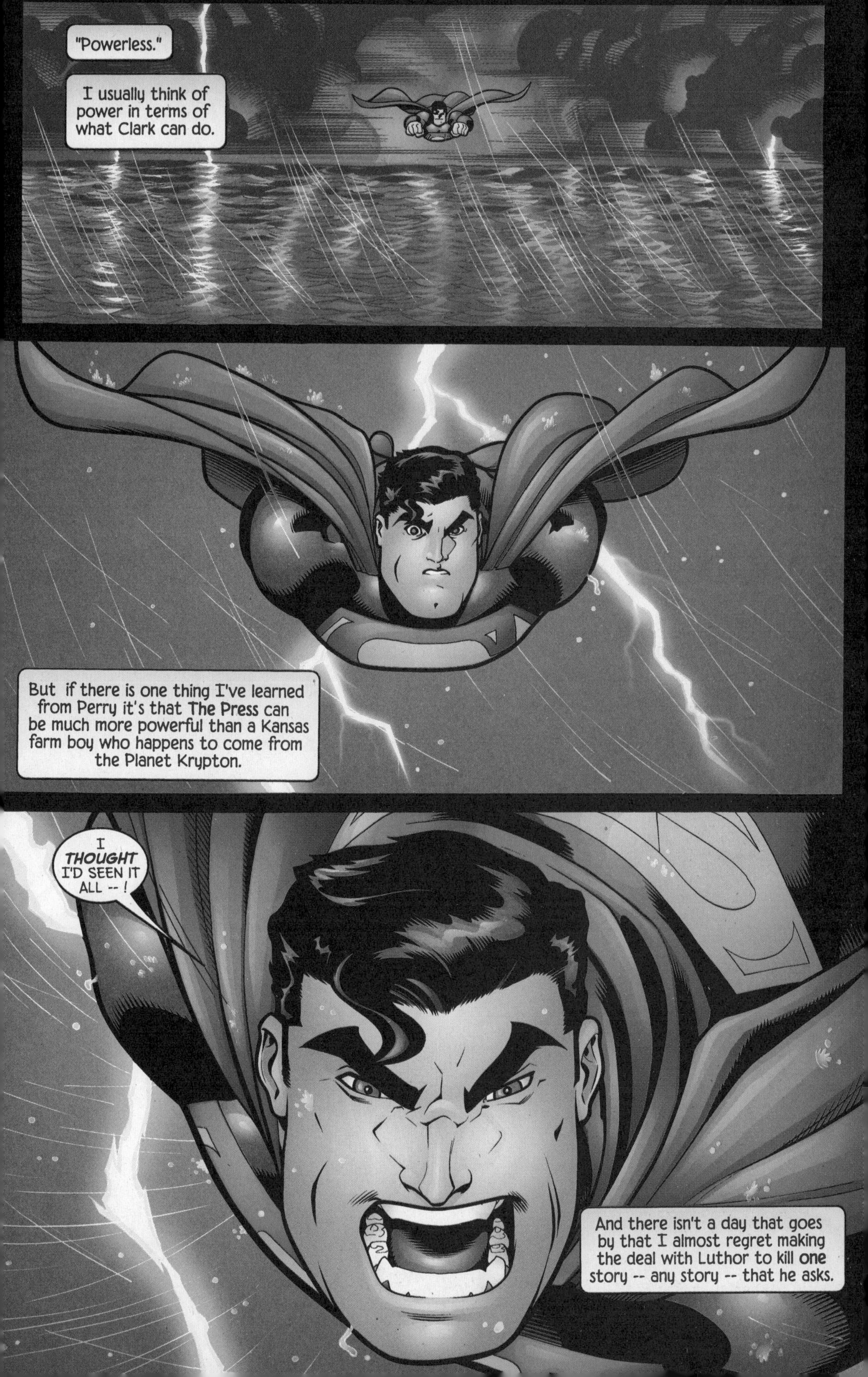
"Powerless."
I usually think of power in terms of what Clark can do.
But if there is one thing I've learned from Perry it's that The Press can be much more powerful than a Kansas farm boy who happens to come from the Planet Krypton.
I THOUGHT I'D SEEN IT ALL -- !
And there isn't a day that goes by that I almost regret making the deal with Luthor to kill one story -- any story -- that he asks.

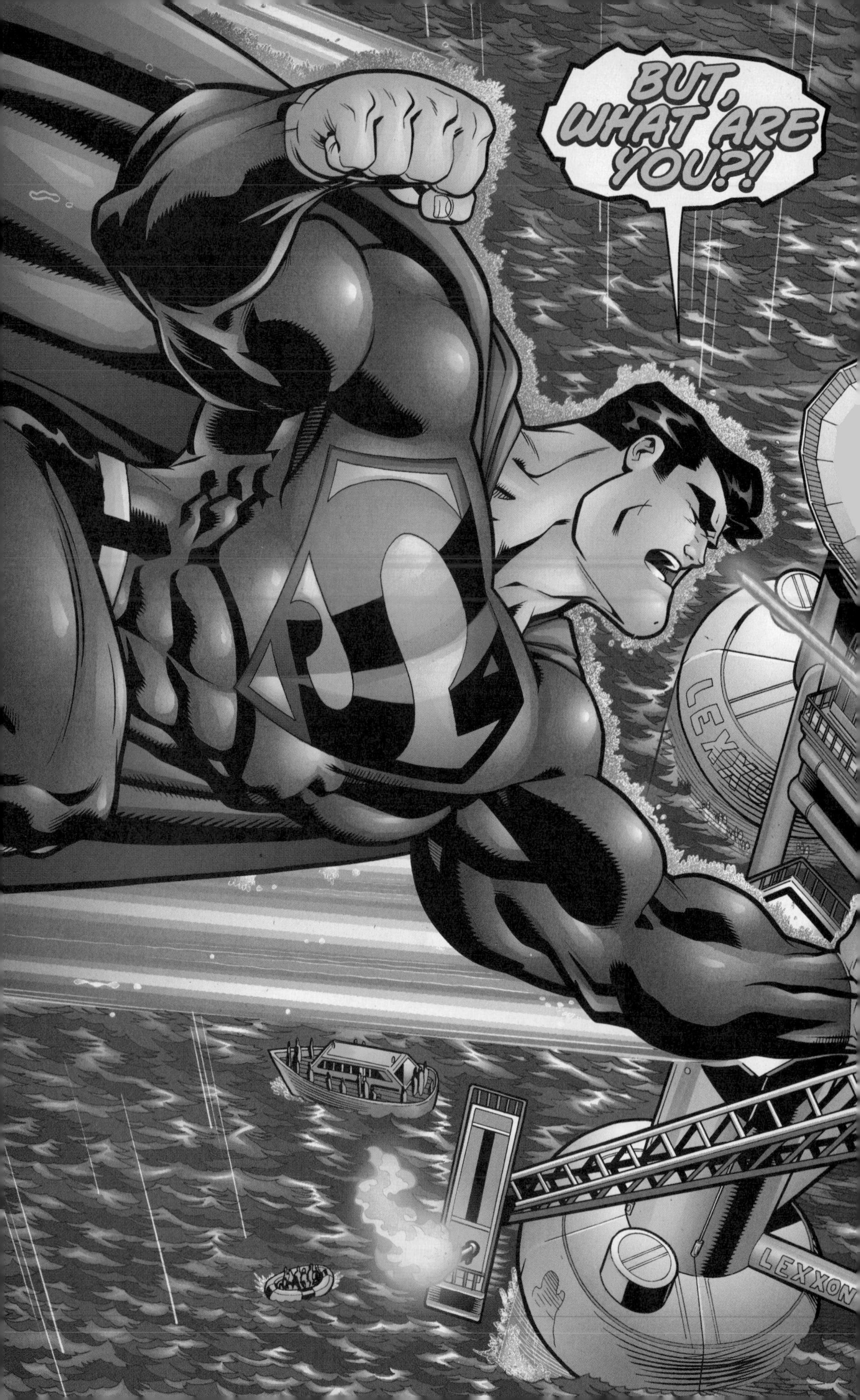
BUT, WHAT ARE YOU?!
LEXXON
LEXXON

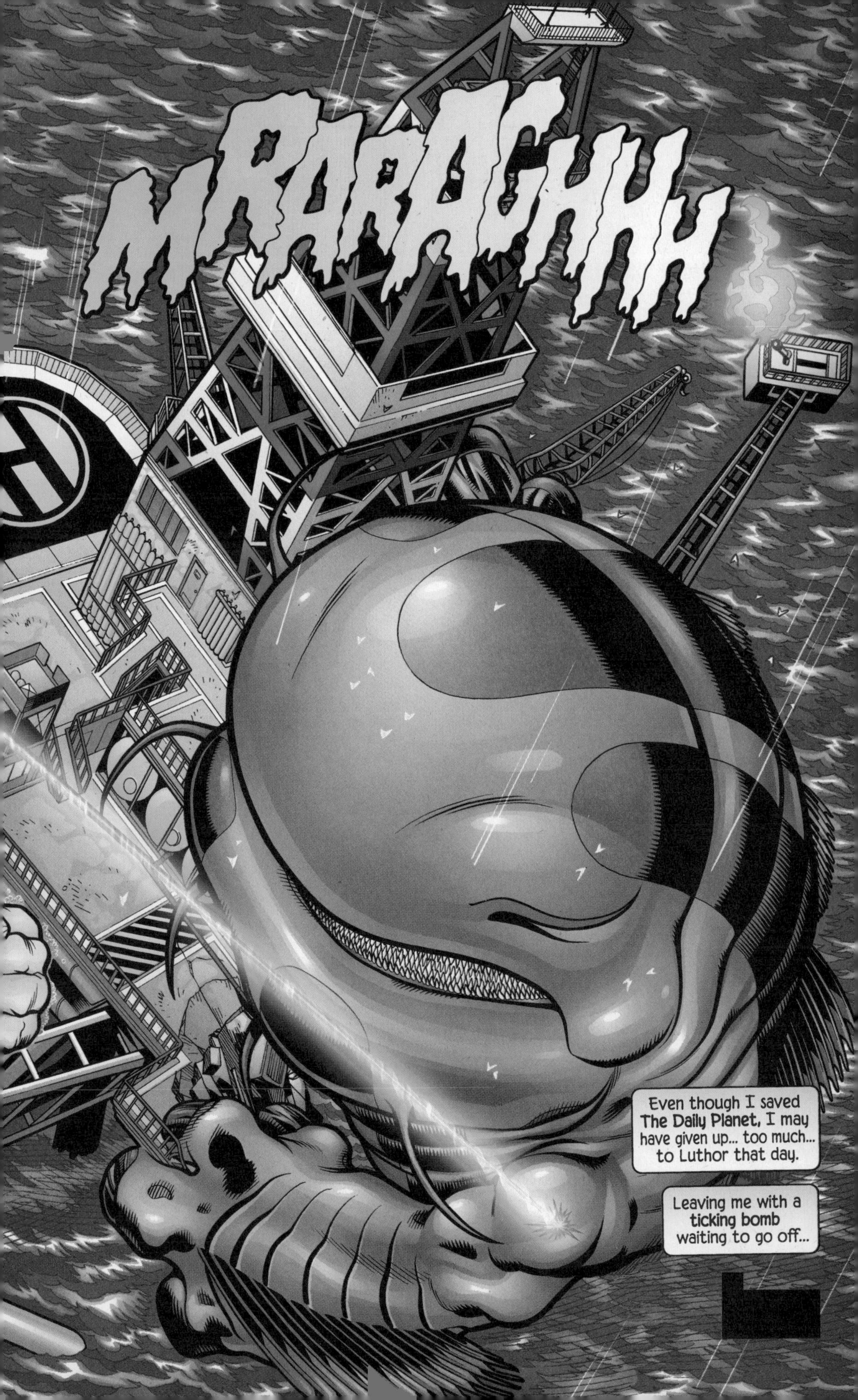
MRRRAGHHH
Even though I saved The Daily Planet, I may have given up... too much... to Luthor that day.
Leaving me with a ticking bomb waiting to go off...

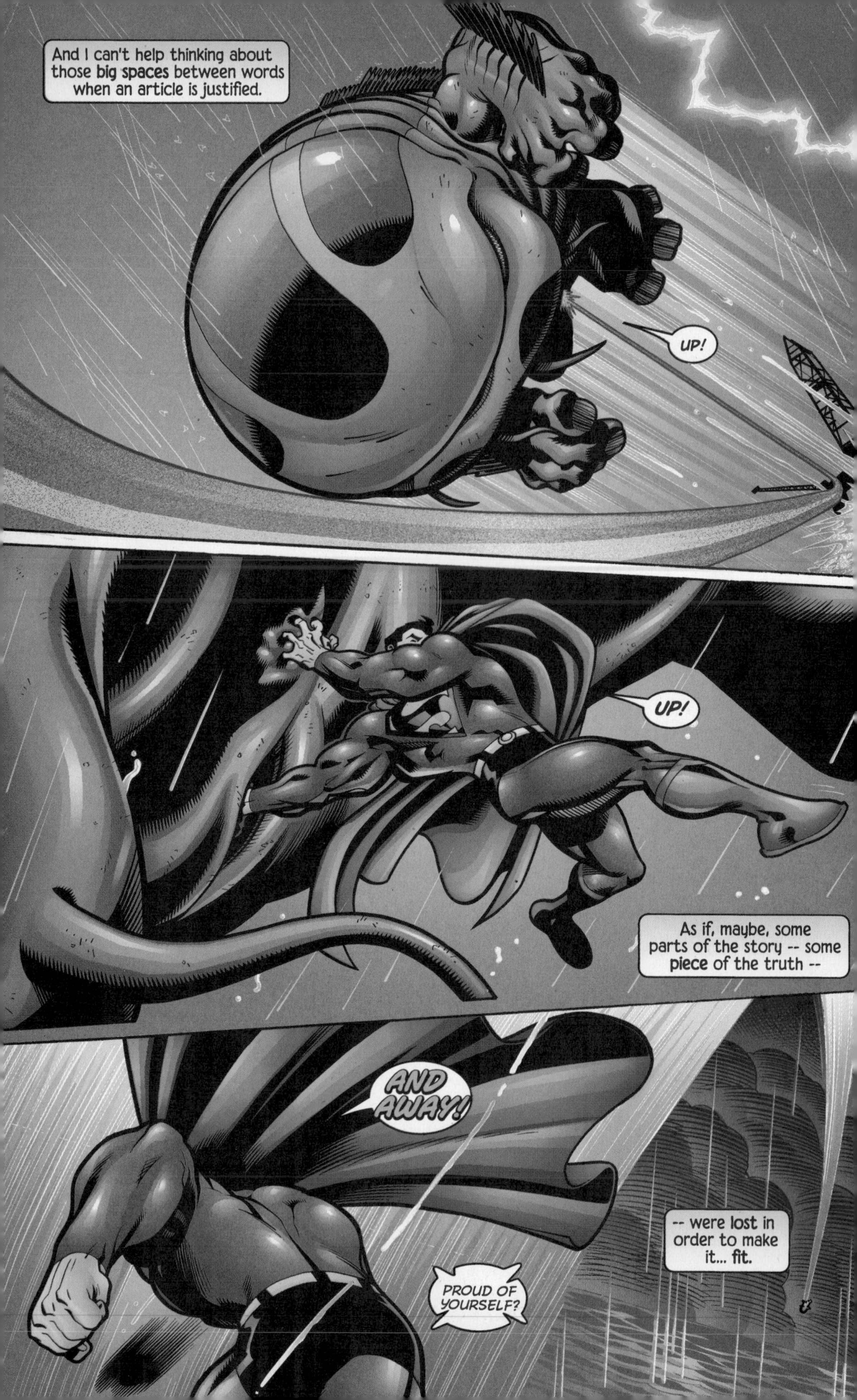
And I can't help thinking about those big spaces between words when an article is justified.
UP!
UP!
As if, maybe, some parts of the story -- some piece of the truth --
AND AWAY!
-- were lost in order to make it... fit.
PROUD OF YOURSELF?

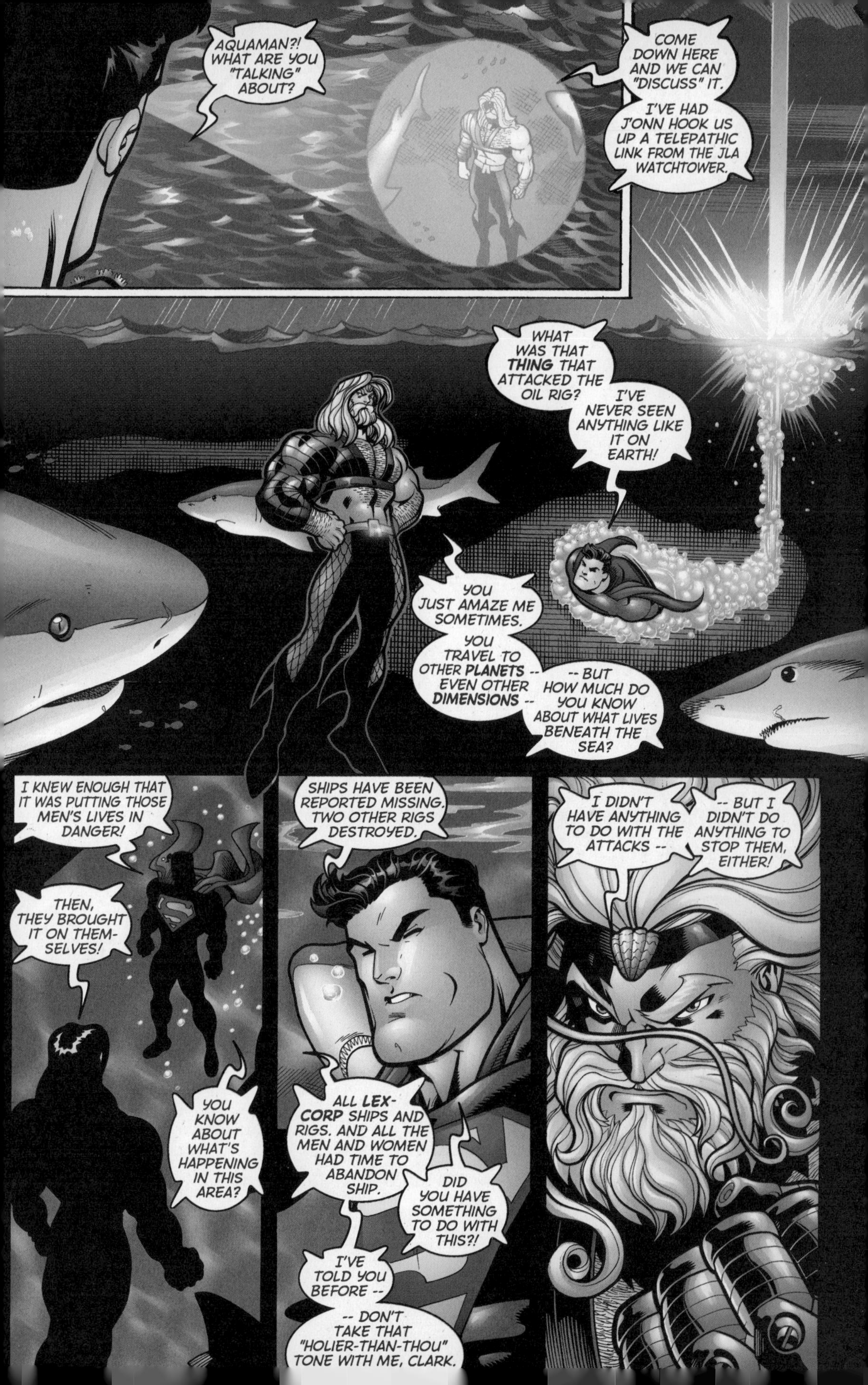

AQUAMAN?! WHAT ARE YOU "TALKING" ABOUT?
COME DOWN HERE AND WE CAN "DISCUSS" IT.
I'VE HAD J'ONN HOOK US UP A TELEPATHIC LINK FROM THE JLA WATCHTOWER.
WHAT WAS THAT THING THAT ATTACKED THE OIL RIG?
I'VE NEVER SEEN ANYTHING LIKE IT ON EARTH!
YOU JUST AMAZE ME SOMETIMES.
YOU TRAVEL TO OTHER PLANETS -- EVEN OTHER DIMENSIONS --
-- BUT HOW MUCH DO YOU KNOW ABOUT WHAT LIVES BENEATH THE SEA?
I KNEW ENOUGH THAT IT WAS PUTTING THOSE MEN'S LIVES IN DANGER!
THEN, THEY BROUGHT IT ON THEMSELVES!
YOU KNOW ABOUT WHAT'S HAPPENING IN THIS AREA?
SHIPS HAVE BEEN REPORTED MISSING. TWO OTHER RIGS DESTROYED.
ALL LEXCORP SHIPS AND RIGS. AND ALL THE MEN AND WOMEN HAD TIME TO ABANDON SHIP.
DID YOU HAVE SOMETHING TO DO WITH THIS?!
I'VE TOLD YOU BEFORE --
-- DON'T TAKE THAT "HOLIER-THAN-THOU" TONE WITH ME, CLARK.
I DIDN'T HAVE ANYTHING TO DO WITH THE ATTACKS --
-- BUT I DIDN'T DO ANYTHING TO STOP THEM, EITHER!

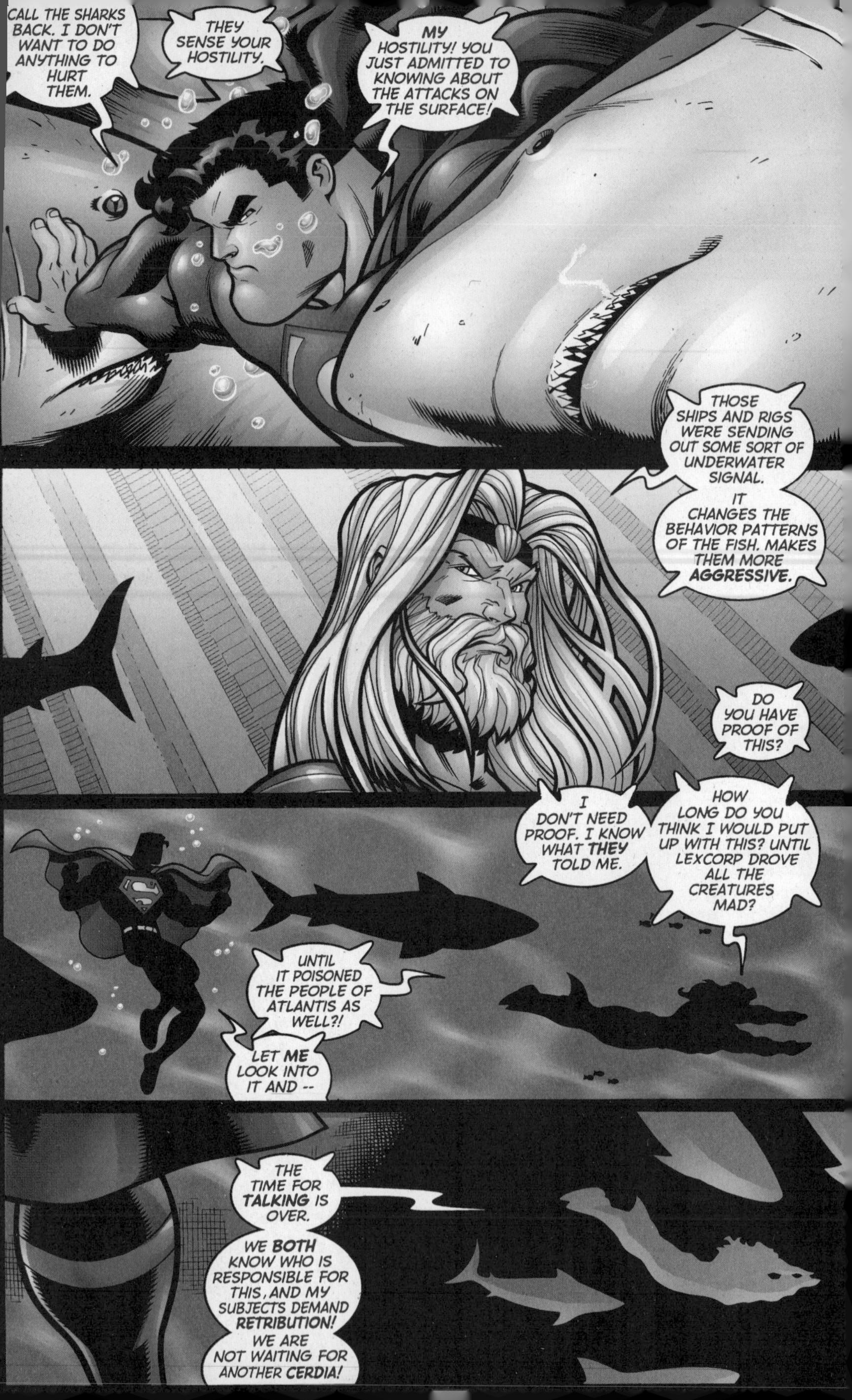

CALL THE SHARKS BACK. I DON'T WANT TO DO ANYTHING TO HURT THEM.
THEY SENSE YOUR HOSTILITY.
MY HOSTILITY! YOU JUST ADMITTED TO KNOWING ABOUT THE ATTACKS ON THE SURFACE!
THOSE SHIPS AND RIGS WERE SENDING OUT SOME SORT OF UNDERWATER SIGNAL.
IT CHANGES THE BEHAVIOR PATTERNS OF THE FISH. MAKES THEM MORE AGGRESSIVE.
DO YOU HAVE PROOF OF THIS?
I DON'T NEED PROOF. I KNOW WHAT THEY TOLD ME.
HOW LONG DO YOU THINK I WOULD PUT UP WITH THIS? UNTIL LEXCORP DROVE ALL THE CREATURES MAD?
UNTIL IT POISONED THE PEOPLE OF ATLANTIS AS WELL?!
LET ME LOOK INTO IT AND --
THE TIME FOR TALKING IS OVER.
WE BOTH KNOW WHO IS RESPONSIBLE FOR THIS, AND MY SUBJECTS DEMAND RETRIBUTION!
WE ARE NOT WAITING FOR ANOTHER CERDIA!

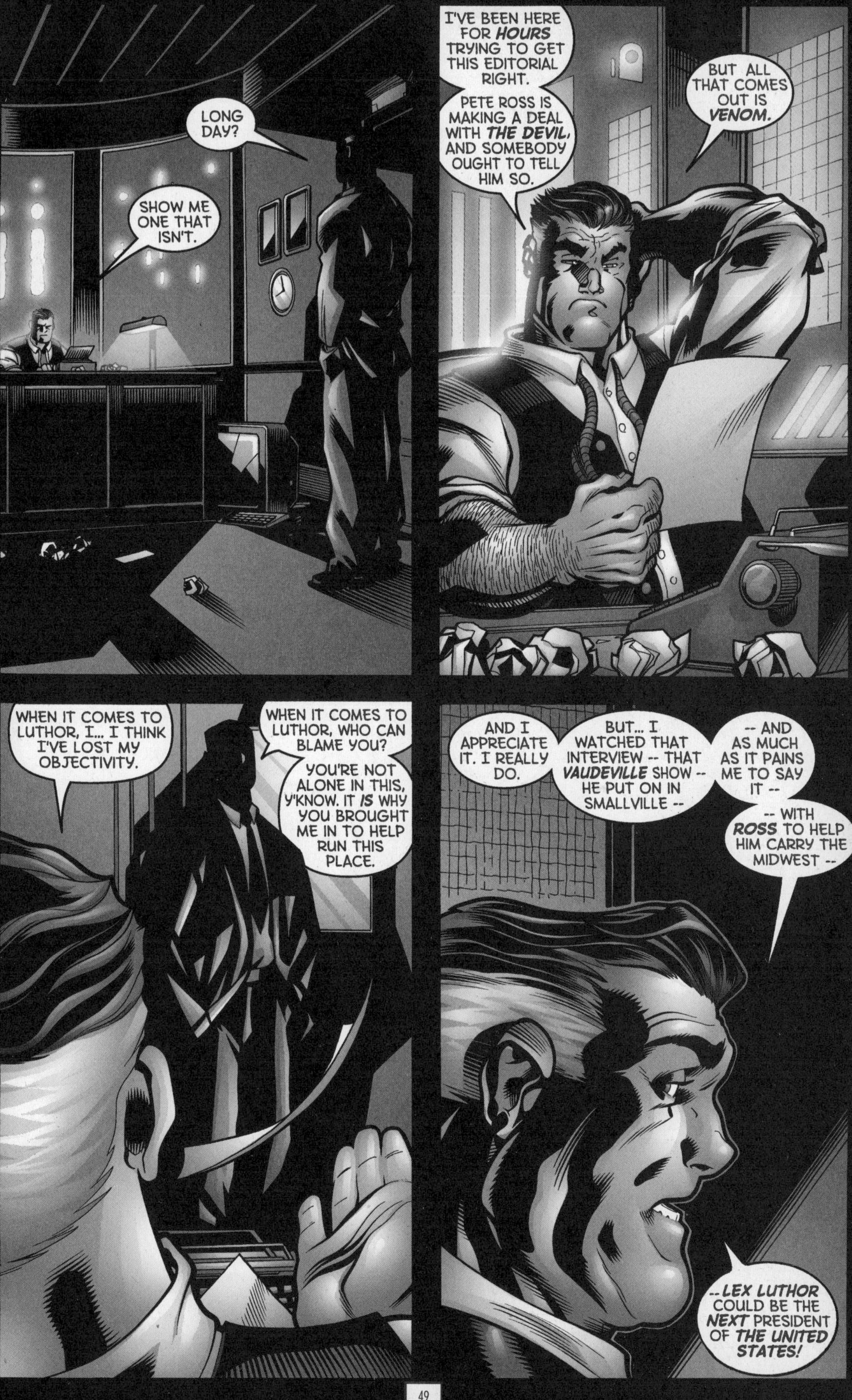
LONG DAY?
SHOW ME ONE THAT ISN'T.
I'VE BEEN HERE FOR HOURS TRYING TO GET THIS EDITORIAL RIGHT.
PETE ROSS IS MAKING A DEAL WITH THE DEVIL, AND SOMEBODY OUGHT TO TELL HIM SO.
BUT ALL THAT COMES OUT IS VENOM.
WHEN IT COMES TO LUTHOR, I... I THINK I'VE LOST MY OBJECTIVITY.
WHEN IT COMES TO LUTHOR, WHO CAN BLAME YOU?
YOU'RE NOT ALONE IN THIS, Y'KNOW. IT IS WHY YOU BROUGHT ME IN TO HELP RUN THIS PLACE.
AND I APPRECIATE IT. I REALLY DO.
BUT... I WATCHED THAT INTERVIEW -- THAT VAUDEVILLE SHOW -- HE PUT ON IN SMALLVILLE --
-- AND AS MUCH AS IT PAINS ME TO SAY IT --
-- WITH ROSS TO HELP HIM CARRY THE MIDWEST --
-- LEX LUTHOR COULD BE THE NEXT PRESIDENT OF THE UNITED STATES!

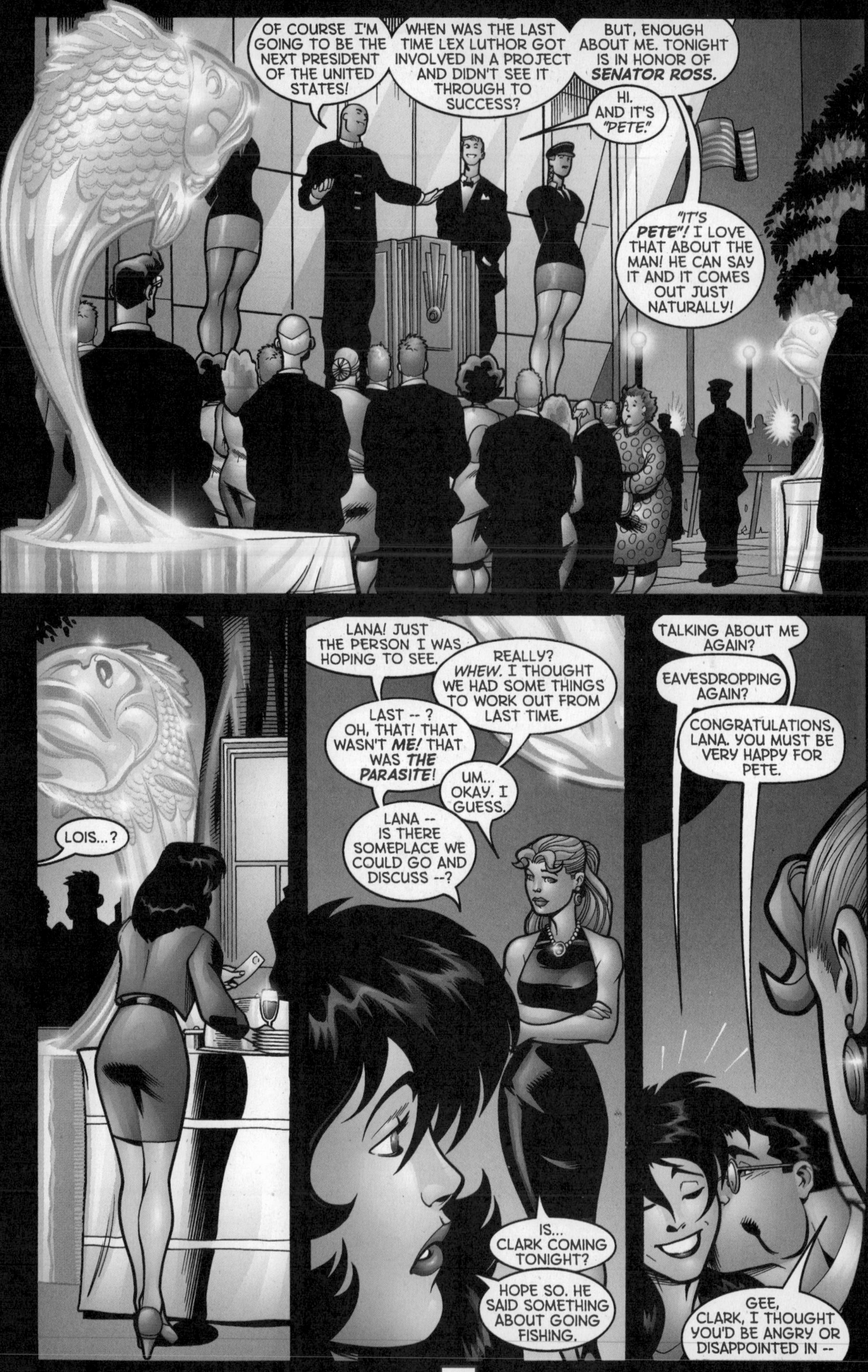
OF COURSE I'M GOING TO BE THE NEXT PRESIDENT OF THE UNITED STATES!
WHEN WAS THE LAST TIME LEX LUTHOR GOT INVOLVED IN A PROJECT AND DIDN'T SEE IT THROUGH TO SUCCESS?
BUT, ENOUGH ABOUT ME. TONIGHT IS IN HONOR OF SENATOR ROSS.
HI. AND IT'S "PETE."
"IT'S PETE"! I LOVE THAT ABOUT THE MAN! HE CAN SAY IT AND IT COMES OUT JUST NATURALLY!
LOIS...?
LANA! JUST THE PERSON I WAS HOPING TO SEE.
REALLY? WHEW. I THOUGHT WE HAD SOME THINGS TO WORK OUT FROM LAST TIME.
LAST -- ? OH, THAT! THAT WASN'T ME! THAT WAS THE PARASITE!
UM... OKAY. I GUESS.
LANA -- IS THERE SOMEPLACE WE COULD GO AND DISCUSS --?
IS... CLARK COMING TONIGHT?
HOPE SO. HE SAID SOMETHING ABOUT GOING FISHING.
TALKING ABOUT ME AGAIN?
EAVESDROPPING AGAIN?
CONGRATULATIONS, LANA. YOU MUST BE VERY HAPPY FOR PETE.
GEE, CLARK, I THOUGHT YOU'D BE ANGRY OR DISAPPOINTED IN --

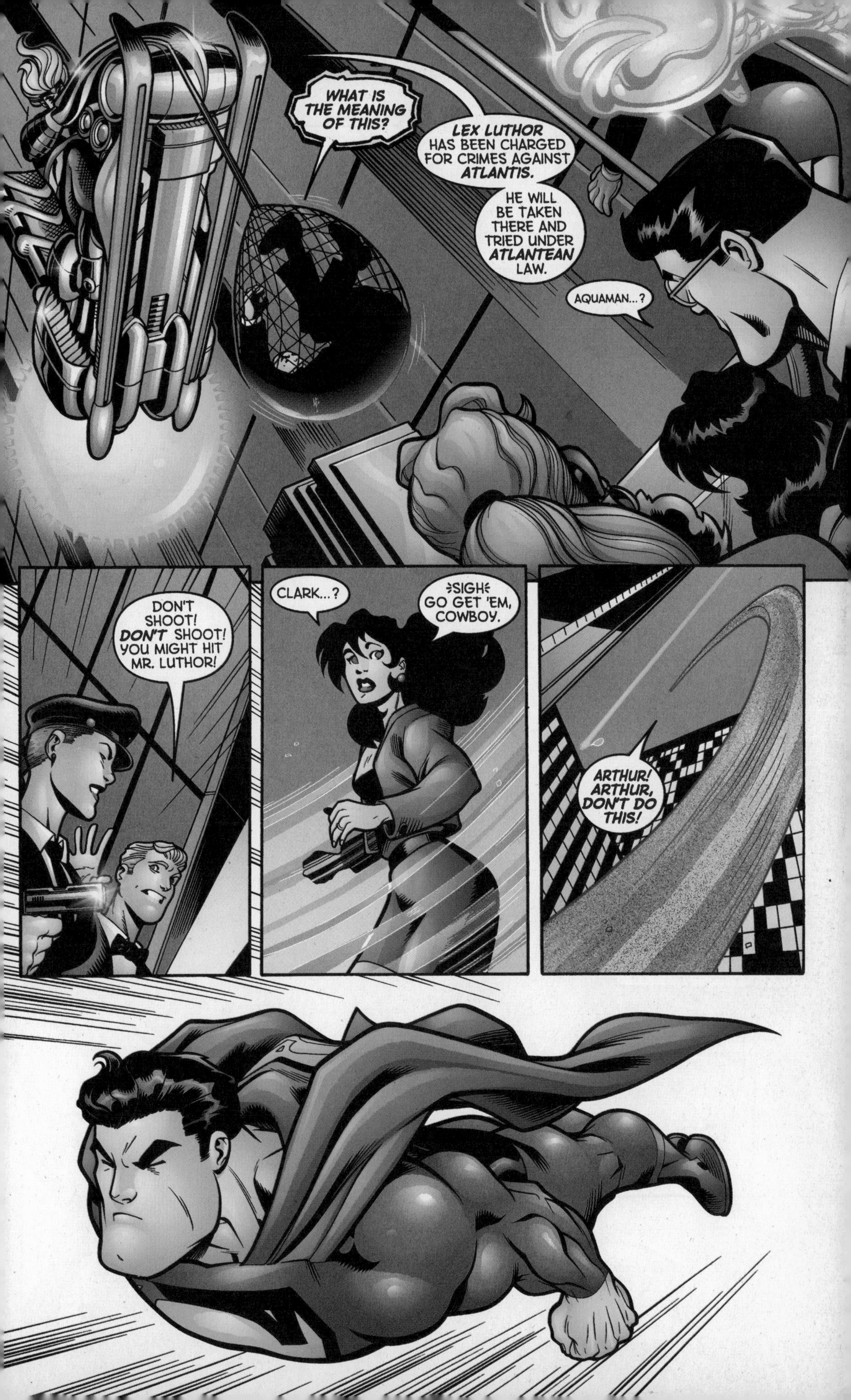
WHAT IS THE MEANING OF THIS?
LEX LUTHOR HAS BEEN CHARGED FOR CRIMES AGAINST ATLANTIS.
HE WILL BE TAKEN THERE AND TRIED UNDER ATLANTEAN LAW.
AQUAMAN...?
DON'T SHOOT! DON'T SHOOT! YOU MIGHT HIT MR. LUTHOR!
CLARK...?
SIGH
GO GET 'EM, COWBOY.
ARTHUR! ARTHUR, DON'T DO THIS!

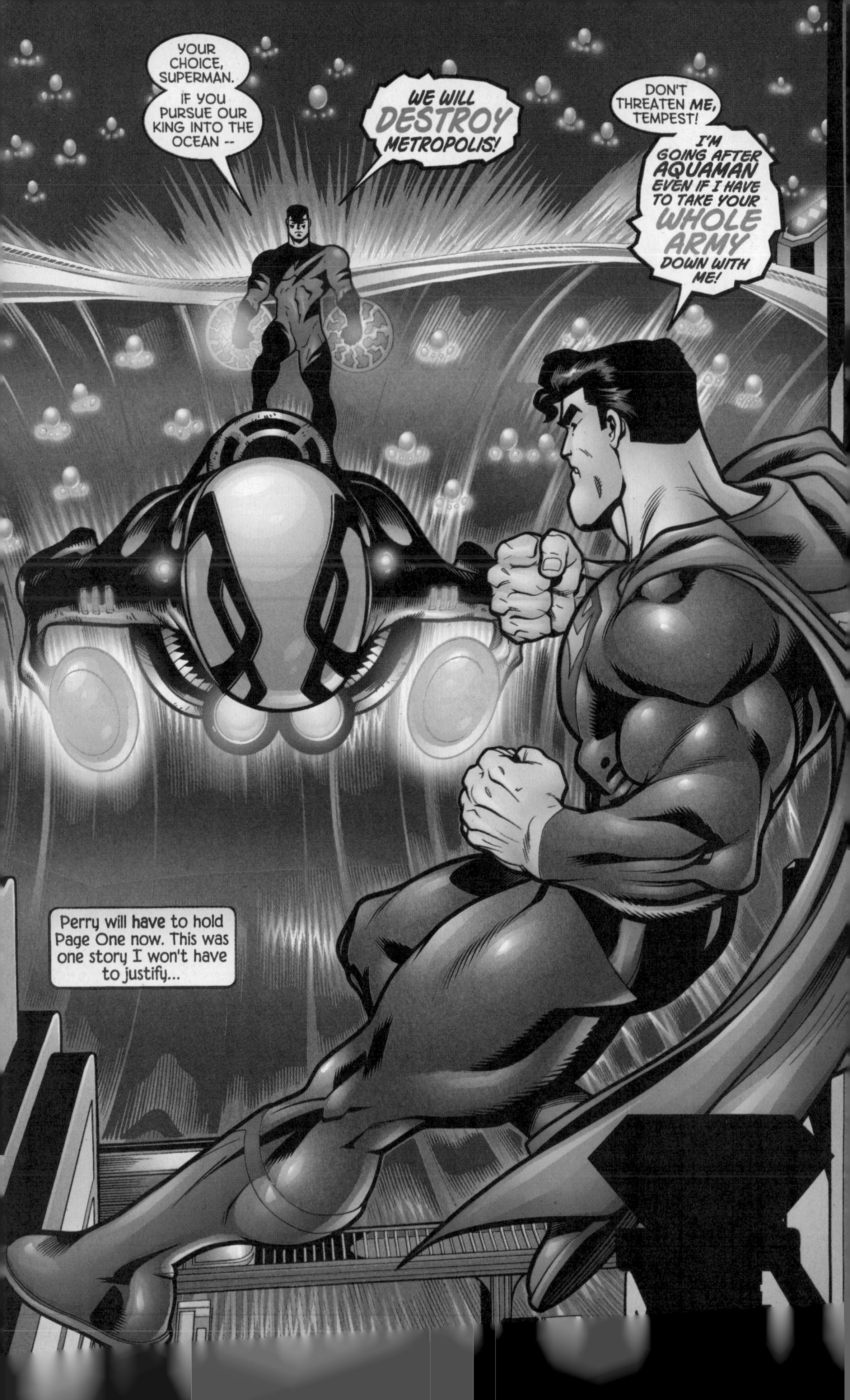
YOUR CHOICE, SUPERMAN.
IF YOU PURSUE OUR KING INTO THE OCEAN --
WE WILL DESTROY METROPOLIS!
DON'T THREATEN ME, TEMPEST!
I'M GOING AFTER AQUAMAN EVEN IF I HAVE TO TAKE YOUR WHOLE ARMY DOWN WITH ME!
Perry will have to hold Page One now. This was one story I won't have to justify...

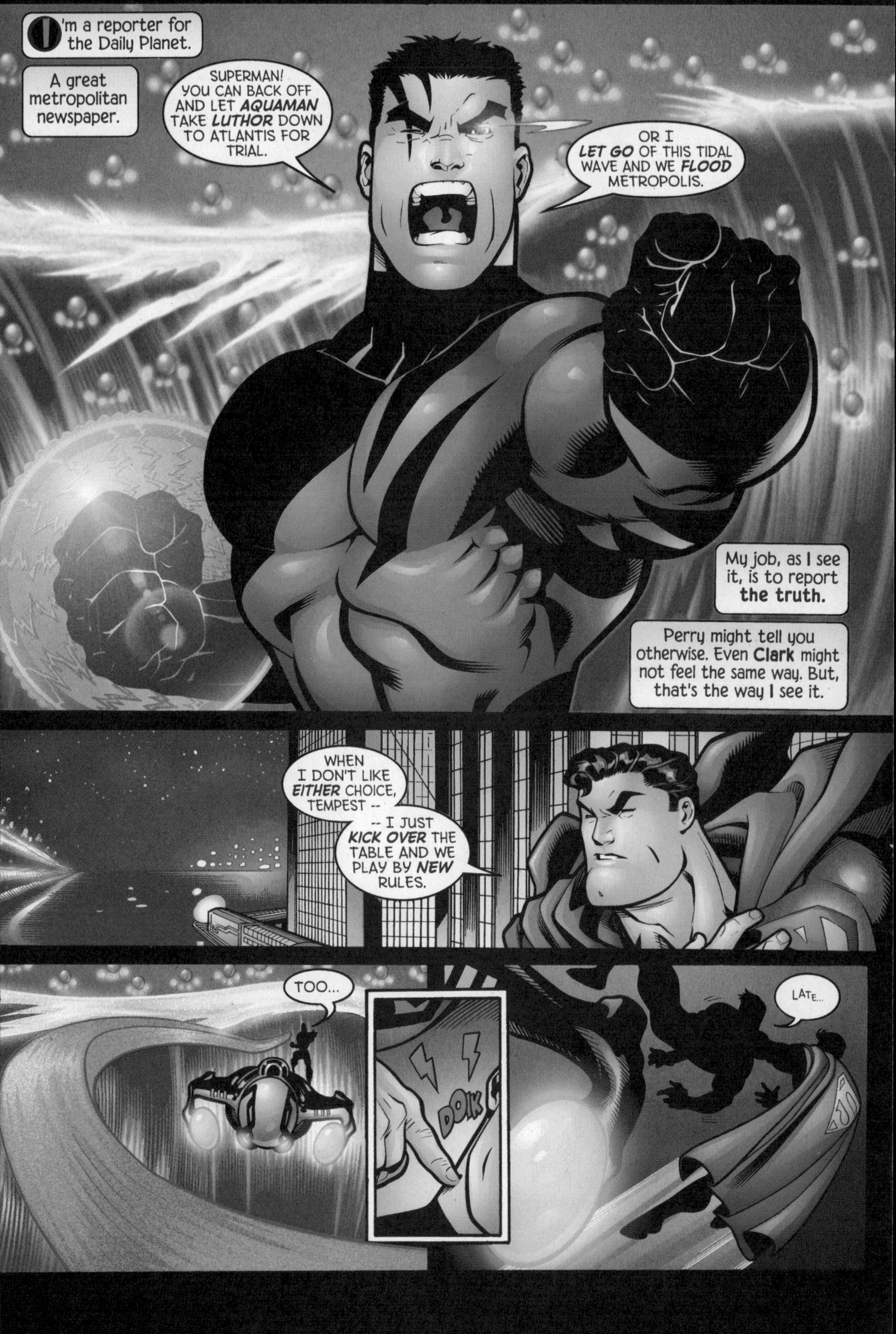
I'm a reporter for the Daily Planet.
A great metropolitan newspaper.
SUPERMAN! YOU CAN BACK OFF AND LET AQUAMAN TAKE LUTHOR DOWN TO ATLANTIS FOR TRIAL.
OR I LET GO OF THIS TIDAL WAVE AND WE FLOOD METROPOLIS.
My job, as I see it, is to report the truth.
Perry might tell you otherwise. Even Clark might not feel the same way. But, that's the way I see it.
WHEN I DON'T LIKE EITHER CHOICE, TEMPEST --
-- I JUST KICK OVER THE TABLE AND WE PLAY BY NEW RULES.
TOO...
DOIK
LATE...

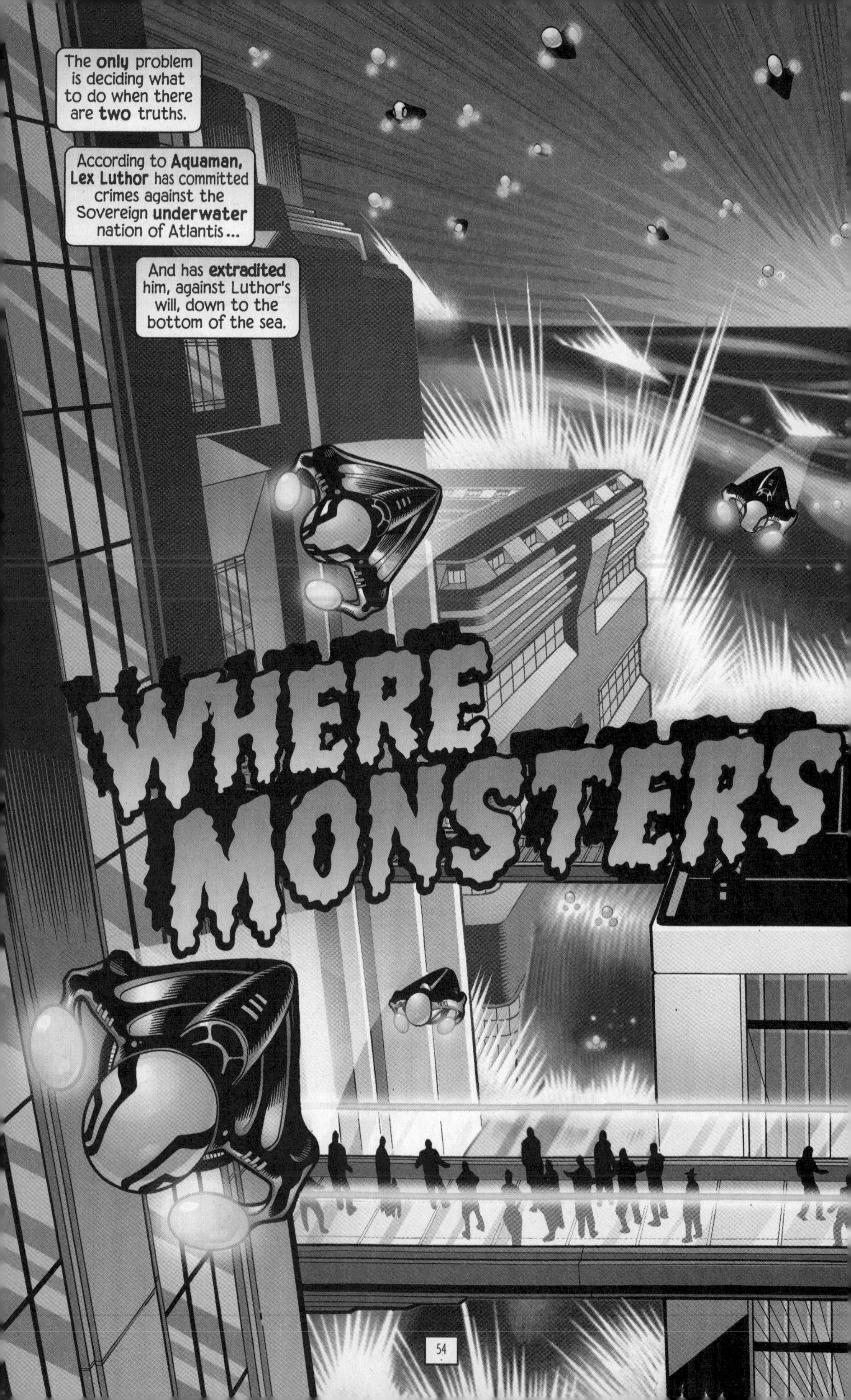
The **only** problem is deciding what to do when there are **two** truths.
According to **Aquaman, Lex Luthor** has committed crimes against the Sovereign **underwater** nation of Atlantis...
And has **extradited** him, against Luthor's will, down to the bottom of the sea.
WHERE MONSTERS

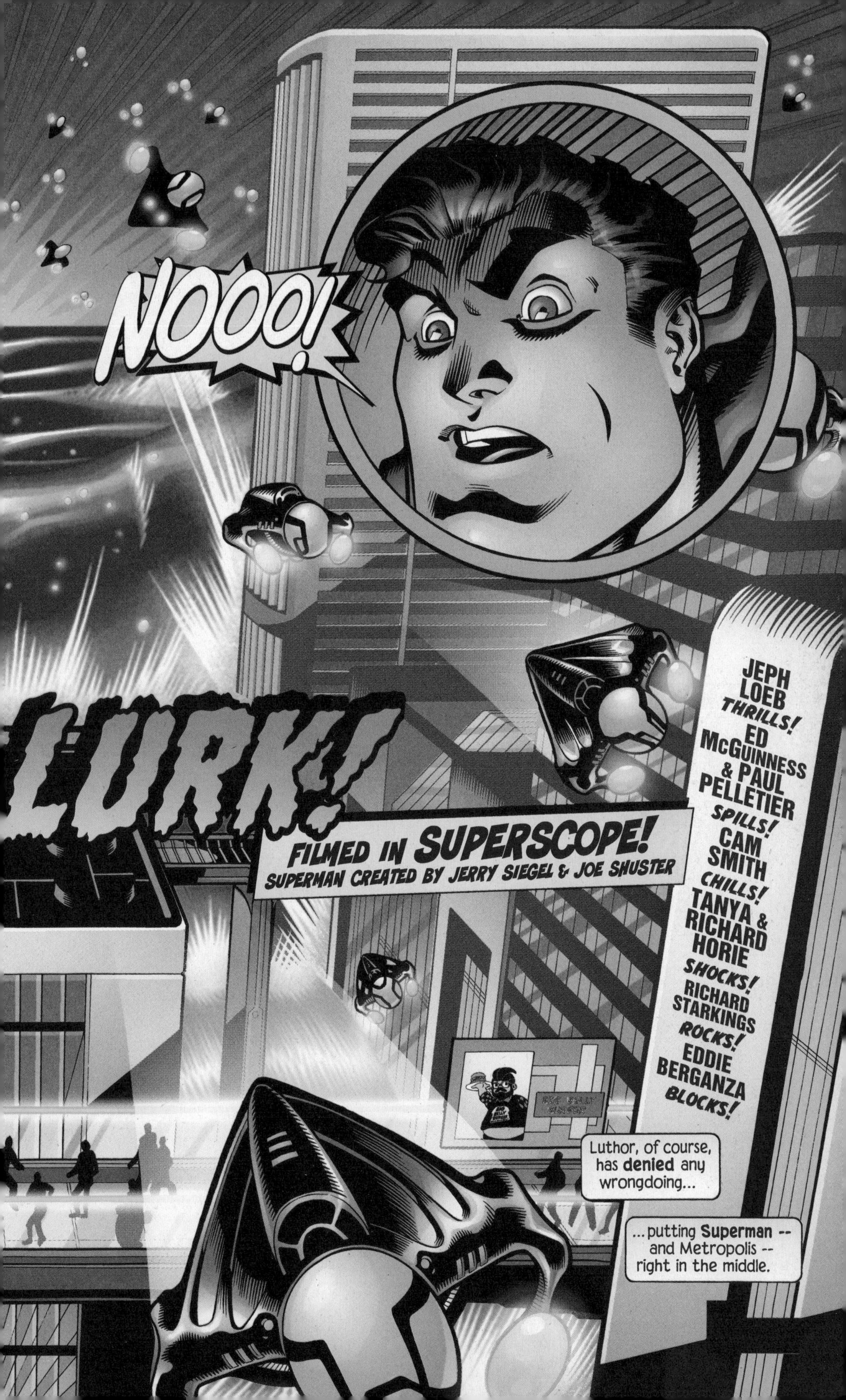
NOOO!
LURK!
FILMED IN SUPERSCOPE!
SUPERMAN CREATED BY JERRY SIEGEL & JOE SHUSTER
JEPH LOEB THRILLS!
ED McGUINNESS & PAUL PELLETIER SPILLS!
CAM SMITH CHILLS!
TANYA & RICHARD HORIE SHOCKS!
RICHARD STARKINGS ROCKS!
EDDIE BERGANZA BLOCKS!
Luthor, of course, has denied any wrongdoing...
...putting Superman -- and Metropolis -- right in the middle.

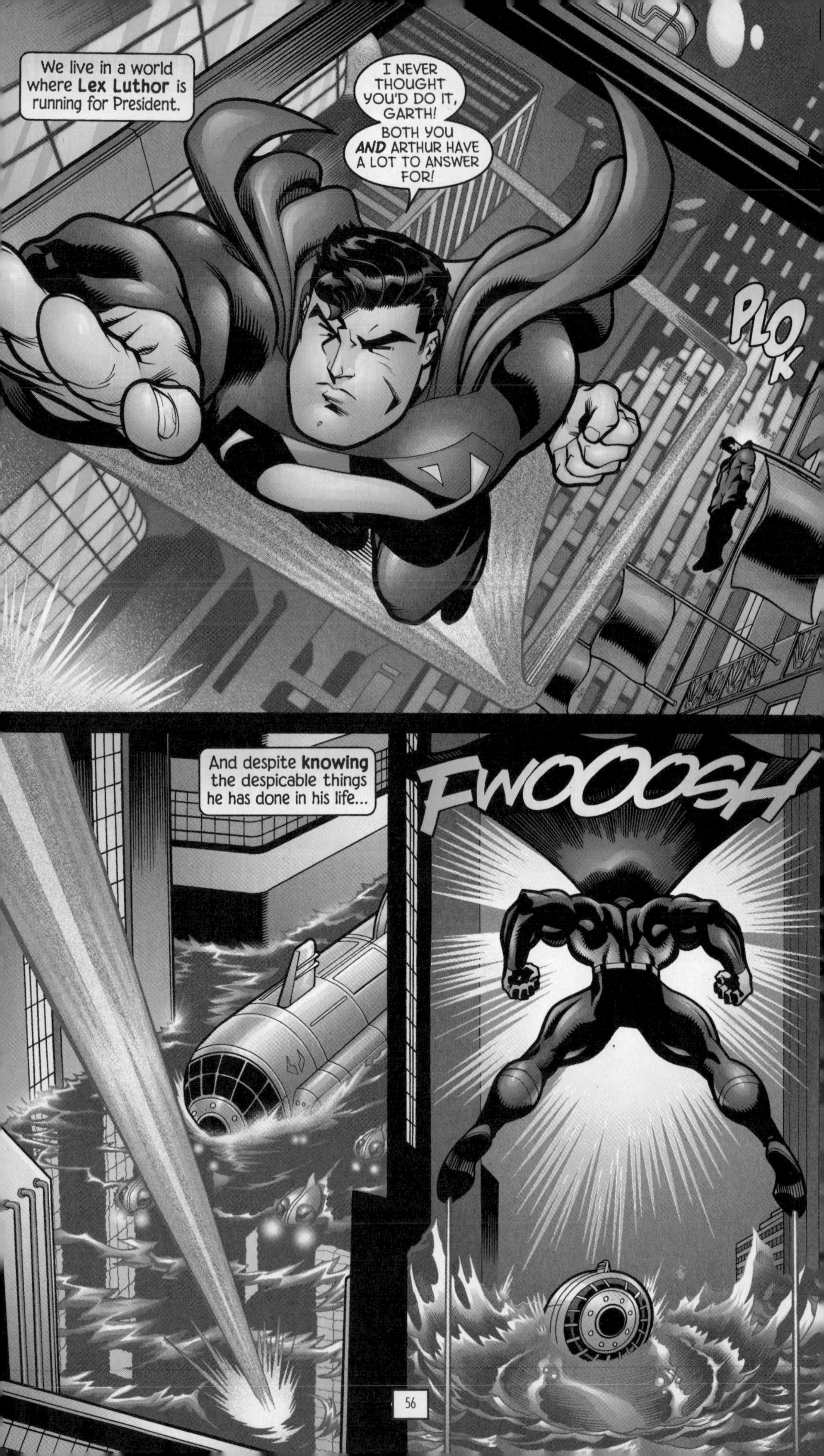
We live in a world where **Lex Luthor** is running for President.
I NEVER THOUGHT YOU'D DO IT, GARTH! BOTH YOU **AND** ARTHUR HAVE A LOT TO ANSWER FOR!
PLOK
And despite **knowing** the despicable things he has done in his life...
FWOOOSH

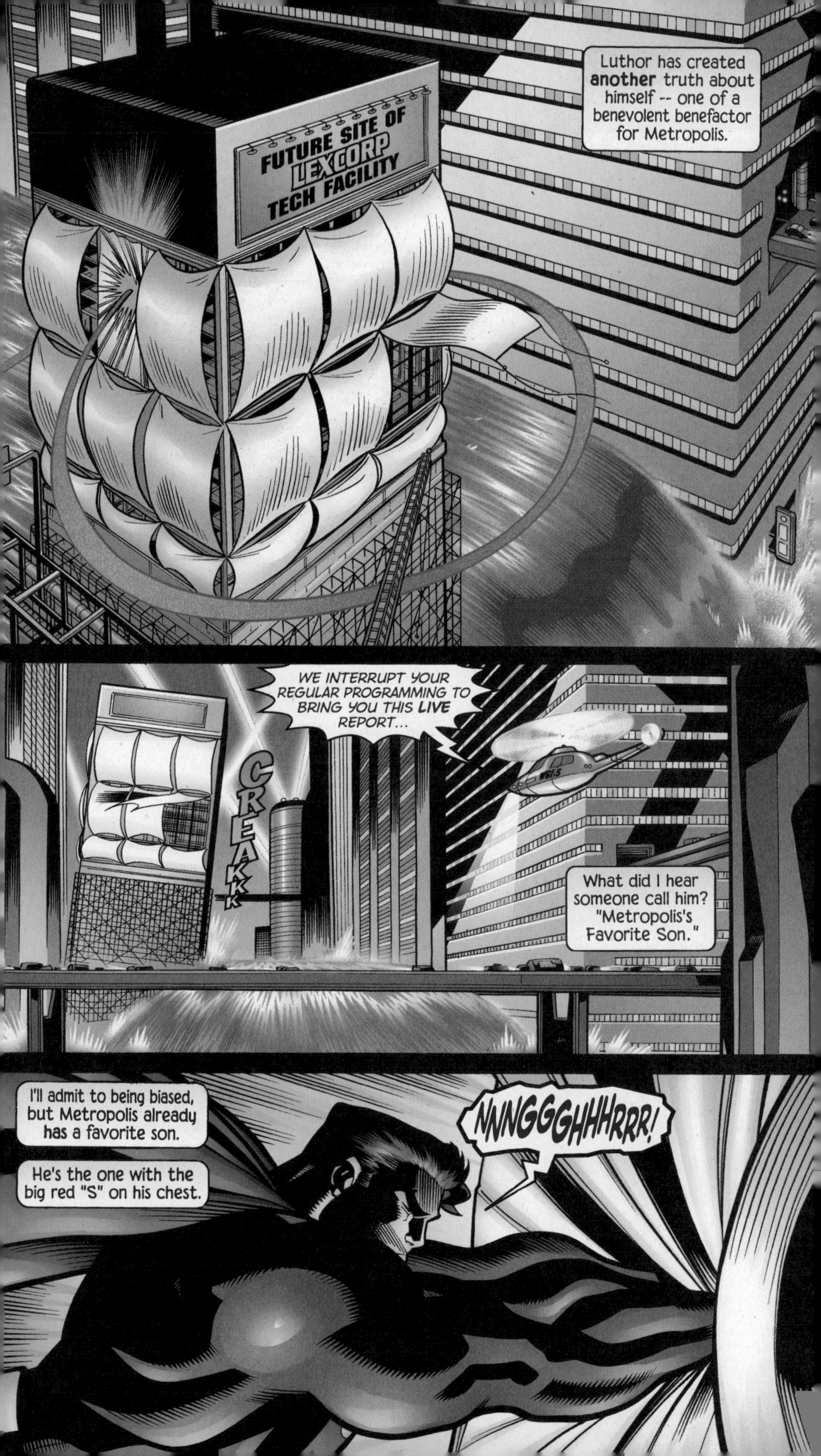
FUTURE SITE OF LEXCORP TECH FACILITY
Luthor has created **another** truth about himself -- one of a benevolent benefactor for Metropolis.
WE INTERRUPT YOUR REGULAR PROGRAMMING TO BRING YOU THIS **LIVE** REPORT...
CREAKKK
What did I hear someone call him? "Metropolis's Favorite Son."
I'll admit to being biased, but Metropolis already **has** a favorite son.
He's the one with the big red "S" on his chest.
NNNGGGHHHRRR!

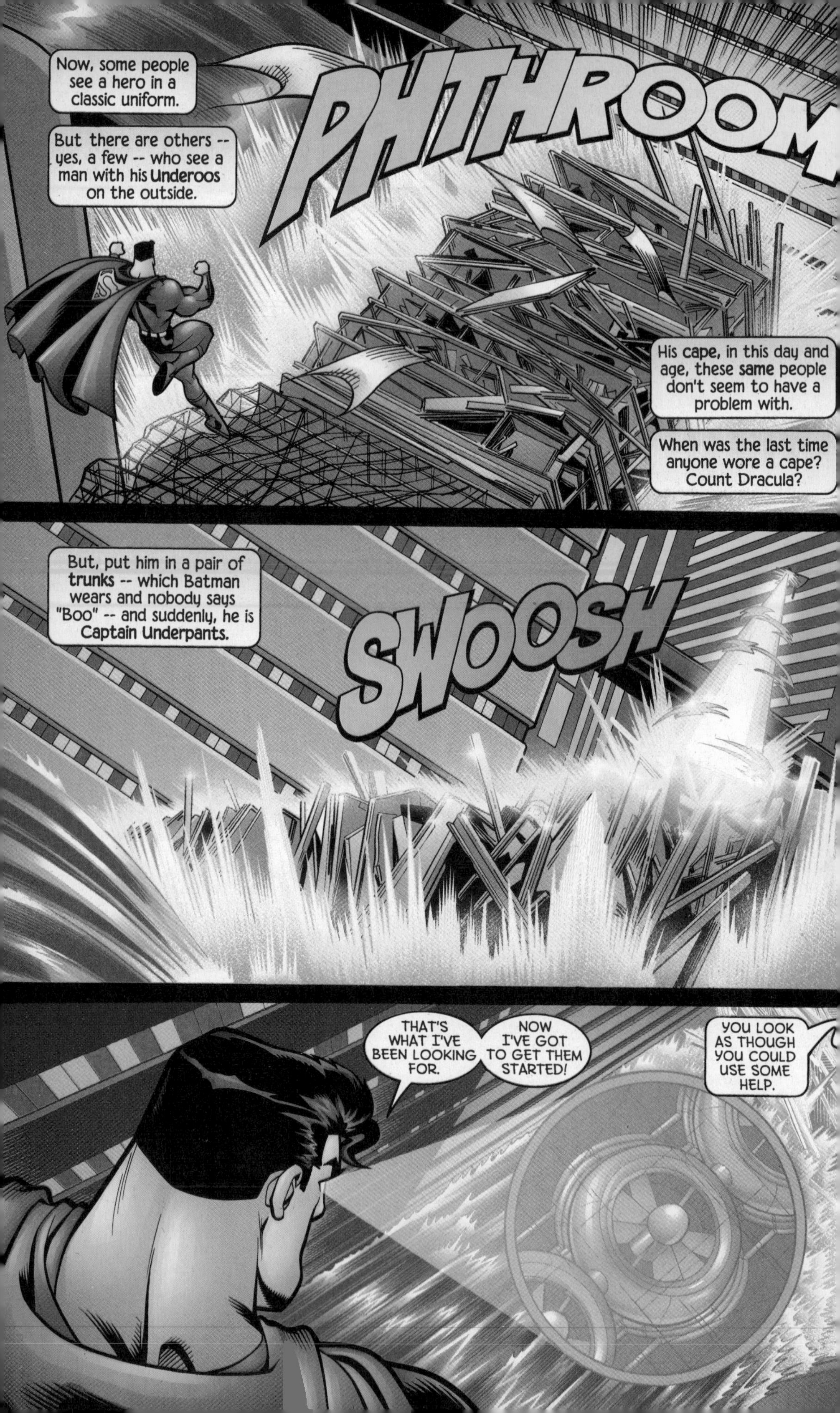
Now, some people see a hero in a classic uniform.
But there are others -- yes, a few -- who see a man with his Underoos on the outside.
PHTHROOM
His cape, in this day and age, these same people don't seem to have a problem with.
When was the last time anyone wore a cape? Count Dracula?
But, put him in a pair of trunks -- which Batman wears and nobody says "Boo" -- and suddenly, he is Captain Underpants.
SWOOSH
THAT'S WHAT I'VE BEEN LOOKING FOR.
NOW I'VE GOT TO GET THEM STARTED!
YOU LOOK AS THOUGH YOU COULD USE SOME HELP.

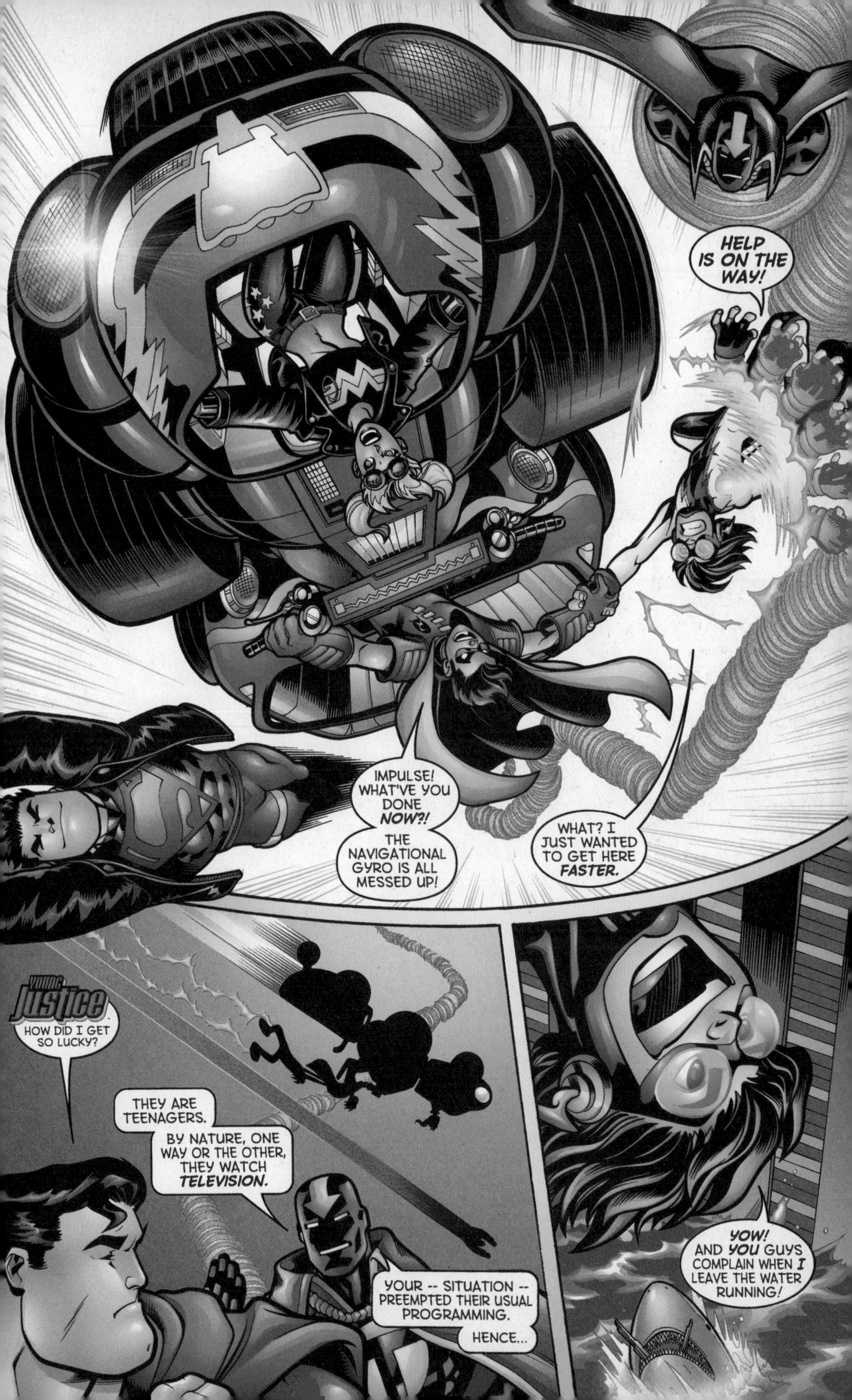
HELP IS ON THE WAY!
IMPULSE! WHAT'VE YOU DONE NOW?!
THE NAVIGATIONAL GYRO IS ALL MESSED UP!
WHAT? I JUST WANTED TO GET HERE FASTER.
YOUNG JUSTICE
HOW DID I GET SO LUCKY?
THEY ARE TEENAGERS.
BY NATURE, ONE WAY OR THE OTHER, THEY WATCH TELEVISION.
YOUR -- SITUATION -- PREEMPTED THEIR USUAL PROGRAMMING.
HENCE...
YOW! AND YOU GUYS COMPLAIN WHEN I LEAVE THE WATER RUNNING!

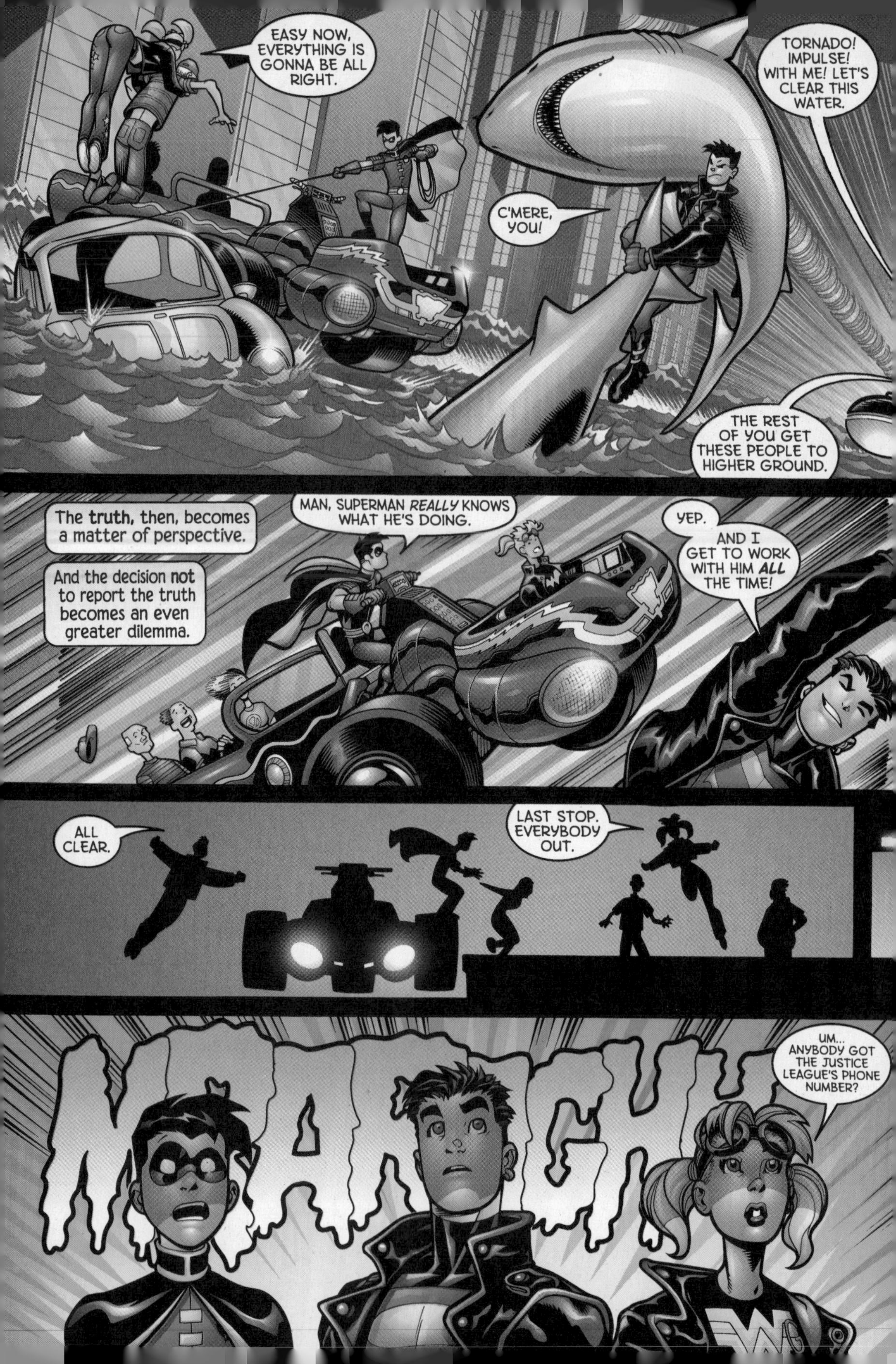
EASY NOW, EVERYTHING IS GONNA BE ALL RIGHT.
TORNADO! IMPULSE! WITH ME! LET'S CLEAR THIS WATER.
C'MERE, YOU!
THE REST OF YOU GET THESE PEOPLE TO HIGHER GROUND.
The truth, then, becomes a matter of perspective.
And the decision not to report the truth becomes an even greater dilemma.
MAN, SUPERMAN REALLY KNOWS WHAT HE'S DOING.
YEP.
AND I GET TO WORK WITH HIM ALL THE TIME!
ALL CLEAR.
LAST STOP. EVERYBODY OUT.
UM... ANYBODY GOT THE JUSTICE LEAGUE'S PHONE NUMBER?

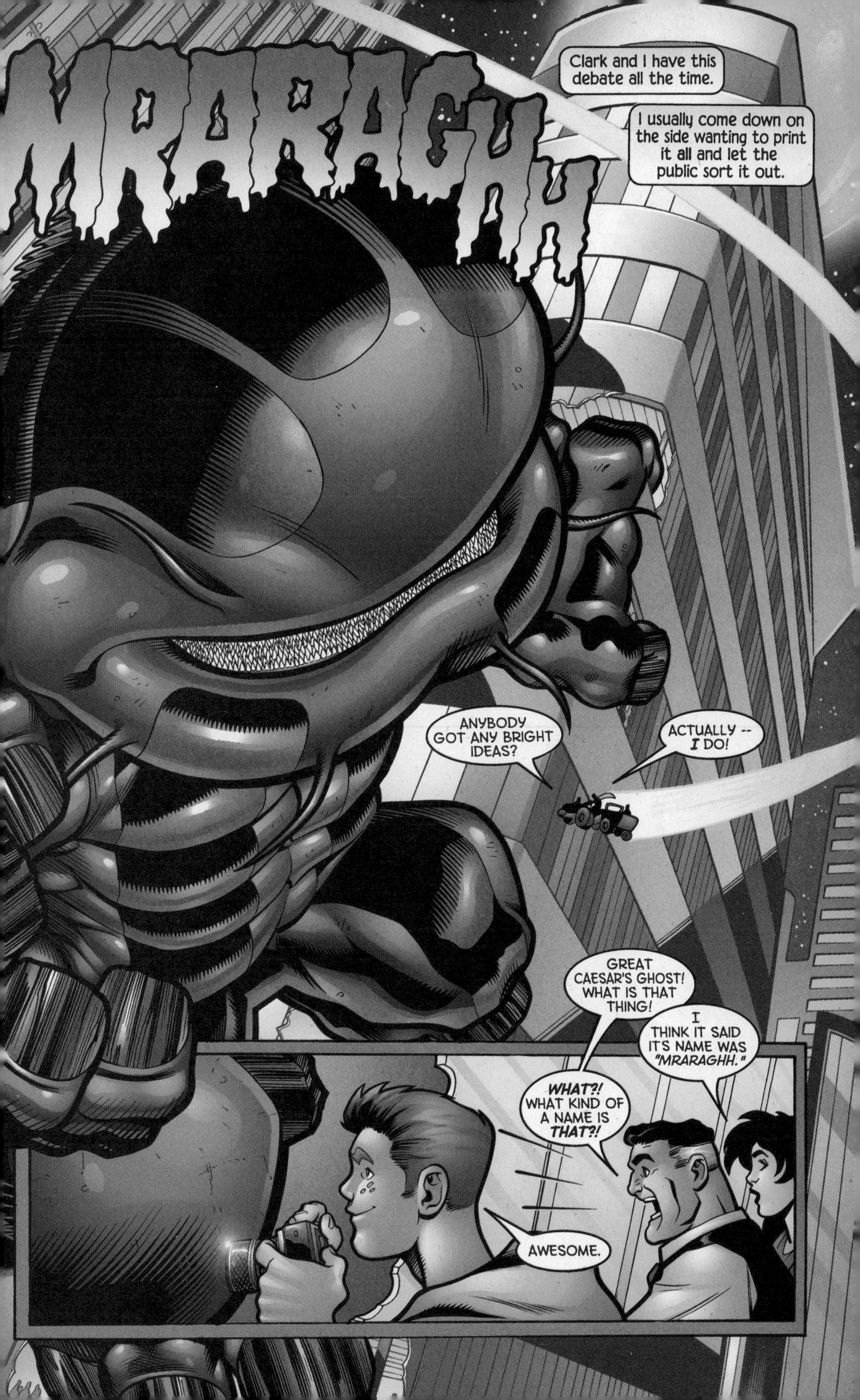
MRARAGHH
Clark and I have this debate all the time.
I usually come down on the side wanting to print it all and let the public sort it out.
ANYBODY GOT ANY BRIGHT IDEAS?
ACTUALLY -- I DO!
GREAT CAESAR'S GHOST! WHAT IS THAT THING!
I THINK IT SAID ITS NAME WAS "MRARAGHH."
WHAT?! WHAT KIND OF A NAME IS THAT?!
AWESOME.

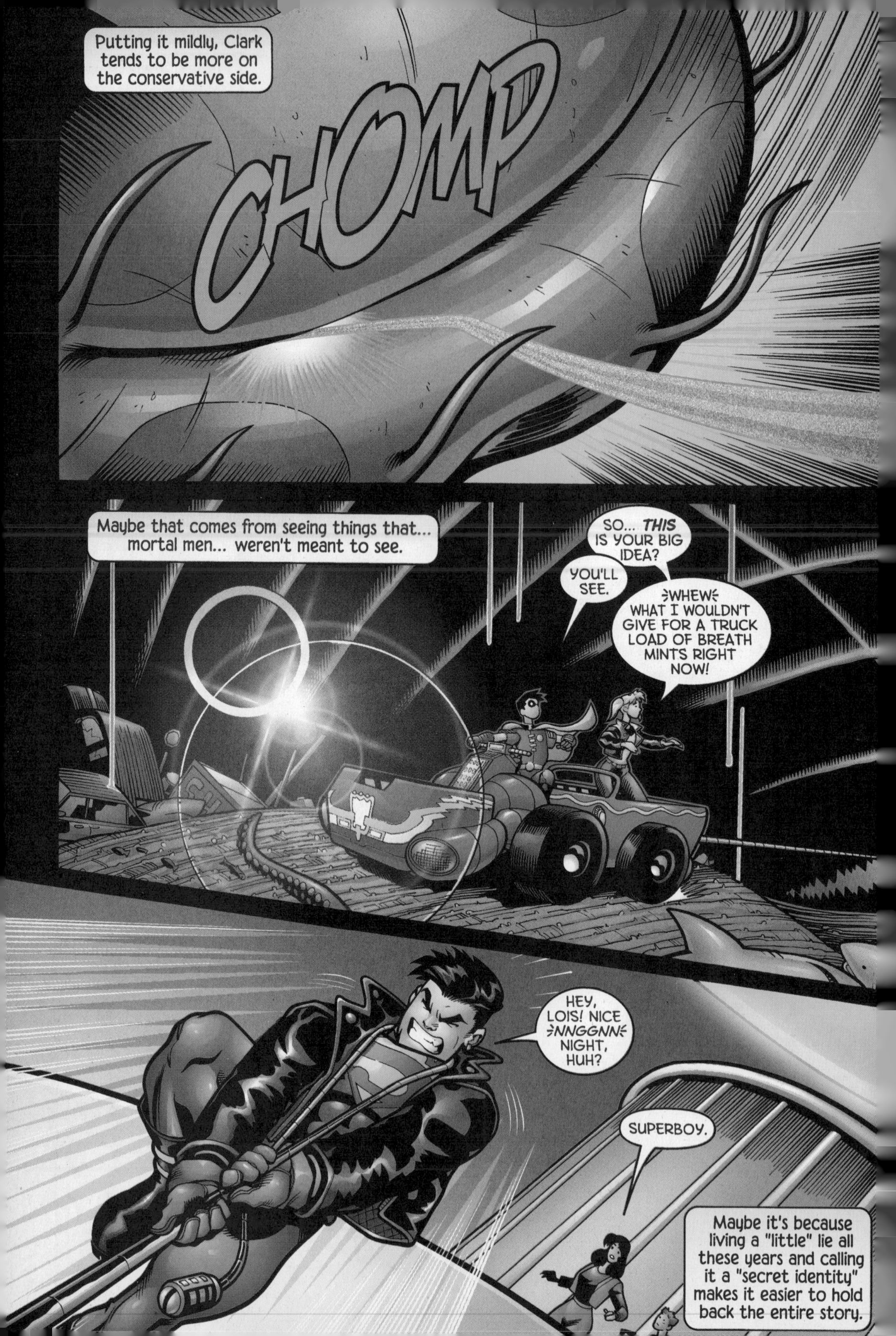
Putting it mildly, Clark tends to be more on the conservative side.
CHOMP
Maybe that comes from seeing things that... mortal men... weren't meant to see.
SO... THIS IS YOUR BIG IDEA?
YOU'LL SEE.
WHEW WHAT I WOULDN'T GIVE FOR A TRUCK LOAD OF BREATH MINTS RIGHT NOW!
HEY, LOIS! NICE NNGGNN NIGHT, HUH?
SUPERBOY.
Maybe it's because living a "little" lie all these years and calling it a "secret identity" makes it easier to hold back the entire story.

WE HAVEN'T GOT MUCH TIME BEFORE THAT WATER RUSHES BACK. MY FRIEND *STEEL* TOLD ME ABOUT THESE HYDRAULIC *PUMPS* WHICH ARE SCATTERED THROUGHOUT THE CITY.

ANOTHER *"GIFT"* FROM THE B13 VIRUS THAT UPGRADED METROPOLIS OVERNIGHT.

THEY SHOULD'VE STARTED *AUTOMATICALLY*, BUT NOW THAT'S *OUR JOB!*

I've never questioned Clark's need to put on glasses and change his voice an octave.

SZZZRAK

SZZZRAK

FWIZZ

ZIP ZIP ZIP
ZIP ZIP ZIP
ZIP ZIP
ZIP

FOUND THEM!

ONE, TWO, THREE, GO!

And now being one of the few who gets to know "the secret," I can't argue how it protects me -- all of us who know him.

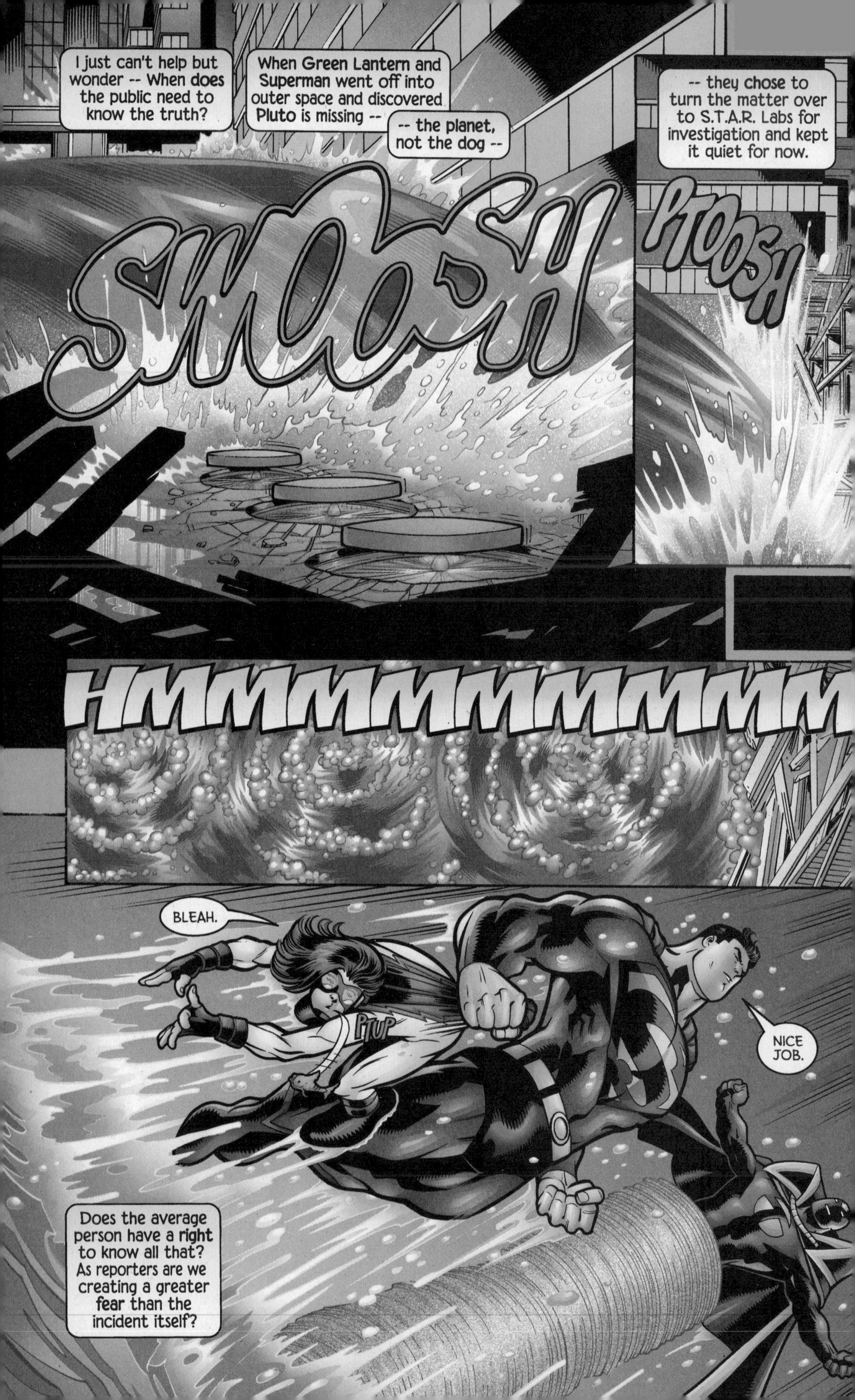
I just can't help but wonder -- When does the public need to know the truth?
When Green Lantern and Superman went off into outer space and discovered Pluto is missing --
-- the planet, not the dog --
-- they chose to turn the matter over to S.T.A.R. Labs for investigation and kept it quiet for now.
SHOOSH
PTOOSH
HMMMMMMMMMM
BLEAH.
PTUP
NICE JOB.
Does the average person have a right to know all that? As reporters are we creating a greater fear than the incident itself?

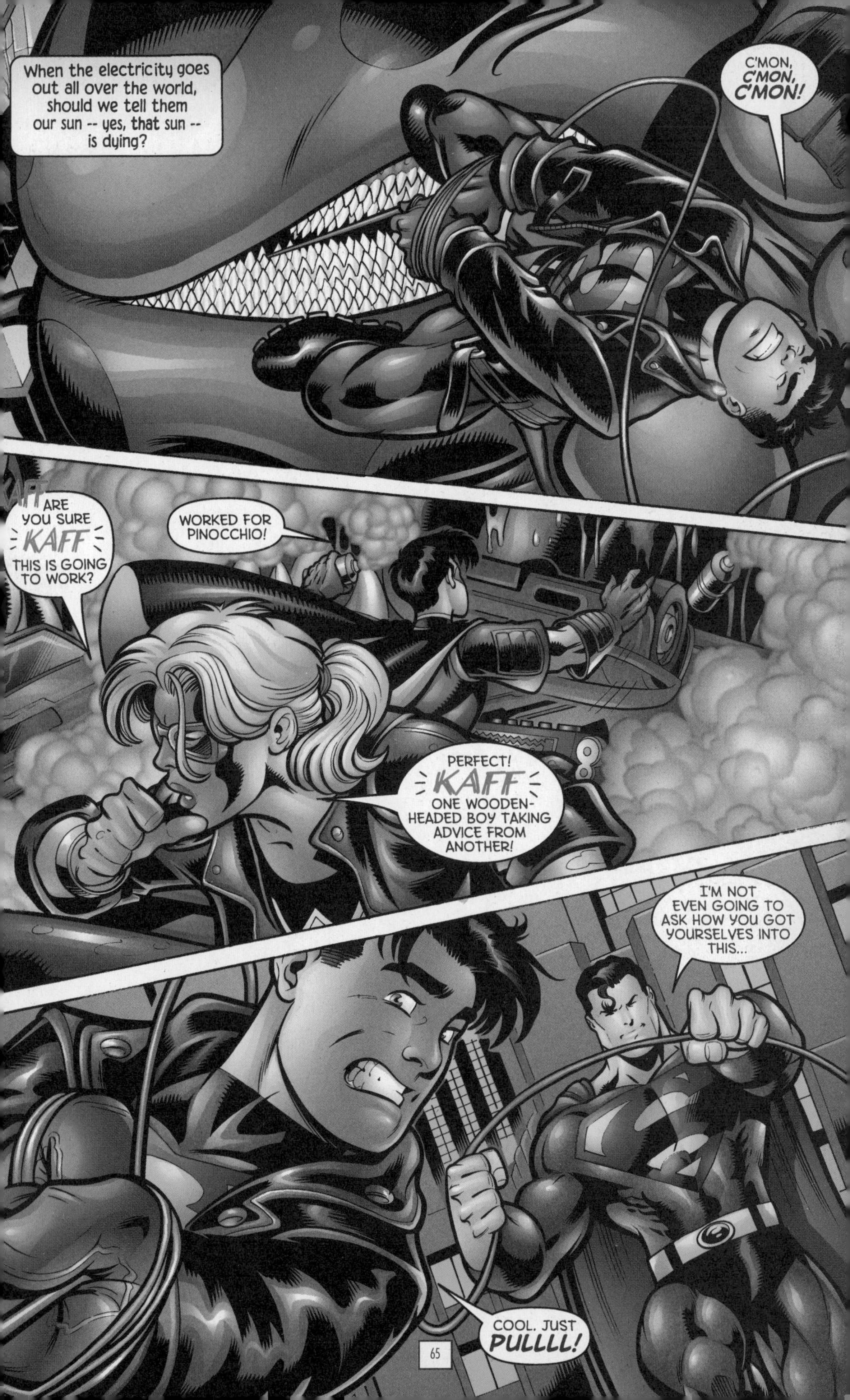
When the electricity goes out all over the world, should we tell them our sun -- yes, that sun -- is dying?
C'MON, C'MON, C'MON!
KAFF ARE YOU SURE KAFF THIS IS GOING TO WORK?
WORKED FOR PINOCCHIO!
PERFECT! KAFF ONE WOODEN-HEADED BOY TAKING ADVICE FROM ANOTHER!
I'M NOT EVEN GOING TO ASK HOW YOU GOT YOURSELVES INTO THIS...
COOL. JUST PULLLL!

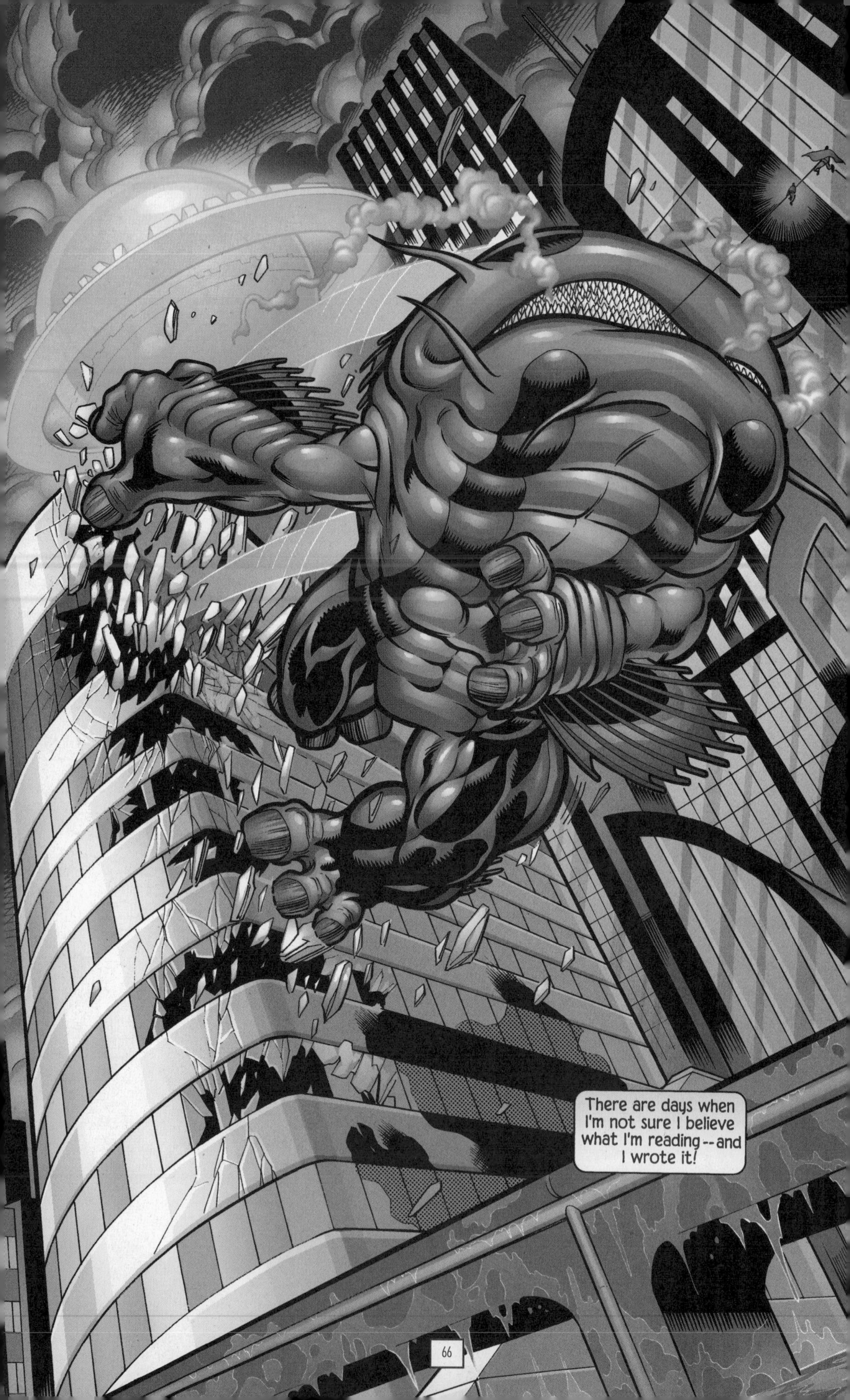
There are days when I'm not sure I believe what I'm reading--and I wrote it!

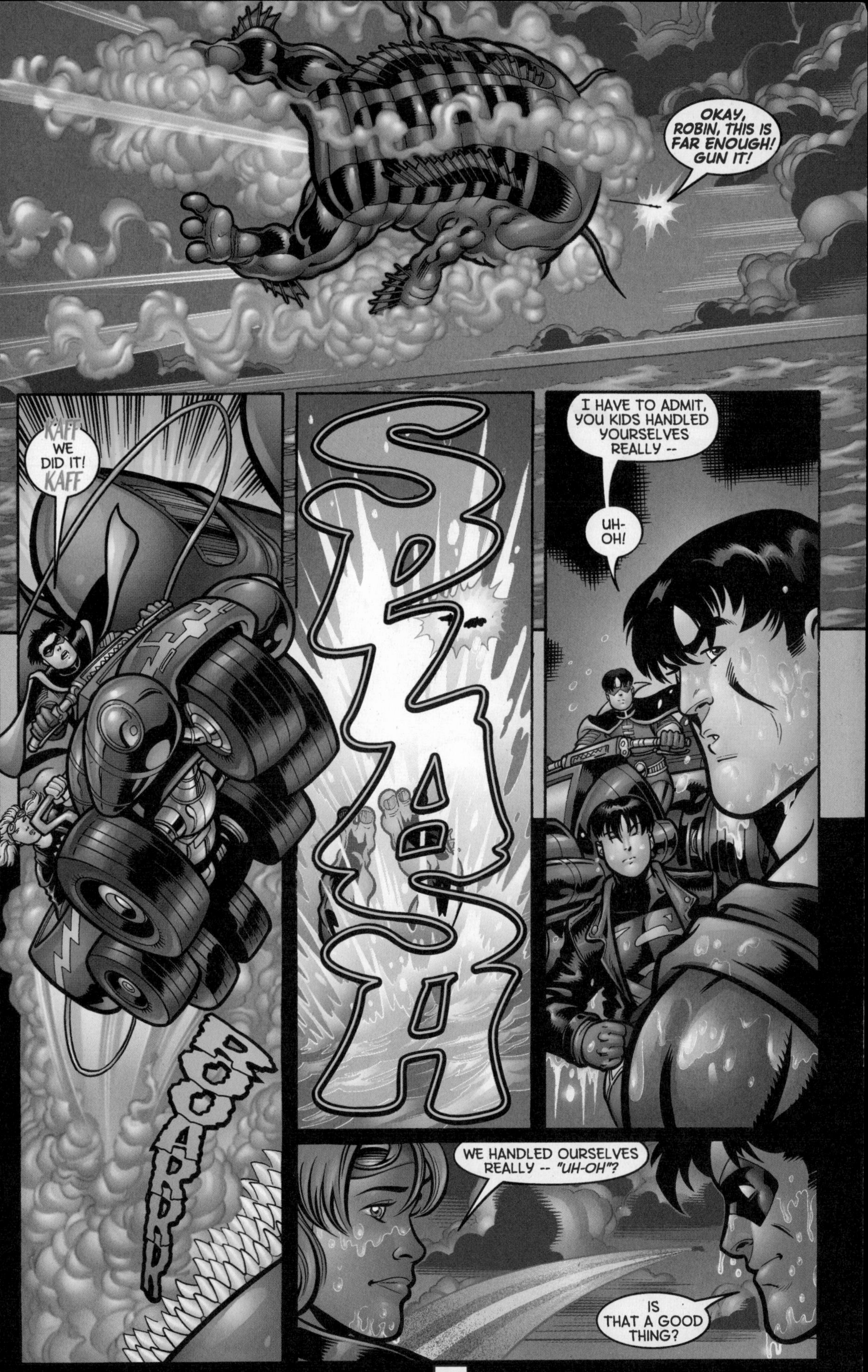
OKAY, ROBIN, THIS IS FAR ENOUGH! GUN IT!
KAFF WE DID IT! KAFF
SPLASH
I HAVE TO ADMIT, YOU KIDS HANDLED YOURSELVES REALLY --
UH-OH!
BOOADRRP
WE HANDLED OURSELVES REALLY -- "UH-OH"?
IS THAT A GOOD THING?

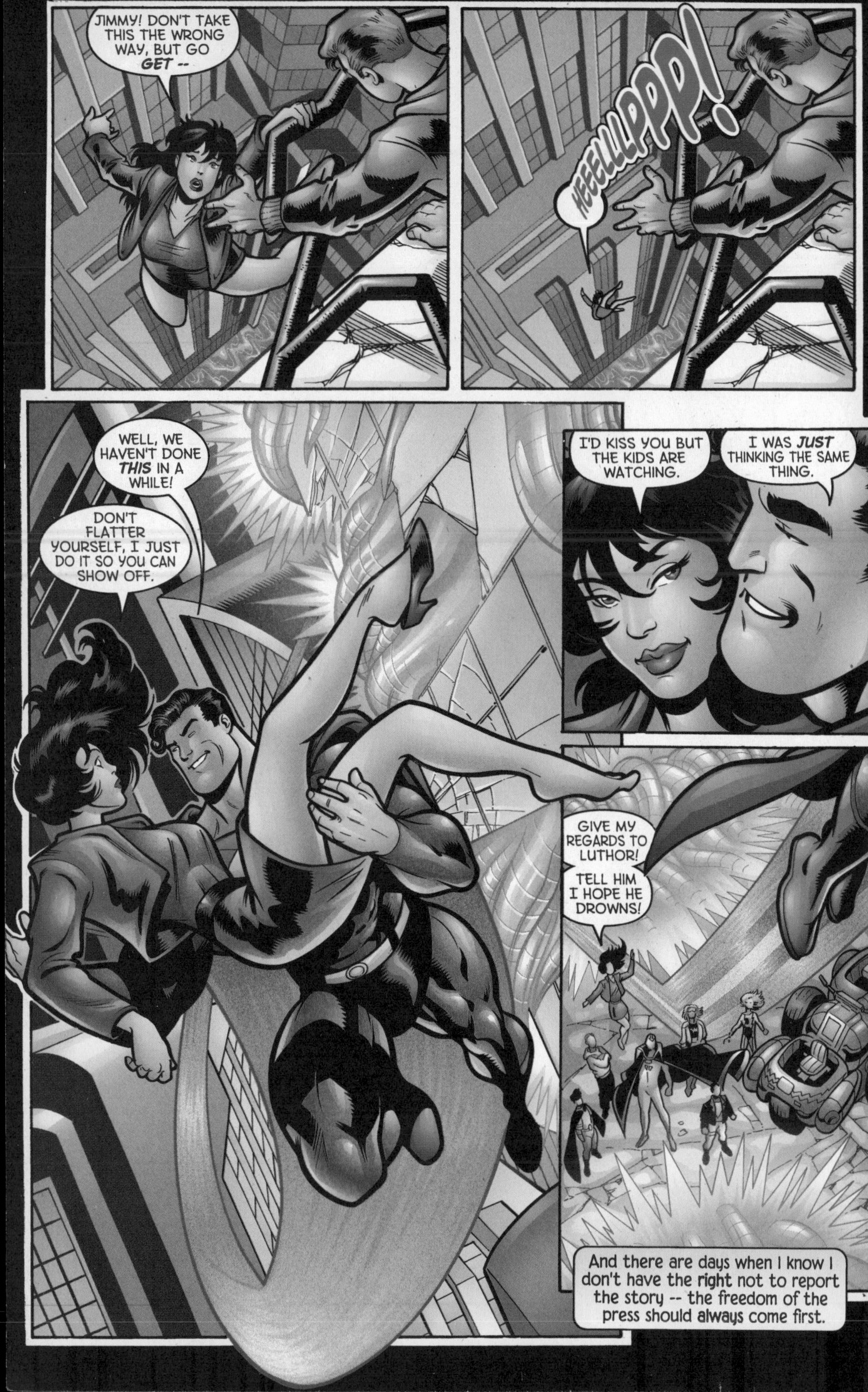
JIMMY! DON'T TAKE THIS THE WRONG WAY, BUT GO *GET* --
HEEELLLPPP!
WELL, WE HAVEN'T DONE *THIS* IN A WHILE!
DON'T FLATTER YOURSELF, I JUST DO IT SO YOU CAN SHOW OFF.
I'D KISS YOU BUT THE KIDS ARE WATCHING.
I WAS *JUST* THINKING THE SAME THING.
GIVE MY REGARDS TO LUTHOR!
TELL HIM I HOPE HE DROWNS!
And there are days when I know I don't have the right not to report the story -- the freedom of the press should always come first.

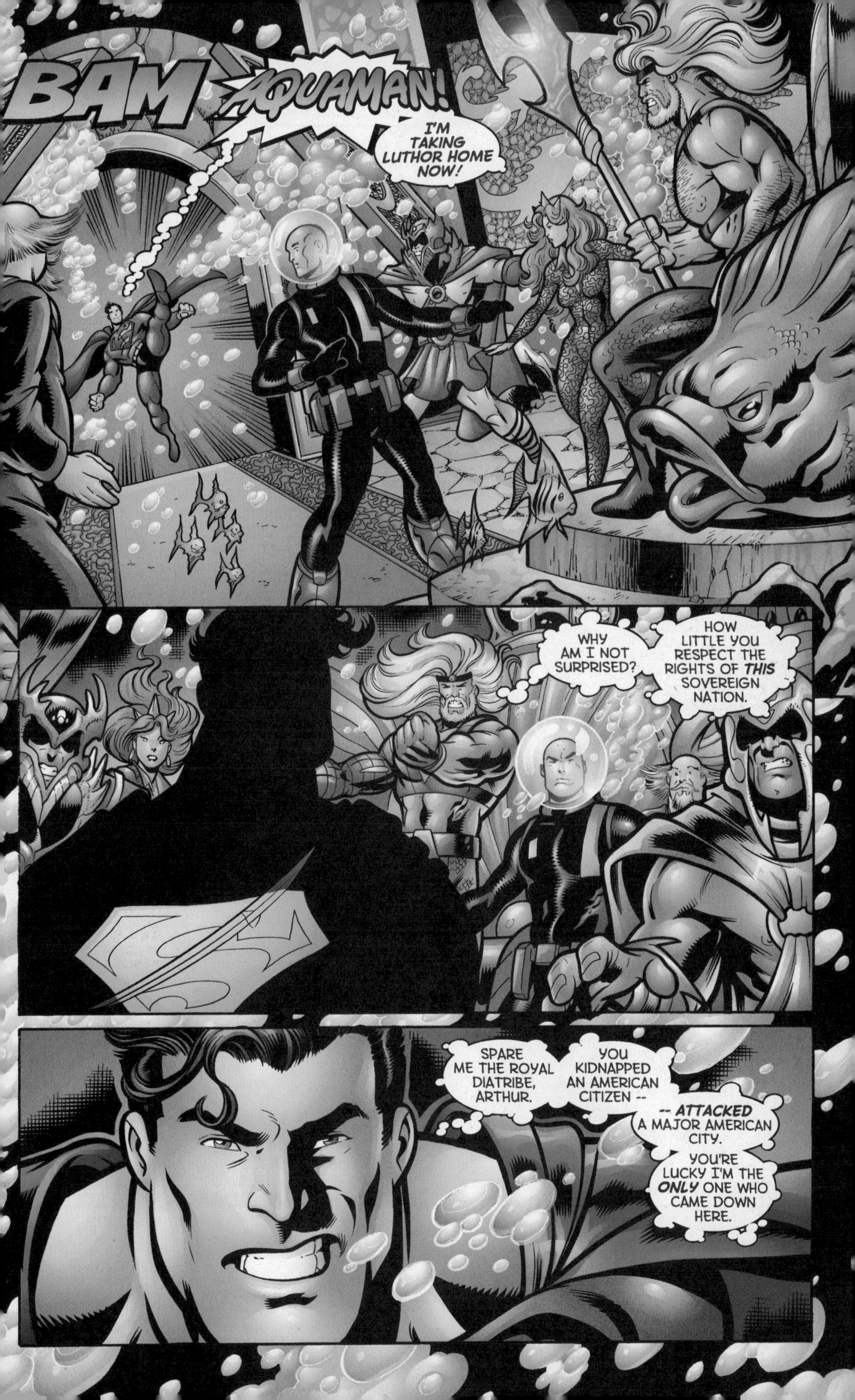
BAM
AQUAMAN!
I'M TAKING LUTHOR HOME NOW!
WHY AM I NOT SURPRISED?
HOW LITTLE YOU RESPECT THE RIGHTS OF THIS SOVEREIGN NATION.
SPARE ME THE ROYAL DIATRIBE, ARTHUR.
YOU KIDNAPPED AN AMERICAN CITIZEN --
-- ATTACKED A MAJOR AMERICAN CITY.
YOU'RE LUCKY I'M THE ONLY ONE WHO CAME DOWN HERE.

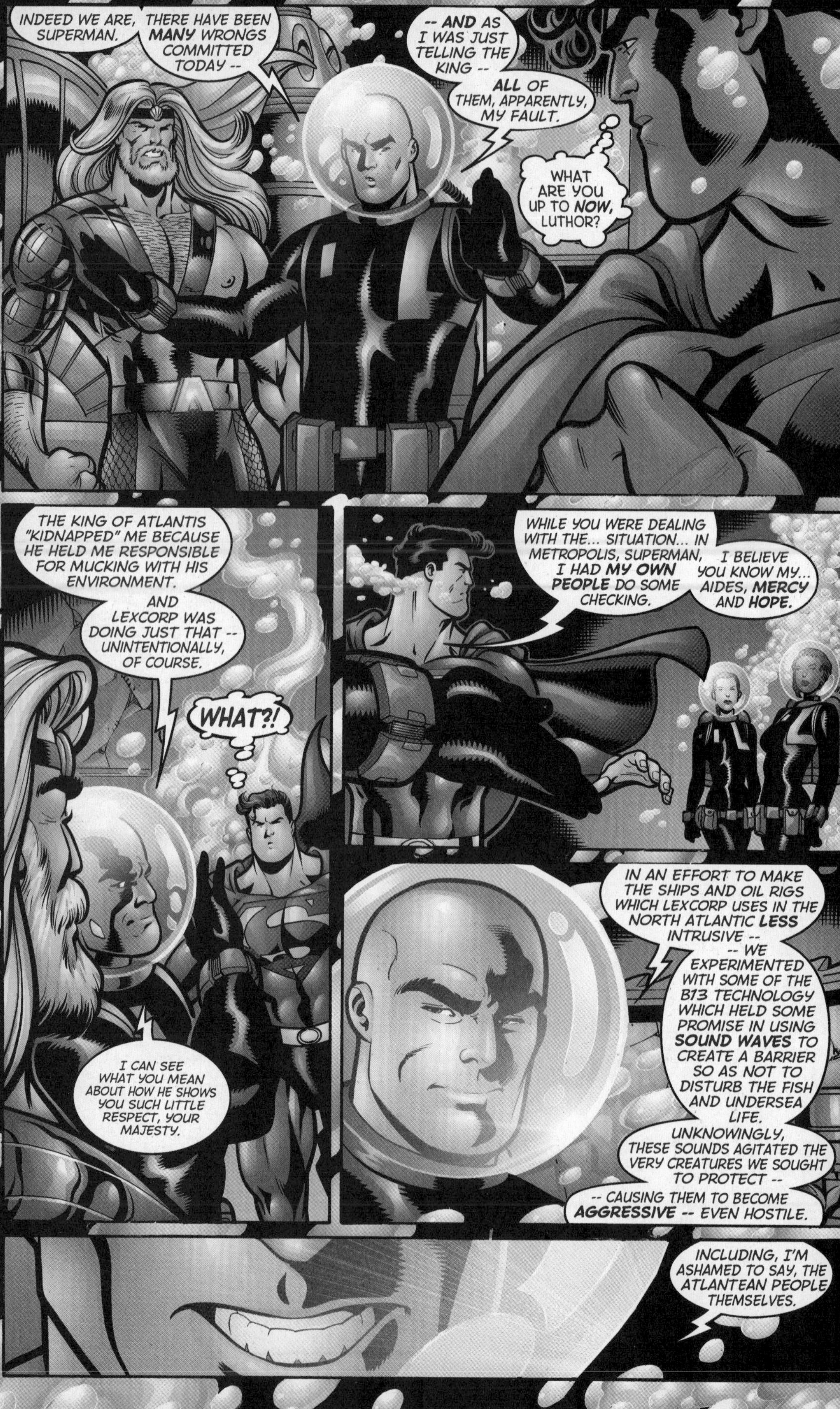

INDEED WE ARE, SUPERMAN.
THERE HAVE BEEN MANY WRONGS COMMITTED TODAY --
-- AND AS I WAS JUST TELLING THE KING --
ALL OF THEM, APPARENTLY, MY FAULT.
WHAT ARE YOU UP TO NOW, LUTHOR?
THE KING OF ATLANTIS "KIDNAPPED" ME BECAUSE HE HELD ME RESPONSIBLE FOR MUCKING WITH HIS ENVIRONMENT.
AND LEXCORP WAS DOING JUST THAT -- UNINTENTIONALLY, OF COURSE.
WHAT?!
I CAN SEE WHAT YOU MEAN ABOUT HOW HE SHOWS YOU SUCH LITTLE RESPECT, YOUR MAJESTY.
WHILE YOU WERE DEALING WITH THE... SITUATION... IN METROPOLIS, SUPERMAN, I HAD MY OWN PEOPLE DO SOME CHECKING.
I BELIEVE YOU KNOW MY... AIDES, MERCY AND HOPE.
IN AN EFFORT TO MAKE THE SHIPS AND OIL RIGS WHICH LEXCORP USES IN THE NORTH ATLANTIC LESS INTRUSIVE --
-- WE EXPERIMENTED WITH SOME OF THE B13 TECHNOLOGY WHICH HELD SOME PROMISE IN USING SOUND WAVES TO CREATE A BARRIER SO AS NOT TO DISTURB THE FISH AND UNDERSEA LIFE.
UNKNOWINGLY, THESE SOUNDS AGITATED THE VERY CREATURES WE SOUGHT TO PROTECT --
-- CAUSING THEM TO BECOME AGGRESSIVE -- EVEN HOSTILE.
INCLUDING, I'M ASHAMED TO SAY, THE ATLANTEAN PEOPLE THEMSELVES.

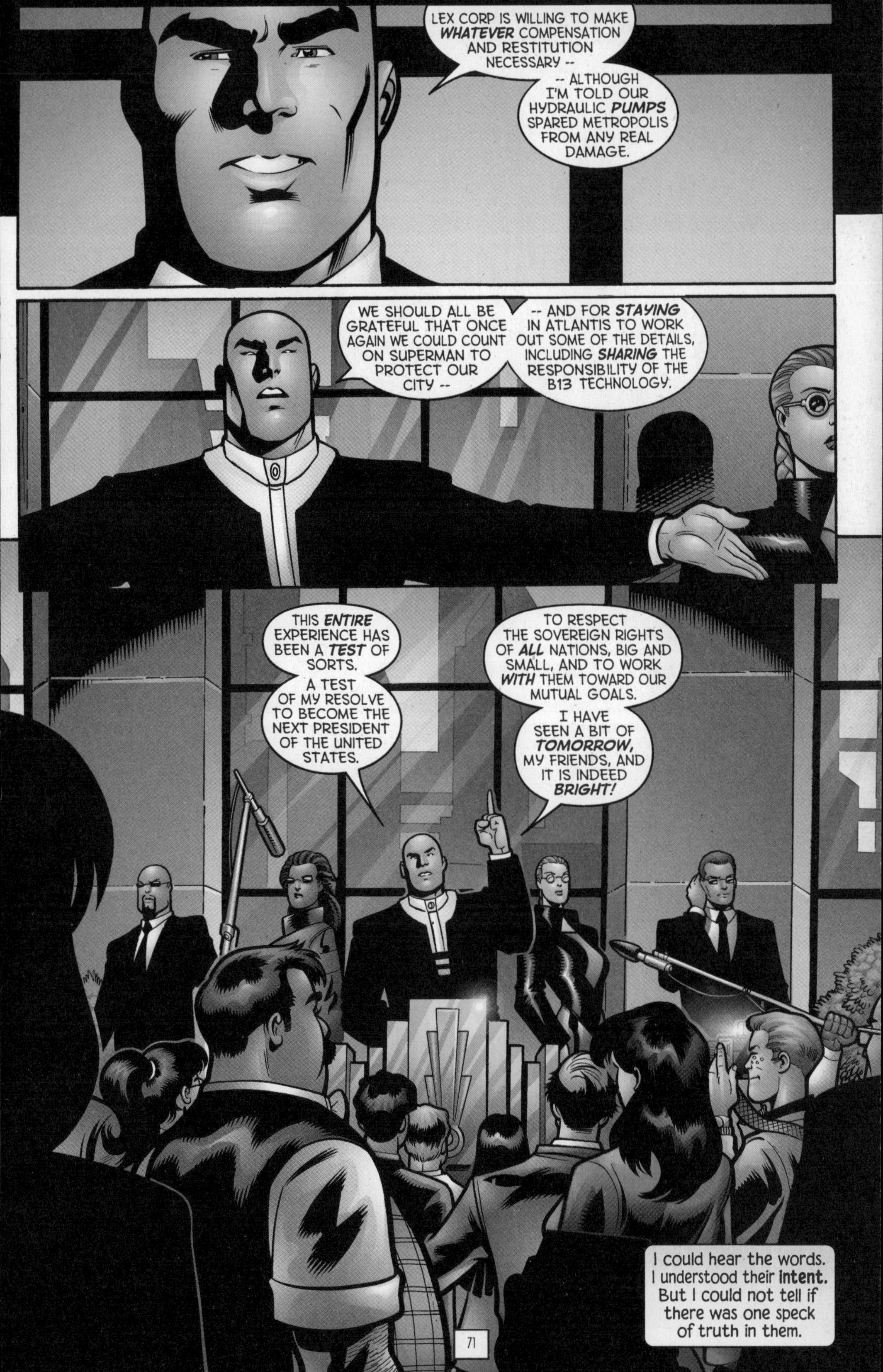
LEX CORP IS WILLING TO MAKE WHATEVER COMPENSATION AND RESTITUTION NECESSARY --
-- ALTHOUGH I'M TOLD OUR HYDRAULIC PUMPS SPARED METROPOLIS FROM ANY REAL DAMAGE.
WE SHOULD ALL BE GRATEFUL THAT ONCE AGAIN WE COULD COUNT ON SUPERMAN TO PROTECT OUR CITY --
-- AND FOR STAYING IN ATLANTIS TO WORK OUT SOME OF THE DETAILS, INCLUDING SHARING THE RESPONSIBILITY OF THE B13 TECHNOLOGY.
THIS ENTIRE EXPERIENCE HAS BEEN A TEST OF SORTS.
A TEST OF MY RESOLVE TO BECOME THE NEXT PRESIDENT OF THE UNITED STATES.
TO RESPECT THE SOVEREIGN RIGHTS OF ALL NATIONS, BIG AND SMALL, AND TO WORK WITH THEM TOWARD OUR MUTUAL GOALS.
I HAVE SEEN A BIT OF TOMORROW, MY FRIENDS, AND IT IS INDEED BRIGHT!
I could hear the words. I understood their intent. But I could not tell if there was one speck of truth in them.

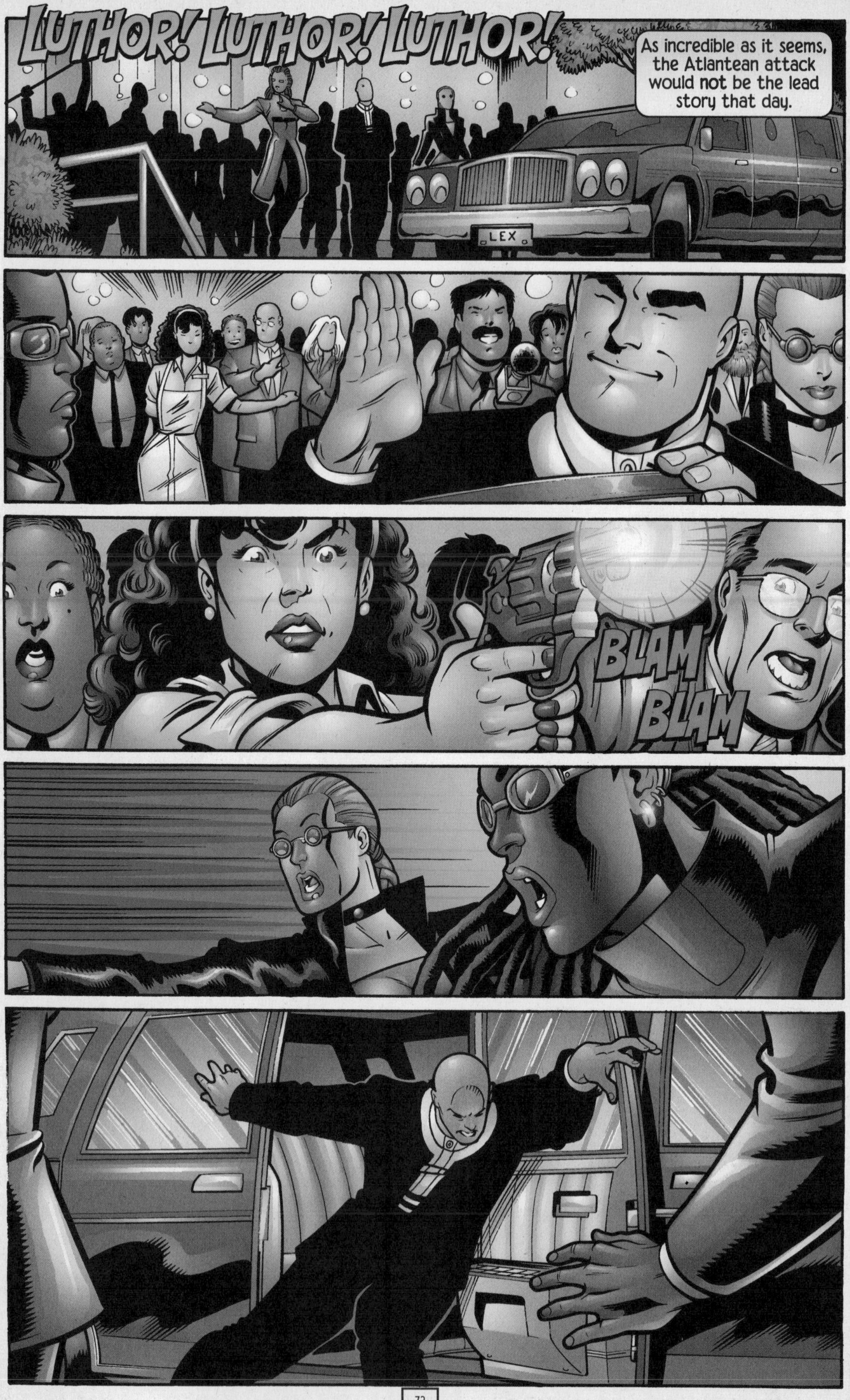
LUTHOR! LUTHOR! LUTHOR!
As incredible as it seems, the Atlantean attack would not be the lead story that day.
LEX
BLAM
BLAM

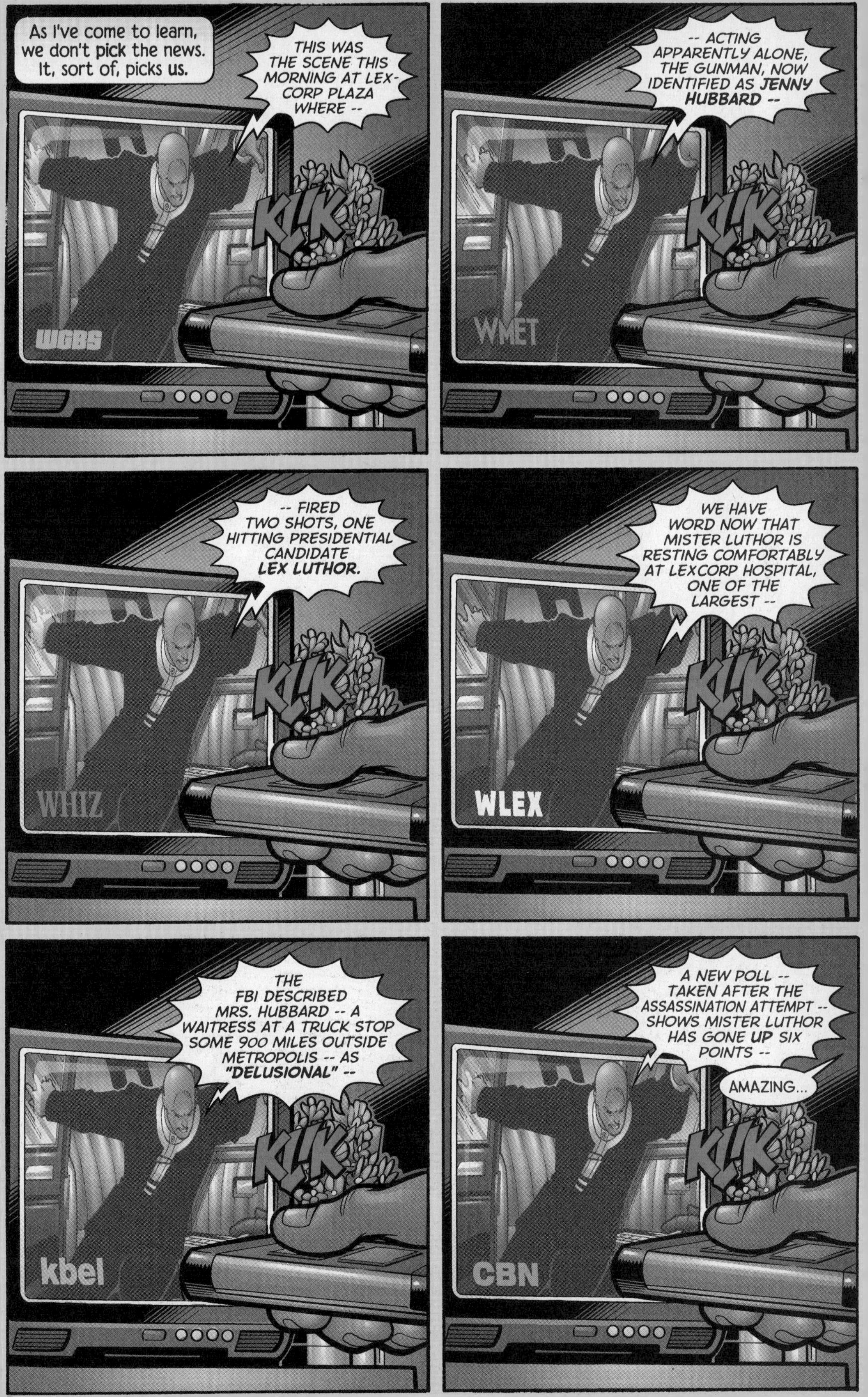
As I've come to learn, we don't pick the news. It, sort of, picks us.
THIS WAS THE SCENE THIS MORNING AT LEX-CORP PLAZA WHERE --
KL'K
WGBS
-- ACTING APPARENTLY ALONE, THE GUNMAN, NOW IDENTIFIED AS JENNY HUBBARD --
KL'K
WMET
-- FIRED TWO SHOTS, ONE HITTING PRESIDENTIAL CANDIDATE LEX LUTHOR.
KL'K
WHIZ
WE HAVE WORD NOW THAT MISTER LUTHOR IS RESTING COMFORTABLY AT LEXCORP HOSPITAL, ONE OF THE LARGEST --
KL'K
WLEX
THE FBI DESCRIBED MRS. HUBBARD -- A WAITRESS AT A TRUCK STOP SOME 900 MILES OUTSIDE METROPOLIS -- AS "DELUSIONAL" --
KL'K
kbel
A NEW POLL -- TAKEN AFTER THE ASSASSINATION ATTEMPT -- SHOWS MISTER LUTHOR HAS GONE UP SIX POINTS --
AMAZING...
KL'K
CBN

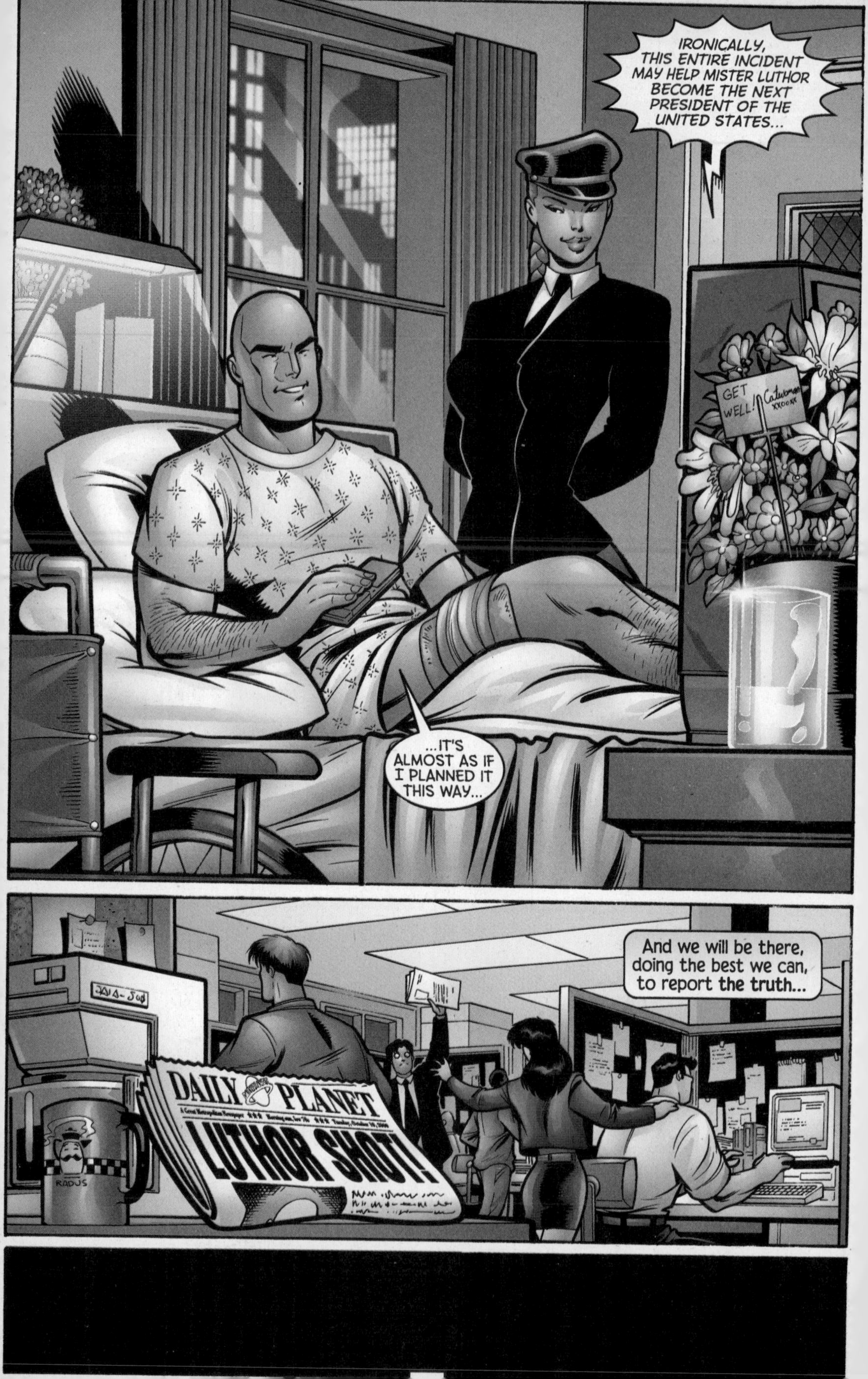
IRONICALLY, THIS ENTIRE INCIDENT MAY HELP MISTER LUTHOR BECOME THE NEXT PRESIDENT OF THE UNITED STATES...
GET WELL! Catwoman XXOOXX
...IT'S ALMOST AS IF I PLANNED IT THIS WAY...
And we will be there, doing the best we can, to report the truth...
DAILY PLANET
LUTHOR SHOT!
RADUS

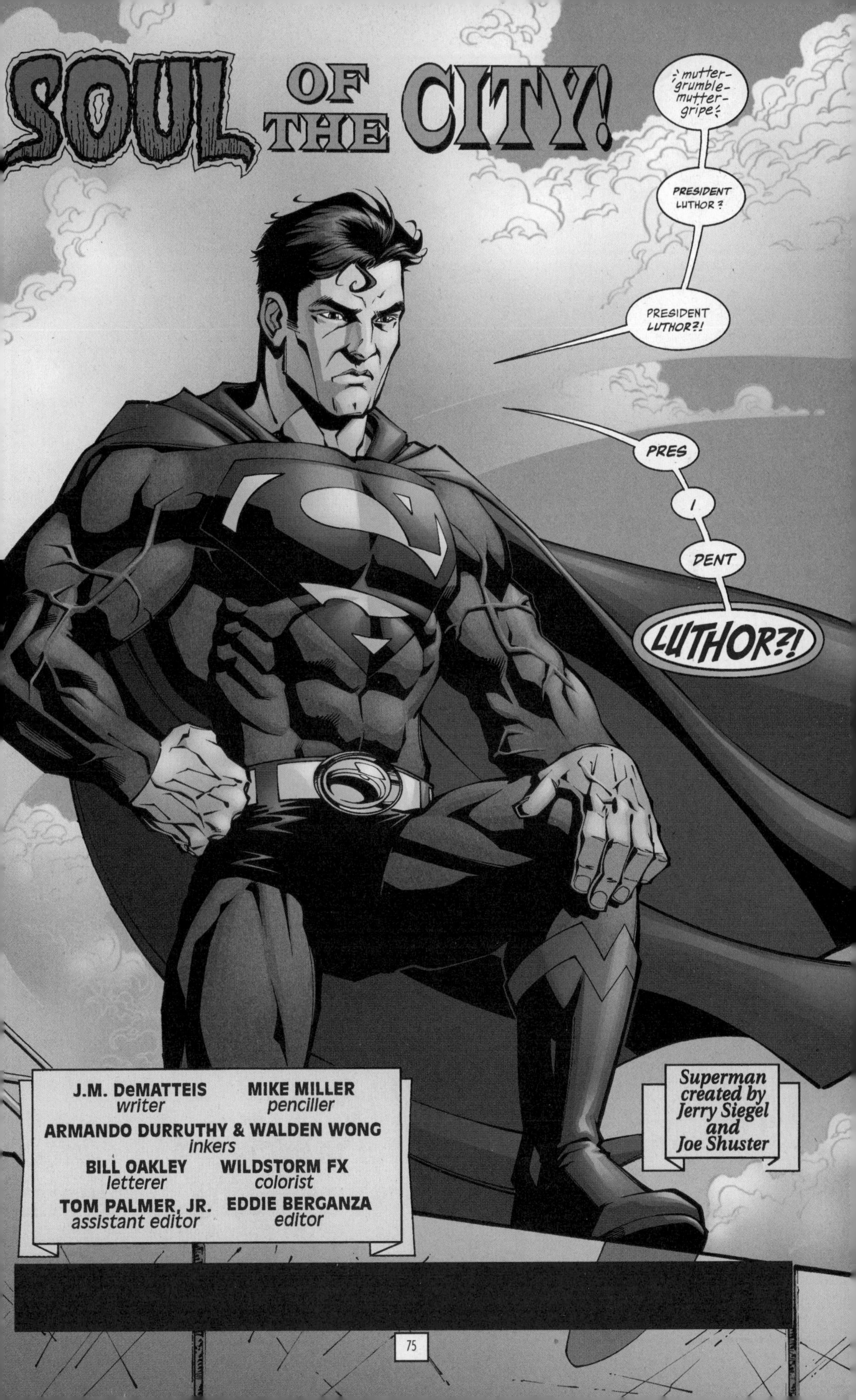
SOUL OF THE CITY!
mutter-grumble-mutter-gripe
PRESIDENT LUTHOR?
PRESIDENT LUTHOR?!
PRES
I
DENT
LUTHOR?!
J.M. DeMATTEIS writer
MIKE MILLER penciller
ARMANDO DURRUTHY & WALDEN WONG inkers
BILL OAKLEY letterer
WILDSTORM FX colorist
TOM PALMER, JR. assistant editor
EDDIE BERGANZA editor
Superman created by Jerry Siegel and Joe Shuster

LEX LUTHOR FOR PRESIDENT

LUTHOR

TOMORROW IS OURS!

LUTH
PRE

OR
ENT!

LUTHO FOR PREZ!

LUTHOR!

I... I JUST CAME BY TO SAY--

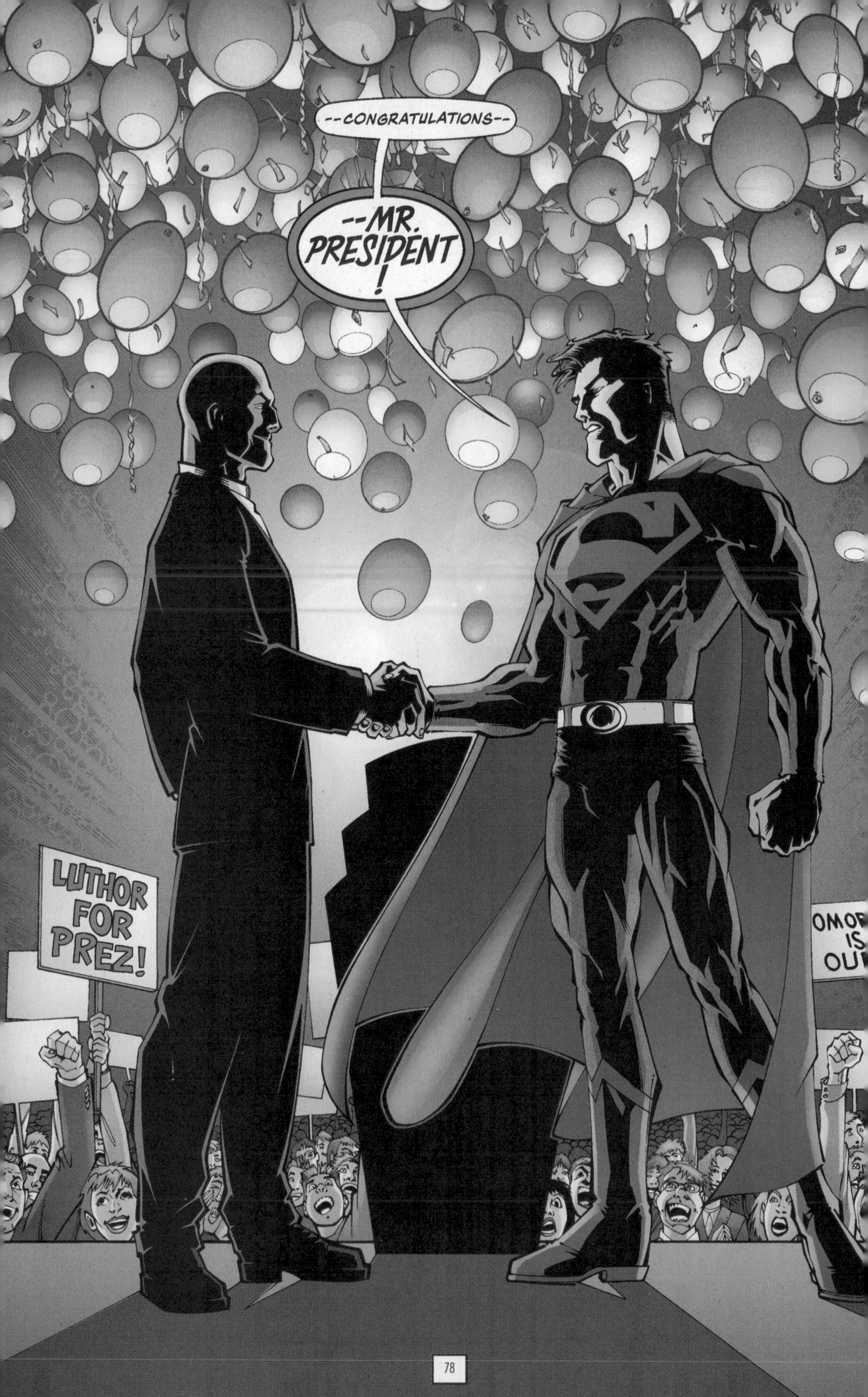
--CONGRATULATIONS--
--MR. PRESIDENT!
LUTHOR FOR PREZ!

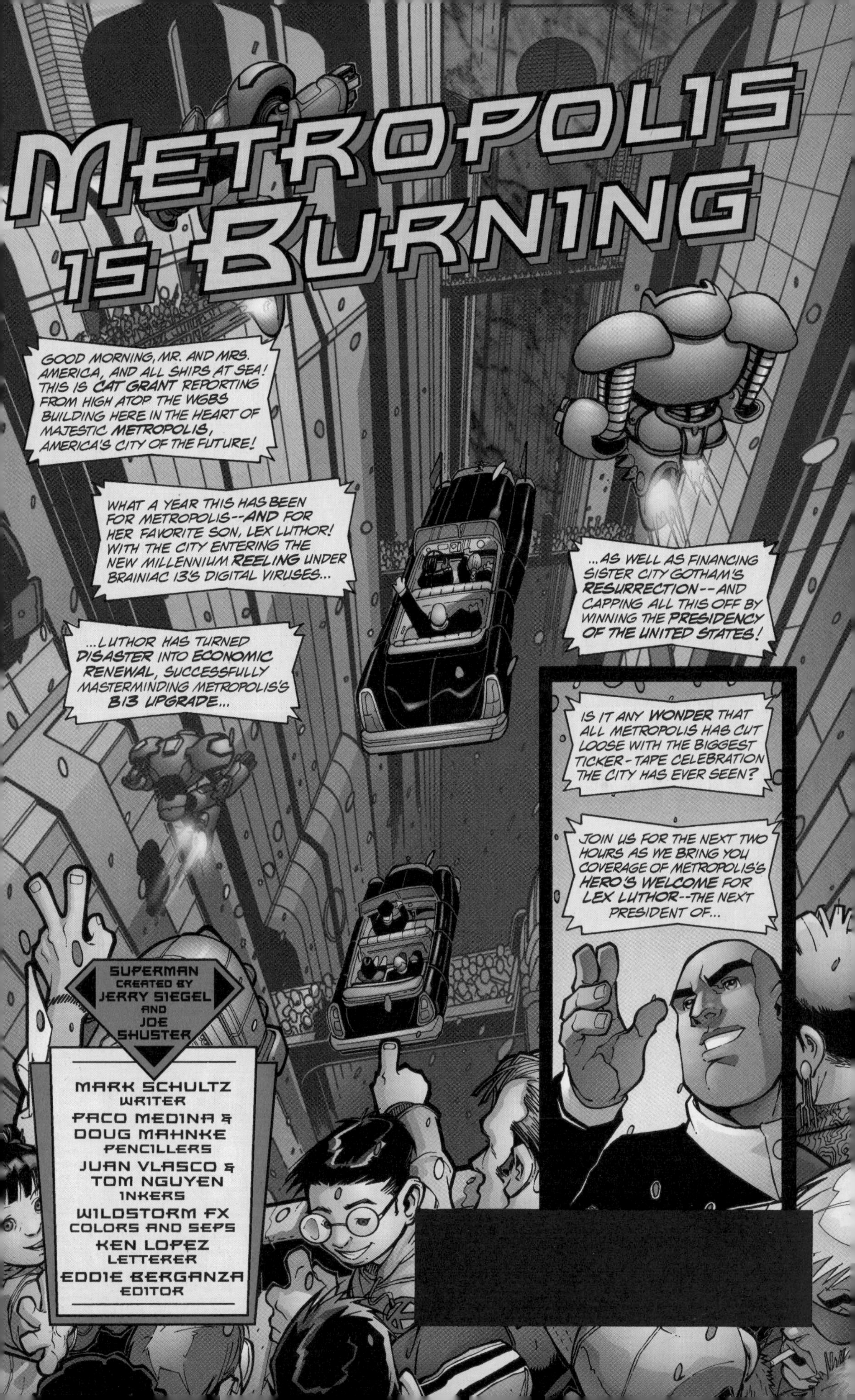
METROPOLIS IS BURNING
GOOD MORNING, MR. AND MRS. AMERICA, AND ALL SHIPS AT SEA! THIS IS CAT GRANT REPORTING FROM HIGH ATOP THE WGBS BUILDING HERE IN THE HEART OF MAJESTIC METROPOLIS, AMERICA'S CITY OF THE FUTURE!
WHAT A YEAR THIS HAS BEEN FOR METROPOLIS--AND FOR HER FAVORITE SON, LEX LUTHOR! WITH THE CITY ENTERING THE NEW MILLENNIUM REELING UNDER BRAINIAC 13'S DIGITAL VIRUSES...
...LUTHOR HAS TURNED DISASTER INTO ECONOMIC RENEWAL, SUCCESSFULLY MASTERMINDING METROPOLIS'S B13 UPGRADE...
...AS WELL AS FINANCING SISTER CITY GOTHAM'S RESURRECTION--AND CAPPING ALL THIS OFF BY WINNING THE PRESIDENCY OF THE UNITED STATES!
IS IT ANY WONDER THAT ALL METROPOLIS HAS CUT LOOSE WITH THE BIGGEST TICKER-TAPE CELEBRATION THE CITY HAS EVER SEEN?
JOIN US FOR THE NEXT TWO HOURS AS WE BRING YOU COVERAGE OF METROPOLIS'S HERO'S WELCOME FOR LEX LUTHOR--THE NEXT PRESIDENT OF...
SUPERMAN CREATED BY JERRY SIEGEL AND JOE SHUSTER
MARK SCHULTZ WRITER
PACO MEDINA & DOUG MAHNKE PENCILLERS
JUAN VLASCO & TOM NGUYEN INKERS
WILDSTORM FX COLORS AND SEPS
KEN LOPEZ LETTERER
EDDIE BERGANZA EDITOR

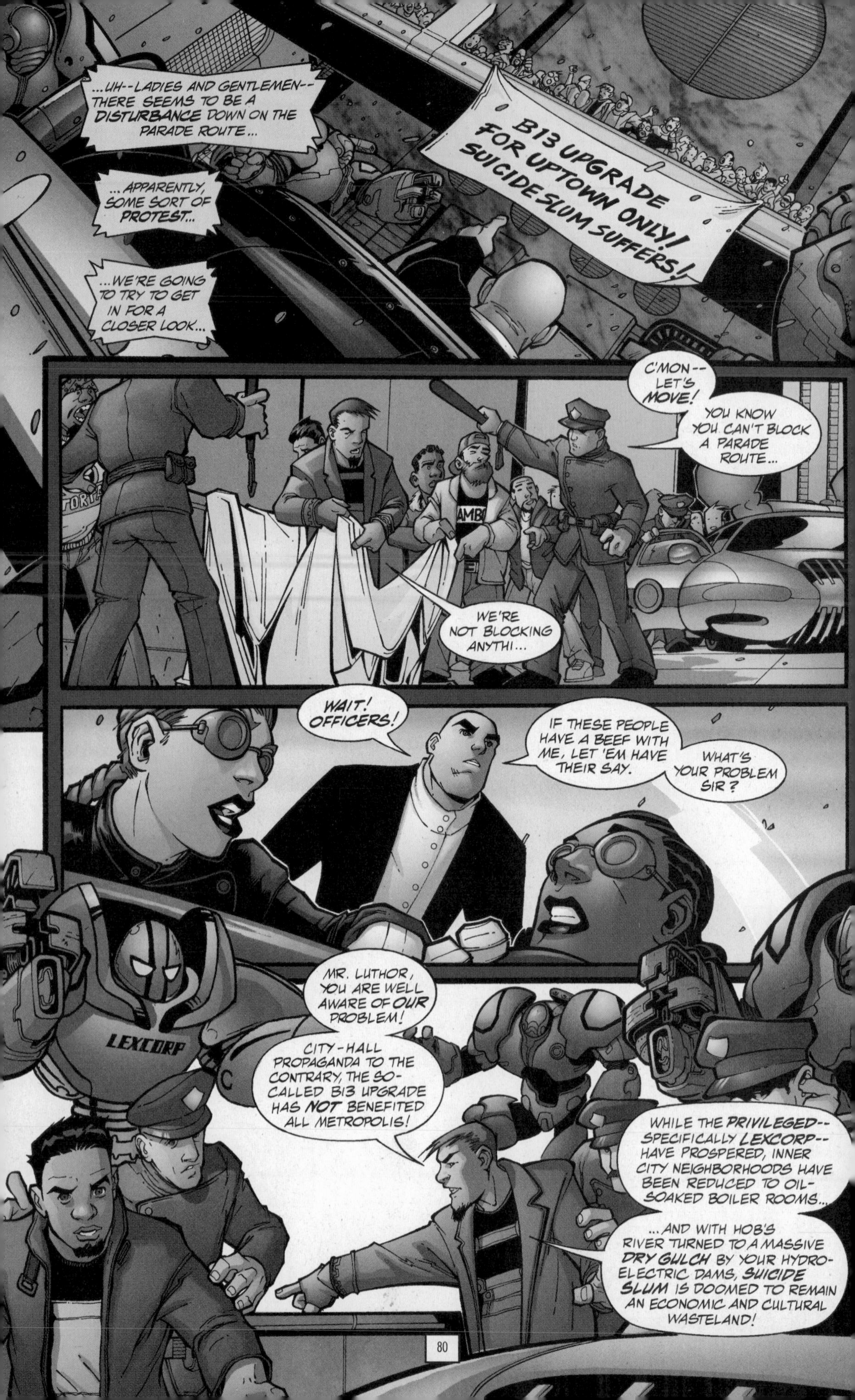
...UH--LADIES AND GENTLEMEN--
THERE SEEMS TO BE A DISTURBANCE DOWN ON THE PARADE ROUTE...
...APPARENTLY, SOME SORT OF PROTEST...
...WE'RE GOING TO TRY TO GET IN FOR A CLOSER LOOK...
B13 UPGRADE FOR UPTOWN ONLY! SUICIDE SLUM SUFFERS!
C'MON--LET'S MOVE!
YOU KNOW YOU CAN'T BLOCK A PARADE ROUTE...
WE'RE NOT BLOCKING ANYTHI...
WAIT! OFFICERS!
IF THESE PEOPLE HAVE A BEEF WITH ME, LET 'EM HAVE THEIR SAY.
WHAT'S YOUR PROBLEM SIR?
MR. LUTHOR, YOU ARE WELL AWARE OF OUR PROBLEM!
CITY-HALL PROPAGANDA TO THE CONTRARY, THE SO-CALLED B13 UPGRADE HAS NOT BENEFITED ALL METROPOLIS!
LEXCORP
WHILE THE PRIVILEGED--SPECIFICALLY LEXCORP--HAVE PROSPERED, INNER CITY NEIGHBORHOODS HAVE BEEN REDUCED TO OIL-SOAKED BOILER ROOMS...
...AND WITH HOB'S RIVER TURNED TO A MASSIVE DRY GULCH BY YOUR HYDRO-ELECTRIC DAMS, SUICIDE SLUM IS DOOMED TO REMAIN AN ECONOMIC AND CULTURAL WASTELAND!

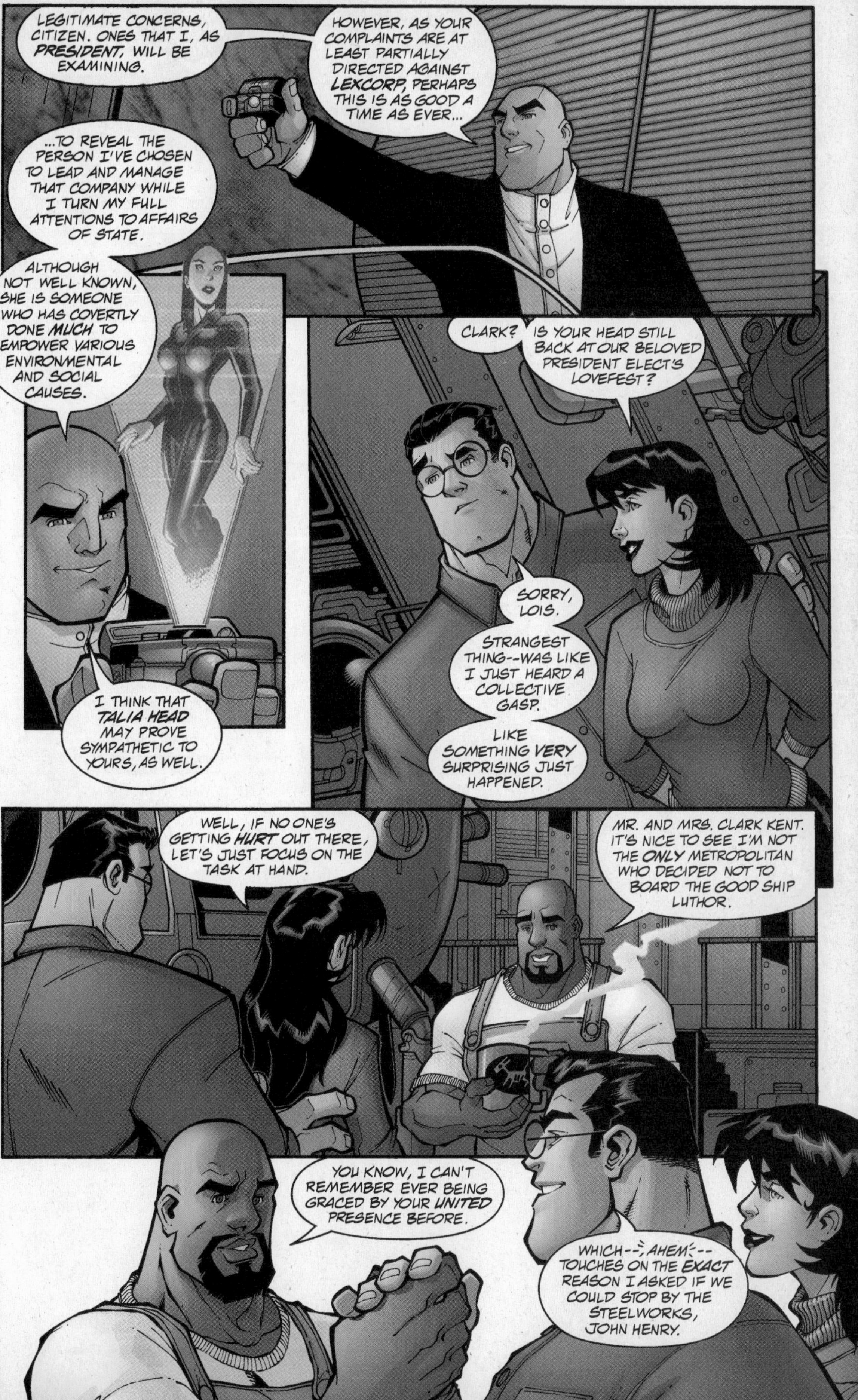
LEGITIMATE CONCERNS, CITIZEN. ONES THAT I, AS PRESIDENT, WILL BE EXAMINING.
HOWEVER, AS YOUR COMPLAINTS ARE AT LEAST PARTIALLY DIRECTED AGAINST LEXCORP, PERHAPS THIS IS AS GOOD A TIME AS EVER...
...TO REVEAL THE PERSON I'VE CHOSEN TO LEAD AND MANAGE THAT COMPANY WHILE I TURN MY FULL ATTENTIONS TO AFFAIRS OF STATE.
ALTHOUGH NOT WELL KNOWN, SHE IS SOMEONE WHO HAS COVERTLY DONE MUCH TO EMPOWER VARIOUS ENVIRONMENTAL AND SOCIAL CAUSES.
I THINK THAT TALIA HEAD MAY PROVE SYMPATHETIC TO YOURS, AS WELL.
CLARK?
IS YOUR HEAD STILL BACK AT OUR BELOVED PRESIDENT ELECT'S LOVEFEST?
SORRY, LOIS.
STRANGEST THING--WAS LIKE I JUST HEARD A COLLECTIVE GASP.
LIKE SOMETHING VERY SURPRISING JUST HAPPENED.
WELL, IF NO ONE'S GETTING HURT OUT THERE, LET'S JUST FOCUS ON THE TASK AT HAND.
MR. AND MRS. CLARK KENT. IT'S NICE TO SEE I'M NOT THE ONLY METROPOLITAN WHO DECIDED NOT TO BOARD THE GOOD SHIP LUTHOR.
YOU KNOW, I CAN'T REMEMBER EVER BEING GRACED BY YOUR UNITED PRESENCE BEFORE.
WHICH--AHEM--TOUCHES ON THE EXACT REASON I ASKED IF WE COULD STOP BY THE STEELWORKS, JOHN HENRY.

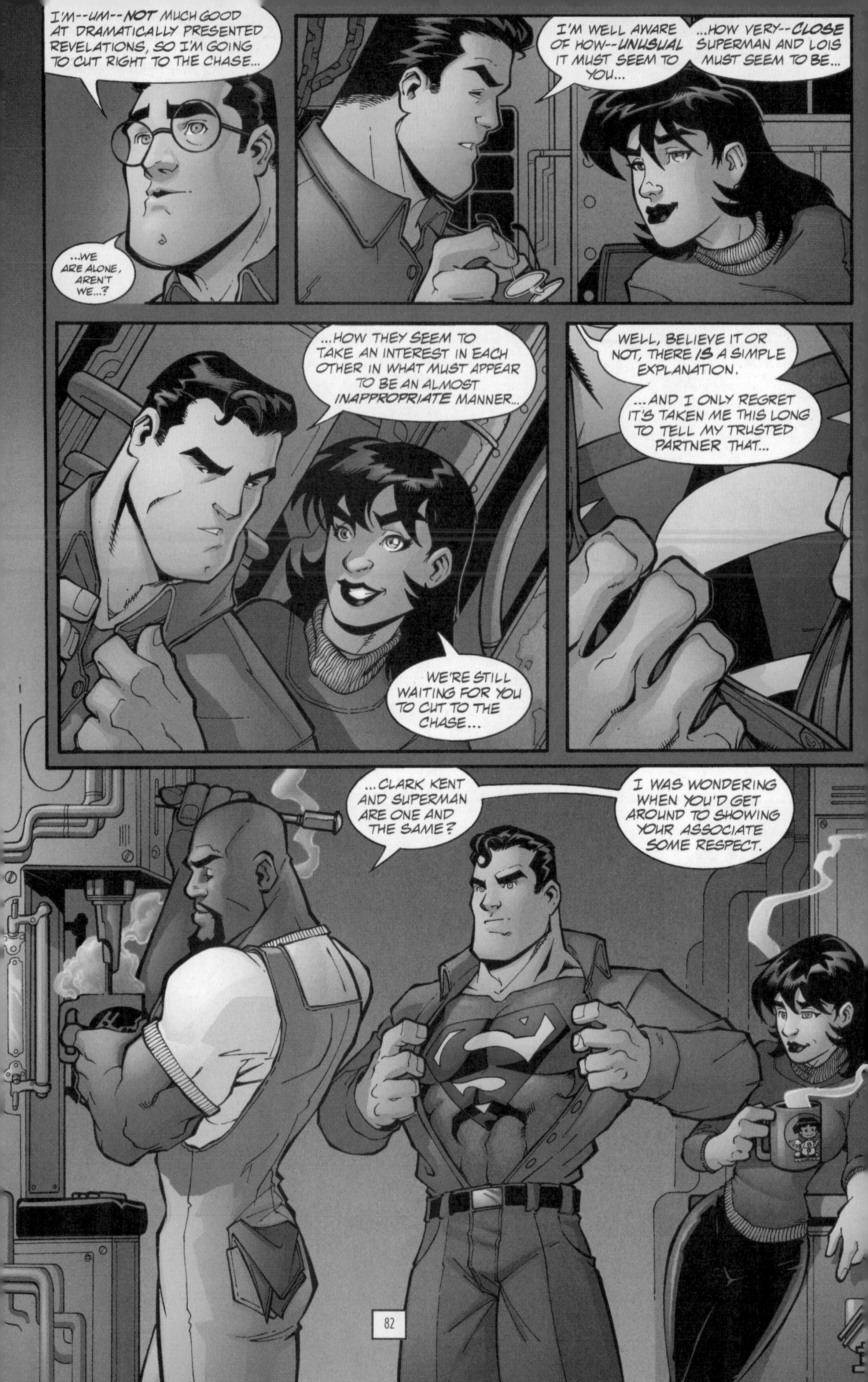
I'M--UM--NOT MUCH GOOD AT DRAMATICALLY PRESENTED REVELATIONS, SO I'M GOING TO CUT RIGHT TO THE CHASE...
...WE ARE ALONE, AREN'T WE...?
I'M WELL AWARE OF HOW--UNUSUAL IT MUST SEEM TO YOU...
...HOW VERY--CLOSE SUPERMAN AND LOIS MUST SEEM TO BE...
...HOW THEY SEEM TO TAKE AN INTEREST IN EACH OTHER IN WHAT MUST APPEAR TO BE AN ALMOST INAPPROPRIATE MANNER...
WE'RE STILL WAITING FOR YOU TO CUT TO THE CHASE...
WELL, BELIEVE IT OR NOT, THERE IS A SIMPLE EXPLANATION.
...AND I ONLY REGRET IT'S TAKEN ME THIS LONG TO TELL MY TRUSTED PARTNER THAT...
...CLARK KENT AND SUPERMAN ARE ONE AND THE SAME?
I WAS WONDERING WHEN YOU'D GET AROUND TO SHOWING YOUR ASSOCIATE SOME RESPECT.

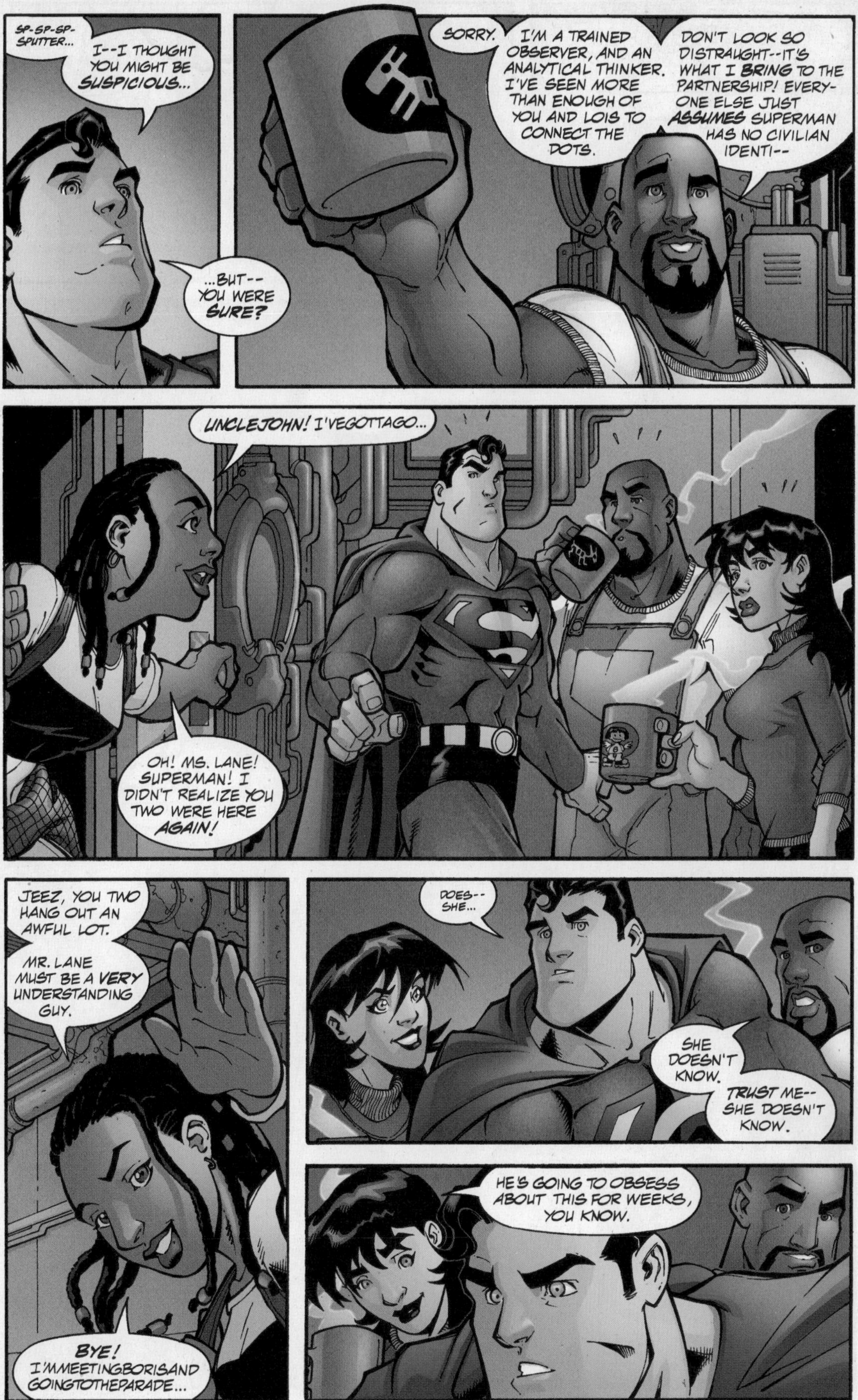
SP-SP-SP-SPUTTER...
I--I THOUGHT YOU MIGHT BE SUSPICIOUS...
...BUT--YOU WERE SURE?
SORRY.
I'M A TRAINED OBSERVER, AND AN ANALYTICAL THINKER. I'VE SEEN MORE THAN ENOUGH OF YOU AND LOIS TO CONNECT THE DOTS.
DON'T LOOK SO DISTRAUGHT--IT'S WHAT I BRING TO THE PARTNERSHIP! EVERY-ONE ELSE JUST ASSUMES SUPERMAN HAS NO CIVILIAN IDENTI--
UNCLEJOHN! I'VEGOTTAGO...
OH! MS. LANE! SUPERMAN! I DIDN'T REALIZE YOU TWO WERE HERE AGAIN!
JEEZ, YOU TWO HANG OUT AN AWFUL LOT.
MR. LANE MUST BE A VERY UNDERSTANDING GUY.
BYE! I'MMEETINGBORISAND GOINGTOTHEPARADE...
DOES--SHE...
SHE DOESN'T KNOW.
TRUST ME--SHE DOESN'T KNOW.
HE'S GOING TO OBSESS ABOUT THIS FOR WEEKS, YOU KNOW.

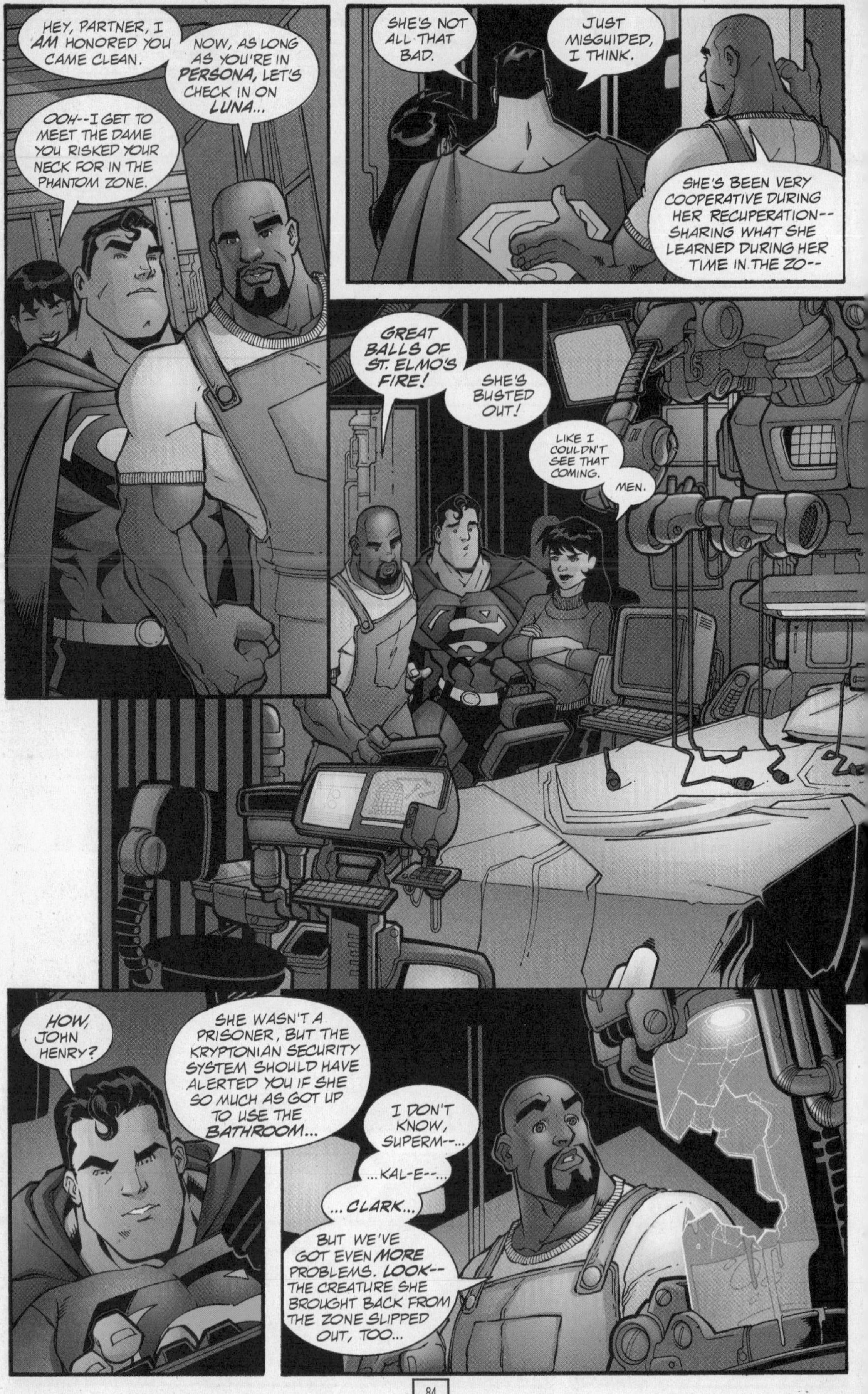
HEY, PARTNER, I AM HONORED YOU CAME CLEAN.
NOW, AS LONG AS YOU'RE IN PERSONA, LET'S CHECK IN ON LUNA...
OOH--I GET TO MEET THE DAME YOU RISKED YOUR NECK FOR IN THE PHANTOM ZONE.
SHE'S NOT ALL THAT BAD.
JUST MISGUIDED, I THINK.
SHE'S BEEN VERY COOPERATIVE DURING HER RECUPERATION--SHARING WHAT SHE LEARNED DURING HER TIME IN THE ZO--
GREAT BALLS OF ST. ELMO'S FIRE!
SHE'S BUSTED OUT!
LIKE I COULDN'T SEE THAT COMING.
MEN.
HOW, JOHN HENRY?
SHE WASN'T A PRISONER, BUT THE KRYPTONIAN SECURITY SYSTEM SHOULD HAVE ALERTED YOU IF SHE SO MUCH AS GOT UP TO USE THE BATHROOM...
I DON'T KNOW, SUPERM--...
...KAL-E--...
...CLARK...
BUT WE'VE GOT EVEN MORE PROBLEMS. LOOK--THE CREATURE SHE BROUGHT BACK FROM THE ZONE SLIPPED OUT, TOO...

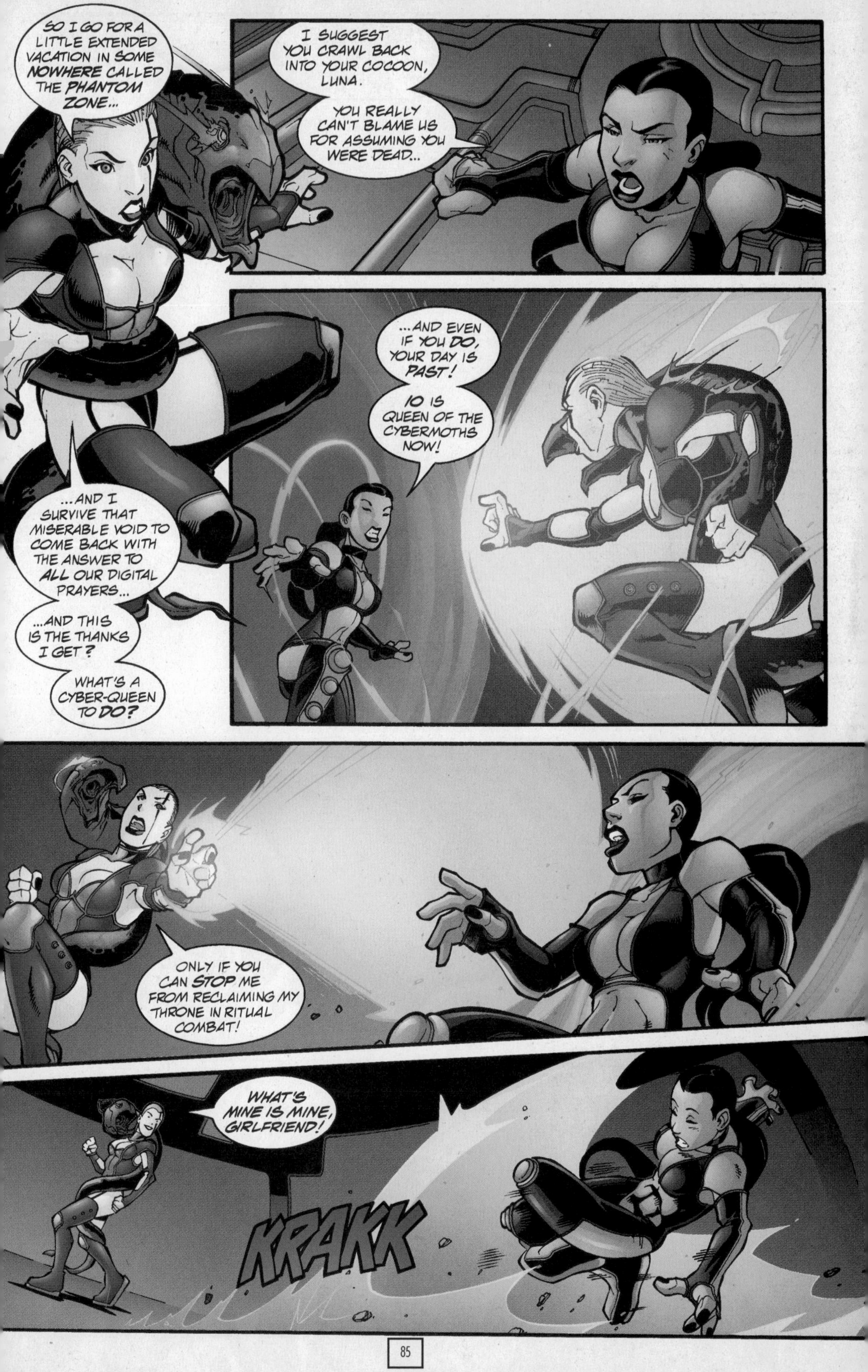
SO I GO FOR A LITTLE EXTENDED VACATION IN SOME NOWHERE CALLED THE PHANTOM ZONE...
I SUGGEST YOU CRAWL BACK INTO YOUR COCOON, LUNA.
YOU REALLY CAN'T BLAME US FOR ASSUMING YOU WERE DEAD...
...AND I SURVIVE THAT MISERABLE VOID TO COME BACK WITH THE ANSWER TO ALL OUR DIGITAL PRAYERS...
...AND THIS IS THE THANKS I GET?
WHAT'S A CYBER-QUEEN TO DO?
...AND EVEN IF YOU DO, YOUR DAY IS PAST!
IO IS QUEEN OF THE CYBERMOTHS NOW!
ONLY IF YOU CAN STOP ME FROM RECLAIMING MY THRONE IN RITUAL COMBAT!
WHAT'S MINE IS MINE, GIRLFRIEND!
KRAKK

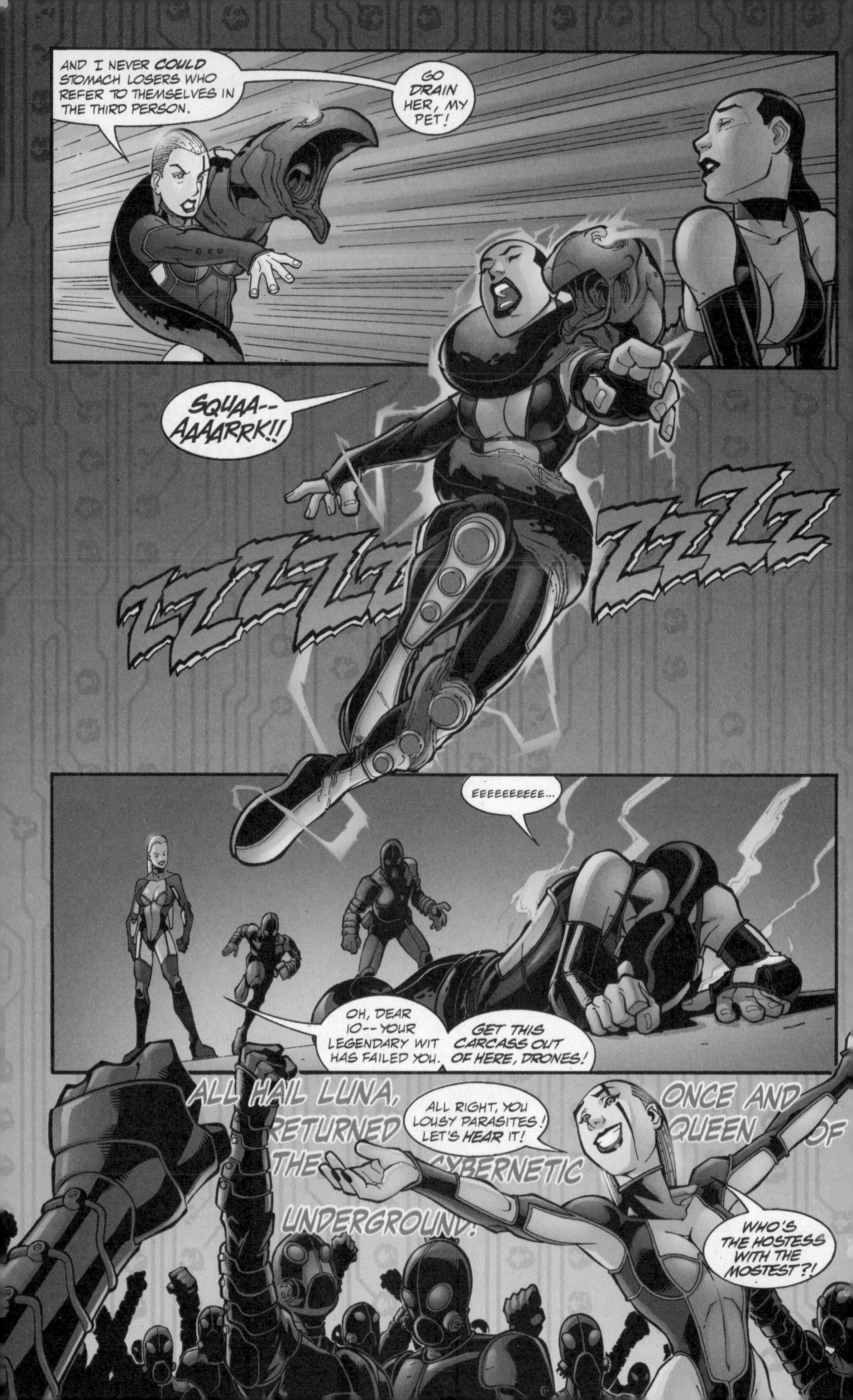
AND I NEVER COULD STOMACH LOSERS WHO REFER TO THEMSELVES IN THE THIRD PERSON.
GO DRAIN HER, MY PET!
SQUAA-- AAAARRK!!
ZZZZZZZZZZZ
EEEEEEEEEE...
OH, DEAR IO-- YOUR LEGENDARY WIT HAS FAILED YOU.
GET THIS CARCASS OUT OF HERE, DRONES!
ALL RIGHT, YOU LOUSY PARASITES! LET'S HEAR IT!
ALL HAIL LUNA, RETURNED ONCE AND QUEEN OF THE CYBERNETIC UNDERGROUND!
WHO'S THE HOSTESS WITH THE MOSTEST?!

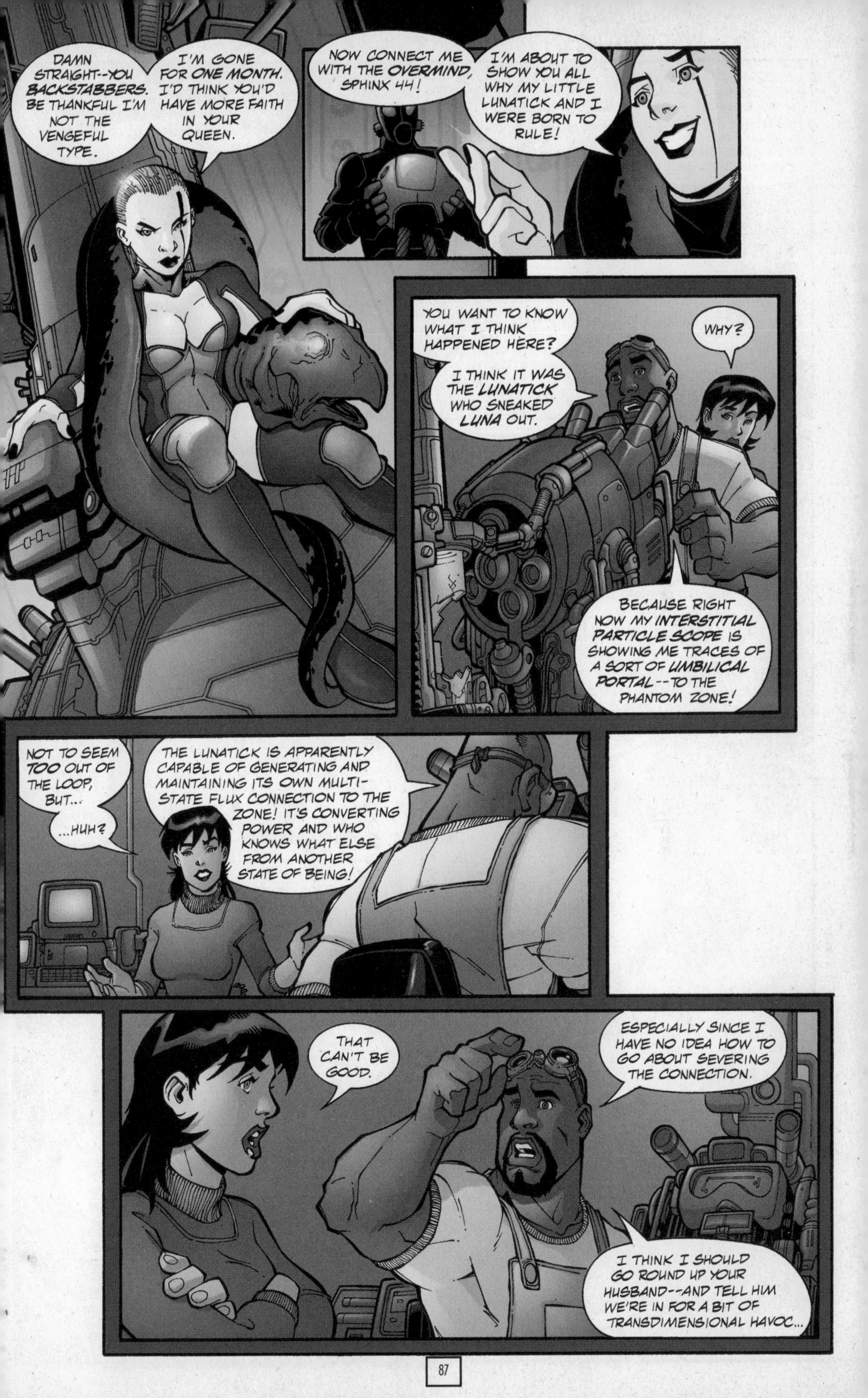
DAMN STRAIGHT--YOU BACKSTABBERS. BE THANKFUL I'M NOT THE VENGEFUL TYPE.
I'M GONE FOR ONE MONTH. I'D THINK YOU'D HAVE MORE FAITH IN YOUR QUEEN.
NOW CONNECT ME WITH THE OVERMIND, SPHINX 44!
I'M ABOUT TO SHOW YOU ALL WHY MY LITTLE LUNATICK AND I WERE BORN TO RULE!
YOU WANT TO KNOW WHAT I THINK HAPPENED HERE?
I THINK IT WAS THE LUNATICK WHO SNEAKED LUNA OUT.
WHY?
BECAUSE RIGHT NOW MY INTERSTITIAL PARTICLE SCOPE IS SHOWING ME TRACES OF A SORT OF UMBILICAL PORTAL--TO THE PHANTOM ZONE!
NOT TO SEEM TOO OUT OF THE LOOP, BUT...
...HUH?
THE LUNATICK IS APPARENTLY CAPABLE OF GENERATING AND MAINTAINING ITS OWN MULTI-STATE FLUX CONNECTION TO THE ZONE! IT'S CONVERTING POWER AND WHO KNOWS WHAT ELSE FROM ANOTHER STATE OF BEING!
THAT CAN'T BE GOOD.
ESPECIALLY SINCE I HAVE NO IDEA HOW TO GO ABOUT SEVERING THE CONNECTION.
I THINK I SHOULD GO ROUND UP YOUR HUSBAND--AND TELL HIM WE'RE IN FOR A BIT OF TRANSDIMENSIONAL HAVOC...

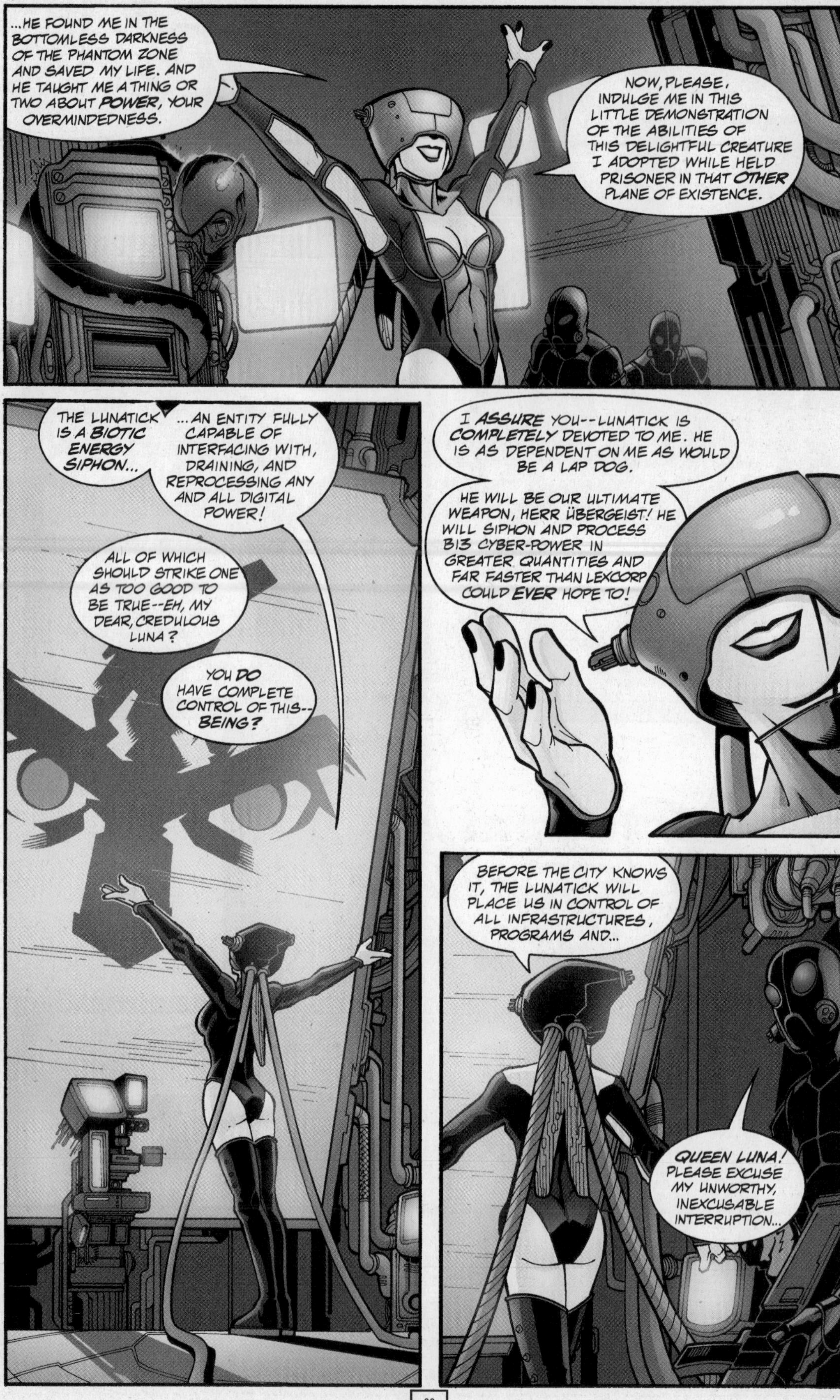
...HE FOUND ME IN THE BOTTOMLESS DARKNESS OF THE PHANTOM ZONE AND SAVED MY LIFE. AND HE TAUGHT ME A THING OR TWO ABOUT POWER, YOUR OVERMINDEDNESS.
NOW, PLEASE, INDULGE ME IN THIS LITTLE DEMONSTRATION OF THE ABILITIES OF THIS DELIGHTFUL CREATURE I ADOPTED WHILE HELD PRISONER IN THAT OTHER PLANE OF EXISTENCE.
THE LUNATICK IS A BIOTIC ENERGY SIPHON...
...AN ENTITY FULLY CAPABLE OF INTERFACING WITH, DRAINING, AND REPROCESSING ANY AND ALL DIGITAL POWER!
ALL OF WHICH SHOULD STRIKE ONE AS TOO GOOD TO BE TRUE--EH, MY DEAR, CREDULOUS LUNA?
YOU DO HAVE COMPLETE CONTROL OF THIS--BEING?
I ASSURE YOU--LUNATICK IS COMPLETELY DEVOTED TO ME. HE IS AS DEPENDENT ON ME AS WOULD BE A LAP DOG.
HE WILL BE OUR ULTIMATE WEAPON, HERR ÜBERGEIST! HE WILL SIPHON AND PROCESS B13 CYBER-POWER IN GREATER QUANTITIES AND FAR FASTER THAN LEXCORP COULD EVER HOPE TO!
BEFORE THE CITY KNOWS IT, THE LUNATICK WILL PLACE US IN CONTROL OF ALL INFRASTRUCTURES, PROGRAMS AND...
QUEEN LUNA! PLEASE EXCUSE MY UNWORTHY, INEXCUSABLE INTERRUPTION...

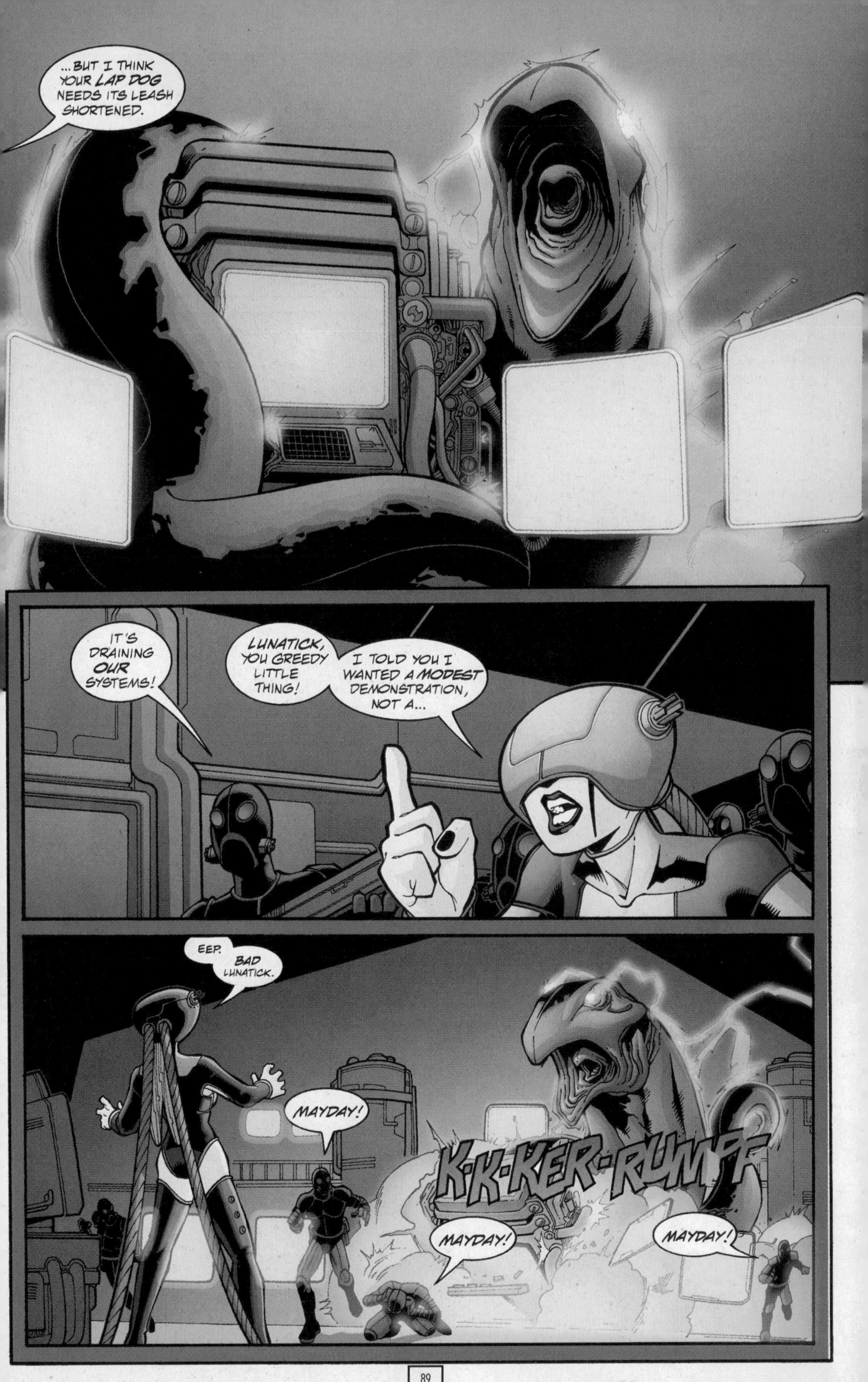

...BUT I THINK YOUR LAP DOG NEEDS ITS LEASH SHORTENED.
IT'S DRAINING OUR SYSTEMS!
LUNATICK, YOU GREEDY LITTLE THING!
I TOLD YOU I WANTED A MODEST DEMONSTRATION, NOT A...
EEP.
BAD LUNATICK.
MAYDAY!
K-K-KER-RUMPF
MAYDAY!
MAYDAY!

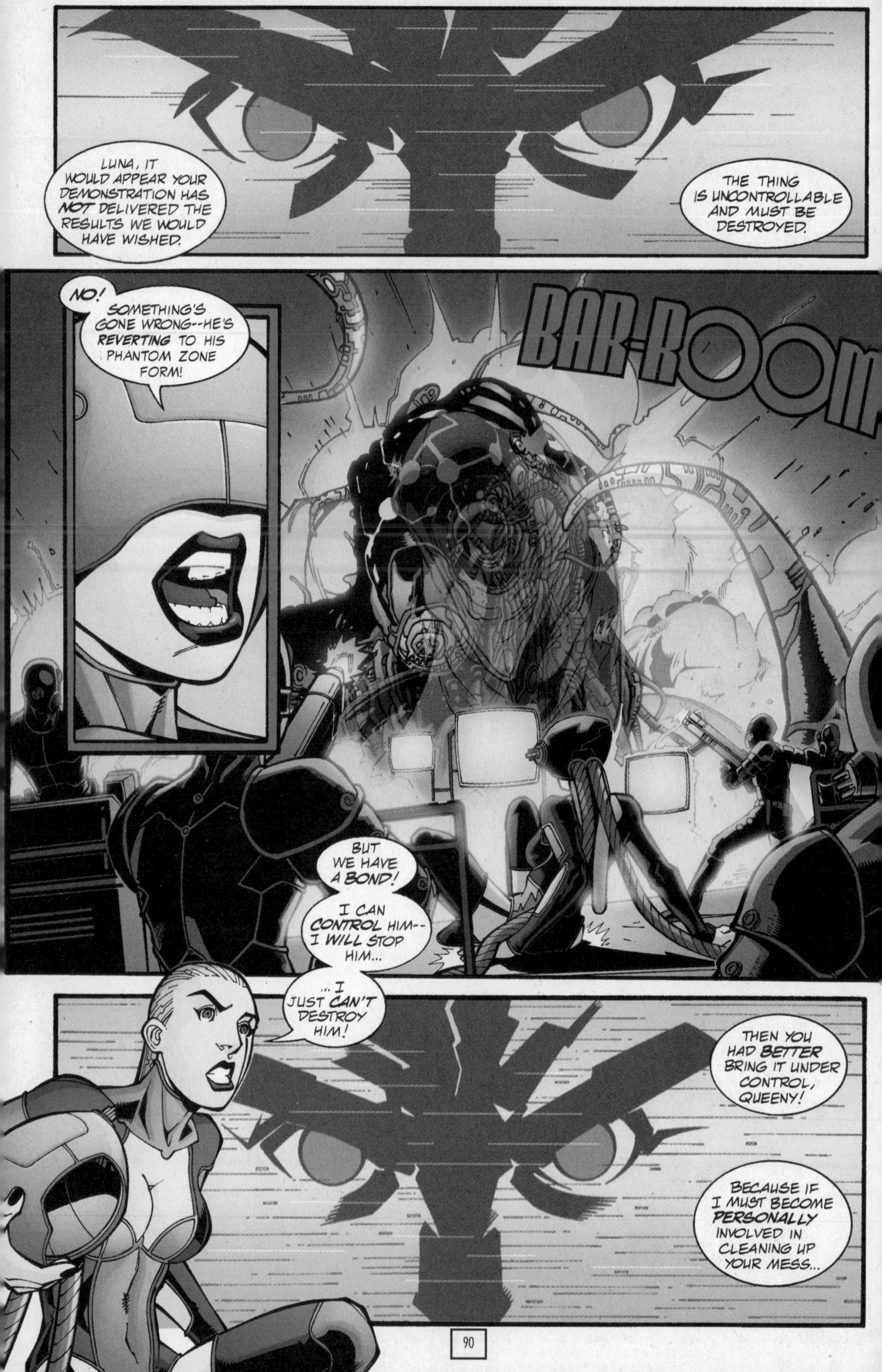
LUNA, IT WOULD APPEAR YOUR DEMONSTRATION HAS NOT DELIVERED THE RESULTS WE WOULD HAVE WISHED.
THE THING IS UNCONTROLLABLE AND MUST BE DESTROYED.
NO! SOMETHING'S GONE WRONG--HE'S REVERTING TO HIS PHANTOM ZONE FORM!
BAR-ROOM
BUT WE HAVE A BOND!
I CAN CONTROL HIM-- I WILL STOP HIM...
... I JUST CAN'T DESTROY HIM!
THEN YOU HAD BETTER BRING IT UNDER CONTROL, QUEENY!
BECAUSE IF I MUST BECOME PERSONALLY INVOLVED IN CLEANING UP YOUR MESS...

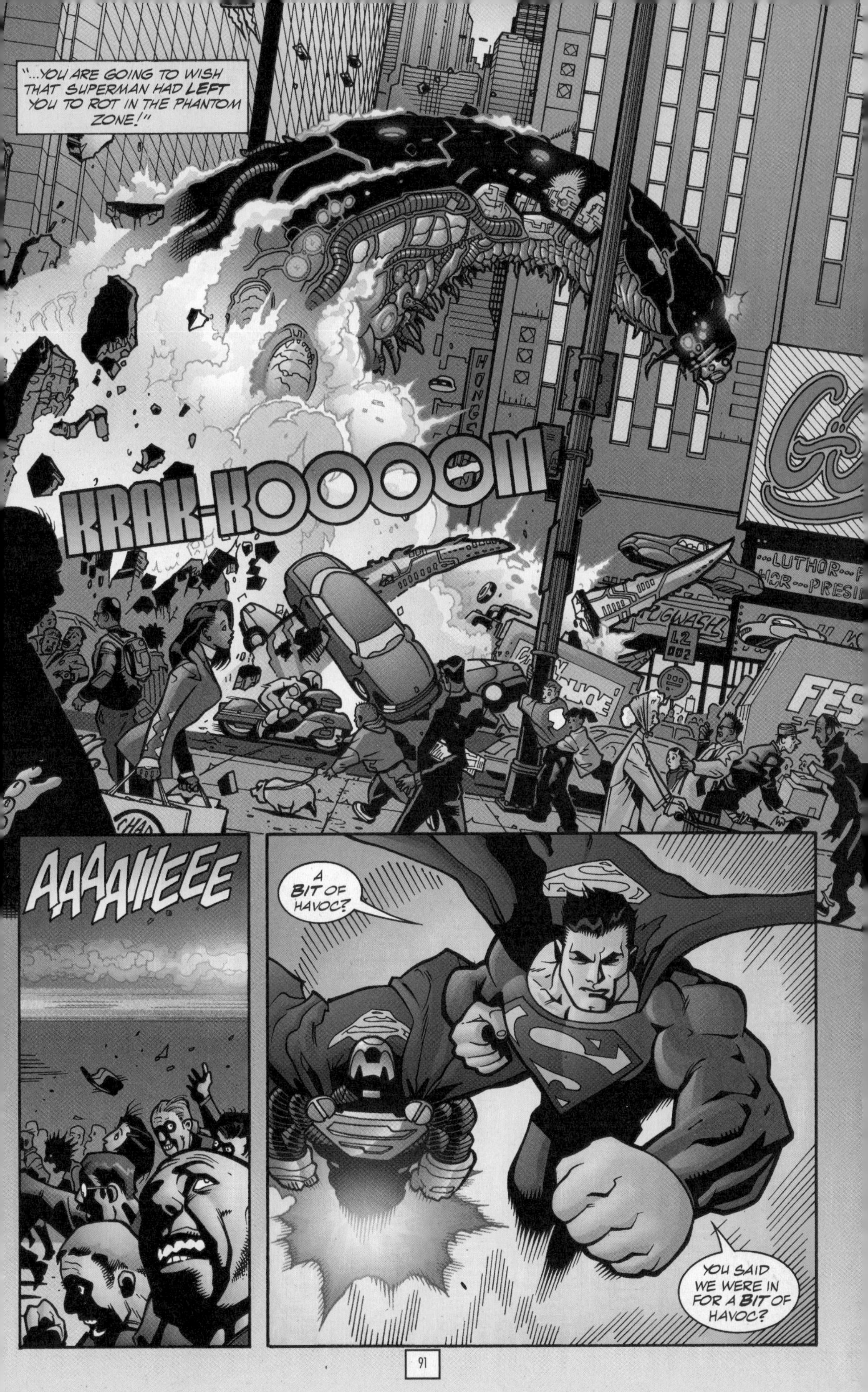
"...YOU ARE GOING TO WISH THAT SUPERMAN HAD LEFT YOU TO ROT IN THE PHANTOM ZONE!"
KRAK-KOOOOOM
...LUTHOR...F
HOR...PRESI
FES
AAAAIIIEEE
A BIT OF HAVOC?
YOU SAID WE WERE IN FOR A BIT OF HAVOC?

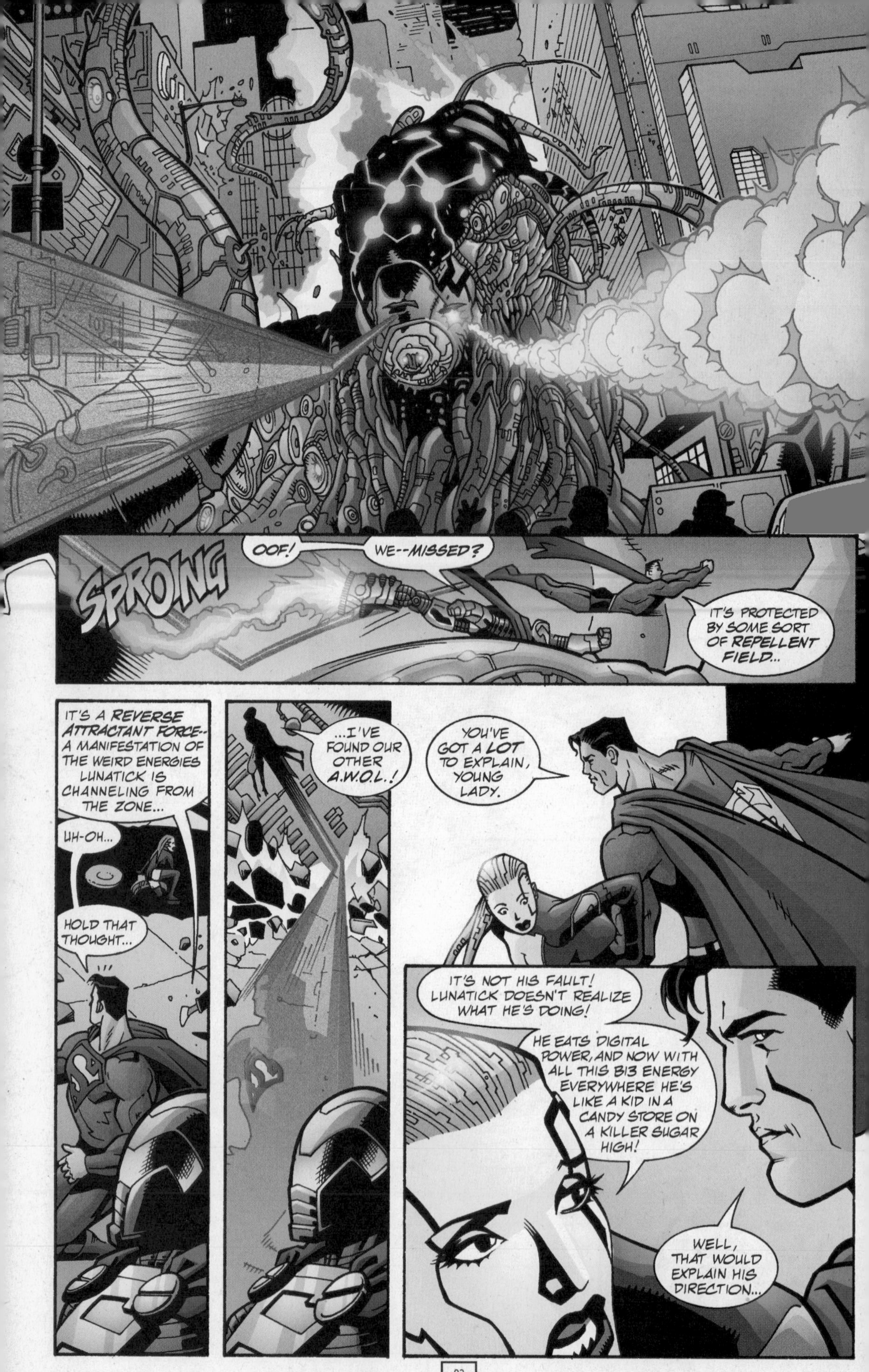
SPROING
OOF!
WE--MISSED?
IT'S PROTECTED BY SOME SORT OF REPELLENT FIELD...
IT'S A REVERSE ATTRACTANT FORCE-- A MANIFESTATION OF THE WEIRD ENERGIES LUNATICK IS CHANNELING FROM THE ZONE...
UH-OH...
HOLD THAT THOUGHT...
...I'VE FOUND OUR OTHER A.W.O.L.!
YOU'VE GOT A LOT TO EXPLAIN, YOUNG LADY.
IT'S NOT HIS FAULT! LUNATICK DOESN'T REALIZE WHAT HE'S DOING!
HE EATS DIGITAL POWER, AND NOW WITH ALL THIS B13 ENERGY EVERYWHERE HE'S LIKE A KID IN A CANDY STORE ON A KILLER SUGAR HIGH!
WELL, THAT WOULD EXPLAIN HIS DIRECTION...

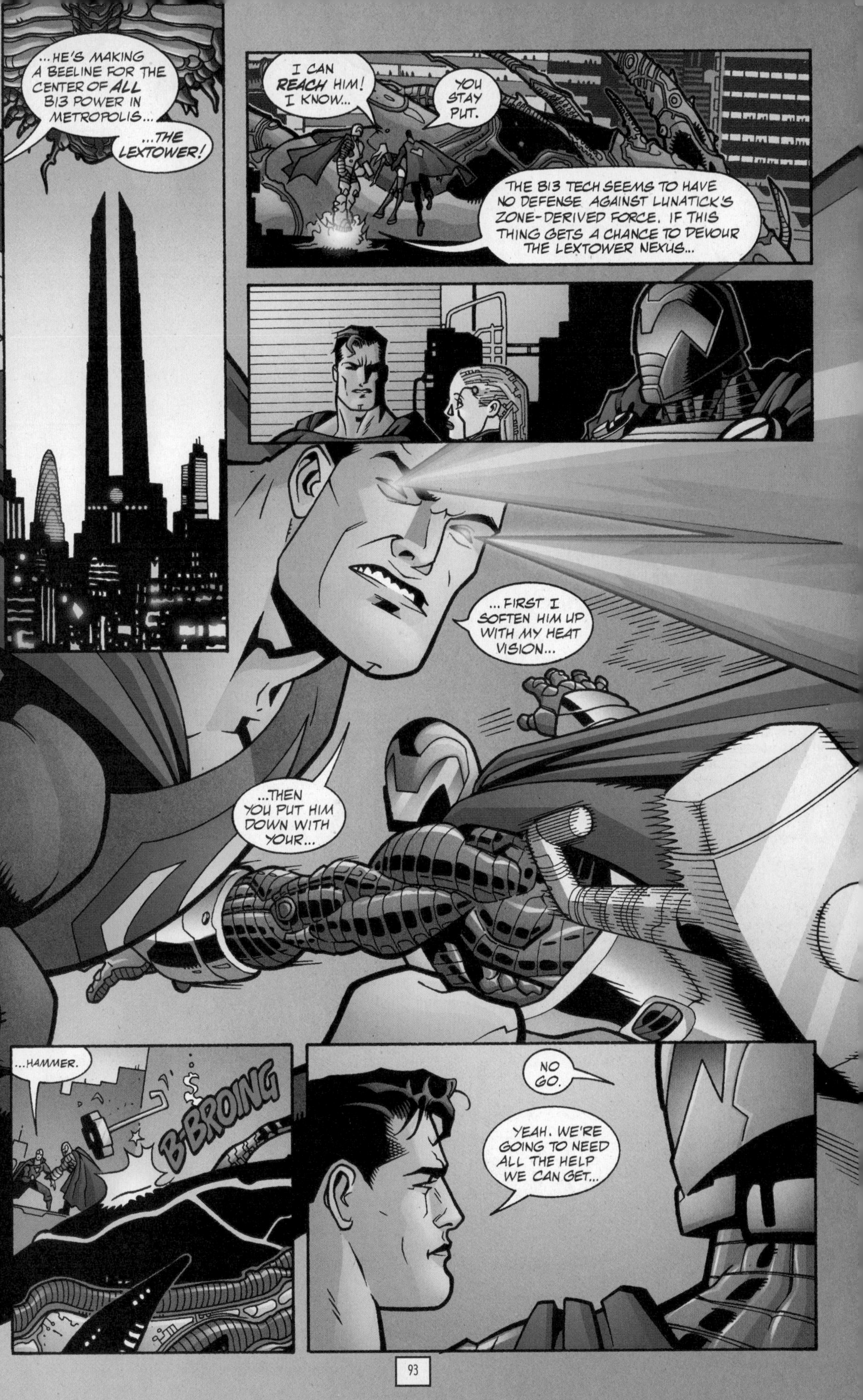
...HE'S MAKING A BEELINE FOR THE CENTER OF ALL B13 POWER IN METROPOLIS...
...THE LEXTOWER!
I CAN REACH HIM! I KNOW...
YOU STAY PUT.
THE B13 TECH SEEMS TO HAVE NO DEFENSE AGAINST LUNATICK'S ZONE-DERIVED FORCE. IF THIS THING GETS A CHANCE TO DEVOUR THE LEXTOWER NEXUS...
...FIRST I SOFTEN HIM UP WITH MY HEAT VISION...
...THEN YOU PUT HIM DOWN WITH YOUR...
...HAMMER.
B-BROING
NO GO.
YEAH. WE'RE GOING TO NEED ALL THE HELP WE CAN GET...

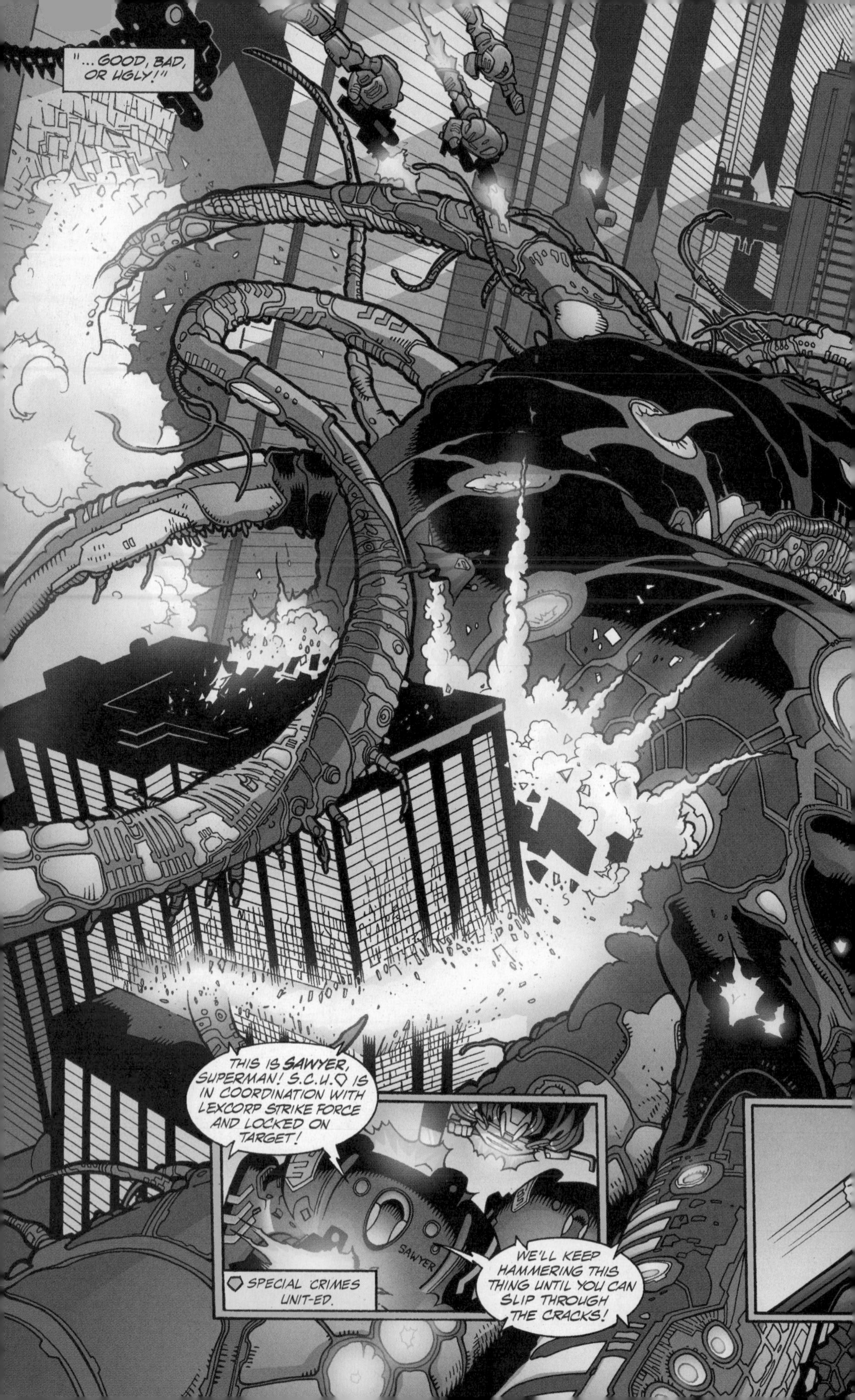
"...GOOD, BAD, OR UGLY!"
THIS IS SAWYER, SUPERMAN! S.C.U.◊ IS IN COORDINATION WITH LEXCORP STRIKE FORCE AND LOCKED ON TARGET!
SAWYER
◊ SPECIAL CRIMES UNIT-ED.
WE'LL KEEP HAMMERING THIS THING UNTIL YOU CAN SLIP THROUGH THE CRACKS!

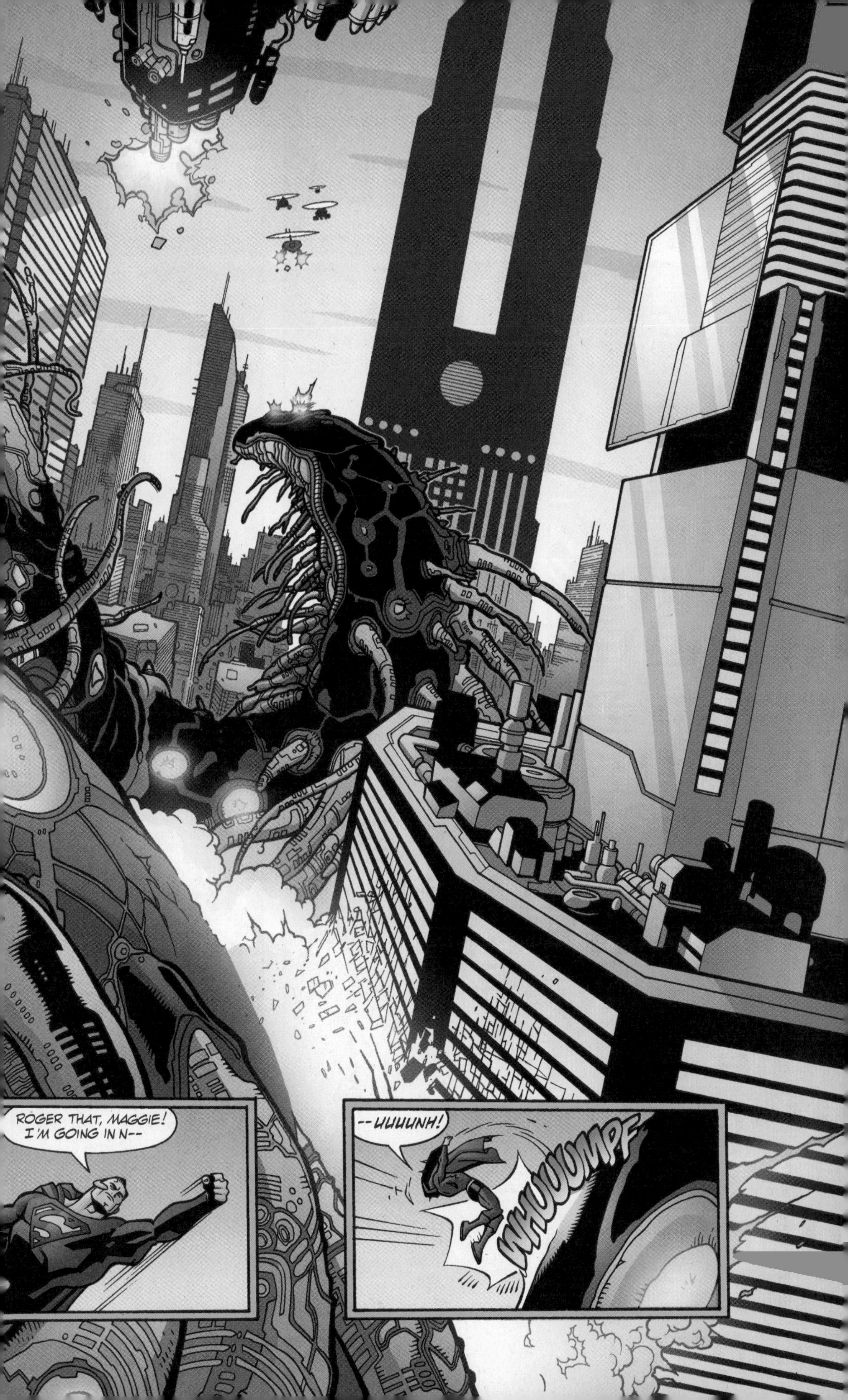
ROGER THAT, MAGGIE! I'M GOING IN N--
--UUUUNH!
WHUUUMPF

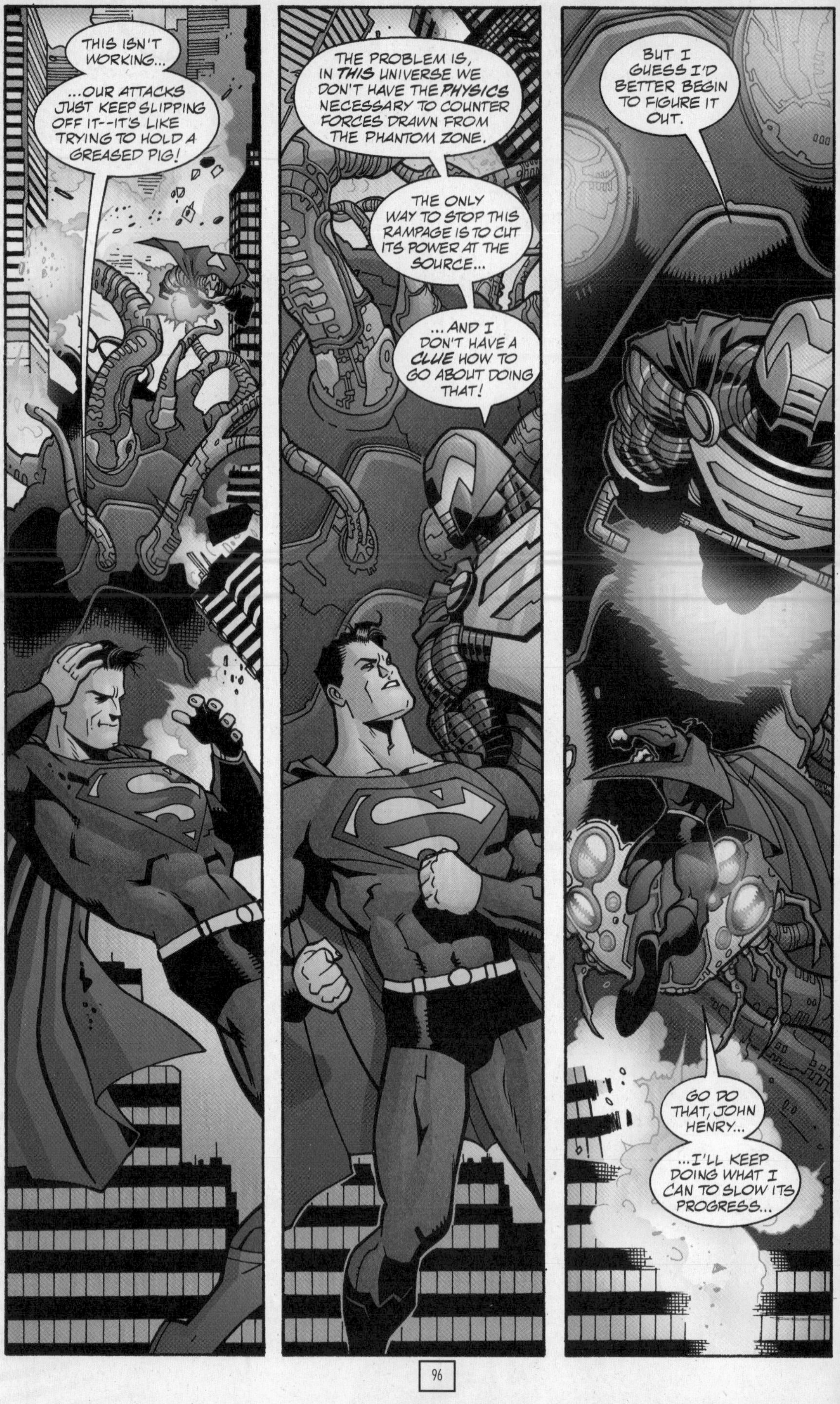
THIS ISN'T WORKING...
...OUR ATTACKS JUST KEEP SLIPPING OFF IT--IT'S LIKE TRYING TO HOLD A GREASED PIG!
THE PROBLEM IS, IN THIS UNIVERSE WE DON'T HAVE THE PHYSICS NECESSARY TO COUNTER FORCES DRAWN FROM THE PHANTOM ZONE.
THE ONLY WAY TO STOP THIS RAMPAGE IS TO CUT ITS POWER AT THE SOURCE...
...AND I DON'T HAVE A CLUE HOW TO GO ABOUT DOING THAT!
BUT I GUESS I'D BETTER BEGIN TO FIGURE IT OUT.
GO DO THAT, JOHN HENRY...
...I'LL KEEP DOING WHAT I CAN TO SLOW ITS PROGRESS...

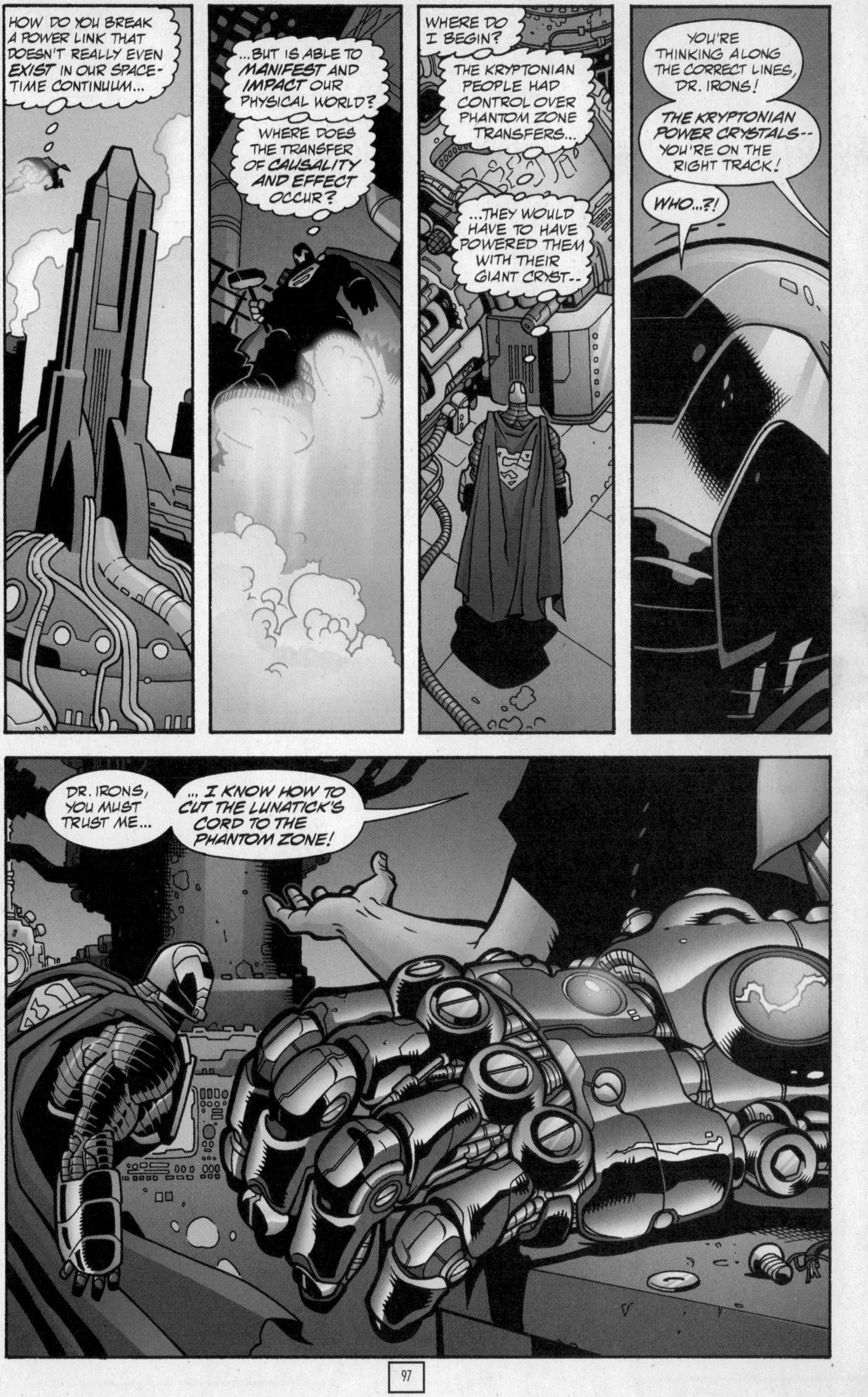
HOW DO YOU BREAK A POWER LINK THAT DOESN'T REALLY EVEN EXIST IN OUR SPACE-TIME CONTINUUM...
...BUT IS ABLE TO MANIFEST AND IMPACT OUR PHYSICAL WORLD?
WHERE DOES THE TRANSFER OF CAUSALITY AND EFFECT OCCUR?
WHERE DO I BEGIN?
THE KRYPTONIAN PEOPLE HAD CONTROL OVER PHANTOM ZONE TRANSFERS...
...THEY WOULD HAVE TO HAVE POWERED THEM WITH THEIR GIANT CRYST--
YOU'RE THINKING ALONG THE CORRECT LINES, DR. IRONS!
THE KRYPTONIAN POWER CRYSTALS-- YOU'RE ON THE RIGHT TRACK!
WHO...?!
DR. IRONS, YOU MUST TRUST ME...
... I KNOW HOW TO CUT THE LUNATICK'S CORD TO THE PHANTOM ZONE!

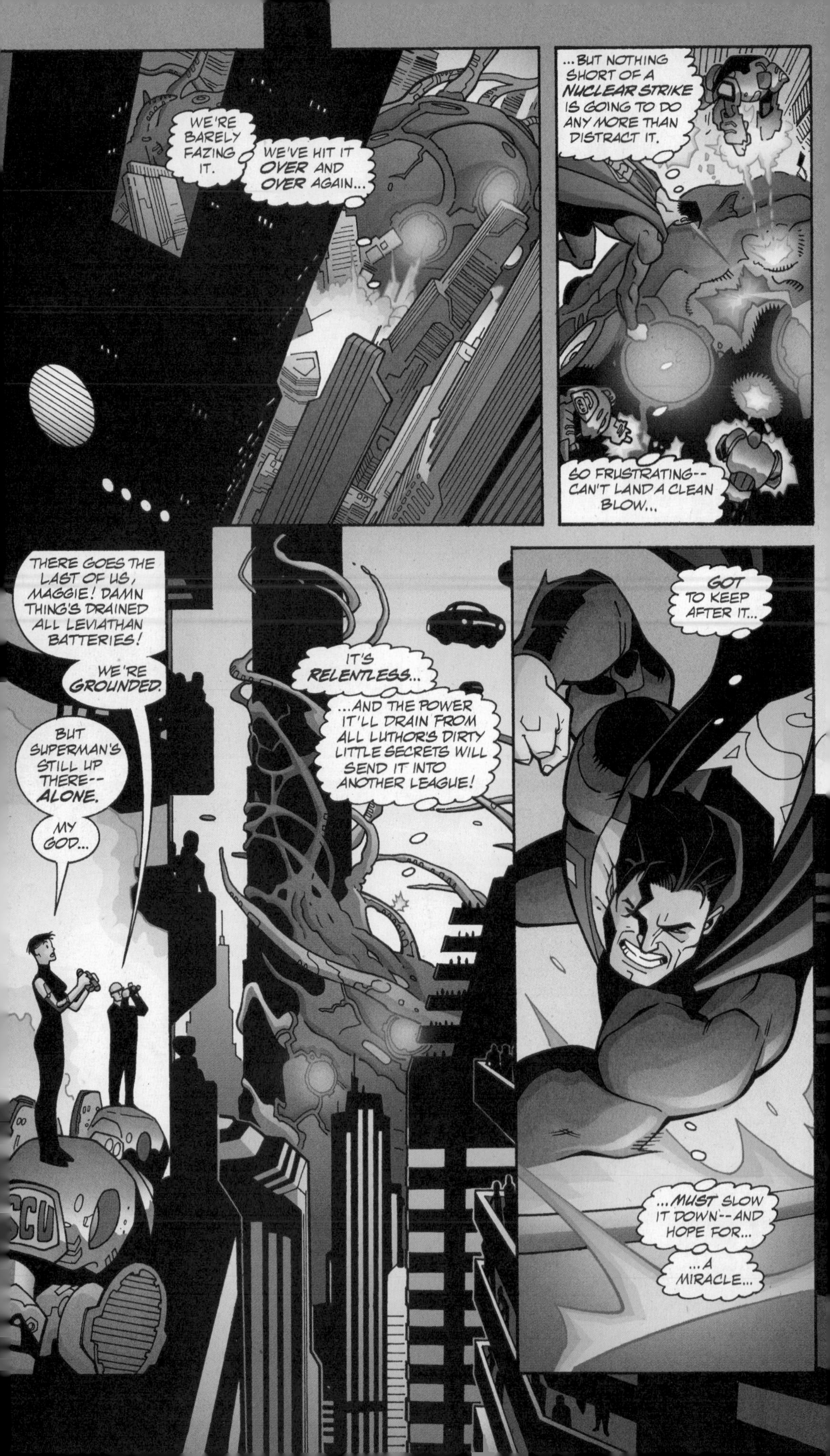
WE'RE BARELY FAZING IT.
WE'VE HIT IT OVER AND OVER AGAIN...
...BUT NOTHING SHORT OF A NUCLEAR STRIKE IS GOING TO DO ANY MORE THAN DISTRACT IT.
SO FRUSTRATING-- CAN'T LAND A CLEAN BLOW...
THERE GOES THE LAST OF US, MAGGIE! DAMN THING'S DRAINED ALL LEVIATHAN BATTERIES!
WE'RE GROUNDED.
BUT SUPERMAN'S STILL UP THERE-- ALONE.
MY GOD...
SCU
IT'S RELENTLESS...
...AND THE POWER IT'LL DRAIN FROM ALL LUTHOR'S DIRTY LITTLE SECRETS WILL SEND IT INTO ANOTHER LEAGUE!
GOT TO KEEP AFTER IT...
...MUST SLOW IT DOWN--AND HOPE FOR...
...A MIRACLE...

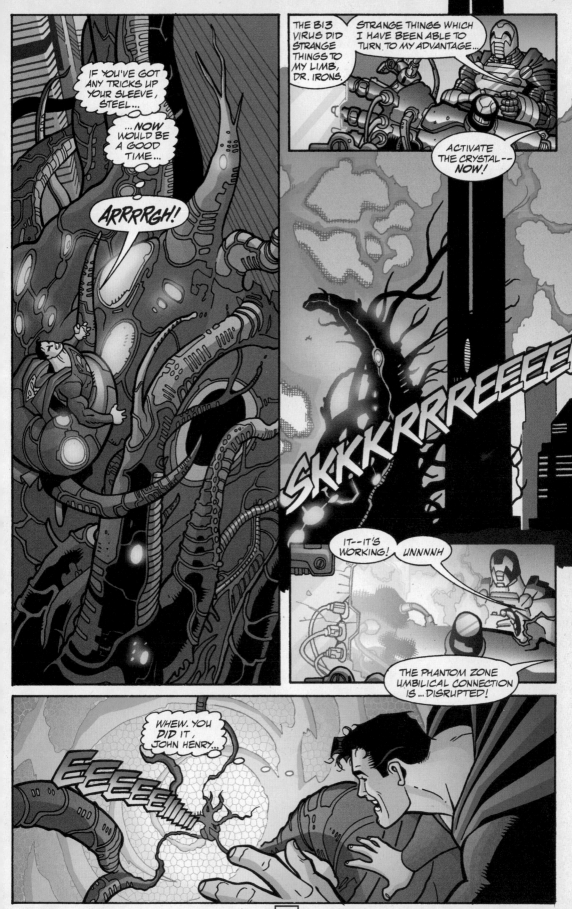

IF YOU'VE GOT ANY TRICKS UP YOUR SLEEVE, STEEL...

...NOW WOULD BE A GOOD TIME...

ARRRRGH!

THE B13 VIRUS DID STRANGE THINGS TO MY LIMB, DR. IRONS.

STRANGE THINGS WHICH I HAVE BEEN ABLE TO TURN TO MY ADVANTAGE...

ACTIVATE THE CRYSTAL-- NOW!

SKKKRRRREEEEE

IT--IT'S WORKING!

UNNNNH

THE PHANTOM ZONE UMBILICAL CONNECTION IS ...DISRUPTED!

WHEW. YOU DID IT, JOHN HENRY...

EEEEEEE

99

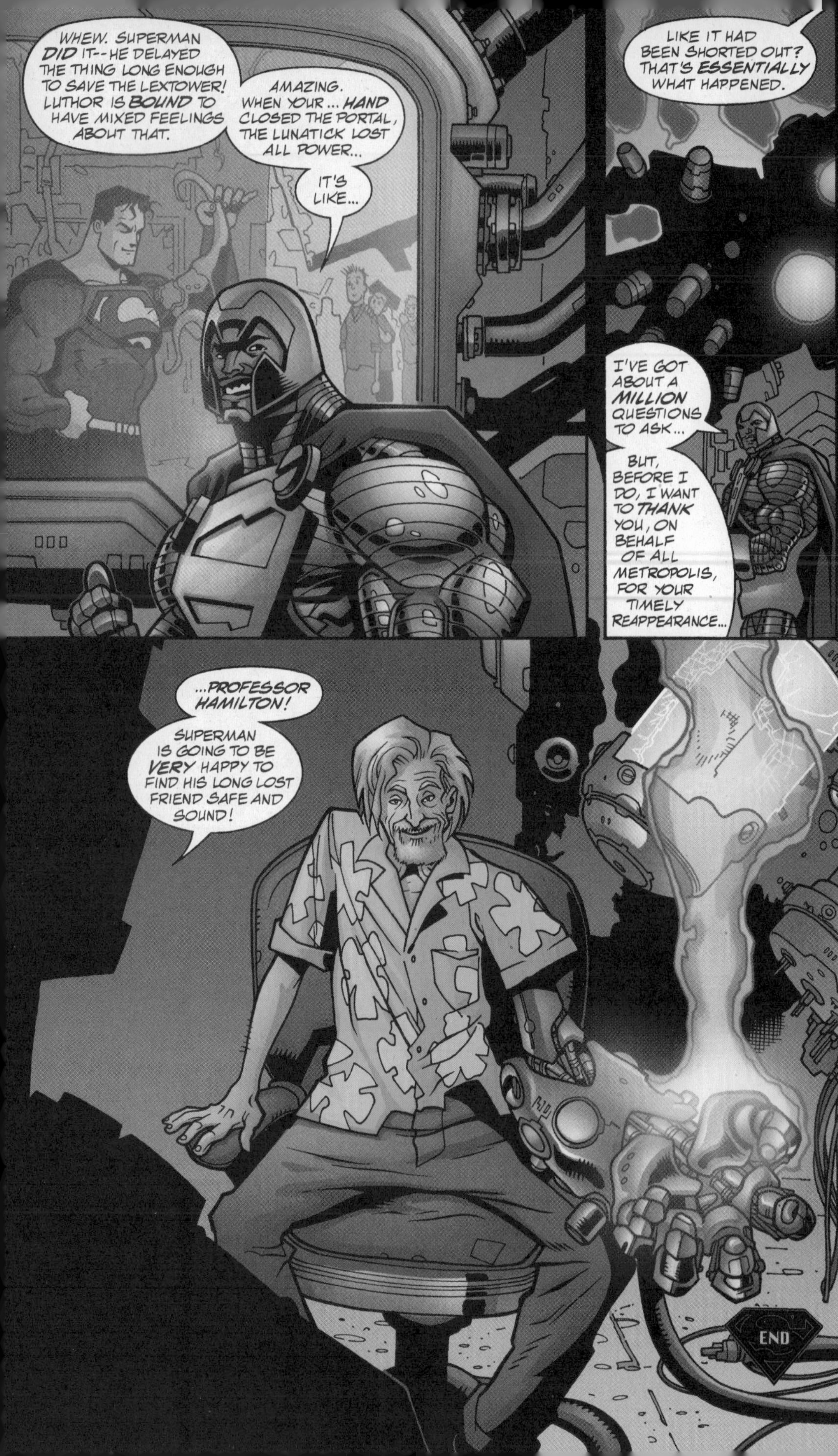
WHEW. SUPERMAN DID IT--HE DELAYED THE THING LONG ENOUGH TO SAVE THE LEXTOWER! LUTHOR IS BOUND TO HAVE MIXED FEELINGS ABOUT THAT.
AMAZING. WHEN YOUR... HAND CLOSED THE PORTAL, THE LUNATICK LOST ALL POWER...
IT'S LIKE...
LIKE IT HAD BEEN SHORTED OUT? THAT'S ESSENTIALLY WHAT HAPPENED.
I'VE GOT ABOUT A MILLION QUESTIONS TO ASK...
BUT, BEFORE I DO, I WANT TO THANK YOU, ON BEHALF OF ALL METROPOLIS, FOR YOUR TIMELY REAPPEARANCE...
...PROFESSOR HAMILTON!
SUPERMAN IS GOING TO BE VERY HAPPY TO FIND HIS LONG LOST FRIEND SAFE AND SOUND!
END

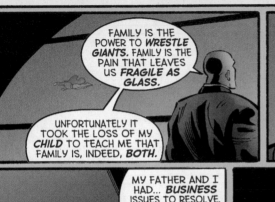

FAMILY IS THE POWER TO **WRESTLE GIANTS**. FAMILY IS THE PAIN THAT LEAVES US **FRAGILE AS GLASS**.

UNFORTUNATELY IT TOOK THE LOSS OF MY **CHILD** TO TEACH ME THAT FAMILY IS, INDEED, **BOTH**.

I'M SORRY... HAVE I TAKEN OVER THE **CONVERSATION**?

YOU WERE EXPLAINING **WHY** I SHOULD TAKE YOU BACK WHEN YOU MISSED THE MOST **IMPORTANT** PRESS CONFERENCE SINCE **MOSES** CAME DOWN FROM THE MOUNTAIN?

MY FATHER AND I HAD... **BUSINESS** ISSUES TO RESOLVE. FAMILIAL **PHILOSOPHY** REGARDING MY MOVE INTO THE PUBLIC EYE.

THE DISCUSSION WAS LONG IN COMING, DRAWN OUT BY AN UNFORTUNATE **ILLNESS** --

HE **KICKED** YOU OUT, DIDN'T HE?

...

NEVER **MET** THE MAN, BUT WE HEAR **STORIES**.

I'M TOLD HE PROBABLY WOULDN'T STAND FOR HIS **DAUGHTER** COMING TO WORK FOR A LOWLY **AMERICAN** --

NOTHING WAS KICKED. I LEFT... WITH **THESE**.

FORTY **DAYS'** WORTH OF **SITAR** MUSIC?

THREE **HUNDRED** YEARS OF SOCIOLOGICAL, GENETIC, CHEMICAL, AND POLITICAL RESEARCH. THE **HEART** OF MY FATHER'S CORPORATION...

NOT TO MENTION THE **PASSCODES** FOR HIS EVERY ACCOUNT. HIS CONTACTS, **LEGITIMATE** AND OTHERWISE, AND THE **BLACKMAIL** DOSSIER HE HAD ON EACH ONE.

YOU'RE **KIDDING**.

I SERIOUSLY **DOUBT** IT.

I HAVE WATCHED MY FATHER FIGHT AN **ENDLESS** BATTLE, ALONE AGAINST A **LEGION** OF ENEMIES. HE HAS COME **CLOSE** TO SUCCESS MANY TIMES --

-- BUT **ULTIMATE** GLORY ESCAPES HIM.

I WILL **NOT** BE THAT PERSON. IF I AM LOSING **ONE** FAMILY... I WILL BUILD A **NEW** ONE...

...FROM THE **BEST** OF ALL POSSIBLE PARTS.

...

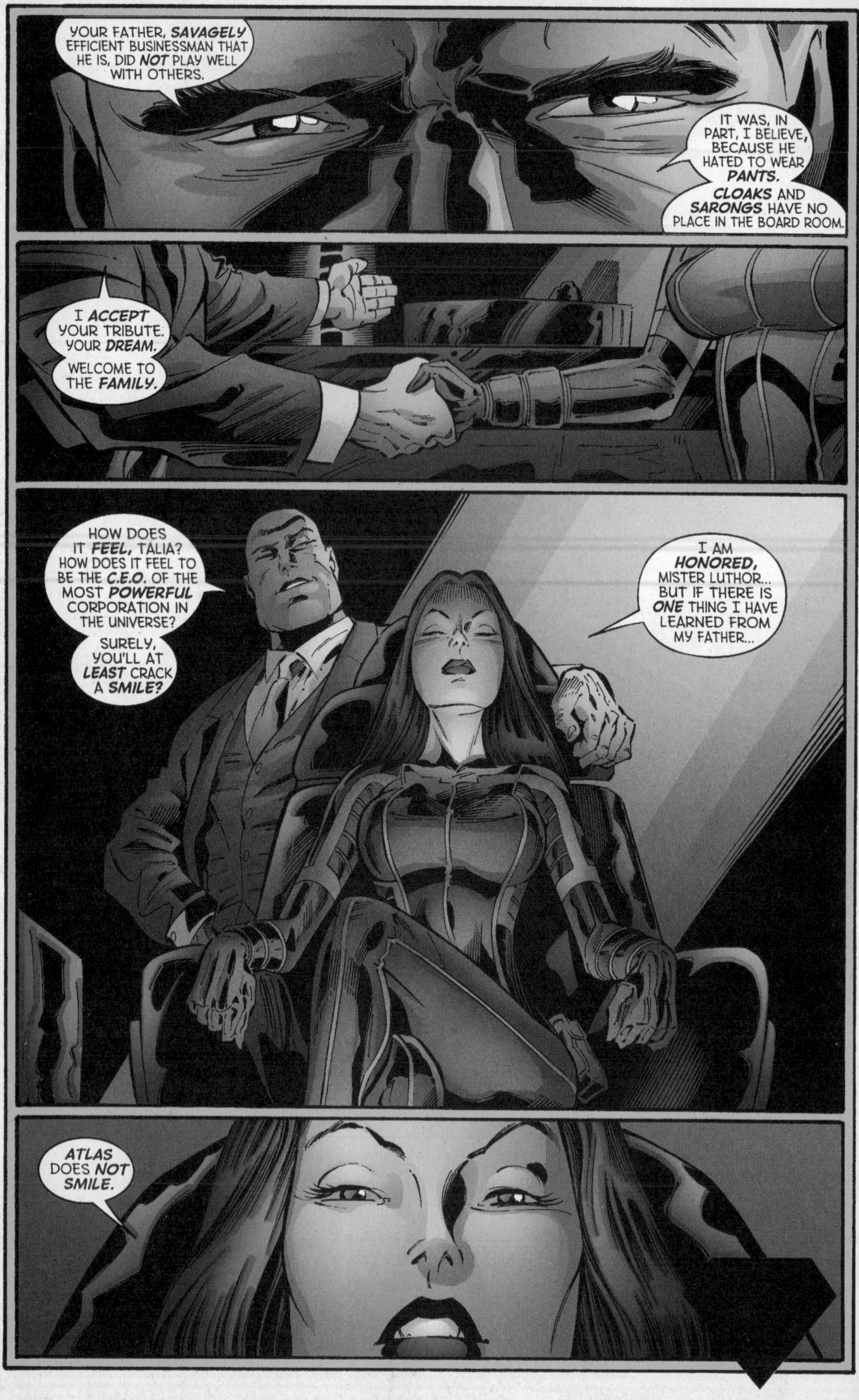

YOUR FATHER, SAVAGELY EFFICIENT BUSINESSMAN THAT HE IS, DID NOT PLAY WELL WITH OTHERS.
IT WAS, IN PART, I BELIEVE, BECAUSE HE HATED TO WEAR PANTS.
CLOAKS AND SARONGS HAVE NO PLACE IN THE BOARD ROOM.
I ACCEPT YOUR TRIBUTE. YOUR DREAM.
WELCOME TO THE FAMILY.
HOW DOES IT FEEL, TALIA? HOW DOES IT FEEL TO BE THE C.E.O. OF THE MOST POWERFUL CORPORATION IN THE UNIVERSE?
SURELY, YOU'LL AT LEAST CRACK A SMILE?
I AM HONORED, MISTER LUTHOR... BUT IF THERE IS ONE THING I HAVE LEARNED FROM MY FATHER...
ATLAS DOES NOT SMILE.

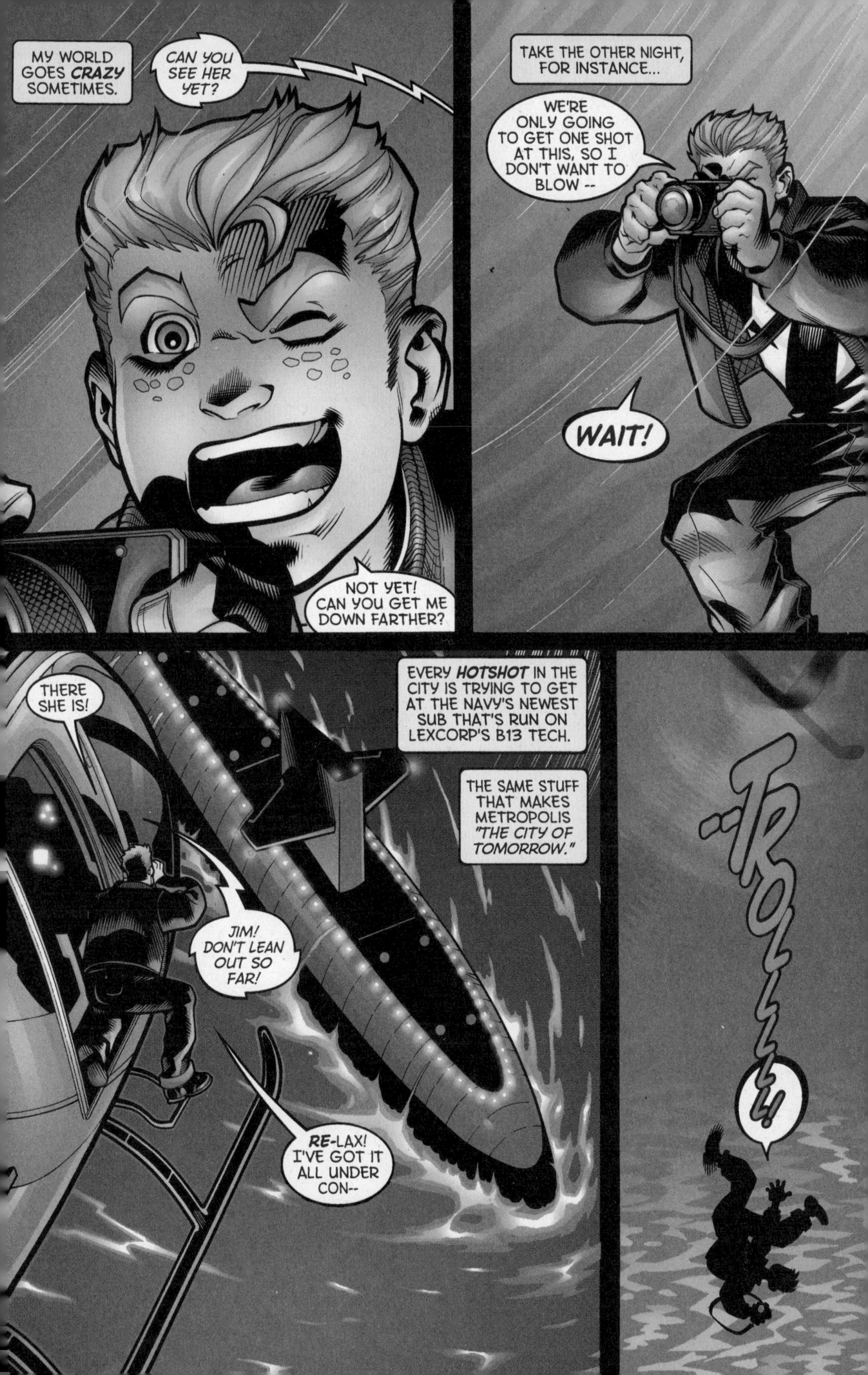
MY WORLD GOES CRAZY SOMETIMES.
CAN YOU SEE HER YET?
NOT YET! CAN YOU GET ME DOWN FARTHER?
TAKE THE OTHER NIGHT, FOR INSTANCE...
WE'RE ONLY GOING TO GET ONE SHOT AT THIS, SO I DON'T WANT TO BLOW --
WAIT!
THERE SHE IS!
EVERY HOTSHOT IN THE CITY IS TRYING TO GET AT THE NAVY'S NEWEST SUB THAT'S RUN ON LEXCORP'S B13 TECH.
THE SAME STUFF THAT MAKES METROPOLIS "THE CITY OF TOMORROW."
JIM! DON'T LEAN OUT SO FAR!
RE-LAX! I'VE GOT IT ALL UNDER CON--
--TROLLLL!

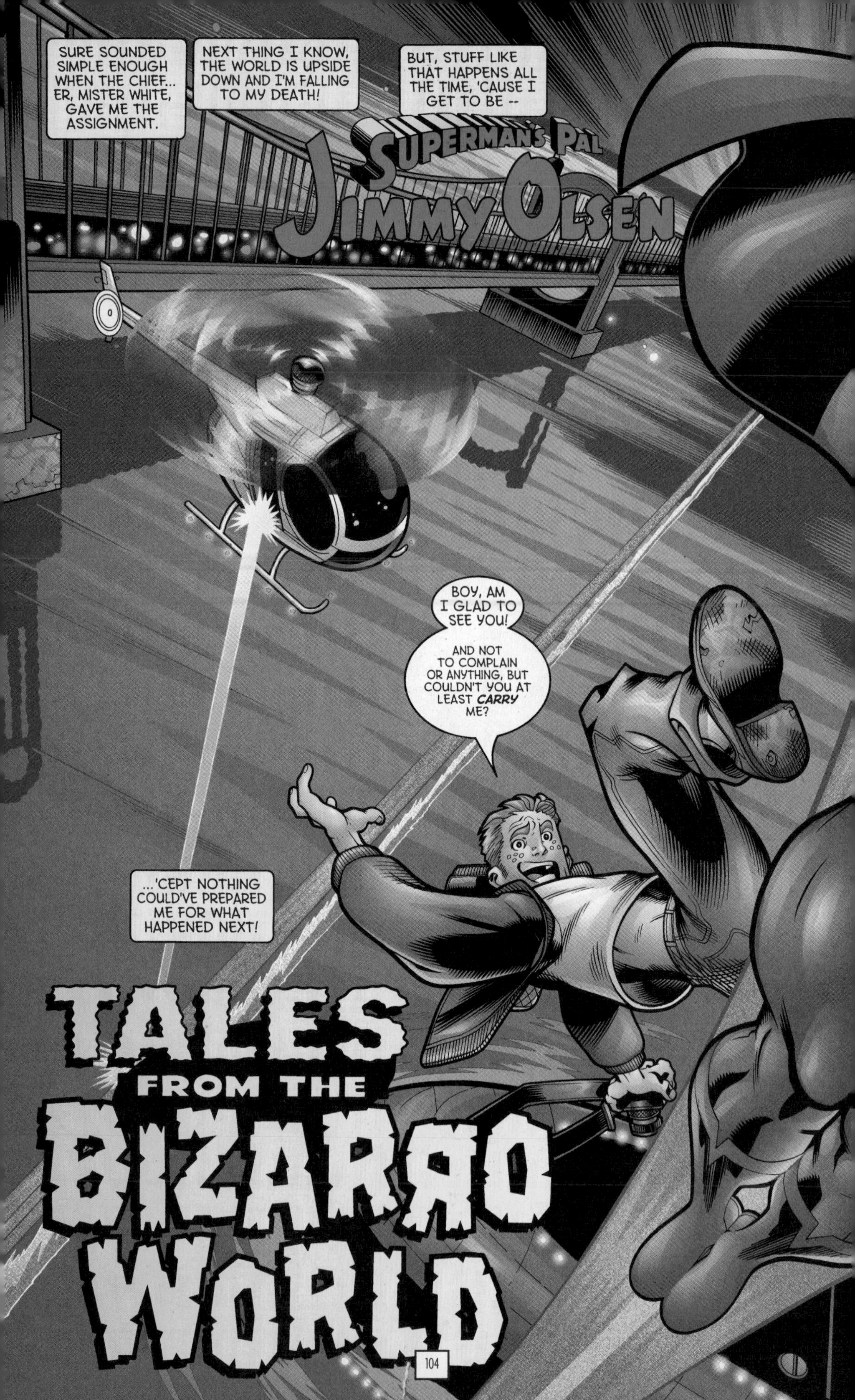

SURE SOUNDED SIMPLE ENOUGH WHEN THE CHIEF... ER, MISTER WHITE, GAVE ME THE ASSIGNMENT.
NEXT THING I KNOW, THE WORLD IS UPSIDE DOWN AND I'M FALLING TO MY DEATH!
BUT, STUFF LIKE THAT HAPPENS ALL THE TIME, 'CAUSE I GET TO BE --
SUPERMAN'S PAL JIMMY OLSEN
BOY, AM I GLAD TO SEE YOU!
AND NOT TO COMPLAIN OR ANYTHING, BUT COULDN'T YOU AT LEAST CARRY ME?
...'CEPT NOTHING COULD'VE PREPARED ME FOR WHAT HAPPENED NEXT!
TALES FROM THE BIZARRO WORLD

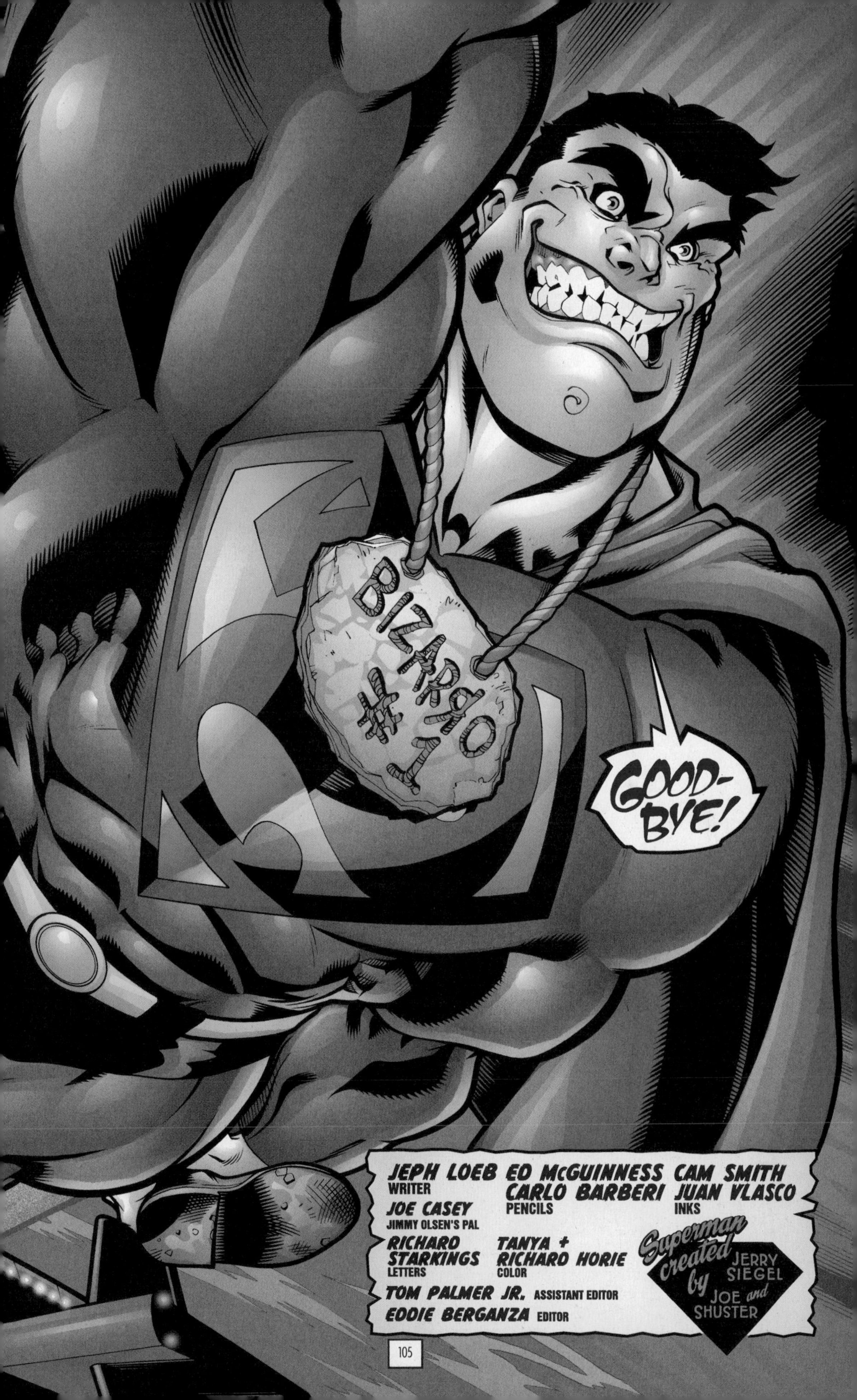
BIZARRO #1
GOOD-BYE!
JEPH LOEB WRITER
ED McGUINNESS CARLO BARBERI PENCILS
CAM SMITH JUAN VLASCO INKS
JOE CASEY JIMMY OLSEN'S PAL
RICHARD STARKINGS LETTERS
TANYA + RICHARD HORIE COLOR
TOM PALMER JR. ASSISTANT EDITOR
EDDIE BERGANZA EDITOR
Superman created by JERRY SIEGEL and JOE SHUSTER

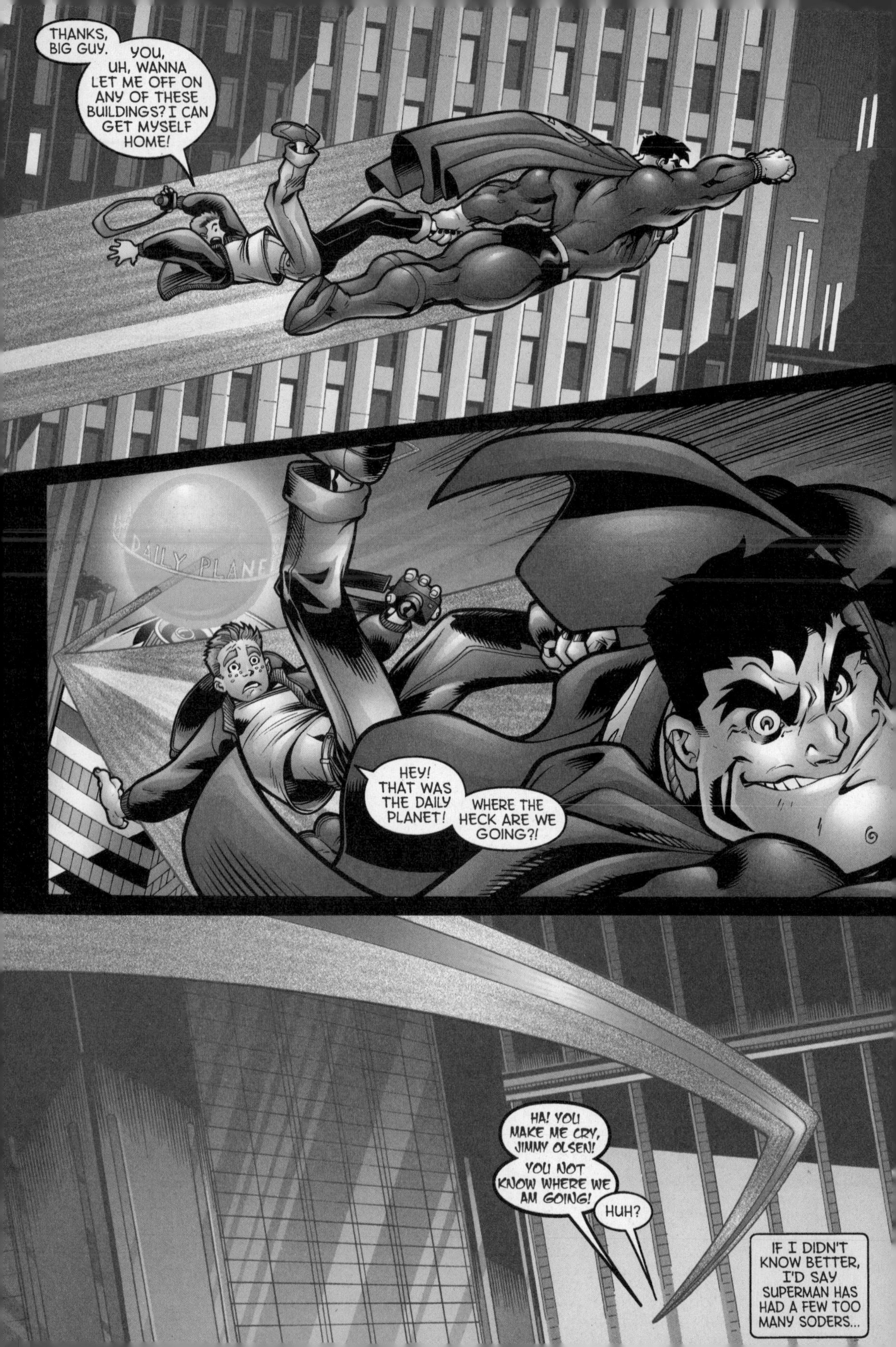
THANKS, BIG GUY.
YOU, UH, WANNA LET ME OFF ON ANY OF THESE BUILDINGS? I CAN GET MYSELF HOME!
DAILY PLANET
HEY! THAT WAS THE DAILY PLANET!
WHERE THE HECK ARE WE GOING?!
HA! YOU MAKE ME CRY, JIMMY OLSEN!
YOU NOT KNOW WHERE WE AM GOING!
HUH?
IF I DIDN'T KNOW BETTER, I'D SAY SUPERMAN HAS HAD A FEW TOO MANY SODERS...

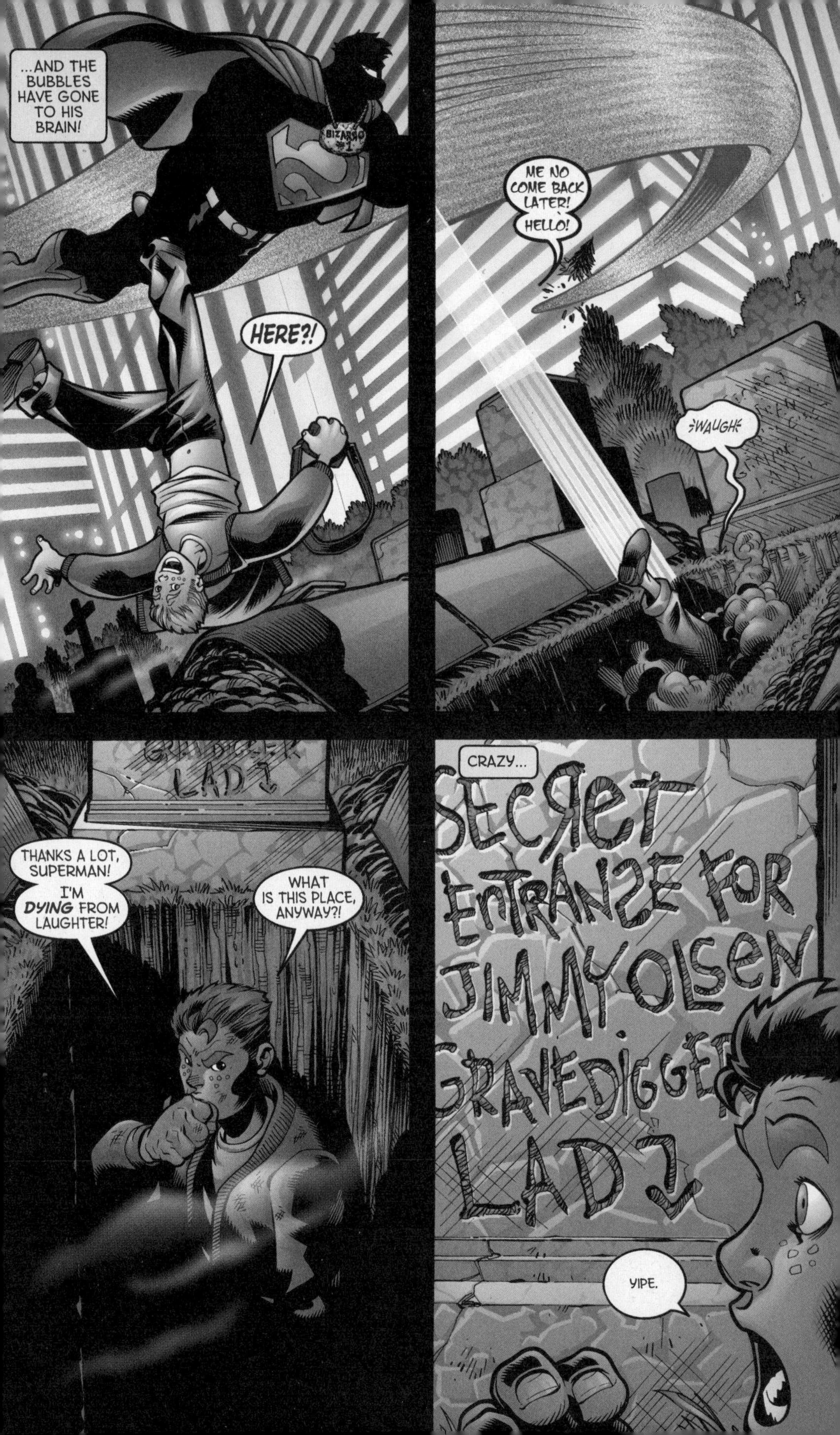
...AND THE BUBBLES HAVE GONE TO HIS BRAIN!
BIZARRO #1
HERE?!
ME NO COME BACK LATER!
HELLO!
WAUGH
THANKS A LOT, SUPERMAN! I'M DYING FROM LAUGHTER!
WHAT IS THIS PLACE, ANYWAY?!
CRAZY...
SECRET ENTRANZE FOR JIMMY OLSEN GRAVEDIGGER LAD
YIPE.

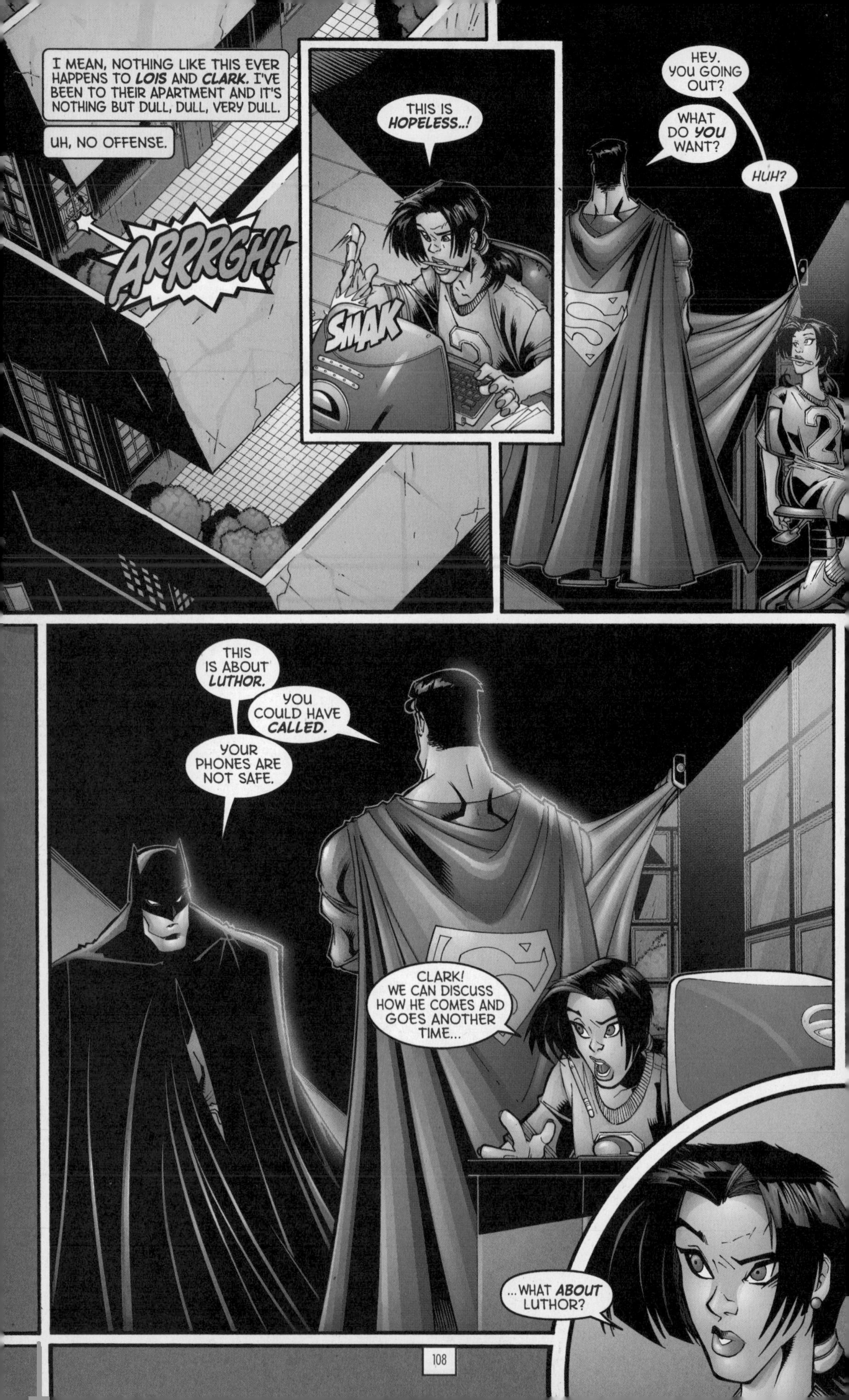
I MEAN, NOTHING LIKE THIS EVER HAPPENS TO LOIS AND CLARK. I'VE BEEN TO THEIR APARTMENT AND IT'S NOTHING BUT DULL, DULL, VERY DULL.
UH, NO OFFENSE.
ARRRGH!
THIS IS HOPELESS..!
SMAK
HEY. YOU GOING OUT?
WHAT DO YOU WANT?
HUH?
THIS IS ABOUT LUTHOR.
YOU COULD HAVE CALLED.
YOUR PHONES ARE NOT SAFE.
CLARK! WE CAN DISCUSS HOW HE COMES AND GOES ANOTHER TIME...
...WHAT ABOUT LUTHOR?

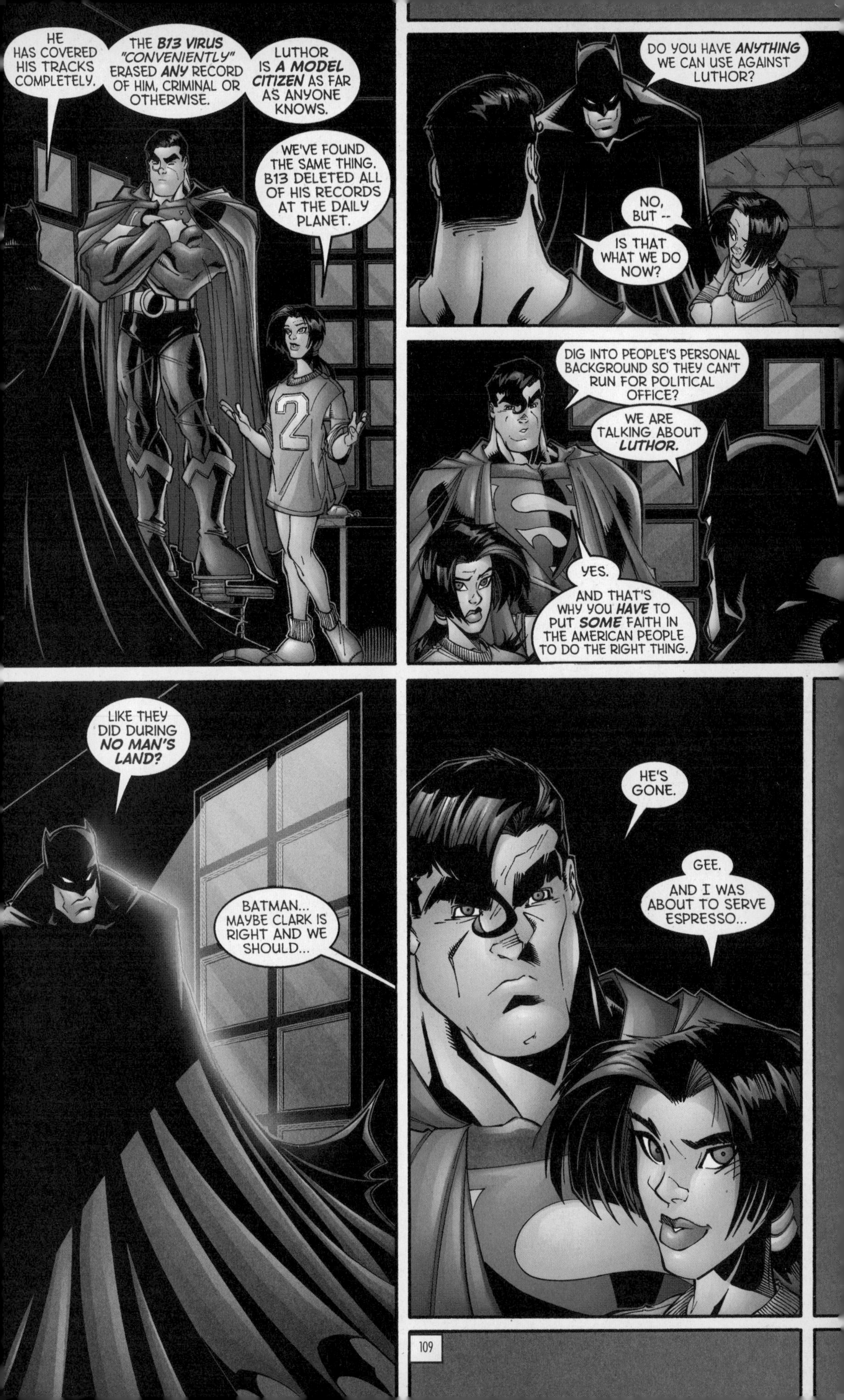
HE HAS COVERED HIS TRACKS COMPLETELY.
THE B13 VIRUS "CONVENIENTLY" ERASED ANY RECORD OF HIM, CRIMINAL OR OTHERWISE.
LUTHOR IS A MODEL CITIZEN AS FAR AS ANYONE KNOWS.
WE'VE FOUND THE SAME THING. B13 DELETED ALL OF HIS RECORDS AT THE DAILY PLANET.
DO YOU HAVE ANYTHING WE CAN USE AGAINST LUTHOR?
NO, BUT --
IS THAT WHAT WE DO NOW?
DIG INTO PEOPLE'S PERSONAL BACKGROUND SO THEY CAN'T RUN FOR POLITICAL OFFICE?
WE ARE TALKING ABOUT LUTHOR.
YES.
AND THAT'S WHY YOU HAVE TO PUT SOME FAITH IN THE AMERICAN PEOPLE TO DO THE RIGHT THING.
LIKE THEY DID DURING NO MAN'S LAND?
BATMAN... MAYBE CLARK IS RIGHT AND WE SHOULD...
HE'S GONE.
GEE.
AND I WAS ABOUT TO SERVE ESPRESSO...

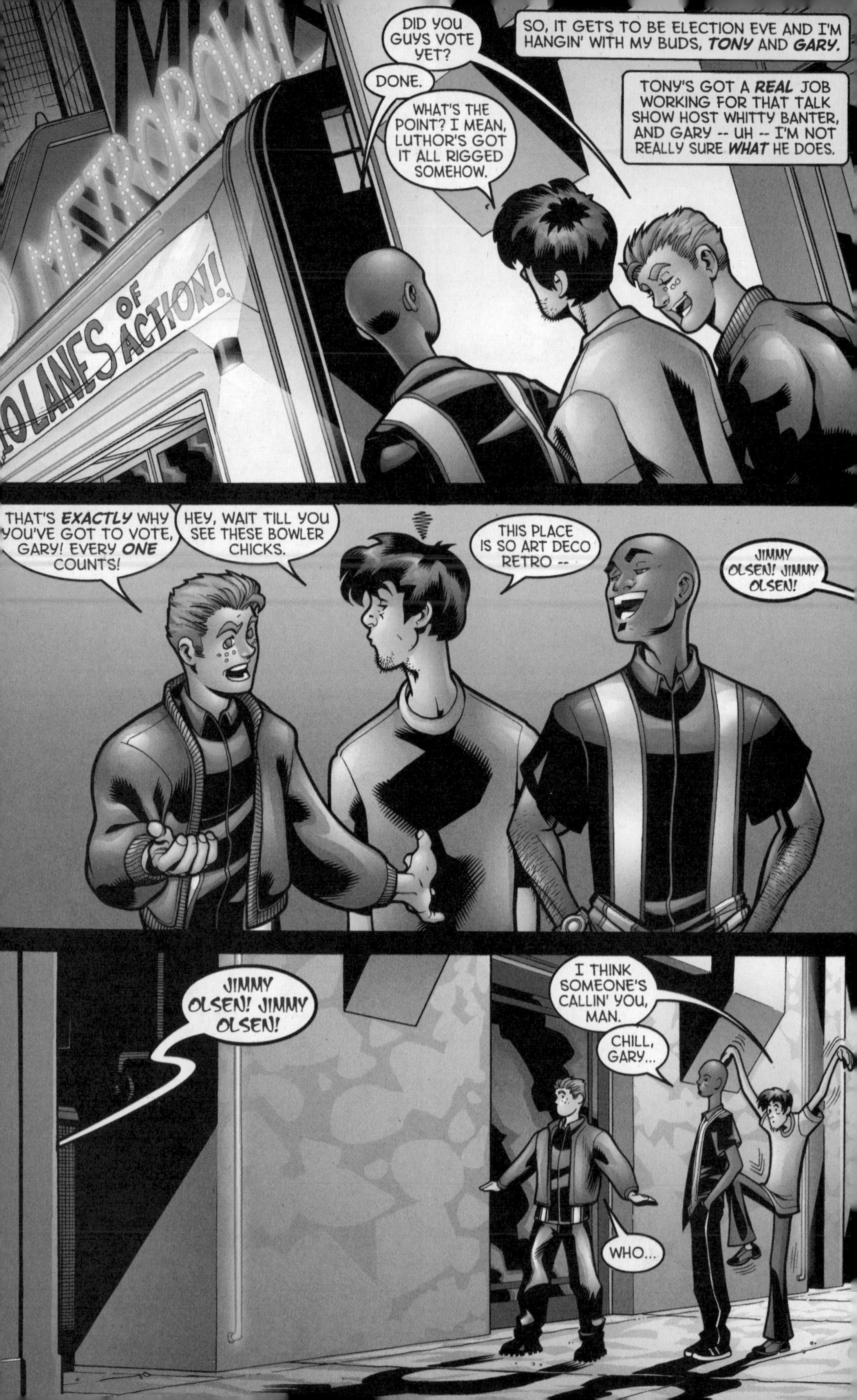
METROBOWL
10 LANES OF ACTION!
SO, IT GETS TO BE ELECTION EVE AND I'M HANGIN' WITH MY BUDS, TONY AND GARY.
TONY'S GOT A REAL JOB WORKING FOR THAT TALK SHOW HOST WHITTY BANTER, AND GARY -- UH -- I'M NOT REALLY SURE WHAT HE DOES.
DID YOU GUYS VOTE YET?
DONE.
WHAT'S THE POINT? I MEAN, LUTHOR'S GOT IT ALL RIGGED SOMEHOW.
THAT'S EXACTLY WHY YOU'VE GOT TO VOTE, GARY! EVERY ONE COUNTS!
HEY, WAIT TILL YOU SEE THESE BOWLER CHICKS.
THIS PLACE IS SO ART DECO RETRO --
JIMMY OLSEN! JIMMY OLSEN!
JIMMY OLSEN! JIMMY OLSEN!
I THINK SOMEONE'S CALLIN' YOU, MAN.
CHILL, GARY...
WHO...

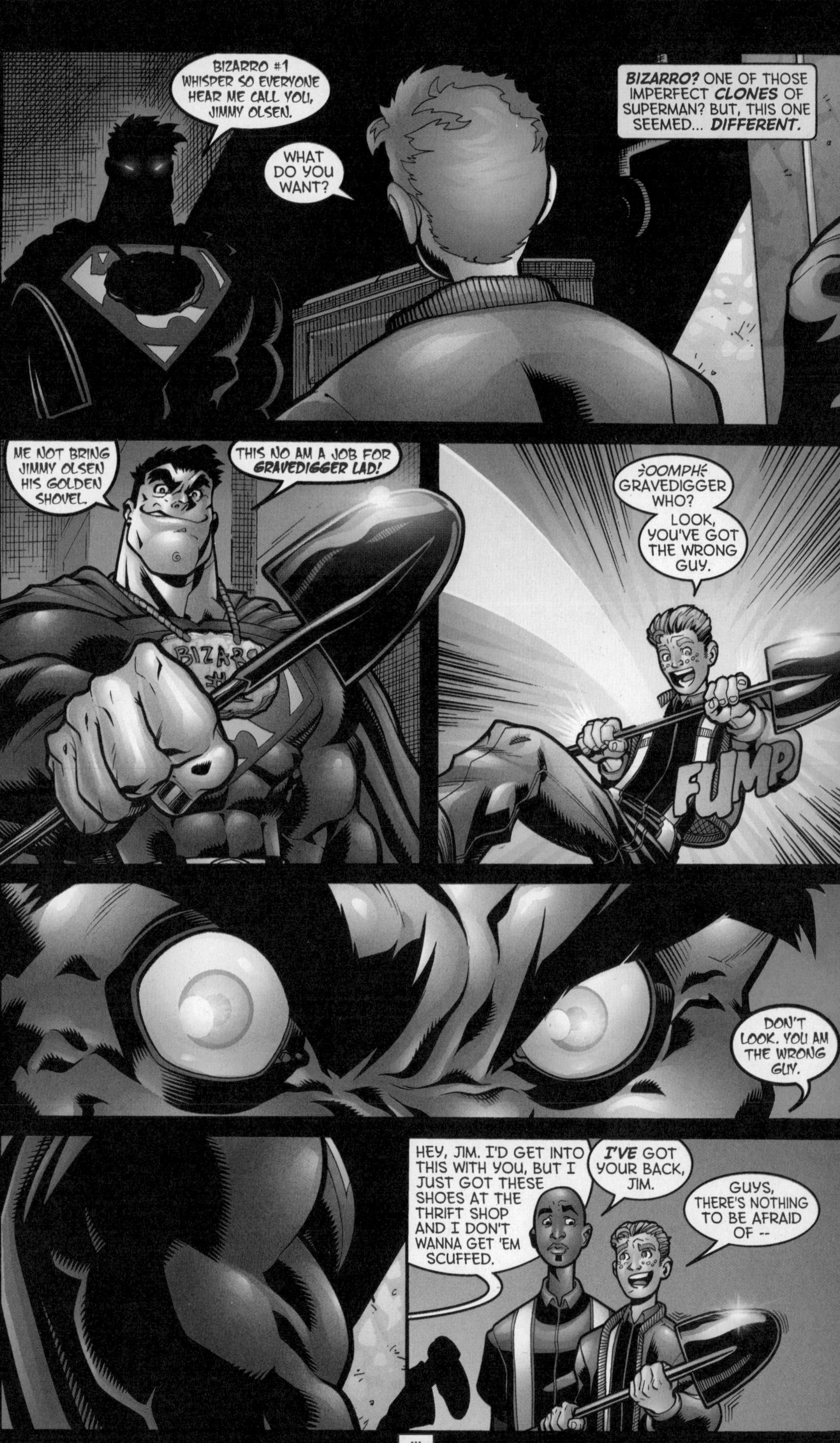
BIZARRO #1 WHISPER SO EVERYONE HEAR ME CALL YOU, JIMMY OLSEN.
WHAT DO YOU WANT?
BIZARRO? ONE OF THOSE IMPERFECT CLONES OF SUPERMAN? BUT, THIS ONE SEEMED... DIFFERENT.
ME NOT BRING JIMMY OLSEN HIS GOLDEN SHOVEL.
THIS NO AM A JOB FOR GRAVEDIGGER LAD!
BIZARRO #1
OOMPH GRAVEDIGGER WHO?
LOOK, YOU'VE GOT THE WRONG GUY.
FUMP
DON'T LOOK. YOU AM THE WRONG GUY.
HEY, JIM. I'D GET INTO THIS WITH YOU, BUT I JUST GOT THESE SHOES AT THE THRIFT SHOP AND I DON'T WANNA GET 'EM SCUFFED.
I'VE GOT YOUR BACK, JIM.
GUYS, THERE'S NOTHING TO BE AFRAID OF --

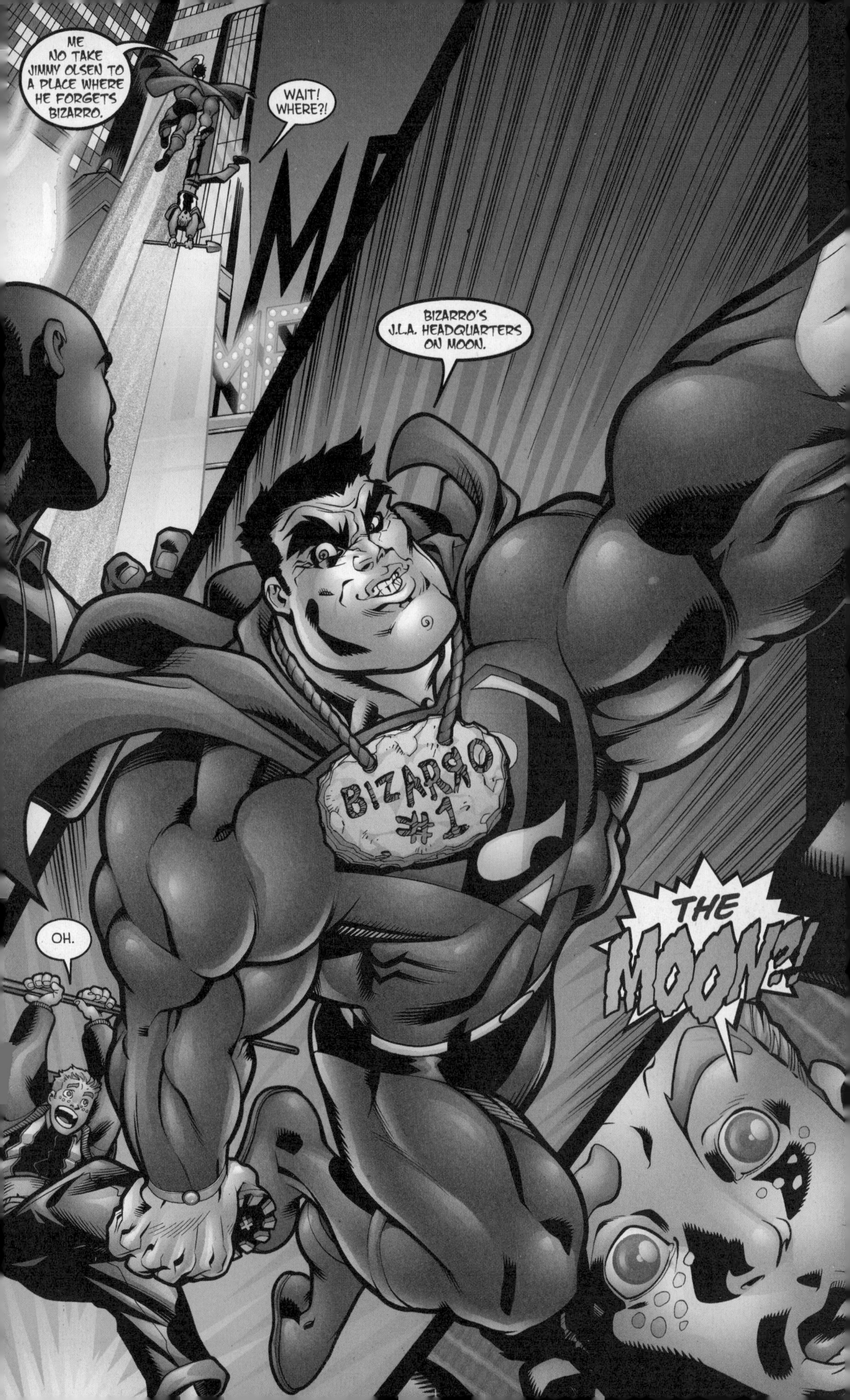
ME NO TAKE JIMMY OLSEN TO A PLACE WHERE HE FORGETS BIZARRO.
WAIT! WHERE?!
BIZARRO'S J.L.A. HEADQUARTERS ON MOON.
BIZARRO #1
OH.
THE MOON?!

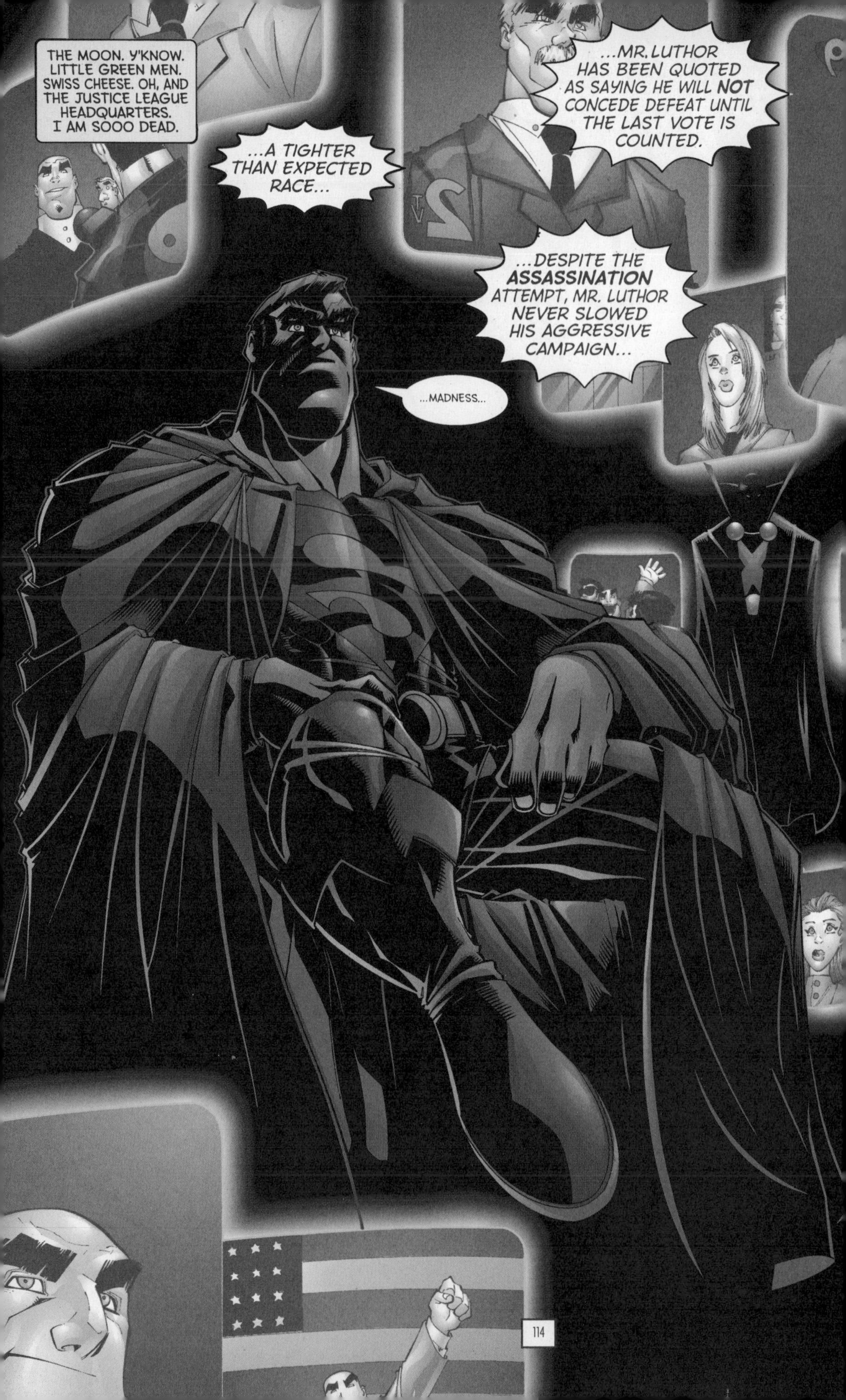
THE MOON. Y'KNOW. LITTLE GREEN MEN. SWISS CHEESE. OH, AND THE JUSTICE LEAGUE HEADQUARTERS. I AM SOOO DEAD.
...A TIGHTER THAN EXPECTED RACE...
...MR. LUTHOR HAS BEEN QUOTED AS SAYING HE WILL NOT CONCEDE DEFEAT UNTIL THE LAST VOTE IS COUNTED.
...DESPITE THE ASSASSINATION ATTEMPT, MR. LUTHOR NEVER SLOWED HIS AGGRESSIVE CAMPAIGN...
...MADNESS...

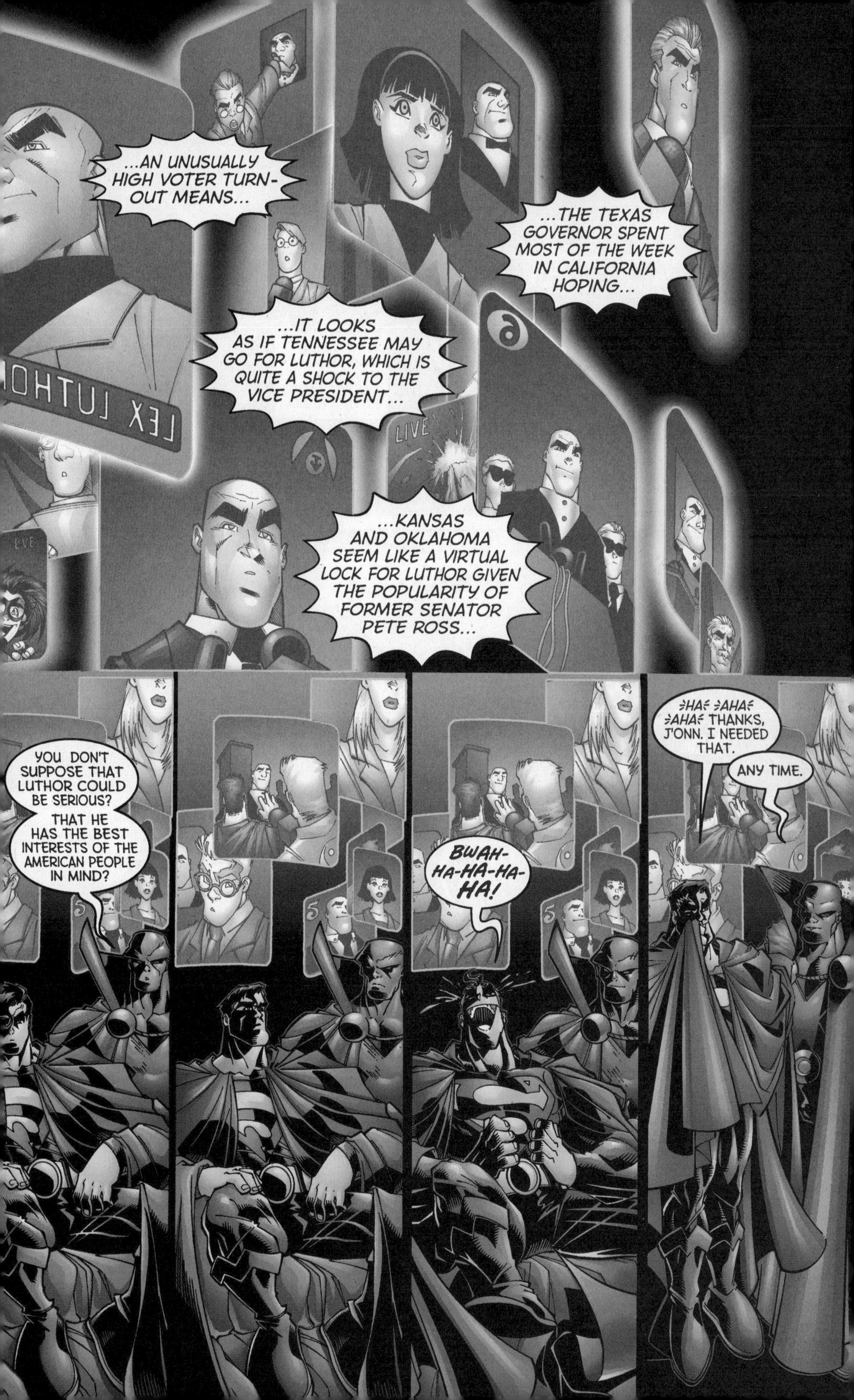
...AN UNUSUALLY HIGH VOTER TURN-OUT MEANS...
...THE TEXAS GOVERNOR SPENT MOST OF THE WEEK IN CALIFORNIA HOPING...
...IT LOOKS AS IF TENNESSEE MAY GO FOR LUTHOR, WHICH IS QUITE A SHOCK TO THE VICE PRESIDENT...
LEX LUTHOR
LIVE
...KANSAS AND OKLAHOMA SEEM LIKE A VIRTUAL LOCK FOR LUTHOR GIVEN THE POPULARITY OF FORMER SENATOR PETE ROSS...
YOU DON'T SUPPOSE THAT LUTHOR COULD BE SERIOUS?
THAT HE HAS THE BEST INTERESTS OF THE AMERICAN PEOPLE IN MIND?
BWAH-HA-HA-HA-HA!
HA AHA AHA THANKS, J'ONN. I NEEDED THAT.
ANY TIME.

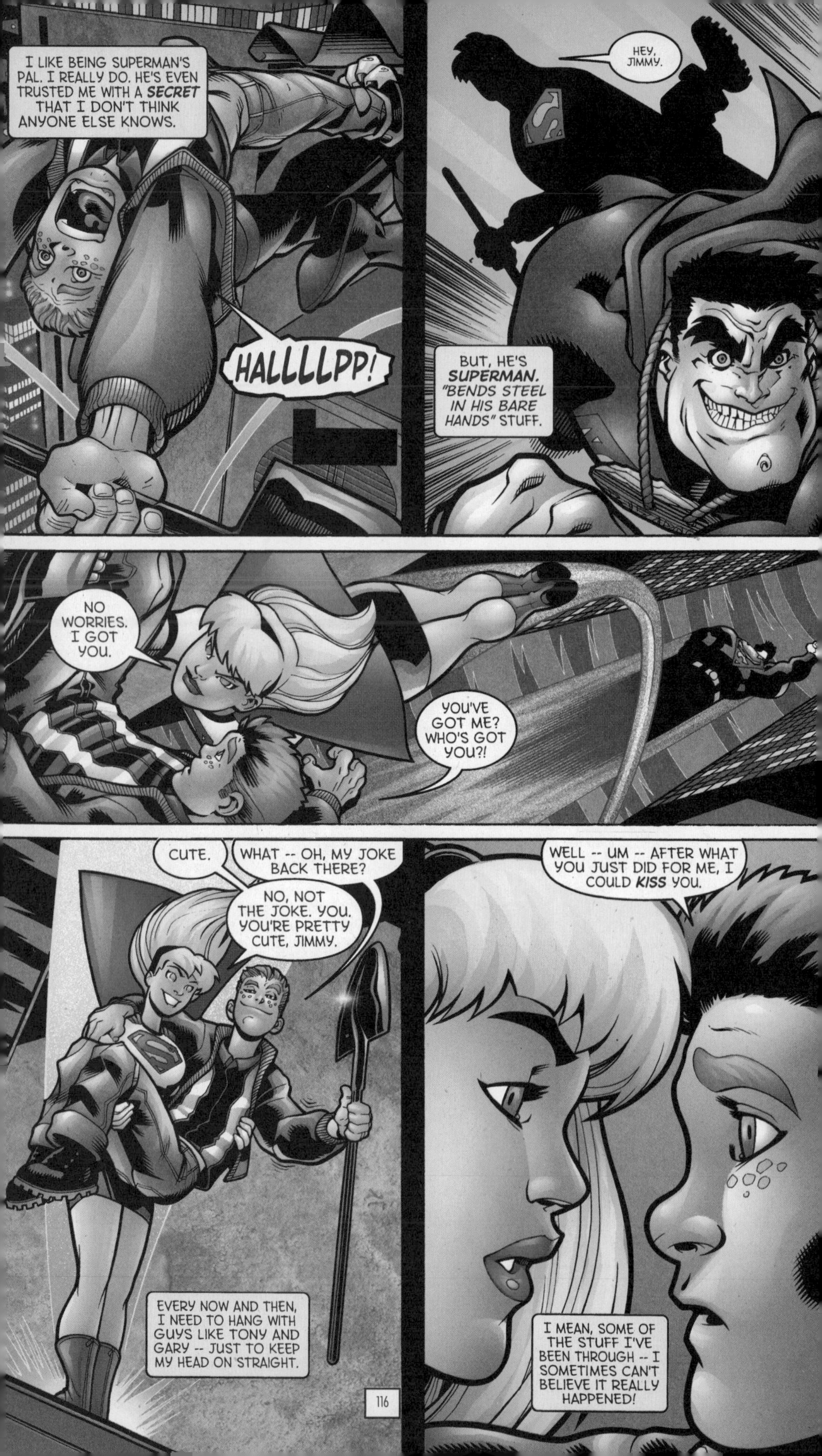
I LIKE BEING SUPERMAN'S PAL. I REALLY DO. HE'S EVEN TRUSTED ME WITH A SECRET THAT I DON'T THINK ANYONE ELSE KNOWS.
HALLLLPP!
HEY, JIMMY.
BUT, HE'S SUPERMAN. "BENDS STEEL IN HIS BARE HANDS" STUFF.
NO WORRIES. I GOT YOU.
YOU'VE GOT ME? WHO'S GOT YOU?!
CUTE.
WHAT -- OH, MY JOKE BACK THERE?
NO, NOT THE JOKE. YOU. YOU'RE PRETTY CUTE, JIMMY.
EVERY NOW AND THEN, I NEED TO HANG WITH GUYS LIKE TONY AND GARY -- JUST TO KEEP MY HEAD ON STRAIGHT.
WELL -- UM -- AFTER WHAT YOU JUST DID FOR ME, I COULD KISS YOU.
I MEAN, SOME OF THE STUFF I'VE BEEN THROUGH -- I SOMETIMES CAN'T BELIEVE IT REALLY HAPPENED!

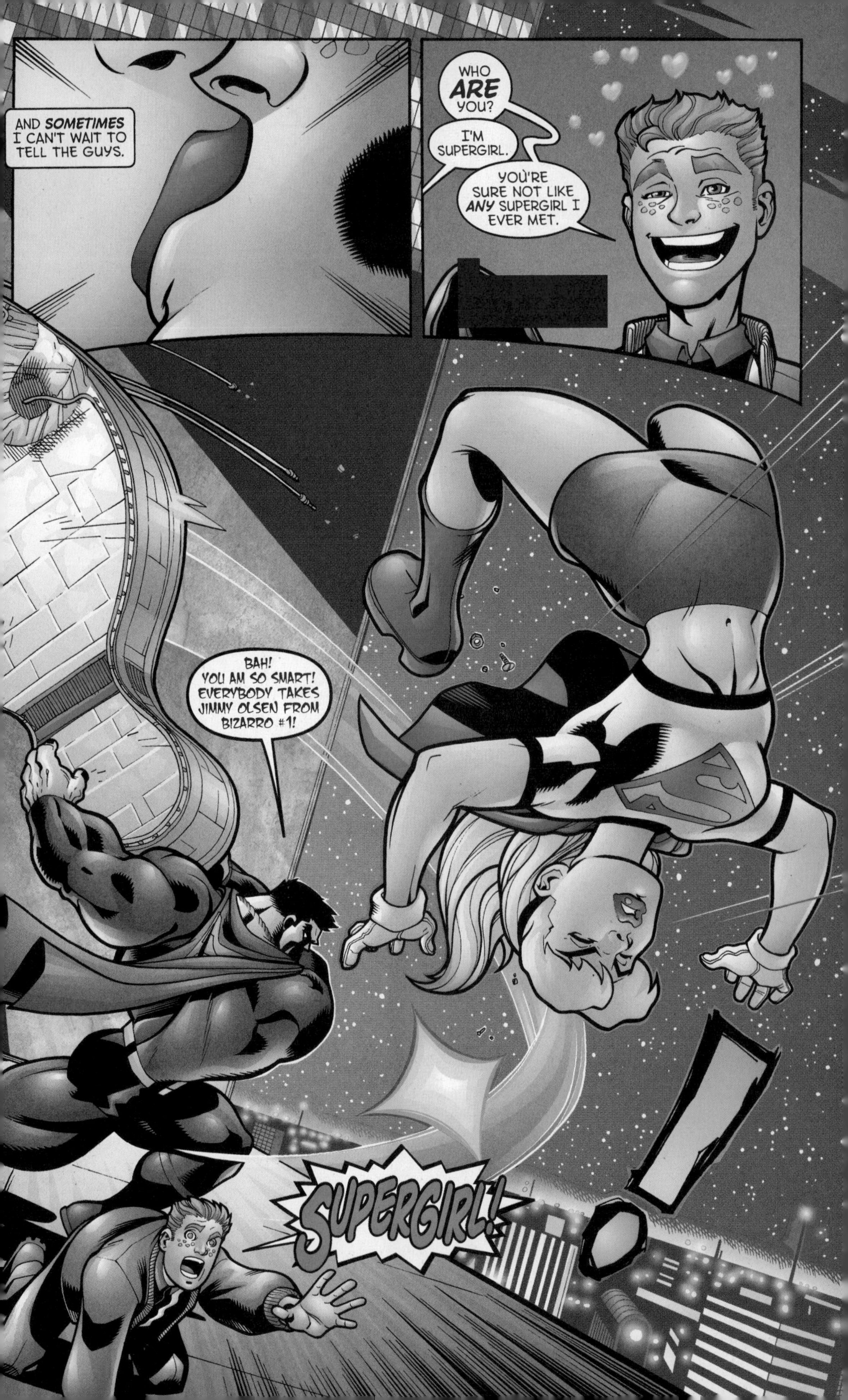
AND SOMETIMES I CAN'T WAIT TO TELL THE GUYS.
WHO ARE YOU?
I'M SUPERGIRL.
YOU'RE SURE NOT LIKE ANY SUPERGIRL I EVER MET.
[redacted]
BAH! YOU AM SO SMART! EVERYBODY TAKES JIMMY OLSEN FROM BIZARRO #1!
SUPERGIRL!

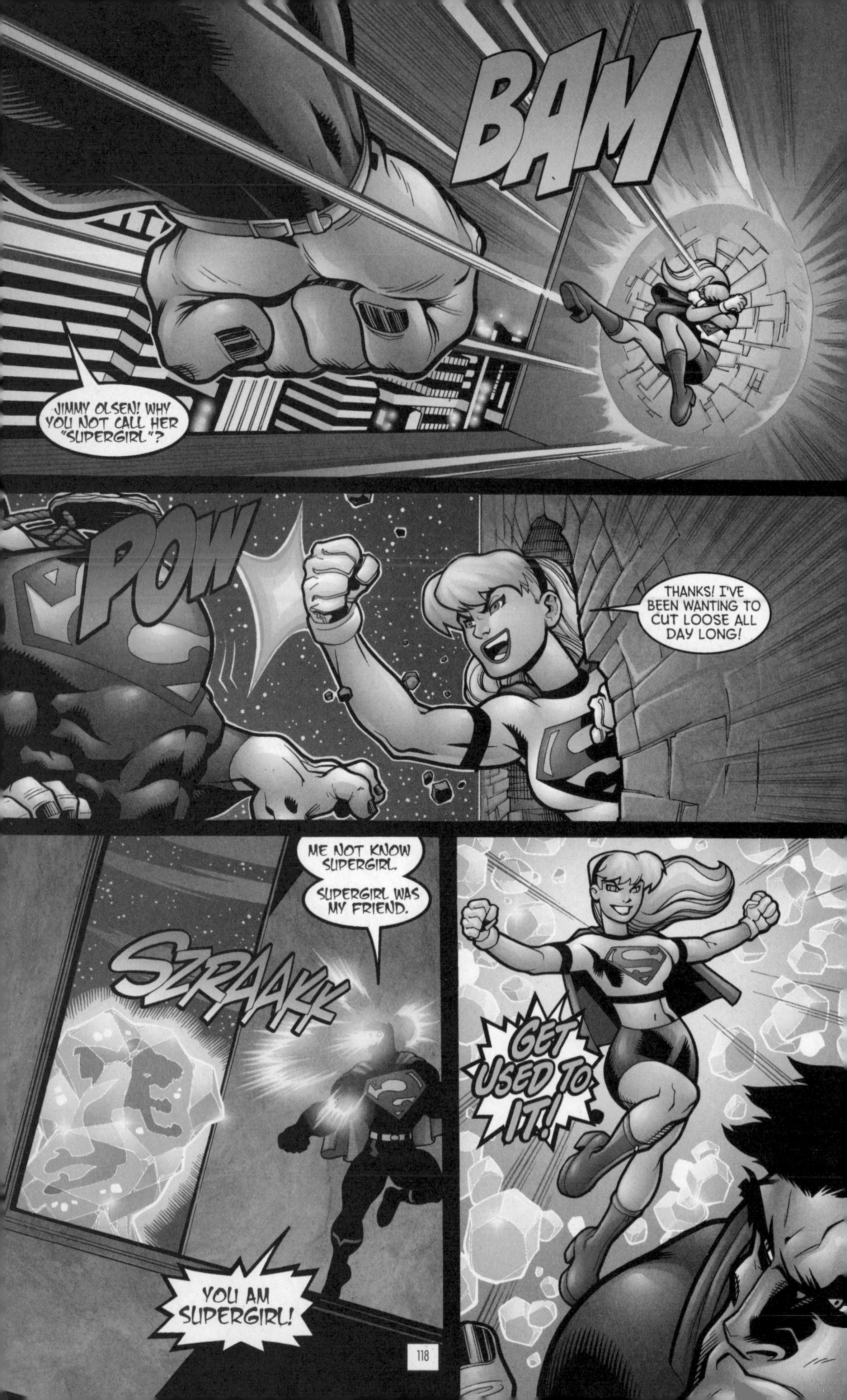
BAM
JIMMY OLSEN! WHY YOU NOT CALL HER "SUPERGIRL"?
POW
THANKS! I'VE BEEN WANTING TO CUT LOOSE ALL DAY LONG!
ME NOT KNOW SUPERGIRL.
SUPERGIRL WAS MY FRIEND.
SZRAAKK
YOU AM SUPERGIRL!
GET USED TO IT!

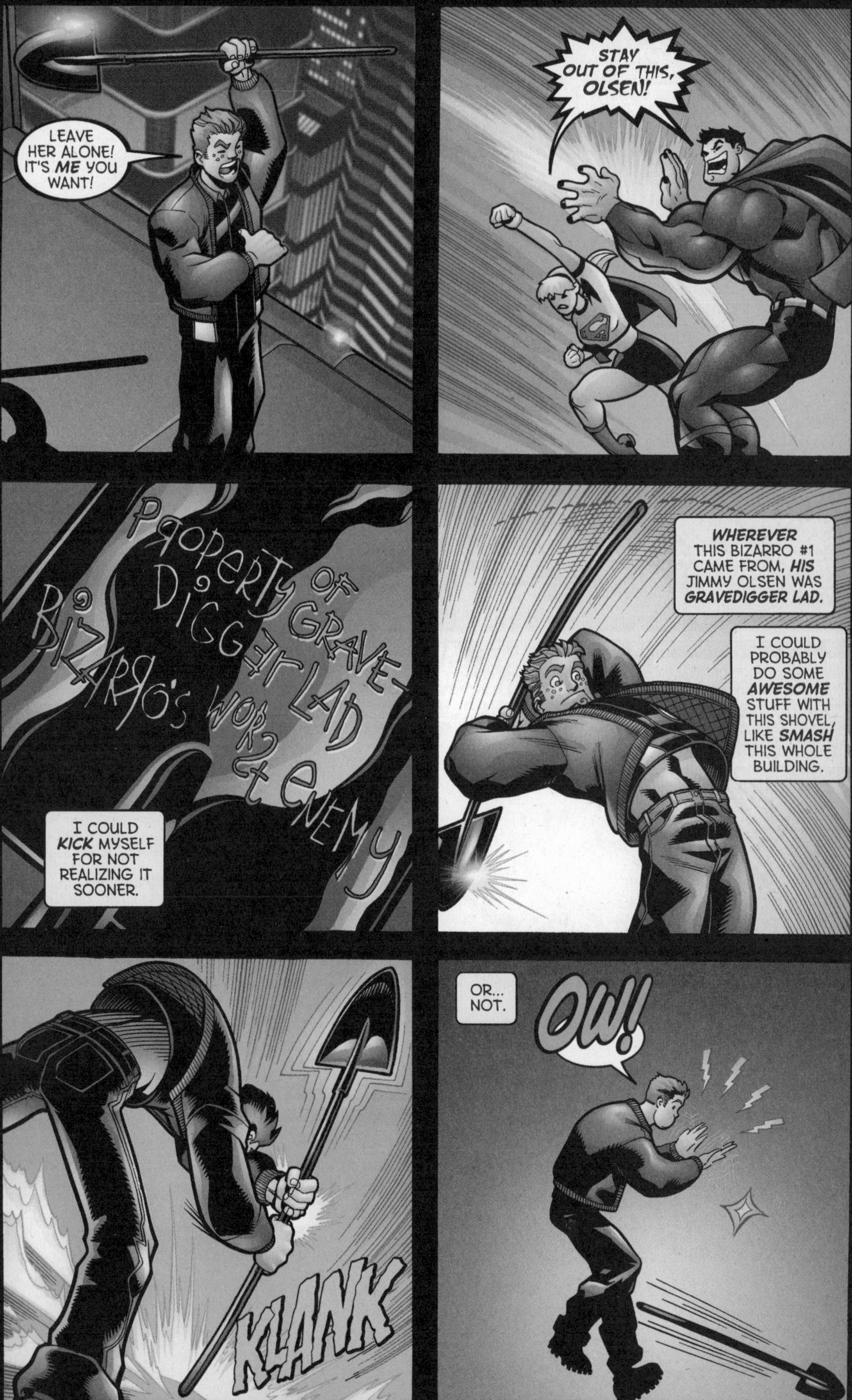

LEAVE HER ALONE! IT'S ME YOU WANT!
STAY OUT OF THIS, OLSEN!
PROPERTY OF GRAVE-DIGGER LAD
BIZARRO'S WORZT ENEMY
I COULD KICK MYSELF FOR NOT REALIZING IT SOONER.
WHEREVER THIS BIZARRO #1 CAME FROM, HIS JIMMY OLSEN WAS GRAVEDIGGER LAD.
I COULD PROBABLY DO SOME AWESOME STUFF WITH THIS SHOVEL, LIKE SMASH THIS WHOLE BUILDING.
KLANK
OR... NOT.
OW!

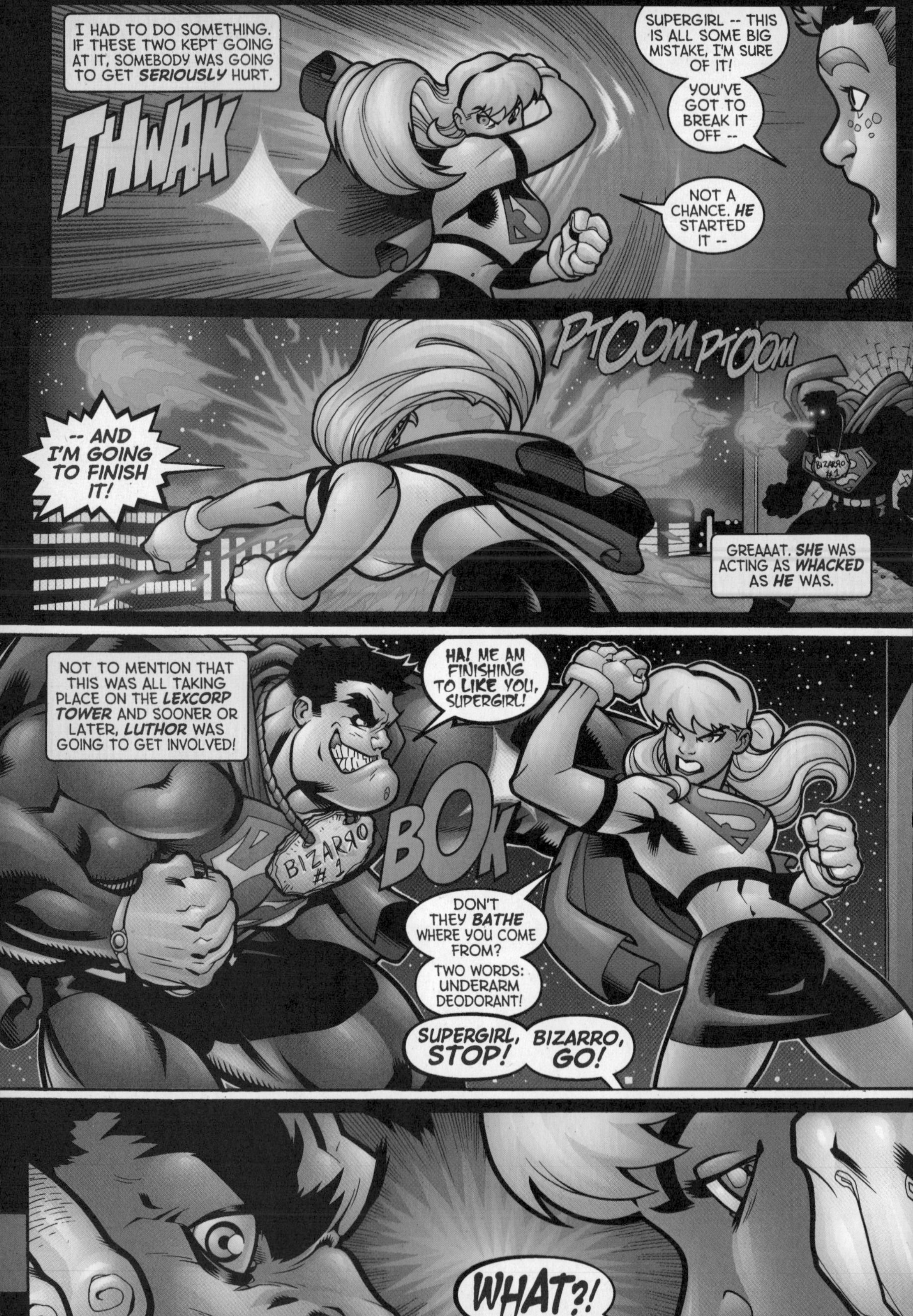

I HAD TO DO SOMETHING. IF THESE TWO KEPT GOING AT IT, SOMEBODY WAS GOING TO GET SERIOUSLY HURT.
THWAK
SUPERGIRL -- THIS IS ALL SOME BIG MISTAKE, I'M SURE OF IT!
YOU'VE GOT TO BREAK IT OFF --
NOT A CHANCE. HE STARTED IT --
PTOOM PTOOM
-- AND I'M GOING TO FINISH IT!
BIZARRO #1
GREAAAT. SHE WAS ACTING AS WHACKED AS HE WAS.
NOT TO MENTION THAT THIS WAS ALL TAKING PLACE ON THE LEXCORP TOWER AND SOONER OR LATER, LUTHOR WAS GOING TO GET INVOLVED!
HA! ME AM FINISHING TO LIKE YOU, SUPERGIRL!
BIZARRO #1
BOK
DON'T THEY BATHE WHERE YOU COME FROM?
TWO WORDS: UNDERARM DEODORANT!
SUPERGIRL, STOP!
BIZARRO, GO!
WHAT?!

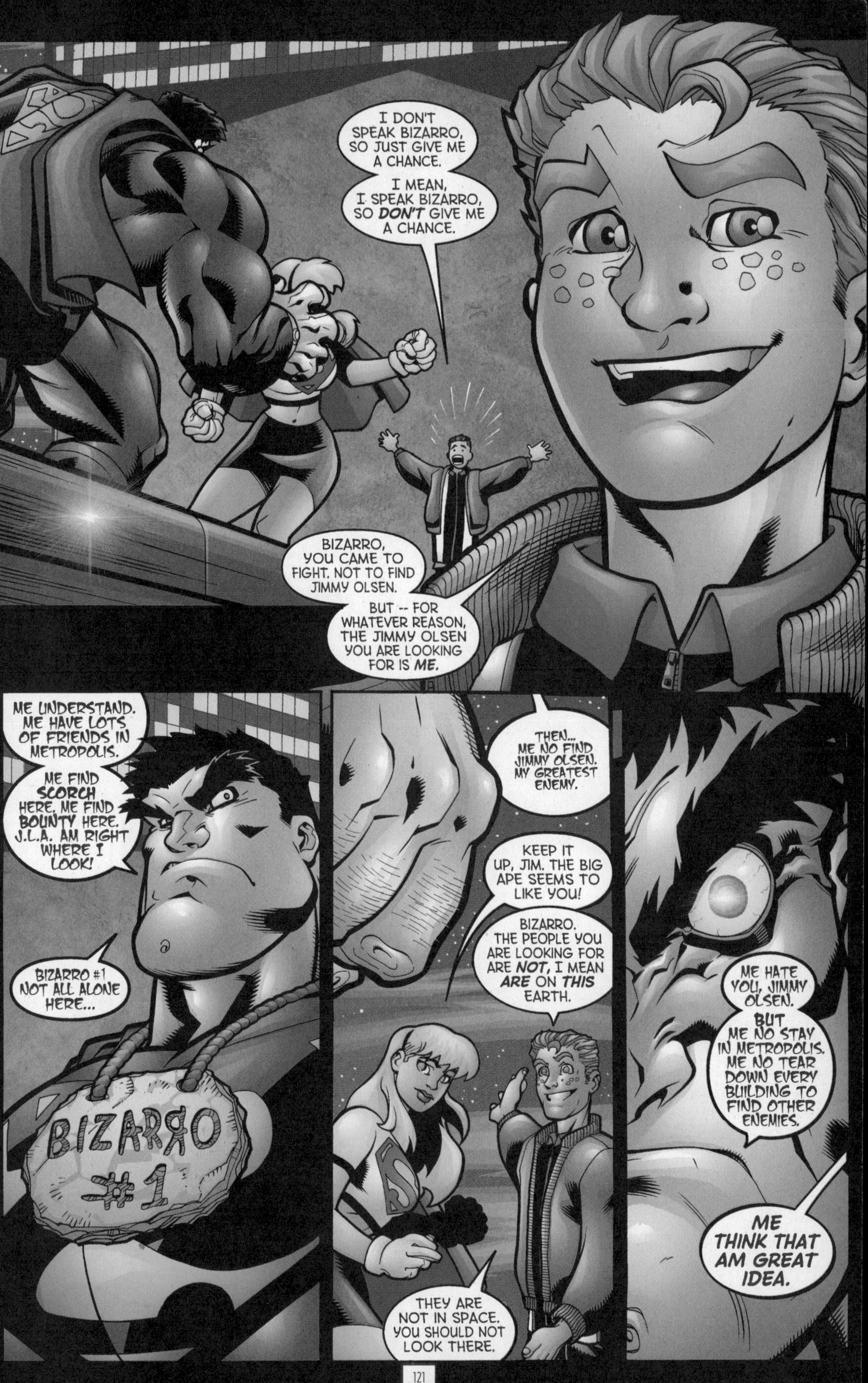
I DON'T SPEAK BIZARRO, SO JUST GIVE ME A CHANCE.
I MEAN, I SPEAK BIZARRO, SO DON'T GIVE ME A CHANCE.
BIZARRO, YOU CAME TO FIGHT. NOT TO FIND JIMMY OLSEN.
BUT -- FOR WHATEVER REASON, THE JIMMY OLSEN YOU ARE LOOKING FOR IS ME.
ME UNDERSTAND. ME HAVE LOTS OF FRIENDS IN METROPOLIS.
ME FIND SCORCH HERE. ME FIND BOUNTY HERE. J.L.A. AM RIGHT WHERE I LOOK!
BIZARRO #1 NOT ALL ALONE HERE...
BIZARRO #1
THEN... ME NO FIND JIMMY OLSEN. MY GREATEST ENEMY.
KEEP IT UP, JIM. THE BIG APE SEEMS TO LIKE YOU!
BIZARRO. THE PEOPLE YOU ARE LOOKING FOR ARE NOT, I MEAN ARE ON THIS EARTH.
THEY ARE NOT IN SPACE. YOU SHOULD NOT LOOK THERE.
ME HATE YOU, JIMMY OLSEN.
BUT ME NO STAY IN METROPOLIS. ME NO TEAR DOWN EVERY BUILDING TO FIND OTHER ENEMIES.
ME THINK THAT AM GREAT IDEA.

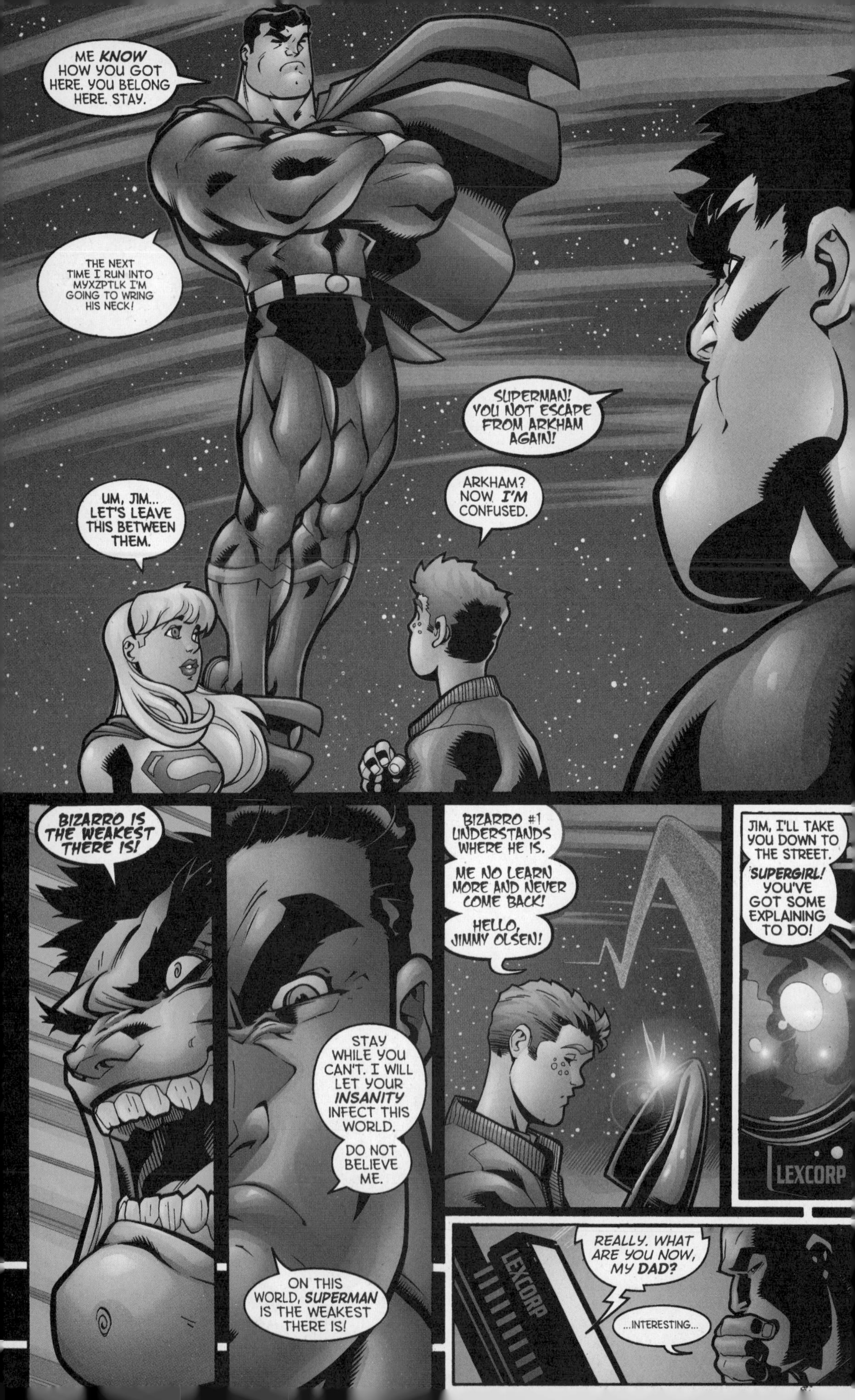

ME KNOW HOW YOU GOT HERE. YOU BELONG HERE. STAY.
THE NEXT TIME I RUN INTO MYXZPTLK I'M GOING TO WRING HIS NECK!
SUPERMAN! YOU NOT ESCAPE FROM ARKHAM AGAIN!
UM, JIM... LET'S LEAVE THIS BETWEEN THEM.
ARKHAM? NOW I'M CONFUSED.
BIZARRO IS THE WEAKEST THERE IS!
STAY WHILE YOU CAN'T. I WILL LET YOUR INSANITY INFECT THIS WORLD.
DO NOT BELIEVE ME.
ON THIS WORLD, SUPERMAN IS THE WEAKEST THERE IS!
BIZARRO #1 UNDERSTANDS WHERE HE IS.
ME NO LEARN MORE AND NEVER COME BACK!
HELLO, JIMMY OLSEN!
JIM, I'LL TAKE YOU DOWN TO THE STREET.
SUPERGIRL! YOU'VE GOT SOME EXPLAINING TO DO!
LEXCORP
LEXCORP
REALLY. WHAT ARE YOU NOW, MY DAD?
...INTERESTING...

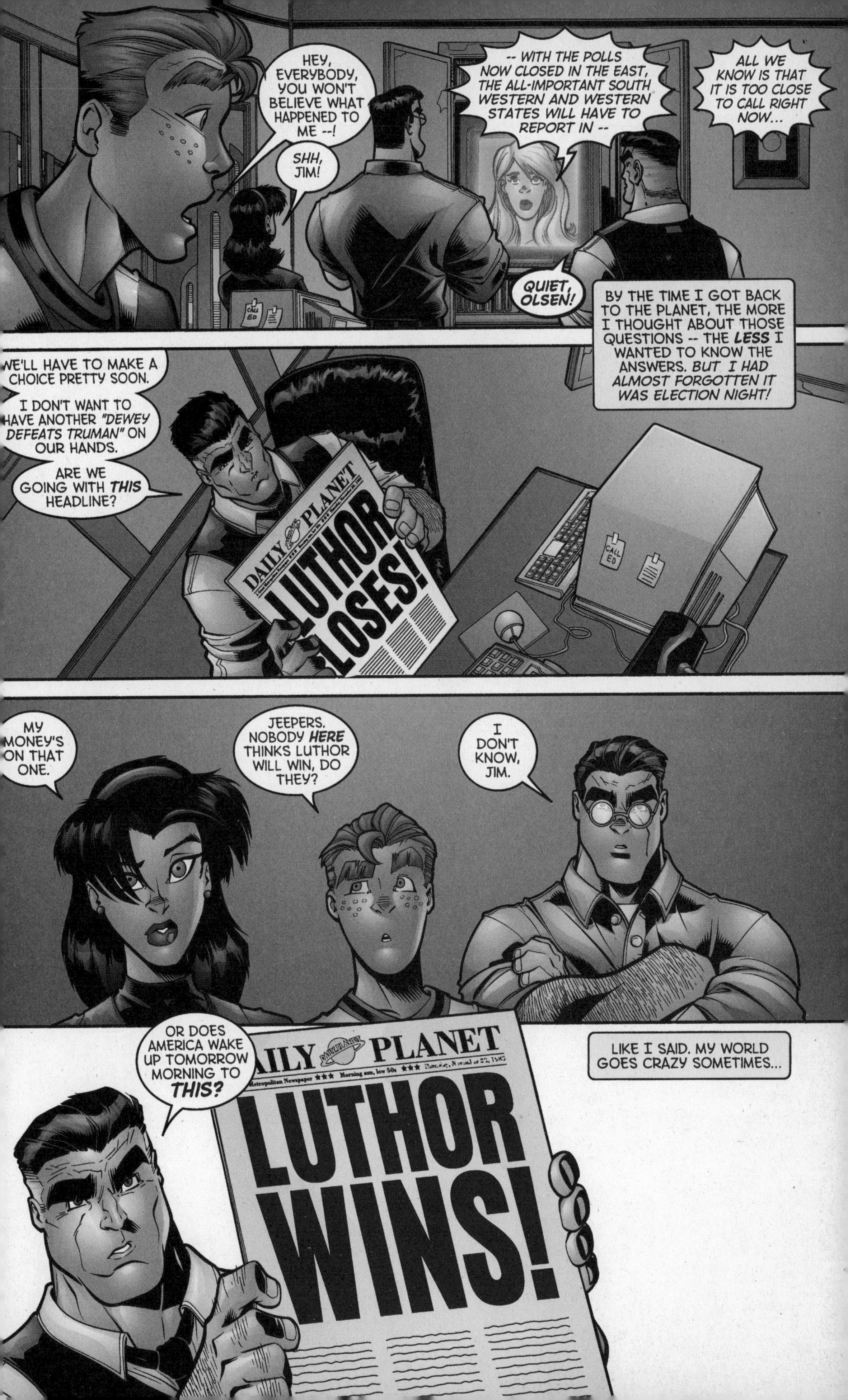
HEY, EVERYBODY, YOU WON'T BELIEVE WHAT HAPPENED TO ME --!
SHH, JIM!
-- WITH THE POLLS NOW CLOSED IN THE EAST, THE ALL-IMPORTANT SOUTH WESTERN AND WESTERN STATES WILL HAVE TO REPORT IN --
ALL WE KNOW IS THAT IT IS TOO CLOSE TO CALL RIGHT NOW...
QUIET, OLSEN!
BY THE TIME I GOT BACK TO THE PLANET, THE MORE I THOUGHT ABOUT THOSE QUESTIONS -- THE LESS I WANTED TO KNOW THE ANSWERS. BUT I HAD ALMOST FORGOTTEN IT WAS ELECTION NIGHT!
WE'LL HAVE TO MAKE A CHOICE PRETTY SOON.
I DON'T WANT TO HAVE ANOTHER "DEWEY DEFEATS TRUMAN" ON OUR HANDS.
ARE WE GOING WITH THIS HEADLINE?
DAILY PLANET
LUTHOR LOSES!
MY MONEY'S ON THAT ONE.
JEEPERS. NOBODY HERE THINKS LUTHOR WILL WIN, DO THEY?
I DON'T KNOW, JIM.
OR DOES AMERICA WAKE UP TOMORROW MORNING TO THIS?
DAILY PLANET
Metropolitan Newspaper ★★★ Morning sun, low 50s ★★★
LUTHOR WINS!
LIKE I SAID. MY WORLD GOES CRAZY SOMETIMES...

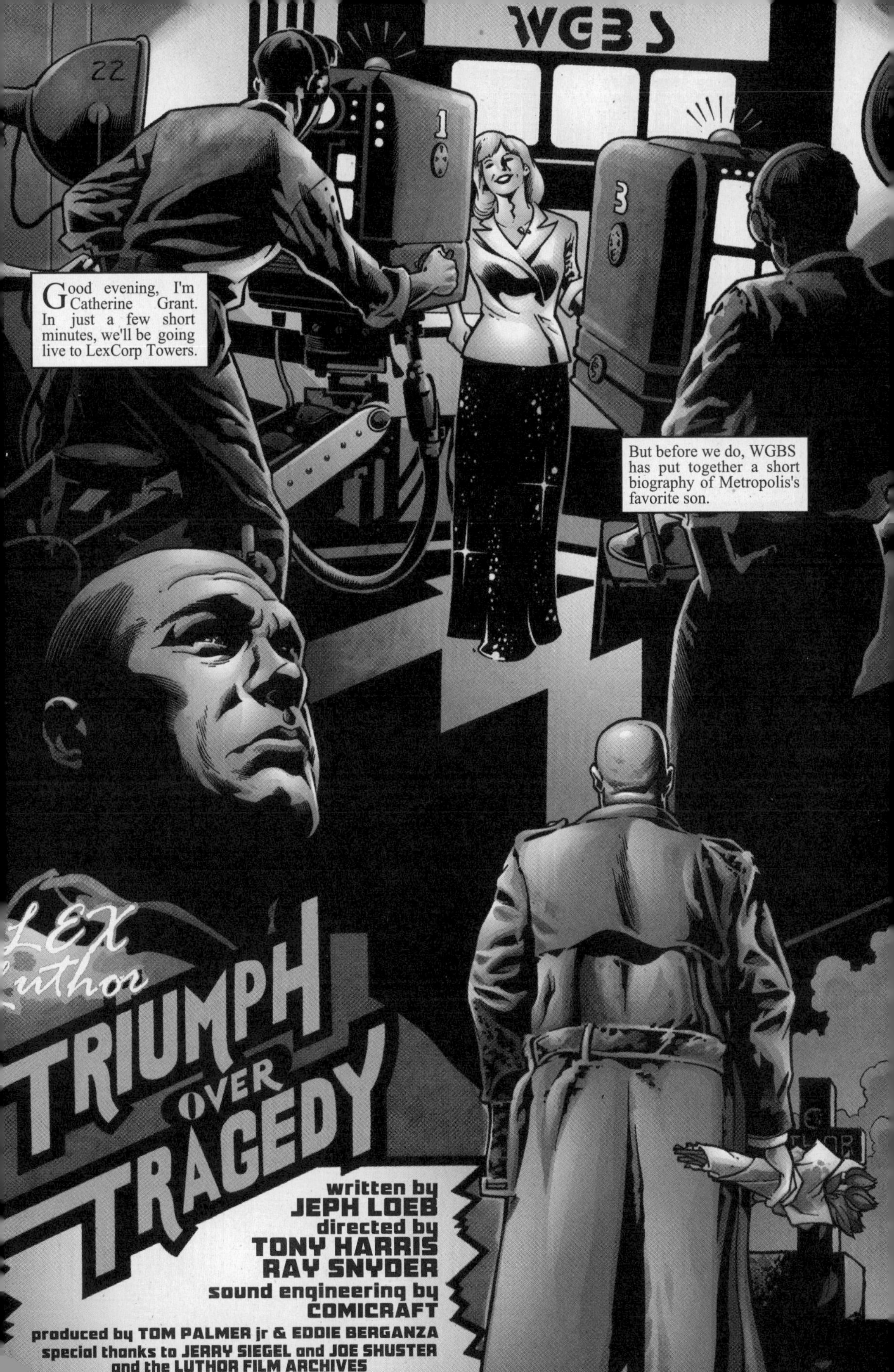
WGBS
Good evening, I'm Catherine Grant. In just a few short minutes, we'll be going live to LexCorp Towers.
But before we do, WGBS has put together a short biography of Metropolis's favorite son.
LEX Luthor
TRIUMPH OVER TRAGEDY
written by JEPH LOEB
directed by TONY HARRIS RAY SNYDER
sound engineering by COMICRAFT
produced by TOM PALMER jr & EDDIE BERGANZA
special thanks to JERRY SIEGEL and JOE SHUSTER and the LUTHOR FILM ARCHIVES

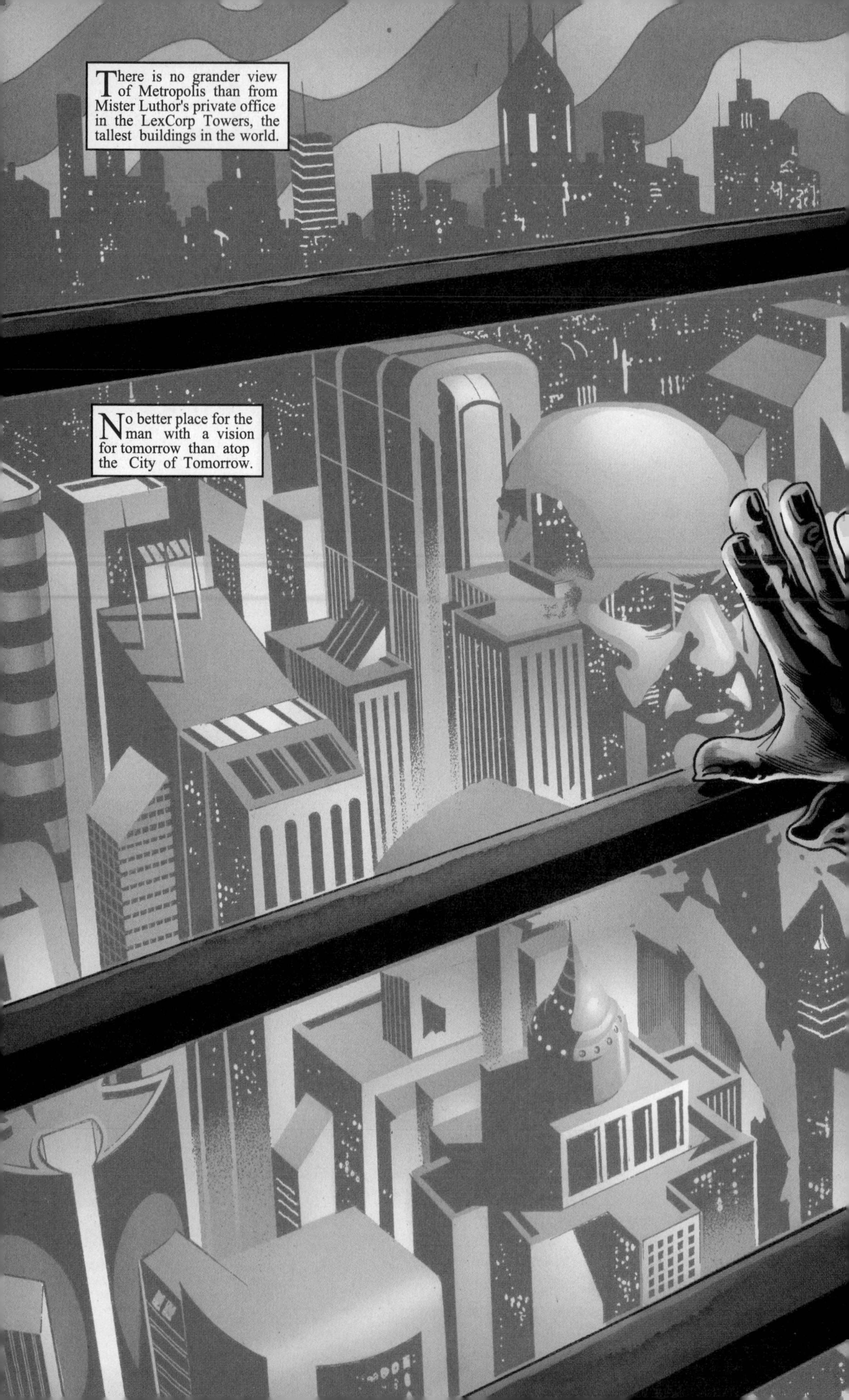
There is no grander view of Metropolis than from Mister Luthor's private office in the LexCorp Towers, the tallest buildings in the world.
No better place for the man with a vision for tomorrow than atop the City of Tomorrow.

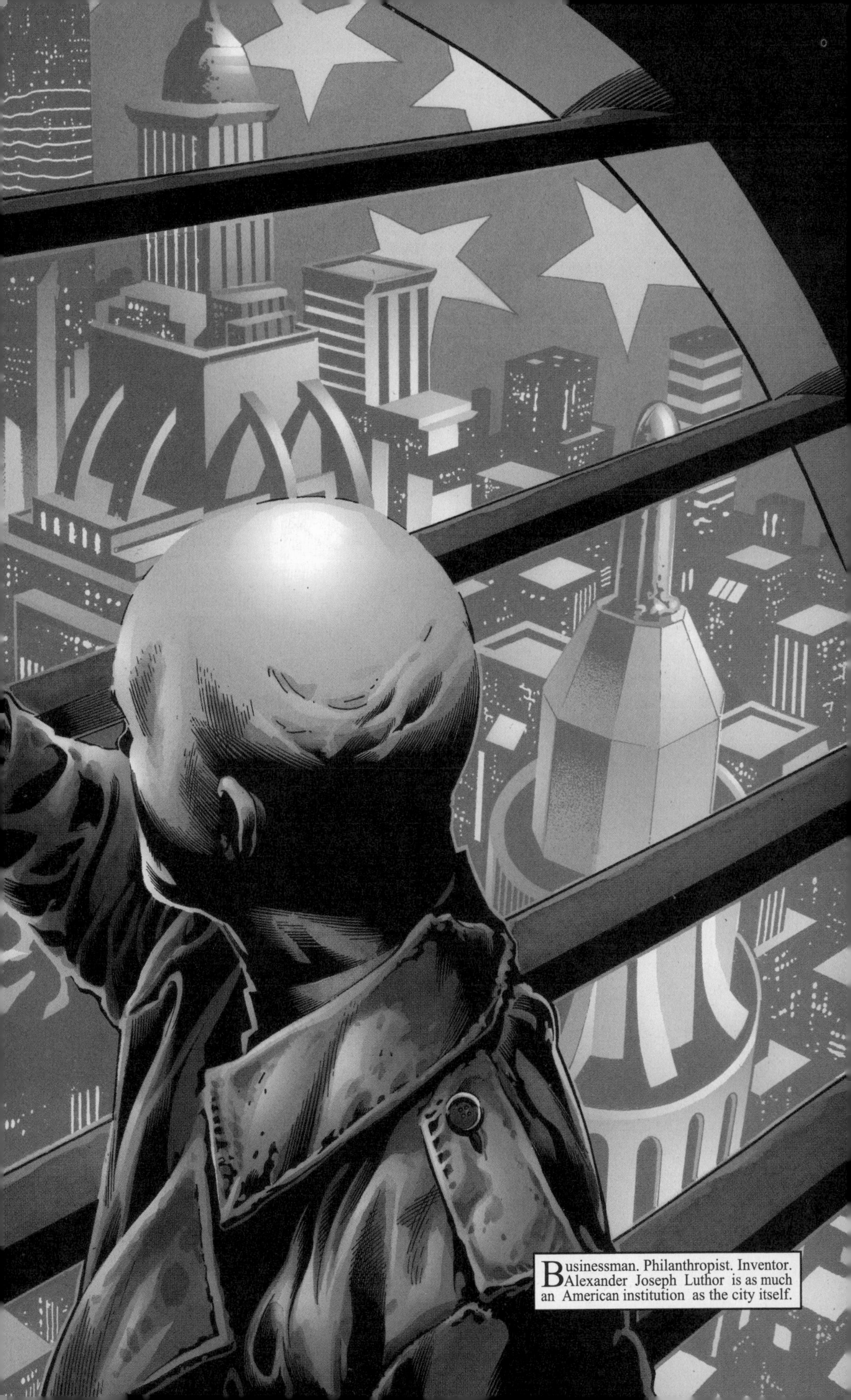
Businessman. Philanthropist. Inventor. Alexander Joseph Luthor is as much an American institution as the city itself.

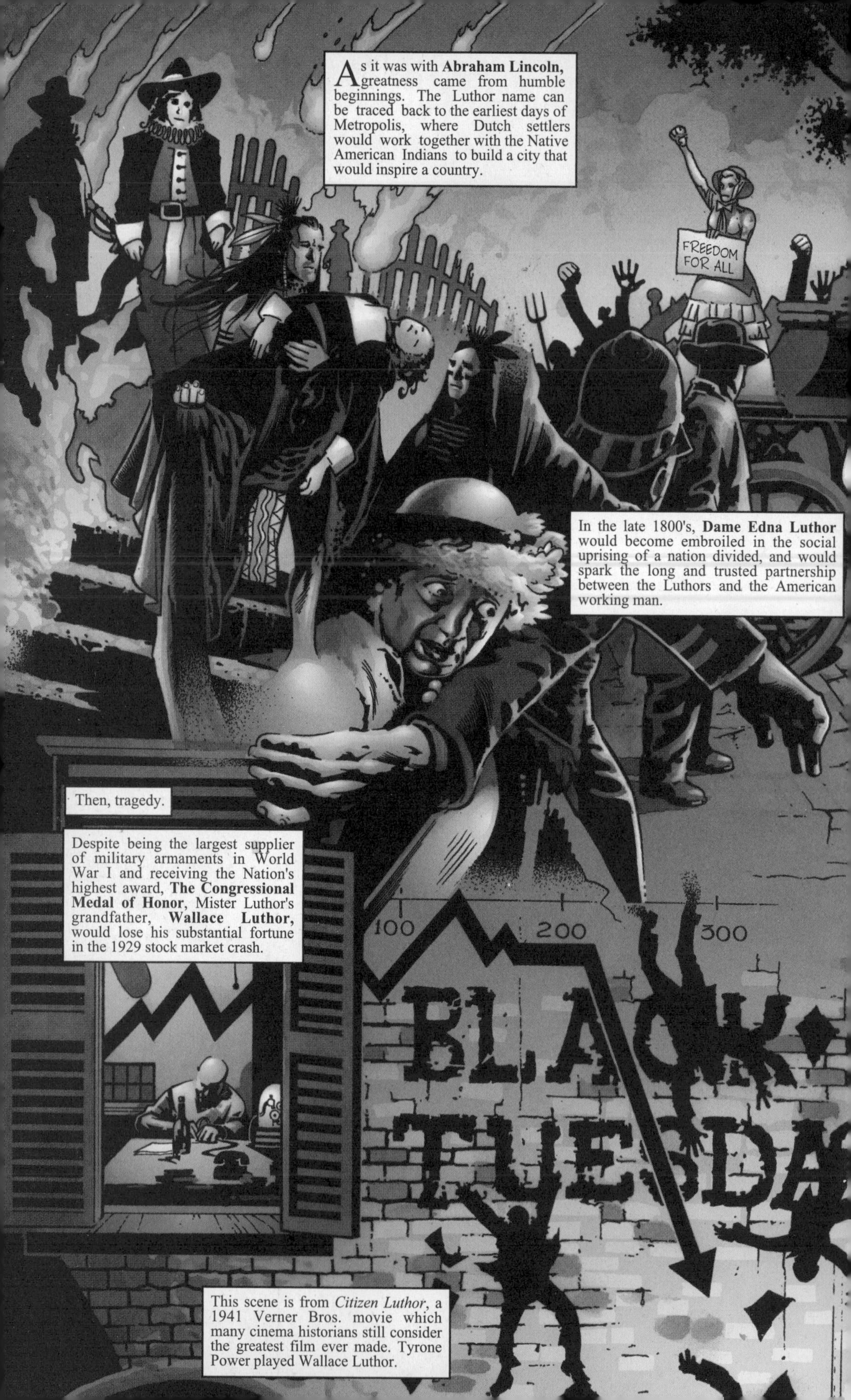
As it was with **Abraham Lincoln,** greatness came from humble beginnings. The Luthor name can be traced back to the earliest days of Metropolis, where Dutch settlers would work together with the Native American Indians to build a city that would inspire a country.
FREEDOM FOR ALL
In the late 1800's, **Dame Edna Luthor** would become embroiled in the social uprising of a nation divided, and would spark the long and trusted partnership between the Luthors and the American working man.
Then, tragedy.
Despite being the largest supplier of military armaments in World War I and receiving the Nation's highest award, **The Congressional Medal of Honor**, Mister Luthor's grandfather, **Wallace Luthor,** would lose his substantial fortune in the 1929 stock market crash.
100
200
300
This scene is from *Citizen Luthor*, a 1941 Verner Bros. movie which many cinema historians still consider the greatest film ever made. Tyrone Power played Wallace Luthor.

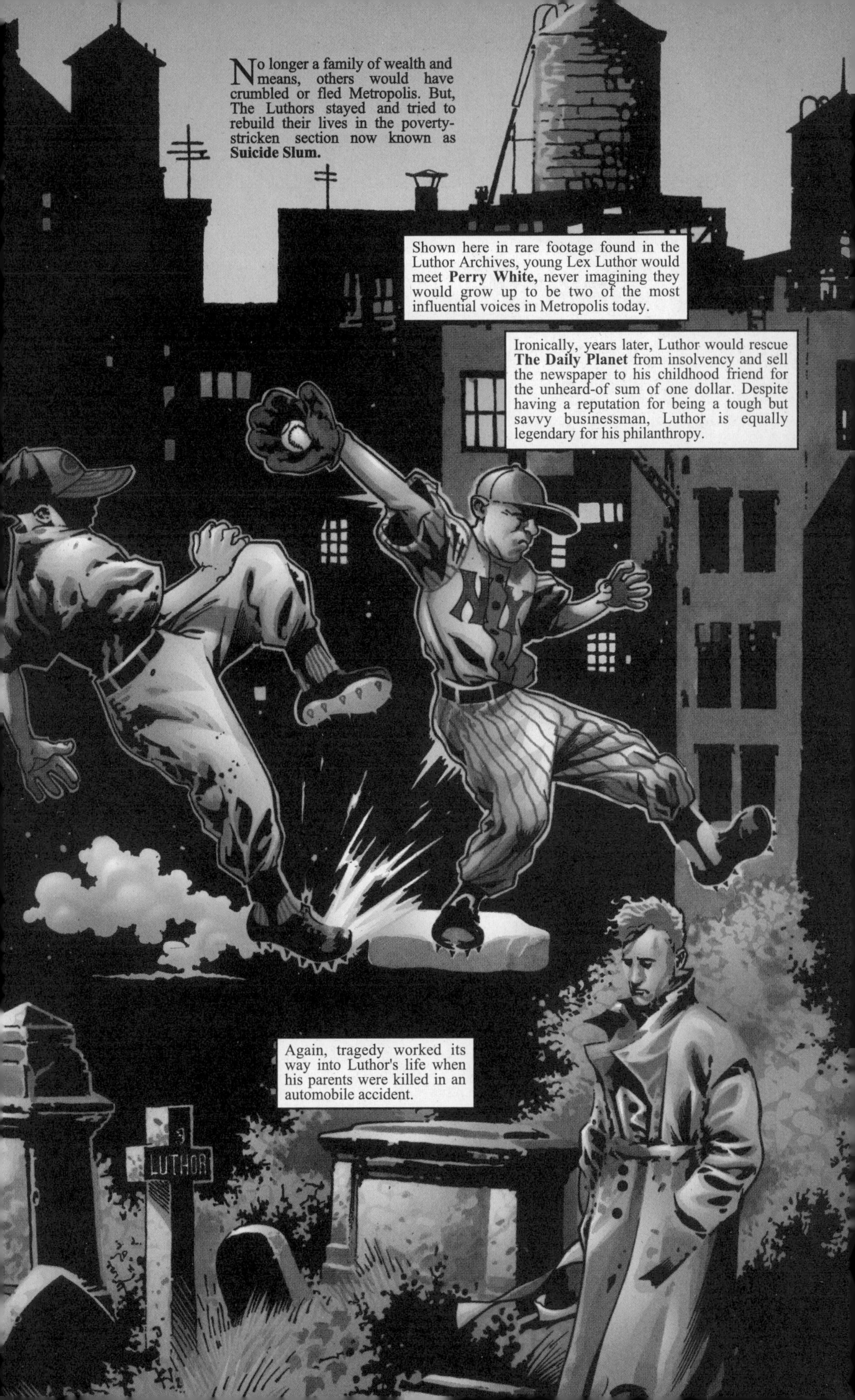
No longer a family of wealth and means, others would have crumbled or fled Metropolis. But, The Luthors stayed and tried to rebuild their lives in the poverty-stricken section now known as **Suicide Slum.**
Shown here in rare footage found in the Luthor Archives, young Lex Luthor would meet **Perry White,** never imagining they would grow up to be two of the most influential voices in Metropolis today.
Ironically, years later, Luthor would rescue **The Daily Planet** from insolvency and sell the newspaper to his childhood friend for the unheard-of sum of one dollar. Despite having a reputation for being a tough but savvy businessman, Luthor is equally legendary for his philanthropy.
Again, tragedy worked its way into Luthor's life when his parents were killed in an automobile accident.
LUTHOR

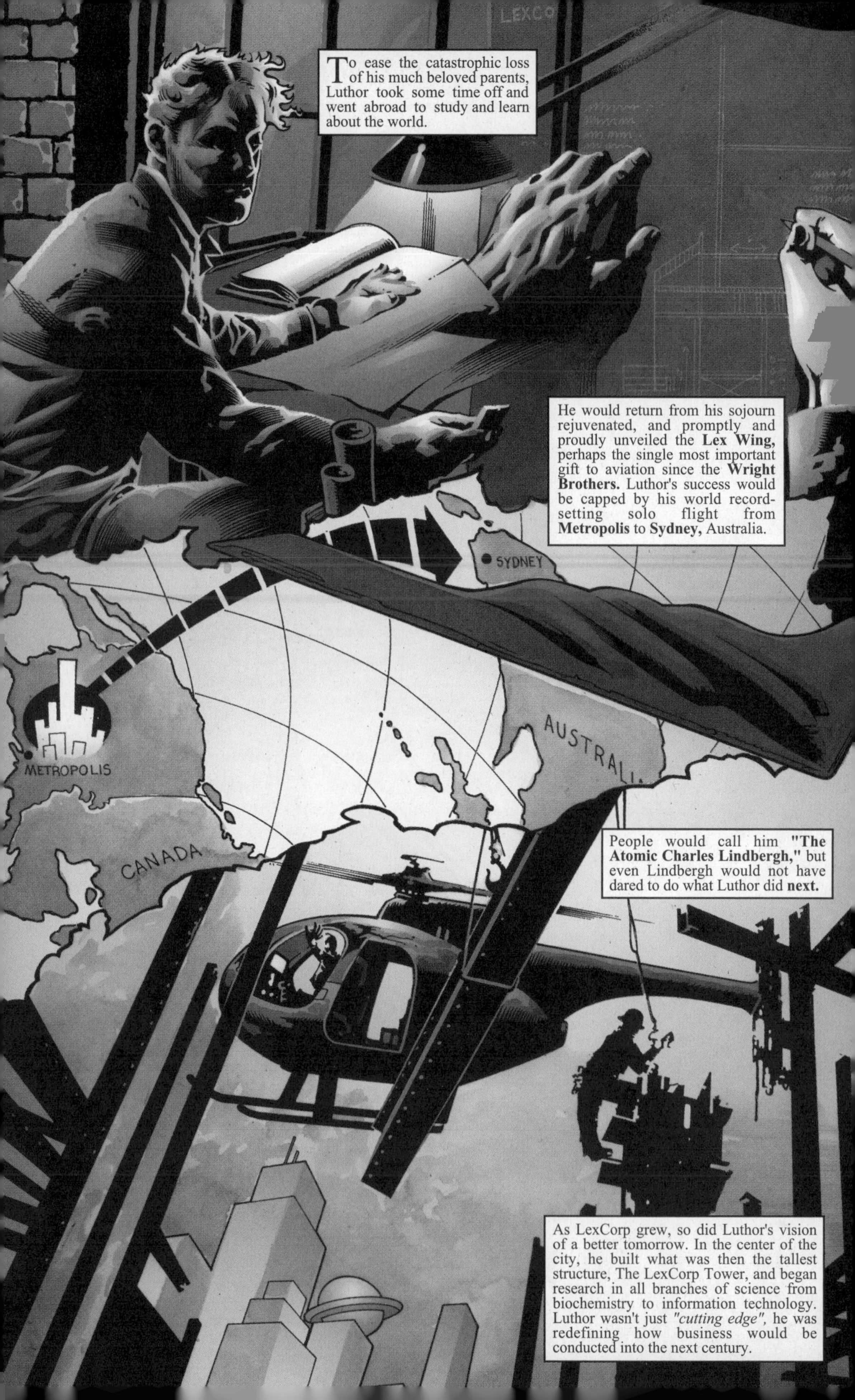

LEXCO
To ease the catastrophic loss of his much beloved parents, Luthor took some time off and went abroad to study and learn about the world.
He would return from his sojourn rejuvenated, and promptly and proudly unveiled the **Lex Wing,** perhaps the single most important gift to aviation since the **Wright Brothers.** Luthor's success would be capped by his world record-setting solo flight from **Metropolis** to **Sydney,** Australia.
SYDNEY
METROPOLIS
AUSTRALI
CANADA
People would call him **"The Atomic Charles Lindbergh,"** but even Lindbergh would not have dared to do what Luthor did **next.**
As LexCorp grew, so did Luthor's vision of a better tomorrow. In the center of the city, he built what was then the tallest structure, The LexCorp Tower, and began research in all branches of science from biochemistry to information technology. Luthor wasn't just *"cutting edge"*, he was redefining how business would be conducted into the next century.

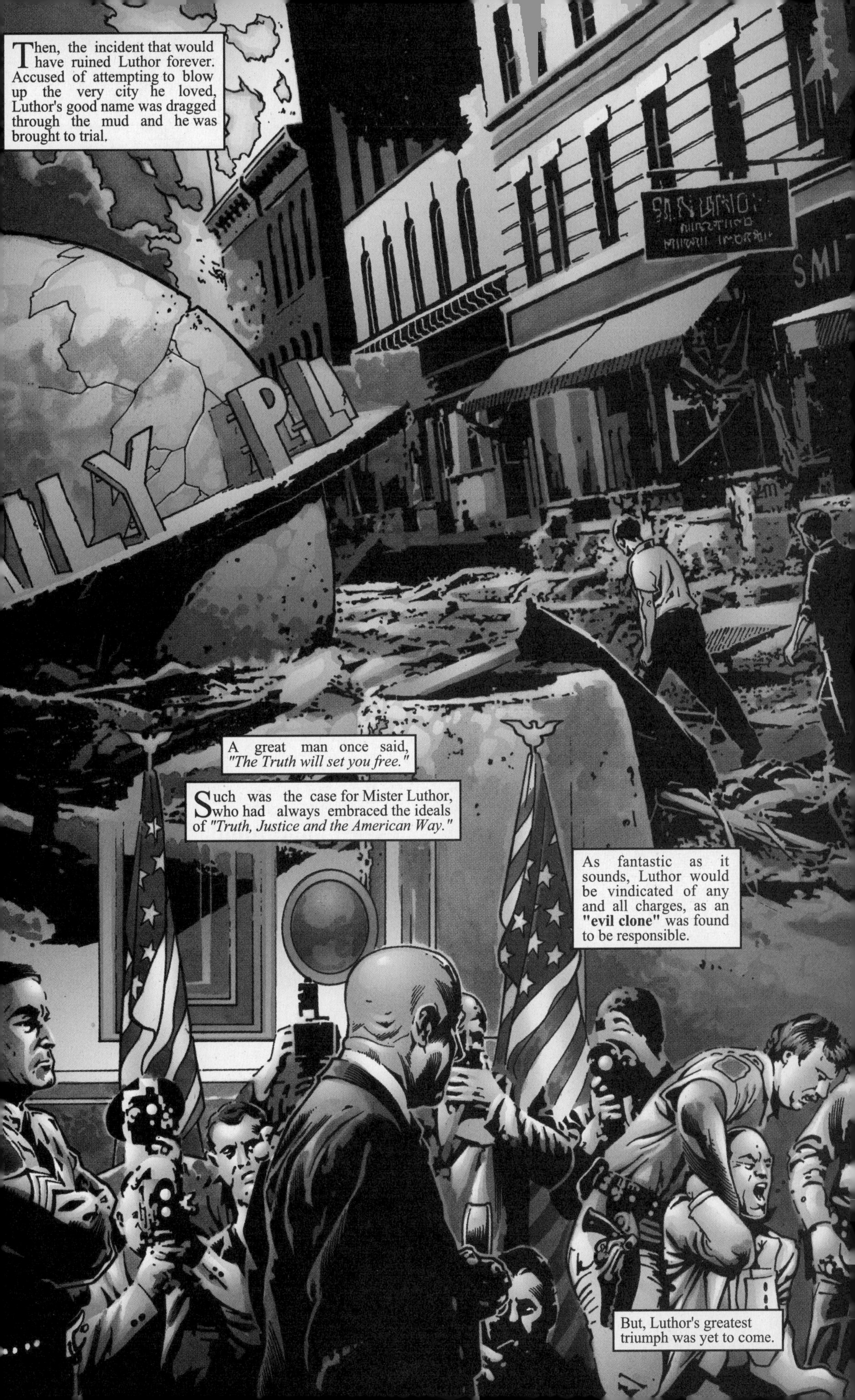
Then, the incident that would have ruined Luthor forever. Accused of attempting to blow up the very city he loved, Luthor's good name was dragged through the mud and he was brought to trial.
A great man once said, *"The Truth will set you free."*
Such was the case for Mister Luthor, who had always embraced the ideals of *"Truth, Justice and the American Way."*
As fantastic as it sounds, Luthor would be vindicated of any and all charges, as an **"evil clone"** was found to be responsible.
But, Luthor's greatest triumph was yet to come.

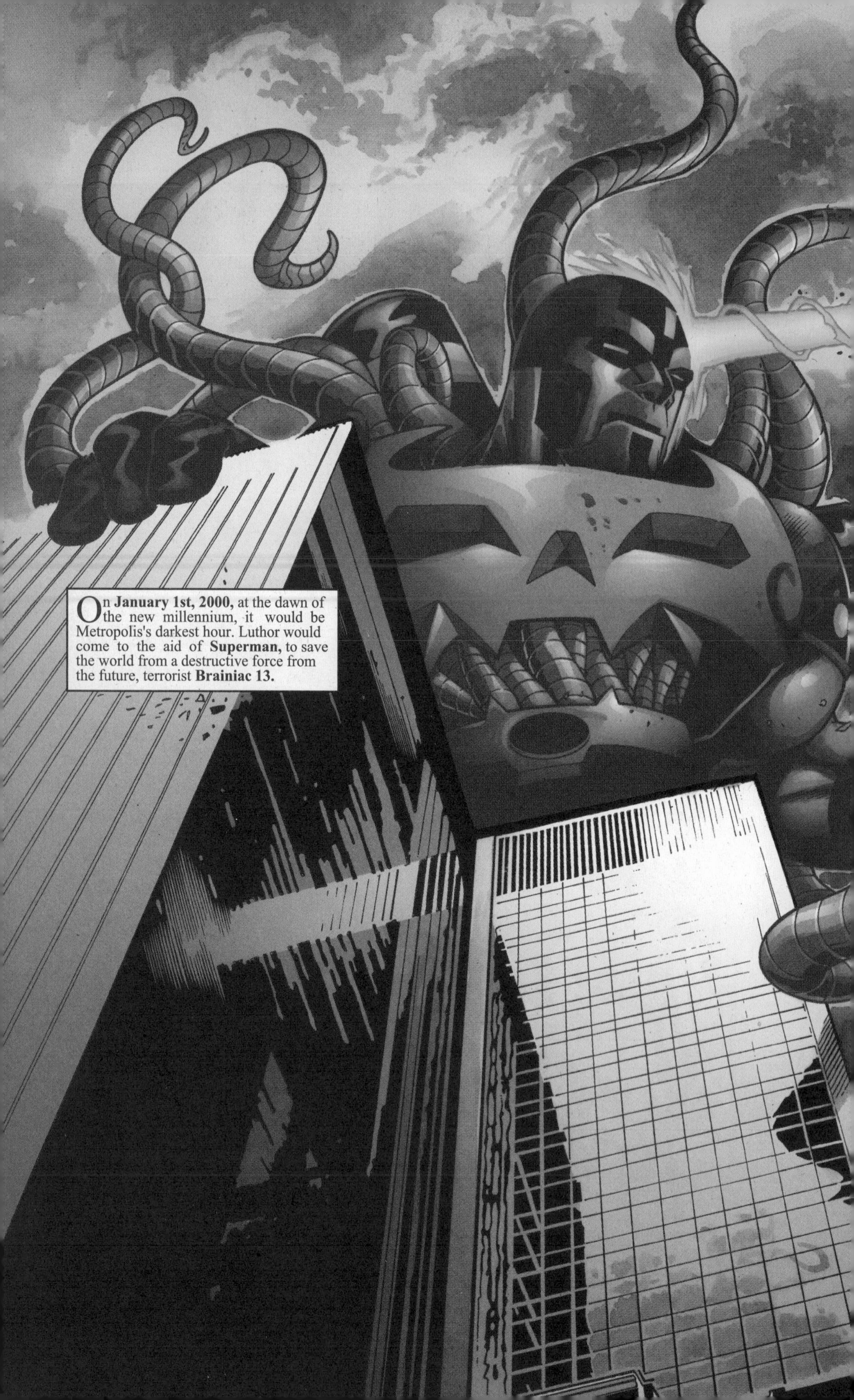
On January 1st, 2000, at the dawn of the new millennium, it would be Metropolis's darkest hour. Luthor would come to the aid of Superman, to save the world from a destructive force from the future, terrorist Brainiac 13.

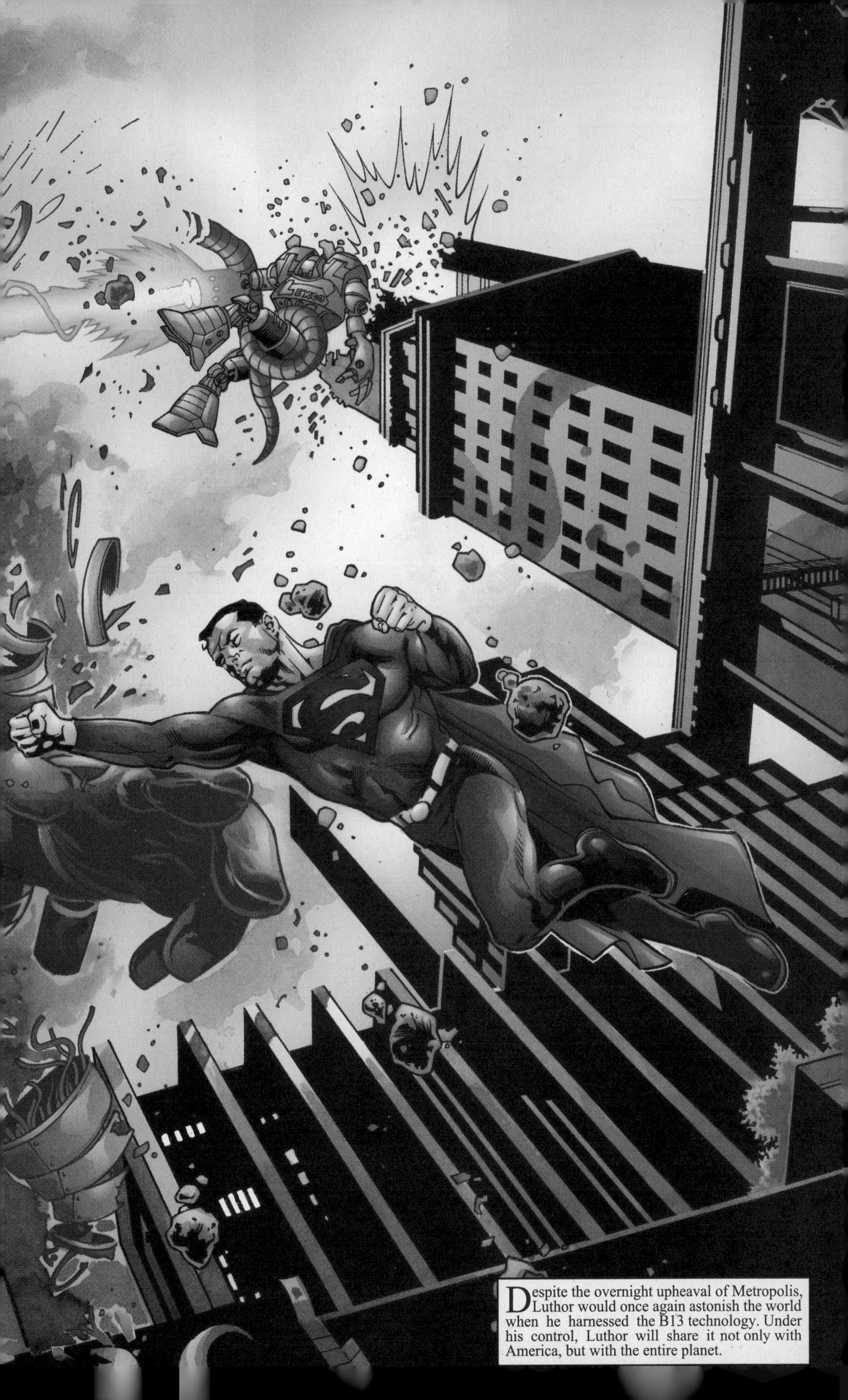

Despite the overnight upheaval of Metropolis, Luthor would once again astonish the world when he harnessed the B13 technology. Under his control, Luthor will share it not only with America, but with the entire planet.

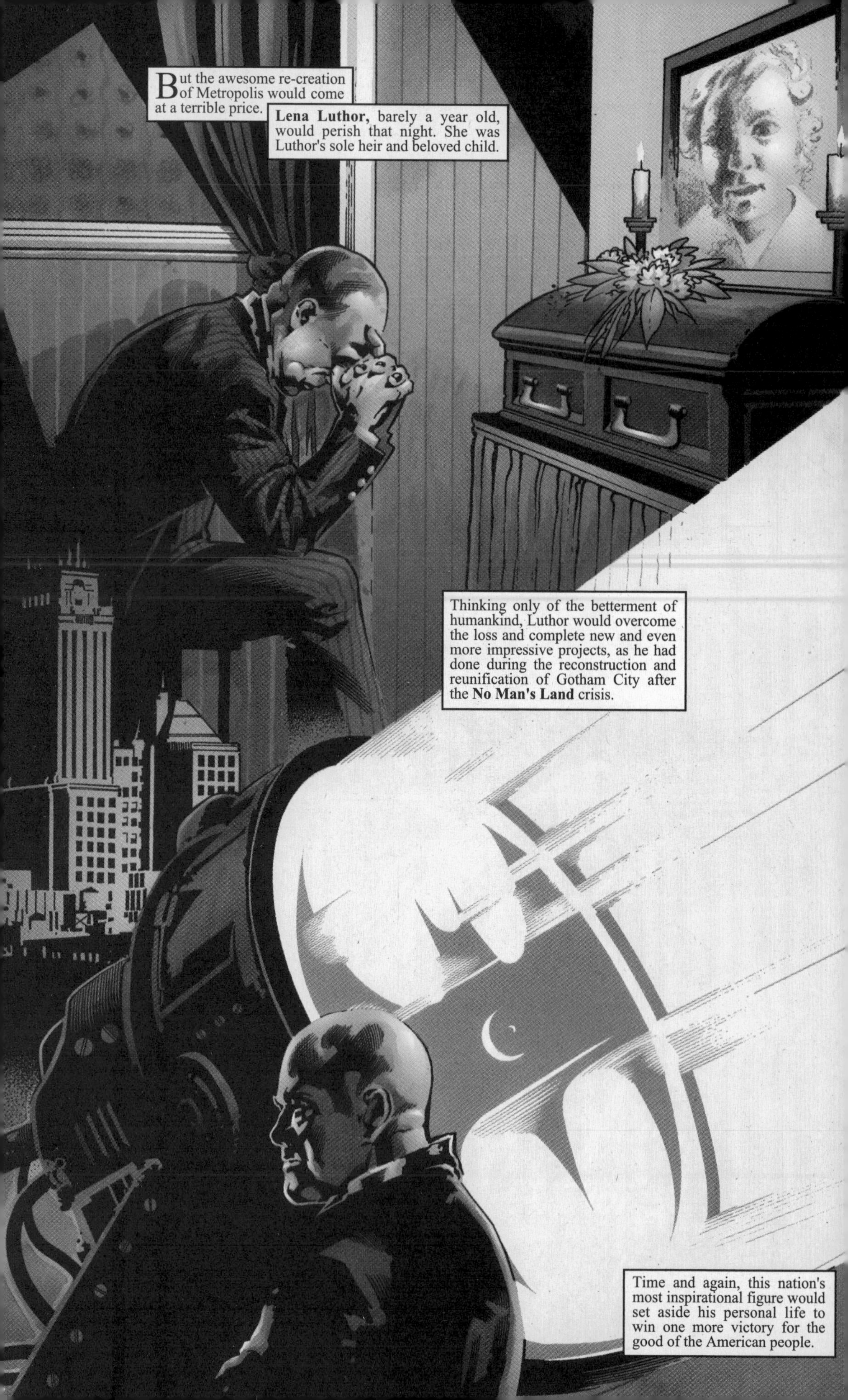
But the awesome re-creation of Metropolis would come at a terrible price.
Lena Luthor, barely a year old, would perish that night. She was Luthor's sole heir and beloved child.
Thinking only of the betterment of humankind, Luthor would overcome the loss and complete new and even more impressive projects, as he had done during the reconstruction and reunification of Gotham City after the **No Man's Land** crisis.
Time and again, this nation's most inspirational figure would set aside his personal life to win one more victory for the good of the American people.

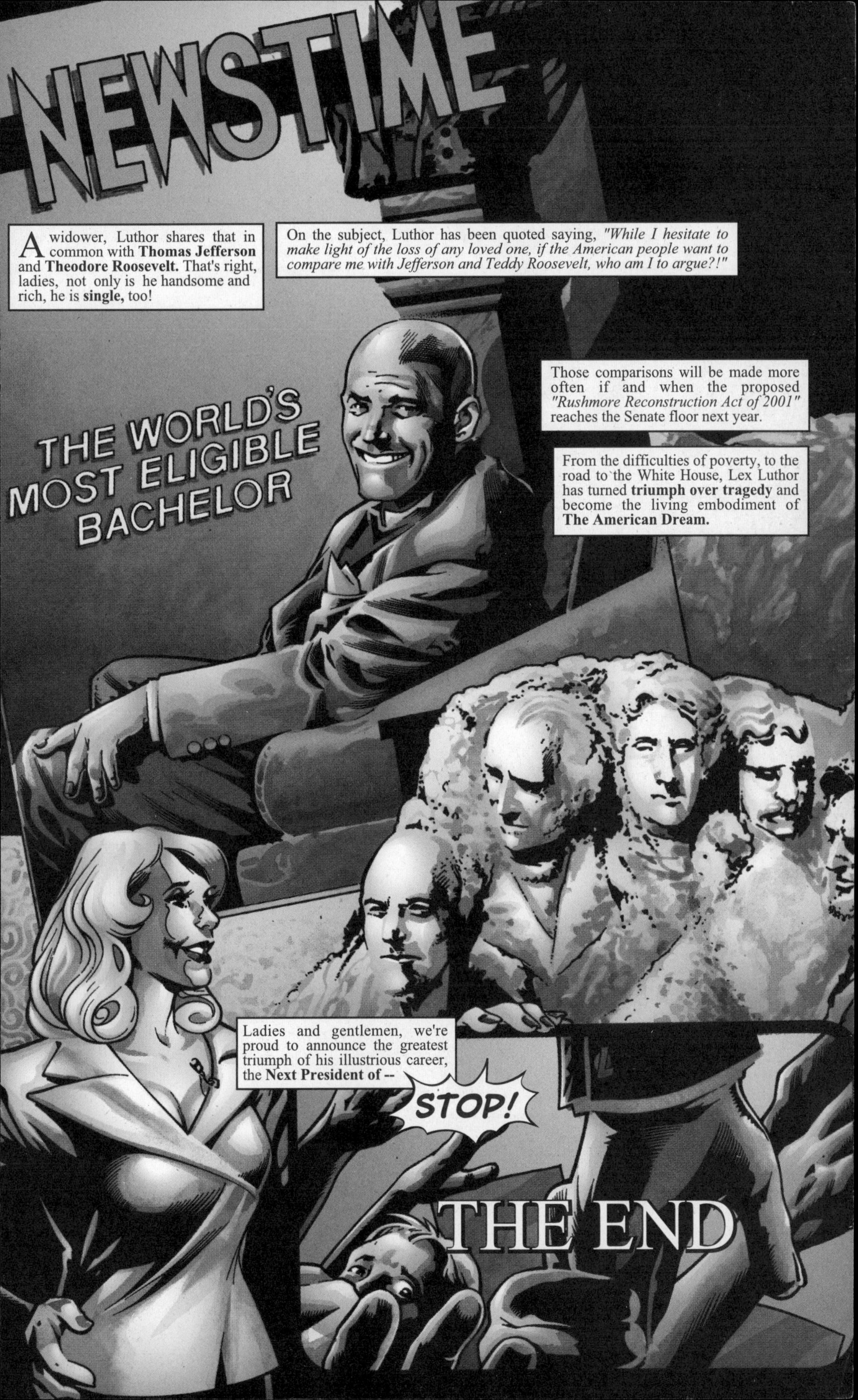
NEWSTIME
A widower, Luthor shares that in common with Thomas Jefferson and Theodore Roosevelt. That's right, ladies, not only is he handsome and rich, he is single, too!
On the subject, Luthor has been quoted saying, "While I hesitate to make light of the loss of any loved one, if the American people want to compare me with Jefferson and Teddy Roosevelt, who am I to argue?!"
THE WORLD'S MOST ELIGIBLE BACHELOR
Those comparisons will be made more often if and when the proposed "Rushmore Reconstruction Act of 2001" reaches the Senate floor next year.
From the difficulties of poverty, to the road to the White House, Lex Luthor has turned triumph over tragedy and become the living embodiment of The American Dream.
Ladies and gentlemen, we're proud to announce the greatest triumph of his illustrious career, the Next President of --
STOP!
THE END

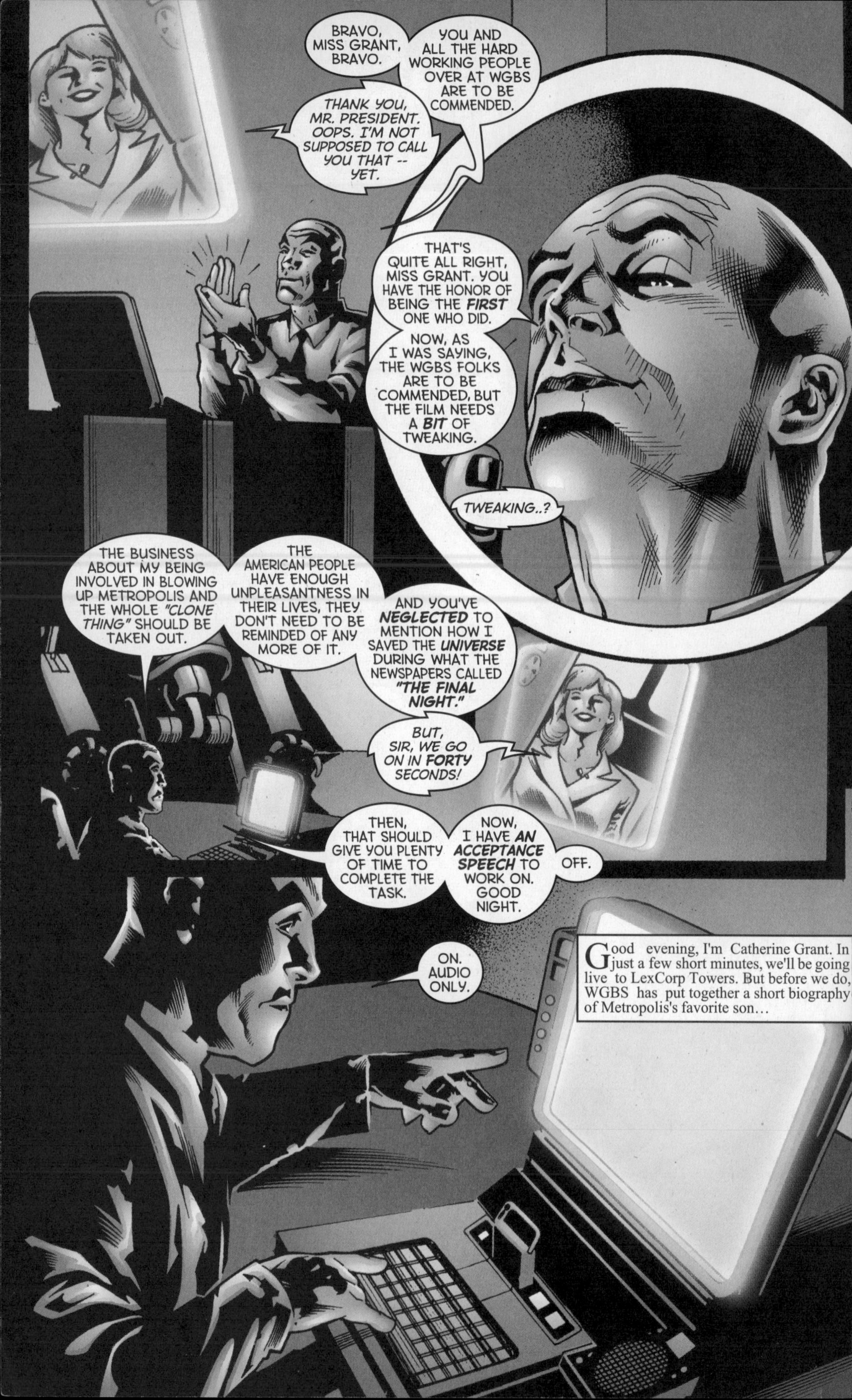
BRAVO, MISS GRANT, BRAVO.
YOU AND ALL THE HARD WORKING PEOPLE OVER AT WGBS ARE TO BE COMMENDED.
THANK YOU, MR. PRESIDENT. OOPS. I'M NOT SUPPOSED TO CALL YOU THAT -- YET.
THAT'S QUITE ALL RIGHT, MISS GRANT. YOU HAVE THE HONOR OF BEING THE FIRST ONE WHO DID.
NOW, AS I WAS SAYING, THE WGBS FOLKS ARE TO BE COMMENDED, BUT THE FILM NEEDS A BIT OF TWEAKING.
TWEAKING..?
THE BUSINESS ABOUT MY BEING INVOLVED IN BLOWING UP METROPOLIS AND THE WHOLE "CLONE THING" SHOULD BE TAKEN OUT.
THE AMERICAN PEOPLE HAVE ENOUGH UNPLEASANTNESS IN THEIR LIVES, THEY DON'T NEED TO BE REMINDED OF ANY MORE OF IT.
AND YOU'VE NEGLECTED TO MENTION HOW I SAVED THE UNIVERSE DURING WHAT THE NEWSPAPERS CALLED "THE FINAL NIGHT."
BUT, SIR, WE GO ON IN FORTY SECONDS!
THEN, THAT SHOULD GIVE YOU PLENTY OF TIME TO COMPLETE THE TASK.
NOW, I HAVE AN ACCEPTANCE SPEECH TO WORK ON. GOOD NIGHT.
OFF.
ON. AUDIO ONLY.
Good evening, I'm Catherine Grant. In just a few short minutes, we'll be going live to LexCorp Towers. But before we do, WGBS has put together a short biography of Metropolis's favorite son…

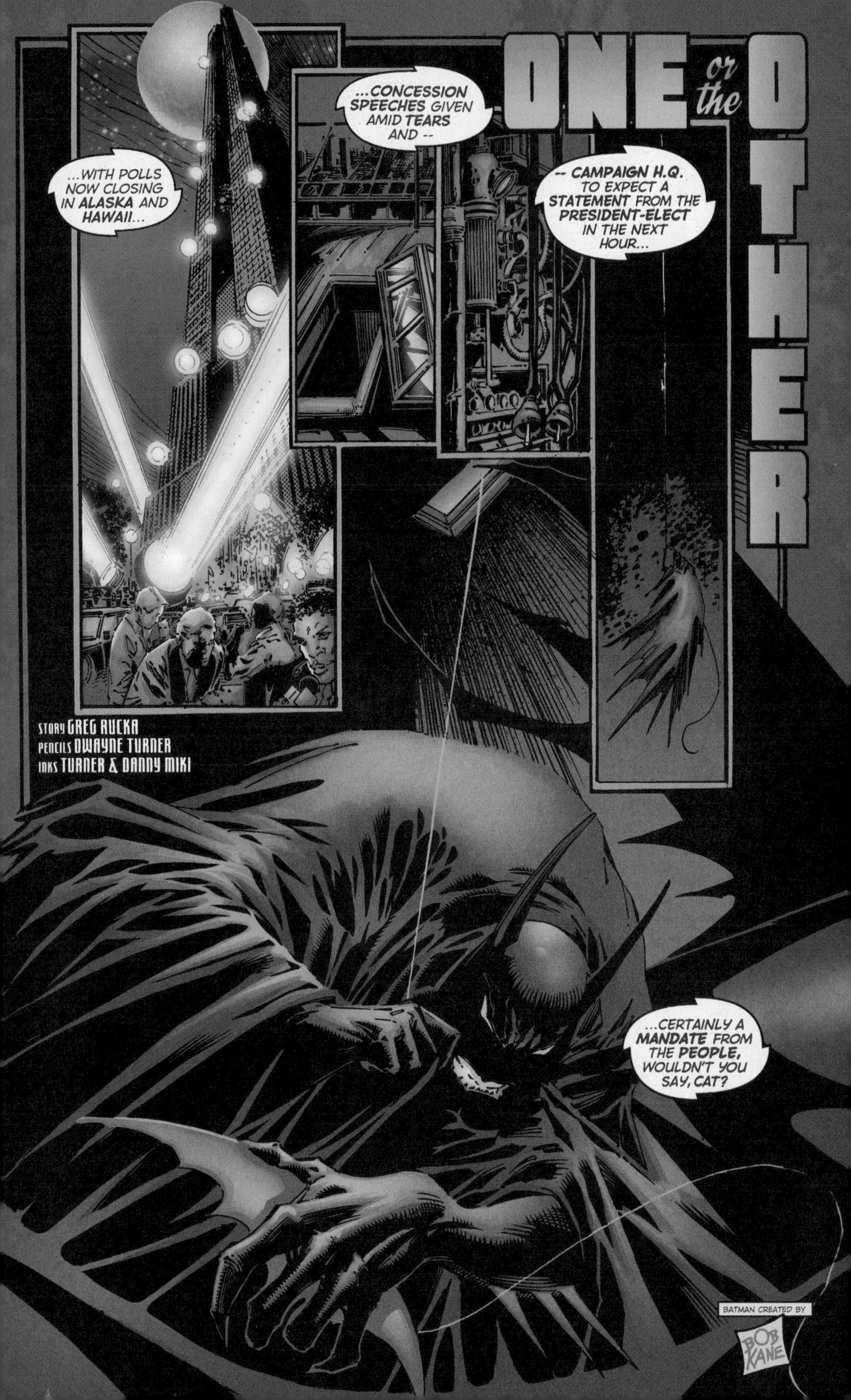
ONE or the OTHER
...WITH POLLS NOW CLOSING IN ALASKA AND HAWAII...
...CONCESSION SPEECHES GIVEN AMID TEARS AND --
-- CAMPAIGN H.Q. TO EXPECT A STATEMENT FROM THE PRESIDENT-ELECT IN THE NEXT HOUR...
STORY GREG RUCKA
PENCILS DWAYNE TURNER
INKS TURNER & DANNY MIKI
...CERTAINLY A MANDATE FROM THE PEOPLE, WOULDN'T YOU SAY, CAT?
BATMAN CREATED BY BOB KANE

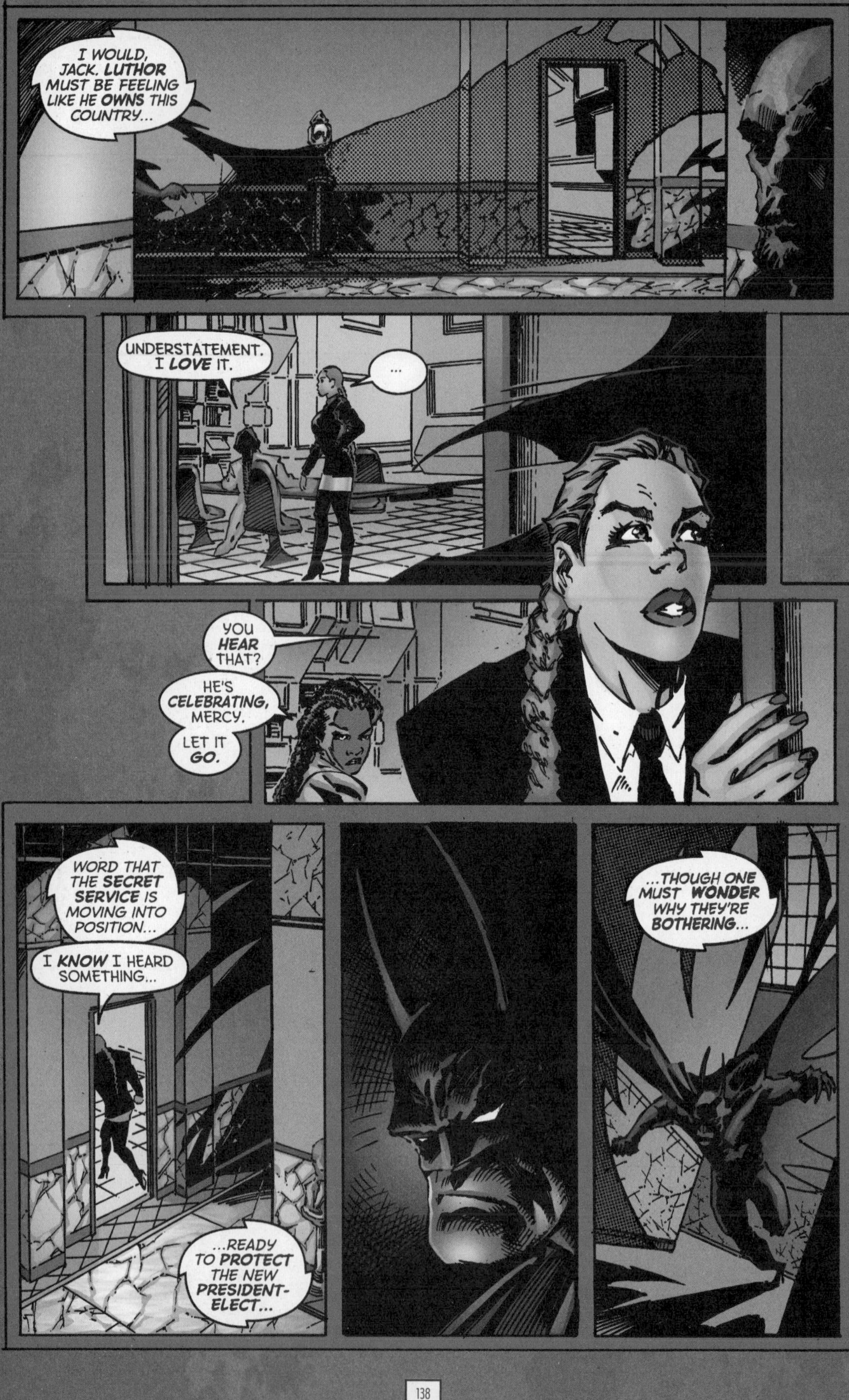
I WOULD, JACK. LUTHOR MUST BE FEELING LIKE HE OWNS THIS COUNTRY...
UNDERSTATEMENT. I LOVE IT.
...
YOU HEAR THAT?
HE'S CELEBRATING, MERCY.
LET IT GO.
WORD THAT THE SECRET SERVICE IS MOVING INTO POSITION...
I KNOW I HEARD SOMETHING...
...READY TO PROTECT THE NEW PRESIDENT-ELECT...
...THOUGH ONE MUST WONDER WHY THEY'RE BOTHERING...

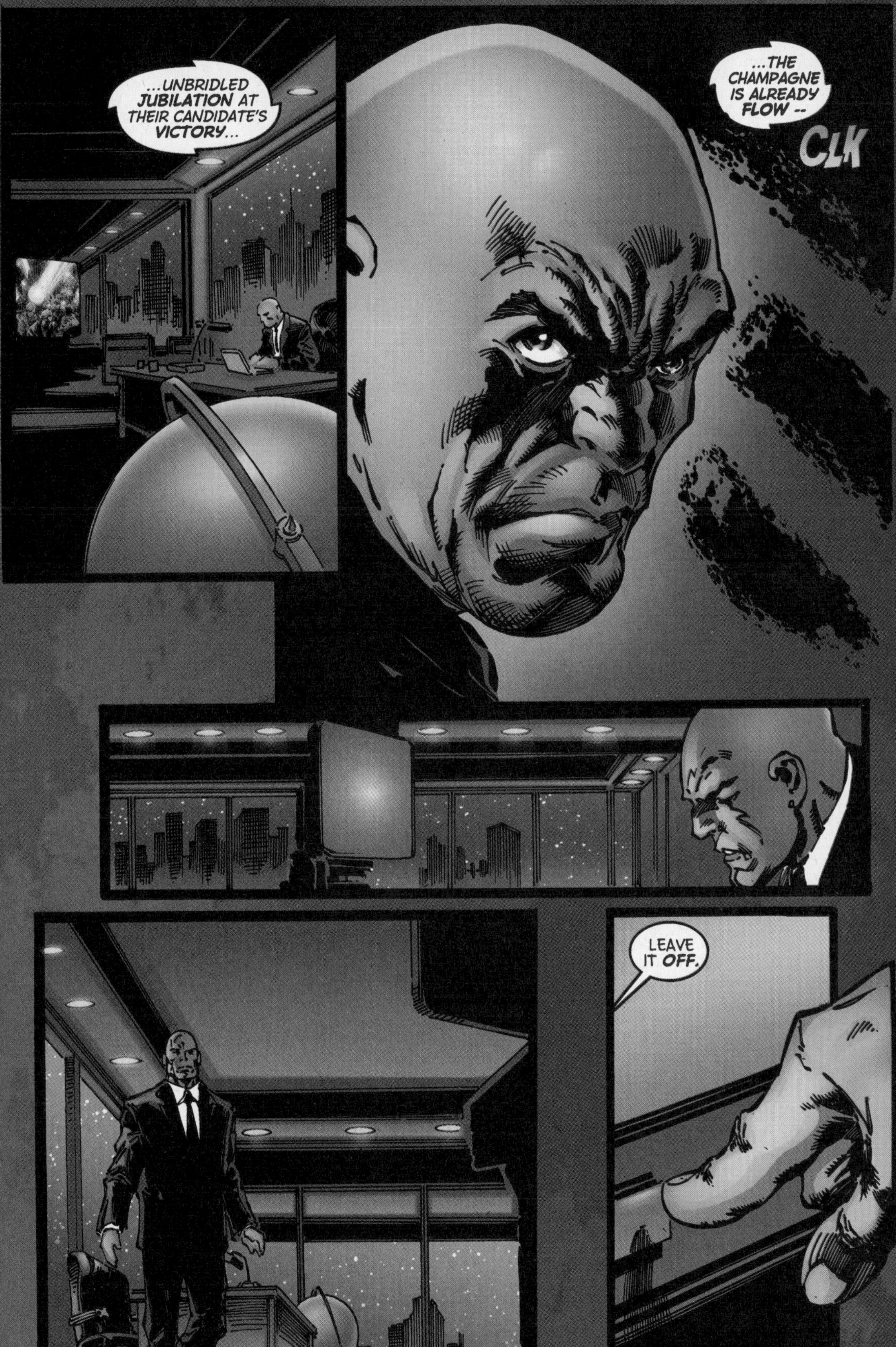
...UNBRIDLED JUBILATION AT THEIR CANDIDATE'S VICTORY...
...THE CHAMPAGNE IS ALREADY FLOW --
CLK
LEAVE IT OFF.

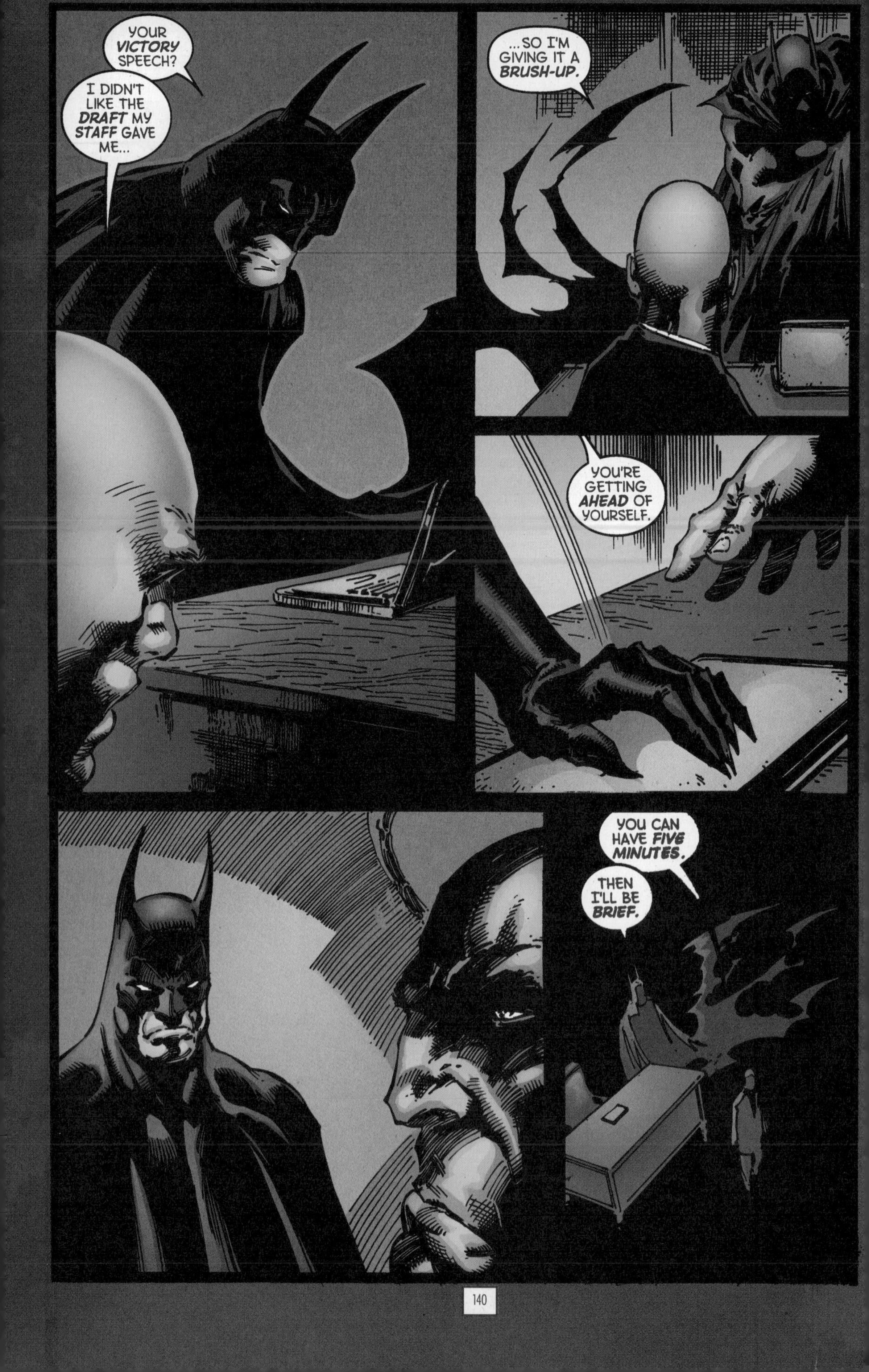
YOUR VICTORY SPEECH?
I DIDN'T LIKE THE DRAFT MY STAFF GAVE ME...
...SO I'M GIVING IT A BRUSH-UP.
YOU'RE GETTING AHEAD OF YOURSELF.
YOU CAN HAVE FIVE MINUTES.
THEN I'LL BE BRIEF.

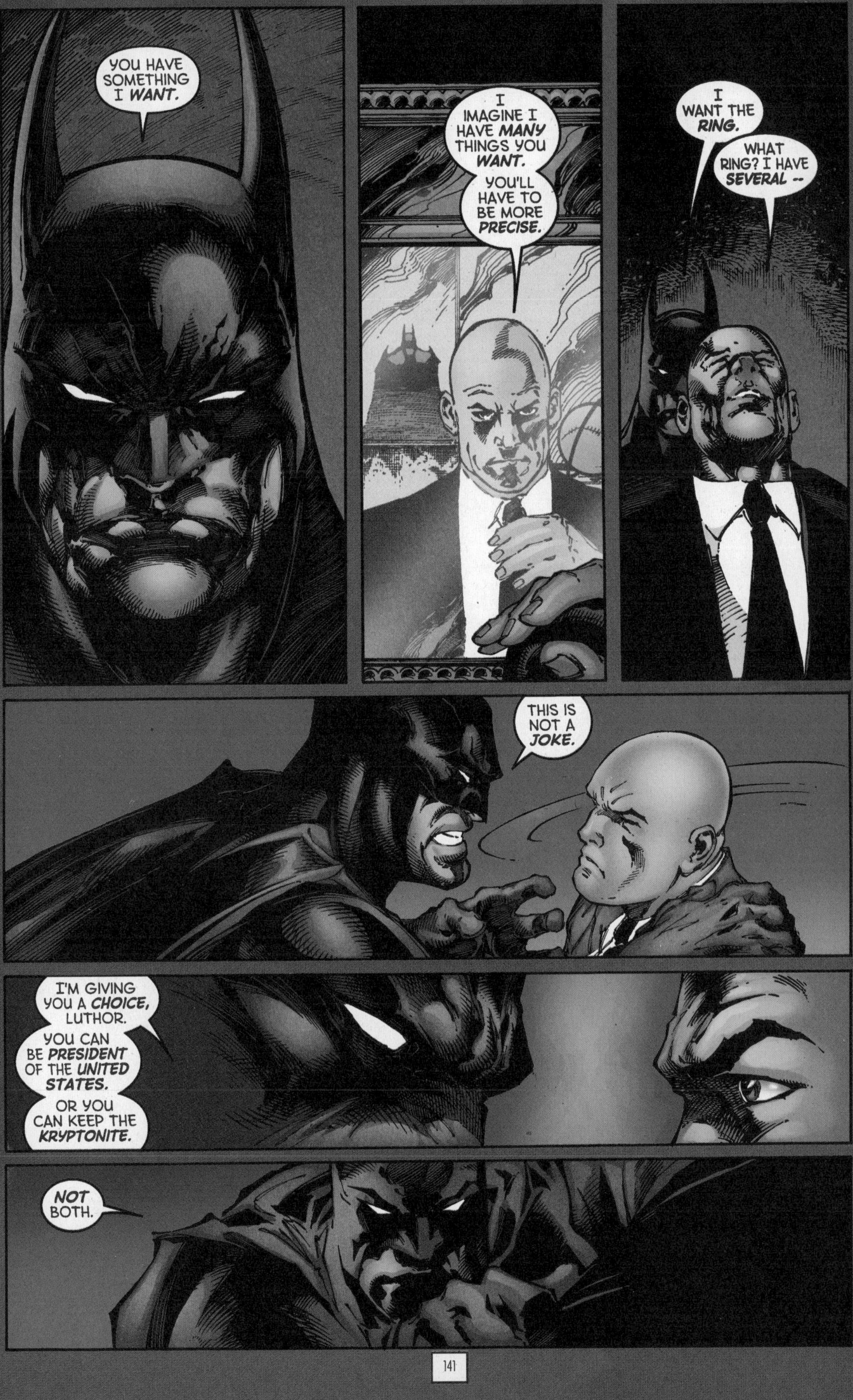
YOU HAVE SOMETHING I *WANT.*
I IMAGINE I HAVE *MANY* THINGS YOU *WANT.*
YOU'LL HAVE TO BE MORE *PRECISE.*
I WANT THE *RING.*
WHAT RING? I HAVE *SEVERAL* --
THIS IS NOT A *JOKE.*
I'M GIVING YOU A *CHOICE,* LUTHOR.
YOU CAN BE *PRESIDENT* OF THE *UNITED STATES.*
OR YOU CAN KEEP THE *KRYPTONITE.*
NOT BOTH.

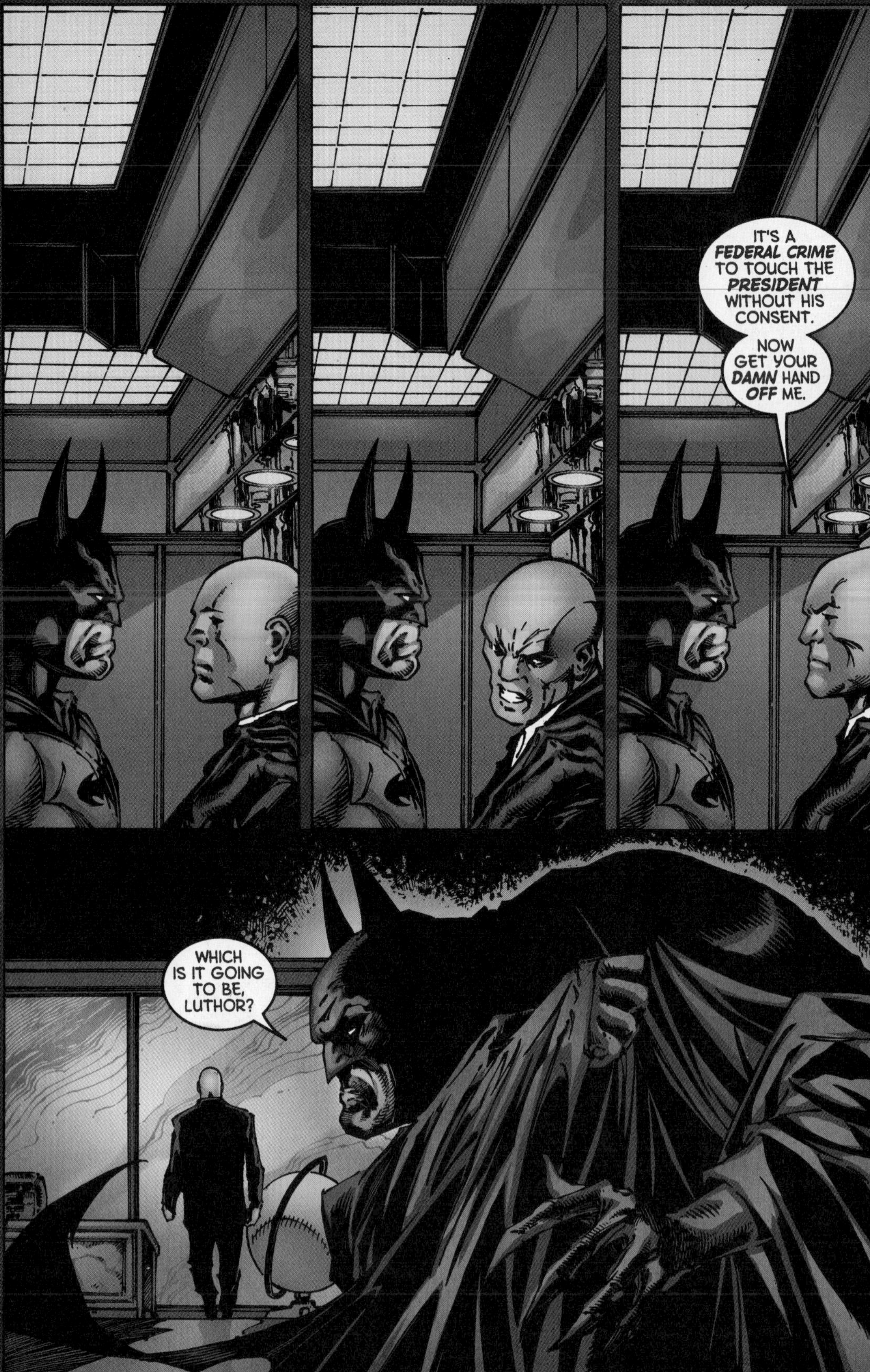
IT'S A FEDERAL CRIME TO TOUCH THE PRESIDENT WITHOUT HIS CONSENT.
NOW GET YOUR DAMN HAND OFF ME.
WHICH IS IT GOING TO BE, LUTHOR?

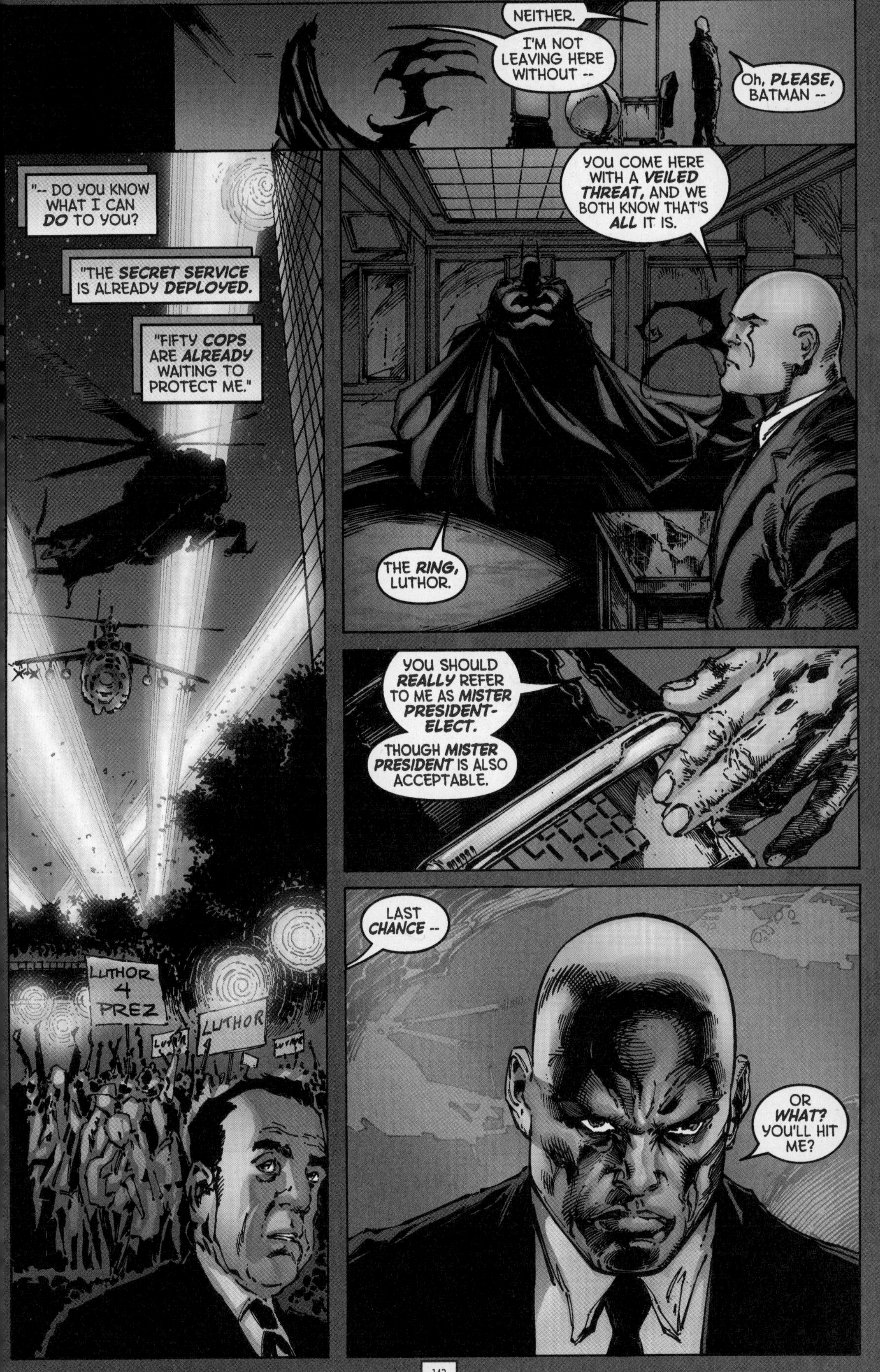
NEITHER.
I'M NOT LEAVING HERE WITHOUT --
Oh, PLEASE, BATMAN --
"-- DO YOU KNOW WHAT I CAN DO TO YOU?
"THE SECRET SERVICE IS ALREADY DEPLOYED.
"FIFTY COPS ARE ALREADY WAITING TO PROTECT ME."
LUTHOR 4 PREZ
LUTHOR
YOU COME HERE WITH A VEILED THREAT, AND WE BOTH KNOW THAT'S ALL IT IS.
THE RING, LUTHOR.
YOU SHOULD REALLY REFER TO ME AS MISTER PRESIDENT-ELECT.
THOUGH MISTER PRESIDENT IS ALSO ACCEPTABLE.
LAST CHANCE --
OR WHAT? YOU'LL HIT ME?

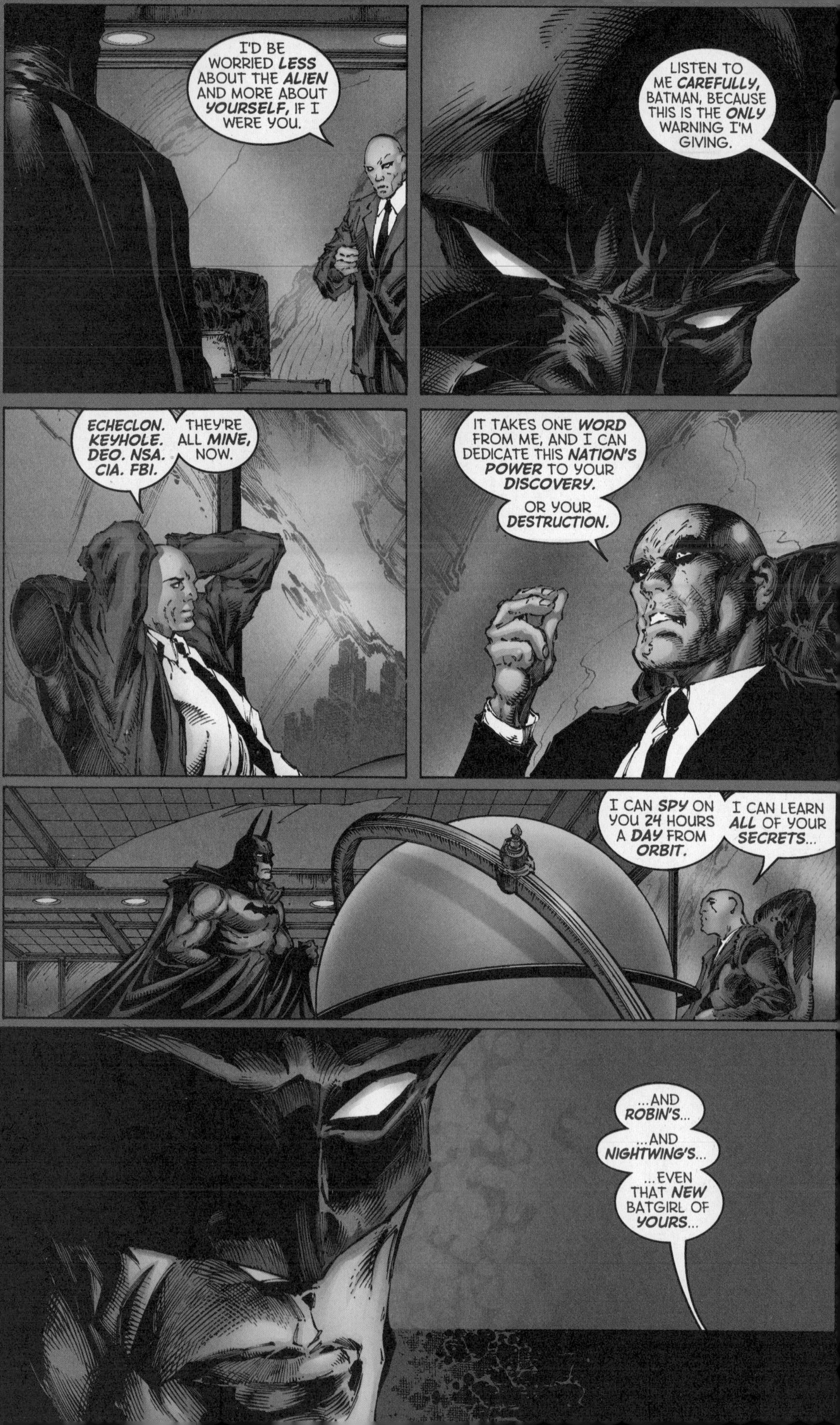
I'D BE WORRIED LESS ABOUT THE ALIEN AND MORE ABOUT YOURSELF, IF I WERE YOU.
LISTEN TO ME CAREFULLY, BATMAN, BECAUSE THIS IS THE ONLY WARNING I'M GIVING.
ECHECLON. KEYHOLE. DEO. NSA. CIA. FBI.
THEY'RE ALL MINE, NOW.
IT TAKES ONE WORD FROM ME, AND I CAN DEDICATE THIS NATION'S POWER TO YOUR DISCOVERY.
OR YOUR DESTRUCTION.
I CAN SPY ON YOU 24 HOURS A DAY FROM ORBIT.
I CAN LEARN ALL OF YOUR SECRETS...
...AND ROBIN'S...
...AND NIGHTWING'S...
...EVEN THAT NEW BATGIRL OF YOURS...

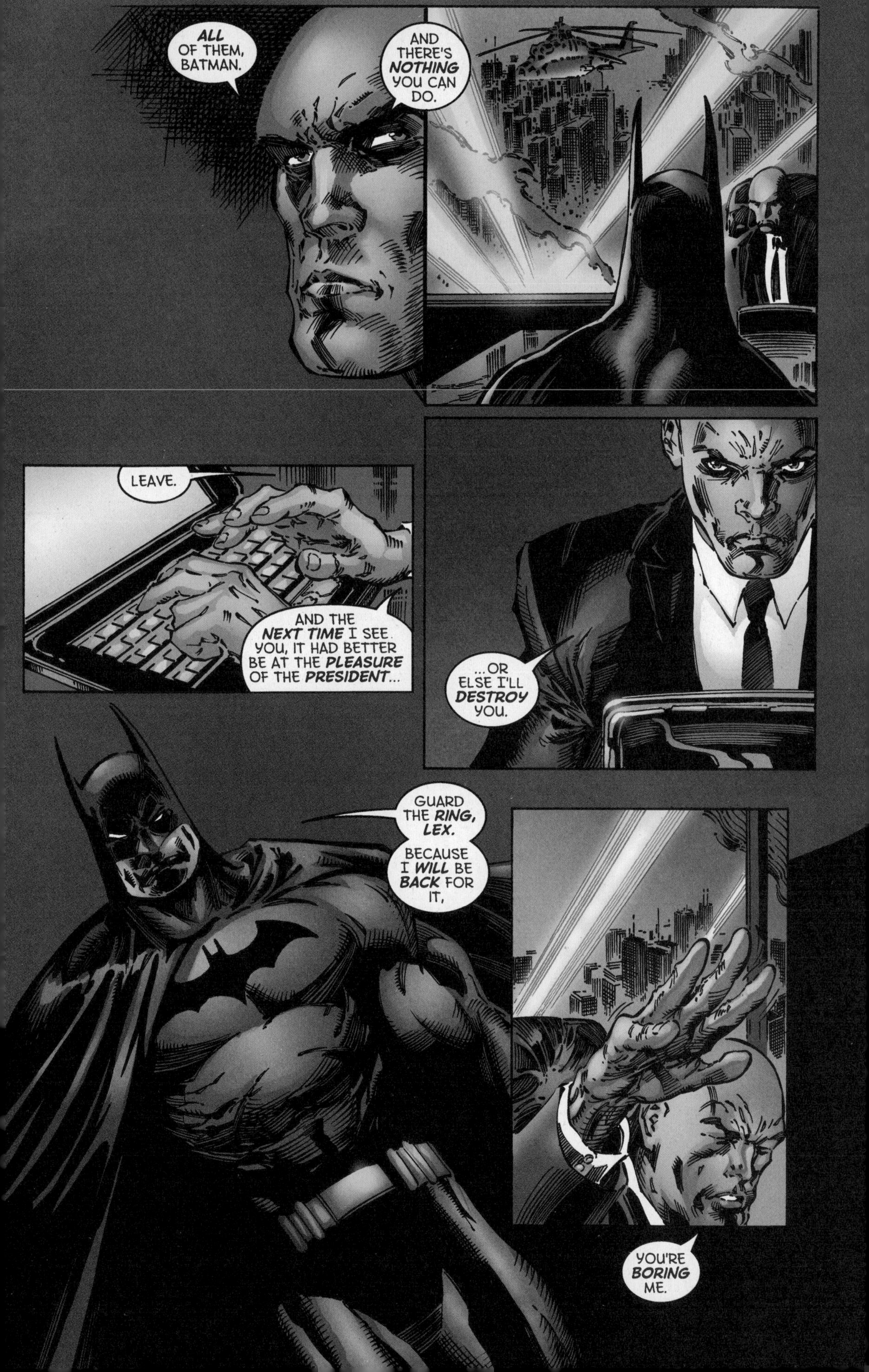
ALL OF THEM, BATMAN.
AND THERE'S NOTHING YOU CAN DO.
LEAVE.
AND THE NEXT TIME I SEE YOU, IT HAD BETTER BE AT THE PLEASURE OF THE PRESIDENT...
...OR ELSE I'LL DESTROY YOU.
GUARD THE RING, LEX.
BECAUSE I WILL BE BACK FOR IT,
YOU'RE BORING ME.

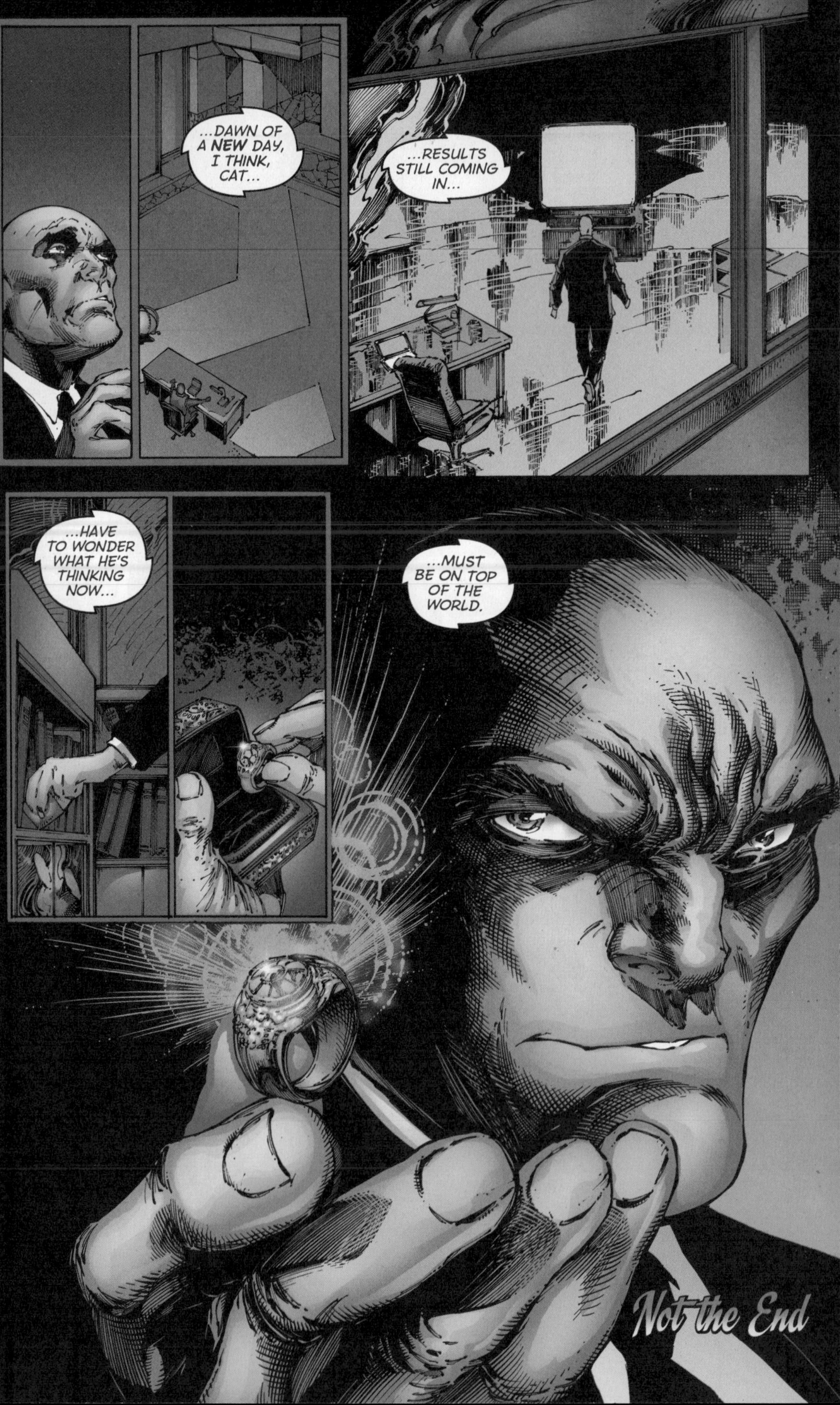

...DAWN OF A NEW DAY, I THINK, CAT...
...RESULTS STILL COMING IN...
...HAVE TO WONDER WHAT HE'S THINKING NOW...
...MUST BE ON TOP OF THE WORLD.
Not the End

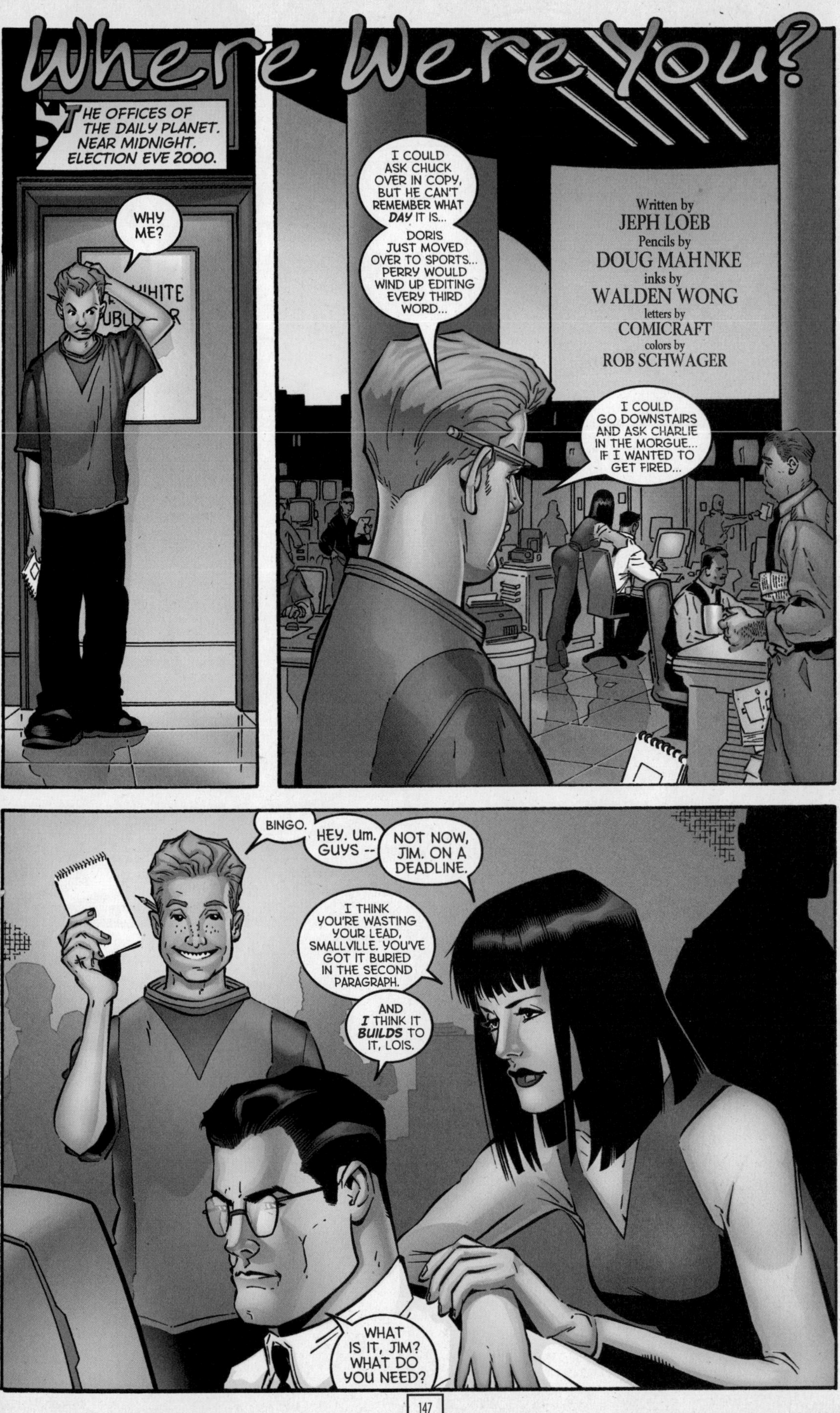
Where Were You?
THE OFFICES OF THE DAILY PLANET. NEAR MIDNIGHT. ELECTION EVE 2000.
WHY ME?
I COULD ASK CHUCK OVER IN COPY, BUT HE CAN'T REMEMBER WHAT DAY IT IS...
DORIS JUST MOVED OVER TO SPORTS... PERRY WOULD WIND UP EDITING EVERY THIRD WORD...
Written by JEPH LOEB
Pencils by DOUG MAHNKE
inks by WALDEN WONG
letters by COMICRAFT
colors by ROB SCHWAGER
I COULD GO DOWNSTAIRS AND ASK CHARLIE IN THE MORGUE... IF I WANTED TO GET FIRED...
BINGO.
HEY. Um. GUYS --
NOT NOW, JIM. ON A DEADLINE.
I THINK YOU'RE WASTING YOUR LEAD, SMALLVILLE. YOU'VE GOT IT BURIED IN THE SECOND PARAGRAPH.
AND I THINK IT BUILDS TO IT, LOIS.
WHAT IS IT, JIM? WHAT DO YOU NEED?

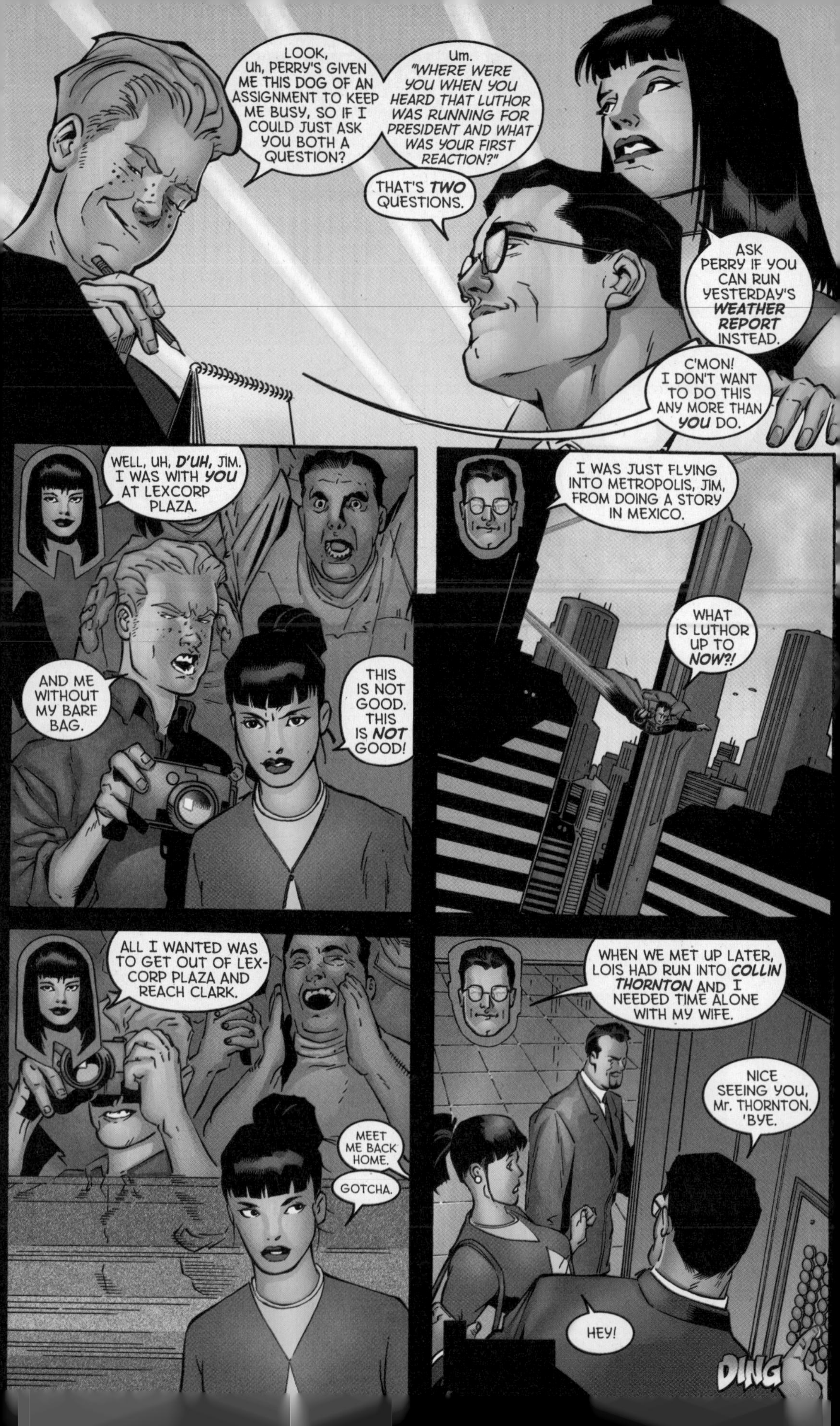
LOOK, Uh, PERRY'S GIVEN ME THIS DOG OF AN ASSIGNMENT TO KEEP ME BUSY, SO IF I COULD JUST ASK YOU BOTH A QUESTION?
Um. "WHERE WERE YOU WHEN YOU HEARD THAT LUTHOR WAS RUNNING FOR PRESIDENT AND WHAT WAS YOUR FIRST REACTION?"
THAT'S TWO QUESTIONS.
ASK PERRY IF YOU CAN RUN YESTERDAY'S WEATHER REPORT INSTEAD.
C'MON! I DON'T WANT TO DO THIS ANY MORE THAN YOU DO.
WELL, UH, D'UH, JIM. I WAS WITH YOU AT LEXCORP PLAZA.
AND ME WITHOUT MY BARF BAG.
THIS IS NOT GOOD. THIS IS NOT GOOD!
I WAS JUST FLYING INTO METROPOLIS, JIM, FROM DOING A STORY IN MEXICO.
WHAT IS LUTHOR UP TO NOW?!
ALL I WANTED WAS TO GET OUT OF LEXCORP PLAZA AND REACH CLARK.
MEET ME BACK HOME.
GOTCHA.
WHEN WE MET UP LATER, LOIS HAD RUN INTO COLLIN THORNTON AND I NEEDED TIME ALONE WITH MY WIFE.
NICE SEEING YOU, Mr. THORNTON. 'BYE.
HEY!
DING

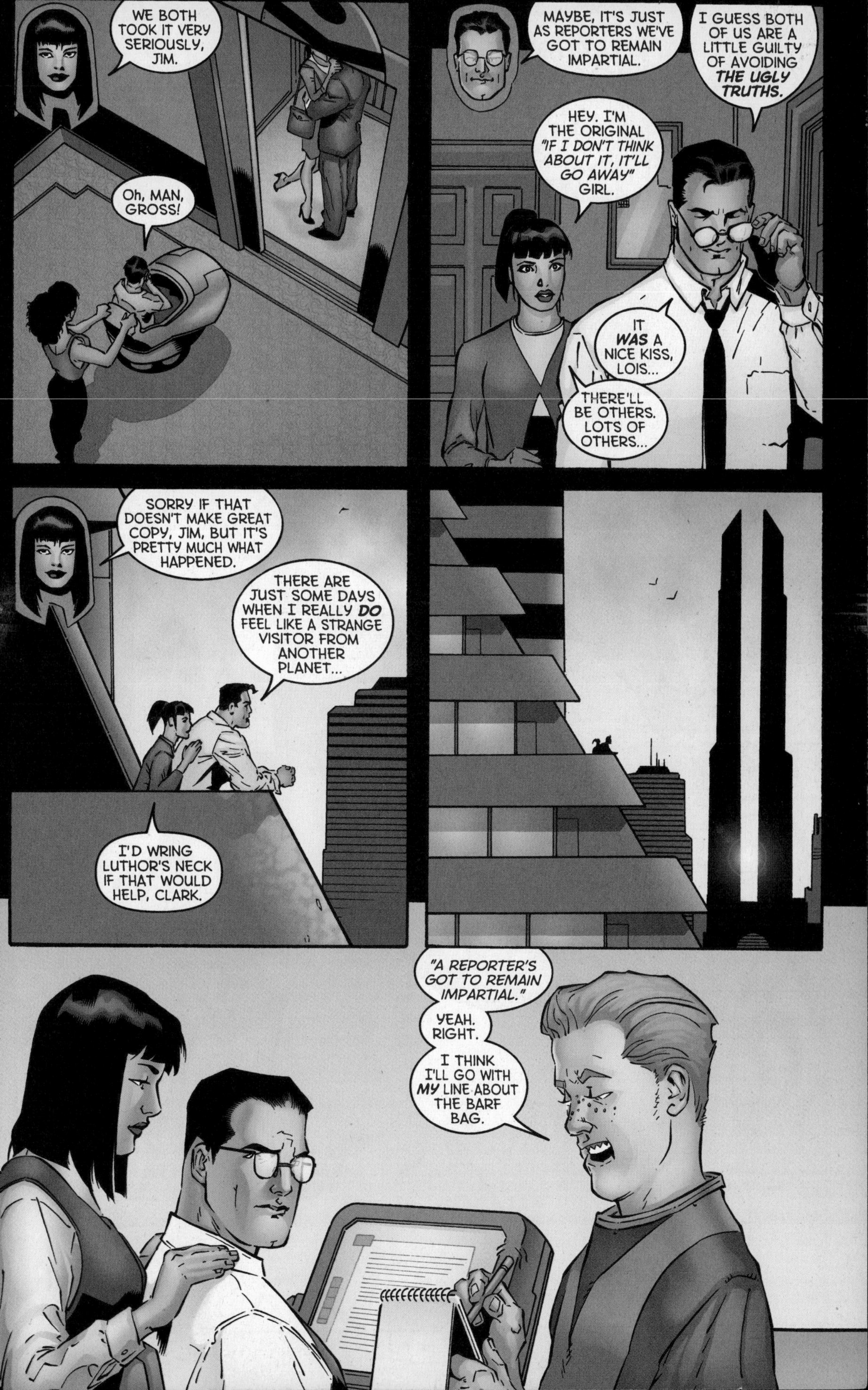
WE BOTH TOOK IT VERY SERIOUSLY, JIM.
Oh, MAN, GROSS!
MAYBE, IT'S JUST AS REPORTERS WE'VE GOT TO REMAIN IMPARTIAL.
I GUESS BOTH OF US ARE A LITTLE GUILTY OF AVOIDING *THE UGLY TRUTHS.*
HEY. I'M THE ORIGINAL *"IF I DON'T THINK ABOUT IT, IT'LL GO AWAY"* GIRL.
IT *WAS* A NICE KISS, LOIS...
THERE'LL BE OTHERS. LOTS OF OTHERS...
SORRY IF THAT DOESN'T MAKE GREAT COPY, JIM, BUT IT'S PRETTY MUCH WHAT HAPPENED.
THERE ARE JUST SOME DAYS WHEN I REALLY *DO* FEEL LIKE A STRANGE VISITOR FROM ANOTHER PLANET...
I'D WRING LUTHOR'S NECK IF THAT WOULD HELP, CLARK.
"A REPORTER'S GOT TO REMAIN IMPARTIAL."
YEAH. RIGHT.
I THINK I'LL GO WITH *MY* LINE ABOUT THE BARF BAG.

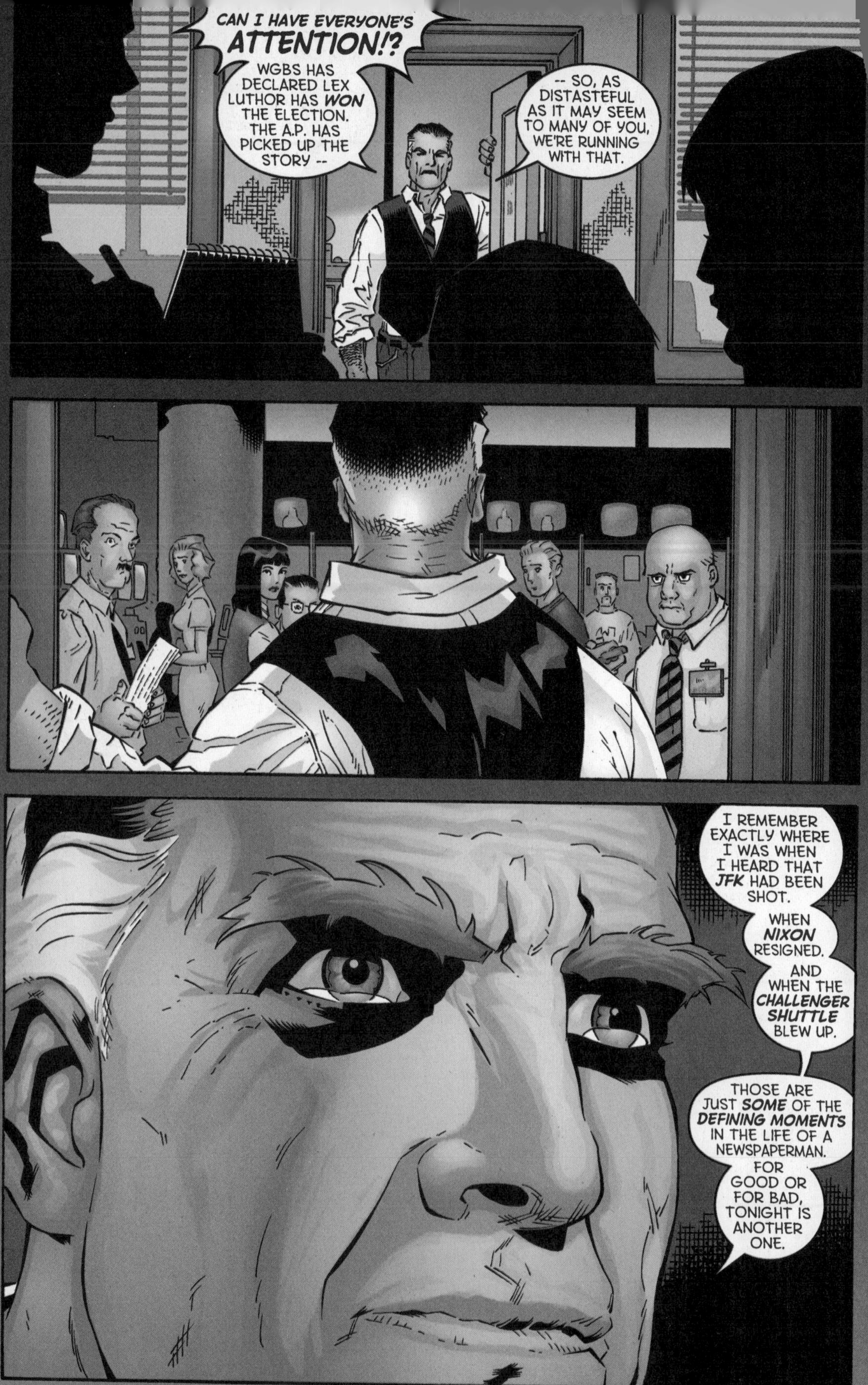
CAN I HAVE EVERYONE'S ATTENTION!?
WGBS HAS DECLARED LEX LUTHOR HAS WON THE ELECTION. THE A.P. HAS PICKED UP THE STORY --
-- SO, AS DISTASTEFUL AS IT MAY SEEM TO MANY OF YOU, WE'RE RUNNING WITH THAT.
I REMEMBER EXACTLY WHERE I WAS WHEN I HEARD THAT JFK HAD BEEN SHOT.
WHEN NIXON RESIGNED.
AND WHEN THE CHALLENGER SHUTTLE BLEW UP.
THOSE ARE JUST SOME OF THE DEFINING MOMENTS IN THE LIFE OF A NEWSPAPERMAN.
FOR GOOD OR FOR BAD, TONIGHT IS ANOTHER ONE.

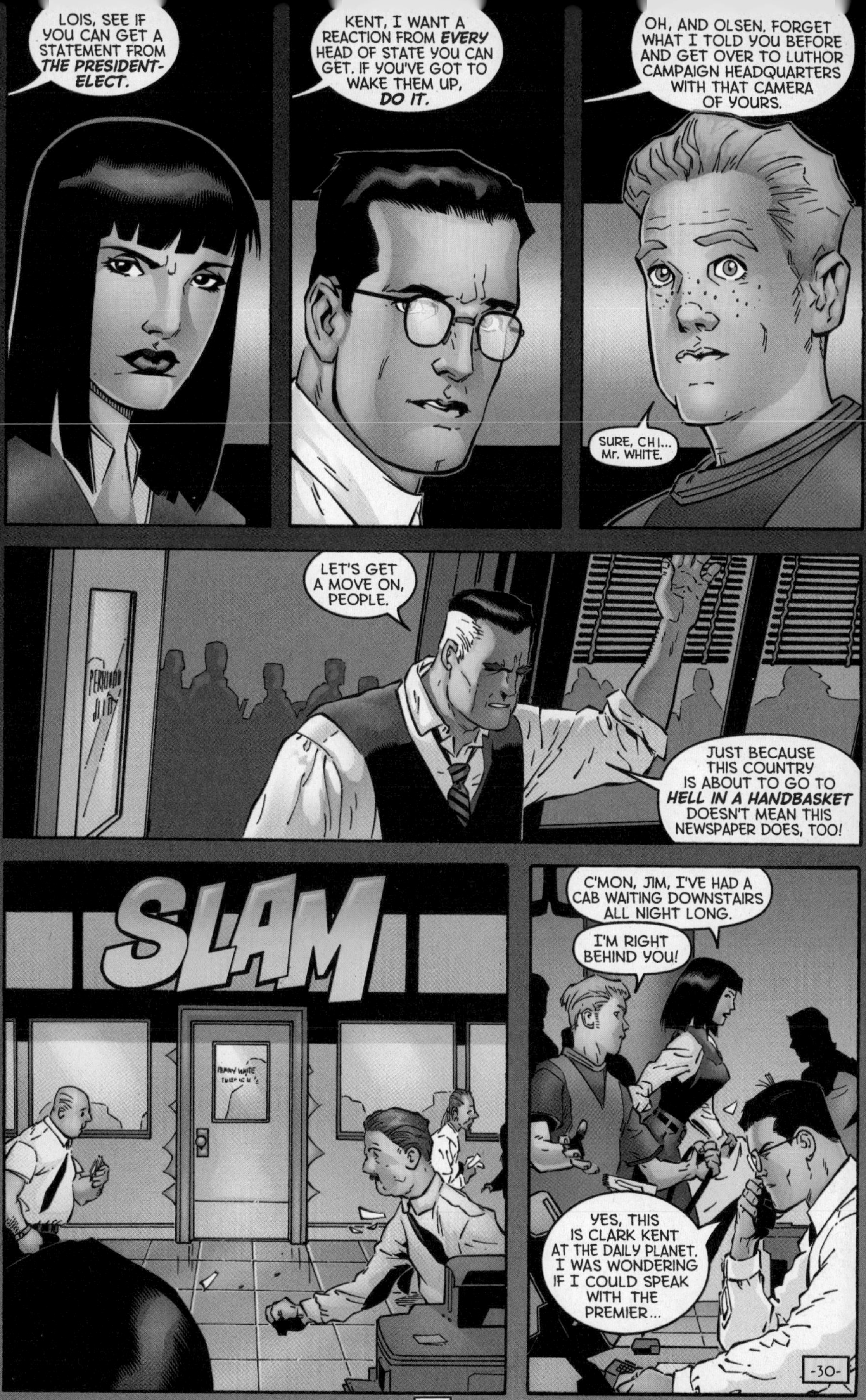
LOIS, SEE IF YOU CAN GET A STATEMENT FROM ***THE PRESIDENT-ELECT.***
KENT, I WANT A REACTION FROM ***EVERY*** HEAD OF STATE YOU CAN GET. IF YOU'VE GOT TO WAKE THEM UP, ***DO IT.***
OH, AND OLSEN. FORGET WHAT I TOLD YOU BEFORE AND GET OVER TO LUTHOR CAMPAIGN HEADQUARTERS WITH THAT CAMERA OF YOURS.
SURE, CHI... Mr. WHITE.
LET'S GET A MOVE ON, PEOPLE.
JUST BECAUSE THIS COUNTRY IS ABOUT TO GO TO ***HELL IN A HANDBASKET*** DOESN'T MEAN THIS NEWSPAPER DOES, TOO!
SLAM
C'MON, JIM, I'VE HAD A CAB WAITING DOWNSTAIRS ALL NIGHT LONG.
I'M RIGHT BEHIND YOU!
YES, THIS IS CLARK KENT AT THE DAILY PLANET. I WAS WONDERING IF I COULD SPEAK WITH THE PREMIER...
-30-

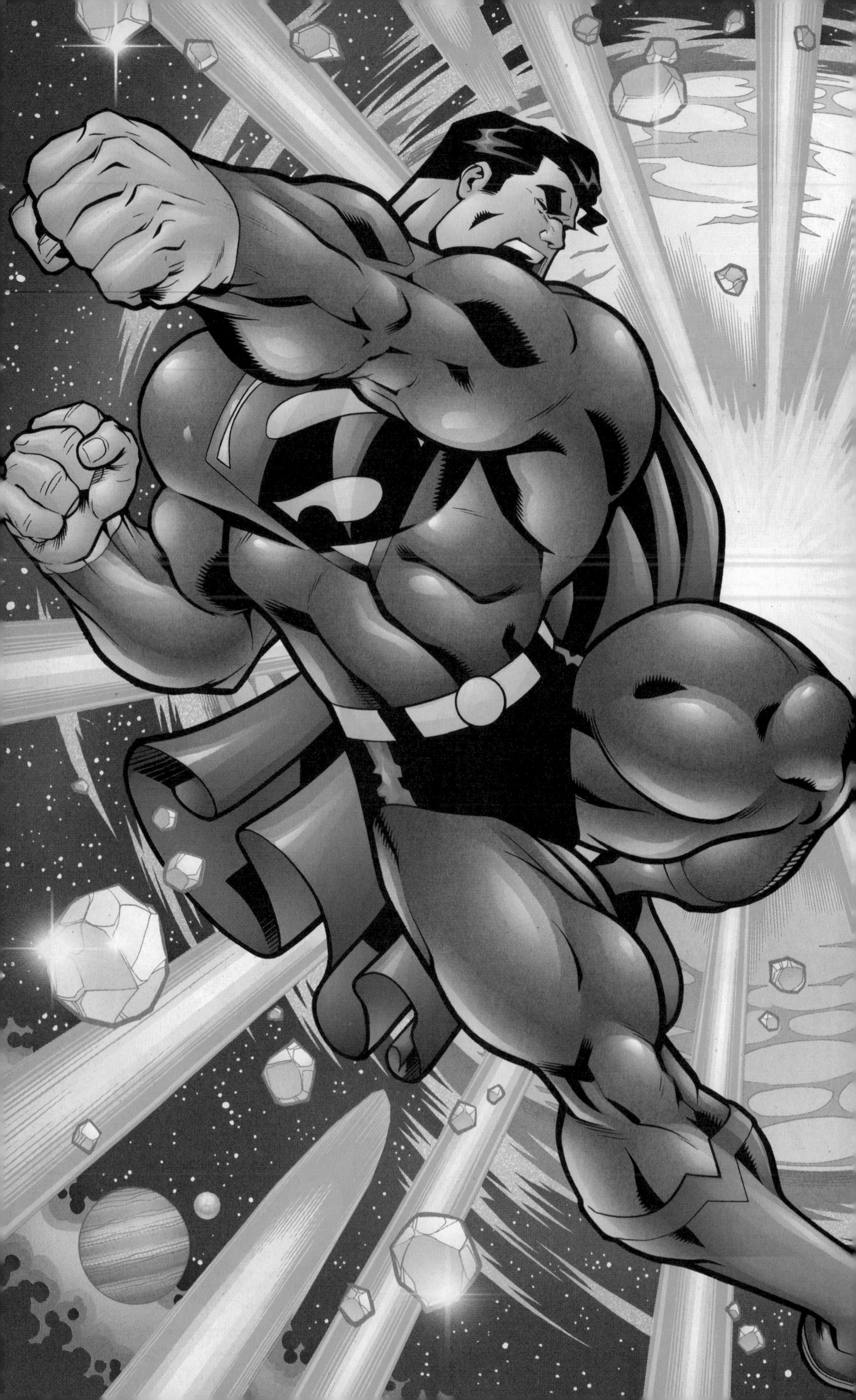

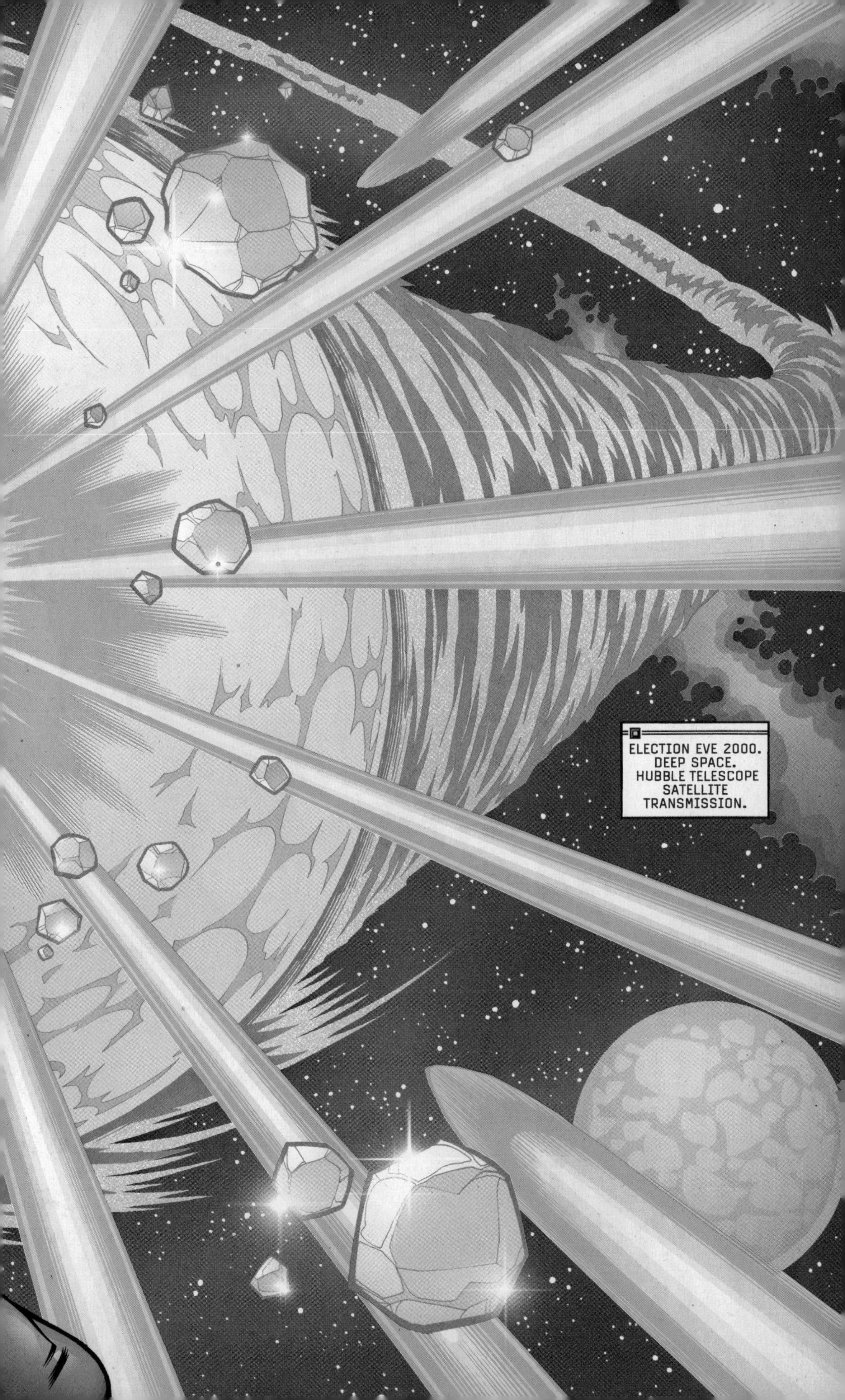
ELECTION EVE 2000.
DEEP SPACE.
HUBBLE TELESCOPE
SATELLITE
TRANSMISSION.

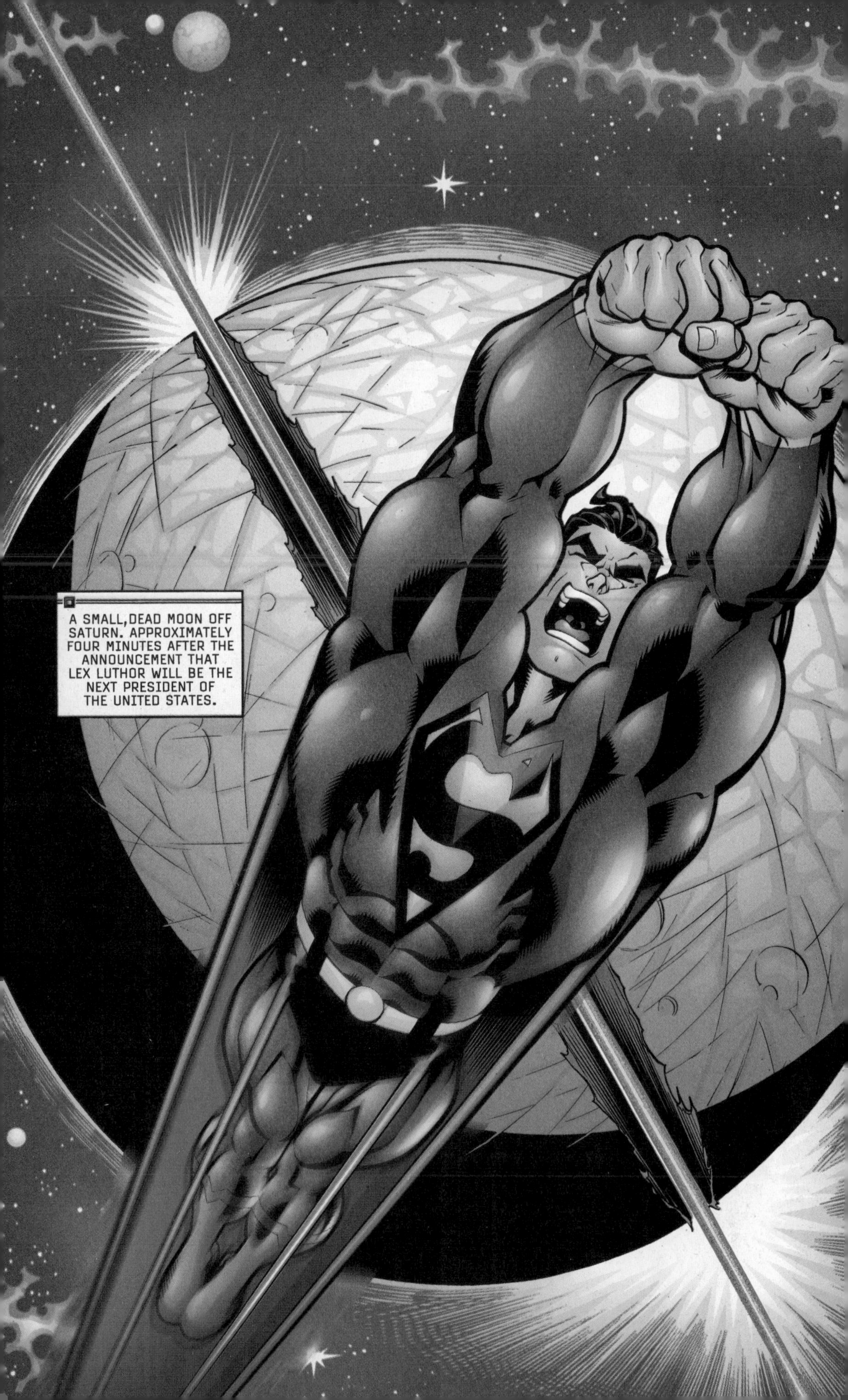
A SMALL, DEAD MOON OFF SATURN. APPROXIMATELY FOUR MINUTES AFTER THE ANNOUNCEMENT THAT LEX LUTHOR WILL BE THE NEXT PRESIDENT OF THE UNITED STATES.

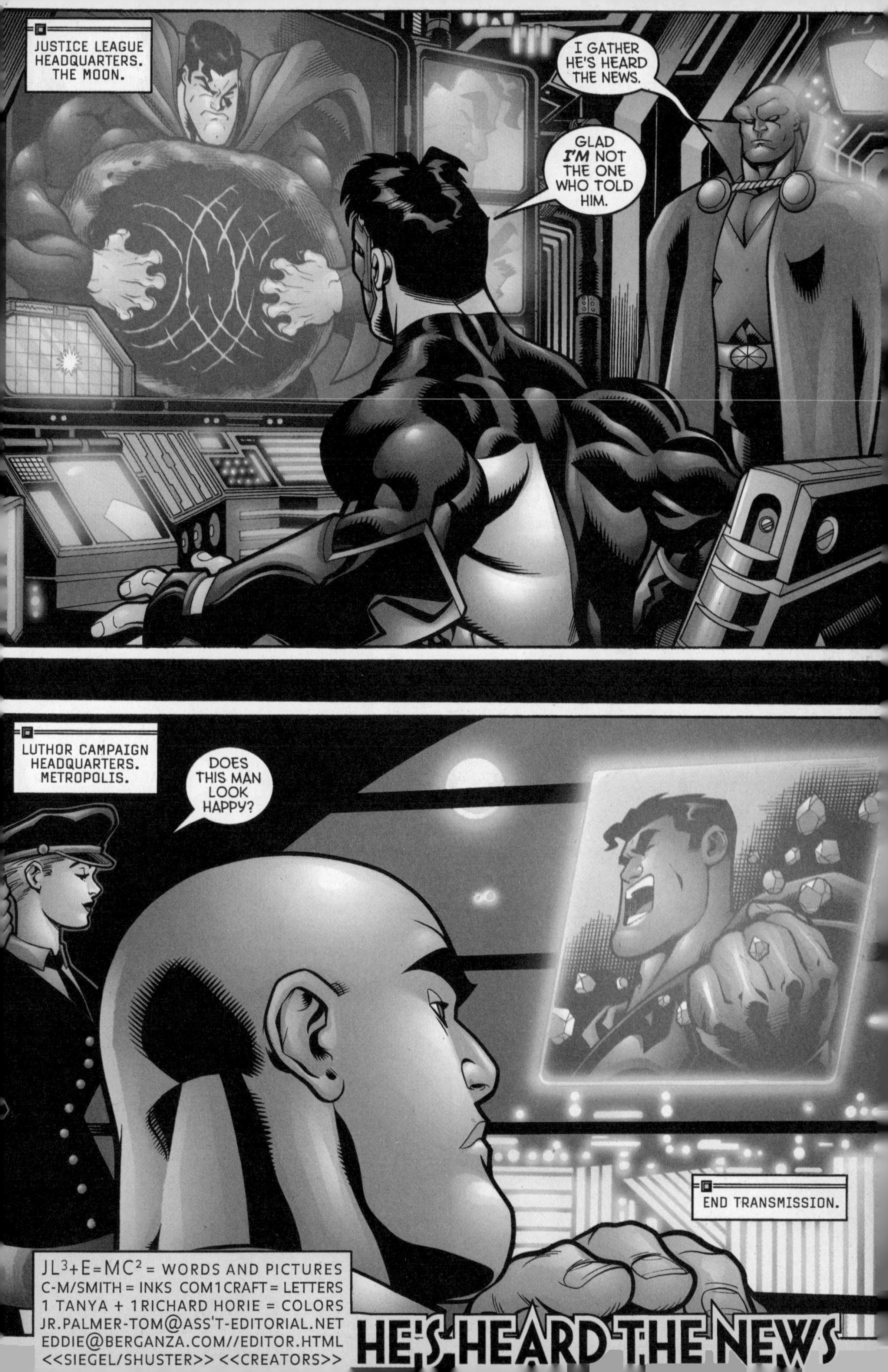

JUSTICE LEAGUE HEADQUARTERS. THE MOON.
I GATHER HE'S HEARD THE NEWS.
GLAD *I'M* NOT THE ONE WHO TOLD HIM.
LUTHOR CAMPAIGN HEADQUARTERS. METROPOLIS.
DOES THIS MAN LOOK HAPPY?
END TRANSMISSION.
$JL^3+E=MC^2$ = WORDS AND PICTURES
C-M/SMITH = INKS COM1CRAFT = LETTERS
1 TANYA + 1RICHARD HORIE = COLORS
JR.PALMER-TOM@ASS'T-EDITORIAL.NET
EDDIE@BERGANZA.COM//EDITOR.HTML
<<SIEGEL/SHUSTER>> <<CREATORS>>
HE'S HEARD THE NEWS

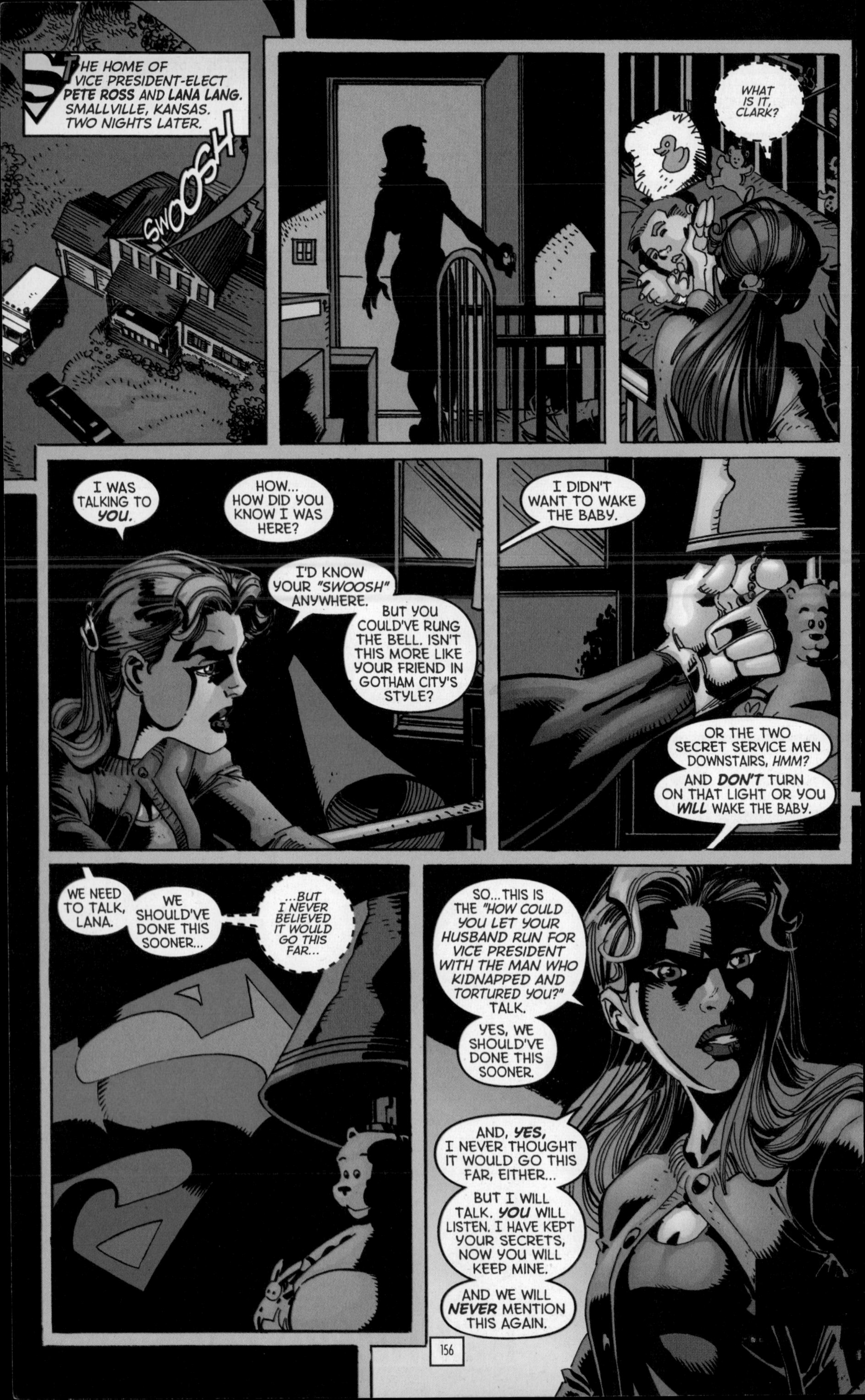
THE HOME OF VICE PRESIDENT-ELECT PETE ROSS AND LANA LANG. SMALLVILLE, KANSAS. TWO NIGHTS LATER.
SWOOSH
WHAT IS IT, CLARK?
I WAS TALKING TO YOU.
HOW... HOW DID YOU KNOW I WAS HERE?
I'D KNOW YOUR "SWOOSH" ANYWHERE.
BUT YOU COULD'VE RUNG THE BELL. ISN'T THIS MORE LIKE YOUR FRIEND IN GOTHAM CITY'S STYLE?
I DIDN'T WANT TO WAKE THE BABY.
OR THE TWO SECRET SERVICE MEN DOWNSTAIRS, HMM?
AND DON'T TURN ON THAT LIGHT OR YOU WILL WAKE THE BABY.
WE NEED TO TALK, LANA.
WE SHOULD'VE DONE THIS SOONER...
...BUT I NEVER BELIEVED IT WOULD GO THIS FAR...
SO...THIS IS THE "HOW COULD YOU LET YOUR HUSBAND RUN FOR VICE PRESIDENT WITH THE MAN WHO KIDNAPPED AND TORTURED YOU?" TALK.
YES, WE SHOULD'VE DONE THIS SOONER.
AND, YES, I NEVER THOUGHT IT WOULD GO THIS FAR, EITHER...
BUT I WILL TALK. YOU WILL LISTEN. I HAVE KEPT YOUR SECRETS, NOW YOU WILL KEEP MINE.
AND WE WILL NEVER MENTION THIS AGAIN.

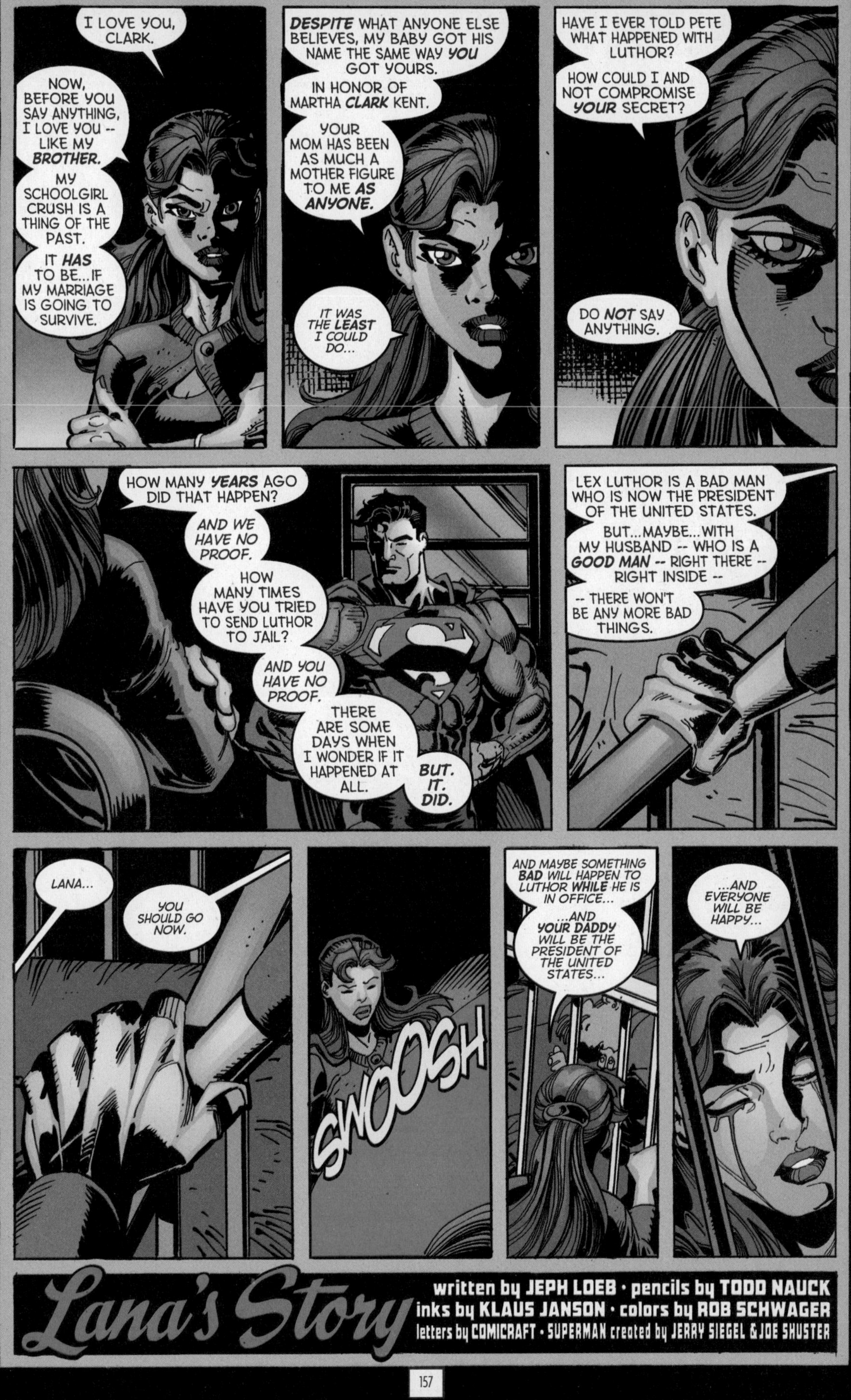
I LOVE YOU, CLARK.
NOW, BEFORE YOU SAY ANYTHING, I LOVE YOU -- LIKE MY BROTHER.
MY SCHOOLGIRL CRUSH IS A THING OF THE PAST.
IT HAS TO BE... IF MY MARRIAGE IS GOING TO SURVIVE.
DESPITE WHAT ANYONE ELSE BELIEVES, MY BABY GOT HIS NAME THE SAME WAY YOU GOT YOURS.
IN HONOR OF MARTHA CLARK KENT.
YOUR MOM HAS BEEN AS MUCH A MOTHER FIGURE TO ME AS ANYONE.
IT WAS THE LEAST I COULD DO...
HAVE I EVER TOLD PETE WHAT HAPPENED WITH LUTHOR?
HOW COULD I AND NOT COMPROMISE YOUR SECRET?
DO NOT SAY ANYTHING.
HOW MANY YEARS AGO DID THAT HAPPEN?
AND WE HAVE NO PROOF.
HOW MANY TIMES HAVE YOU TRIED TO SEND LUTHOR TO JAIL?
AND YOU HAVE NO PROOF.
THERE ARE SOME DAYS WHEN I WONDER IF IT HAPPENED AT ALL.
BUT. IT. DID.
LEX LUTHOR IS A BAD MAN WHO IS NOW THE PRESIDENT OF THE UNITED STATES.
BUT... MAYBE... WITH MY HUSBAND -- WHO IS A GOOD MAN -- RIGHT THERE -- RIGHT INSIDE --
-- THERE WON'T BE ANY MORE BAD THINGS.
LANA...
YOU SHOULD GO NOW.
SWOOSH
AND MAYBE SOMETHING BAD WILL HAPPEN TO LUTHOR WHILE HE IS IN OFFICE...
...AND YOUR DADDY WILL BE THE PRESIDENT OF THE UNITED STATES...
...AND EVERYONE WILL BE HAPPY...

Lana's Story

written by JEPH LOEB · pencils by TODD NAUCK
inks by KLAUS JANSON · colors by ROB SCHWAGER
letters by COMICRAFT · SUPERMAN created by JERRY SIEGEL & JOE SHUSTER

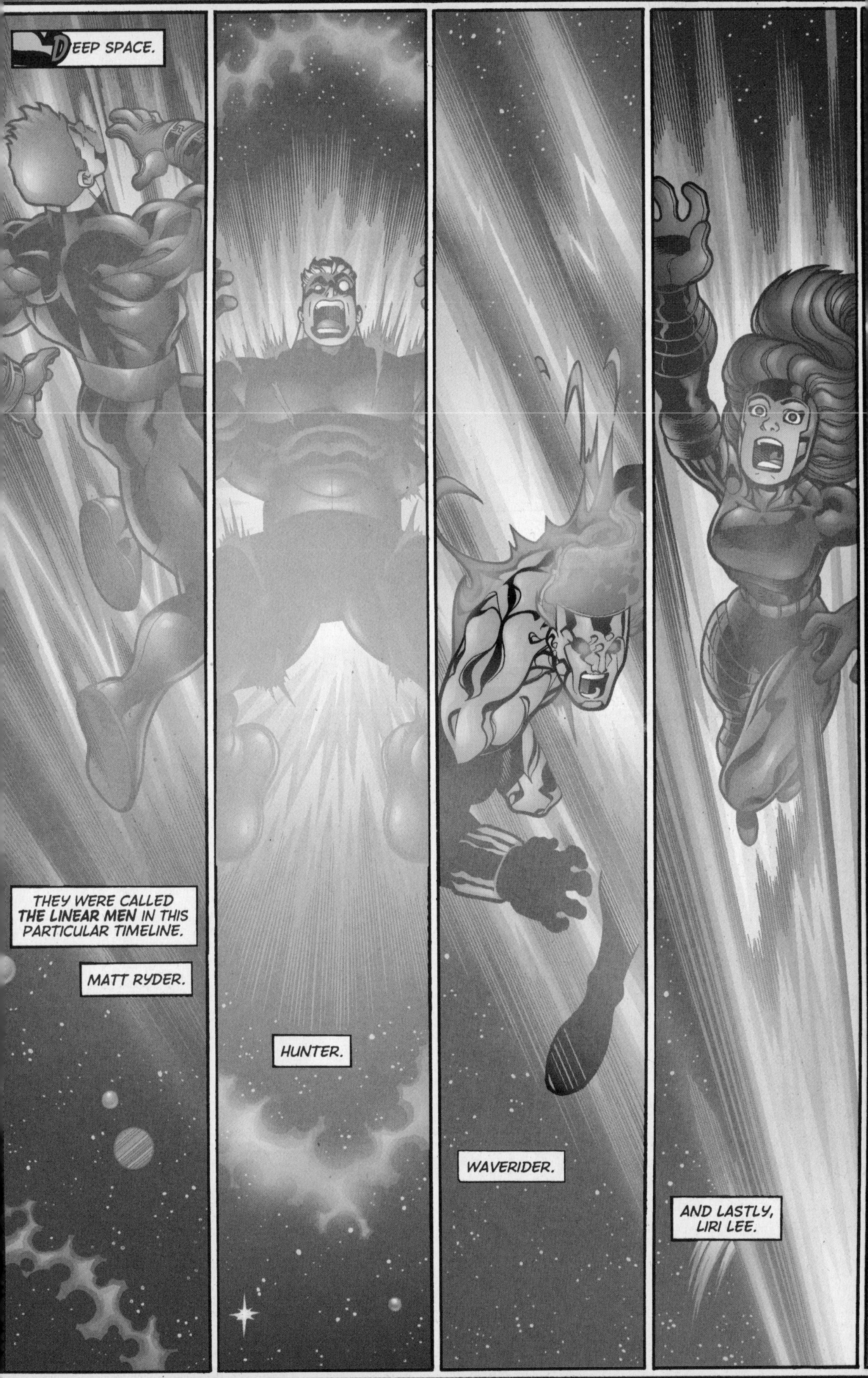
DEEP SPACE.
THEY WERE CALLED THE LINEAR MEN IN THIS PARTICULAR TIMELINE.
MATT RYDER.
HUNTER.
WAVERIDER.
AND LASTLY, LIRI LEE.

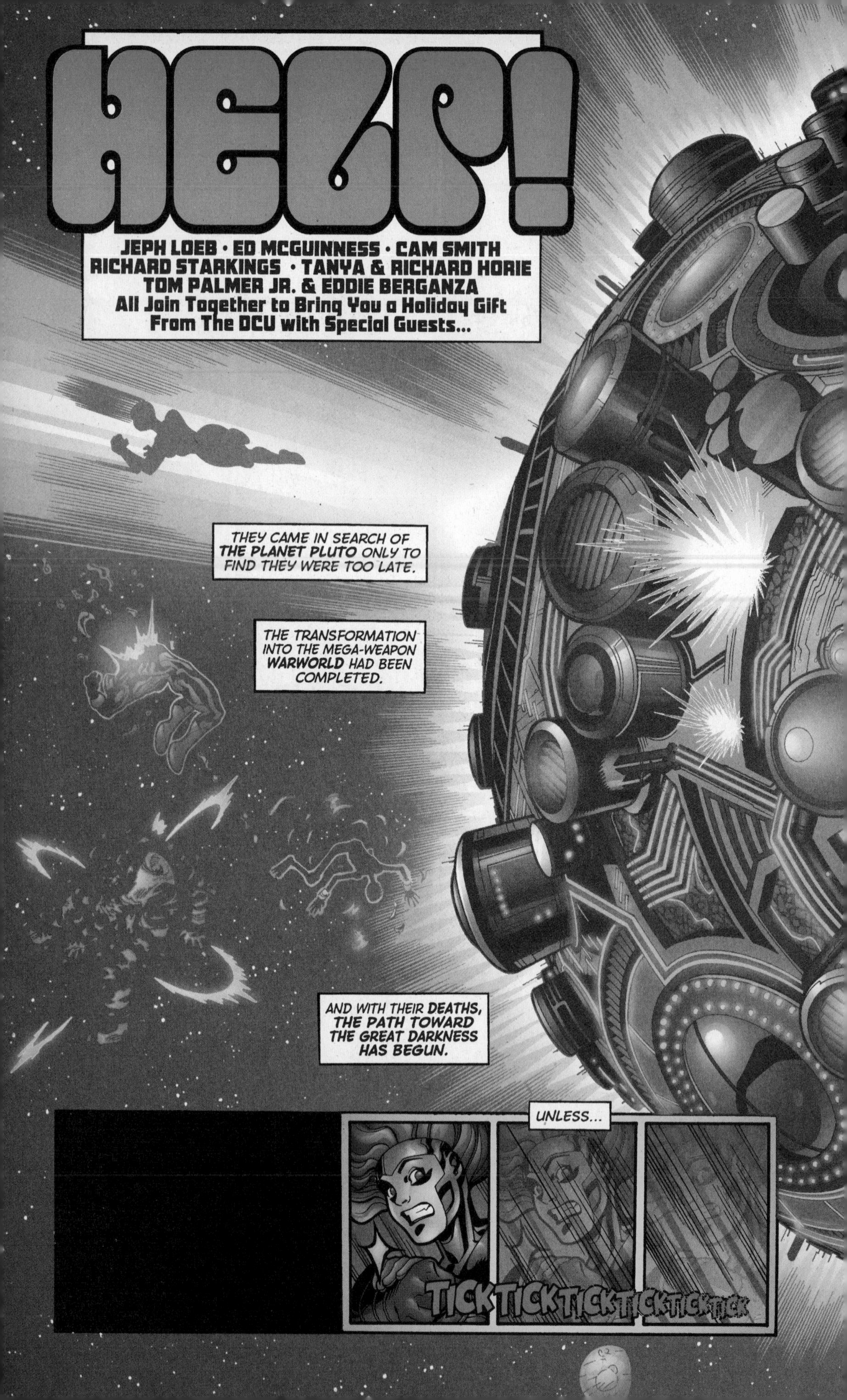
HELP!
JEPH LOEB · ED McGUINNESS · CAM SMITH
RICHARD STARKINGS · TANYA & RICHARD HORIE
TOM PALMER JR. & EDDIE BERGANZA
All Join Together to Bring You a Holiday Gift
From The DCU with Special Guests...
THEY CAME IN SEARCH OF THE PLANET PLUTO ONLY TO FIND THEY WERE TOO LATE.
THE TRANSFORMATION INTO THE MEGA-WEAPON WARWORLD HAD BEEN COMPLETED.
AND WITH THEIR DEATHS, THE PATH TOWARD THE GREAT DARKNESS HAS BEGUN.
UNLESS...
TICK TICK TICK TICK TICK TICK

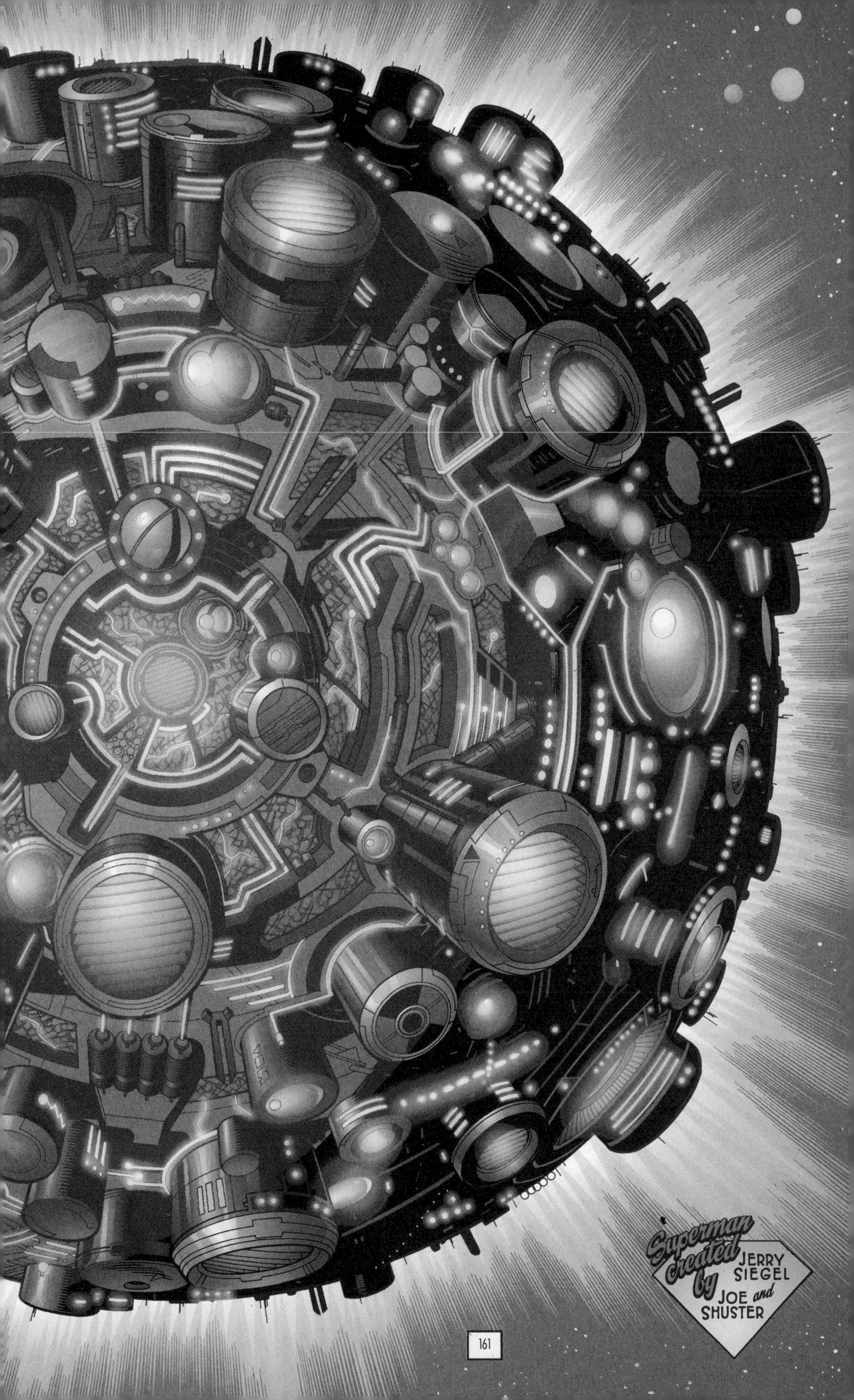
Superman created by JERRY SIEGEL and JOE SHUSTER

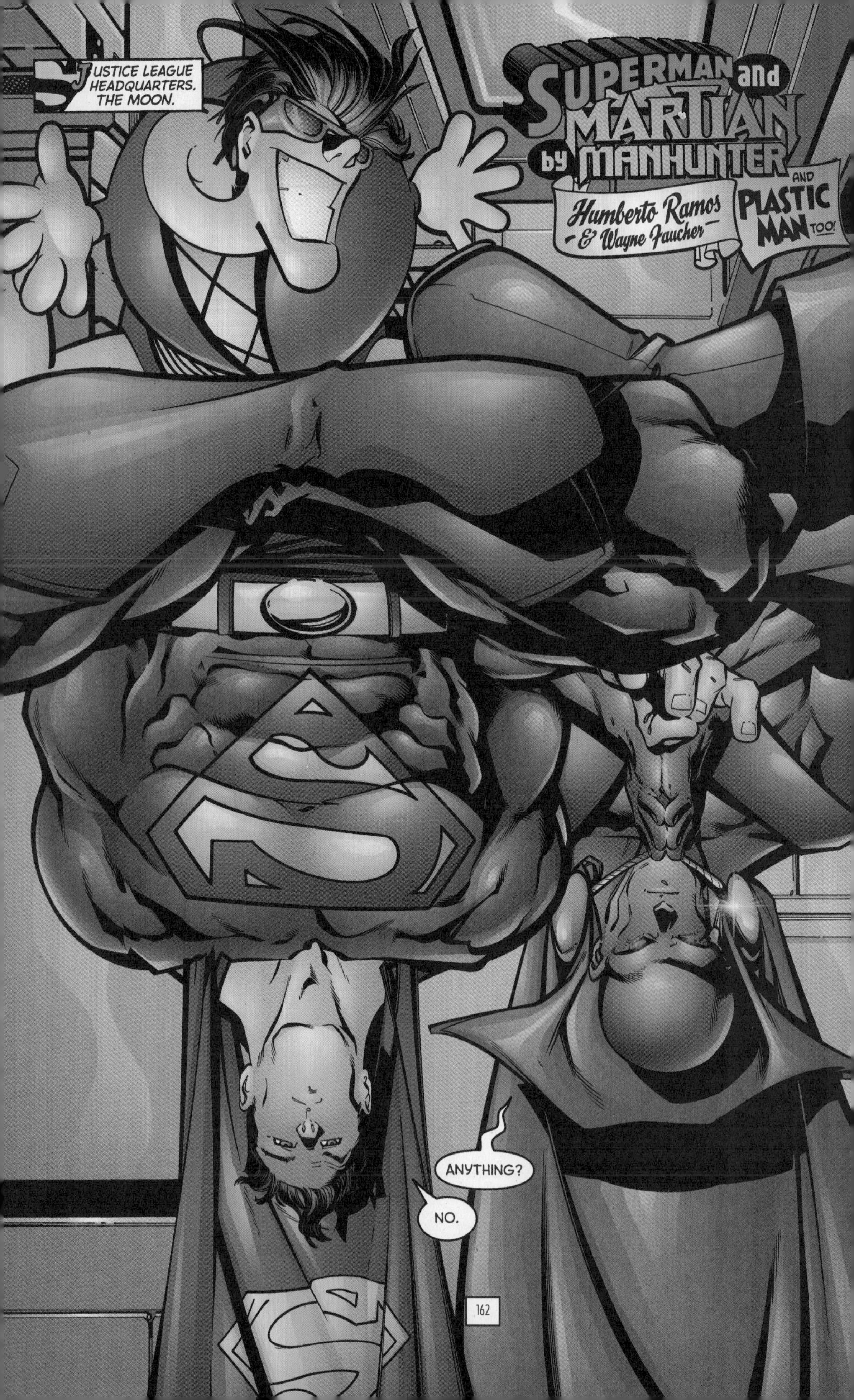

JUSTICE LEAGUE HEADQUARTERS. THE MOON.
SUPERMAN and MARTIAN MANHUNTER
by Humberto Ramos & Wayne Faucher
AND PLASTIC MAN TOO!
ANYTHING?
NO.

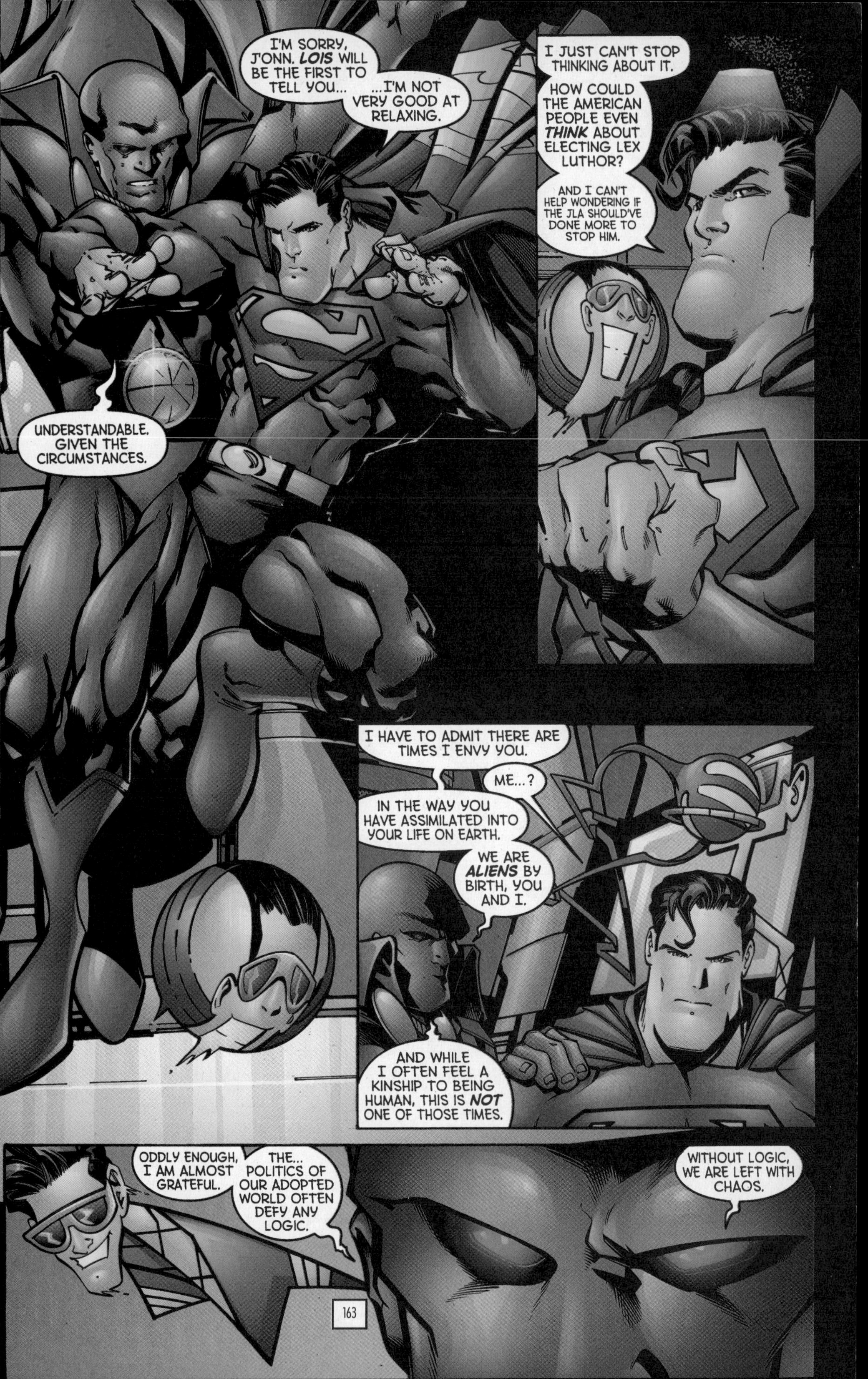
I'M SORRY, J'ONN. LOIS WILL BE THE FIRST TO TELL YOU...
...I'M NOT VERY GOOD AT RELAXING.
UNDERSTANDABLE. GIVEN THE CIRCUMSTANCES.
I JUST CAN'T STOP THINKING ABOUT IT.
HOW COULD THE AMERICAN PEOPLE EVEN THINK ABOUT ELECTING LEX LUTHOR?
AND I CAN'T HELP WONDERING IF THE JLA SHOULD'VE DONE MORE TO STOP HIM.
I HAVE TO ADMIT THERE ARE TIMES I ENVY YOU.
ME...?
IN THE WAY YOU HAVE ASSIMILATED INTO YOUR LIFE ON EARTH.
WE ARE ALIENS BY BIRTH, YOU AND I.
AND WHILE I OFTEN FEEL A KINSHIP TO BEING HUMAN, THIS IS NOT ONE OF THOSE TIMES.
ODDLY ENOUGH, I AM ALMOST GRATEFUL.
THE... POLITICS OF OUR ADOPTED WORLD OFTEN DEFY ANY LOGIC.
WITHOUT LOGIC, WE ARE LEFT WITH CHAOS.

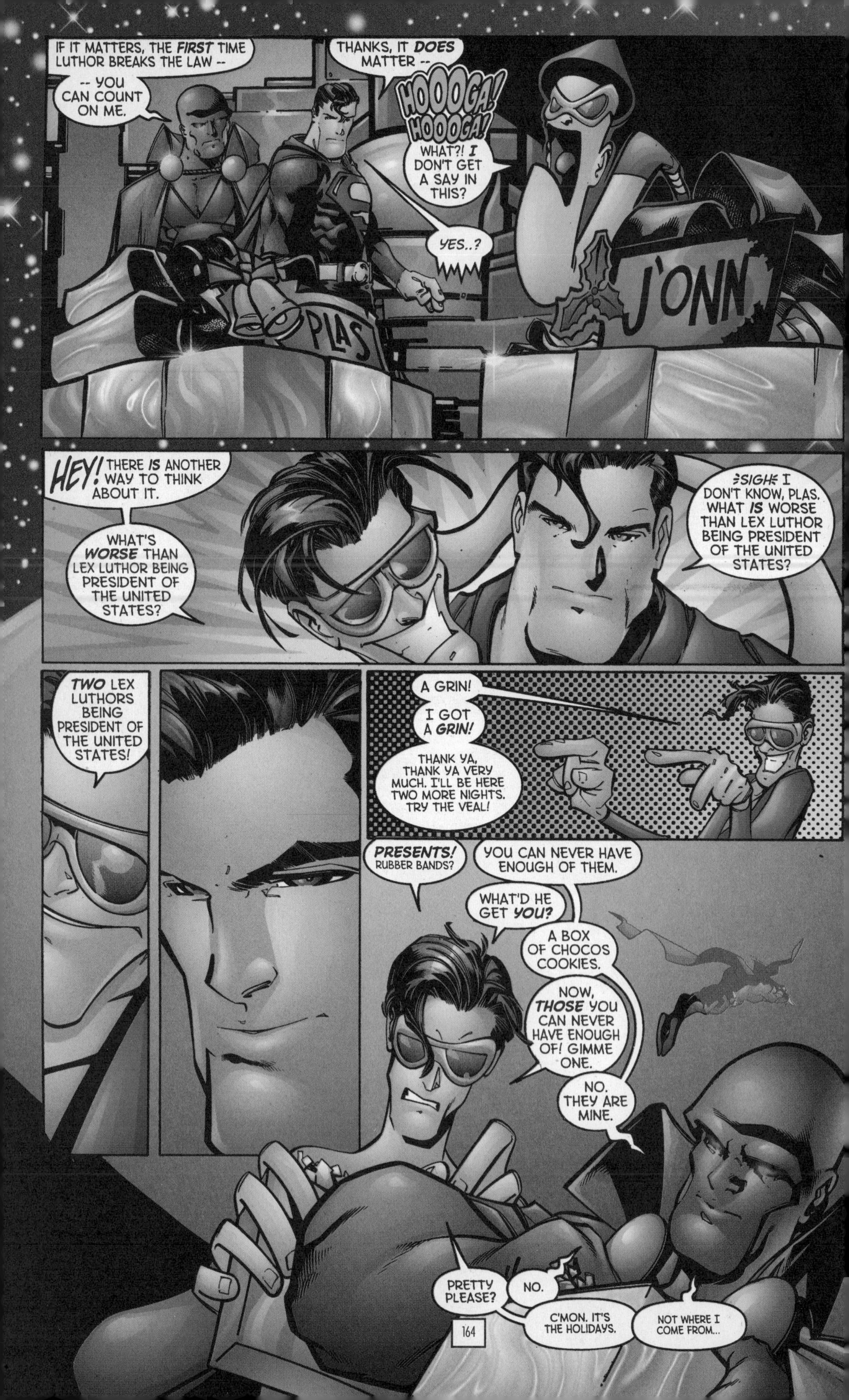

IF IT MATTERS, THE FIRST TIME LUTHOR BREAKS THE LAW --
-- YOU CAN COUNT ON ME.
THANKS, IT DOES MATTER --
HOOOGA! HOOOGA!
WHAT?! I DON'T GET A SAY IN THIS?
YES..?
PLAS
J'ONN
HEY! THERE IS ANOTHER WAY TO THINK ABOUT IT.
WHAT'S WORSE THAN LEX LUTHOR BEING PRESIDENT OF THE UNITED STATES?
SIGH I DON'T KNOW, PLAS. WHAT IS WORSE THAN LEX LUTHOR BEING PRESIDENT OF THE UNITED STATES?
TWO LEX LUTHORS BEING PRESIDENT OF THE UNITED STATES!
A GRIN!
I GOT A GRIN!
THANK YA, THANK YA VERY MUCH. I'LL BE HERE TWO MORE NIGHTS. TRY THE VEAL!
PRESENTS! RUBBER BANDS?
YOU CAN NEVER HAVE ENOUGH OF THEM.
WHAT'D HE GET YOU?
A BOX OF CHOCOS COOKIES.
NOW, THOSE YOU CAN NEVER HAVE ENOUGH OF! GIMME ONE.
NO. THEY ARE MINE.
PRETTY PLEASE?
NO.
C'MON. IT'S THE HOLIDAYS.
NOT WHERE I COME FROM...

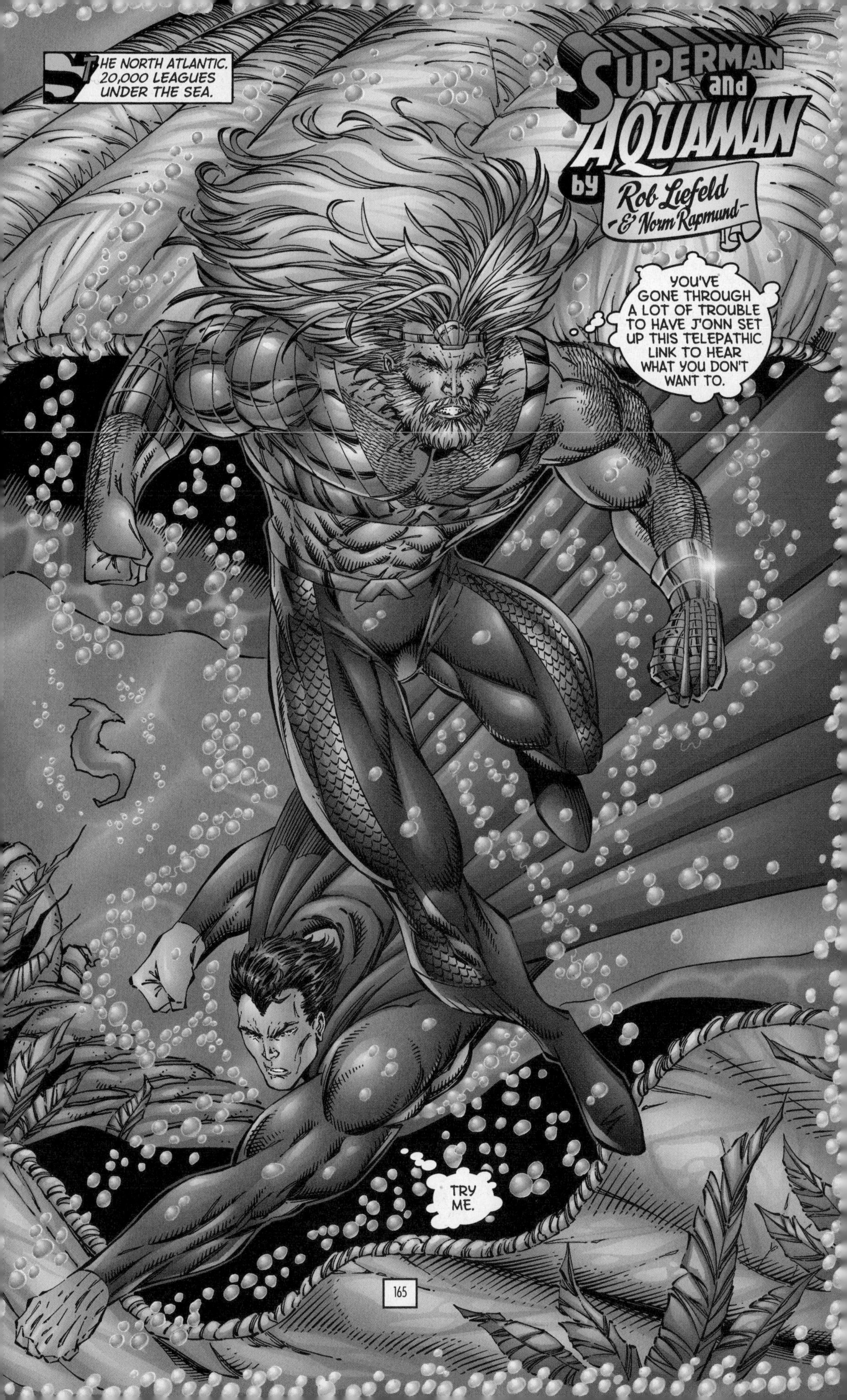

SUPERMAN and AQUAMAN
by Rob Liefeld & Norm Rapmund
THE NORTH ATLANTIC. 20,000 LEAGUES UNDER THE SEA.
YOU'VE GONE THROUGH A LOT OF TROUBLE TO HAVE J'ONN SET UP THIS TELEPATHIC LINK TO HEAR WHAT YOU DON'T WANT TO.
TRY ME.

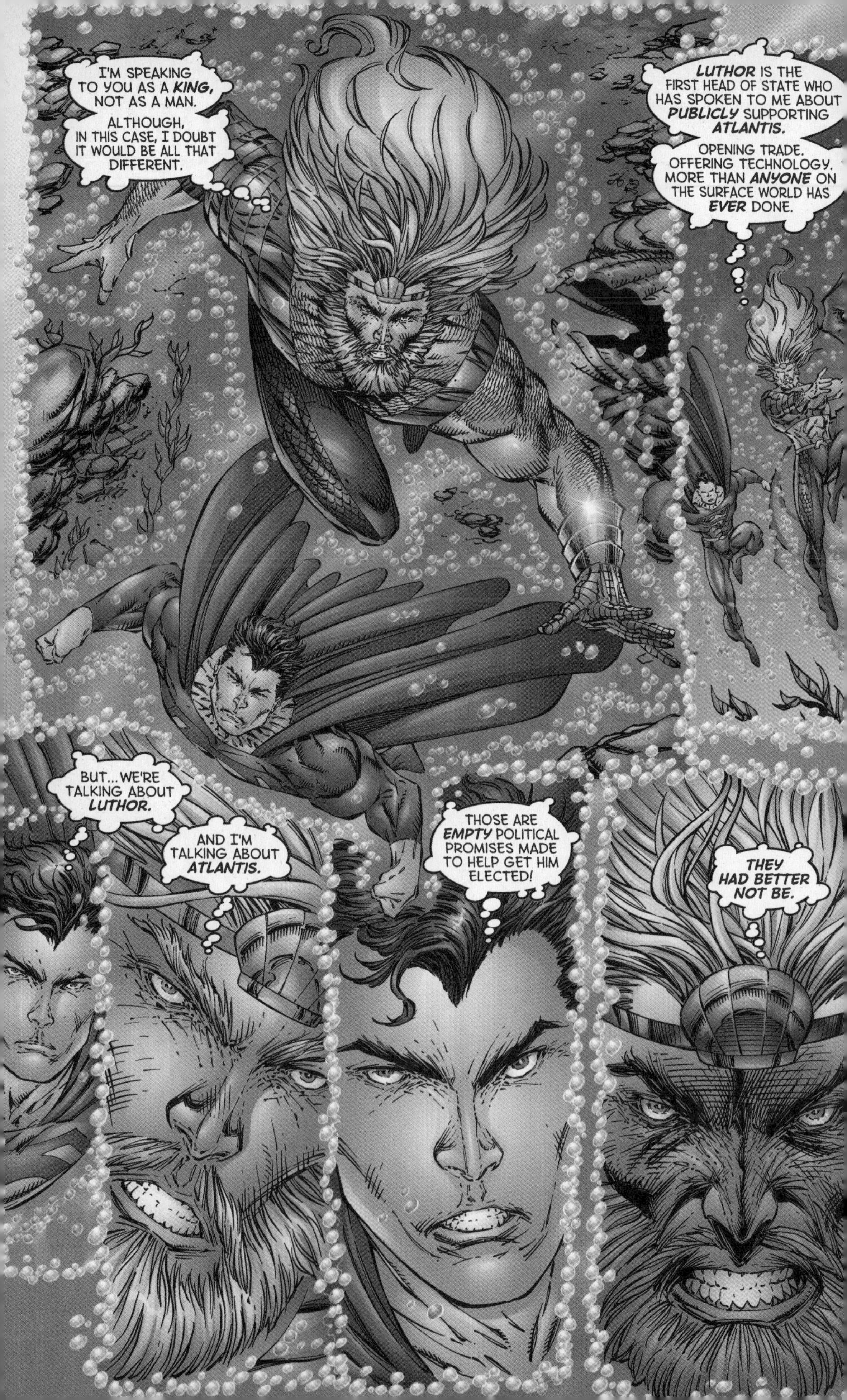
I'M SPEAKING TO YOU AS A KING, NOT AS A MAN.
ALTHOUGH, IN THIS CASE, I DOUBT IT WOULD BE ALL THAT DIFFERENT.
LUTHOR IS THE FIRST HEAD OF STATE WHO HAS SPOKEN TO ME ABOUT PUBLICLY SUPPORTING ATLANTIS.
OPENING TRADE. OFFERING TECHNOLOGY. MORE THAN ANYONE ON THE SURFACE WORLD HAS EVER DONE.
BUT...WE'RE TALKING ABOUT LUTHOR.
AND I'M TALKING ABOUT ATLANTIS.
THOSE ARE EMPTY POLITICAL PROMISES MADE TO HELP GET HIM ELECTED!
THEY HAD BETTER NOT BE.

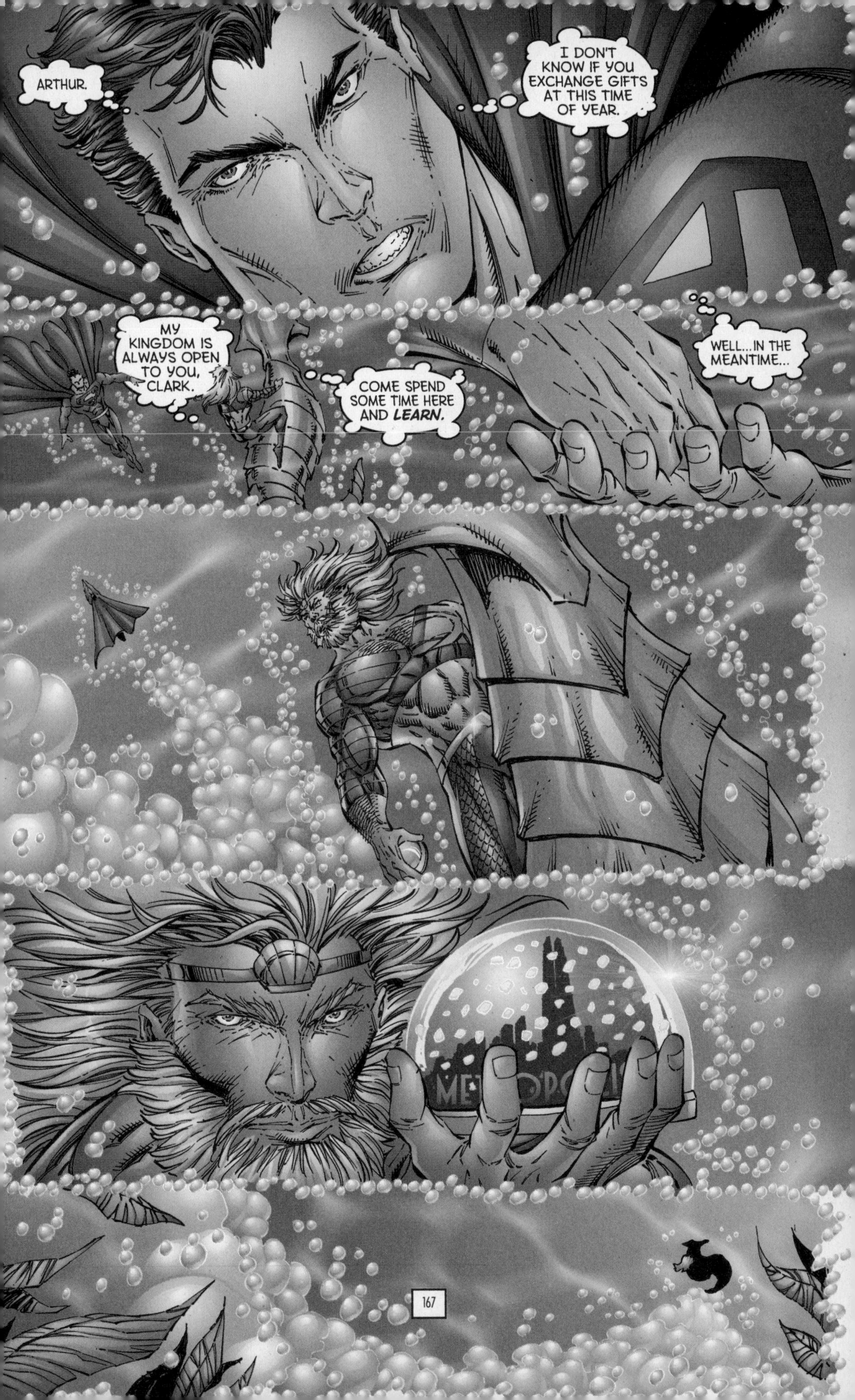
ARTHUR.
I DON'T KNOW IF YOU EXCHANGE GIFTS AT THIS TIME OF YEAR.
MY KINGDOM IS ALWAYS OPEN TO YOU, CLARK.
COME SPEND SOME TIME HERE AND LEARN.
WELL...IN THE MEANTIME...

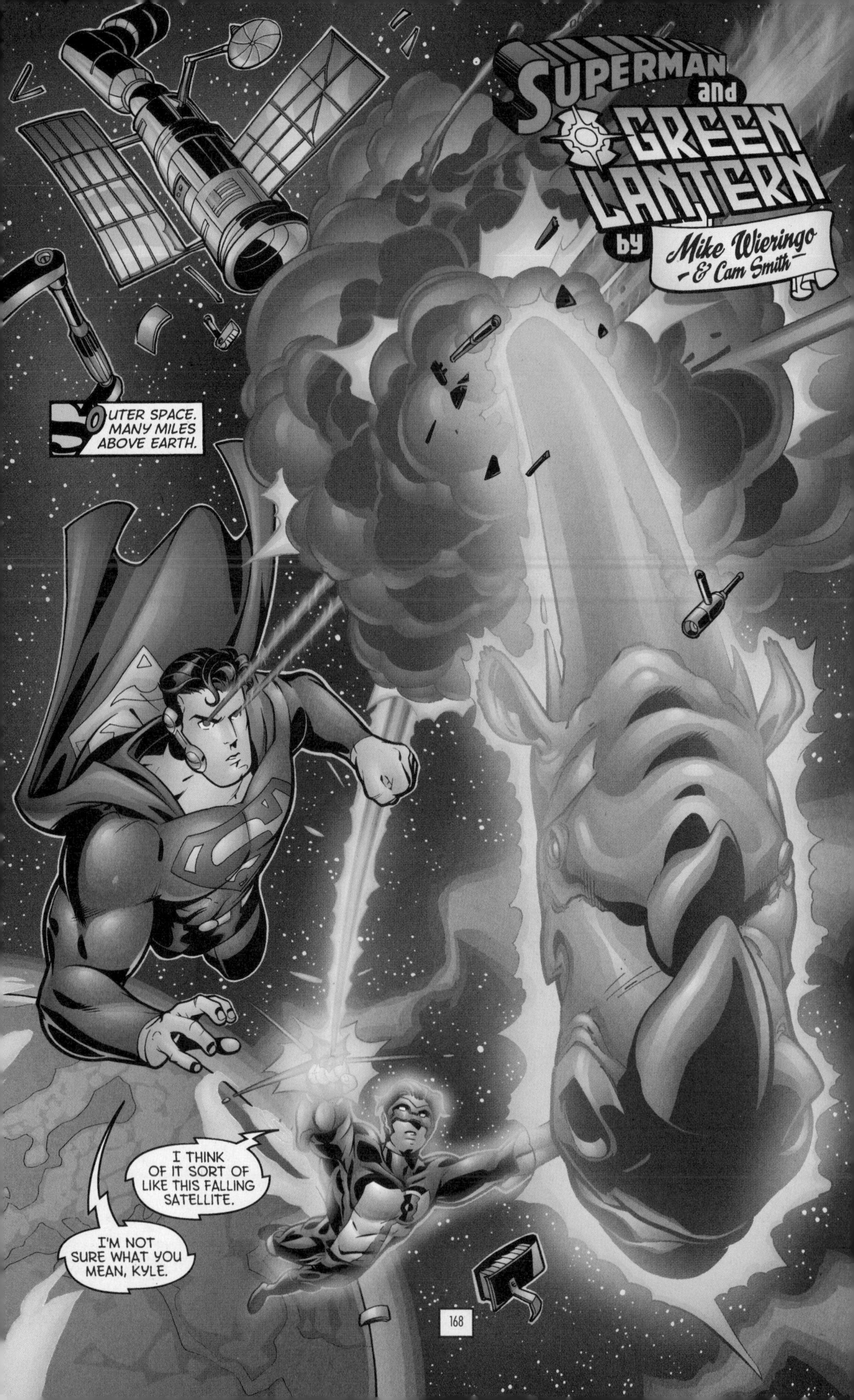
SUPERMAN and GREEN LANTERN
by Mike Wieringo & Cam Smith
OUTER SPACE. MANY MILES ABOVE EARTH.
I THINK OF IT SORT OF LIKE THIS FALLING SATELLITE.
I'M NOT SURE WHAT YOU MEAN, KYLE.

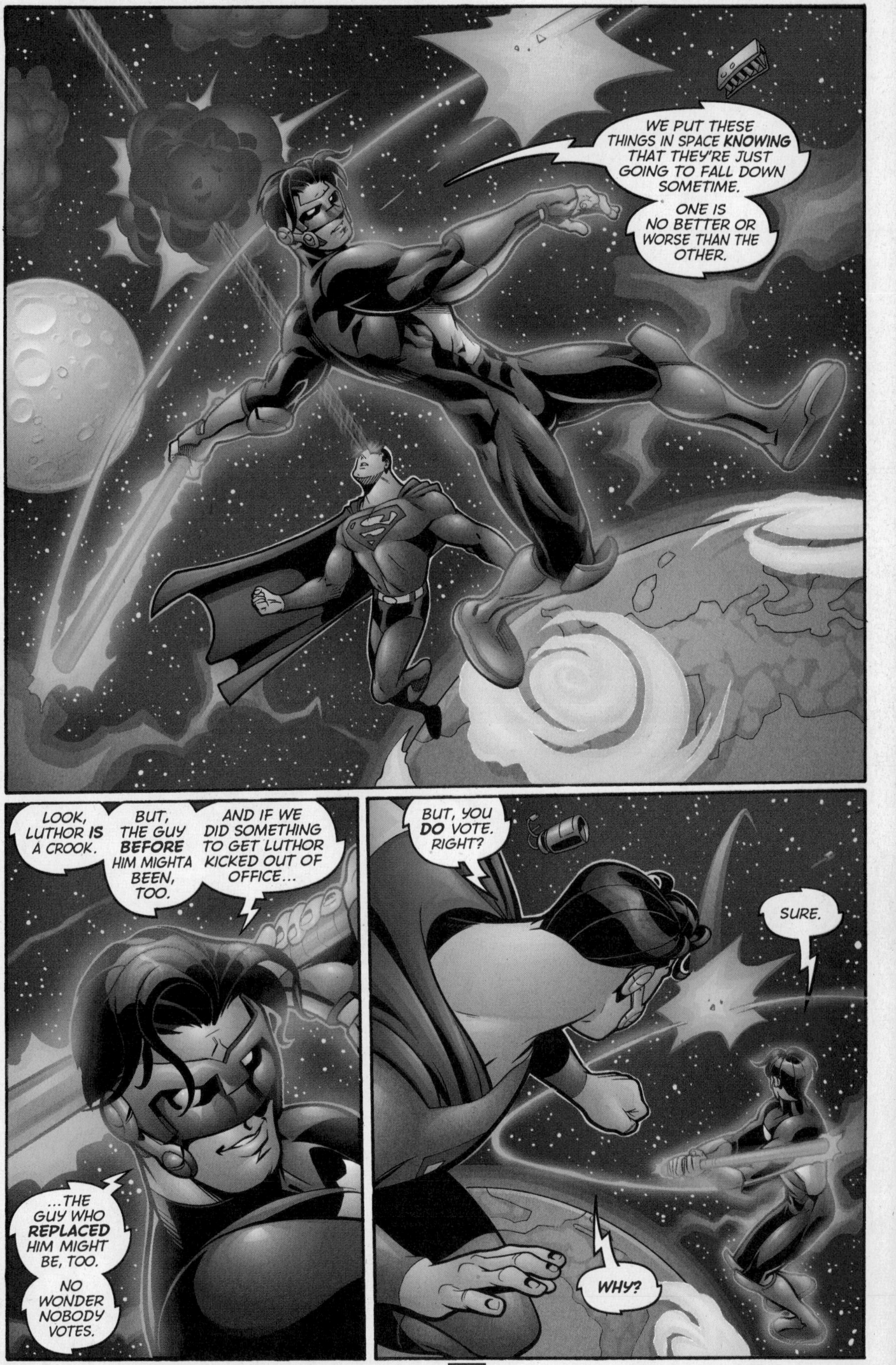
WE PUT THESE THINGS IN SPACE KNOWING THAT THEY'RE JUST GOING TO FALL DOWN SOMETIME.
ONE IS NO BETTER OR WORSE THAN THE OTHER.
LOOK, LUTHOR IS A CROOK.
BUT, THE GUY BEFORE HIM MIGHTA BEEN, TOO.
AND IF WE DID SOMETHING TO GET LUTHOR KICKED OUT OF OFFICE...
...THE GUY WHO REPLACED HIM MIGHT BE, TOO.
NO WONDER NOBODY VOTES.
BUT, YOU DO VOTE. RIGHT?
SURE.
WHY?

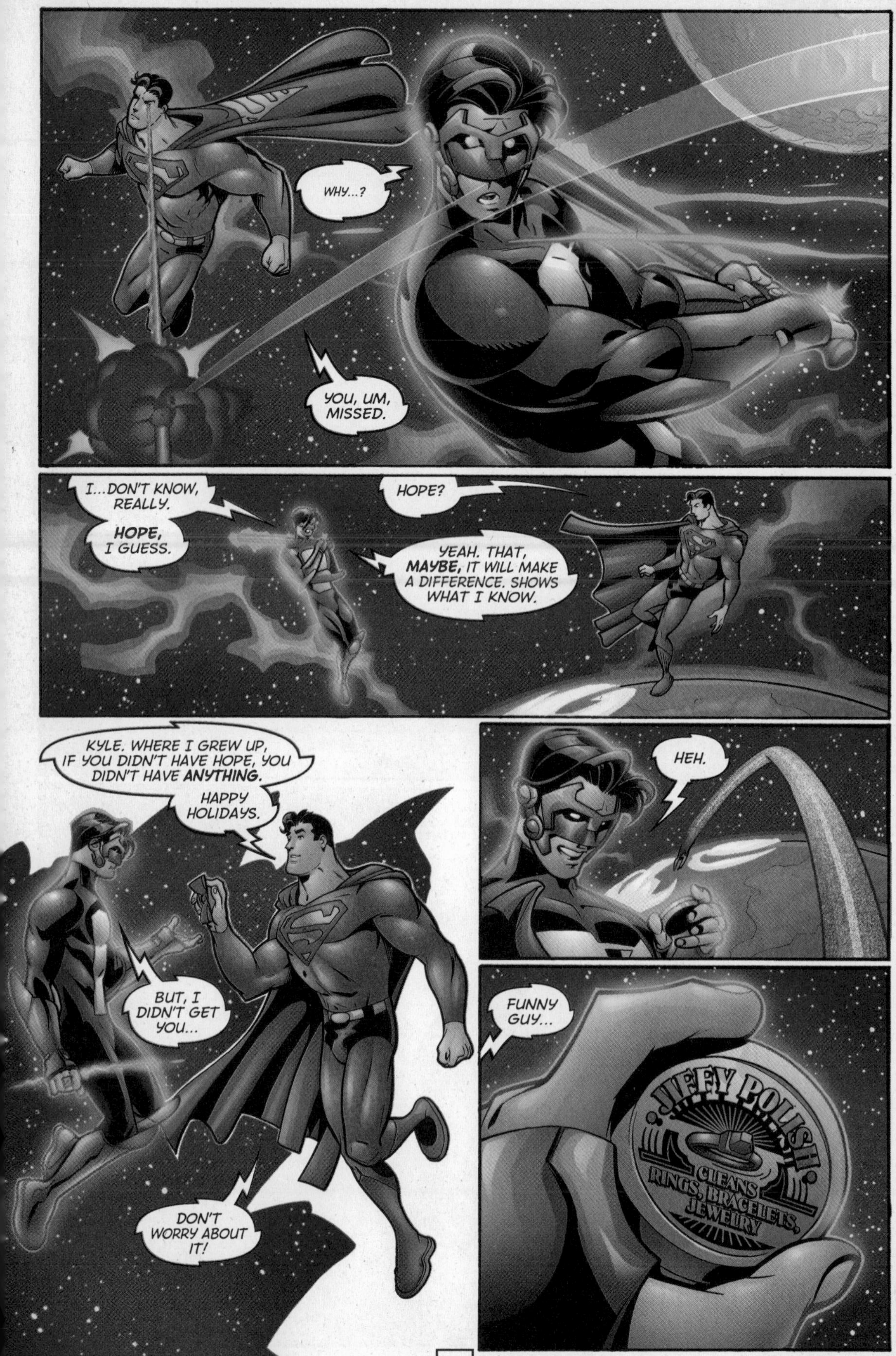
WHY...?
YOU, UM, MISSED.
I...DON'T KNOW, REALLY.
HOPE, I GUESS.
HOPE?
YEAH. THAT, MAYBE, IT WILL MAKE A DIFFERENCE. SHOWS WHAT I KNOW.
KYLE. WHERE I GREW UP, IF YOU DIDN'T HAVE HOPE, YOU DIDN'T HAVE ANYTHING.
HAPPY HOLIDAYS.
BUT, I DIDN'T GET YOU...
DON'T WORRY ABOUT IT!
HEH.
FUNNY GUY...
JIFFY POLISH
CLEANS RINGS, BRACELETS, JEWELRY

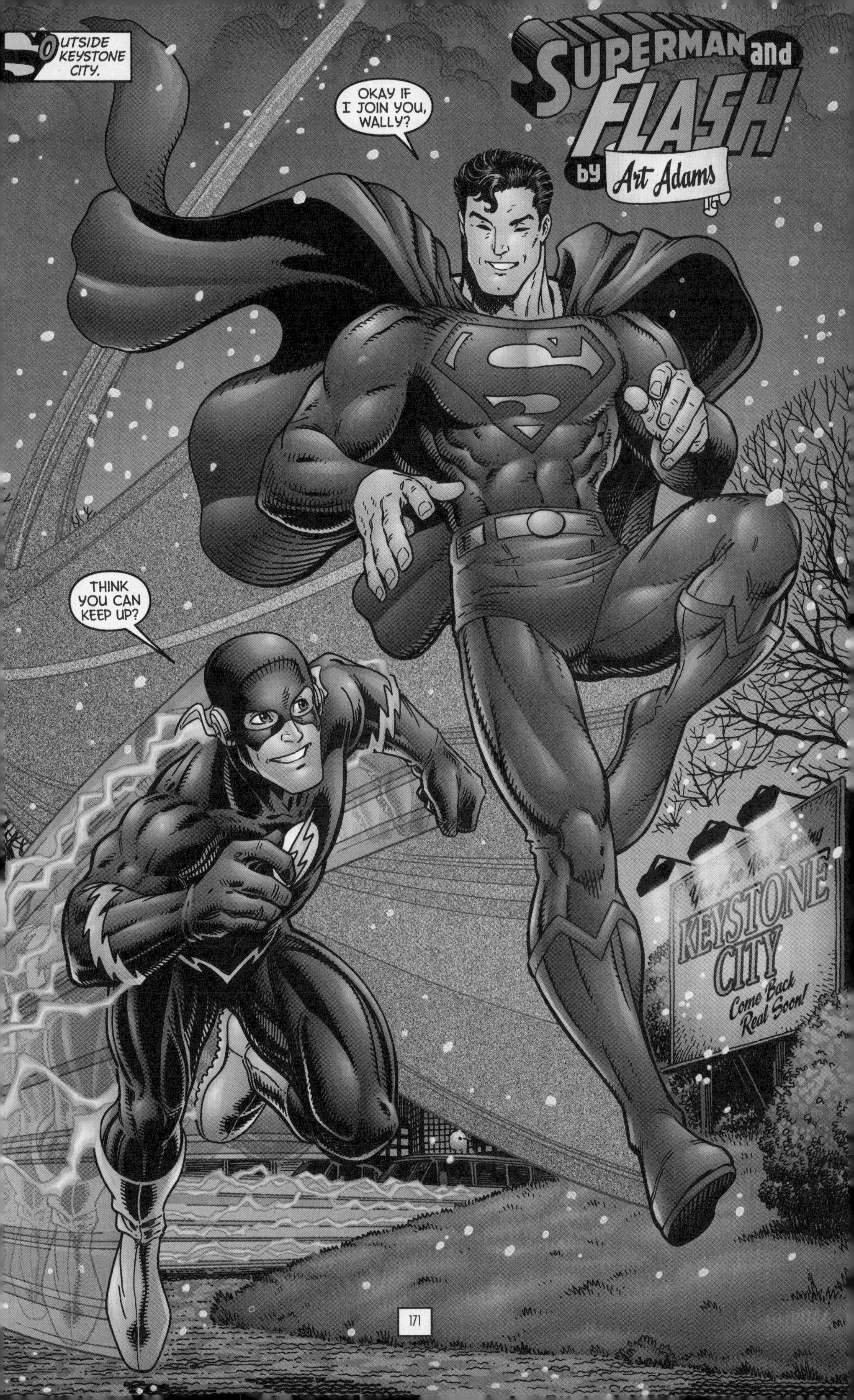

SO OUTSIDE KEYSTONE CITY.
SUPERMAN and FLASH
by Art Adams
OKAY IF I JOIN YOU, WALLY?
THINK YOU CAN KEEP UP?
KEYSTONE CITY
Come Back Real Soon!

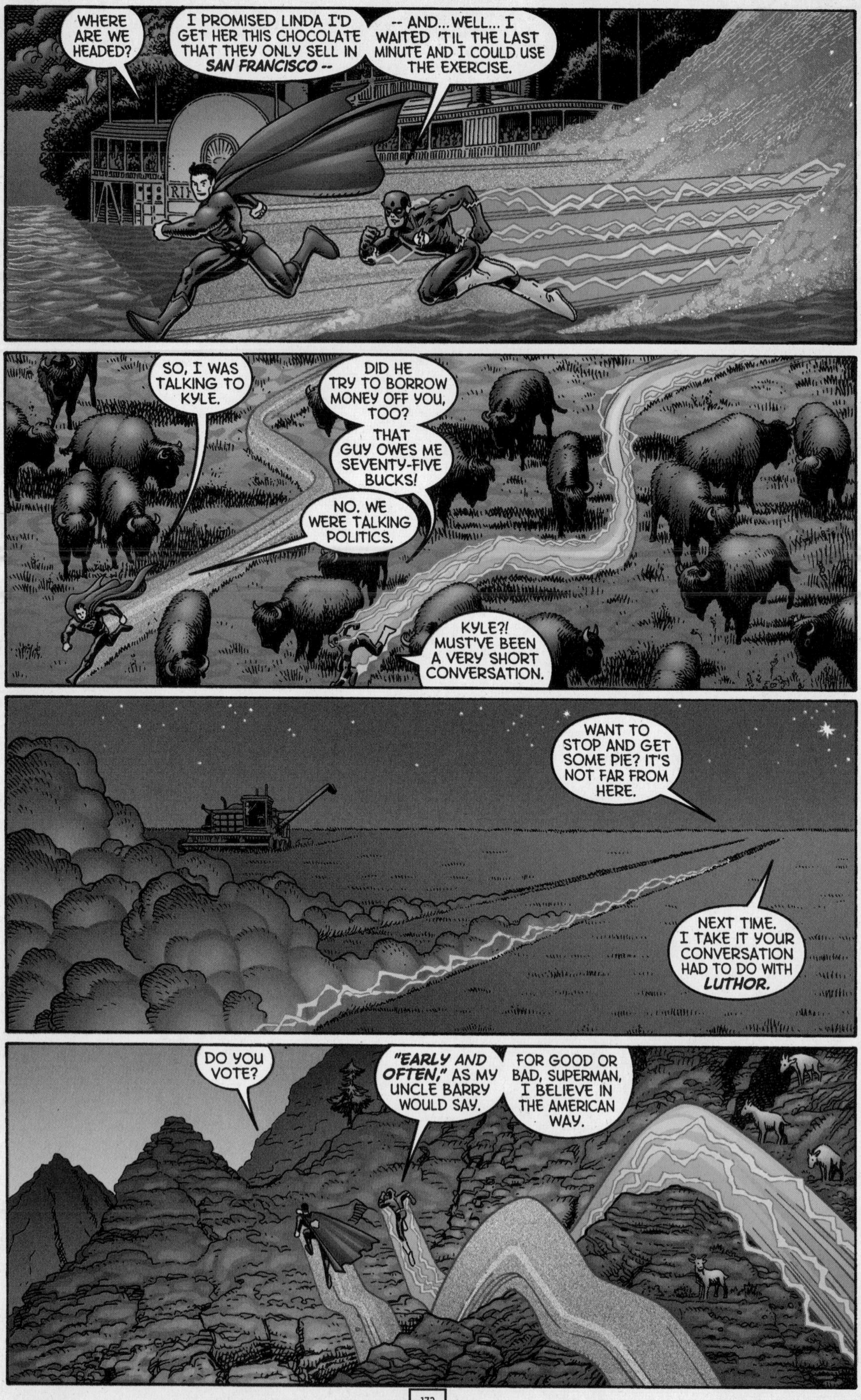

WHERE ARE WE HEADED?
I PROMISED LINDA I'D GET HER THIS CHOCOLATE THAT THEY ONLY SELL IN SAN FRANCISCO --
-- AND... WELL... I WAITED 'TIL THE LAST MINUTE AND I COULD USE THE EXERCISE.
SO, I WAS TALKING TO KYLE.
DID HE TRY TO BORROW MONEY OFF YOU, TOO?
THAT GUY OWES ME SEVENTY-FIVE BUCKS!
NO. WE WERE TALKING POLITICS.
KYLE?! MUST'VE BEEN A VERY SHORT CONVERSATION.
WANT TO STOP AND GET SOME PIE? IT'S NOT FAR FROM HERE.
NEXT TIME. I TAKE IT YOUR CONVERSATION HAD TO DO WITH LUTHOR.
DO YOU VOTE?
"EARLY AND OFTEN," AS MY UNCLE BARRY WOULD SAY.
FOR GOOD OR BAD, SUPERMAN, I BELIEVE IN THE AMERICAN WAY.

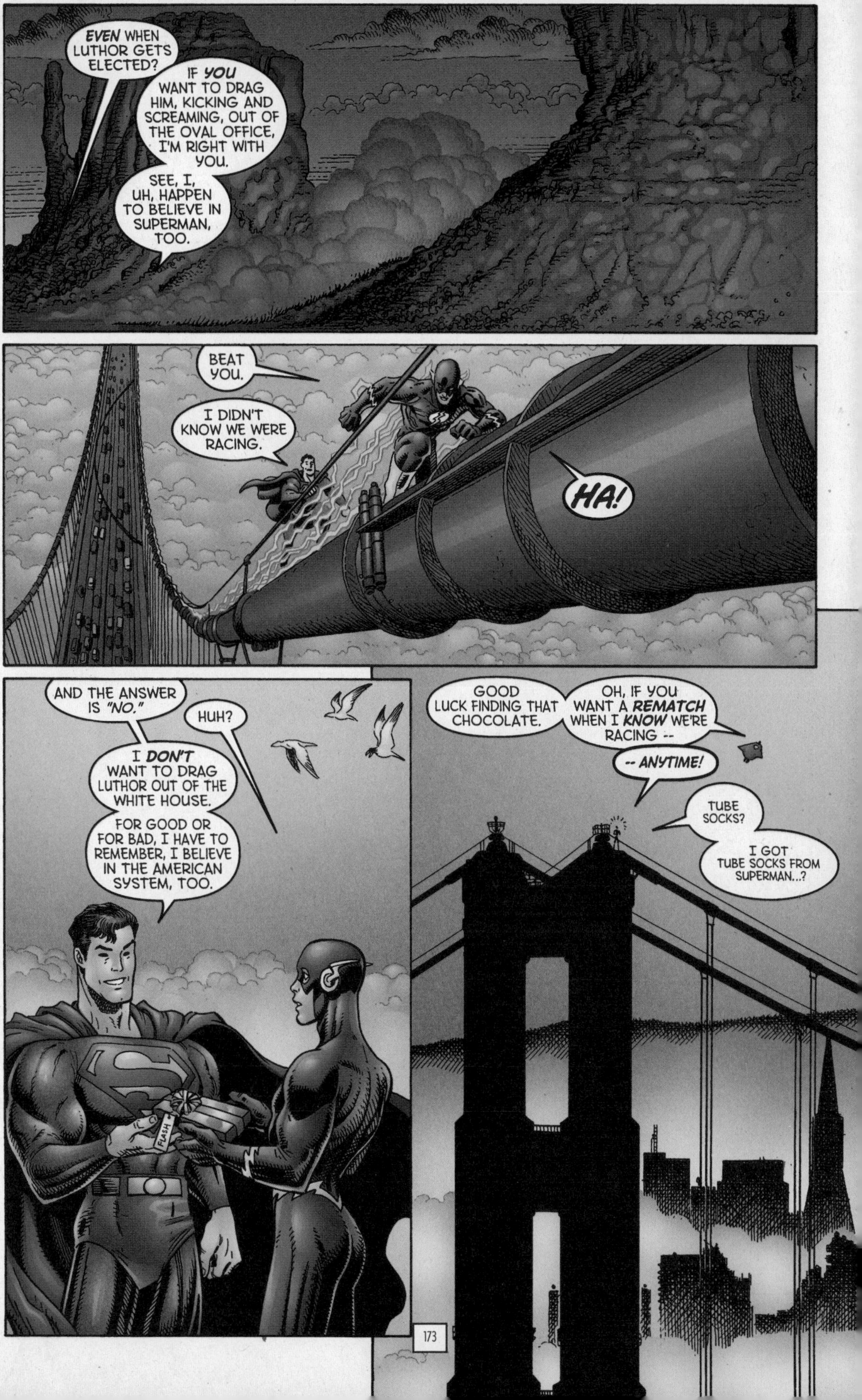
EVEN WHEN LUTHOR GETS ELECTED?
IF YOU WANT TO DRAG HIM, KICKING AND SCREAMING, OUT OF THE OVAL OFFICE, I'M RIGHT WITH YOU.
SEE, I, UH, HAPPEN TO BELIEVE IN SUPERMAN, TOO.
BEAT YOU.
I DIDN'T KNOW WE WERE RACING.
HA!
AND THE ANSWER IS "NO."
HUH?
I DON'T WANT TO DRAG LUTHOR OUT OF THE WHITE HOUSE.
FOR GOOD OR FOR BAD, I HAVE TO REMEMBER, I BELIEVE IN THE AMERICAN SYSTEM, TOO.
FLASH
GOOD LUCK FINDING THAT CHOCOLATE.
OH, IF YOU WANT A REMATCH WHEN I KNOW WE'RE RACING --
-- ANYTIME!
TUBE SOCKS?
I GOT TUBE SOCKS FROM SUPERMAN...?

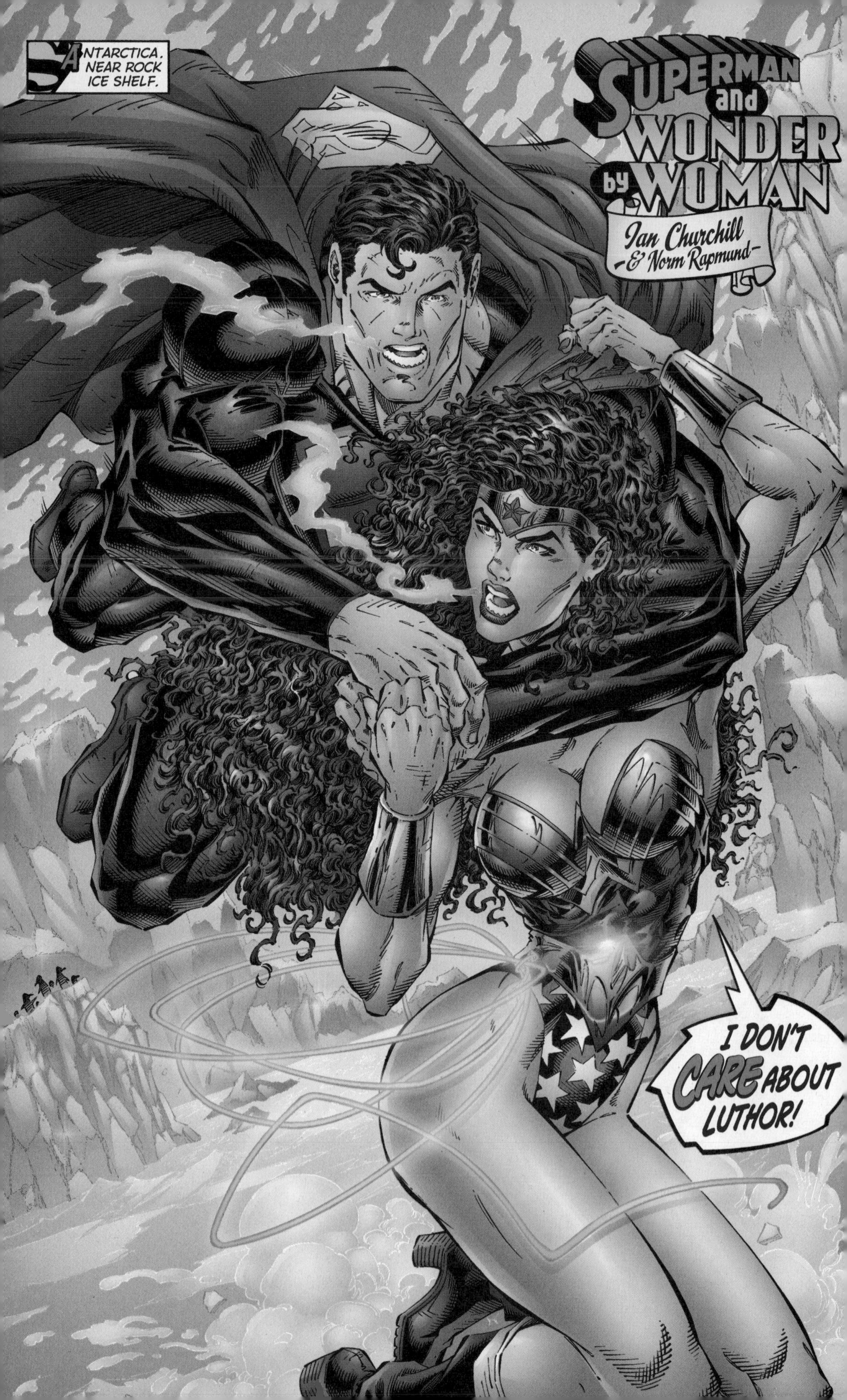
ANTARCTICA. NEAR ROCK ICE SHELF.
SUPERMAN and WONDER WOMAN
by Ian Churchill & Norm Rapmund
I DON'T CARE ABOUT LUTHOR!

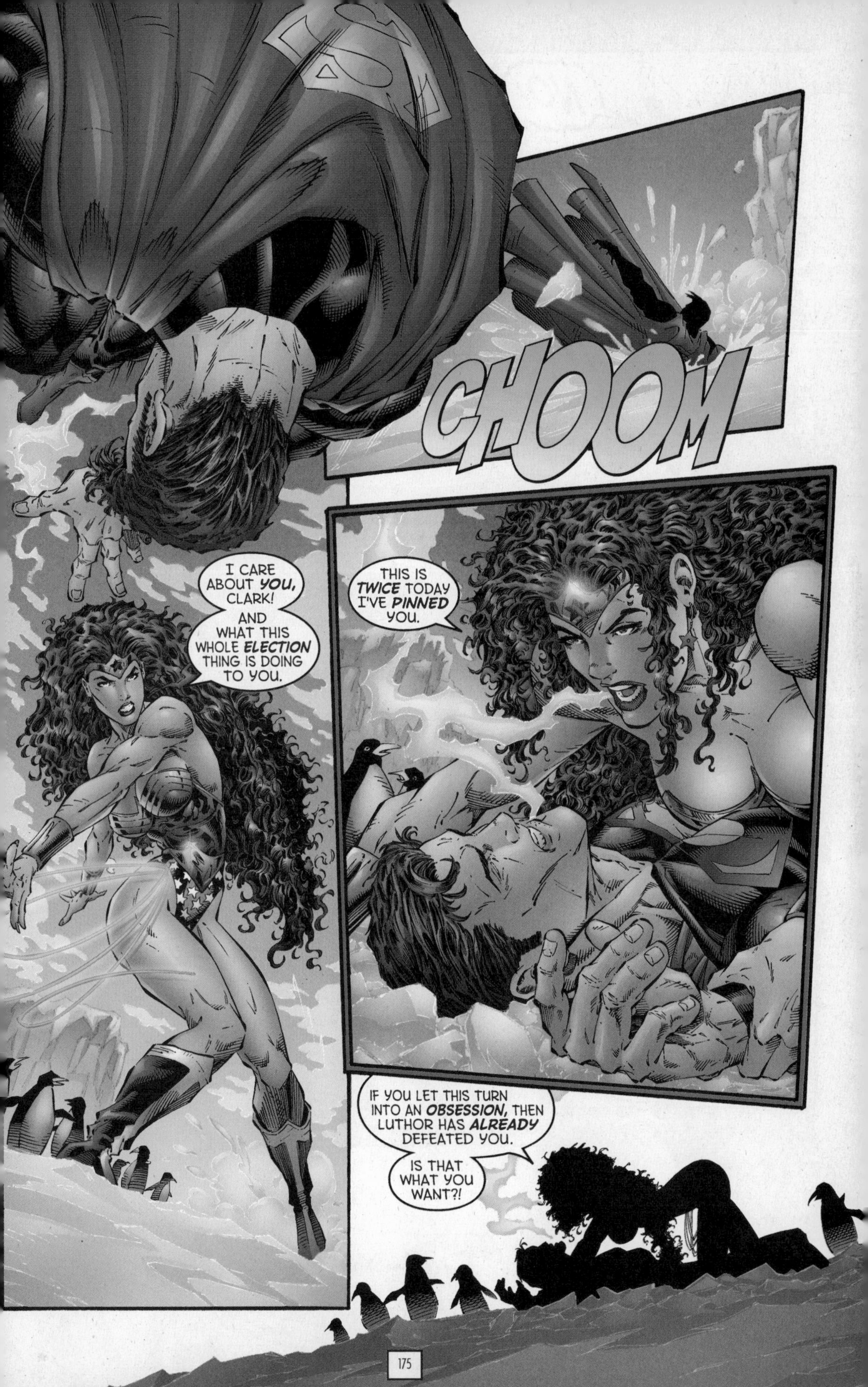
CHOOM
I CARE ABOUT YOU, CLARK!
AND WHAT THIS WHOLE ELECTION THING IS DOING TO YOU.
THIS IS TWICE TODAY I'VE PINNED YOU.
IF YOU LET THIS TURN INTO AN OBSESSION, THEN LUTHOR HAS ALREADY DEFEATED YOU.
IS THAT WHAT YOU WANT?!

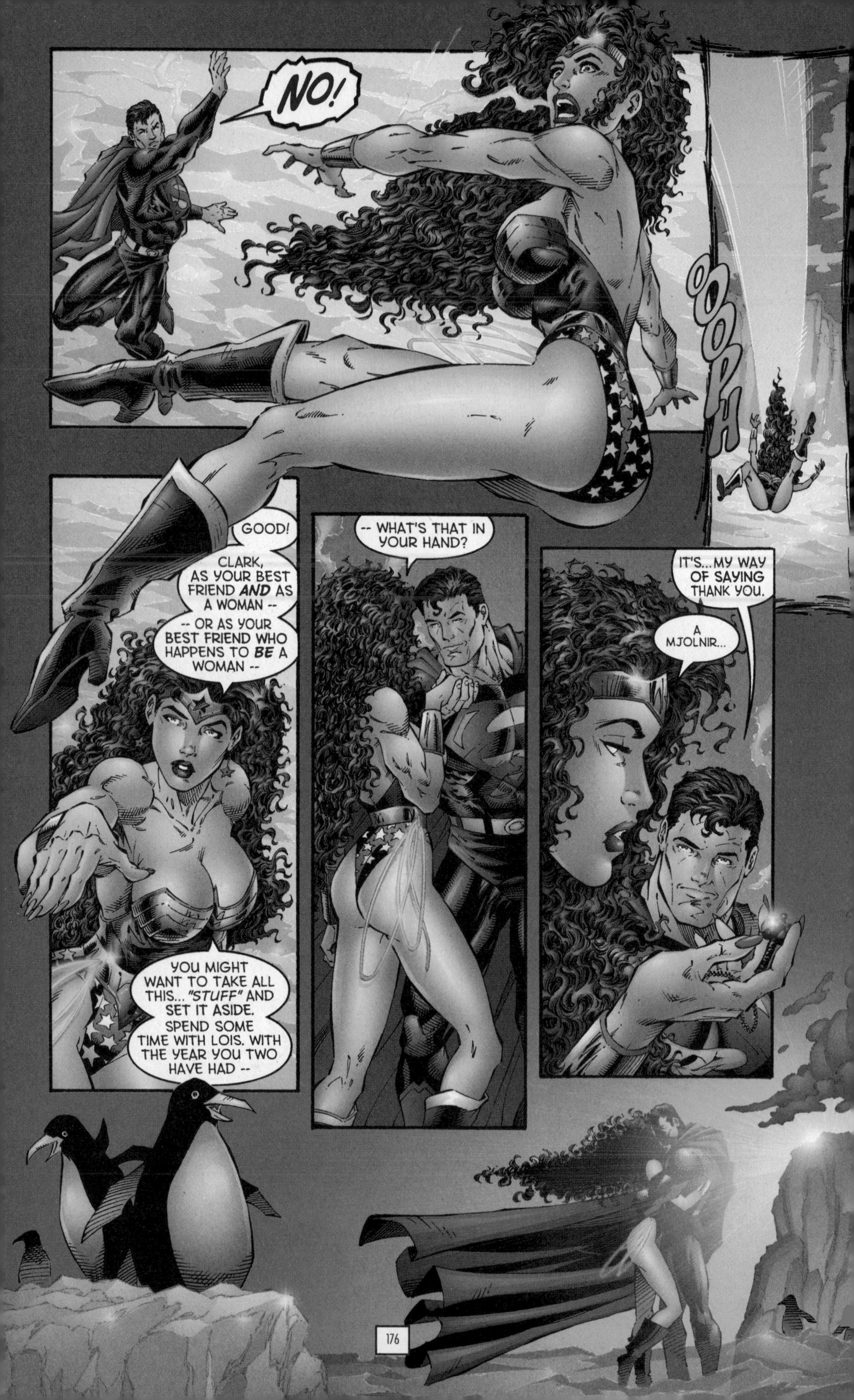
NO!
OOOPH
GOOD!
CLARK, AS YOUR BEST FRIEND AND AS A WOMAN --
-- OR AS YOUR BEST FRIEND WHO HAPPENS TO BE A WOMAN --
YOU MIGHT WANT TO TAKE ALL THIS... "STUFF" AND SET IT ASIDE. SPEND SOME TIME WITH LOIS. WITH THE YEAR YOU TWO HAVE HAD --
-- WHAT'S THAT IN YOUR HAND?
IT'S... MY WAY OF SAYING THANK YOU.
A MJOLNIR...

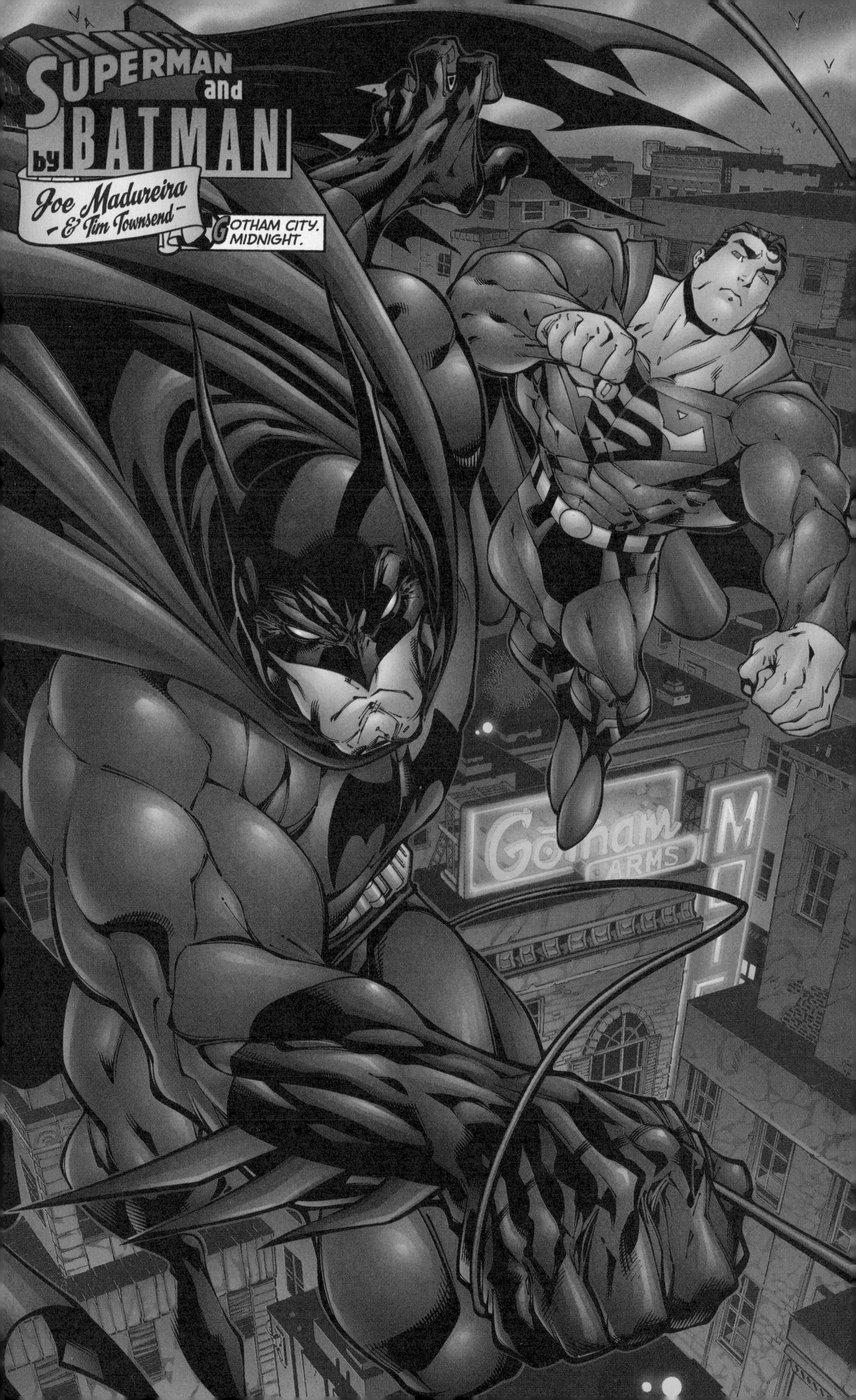
SUPERMAN and BATMAN
by
Joe Madureira
- & Tim Townsend -
GOTHAM CITY. MIDNIGHT.
Gotham
ARMS
M

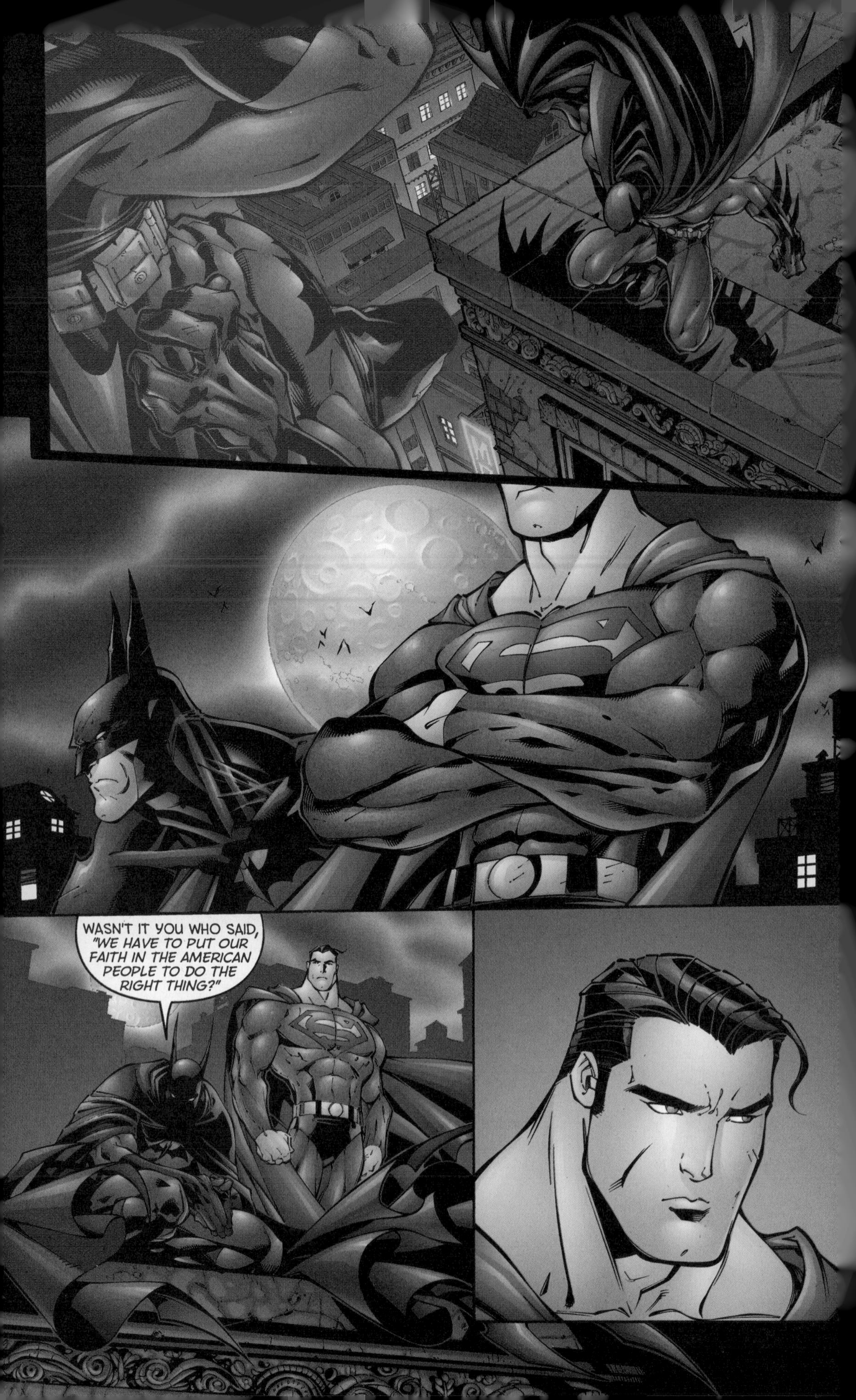
WASN'T IT YOU WHO SAID, "WE HAVE TO PUT OUR FAITH IN THE AMERICAN PEOPLE TO DO THE RIGHT THING?"

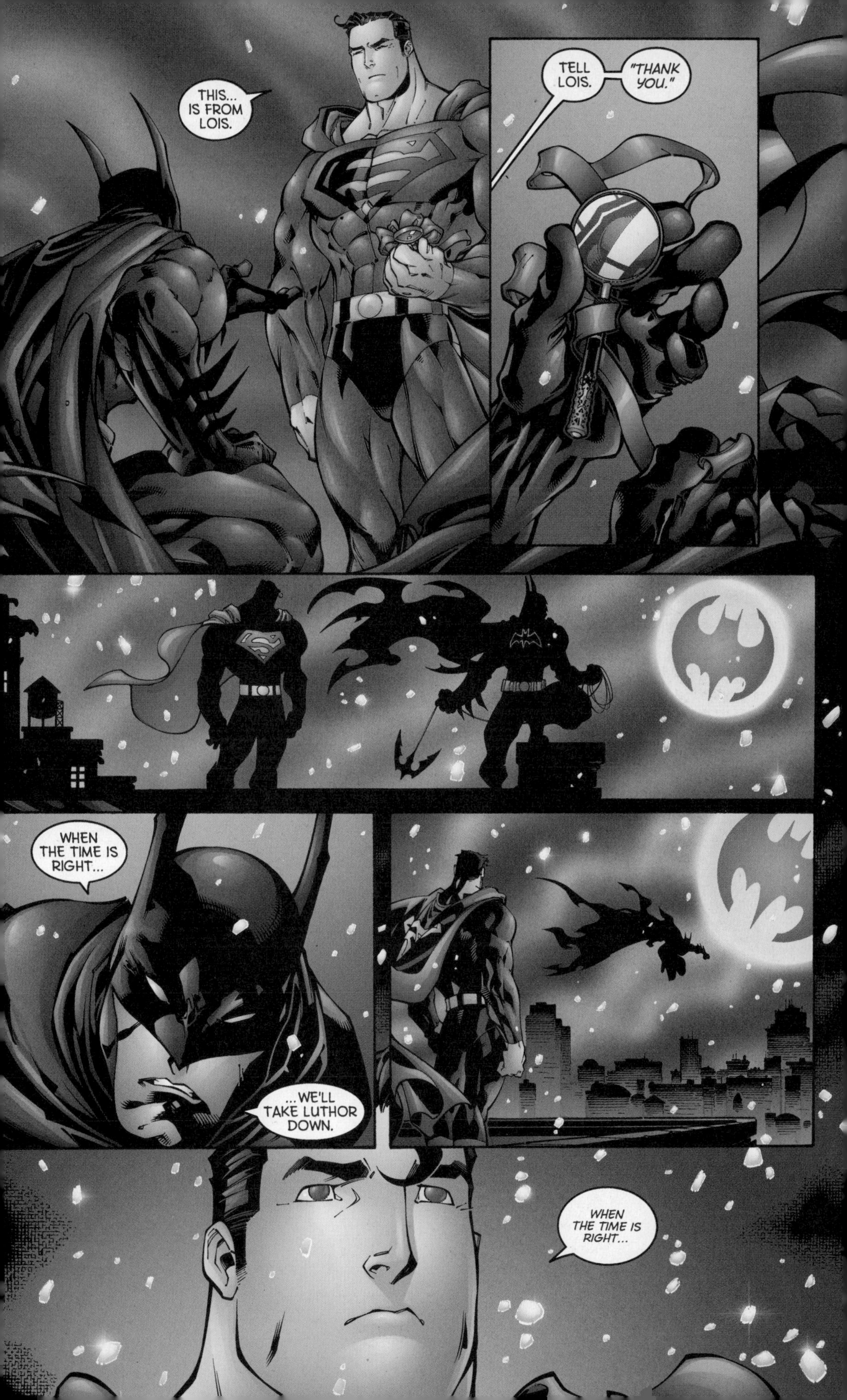
THIS... IS FROM LOIS.
TELL LOIS.
"THANK YOU."
WHEN THE TIME IS RIGHT...
...WE'LL TAKE LUTHOR DOWN.
WHEN THE TIME IS RIGHT...

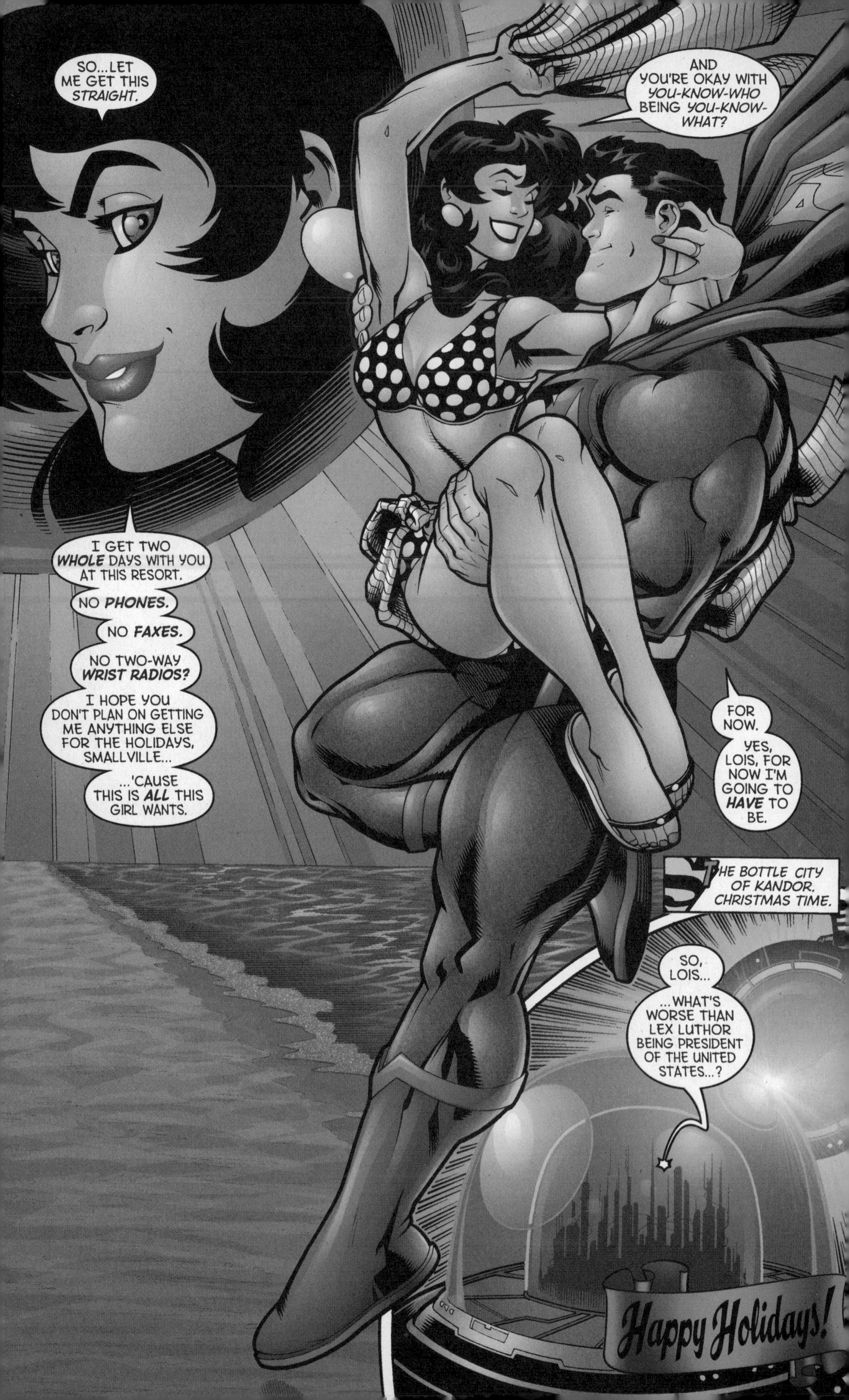
SO...LET ME GET THIS *STRAIGHT.*
AND YOU'RE OKAY WITH *YOU-KNOW-WHO* BEING *YOU-KNOW-WHAT?*
I GET TWO **WHOLE** DAYS WITH YOU AT THIS RESORT.
NO **PHONES.**
NO **FAXES.**
NO TWO-WAY **WRIST RADIOS?**
I HOPE YOU DON'T PLAN ON GETTING ME ANYTHING ELSE FOR THE HOLIDAYS, SMALLVILLE...
...'CAUSE THIS IS **ALL** THIS GIRL WANTS.
FOR NOW.
YES, LOIS, FOR NOW I'M GOING TO **HAVE** TO BE.
THE BOTTLE CITY OF KANDOR. CHRISTMAS TIME.
SO, LOIS...
...WHAT'S WORSE THAN LEX LUTHOR BEING PRESIDENT OF THE UNITED STATES...?
Happy Holidays!

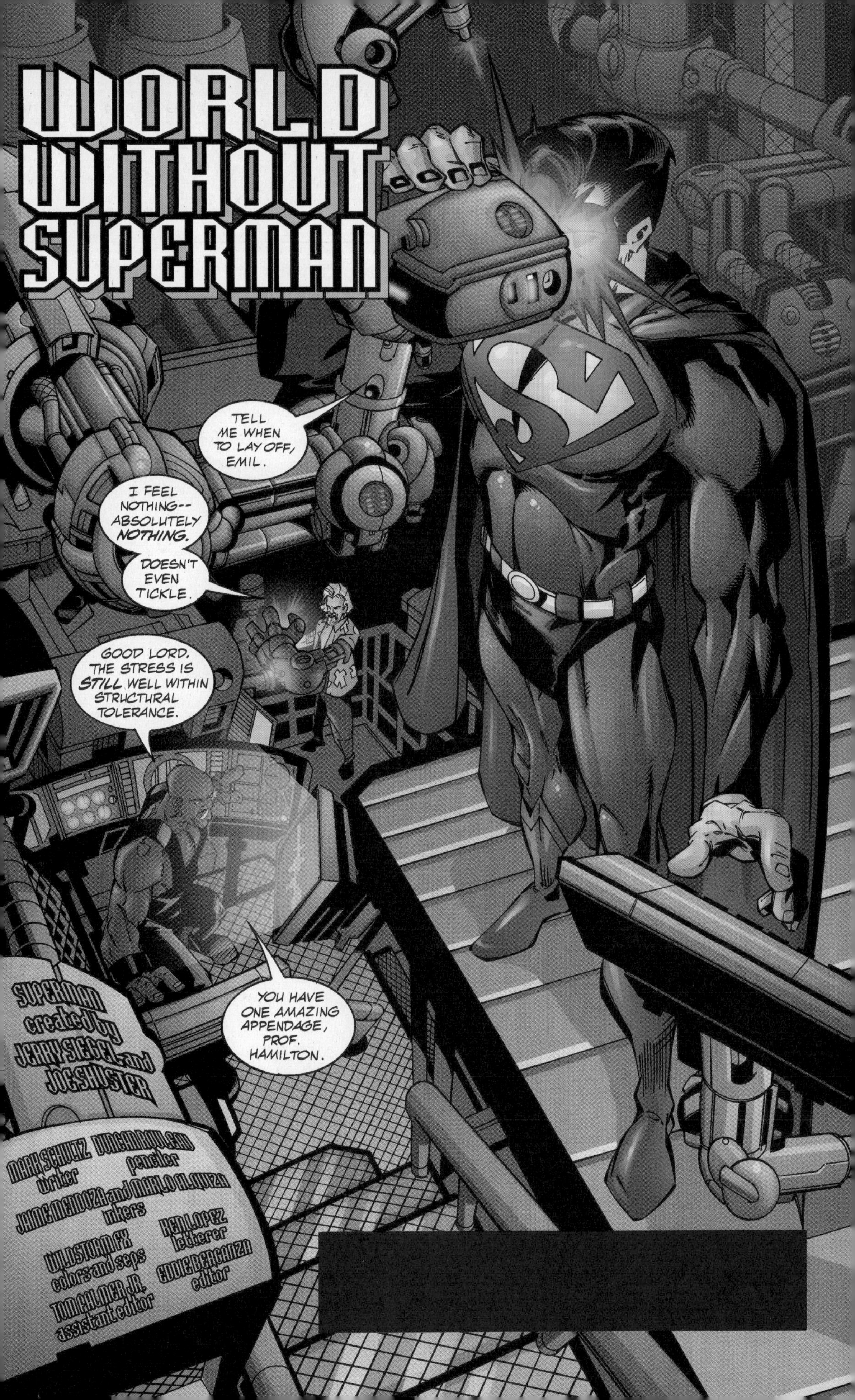
WORLD WITHOUT SUPERMAN
TELL ME WHEN TO LAY OFF, EMIL.
I FEEL NOTHING-- ABSOLUTELY NOTHING.
DOESN'T EVEN TICKLE.
GOOD LORD. THE STRESS IS STILL WELL WITHIN STRUCTURAL TOLERANCE.
YOU HAVE ONE AMAZING APPENDAGE, PROF. HAMILTON.
SUPERMAN created by JERRY SIEGEL and JOE SHUSTER
MARK SCHULTZ writer
DUNCAN ROULEAU penciler
JAIME MENDOZA and MARLO ALQUIZA inkers
WILDSTORM FX colors and seps
KEN LOPEZ letterer
TOM PALMER JR. assistant editor
EDDIE BERGANZA editor
[redacted]

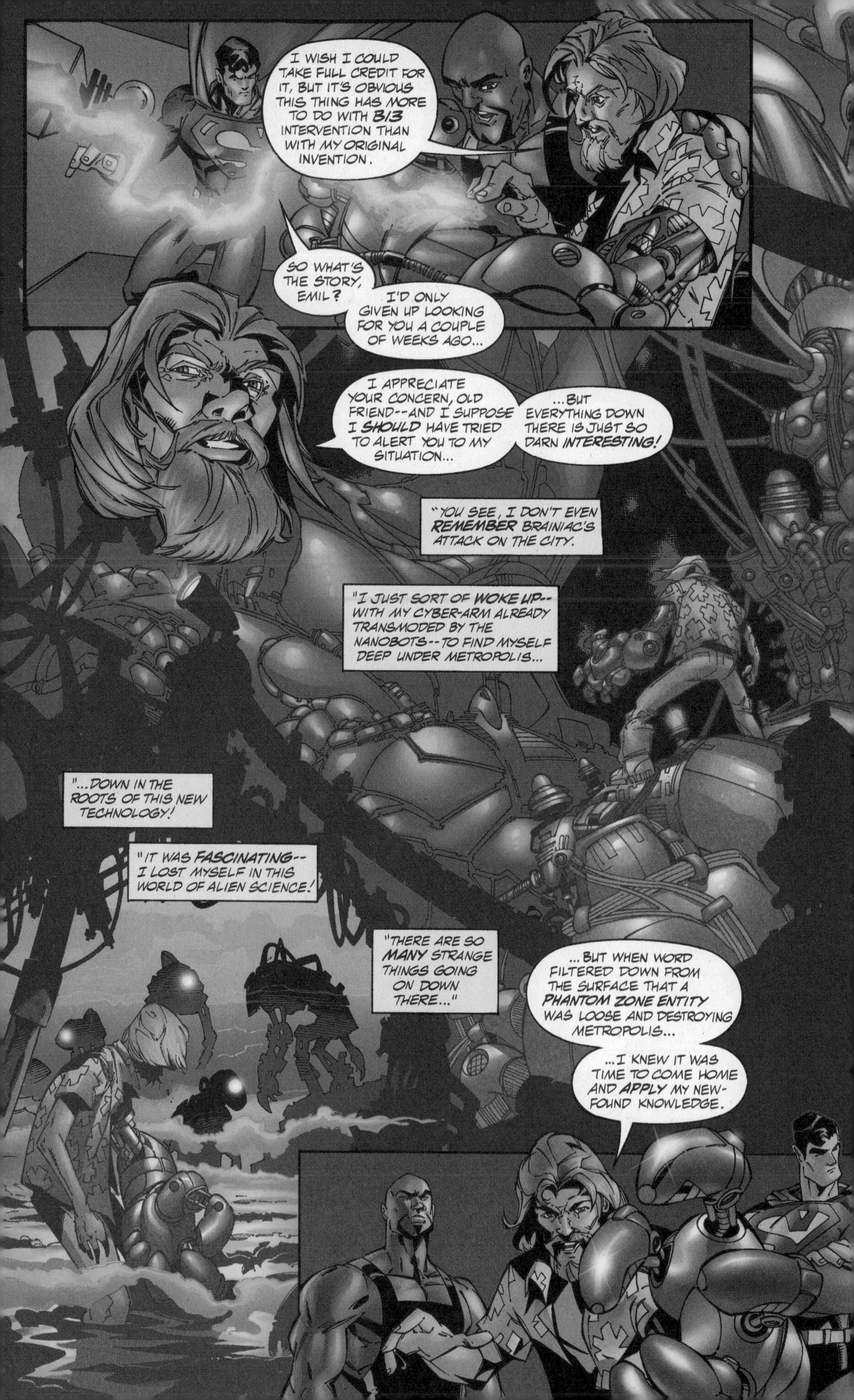
I WISH I COULD TAKE FULL CREDIT FOR IT, BUT IT'S OBVIOUS THIS THING HAS MORE TO DO WITH B13 INTERVENTION THAN WITH MY ORIGINAL INVENTION.
SO WHAT'S THE STORY, EMIL?
I'D ONLY GIVEN UP LOOKING FOR YOU A COUPLE OF WEEKS AGO...
I APPRECIATE YOUR CONCERN, OLD FRIEND--AND I SUPPOSE I SHOULD HAVE TRIED TO ALERT YOU TO MY SITUATION...
...BUT EVERYTHING DOWN THERE IS JUST SO DARN INTERESTING!
"YOU SEE, I DON'T EVEN REMEMBER BRAINIAC'S ATTACK ON THE CITY.
"I JUST SORT OF WOKE UP--WITH MY CYBER-ARM ALREADY TRANSMODED BY THE NANOBOTS--TO FIND MYSELF DEEP UNDER METROPOLIS...
"...DOWN IN THE ROOTS OF THIS NEW TECHNOLOGY!
"IT WAS FASCINATING--I LOST MYSELF IN THIS WORLD OF ALIEN SCIENCE!
"THERE ARE SO MANY STRANGE THINGS GOING ON DOWN THERE..."
...BUT WHEN WORD FILTERED DOWN FROM THE SURFACE THAT A PHANTOM ZONE ENTITY WAS LOOSE AND DESTROYING METROPOLIS...
...I KNEW IT WAS TIME TO COME HOME AND APPLY MY NEW-FOUND KNOWLEDGE.

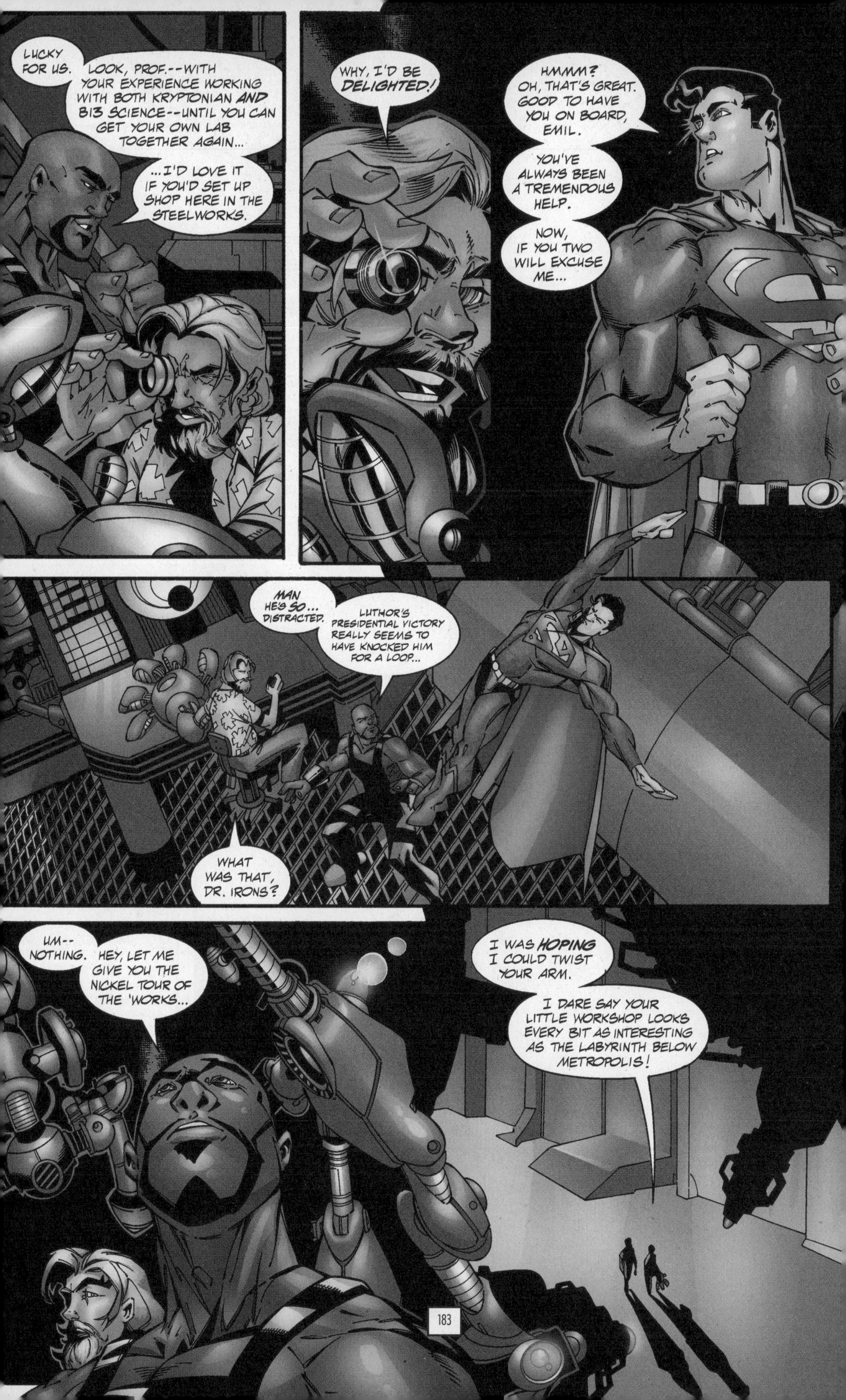
LUCKY FOR US.
LOOK, PROF.--WITH YOUR EXPERIENCE WORKING WITH BOTH KRYPTONIAN AND B13 SCIENCE--UNTIL YOU CAN GET YOUR OWN LAB TOGETHER AGAIN...
...I'D LOVE IT IF YOU'D SET UP SHOP HERE IN THE STEELWORKS.
WHY, I'D BE DELIGHTED!
HMMM? OH, THAT'S GREAT. GOOD TO HAVE YOU ON BOARD, EMIL.
YOU'VE ALWAYS BEEN A TREMENDOUS HELP.
NOW, IF YOU TWO WILL EXCUSE ME...
MAN HE'S SO... DISTRACTED.
LUTHOR'S PRESIDENTIAL VICTORY REALLY SEEMS TO HAVE KNOCKED HIM FOR A LOOP...
WHAT WAS THAT, DR. IRONS?
UM--NOTHING.
HEY, LET ME GIVE YOU THE NICKEL TOUR OF THE 'WORKS...
I WAS HOPING I COULD TWIST YOUR ARM.
I DARE SAY YOUR LITTLE WORKSHOP LOOKS EVERY BIT AS INTERESTING AS THE LABYRINTH BELOW METROPOLIS!

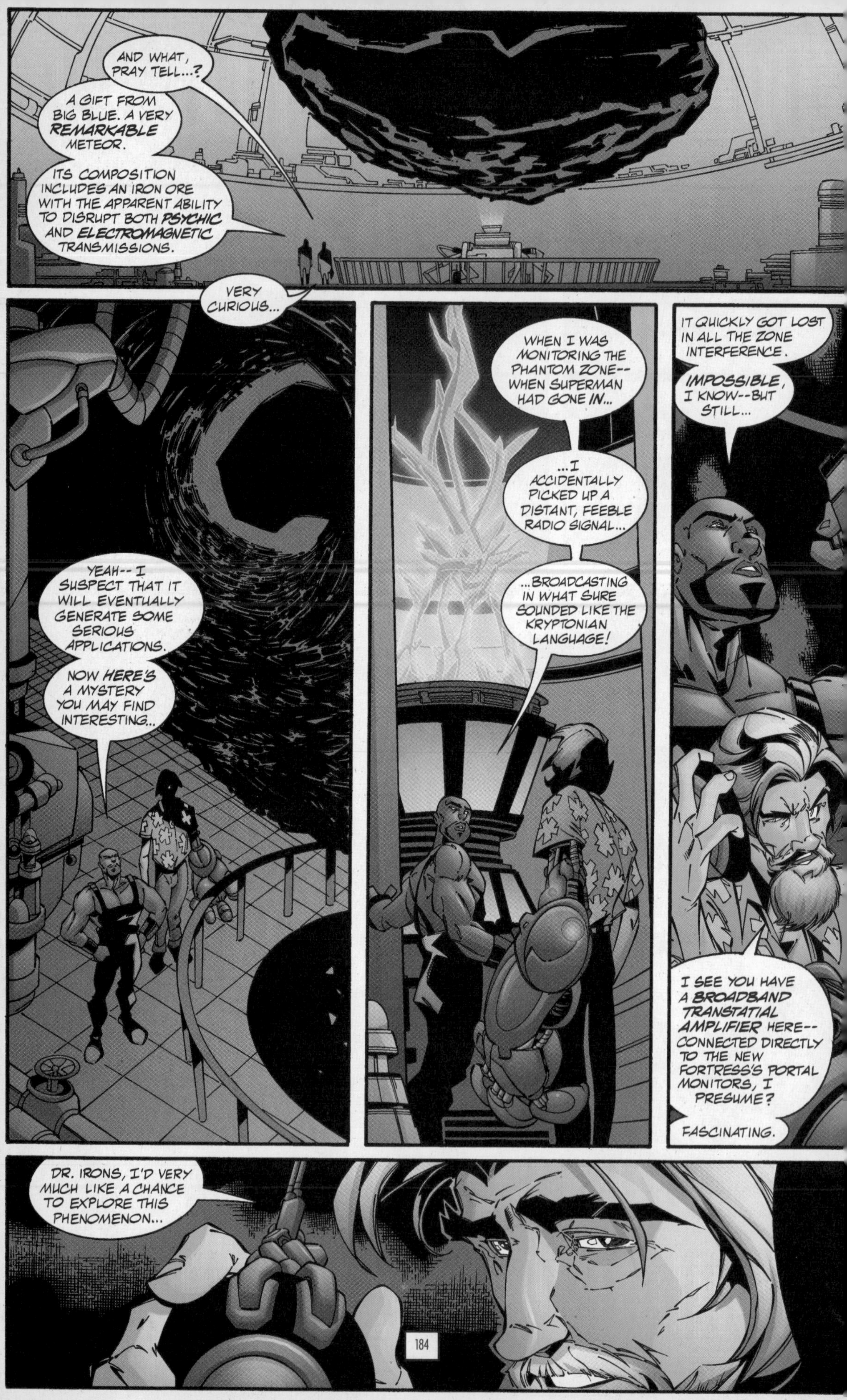
AND WHAT, PRAY TELL...?
A GIFT FROM BIG BLUE. A VERY REMARKABLE METEOR.
ITS COMPOSITION INCLUDES AN IRON ORE WITH THE APPARENT ABILITY TO DISRUPT BOTH PSYCHIC AND ELECTROMAGNETIC TRANSMISSIONS.
VERY CURIOUS...
YEAH-- I SUSPECT THAT IT WILL EVENTUALLY GENERATE SOME SERIOUS APPLICATIONS.
NOW HERE'S A MYSTERY YOU MAY FIND INTERESTING...
WHEN I WAS MONITORING THE PHANTOM ZONE-- WHEN SUPERMAN HAD GONE IN...
...I ACCIDENTALLY PICKED UP A DISTANT, FEEBLE RADIO SIGNAL...
...BROADCASTING IN WHAT SURE SOUNDED LIKE THE KRYPTONIAN LANGUAGE!
IT QUICKLY GOT LOST IN ALL THE ZONE INTERFERENCE.
IMPOSSIBLE, I KNOW--BUT STILL...
I SEE YOU HAVE A BROADBAND TRANSTATIAL AMPLIFIER HERE-- CONNECTED DIRECTLY TO THE NEW FORTRESS'S PORTAL MONITORS, I PRESUME?
FASCINATING.
DR. IRONS, I'D VERY MUCH LIKE A CHANCE TO EXPLORE THIS PHENOMENON...

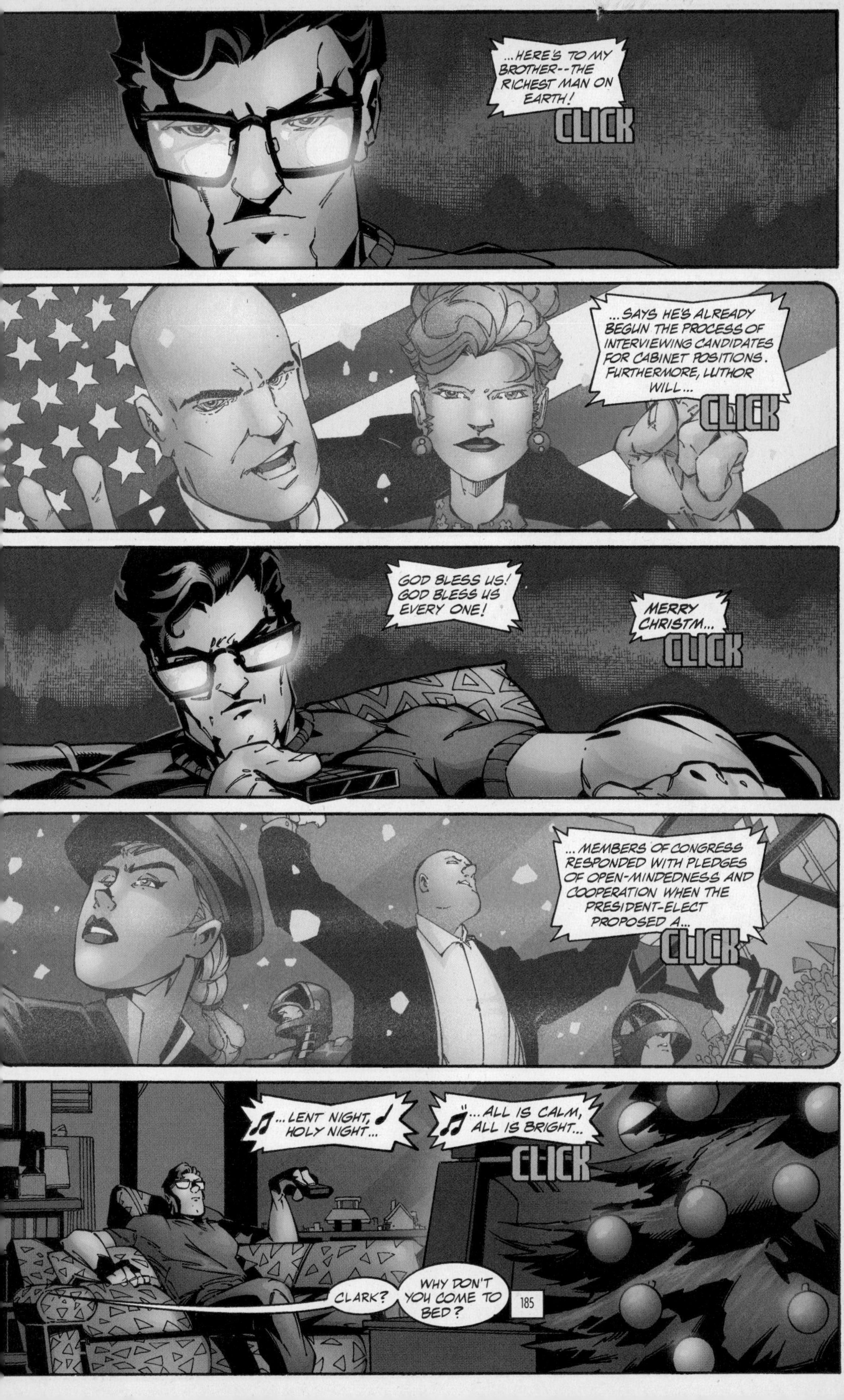
...HERE'S TO MY BROTHER--THE RICHEST MAN ON EARTH!
CLICK
...SAYS HE'S ALREADY BEGUN THE PROCESS OF INTERVIEWING CANDIDATES FOR CABINET POSITIONS. FURTHERMORE, LUTHOR WILL...
CLICK
GOD BLESS US! GOD BLESS US EVERY ONE!
MERRY CHRISTM...
CLICK
...MEMBERS OF CONGRESS RESPONDED WITH PLEDGES OF OPEN-MINDEDNESS AND COOPERATION WHEN THE PRESIDENT-ELECT PROPOSED A...
CLICK
...LENT NIGHT, HOLY NIGHT...
...ALL IS CALM, ALL IS BRIGHT...
CLICK
CLARK?
WHY DON'T YOU COME TO BED?

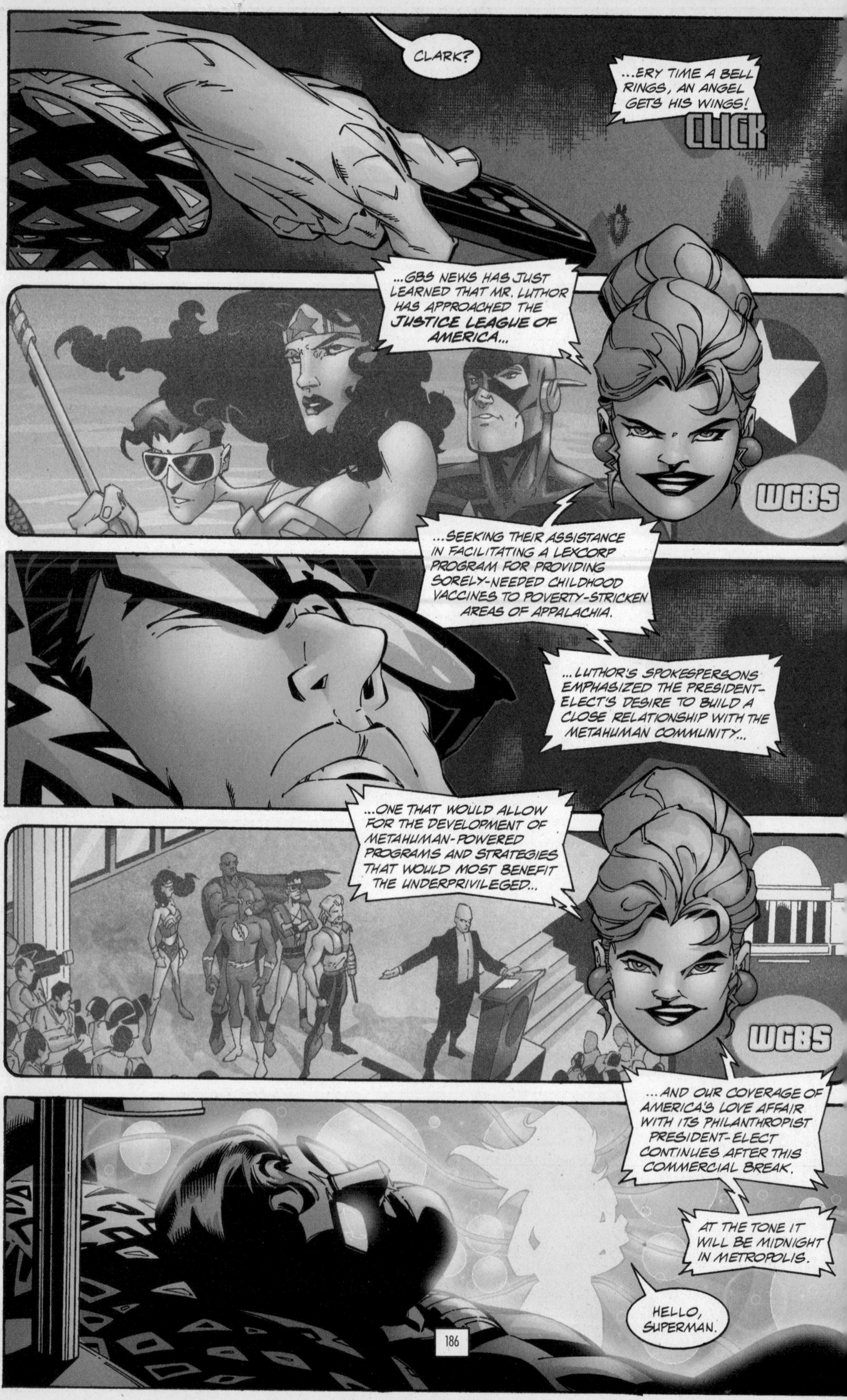
CLARK?
...ERY TIME A BELL RINGS, AN ANGEL GETS HIS WINGS!
CLICK
...GBS NEWS HAS JUST LEARNED THAT MR. LUTHOR HAS APPROACHED THE JUSTICE LEAGUE OF AMERICA...
WGBS
...SEEKING THEIR ASSISTANCE IN FACILITATING A LEXCORP PROGRAM FOR PROVIDING SORELY-NEEDED CHILDHOOD VACCINES TO POVERTY-STRICKEN AREAS OF APPALACHIA.
...LUTHOR'S SPOKESPERSONS EMPHASIZED THE PRESIDENT-ELECT'S DESIRE TO BUILD A CLOSE RELATIONSHIP WITH THE METAHUMAN COMMUNITY...
...ONE THAT WOULD ALLOW FOR THE DEVELOPMENT OF METAHUMAN-POWERED PROGRAMS AND STRATEGIES THAT WOULD MOST BENEFIT THE UNDERPRIVILEGED...
WGBS
...AND OUR COVERAGE OF AMERICA'S LOVE AFFAIR WITH ITS PHILANTHROPIST PRESIDENT-ELECT CONTINUES AFTER THIS COMMERCIAL BREAK.
AT THE TONE IT WILL BE MIDNIGHT IN METROPOLIS.
HELLO, SUPERMAN.

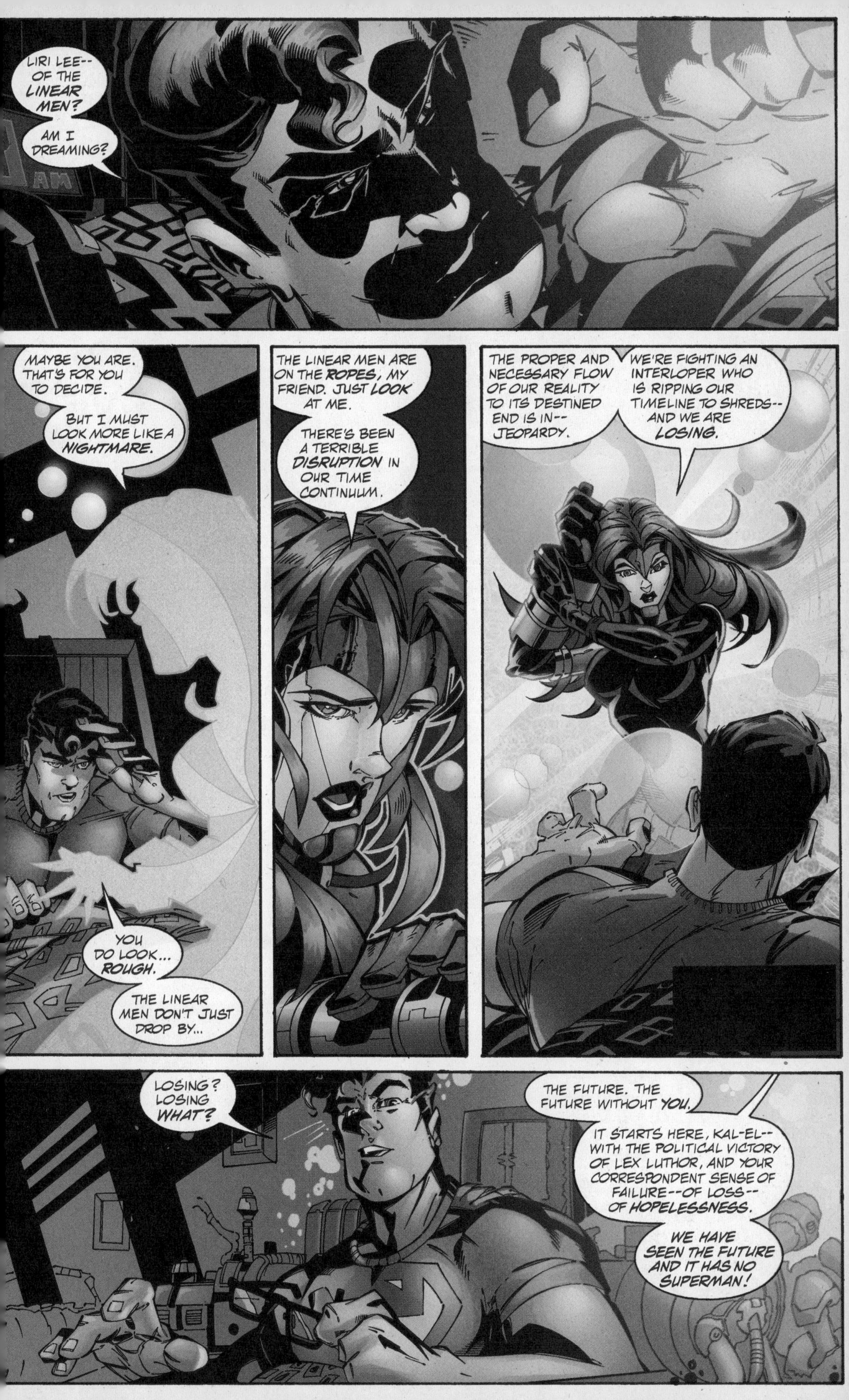

LIRI LEE-- OF THE LINEAR MEN?
AM I DREAMING?
MAYBE YOU ARE. THAT'S FOR YOU TO DECIDE.
BUT I MUST LOOK MORE LIKE A NIGHTMARE.
YOU DO LOOK... ROUGH.
THE LINEAR MEN DON'T JUST DROP BY...
THE LINEAR MEN ARE ON THE ROPES, MY FRIEND. JUST LOOK AT ME.
THERE'S BEEN A TERRIBLE DISRUPTION IN OUR TIME CONTINUUM.
THE PROPER AND NECESSARY FLOW OF OUR REALITY TO ITS DESTINED END IS IN-- JEOPARDY.
WE'RE FIGHTING AN INTERLOPER WHO IS RIPPING OUR TIMELINE TO SHREDS-- AND WE ARE LOSING.
[redacted]
LOSING? LOSING WHAT?
THE FUTURE. THE FUTURE WITHOUT YOU.
IT STARTS HERE, KAL-EL-- WITH THE POLITICAL VICTORY OF LEX LUTHOR, AND YOUR CORRESPONDENT SENSE OF FAILURE--OF LOSS-- OF HOPELESSNESS.
WE HAVE SEEN THE FUTURE AND IT HAS NO SUPERMAN!

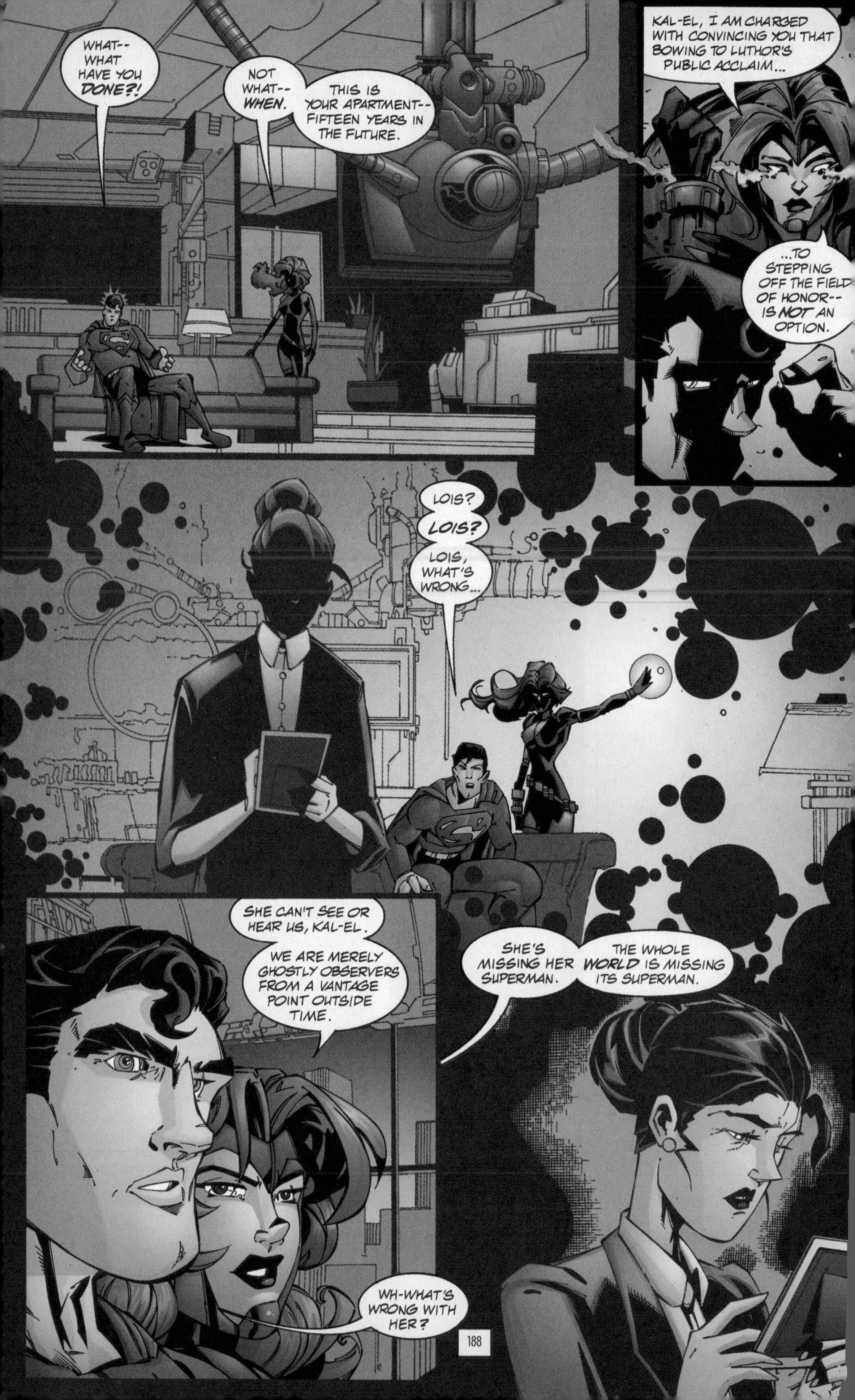
WHAT-- WHAT HAVE YOU DONE?!
NOT WHAT-- WHEN.
THIS IS YOUR APARTMENT-- FIFTEEN YEARS IN THE FUTURE.
KAL-EL, I AM CHARGED WITH CONVINCING YOU THAT BOWING TO LUTHOR'S PUBLIC ACCLAIM...
...TO STEPPING OFF THE FIELD OF HONOR-- IS NOT AN OPTION.
LOIS?
LOIS?
LOIS, WHAT'S WRONG...
SHE CAN'T SEE OR HEAR US, KAL-EL.
WE ARE MERELY GHOSTLY OBSERVERS FROM A VANTAGE POINT OUTSIDE TIME.
WH-WHAT'S WRONG WITH HER?
SHE'S MISSING HER SUPERMAN.
THE WHOLE WORLD IS MISSING ITS SUPERMAN.

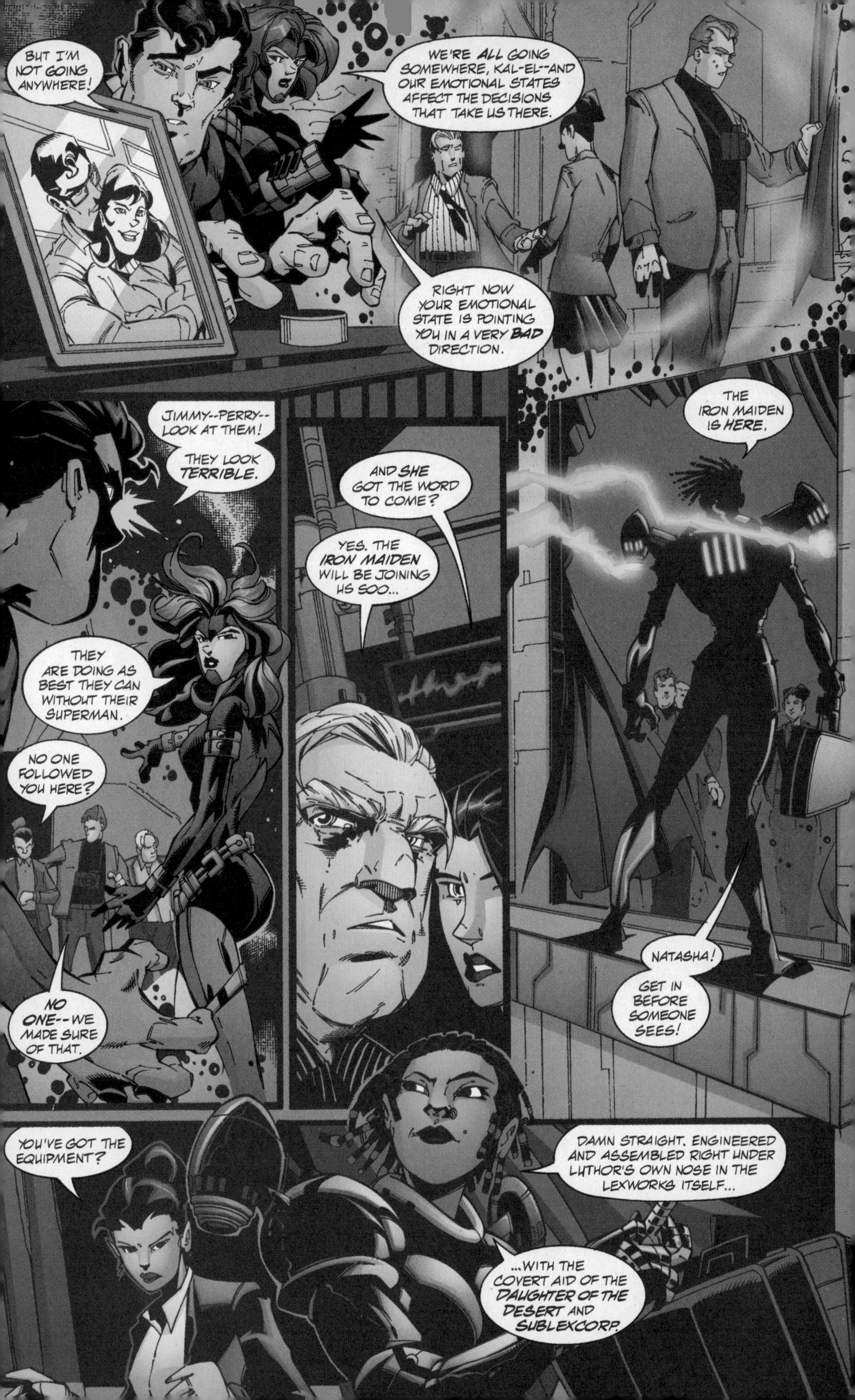
BUT I'M NOT GOING ANYWHERE!
WE'RE ALL GOING SOMEWHERE, KAL-EL--AND OUR EMOTIONAL STATES AFFECT THE DECISIONS THAT TAKE US THERE.
RIGHT NOW YOUR EMOTIONAL STATE IS POINTING YOU IN A VERY BAD DIRECTION.
JIMMY--PERRY--LOOK AT THEM!
THEY LOOK TERRIBLE.
THEY ARE DOING AS BEST THEY CAN WITHOUT THEIR SUPERMAN.
NO ONE FOLLOWED YOU HERE?
NO ONE--WE MADE SURE OF THAT.
AND SHE GOT THE WORD TO COME?
YES. THE IRON MAIDEN WILL BE JOINING US SOO...
THE IRON MAIDEN IS HERE.
NATASHA!
GET IN BEFORE SOMEONE SEES!
YOU'VE GOT THE EQUIPMENT?
DAMN STRAIGHT. ENGINEERED AND ASSEMBLED RIGHT UNDER LUTHOR'S OWN NOSE IN THE LEXWORKS ITSELF...
...WITH THE COVERT AID OF THE DAUGHTER OF THE DESERT AND SUBLEXCORP.

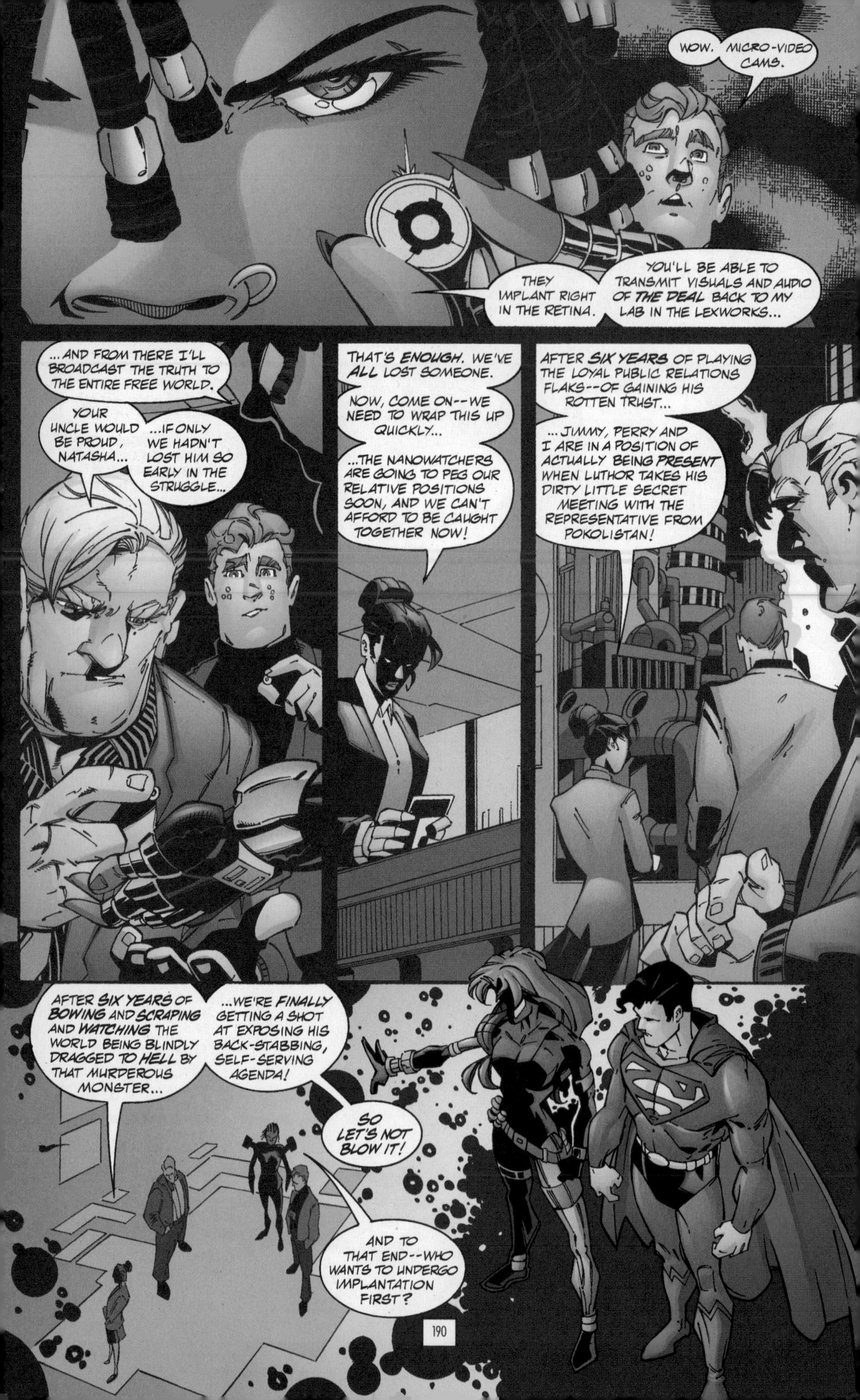
WOW. MICRO-VIDEO CAMS.
THEY IMPLANT RIGHT IN THE RETINA.
YOU'LL BE ABLE TO TRANSMIT VISUALS AND AUDIO OF THE DEAL BACK TO MY LAB IN THE LEXWORKS...
...AND FROM THERE I'LL BROADCAST THE TRUTH TO THE ENTIRE FREE WORLD.
YOUR UNCLE WOULD BE PROUD, NATASHA...
...IF ONLY WE HADN'T LOST HIM SO EARLY IN THE STRUGGLE...
THAT'S ENOUGH. WE'VE ALL LOST SOMEONE.
NOW, COME ON--WE NEED TO WRAP THIS UP QUICKLY...
...THE NANOWATCHERS ARE GOING TO PEG OUR RELATIVE POSITIONS SOON, AND WE CAN'T AFFORD TO BE CAUGHT TOGETHER NOW!
AFTER SIX YEARS OF PLAYING THE LOYAL PUBLIC RELATIONS FLAKS--OF GAINING HIS ROTTEN TRUST...
...JIMMY, PERRY AND I ARE IN A POSITION OF ACTUALLY BEING PRESENT WHEN LUTHOR TAKES HIS DIRTY LITTLE SECRET MEETING WITH THE REPRESENTATIVE FROM POKOLISTAN!
AFTER SIX YEARS OF BOWING AND SCRAPING AND WATCHING THE WORLD BEING BLINDLY DRAGGED TO HELL BY THAT MURDEROUS MONSTER...
...WE'RE FINALLY GETTING A SHOT AT EXPOSING HIS BACK-STABBING, SELF-SERVING AGENDA!
SO LET'S NOT BLOW IT!
AND TO THAT END--WHO WANTS TO UNDERGO IMPLANTATION FIRST?

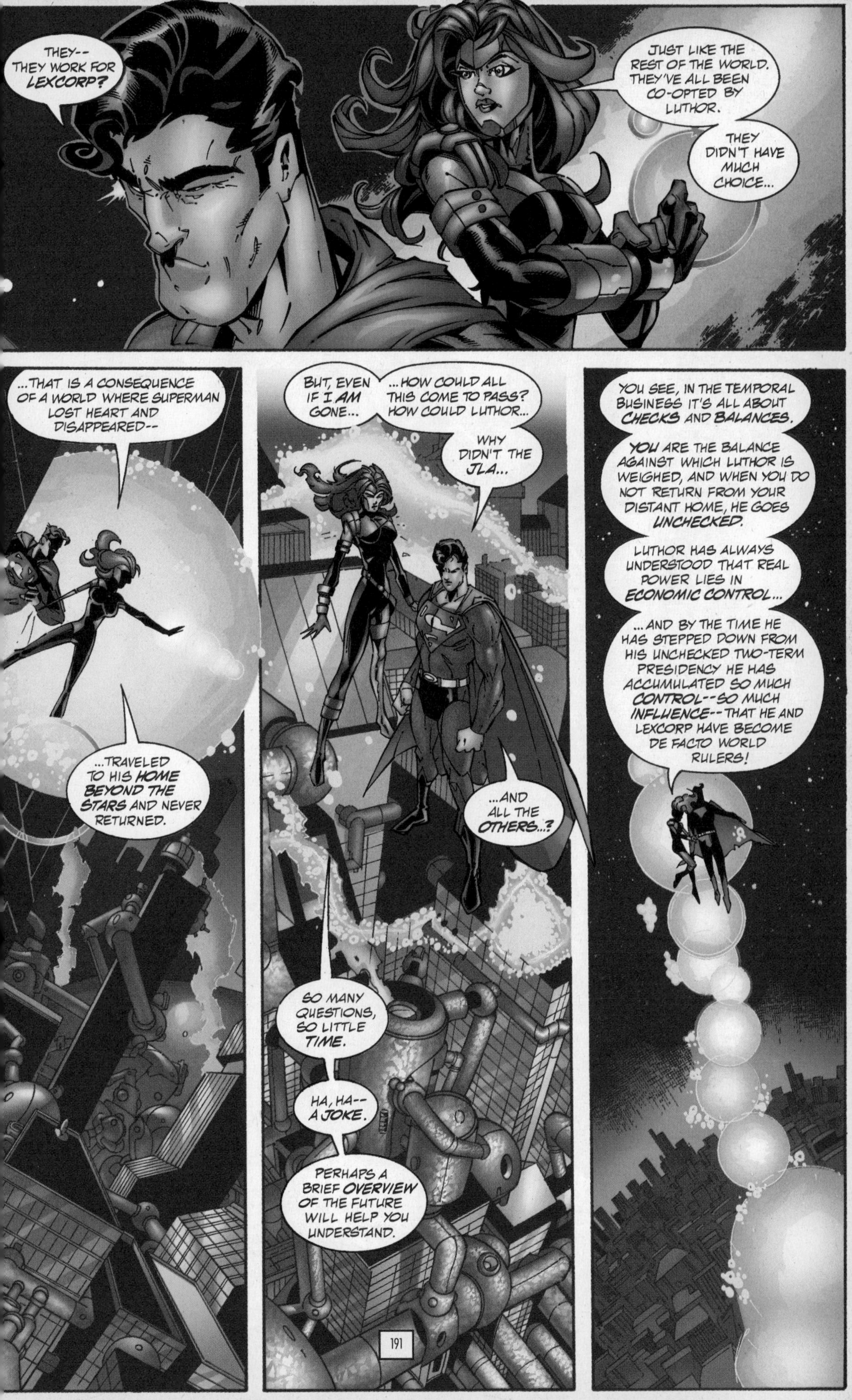
THEY-- THEY WORK FOR LEXCORP?
JUST LIKE THE REST OF THE WORLD. THEY'VE ALL BEEN CO-OPTED BY LUTHOR.
THEY DIDN'T HAVE MUCH CHOICE...
...THAT IS A CONSEQUENCE OF A WORLD WHERE SUPERMAN LOST HEART AND DISAPPEARED--
...TRAVELED TO HIS HOME BEYOND THE STARS AND NEVER RETURNED.
BUT, EVEN IF I AM GONE...
...HOW COULD ALL THIS COME TO PASS? HOW COULD LUTHOR...
WHY DIDN'T THE JLA...
...AND ALL THE OTHERS...?
SO MANY QUESTIONS, SO LITTLE TIME.
HA, HA-- A JOKE.
PERHAPS A BRIEF OVERVIEW OF THE FUTURE WILL HELP YOU UNDERSTAND.
YOU SEE, IN THE TEMPORAL BUSINESS IT'S ALL ABOUT CHECKS AND BALANCES.
YOU ARE THE BALANCE AGAINST WHICH LUTHOR IS WEIGHED, AND WHEN YOU DO NOT RETURN FROM YOUR DISTANT HOME, HE GOES UNCHECKED.
LUTHOR HAS ALWAYS UNDERSTOOD THAT REAL POWER LIES IN ECONOMIC CONTROL...
...AND BY THE TIME HE HAS STEPPED DOWN FROM HIS UNCHECKED TWO-TERM PRESIDENCY HE HAS ACCUMULATED SO MUCH CONTROL--SO MUCH INFLUENCE--THAT HE AND LEXCORP HAVE BECOME DE FACTO WORLD RULERS!

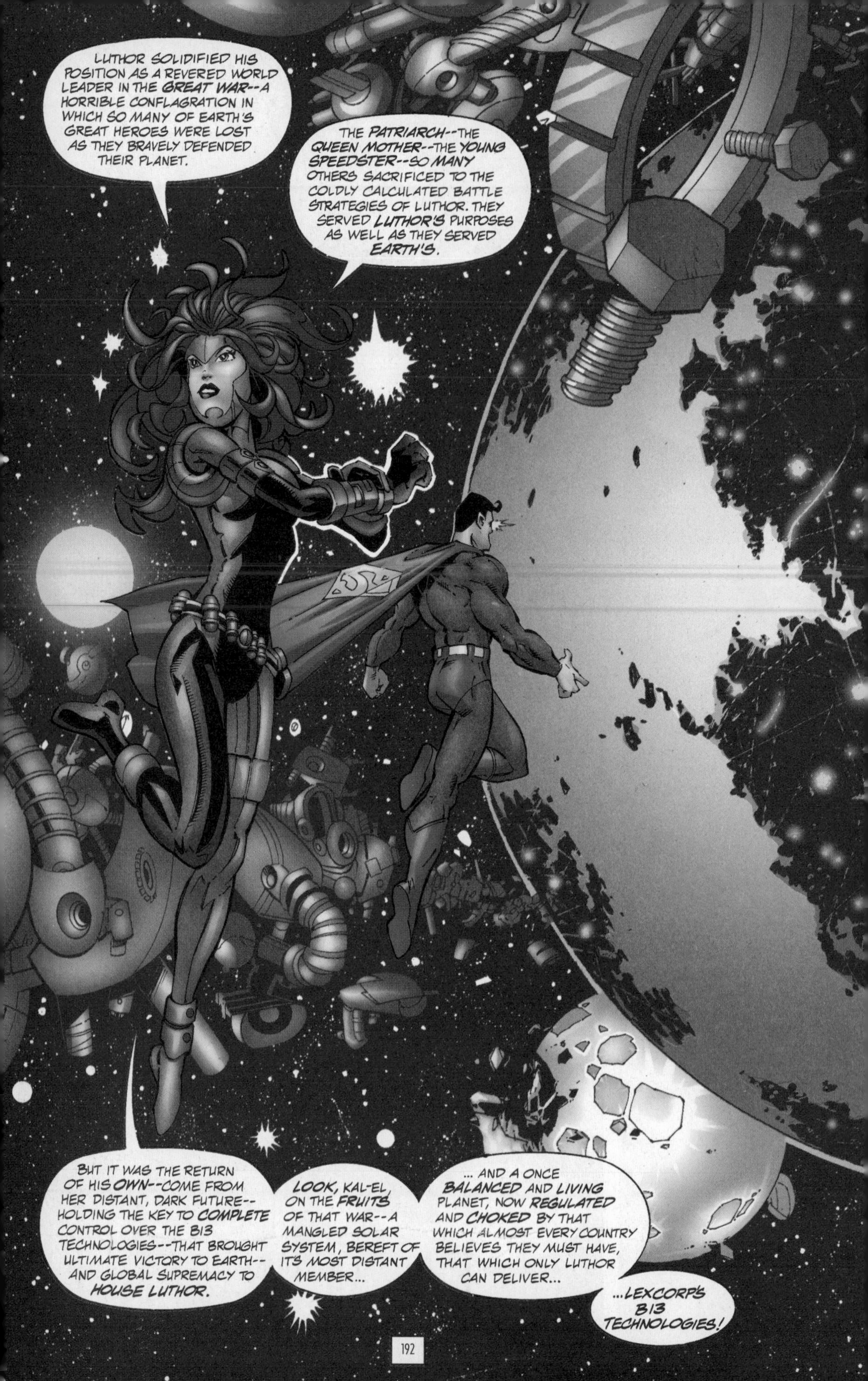
LUTHOR SOLIDIFIED HIS POSITION AS A REVERED WORLD LEADER IN THE GREAT WAR--A HORRIBLE CONFLAGRATION IN WHICH SO MANY OF EARTH'S GREAT HEROES WERE LOST AS THEY BRAVELY DEFENDED THEIR PLANET.
THE PATRIARCH--THE QUEEN MOTHER--THE YOUNG SPEEDSTER--SO MANY OTHERS SACRIFICED TO THE COLDLY CALCULATED BATTLE STRATEGIES OF LUTHOR. THEY SERVED LUTHOR'S PURPOSES AS WELL AS THEY SERVED EARTH'S.
BUT IT WAS THE RETURN OF HIS OWN--COME FROM HER DISTANT, DARK FUTURE--HOLDING THE KEY TO COMPLETE CONTROL OVER THE B13 TECHNOLOGIES--THAT BROUGHT ULTIMATE VICTORY TO EARTH--AND GLOBAL SUPREMACY TO HOUSE LUTHOR.
LOOK, KAL-EL, ON THE FRUITS OF THAT WAR--A MANGLED SOLAR SYSTEM, BEREFT OF IT'S MOST DISTANT MEMBER...
... AND A ONCE BALANCED AND LIVING PLANET, NOW REGULATED AND CHOKED BY THAT WHICH ALMOST EVERY COUNTRY BELIEVES THEY MUST HAVE, THAT WHICH ONLY LUTHOR CAN DELIVER...
...LEXCORP'S B13 TECHNOLOGIES!

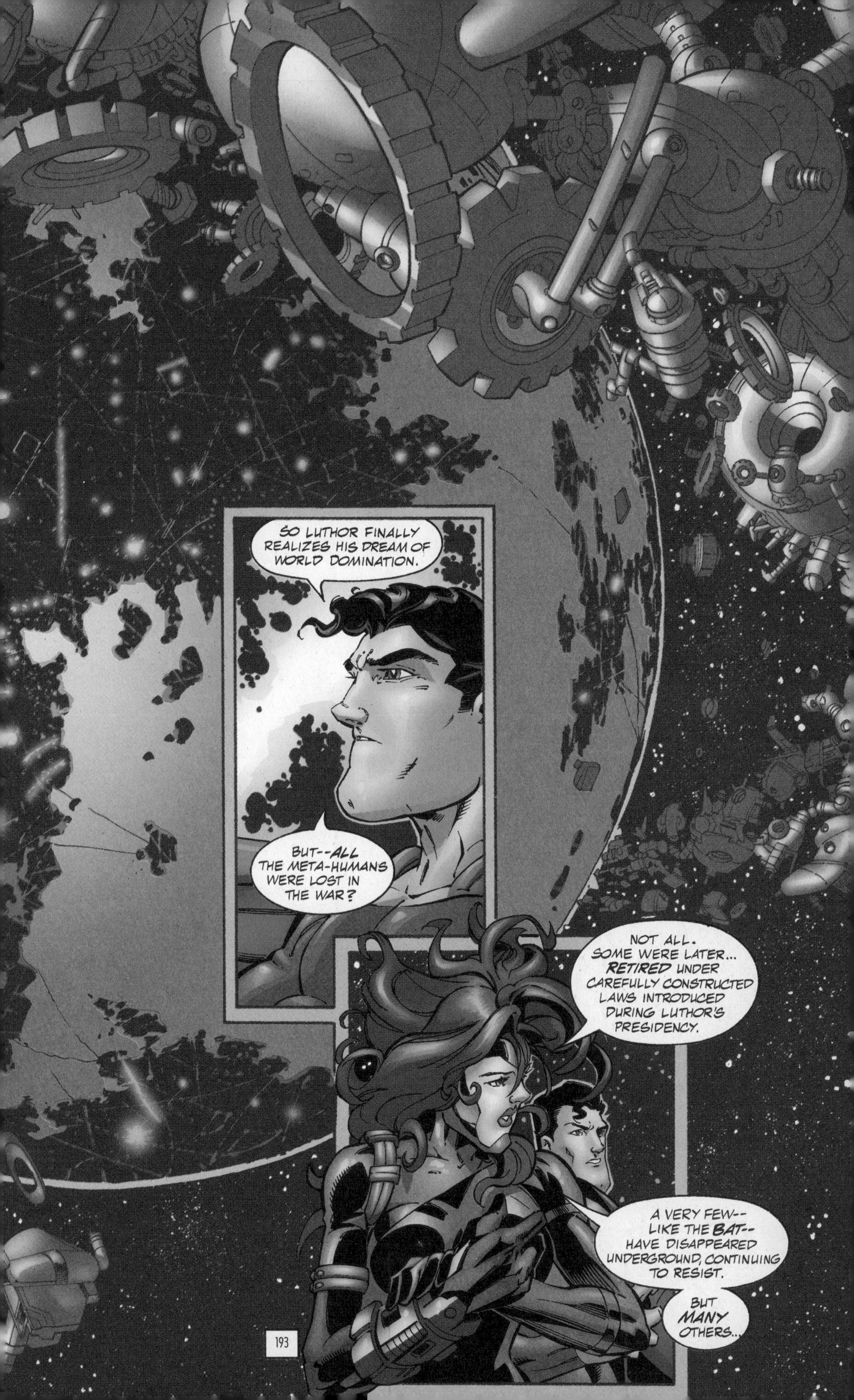
SO LUTHOR FINALLY REALIZES HIS DREAM OF WORLD DOMINATION.
BUT--ALL THE META-HUMANS WERE LOST IN THE WAR?
NOT ALL. SOME WERE LATER... RETIRED UNDER CAREFULLY CONSTRUCTED LAWS INTRODUCED DURING LUTHOR'S PRESIDENCY.
A VERY FEW-- LIKE THE BAT-- HAVE DISAPPEARED UNDERGROUND, CONTINUING TO RESIST.
BUT MANY OTHERS...

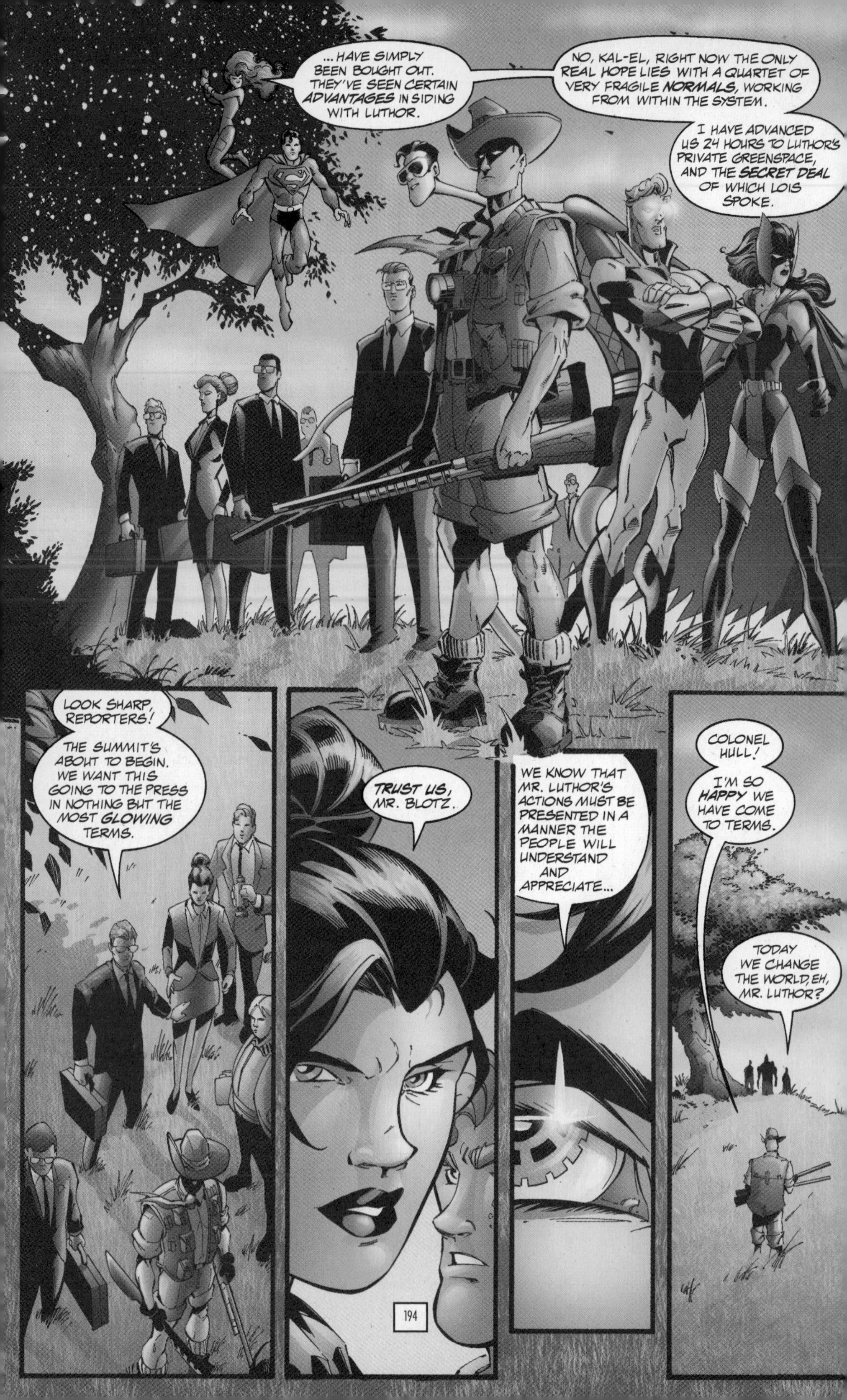
...HAVE SIMPLY BEEN BOUGHT OUT. THEY'VE SEEN CERTAIN ADVANTAGES IN SIDING WITH LUTHOR.
NO, KAL-EL, RIGHT NOW THE ONLY REAL HOPE LIES WITH A QUARTET OF VERY FRAGILE NORMALS, WORKING FROM WITHIN THE SYSTEM.
I HAVE ADVANCED US 24 HOURS TO LUTHOR'S PRIVATE GREENSPACE, AND THE SECRET DEAL OF WHICH LOIS SPOKE.
LOOK SHARP, REPORTERS!
THE SUMMIT'S ABOUT TO BEGIN. WE WANT THIS GOING TO THE PRESS IN NOTHING BUT THE MOST GLOWING TERMS.
TRUST US, MR. BLOTZ.
WE KNOW THAT MR. LUTHOR'S ACTIONS MUST BE PRESENTED IN A MANNER THE PEOPLE WILL UNDERSTAND AND APPRECIATE...
COLONEL HULL!
I'M SO HAPPY WE HAVE COME TO TERMS.
TODAY WE CHANGE THE WORLD, EH, MR. LUTHOR?

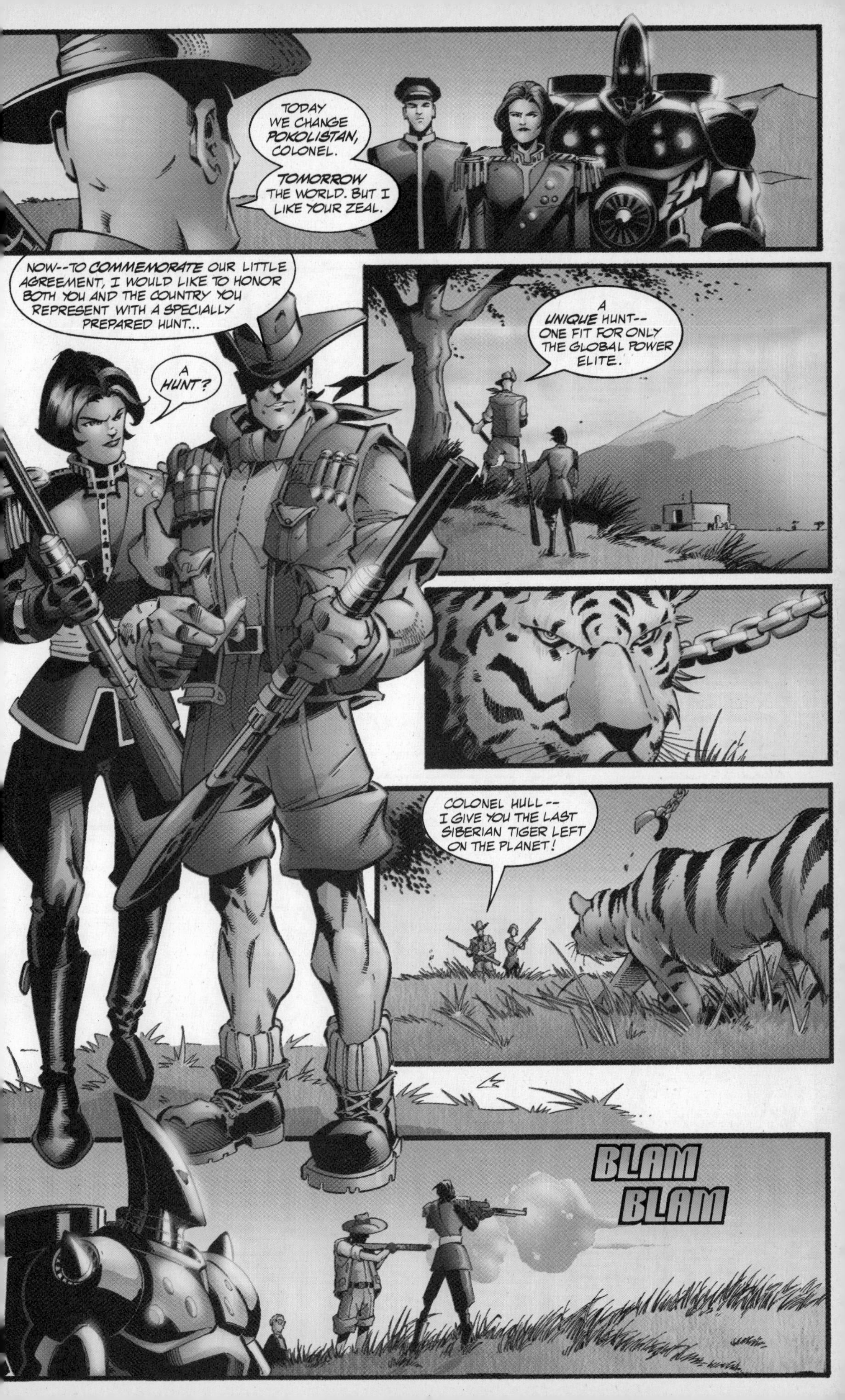
TODAY WE CHANGE POKOLISTAN, COLONEL.
TOMORROW THE WORLD. BUT I LIKE YOUR ZEAL.
NOW--TO COMMEMORATE OUR LITTLE AGREEMENT, I WOULD LIKE TO HONOR BOTH YOU AND THE COUNTRY YOU REPRESENT WITH A SPECIALLY PREPARED HUNT...
A HUNT?
A UNIQUE HUNT-- ONE FIT FOR ONLY THE GLOBAL POWER ELITE.
COLONEL HULL-- I GIVE YOU THE LAST SIBERIAN TIGER LEFT ON THE PLANET!
BLAM
BLAM

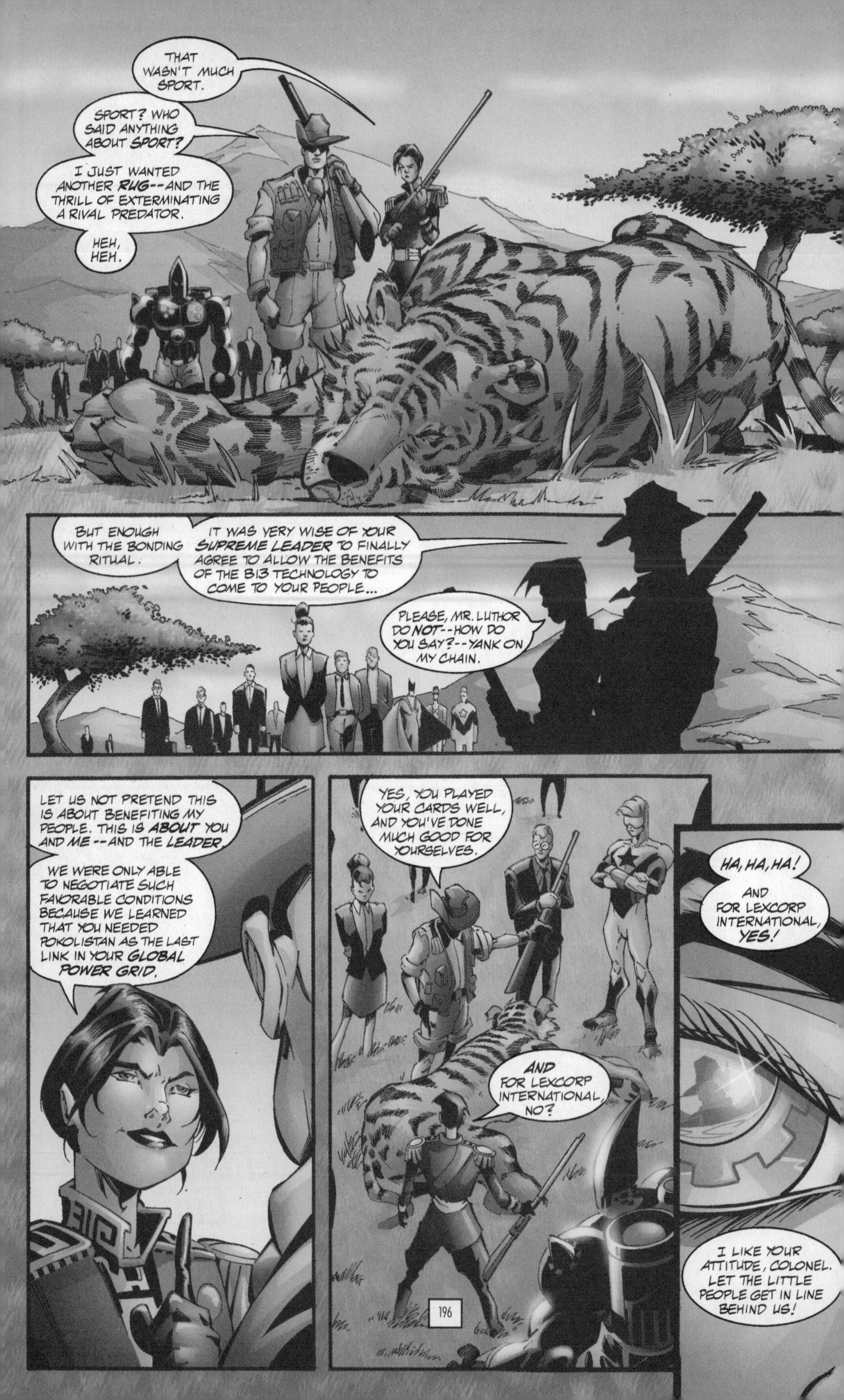
THAT WASN'T MUCH SPORT.
SPORT? WHO SAID ANYTHING ABOUT SPORT?
I JUST WANTED ANOTHER RUG--AND THE THRILL OF EXTERMINATING A RIVAL PREDATOR.
HEH, HEH.
BUT ENOUGH WITH THE BONDING RITUAL.
IT WAS VERY WISE OF YOUR SUPREME LEADER TO FINALLY AGREE TO ALLOW THE BENEFITS OF THE B13 TECHNOLOGY TO COME TO YOUR PEOPLE...
PLEASE, MR. LUTHOR DO NOT--HOW DO YOU SAY?--YANK ON MY CHAIN.
LET US NOT PRETEND THIS IS ABOUT BENEFITING MY PEOPLE. THIS IS ABOUT YOU AND ME--AND THE LEADER.
WE WERE ONLY ABLE TO NEGOTIATE SUCH FAVORABLE CONDITIONS BECAUSE WE LEARNED THAT YOU NEEDED POKOLISTAN AS THE LAST LINK IN YOUR GLOBAL POWER GRID.
YES, YOU PLAYED YOUR CARDS WELL, AND YOU'VE DONE MUCH GOOD FOR YOURSELVES.
AND FOR LEXCORP INTERNATIONAL, NO?
HA, HA, HA!
AND FOR LEXCORP INTERNATIONAL, YES!
I LIKE YOUR ATTITUDE, COLONEL. LET THE LITTLE PEOPLE GET IN LINE BEHIND US!

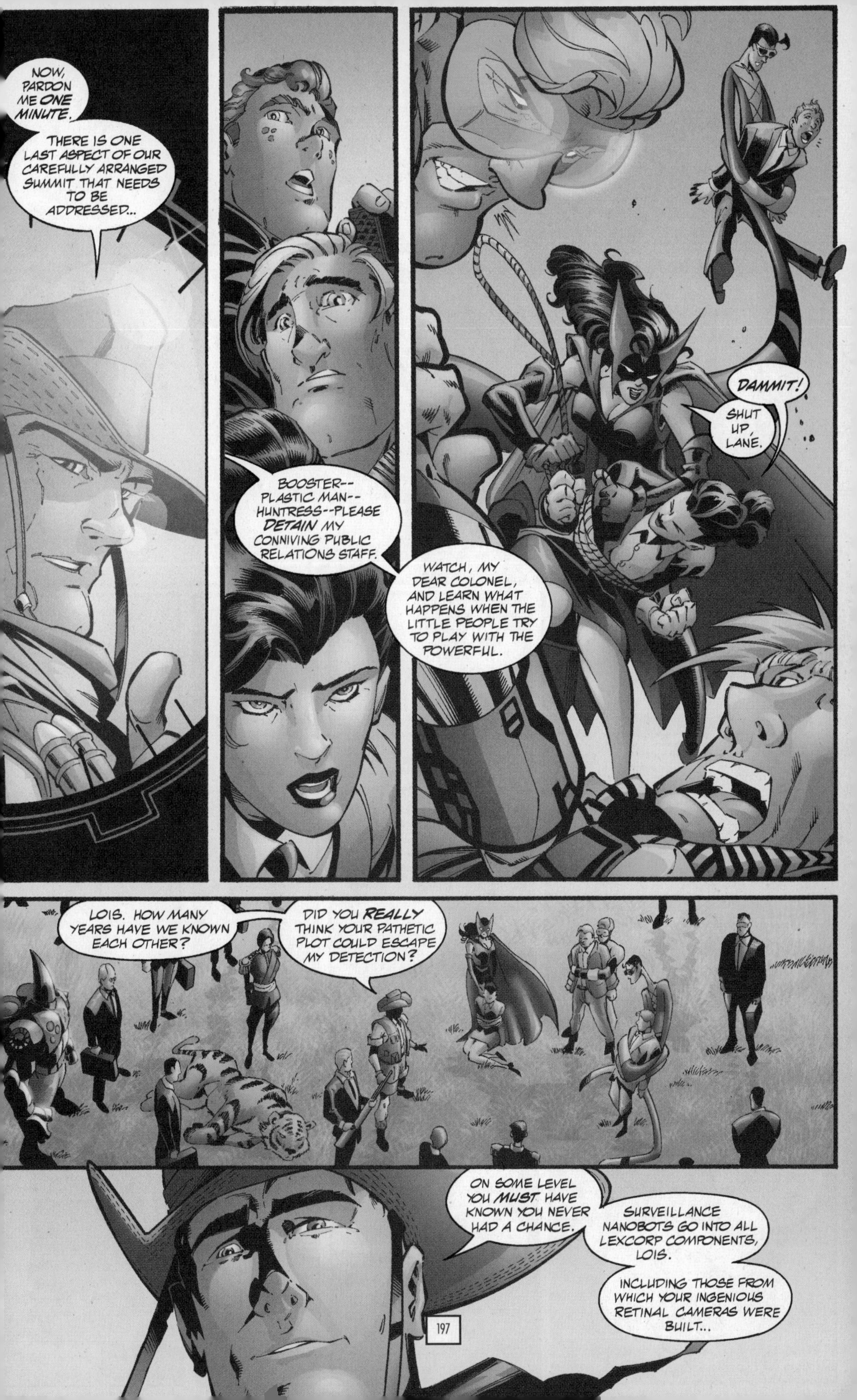
NOW, PARDON ME ONE MINUTE.
THERE IS ONE LAST ASPECT OF OUR CAREFULLY ARRANGED SUMMIT THAT NEEDS TO BE ADDRESSED...
BOOSTER-- PLASTIC MAN-- HUNTRESS--PLEASE DETAIN MY CONNIVING PUBLIC RELATIONS STAFF.
WATCH, MY DEAR COLONEL, AND LEARN WHAT HAPPENS WHEN THE LITTLE PEOPLE TRY TO PLAY WITH THE POWERFUL.
DAMMIT!
SHUT UP, LANE.
LOIS. HOW MANY YEARS HAVE WE KNOWN EACH OTHER?
DID YOU REALLY THINK YOUR PATHETIC PLOT COULD ESCAPE MY DETECTION?
ON SOME LEVEL YOU MUST HAVE KNOWN YOU NEVER HAD A CHANCE.
SURVEILLANCE NANOBOTS GO INTO ALL LEXCORP COMPONENTS, LOIS.
INCLUDING THOSE FROM WHICH YOUR INGENIOUS RETINAL CAMERAS WERE BUILT...

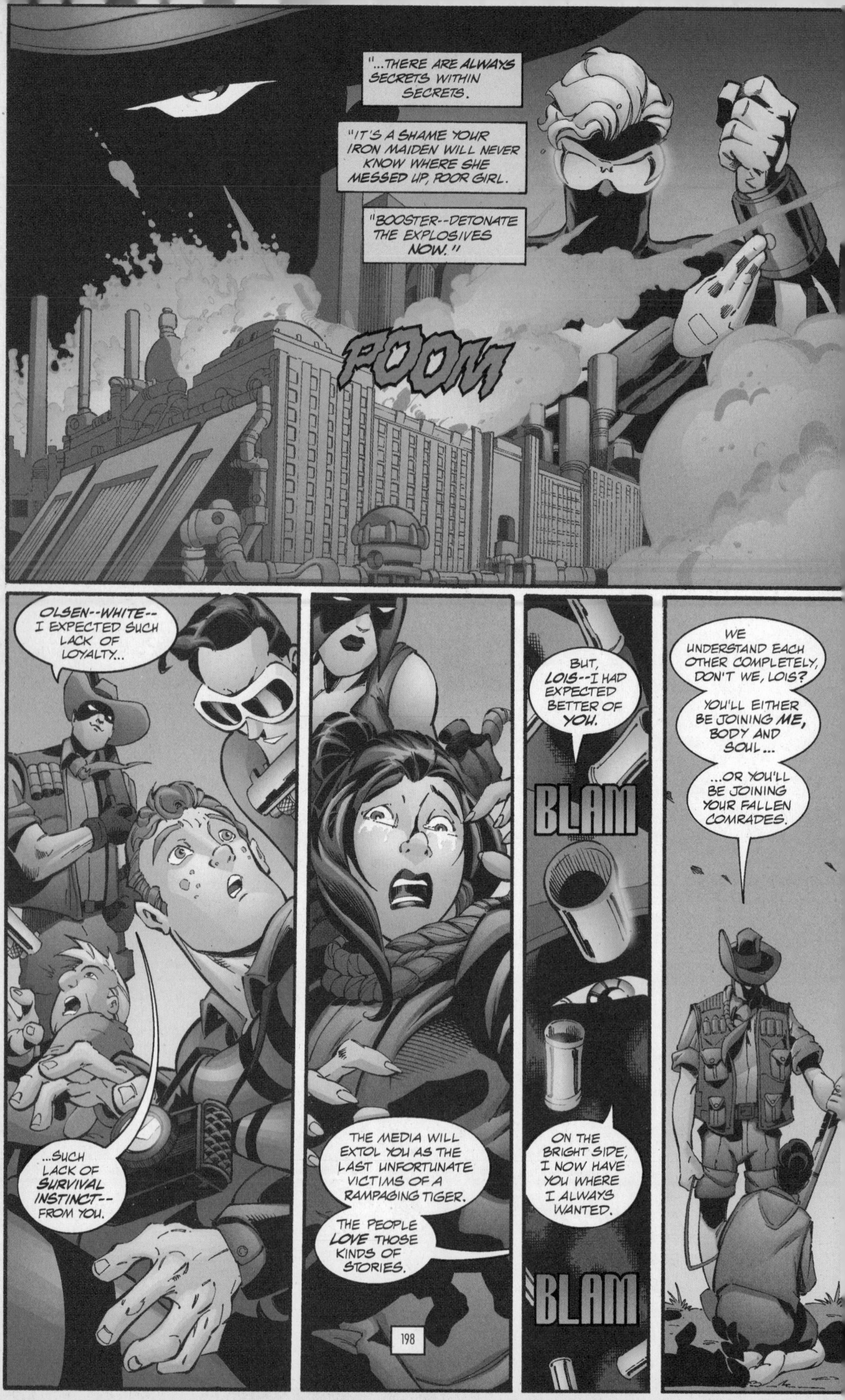
"...THERE ARE ALWAYS SECRETS WITHIN SECRETS.
"IT'S A SHAME YOUR IRON MAIDEN WILL NEVER KNOW WHERE SHE MESSED UP, POOR GIRL.
"BOOSTER--DETONATE THE EXPLOSIVES NOW."
POOM
OLSEN--WHITE--I EXPECTED SUCH LACK OF LOYALTY...
...SUCH LACK OF SURVIVAL INSTINCT--FROM YOU.
THE MEDIA WILL EXTOL YOU AS THE LAST UNFORTUNATE VICTIMS OF A RAMPAGING TIGER.
THE PEOPLE LOVE THOSE KINDS OF STORIES.
BUT, LOIS--I HAD EXPECTED BETTER OF YOU.
BLAM
ON THE BRIGHT SIDE, I NOW HAVE YOU WHERE I ALWAYS WANTED.
BLAM
WE UNDERSTAND EACH OTHER COMPLETELY, DON'T WE, LOIS?
YOU'LL EITHER BE JOINING ME, BODY AND SOUL...
...OR YOU'LL BE JOINING YOUR FALLEN COMRADES.

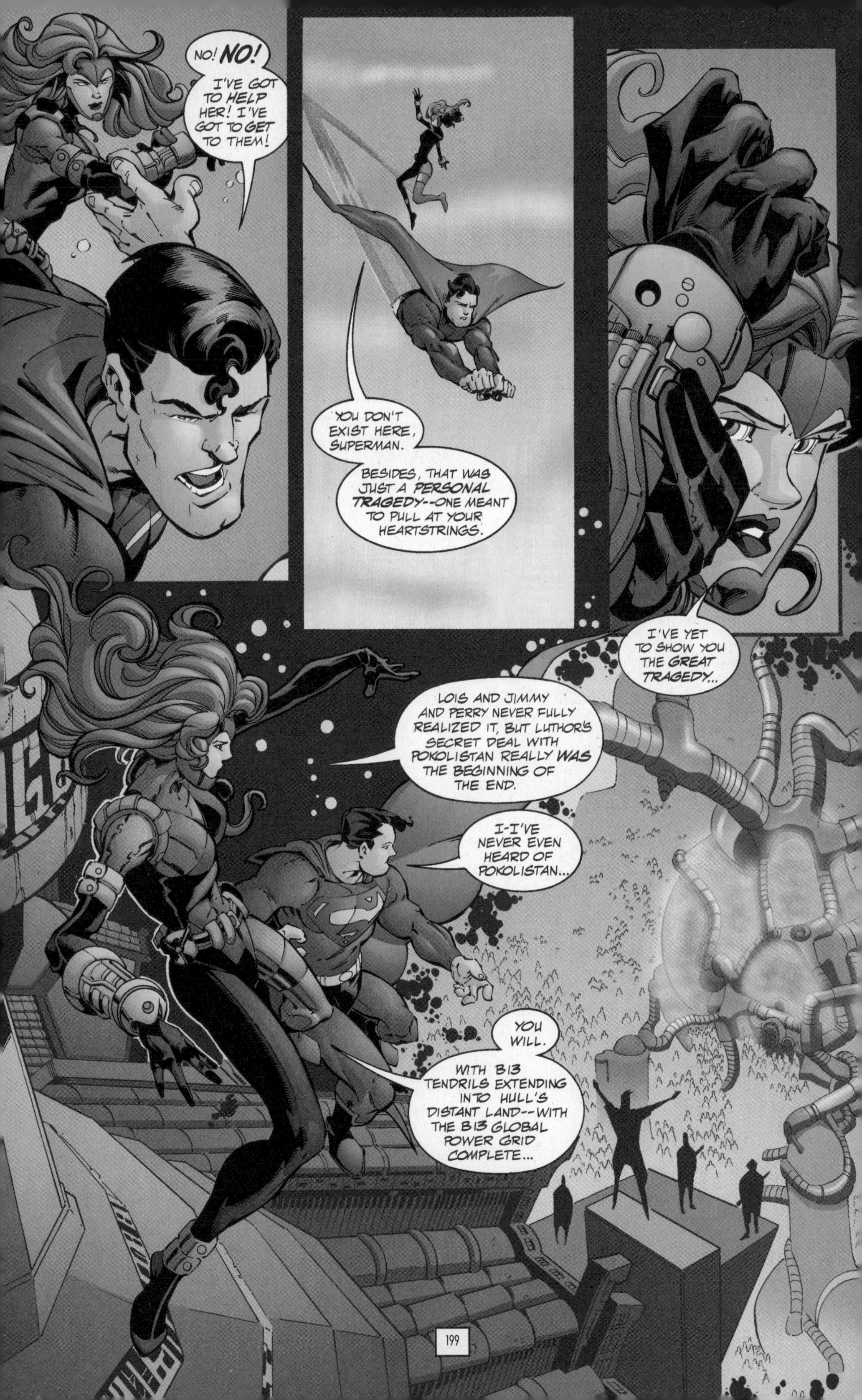
NO! NO!
I'VE GOT TO HELP HER! I'VE GOT TO GET TO THEM!
YOU DON'T EXIST HERE, SUPERMAN.
BESIDES, THAT WAS JUST A PERSONAL TRAGEDY--ONE MEANT TO PULL AT YOUR HEARTSTRINGS.
I'VE YET TO SHOW YOU THE GREAT TRAGEDY...
LOIS AND JIMMY AND PERRY NEVER FULLY REALIZED IT, BUT LUTHOR'S SECRET DEAL WITH POKOLISTAN REALLY WAS THE BEGINNING OF THE END.
I-I'VE NEVER EVEN HEARD OF POKOLISTAN...
YOU WILL.
WITH B13 TENDRILS EXTENDING INTO HULL'S DISTANT LAND--WITH THE B13 GLOBAL POWER GRID COMPLETE...

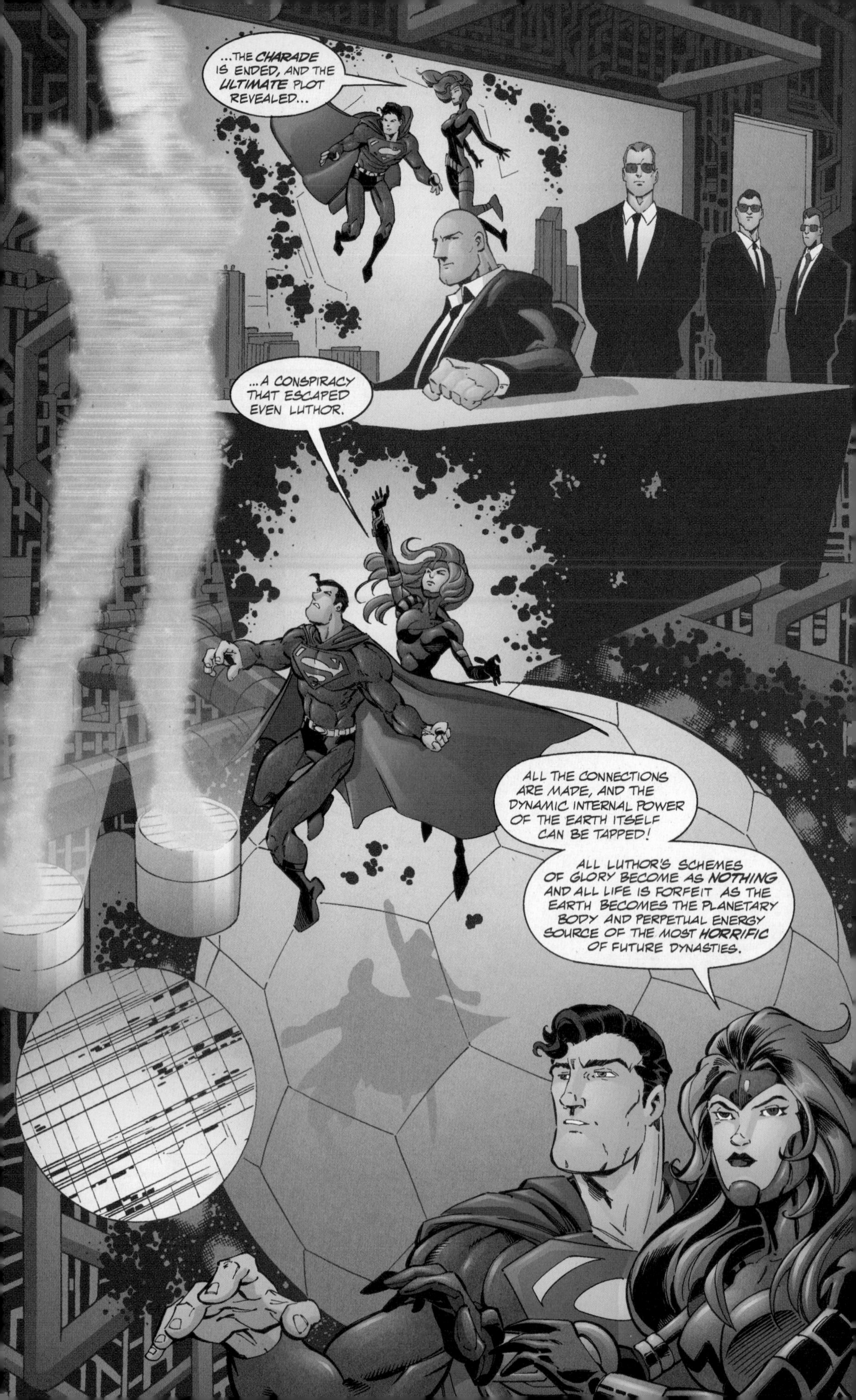
...THE *CHARADE* IS ENDED, AND THE *ULTIMATE* PLOT REVEALED...
...A CONSPIRACY THAT ESCAPED EVEN LUTHOR.
ALL THE CONNECTIONS ARE MADE, AND THE DYNAMIC INTERNAL POWER OF THE EARTH ITSELF CAN BE TAPPED!
ALL LUTHOR'S SCHEMES OF GLORY BECOME AS *NOTHING* AND ALL LIFE IS FORFEIT AS THE EARTH BECOMES THE PLANETARY BODY AND PERPETUAL ENERGY SOURCE OF THE MOST *HORRIFIC* OF FUTURE DYNASTIES.

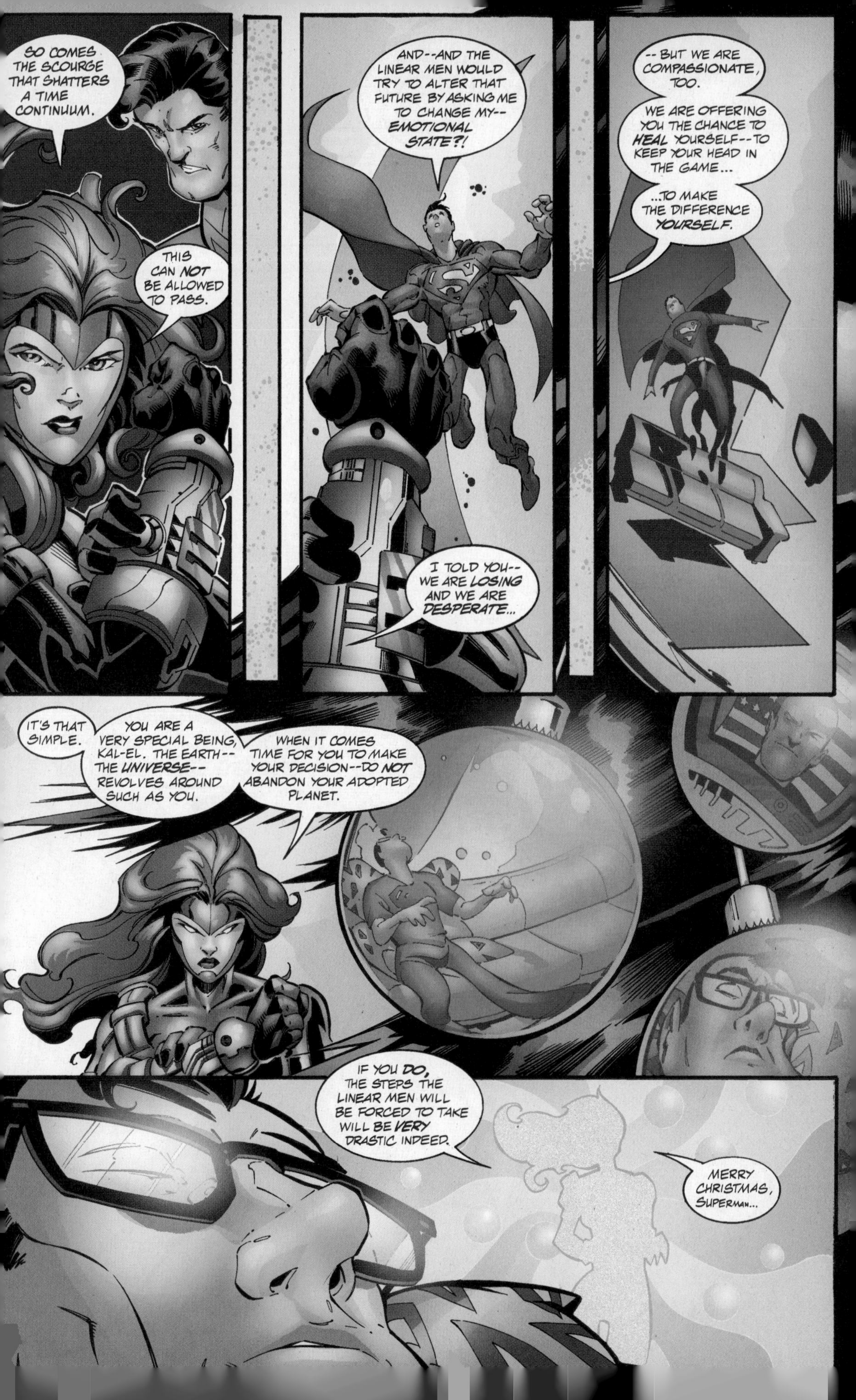
SO COMES THE SCOURGE THAT SHATTERS A TIME CONTINUUM.
THIS CAN *NOT* BE ALLOWED TO PASS.
AND--AND THE LINEAR MEN WOULD TRY TO ALTER THAT FUTURE BY ASKING ME TO CHANGE MY-- *EMOTIONAL STATE?!*
I TOLD YOU-- WE ARE *LOSING* AND WE ARE *DESPERATE*...
-- BUT WE ARE COMPASSIONATE, TOO.
WE ARE OFFERING YOU THE CHANCE TO *HEAL* YOURSELF--TO KEEP YOUR HEAD IN THE GAME...
...TO MAKE THE DIFFERENCE *YOURSELF*.
IT'S THAT SIMPLE.
YOU ARE A VERY SPECIAL BEING, KAL-EL. THE EARTH-- THE *UNIVERSE*-- REVOLVES AROUND SUCH AS YOU.
WHEN IT COMES TIME FOR YOU TO MAKE YOUR DECISION--DO *NOT* ABANDON YOUR ADOPTED PLANET.
IF YOU *DO*, THE STEPS THE LINEAR MEN WILL BE FORCED TO TAKE WILL BE *VERY* DRASTIC INDEED.
MERRY CHRISTMAS, SUPERMAN...

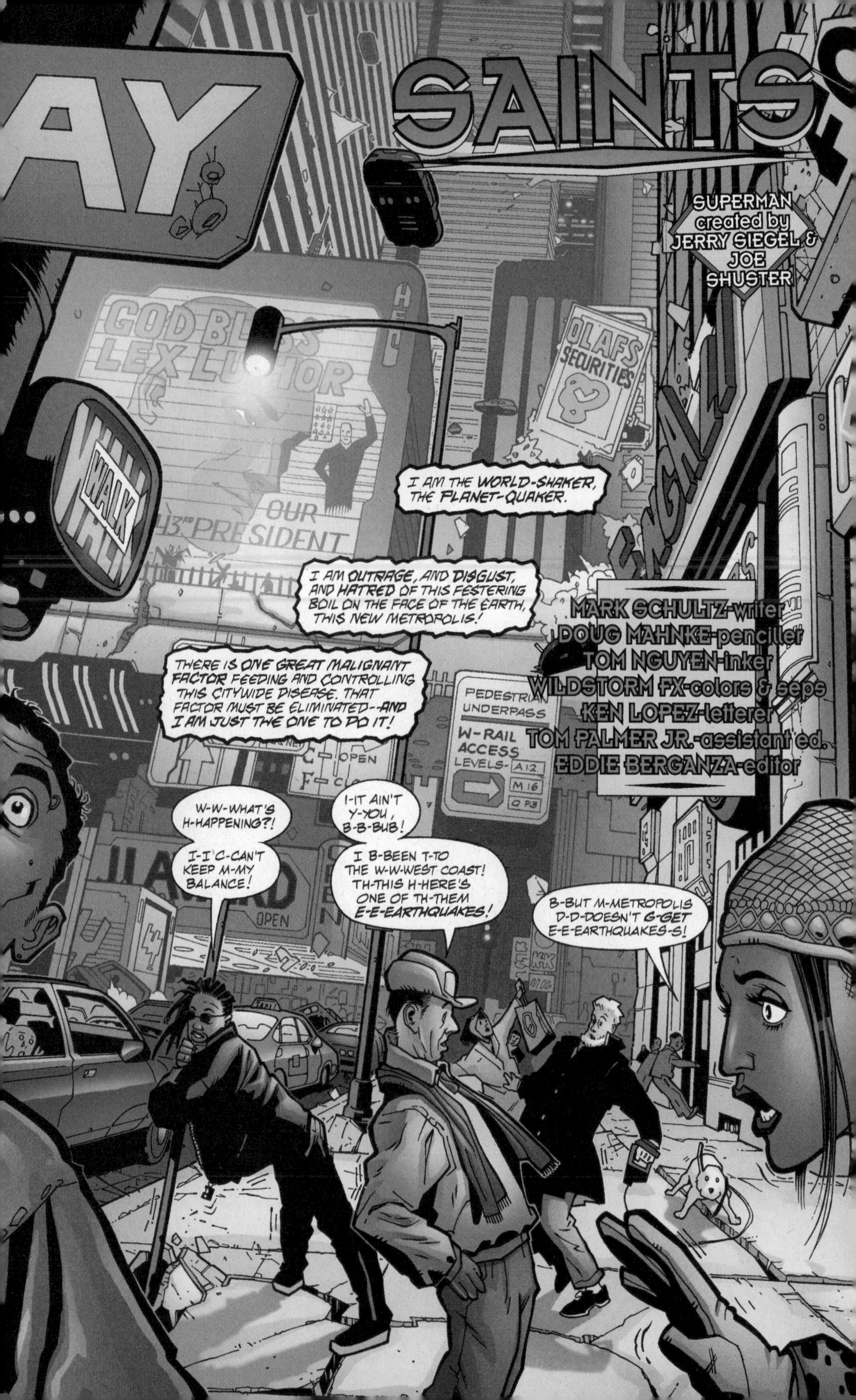
SAINTS
SUPERMAN created by JERRY SIEGEL & JOE SHUSTER
GOD BLESS LEX LUTHOR
OUR 43RD PRESIDENT
WALK
OLAFS SECURITIES
I AM THE WORLD-SHAKER, THE PLANET-QUAKER.
I AM OUTRAGE, AND DISGUST, AND HATRED OF THIS FESTERING BOIL ON THE FACE OF THE EARTH, THIS NEW METROPOLIS!
THERE IS ONE GREAT MALIGNANT FACTOR FEEDING AND CONTROLLING THIS CITYWIDE DISEASE. THAT FACTOR MUST BE ELIMINATED--AND I AM JUST THE ONE TO DO IT!
MARK SCHULTZ-writer
DOUG MAHNKE-penciller
TOM NGUYEN-inker
WILDSTORM FX-colors & seps
KEN LOPEZ-letterer
TOM PALMER JR.-assistant ed.
EDDIE BERGANZA-editor
PEDESTRIAN UNDERPASS
W-RAIL ACCESS LEVELS- A12 M16 Q P3
OPEN
W-W-WHAT'S H-HAPPENING?!
I-I C-CAN'T KEEP M-MY BALANCE!
I-IT AIN'T Y-YOU, B-B-BUB!
I B-BEEN T-TO THE W-W-WEST COAST! TH-THIS H-HERE'S ONE OF TH-THEM E-E-EARTHQUAKES!
B-BUT M-METROPOLIS D-D-DOESN'T G-GET E-E-EARTHQUAKES-S!

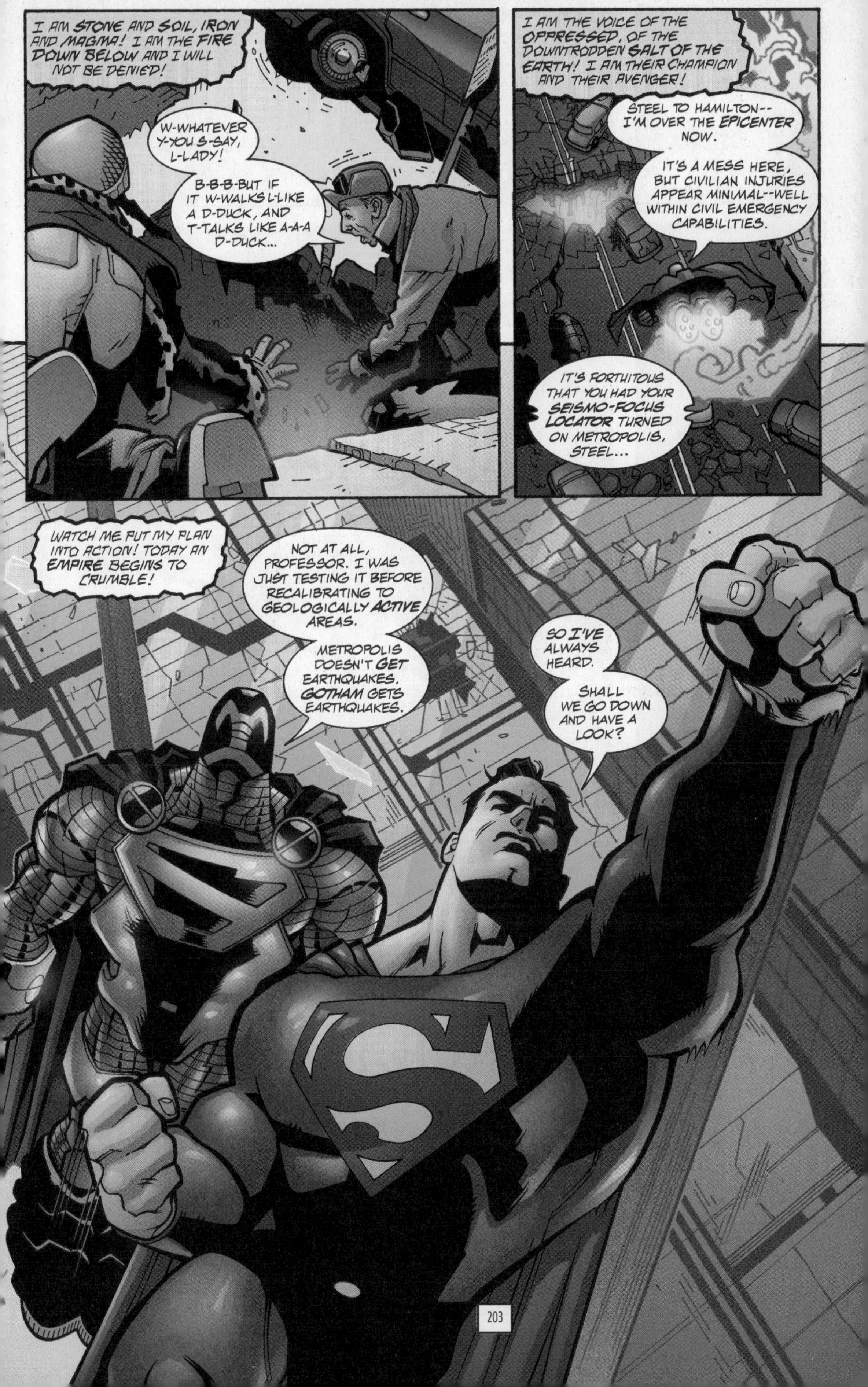
I AM STONE AND SOIL, IRON AND MAGMA! I AM THE FIRE DOWN BELOW AND I WILL NOT BE DENIED!
W-WHATEVER Y-YOU S-SAY, L-LADY!
B-B-B-BUT IF IT W-WALKS L-LIKE A D-DUCK, AND T-TALKS LIKE A-A-A D-DUCK...
I AM THE VOICE OF THE OPPRESSED, OF THE DOWNTRODDEN SALT OF THE EARTH! I AM THEIR CHAMPION AND THEIR AVENGER!
STEEL TO HAMILTON-- I'M OVER THE EPICENTER NOW.
IT'S A MESS HERE, BUT CIVILIAN INJURIES APPEAR MINIMAL--WELL WITHIN CIVIL EMERGENCY CAPABILITIES.
IT'S FORTUITOUS THAT YOU HAD YOUR SEISMO-FOCUS LOCATOR TURNED ON METROPOLIS, STEEL...
WATCH ME PUT MY PLAN INTO ACTION! TODAY AN EMPIRE BEGINS TO CRUMBLE!
NOT AT ALL, PROFESSOR. I WAS JUST TESTING IT BEFORE RECALIBRATING TO GEOLOGICALLY ACTIVE AREAS.
METROPOLIS DOESN'T GET EARTHQUAKES. GOTHAM GETS EARTHQUAKES.
SO I'VE ALWAYS HEARD.
SHALL WE GO DOWN AND HAVE A LOOK?

AFTER *YOU.*

THE *HYPOCENTER--* THE ORIGINATING POINT OF THE QUAKE--SHOULD BE ABOUT 200 METERS STRAIGHT DOWN.

NOT ANYMORE, *STEEL!* BELIEVE IT OR NOT, THE HYPOCENTER FOCUS SEEMS TO BE SHIFTING...

WOW. THE B13 SPIDERBOTS ARE GOING TO HAVE THEIR PALPS FULL REPAIRING ALL THIS.

...APPEARS TO BE MOVING SOUTH-SOUTHWEST AT A STEADY PACE OF 20 KILOMETERS PER HOUR...

ROGER THAT, PROF. I THINK WE'VE PICKED UP ITS TRAIL.

LOOK! THE QUAKE'S ABOUT TO RUPTURE A PRIMARY B13 POWER RELAY!

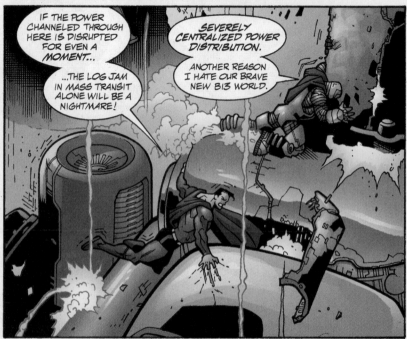

IF THE POWER CHANNELED THROUGH HERE IS DISRUPTED FOR EVEN A *MOMENT...*

...THE LOG JAM IN MASS TRANSIT ALONE WILL BE A NIGHTMARE!

SEVERELY CENTRALIZED POWER DISTRIBUTION.

ANOTHER REASON I HATE OUR BRAVE NEW B13 WORLD.

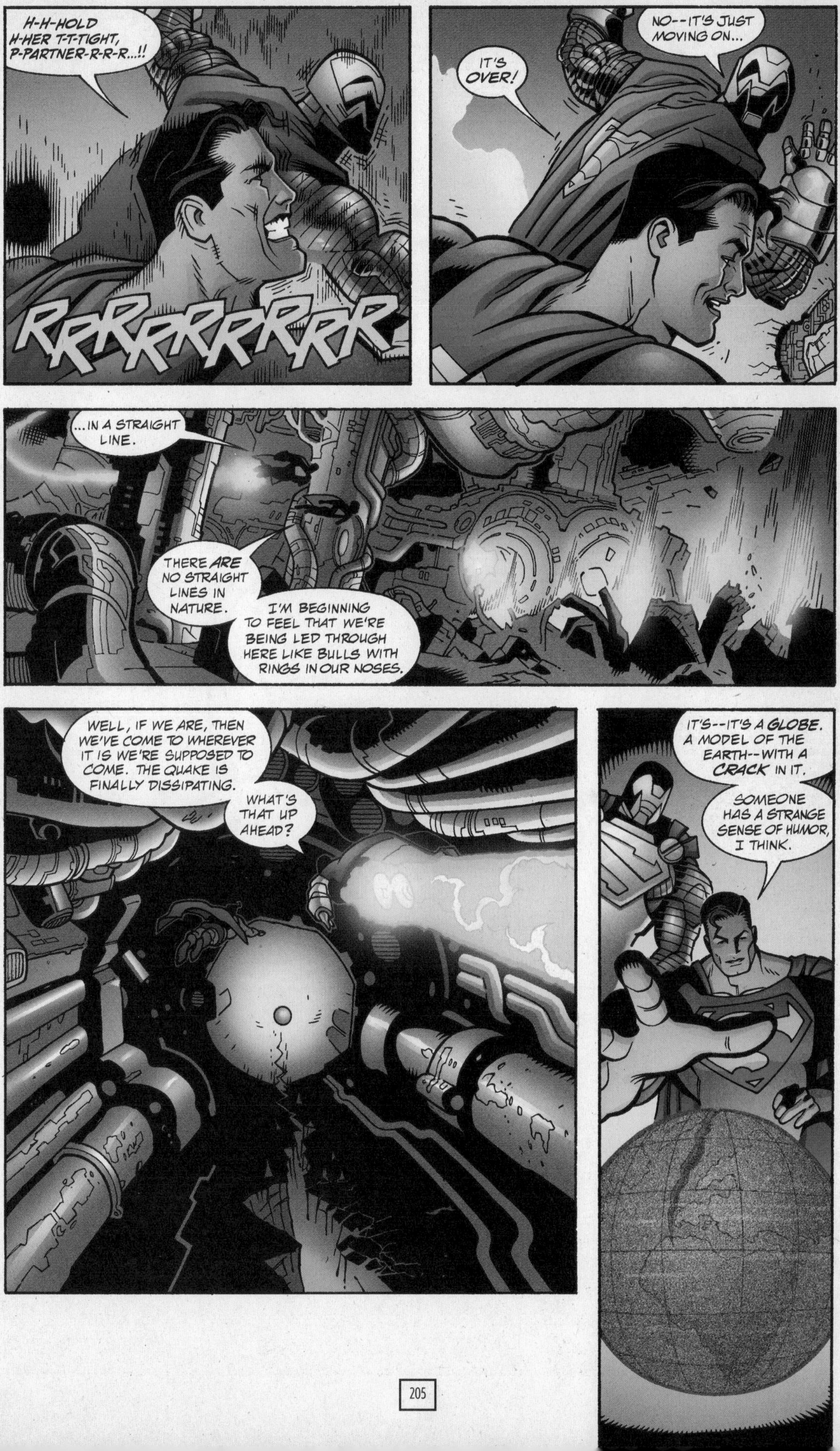
H-H-HOLD H-HER T-T-TIGHT, P-PARTNER-R-R-R...!!
RRRRRRRRRR
IT'S OVER!
NO--IT'S JUST MOVING ON...
...IN A STRAIGHT LINE.
THERE ARE NO STRAIGHT LINES IN NATURE.
I'M BEGINNING TO FEEL THAT WE'RE BEING LED THROUGH HERE LIKE BULLS WITH RINGS IN OUR NOSES.
WELL, IF WE ARE, THEN WE'VE COME TO WHEREVER IT IS WE'RE SUPPOSED TO COME. THE QUAKE IS FINALLY DISSIPATING.
WHAT'S THAT UP AHEAD?
IT'S--IT'S A GLOBE. A MODEL OF THE EARTH--WITH A CRACK IN IT.
SOMEONE HAS A STRANGE SENSE OF HUMOR, I THINK.

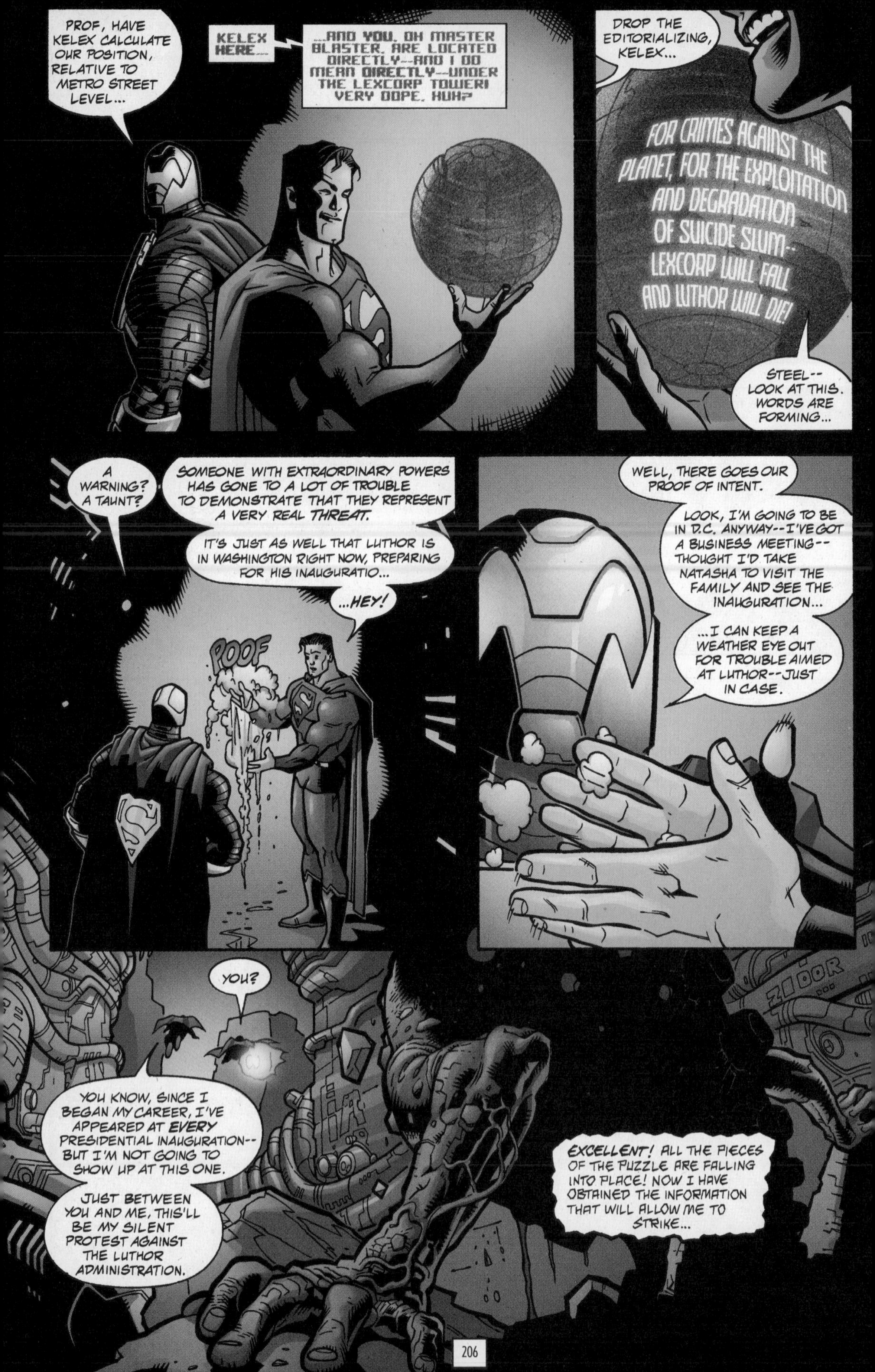
PROF, HAVE KELEX CALCULATE OUR POSITION, RELATIVE TO METRO STREET LEVEL...
KELEX HERE...
...AND YOU, OH MASTER BLASTER, ARE LOCATED DIRECTLY--AND I DO MEAN DIRECTLY--UNDER THE LEXCORP TOWER! VERY DOPE, HUH?
DROP THE EDITORIALIZING, KELEX...
FOR CRIMES AGAINST THE PLANET, FOR THE EXPLOITATION AND DEGRADATION OF SUICIDE SLUM-- LEXCORP WILL FALL AND LUTHOR WILL DIE!
STEEL-- LOOK AT THIS. WORDS ARE FORMING...
A WARNING? A TAUNT?
SOMEONE WITH EXTRAORDINARY POWERS HAS GONE TO A LOT OF TROUBLE TO DEMONSTRATE THAT THEY REPRESENT A VERY REAL THREAT.
IT'S JUST AS WELL THAT LUTHOR IS IN WASHINGTON RIGHT NOW, PREPARING FOR HIS INAUGURATIO...
...HEY!
POOF
WELL, THERE GOES OUR PROOF OF INTENT.
LOOK, I'M GOING TO BE IN D.C. ANYWAY--I'VE GOT A BUSINESS MEETING--THOUGHT I'D TAKE NATASHA TO VISIT THE FAMILY AND SEE THE INAUGURATION...
...I CAN KEEP A WEATHER EYE OUT FOR TROUBLE AIMED AT LUTHOR--JUST IN CASE.
YOU?
YOU KNOW, SINCE I BEGAN MY CAREER, I'VE APPEARED AT EVERY PRESIDENTIAL INAUGURATION--BUT I'M NOT GOING TO SHOW UP AT THIS ONE.
JUST BETWEEN YOU AND ME, THIS'LL BE MY SILENT PROTEST AGAINST THE LUTHOR ADMINISTRATION.
EXCELLENT! ALL THE PIECES OF THE PUZZLE ARE FALLING INTO PLACE! NOW I HAVE OBTAINED THE INFORMATION THAT WILL ALLOW ME TO STRIKE...

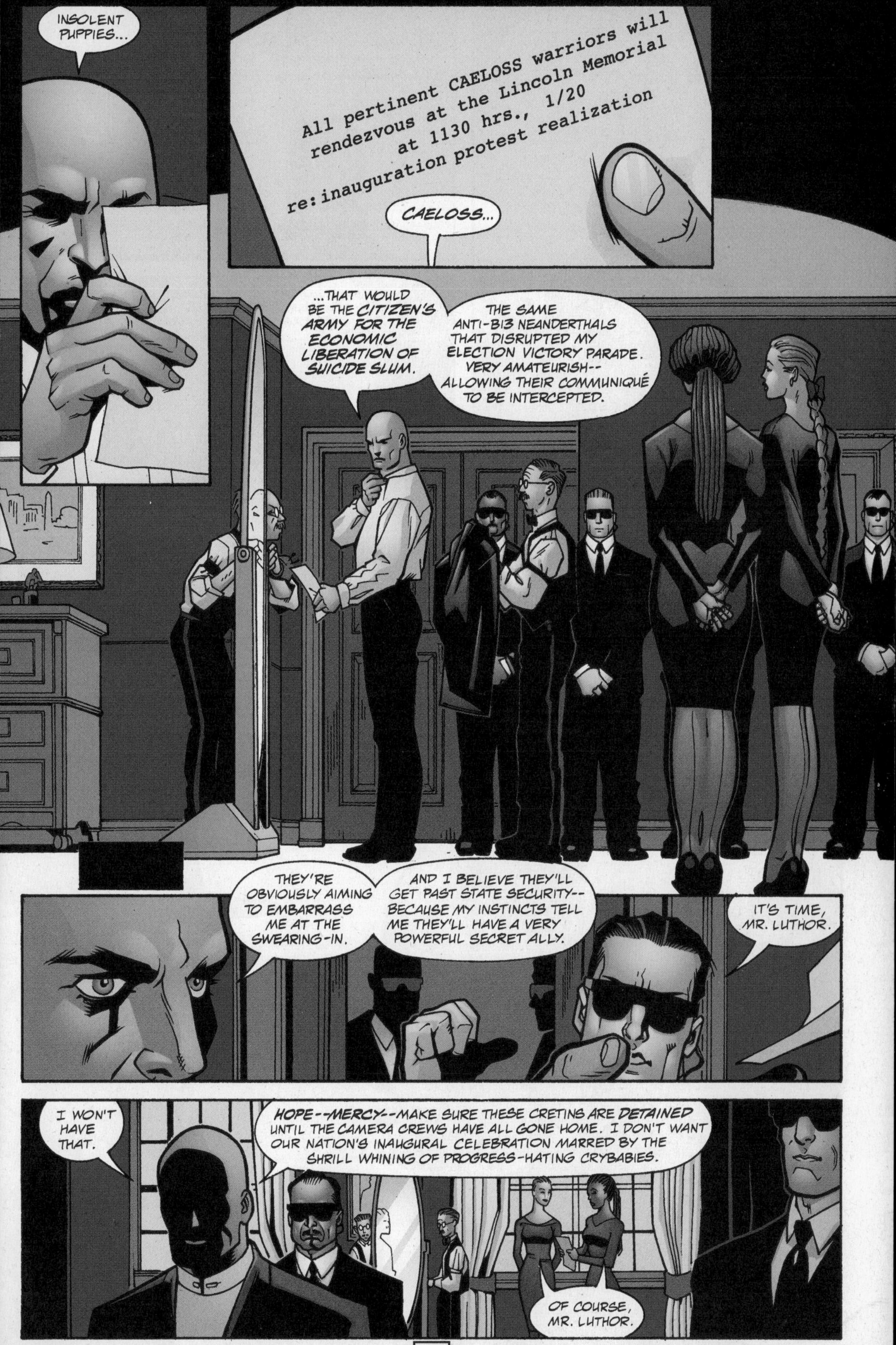
INSOLENT PUPPIES...
All pertinent CAELOSS warriors will rendezvous at the Lincoln Memorial at 1130 hrs., 1/20
re:inauguration protest realization
CAELOSS...
...THAT WOULD BE THE CITIZEN'S ARMY FOR THE ECONOMIC LIBERATION OF SUICIDE SLUM.
THE SAME ANTI-B13 NEANDERTHALS THAT DISRUPTED MY ELECTION VICTORY PARADE. VERY AMATEURISH-- ALLOWING THEIR COMMUNIQUÉ TO BE INTERCEPTED.
THEY'RE OBVIOUSLY AIMING TO EMBARRASS ME AT THE SWEARING-IN.
AND I BELIEVE THEY'LL GET PAST STATE SECURITY-- BECAUSE MY INSTINCTS TELL ME THEY'LL HAVE A VERY POWERFUL SECRET ALLY.
IT'S TIME, MR. LUTHOR.
I WON'T HAVE THAT.
HOPE--MERCY--MAKE SURE THESE CRETINS ARE DETAINED UNTIL THE CAMERA CREWS HAVE ALL GONE HOME. I DON'T WANT OUR NATION'S INAUGURAL CELEBRATION MARRED BY THE SHRILL WHINING OF PROGRESS-HATING CRYBABIES.
OF COURSE, MR. LUTHOR.

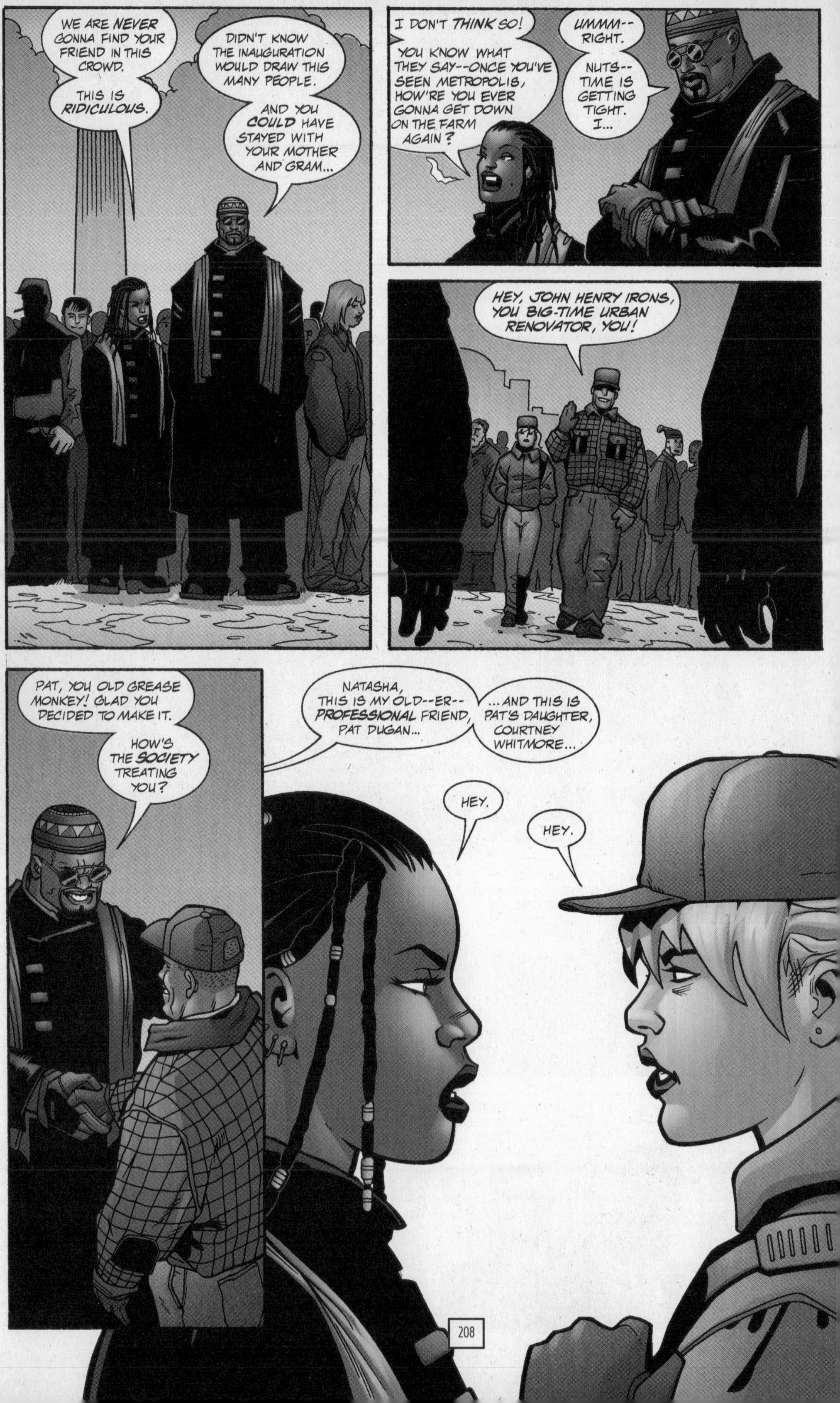
WE ARE NEVER GONNA FIND YOUR FRIEND IN THIS CROWD.
THIS IS RIDICULOUS.
DIDN'T KNOW THE INAUGURATION WOULD DRAW THIS MANY PEOPLE.
AND YOU COULD HAVE STAYED WITH YOUR MOTHER AND GRAM...
I DON'T THINK SO!
YOU KNOW WHAT THEY SAY--ONCE YOU'VE SEEN METROPOLIS, HOW'RE YOU EVER GONNA GET DOWN ON THE FARM AGAIN?
UMMM--RIGHT.
NUTS--TIME IS GETTING TIGHT. I...
HEY, JOHN HENRY IRONS, YOU BIG-TIME URBAN RENOVATOR, YOU!
PAT, YOU OLD GREASE MONKEY! GLAD YOU DECIDED TO MAKE IT.
HOW'S THE SOCIETY TREATING YOU?
NATASHA, THIS IS MY OLD--ER--PROFESSIONAL FRIEND, PAT DUGAN...
...AND THIS IS PAT'S DAUGHTER, COURTNEY WHITMORE...
HEY.
HEY.

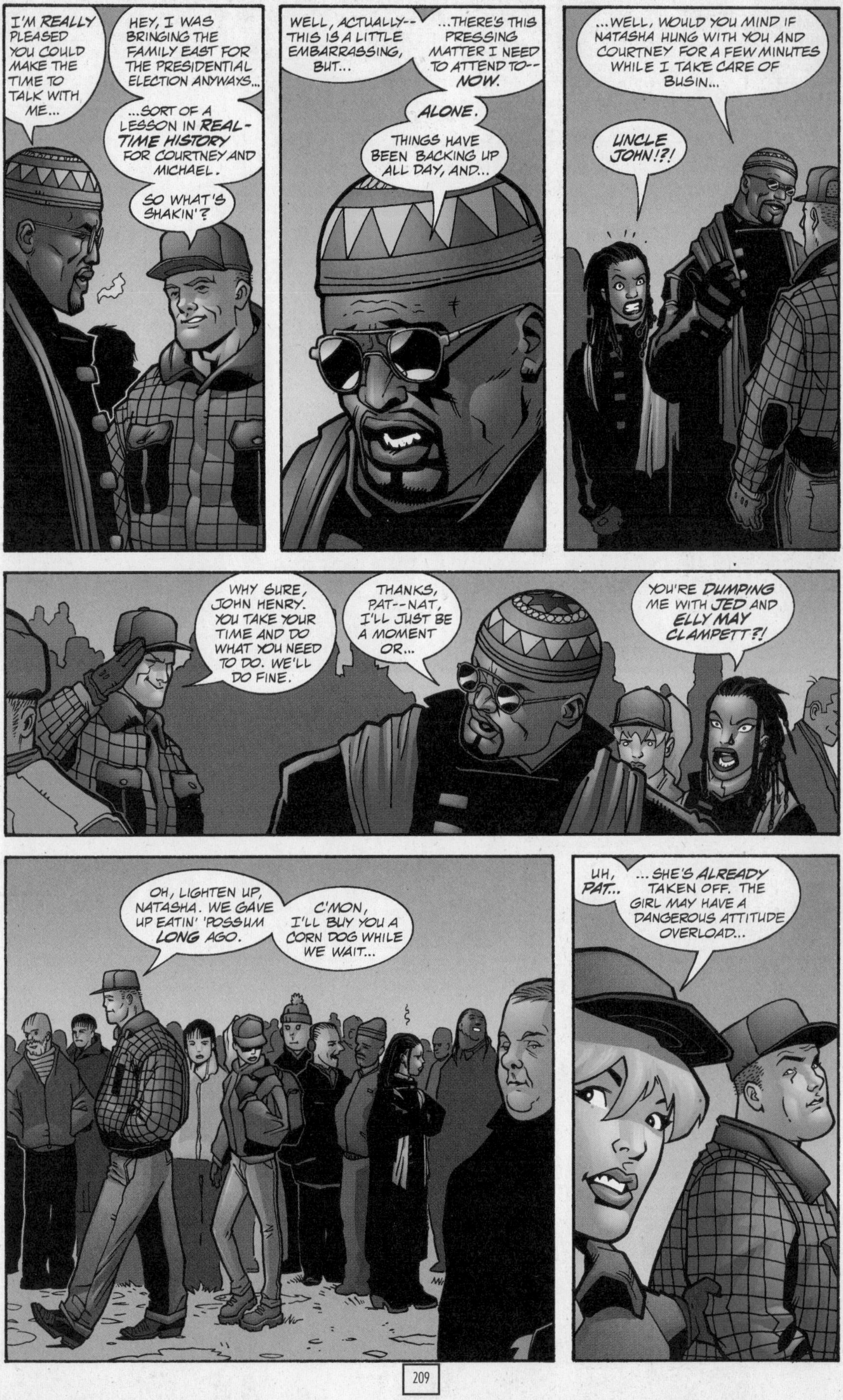
I'M REALLY PLEASED YOU COULD MAKE THE TIME TO TALK WITH ME...
HEY, I WAS BRINGING THE FAMILY EAST FOR THE PRESIDENTIAL ELECTION ANYWAYS...
...SORT OF A LESSON IN REAL-TIME HISTORY FOR COURTNEY AND MICHAEL.
SO WHAT'S SHAKIN'?
WELL, ACTUALLY-- THIS IS A LITTLE EMBARRASSING, BUT...
...THERE'S THIS PRESSING MATTER I NEED TO ATTEND TO-- NOW.
ALONE.
THINGS HAVE BEEN BACKING UP ALL DAY, AND...
...WELL, WOULD YOU MIND IF NATASHA HUNG WITH YOU AND COURTNEY FOR A FEW MINUTES WHILE I TAKE CARE OF BUSIN...
UNCLE JOHN!?!
WHY SURE, JOHN HENRY. YOU TAKE YOUR TIME AND DO WHAT YOU NEED TO DO. WE'LL DO FINE.
THANKS, PAT--NAT, I'LL JUST BE A MOMENT OR...
YOU'RE DUMPING ME WITH JED AND ELLY MAY CLAMPETT?!
OH, LIGHTEN UP, NATASHA. WE GAVE UP EATIN' 'POSSUM LONG AGO.
C'MON, I'LL BUY YOU A CORN DOG WHILE WE WAIT...
UH, PAT...
...SHE'S ALREADY TAKEN OFF. THE GIRL MAY HAVE A DANGEROUS ATTITUDE OVERLOAD...

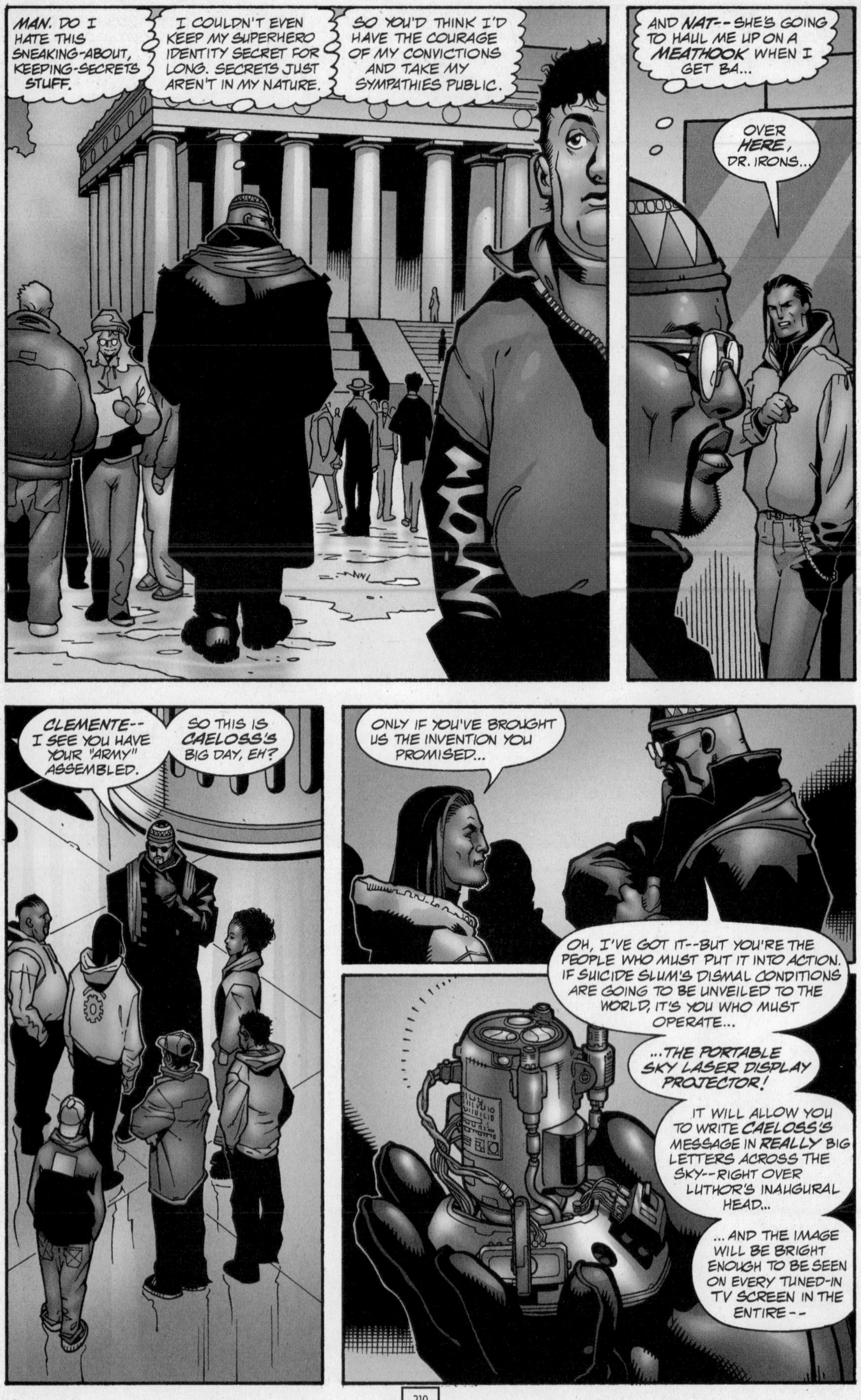

MAN. DO I HATE THIS SNEAKING-ABOUT, KEEPING-SECRETS STUFF.
I COULDN'T EVEN KEEP MY SUPERHERO IDENTITY SECRET FOR LONG. SECRETS JUST AREN'T IN MY NATURE.
SO YOU'D THINK I'D HAVE THE COURAGE OF MY CONVICTIONS AND TAKE MY SYMPATHIES PUBLIC.
AND NAT-- SHE'S GOING TO HAUL ME UP ON A MEATHOOK WHEN I GET BA...
OVER HERE, DR. IRONS...
CLEMENTE-- I SEE YOU HAVE YOUR "ARMY" ASSEMBLED.
SO THIS IS CAELOSS'S BIG DAY, EH?
ONLY IF YOU'VE BROUGHT US THE INVENTION YOU PROMISED...
OH, I'VE GOT IT--BUT YOU'RE THE PEOPLE WHO MUST PUT IT INTO ACTION. IF SUICIDE SLUM'S DISMAL CONDITIONS ARE GOING TO BE UNVEILED TO THE WORLD, IT'S YOU WHO MUST OPERATE...
...THE PORTABLE SKY LASER DISPLAY PROJECTOR!
IT WILL ALLOW YOU TO WRITE CAELOSS'S MESSAGE IN REALLY BIG LETTERS ACROSS THE SKY--RIGHT OVER LUTHOR'S INAUGURAL HEAD...
...AND THE IMAGE WILL BE BRIGHT ENOUGH TO BE SEEN ON EVERY TUNED-IN TV SCREEN IN THE ENTIRE--

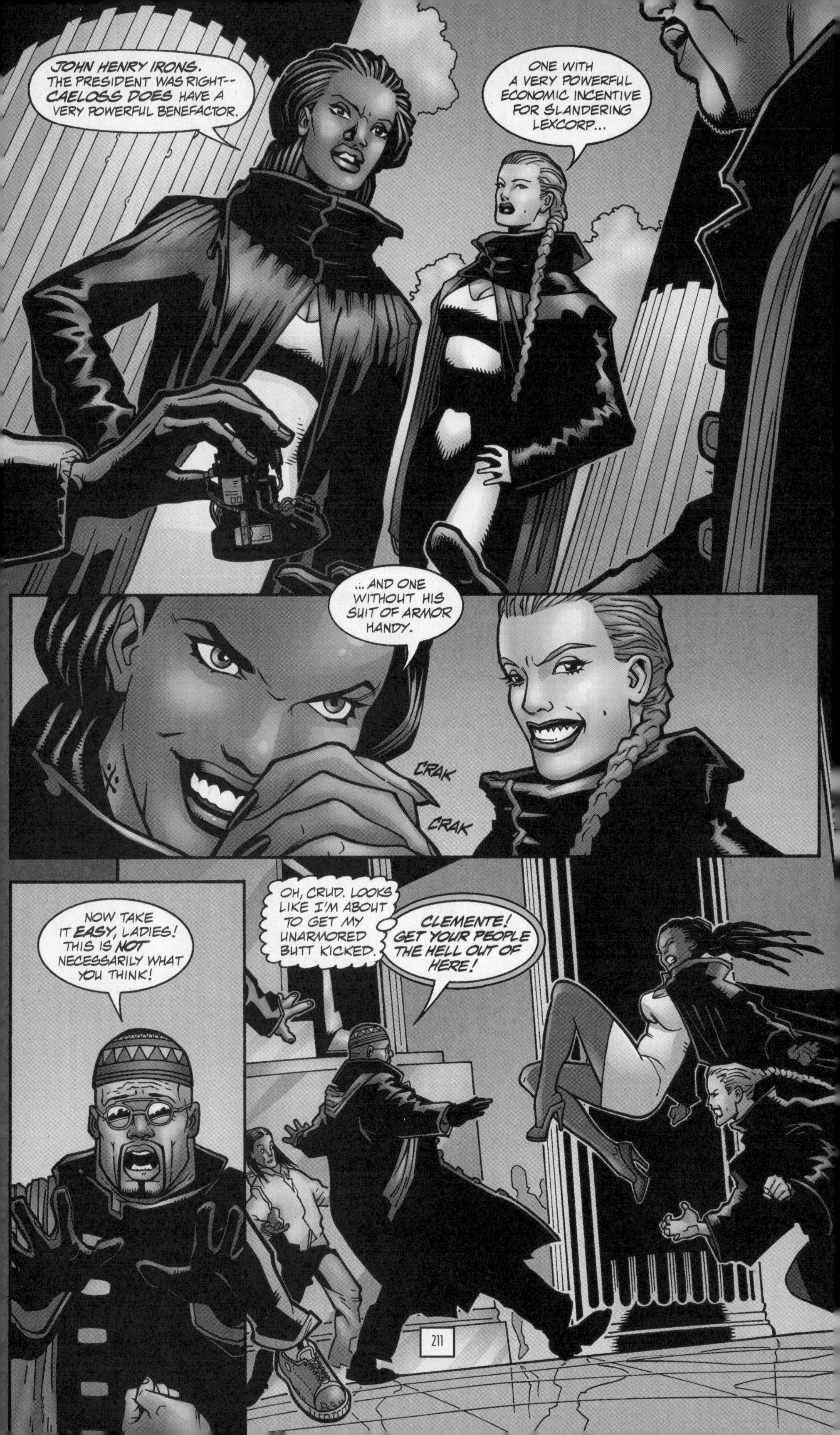
JOHN HENRY IRONS. THE PRESIDENT WAS RIGHT-- CAELOSS DOES HAVE A VERY POWERFUL BENEFACTOR.
ONE WITH A VERY POWERFUL ECONOMIC INCENTIVE FOR SLANDERING LEXCORP...
...AND ONE WITHOUT HIS SUIT OF ARMOR HANDY.
CRAK
CRAK
NOW TAKE IT EASY, LADIES! THIS IS NOT NECESSARILY WHAT YOU THINK!
OH, CRUD. LOOKS LIKE I'M ABOUT TO GET MY UNARMORED BUTT KICKED.
CLEMENTE! GET YOUR PEOPLE THE HELL OUT OF HERE!

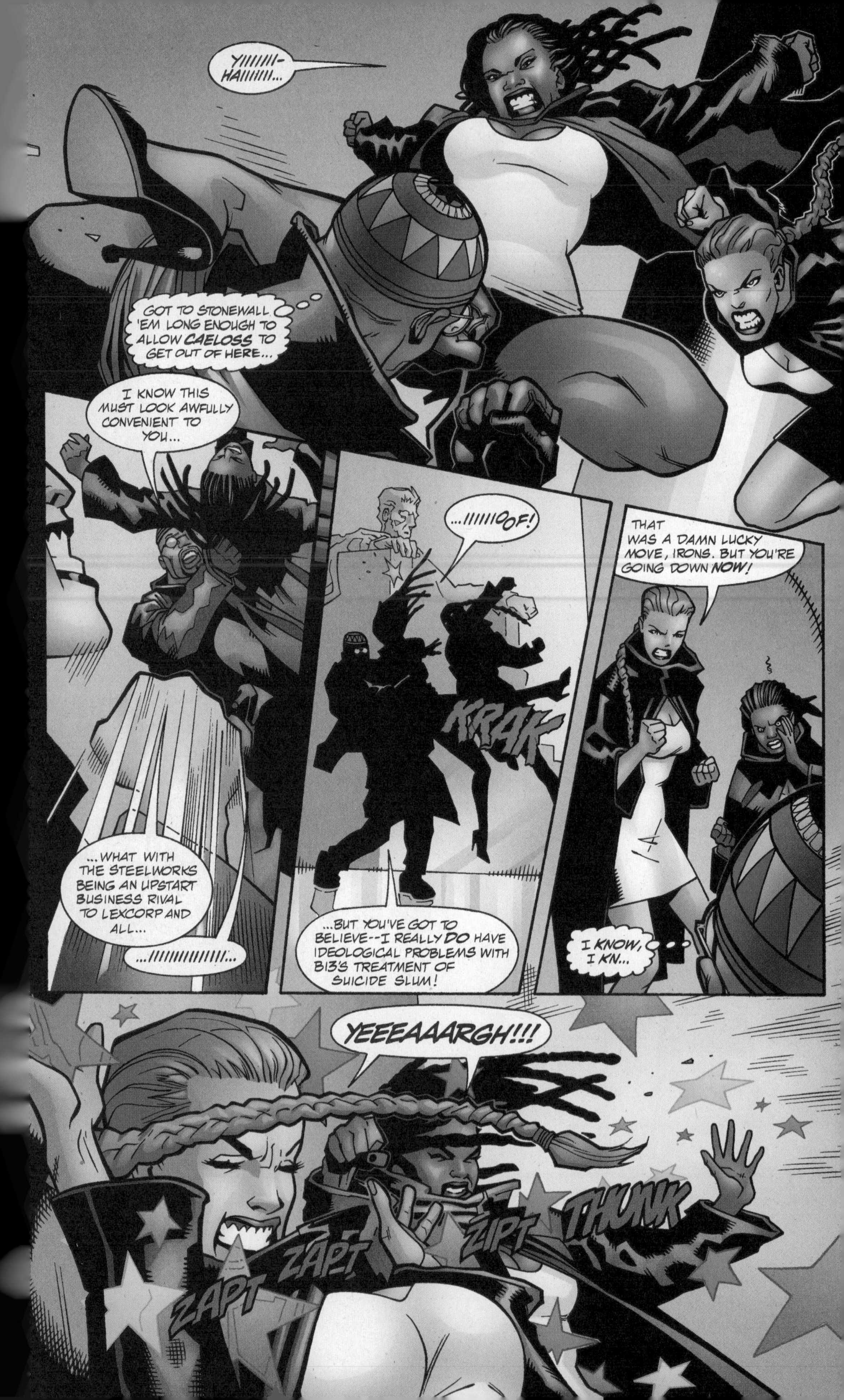

YIIIIIII-HAIIIIIII...
GOT TO STONEWALL 'EM LONG ENOUGH TO ALLOW CAELOSS TO GET OUT OF HERE...
I KNOW THIS MUST LOOK AWFULLY CONVENIENT TO YOU...
...WHAT WITH THE STEELWORKS BEING AN UPSTART BUSINESS RIVAL TO LEXCORP AND ALL...
...IIIIIIIIIIIIII...
...IIIIIIOOF!
KRAK
...BUT YOU'VE GOT TO BELIEVE--I REALLY DO HAVE IDEOLOGICAL PROBLEMS WITH B13'S TREATMENT OF SUICIDE SLUM!
THAT WAS A DAMN LUCKY MOVE, IRONS. BUT YOU'RE GOING DOWN NOW!
I KNOW, I KN...
YEEEAAARGH!!!
ZAPT
ZAPT
ZIPT
THUNK

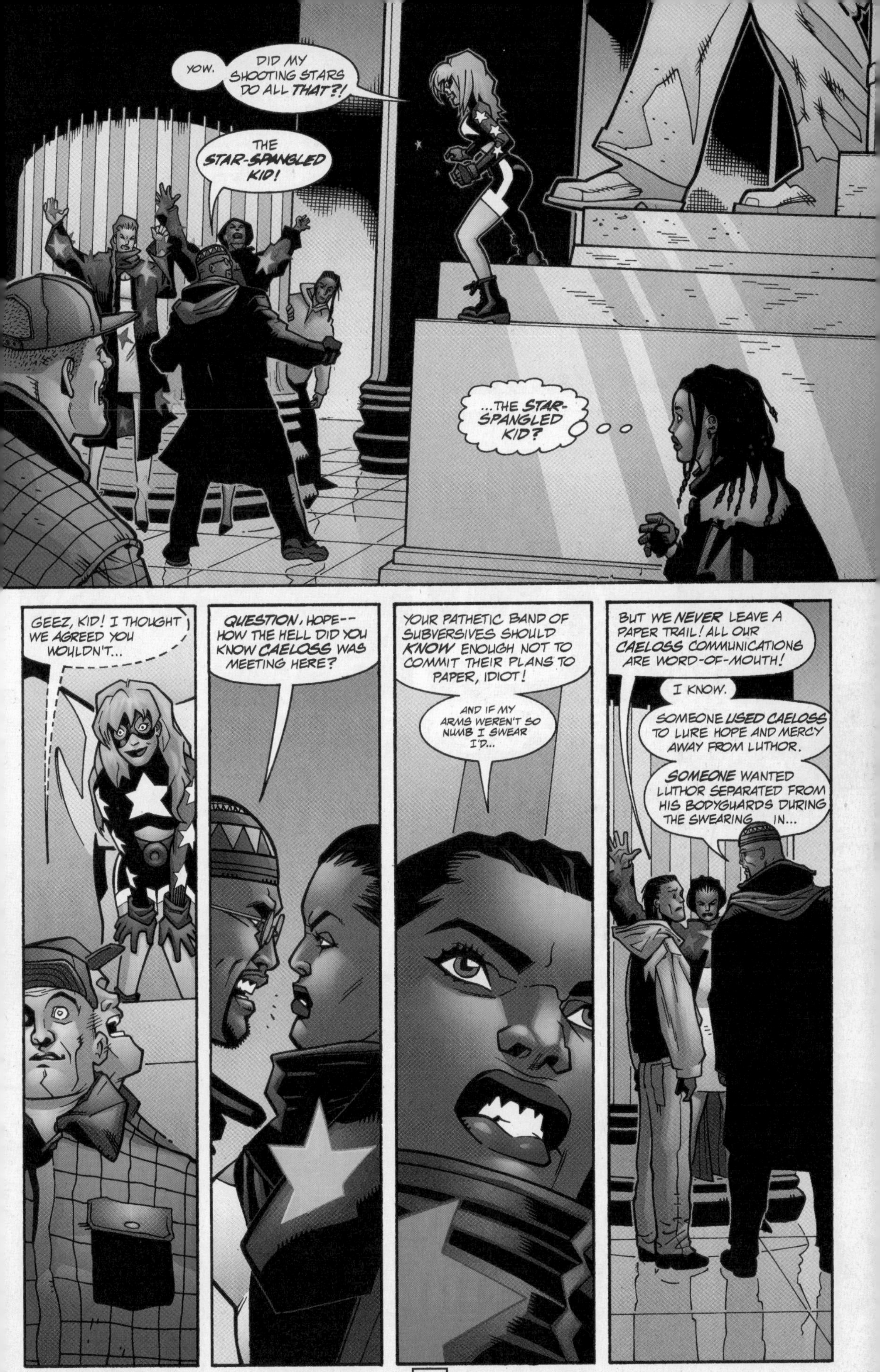
YOW.
DID MY SHOOTING STARS DO ALL THAT?!
THE STAR-SPANGLED KID!
...THE STAR-SPANGLED KID?
GEEZ, KID! I THOUGHT WE AGREED YOU WOULDN'T...
QUESTION, HOPE-- HOW THE HELL DID YOU KNOW CAELOSS WAS MEETING HERE?
YOUR PATHETIC BAND OF SUBVERSIVES SHOULD KNOW ENOUGH NOT TO COMMIT THEIR PLANS TO PAPER, IDIOT!
AND IF MY ARMS WEREN'T SO NUMB I SWEAR I'D...
BUT WE NEVER LEAVE A PAPER TRAIL! ALL OUR CAELOSS COMMUNICATIONS ARE WORD-OF-MOUTH!
I KNOW.
SOMEONE USED CAELOSS TO LURE HOPE AND MERCY AWAY FROM LUTHOR.
SOMEONE WANTED LUTHOR SEPARATED FROM HIS BODYGUARDS DURING THE SWEARING IN...

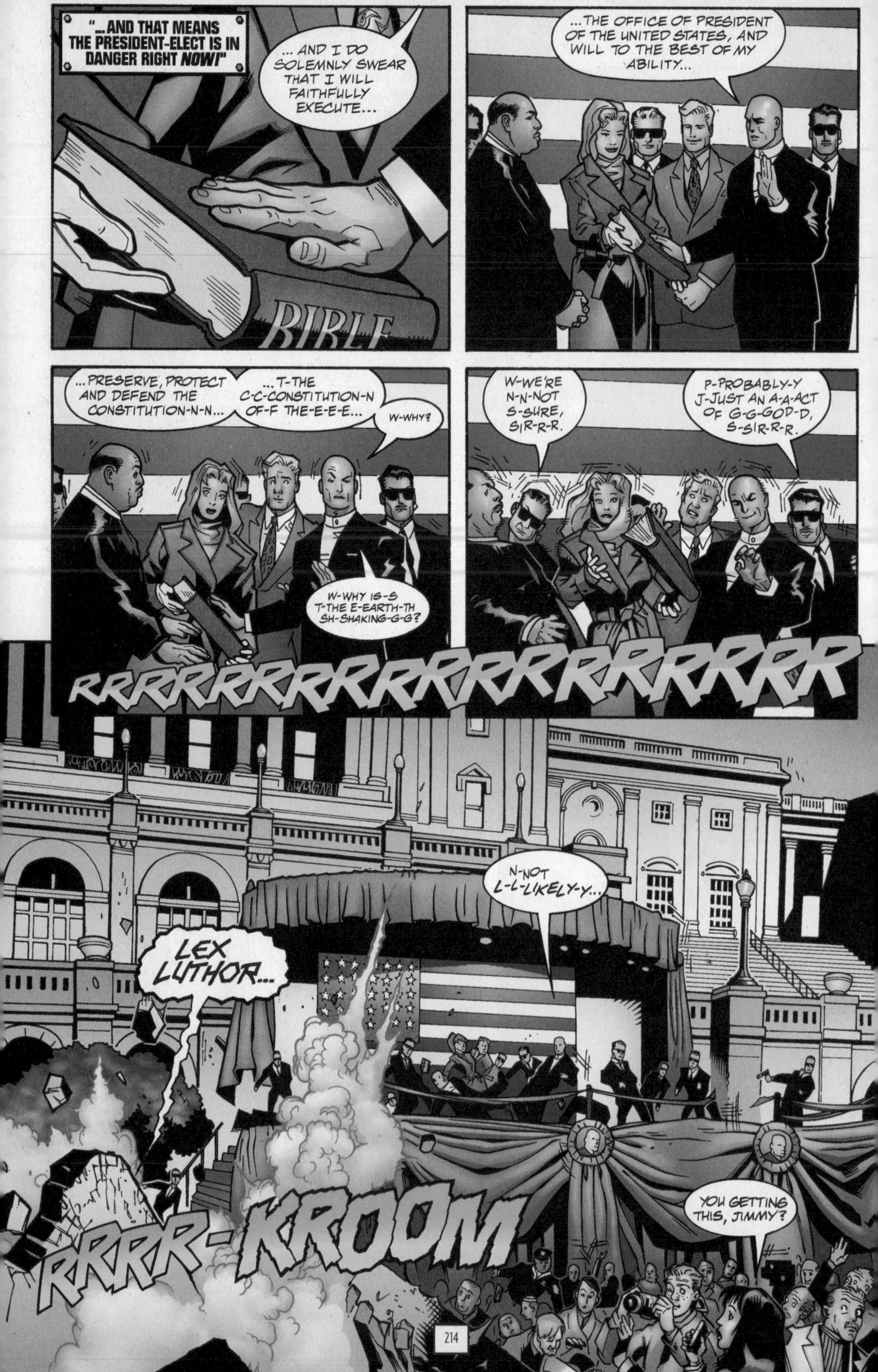

"...AND THAT MEANS THE PRESIDENT-ELECT IS IN DANGER RIGHT NOW!"
...AND I DO SOLEMNLY SWEAR THAT I WILL FAITHFULLY EXECUTE...
BIBLE
...THE OFFICE OF PRESIDENT OF THE UNITED STATES, AND WILL TO THE BEST OF MY ABILITY...
...PRESERVE, PROTECT AND DEFEND THE CONSTITUTION-N-N...
...T-THE C-C-CONSTITUTION-N OF-F THE-E-E-E...
W-WHY?
W-WHY IS-S T-THE E-EARTH-TH SH-SHAKING-G-G?
W-WE'RE N-N-NOT S-SURE, SIR-R-R.
P-PROBABLY-Y J-JUST AN A-A-ACT OF G-G-GOD-D, S-SIR-R-R.
RRRRRRRRRRRRRRRRRRRRRR
N-NOT L-L-LIKELY-Y...
LEX LUTHOR...
RRRR-KROOM
YOU GETTING THIS, JIMMY?

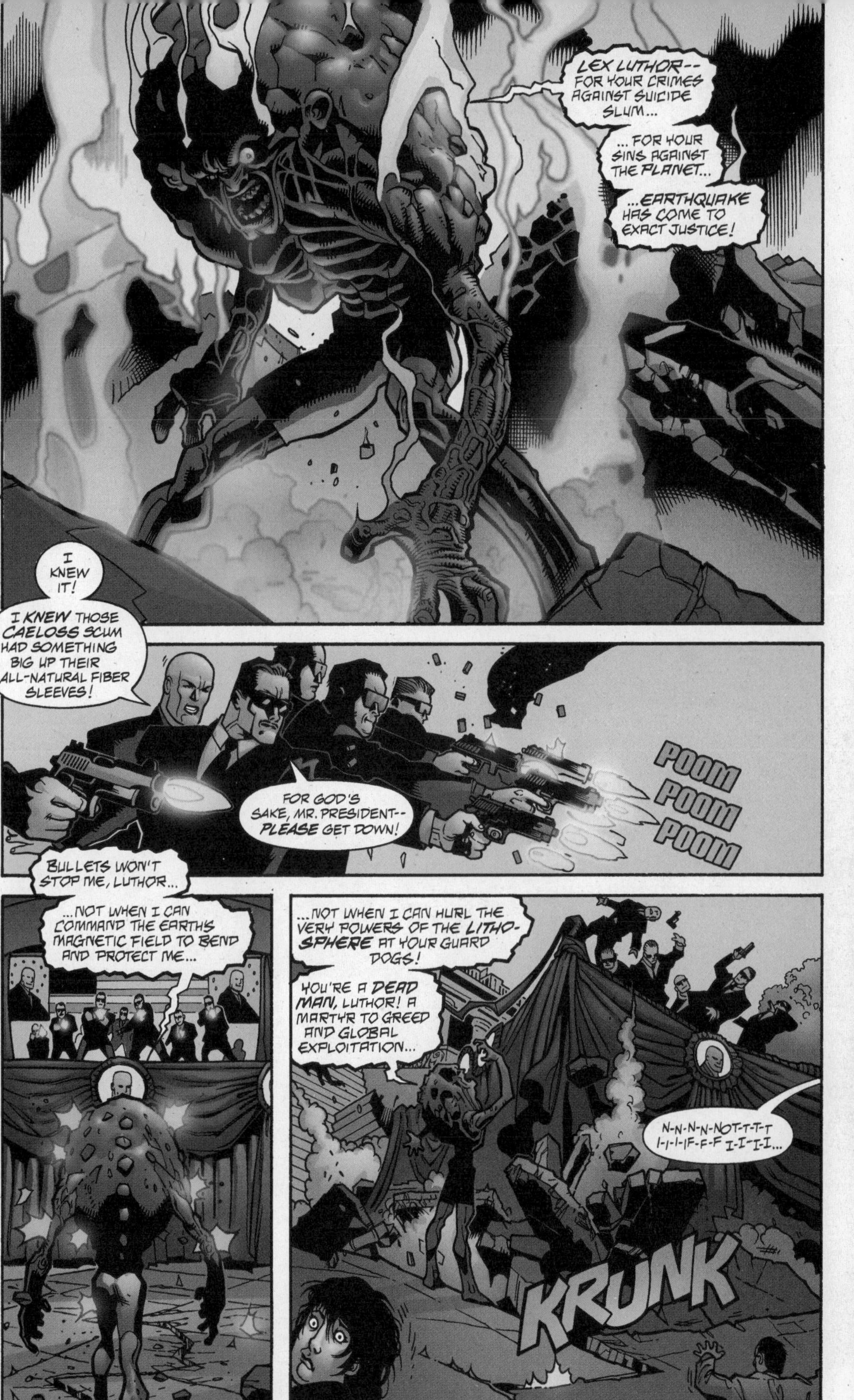
LEX LUTHOR-- FOR YOUR CRIMES AGAINST SUICIDE SLUM...
...FOR YOUR SINS AGAINST THE PLANET...
...EARTHQUAKE HAS COME TO EXACT JUSTICE!
I KNEW IT!
I KNEW THOSE CAELOSS SCUM HAD SOMETHING BIG UP THEIR ALL-NATURAL FIBER SLEEVES!
FOR GOD'S SAKE, MR. PRESIDENT-- PLEASE GET DOWN!
POOM
POOM
POOM
BULLETS WON'T STOP ME, LUTHOR...
...NOT WHEN I CAN COMMAND THE EARTH'S MAGNETIC FIELD TO BEND AND PROTECT ME...
...NOT WHEN I CAN HURL THE VERY POWERS OF THE LITHO-SPHERE AT YOUR GUARD DOGS!
YOU'RE A DEAD MAN, LUTHOR! A MARTYR TO GREED AND GLOBAL EXPLOITATION...
N-N-N-N-NOT-T-T-T I-I-I-IF-F-F I-I-I-I...
KRUNK

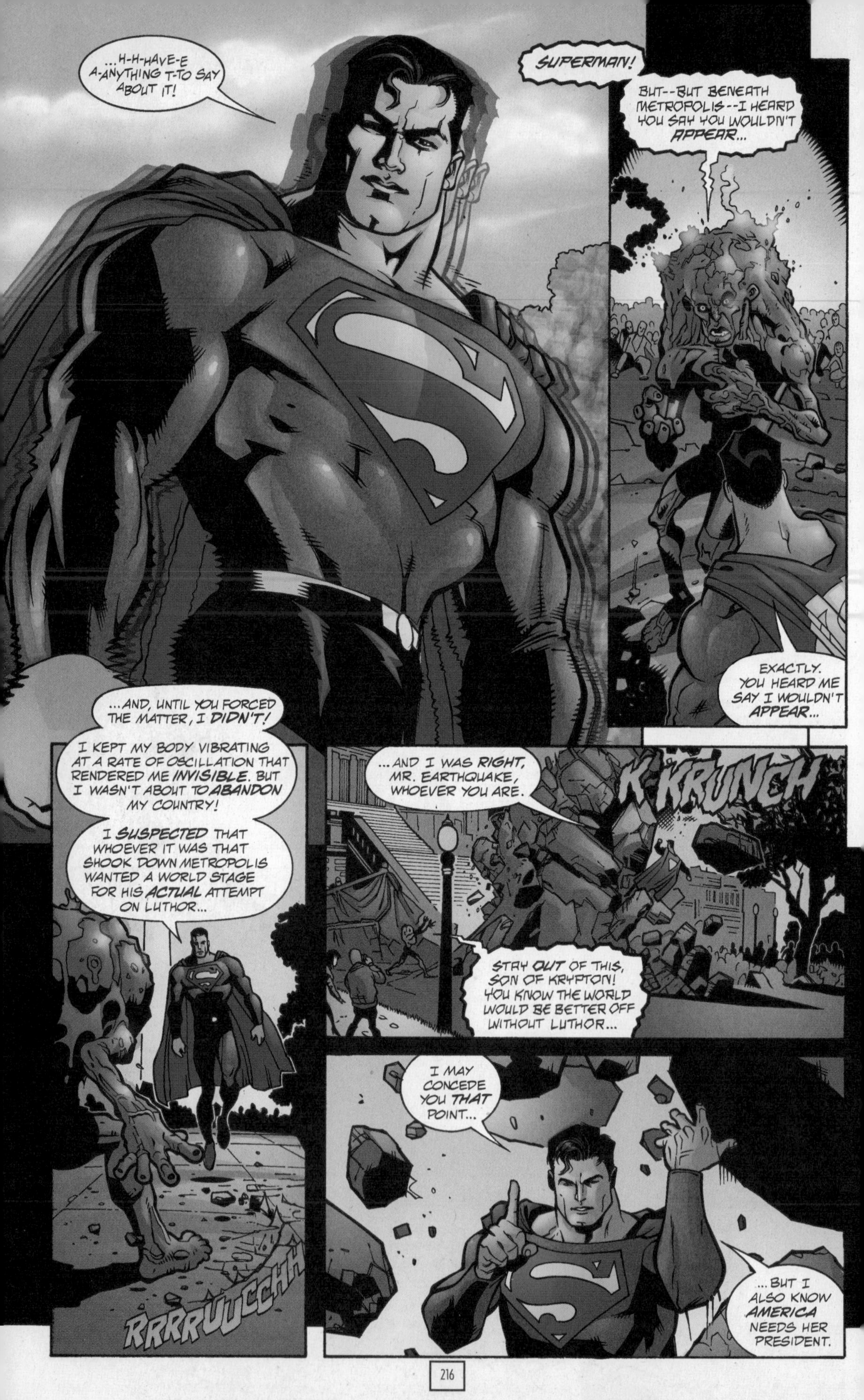
...H-H-HAVE-E A-ANYTHING T-TO SAY ABOUT IT!
SUPERMAN!
BUT--BUT BENEATH METROPOLIS--I HEARD YOU SAY YOU WOULDN'T APPEAR...
EXACTLY. YOU HEARD ME SAY I WOULDN'T APPEAR...
...AND, UNTIL YOU FORCED THE MATTER, I DIDN'T!
I KEPT MY BODY VIBRATING AT A RATE OF OSCILLATION THAT RENDERED ME INVISIBLE. BUT I WASN'T ABOUT TO ABANDON MY COUNTRY!
I SUSPECTED THAT WHOEVER IT WAS THAT SHOOK DOWN METROPOLIS WANTED A WORLD STAGE FOR HIS ACTUAL ATTEMPT ON LUTHOR...
RRRRUUCCHH
...AND I WAS RIGHT, MR. EARTHQUAKE, WHOEVER YOU ARE.
K-KRUNCH
STAY OUT OF THIS, SON OF KRYPTON! YOU KNOW THE WORLD WOULD BE BETTER OFF WITHOUT LUTHOR...
I MAY CONCEDE YOU THAT POINT...
...BUT I ALSO KNOW AMERICA NEEDS HER PRESIDENT.

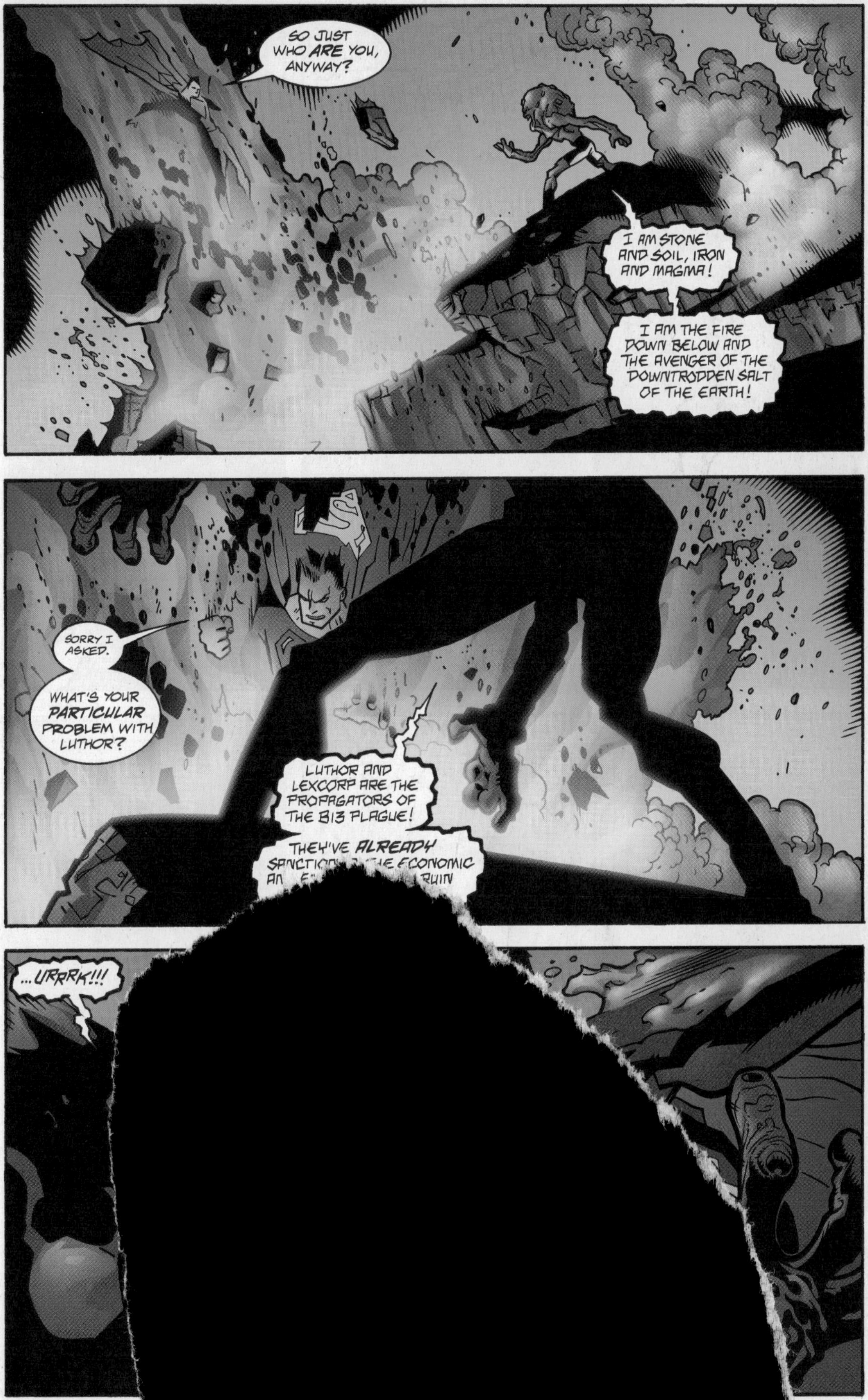
SO JUST WHO ARE YOU, ANYWAY?
I AM STONE AND SOIL, IRON AND MAGMA!
I AM THE FIRE DOWN BELOW AND THE AVENGER OF THE DOWNTRODDEN SALT OF THE EARTH!
SORRY I ASKED.
WHAT'S YOUR PARTICULAR PROBLEM WITH LUTHOR?
LUTHOR AND LEXCORP ARE THE PROPAGATORS OF THE B13 PLAGUE!
THEY'VE ALREADY ... ECONOMIC ... RUIN
...URRRK!!!

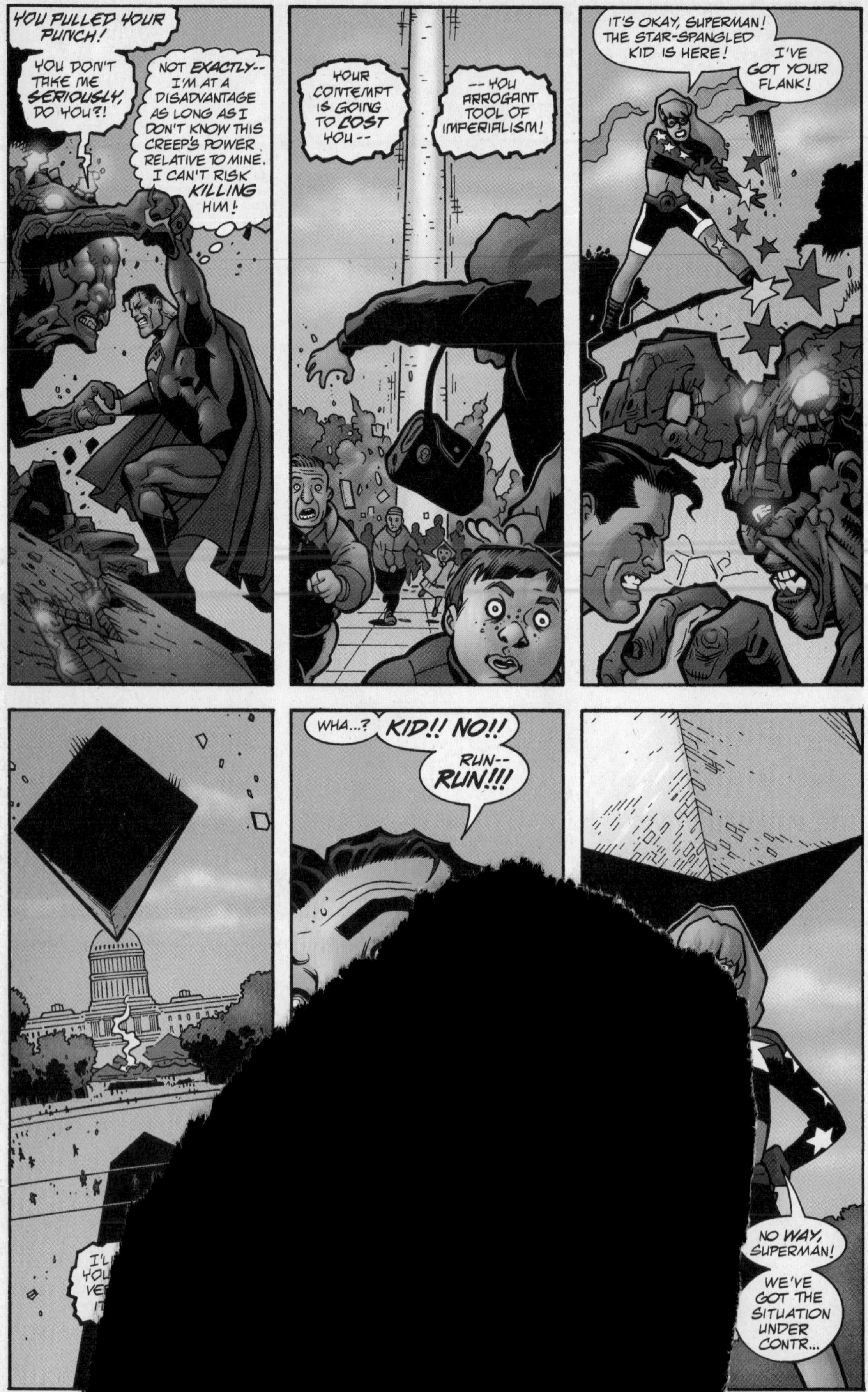
YOU PULLED YOUR PUNCH!
YOU DON'T TAKE ME SERIOUSLY, DO YOU?!
NOT EXACTLY-- I'M AT A DISADVANTAGE AS LONG AS I DON'T KNOW THIS CREEP'S POWER RELATIVE TO MINE. I CAN'T RISK KILLING HIM!
YOUR CONTEMPT IS GOING TO COST YOU --
-- YOU ARROGANT TOOL OF IMPERIALISM!
IT'S OKAY, SUPERMAN! THE STAR-SPANGLED KID IS HERE!
I'VE GOT YOUR FLANK!
WHA...?
KID!! NO!!
RUN-- RUN!!!
NO WAY, SUPERMAN!
WE'VE GOT THE SITUATION UNDER CONTR...

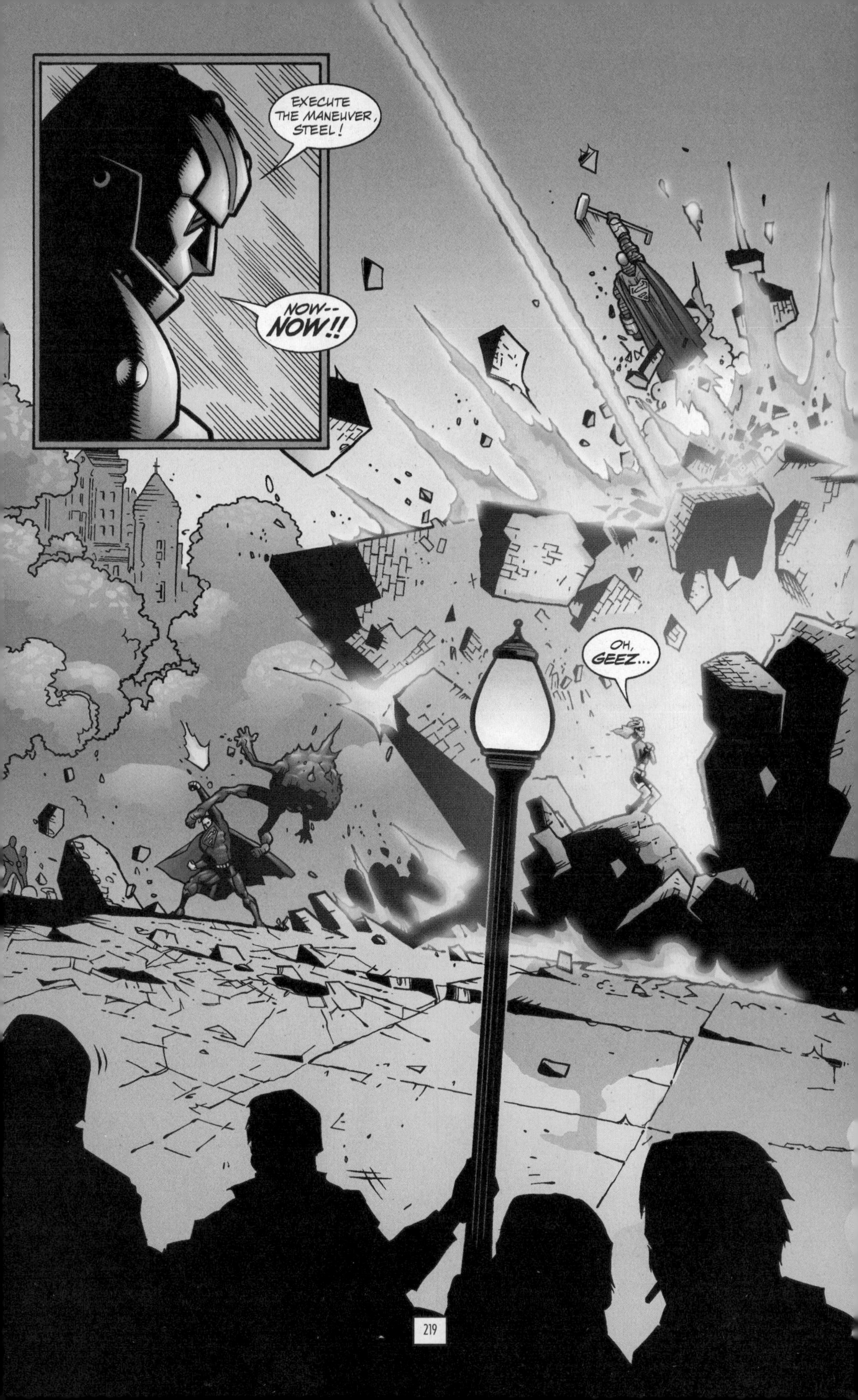
EXECUTE THE MANEUVER, STEEL!
NOW-- NOW!!
OH, GEEZ...

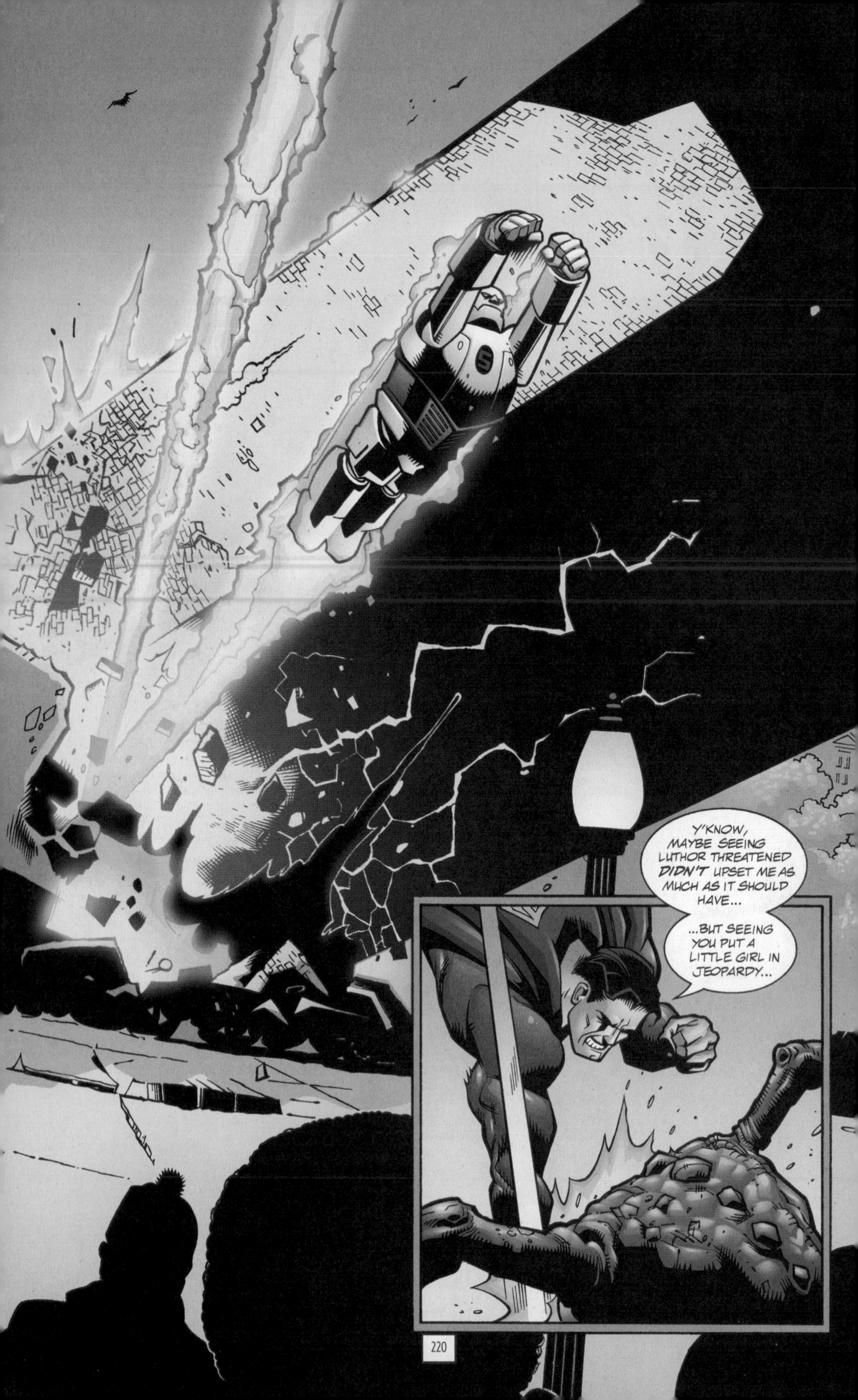
Y'KNOW, MAYBE SEEING LUTHOR THREATENED **DIDN'T** UPSET ME AS MUCH AS IT SHOULD HAVE...
...BUT SEEING YOU PUT A LITTLE GIRL IN JEOPARDY...

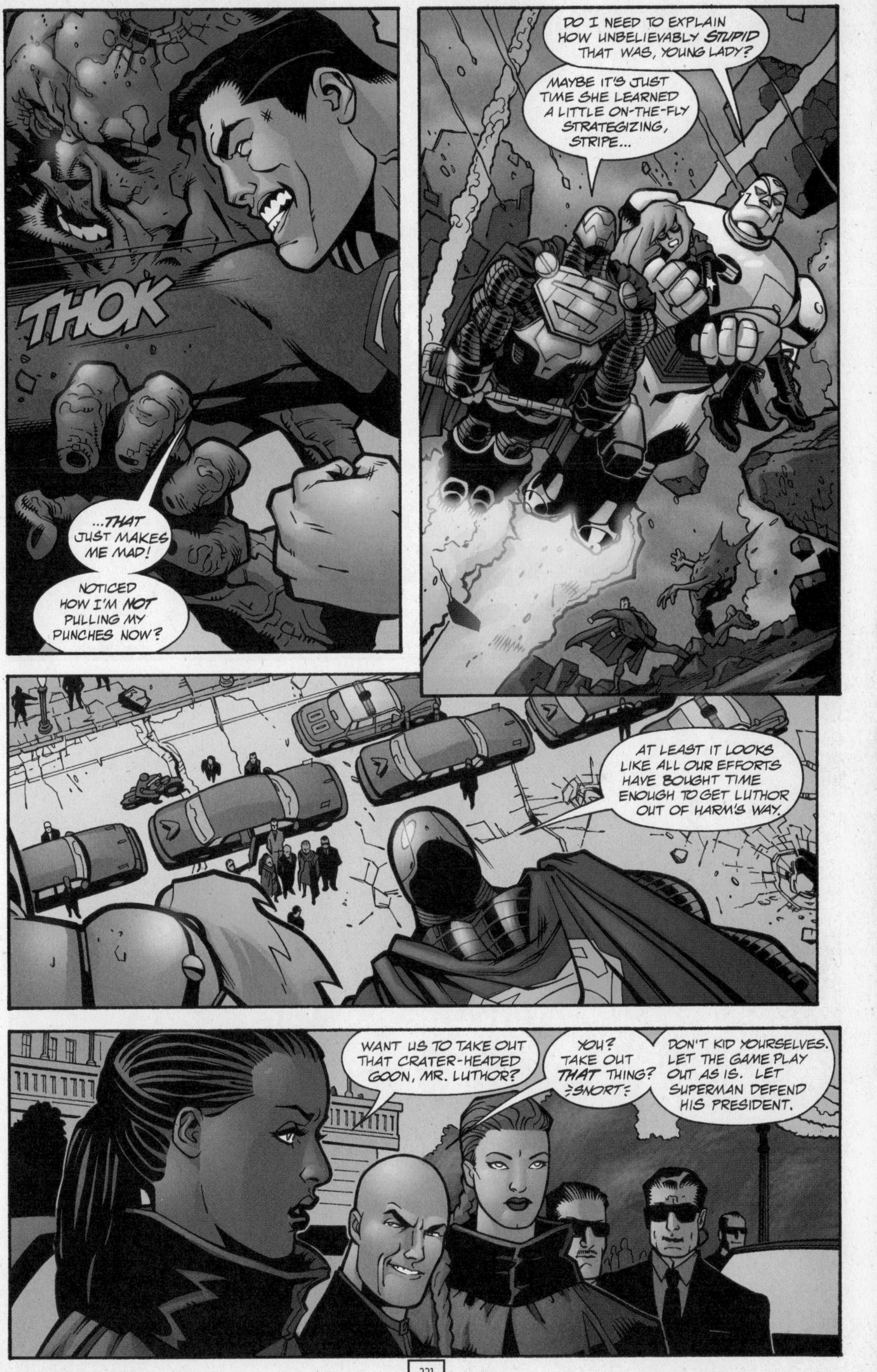
THOK
...THAT JUST MAKES ME MAD!
NOTICED HOW I'M NOT PULLING MY PUNCHES NOW?
DO I NEED TO EXPLAIN HOW UNBELIEVABLY STUPID THAT WAS, YOUNG LADY?
MAYBE IT'S JUST TIME SHE LEARNED A LITTLE ON-THE-FLY STRATEGIZING, STRIPE...
AT LEAST IT LOOKS LIKE ALL OUR EFFORTS HAVE BOUGHT TIME ENOUGH TO GET LUTHOR OUT OF HARM'S WAY.
WANT US TO TAKE OUT THAT CRATER-HEADED GOON, MR. LUTHOR?
YOU? TAKE OUT THAT THING? SNORT
DON'T KID YOURSELVES. LET THE GAME PLAY OUT AS IS. LET SUPERMAN DEFEND HIS PRESIDENT.

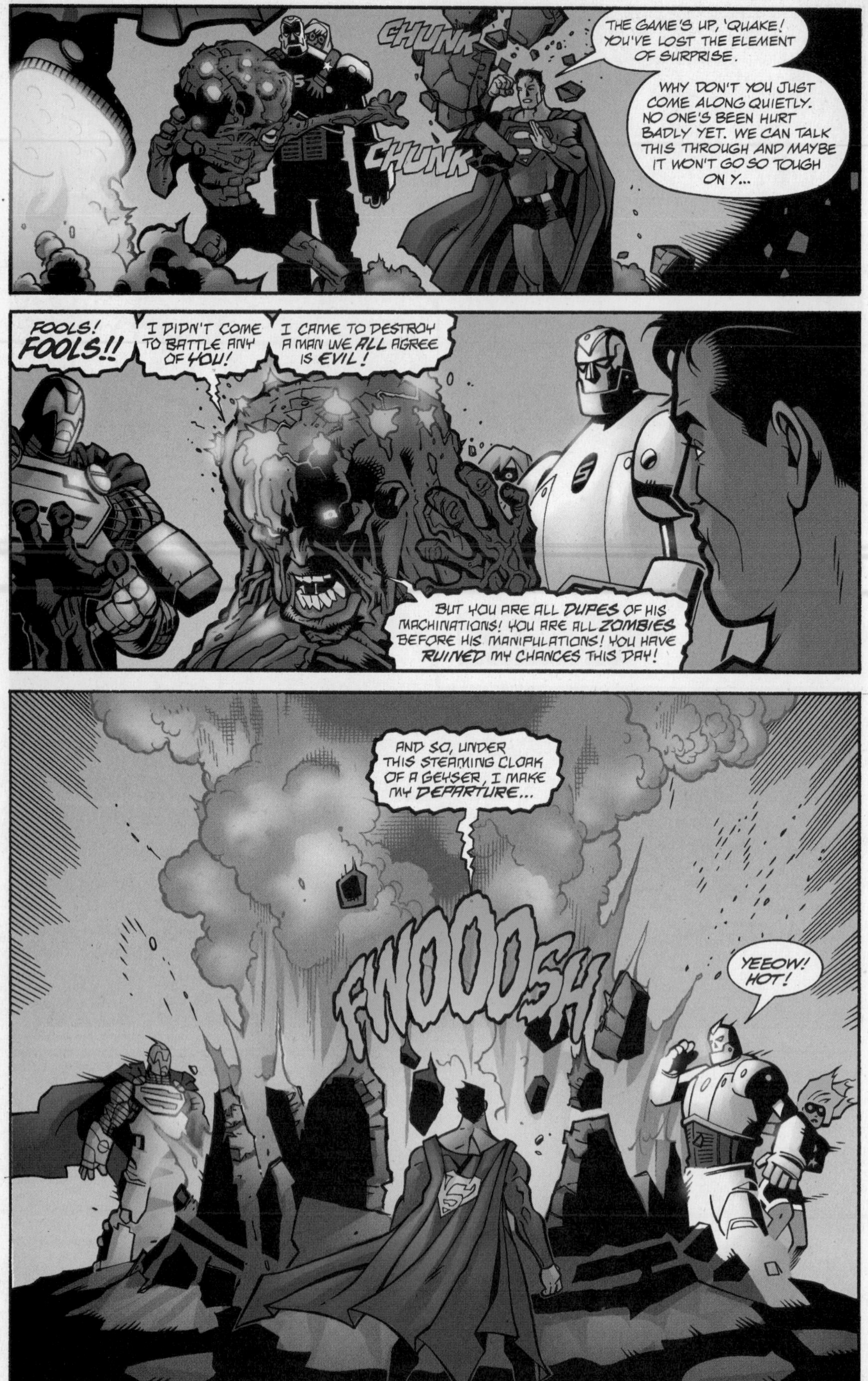
CHUNK
THE GAME'S UP, 'QUAKE! YOU'VE LOST THE ELEMENT OF SURPRISE.
WHY DON'T YOU JUST COME ALONG QUIETLY. NO ONE'S BEEN HURT BADLY YET. WE CAN TALK THIS THROUGH AND MAYBE IT WON'T GO SO TOUGH ON Y...
CHUNK
FOOLS! FOOLS!!
I DIDN'T COME TO BATTLE ANY OF YOU!
I CAME TO DESTROY A MAN WE ALL AGREE IS EVIL!
BUT YOU ARE ALL DUPES OF HIS MACHINATIONS! YOU ARE ALL ZOMBIES BEFORE HIS MANIPULATIONS! YOU HAVE RUINED MY CHANCES THIS DAY!
AND SO, UNDER THIS STEAMING CLOAK OF A GEYSER, I MAKE MY DEPARTURE...
FWOOOSH
YEEOW! HOT!

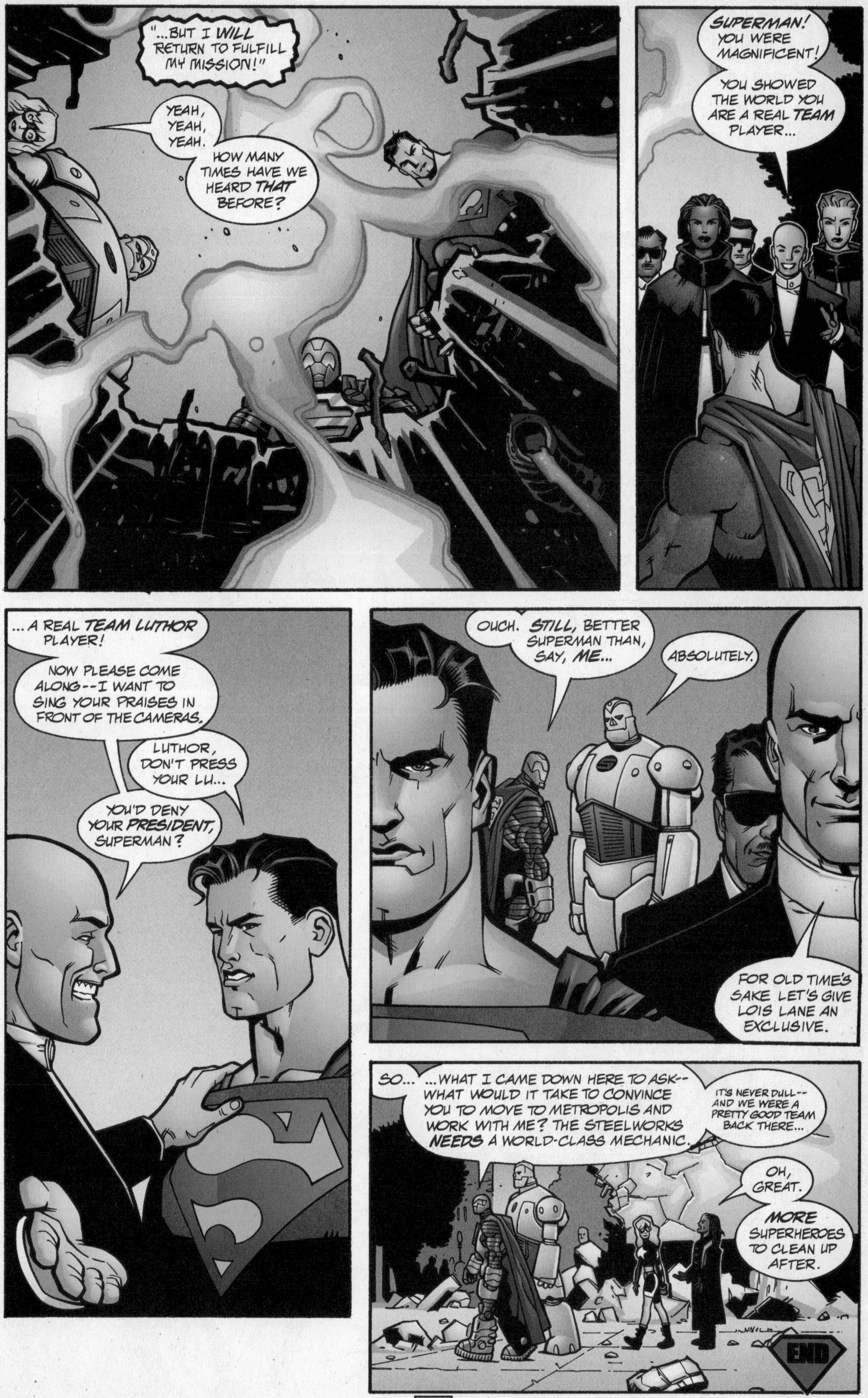
"...BUT I WILL RETURN TO FULFILL MY MISSION!"
YEAH, YEAH, YEAH.
HOW MANY TIMES HAVE WE HEARD THAT BEFORE?
SUPERMAN! YOU WERE MAGNIFICENT!
YOU SHOWED THE WORLD YOU ARE A REAL TEAM PLAYER...
...A REAL TEAM LUTHOR PLAYER!
NOW PLEASE COME ALONG--I WANT TO SING YOUR PRAISES IN FRONT OF THE CAMERAS.
LUTHOR, DON'T PRESS YOUR LU...
YOU'D DENY YOUR PRESIDENT, SUPERMAN?
OUCH. STILL, BETTER SUPERMAN THAN, SAY, ME...
ABSOLUTELY.
FOR OLD TIME'S SAKE LET'S GIVE LOIS LANE AN EXCLUSIVE.
SO...
...WHAT I CAME DOWN HERE TO ASK--WHAT WOULD IT TAKE TO CONVINCE YOU TO MOVE TO METROPOLIS AND WORK WITH ME? THE STEELWORKS NEEDS A WORLD-CLASS MECHANIC.
IT'S NEVER DULL--AND WE WERE A PRETTY GOOD TEAM BACK THERE...
OH, GREAT.
MORE SUPERHEROES TO CLEAN UP AFTER.
END

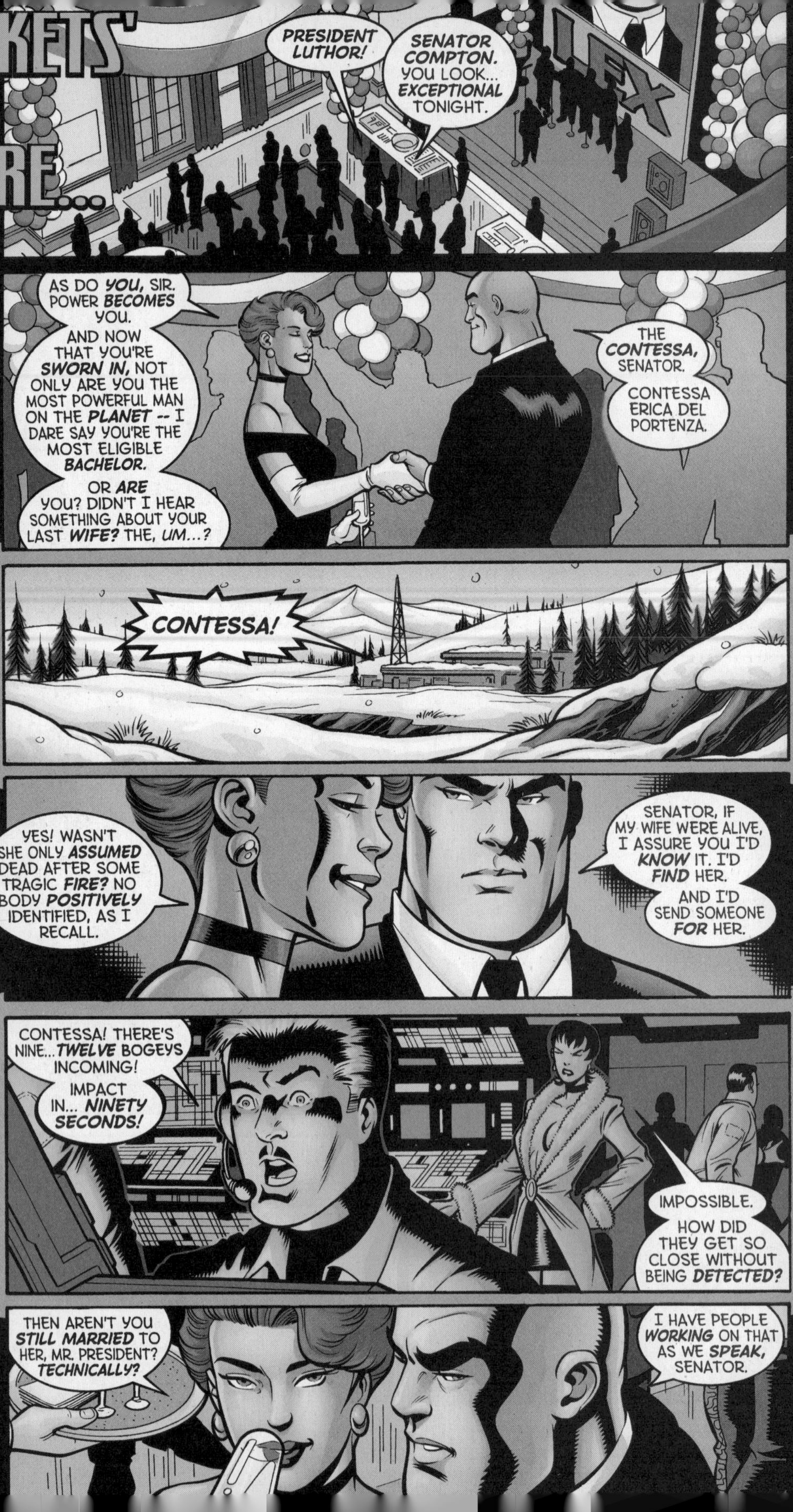
KETS'
RE...
PRESIDENT LUTHOR!
SENATOR COMPTON. YOU LOOK... EXCEPTIONAL TONIGHT.
AS DO YOU, SIR. POWER BECOMES YOU.
AND NOW THAT YOU'RE SWORN IN, NOT ONLY ARE YOU THE MOST POWERFUL MAN ON THE PLANET -- I DARE SAY YOU'RE THE MOST ELIGIBLE BACHELOR.
OR ARE YOU? DIDN'T I HEAR SOMETHING ABOUT YOUR LAST WIFE? THE, UM...?
THE CONTESSA, SENATOR.
CONTESSA ERICA DEL PORTENZA.
CONTESSA!
YES! WASN'T SHE ONLY ASSUMED DEAD AFTER SOME TRAGIC FIRE? NO BODY POSITIVELY IDENTIFIED, AS I RECALL.
SENATOR, IF MY WIFE WERE ALIVE, I ASSURE YOU I'D KNOW IT. I'D FIND HER.
AND I'D SEND SOMEONE FOR HER.
CONTESSA! THERE'S NINE...TWELVE BOGEYS INCOMING!
IMPACT IN... NINETY SECONDS!
IMPOSSIBLE.
HOW DID THEY GET SO CLOSE WITHOUT BEING DETECTED?
THEN AREN'T YOU STILL MARRIED TO HER, MR. PRESIDENT? TECHNICALLY?
I HAVE PEOPLE WORKING ON THAT AS WE SPEAK, SENATOR.

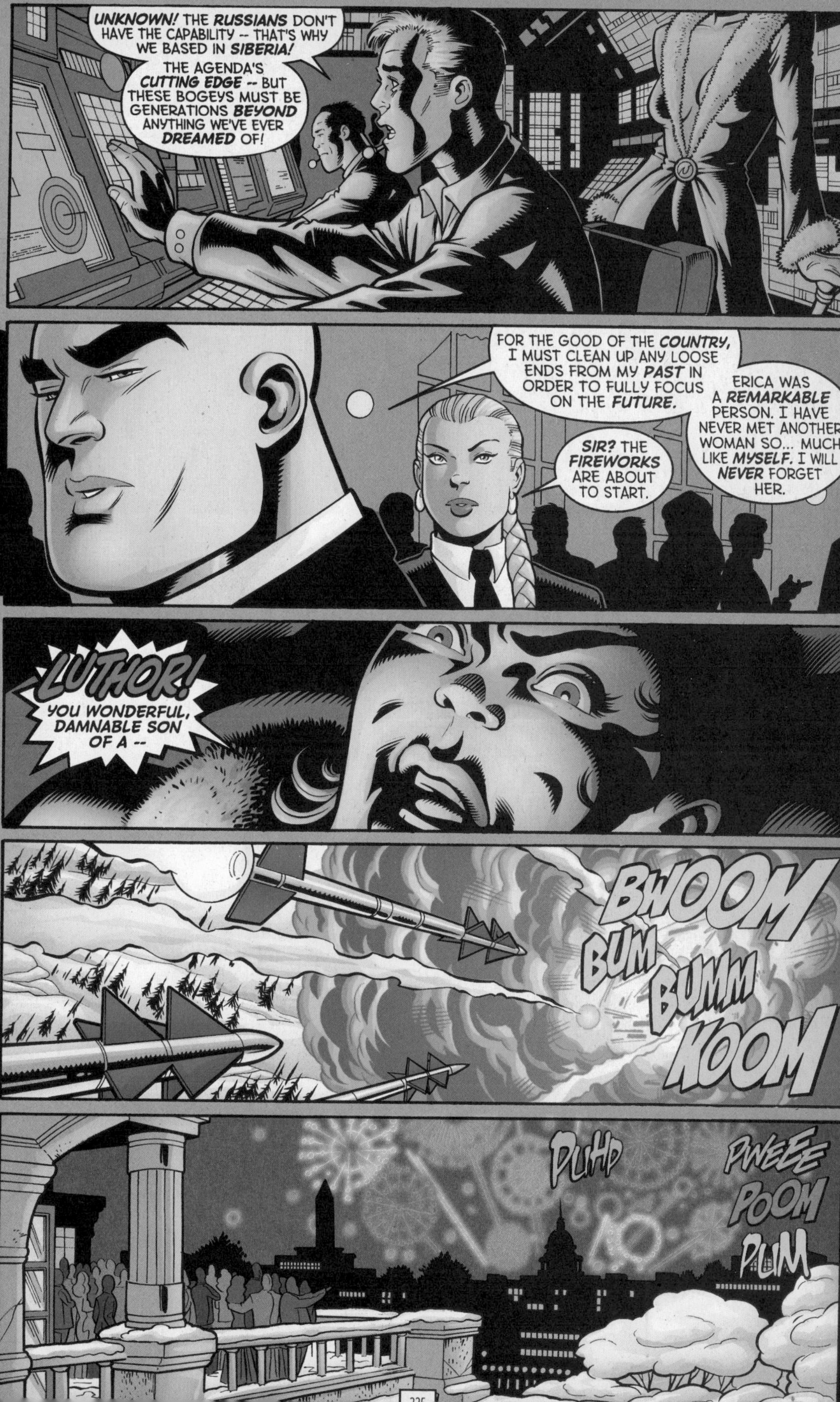
UNKNOWN! THE RUSSIANS DON'T HAVE THE CAPABILITY -- THAT'S WHY WE BASED IN SIBERIA!
THE AGENDA'S CUTTING EDGE -- BUT THESE BOGEYS MUST BE GENERATIONS BEYOND ANYTHING WE'VE EVER DREAMED OF!
FOR THE GOOD OF THE COUNTRY, I MUST CLEAN UP ANY LOOSE ENDS FROM MY PAST IN ORDER TO FULLY FOCUS ON THE FUTURE.
ERICA WAS A REMARKABLE PERSON. I HAVE NEVER MET ANOTHER WOMAN SO... MUCH LIKE MYSELF. I WILL NEVER FORGET HER.
SIR? THE FIREWORKS ARE ABOUT TO START.
LUTHOR! YOU WONDERFUL, DAMNABLE SON OF A --
BWOOM
BUM
BUMM
KOOM
PWEEE
POOM
PLIM

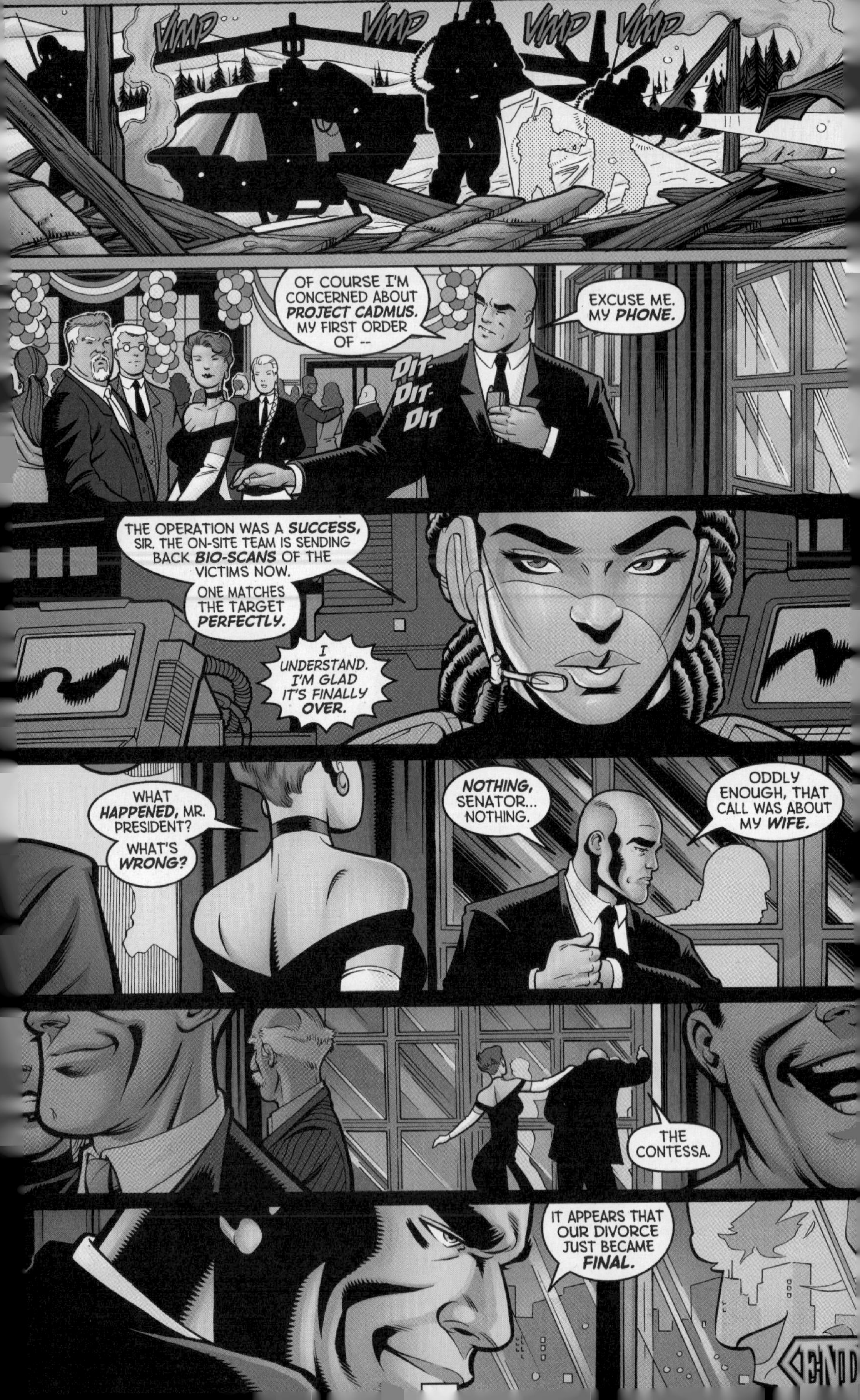
VMP VMP VMP VMP
OF COURSE I'M CONCERNED ABOUT PROJECT CADMUS. MY FIRST ORDER OF --
DIT-DIT-DIT
EXCUSE ME. MY PHONE.
THE OPERATION WAS A SUCCESS, SIR. THE ON-SITE TEAM IS SENDING BACK BIO-SCANS OF THE VICTIMS NOW.
ONE MATCHES THE TARGET PERFECTLY.
I UNDERSTAND. I'M GLAD IT'S FINALLY OVER.
WHAT HAPPENED, MR. PRESIDENT?
WHAT'S WRONG?
NOTHING, SENATOR... NOTHING.
ODDLY ENOUGH, THAT CALL WAS ABOUT MY WIFE.
THE CONTESSA.
IT APPEARS THAT OUR DIVORCE JUST BECAME FINAL.
END

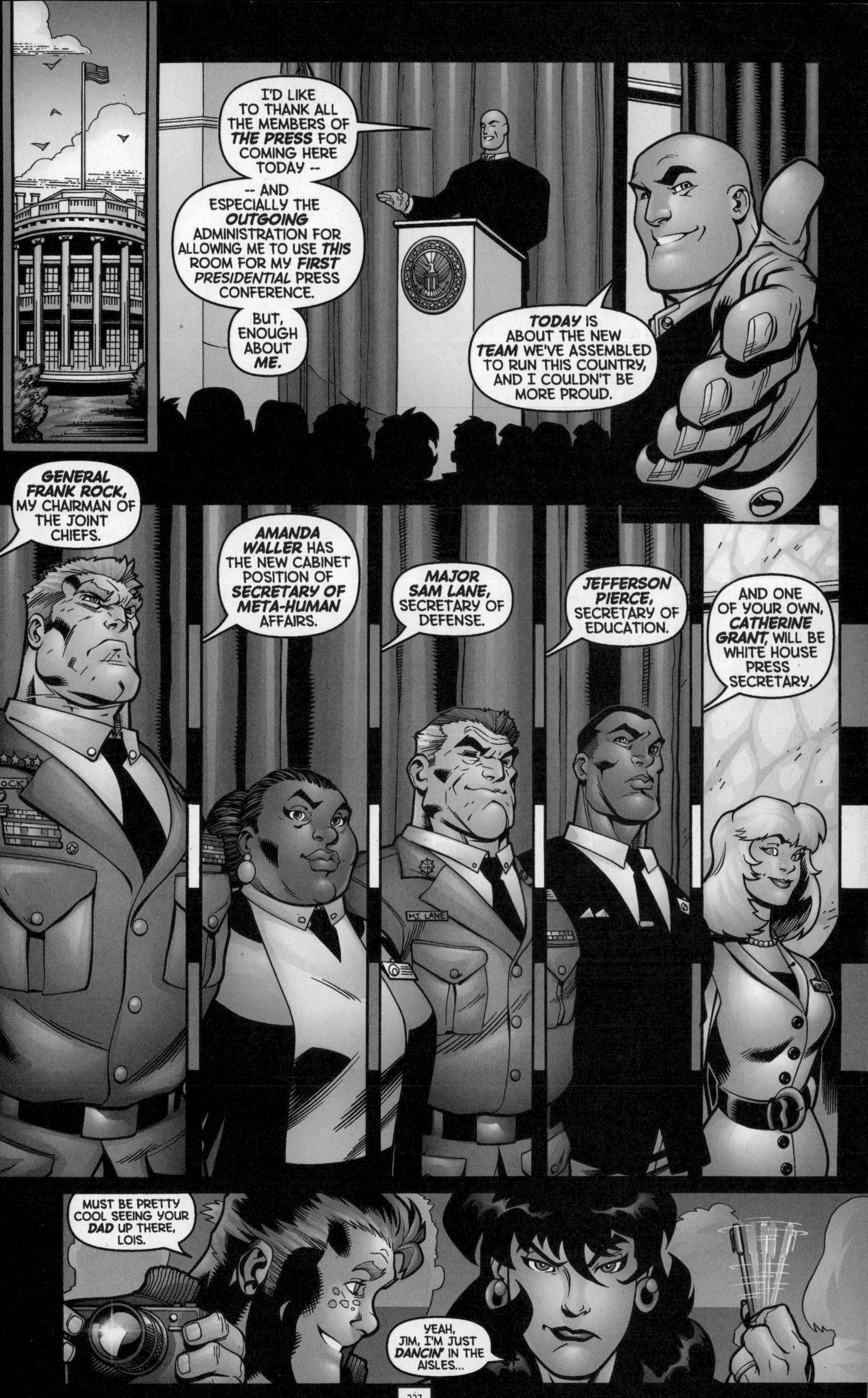

I'D LIKE TO THANK ALL THE MEMBERS OF THE PRESS FOR COMING HERE TODAY --
-- AND ESPECIALLY THE OUTGOING ADMINISTRATION FOR ALLOWING ME TO USE THIS ROOM FOR MY FIRST PRESIDENTIAL PRESS CONFERENCE.
BUT, ENOUGH ABOUT ME.
TODAY IS ABOUT THE NEW TEAM WE'VE ASSEMBLED TO RUN THIS COUNTRY, AND I COULDN'T BE MORE PROUD.
GENERAL FRANK ROCK, MY CHAIRMAN OF THE JOINT CHIEFS.
AMANDA WALLER HAS THE NEW CABINET POSITION OF SECRETARY OF META-HUMAN AFFAIRS.
MAJOR SAM LANE, SECRETARY OF DEFENSE.
JEFFERSON PIERCE, SECRETARY OF EDUCATION.
AND ONE OF YOUR OWN, CATHERINE GRANT, WILL BE WHITE HOUSE PRESS SECRETARY.
MUST BE PRETTY COOL SEEING YOUR DAD UP THERE, LOIS.
YEAH, JIM, I'M JUST DANCIN' IN THE AISLES...

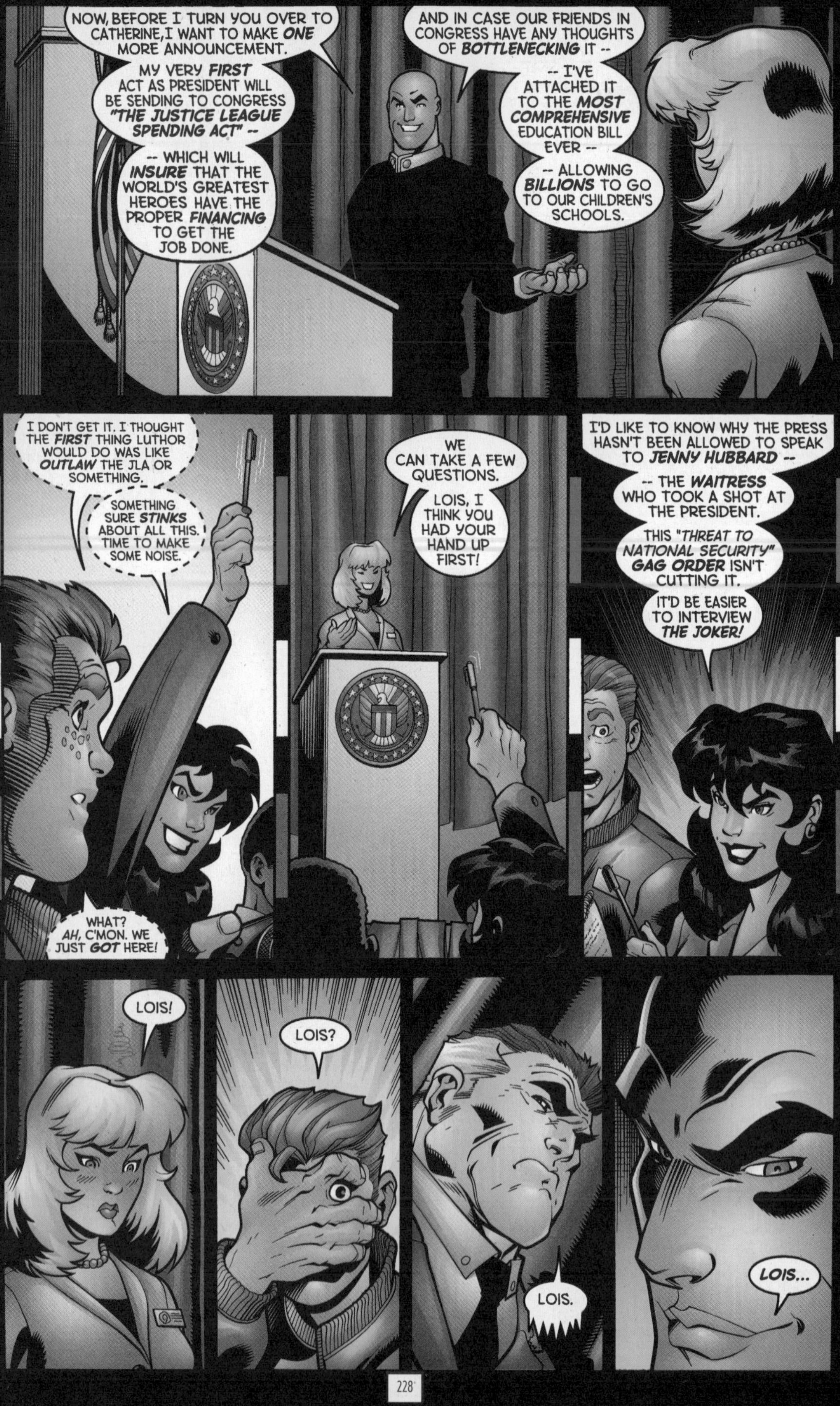
NOW, BEFORE I TURN YOU OVER TO CATHERINE, I WANT TO MAKE ONE MORE ANNOUNCEMENT.
MY VERY FIRST ACT AS PRESIDENT WILL BE SENDING TO CONGRESS "THE JUSTICE LEAGUE SPENDING ACT" --
-- WHICH WILL INSURE THAT THE WORLD'S GREATEST HEROES HAVE THE PROPER FINANCING TO GET THE JOB DONE.
AND IN CASE OUR FRIENDS IN CONGRESS HAVE ANY THOUGHTS OF BOTTLENECKING IT --
-- I'VE ATTACHED IT TO THE MOST COMPREHENSIVE EDUCATION BILL EVER --
-- ALLOWING BILLIONS TO GO TO OUR CHILDREN'S SCHOOLS.
I DON'T GET IT. I THOUGHT THE FIRST THING LUTHOR WOULD DO WAS LIKE OUTLAW THE JLA OR SOMETHING.
SOMETHING SURE STINKS ABOUT ALL THIS. TIME TO MAKE SOME NOISE.
WHAT? AH, C'MON. WE JUST GOT HERE!
WE CAN TAKE A FEW QUESTIONS.
LOIS, I THINK YOU HAD YOUR HAND UP FIRST!
I'D LIKE TO KNOW WHY THE PRESS HASN'T BEEN ALLOWED TO SPEAK TO JENNY HUBBARD --
-- THE WAITRESS WHO TOOK A SHOT AT THE PRESIDENT.
THIS "THREAT TO NATIONAL SECURITY" GAG ORDER ISN'T CUTTING IT.
IT'D BE EASIER TO INTERVIEW THE JOKER!
LOIS!
LOIS?
LOIS.
LOIS...

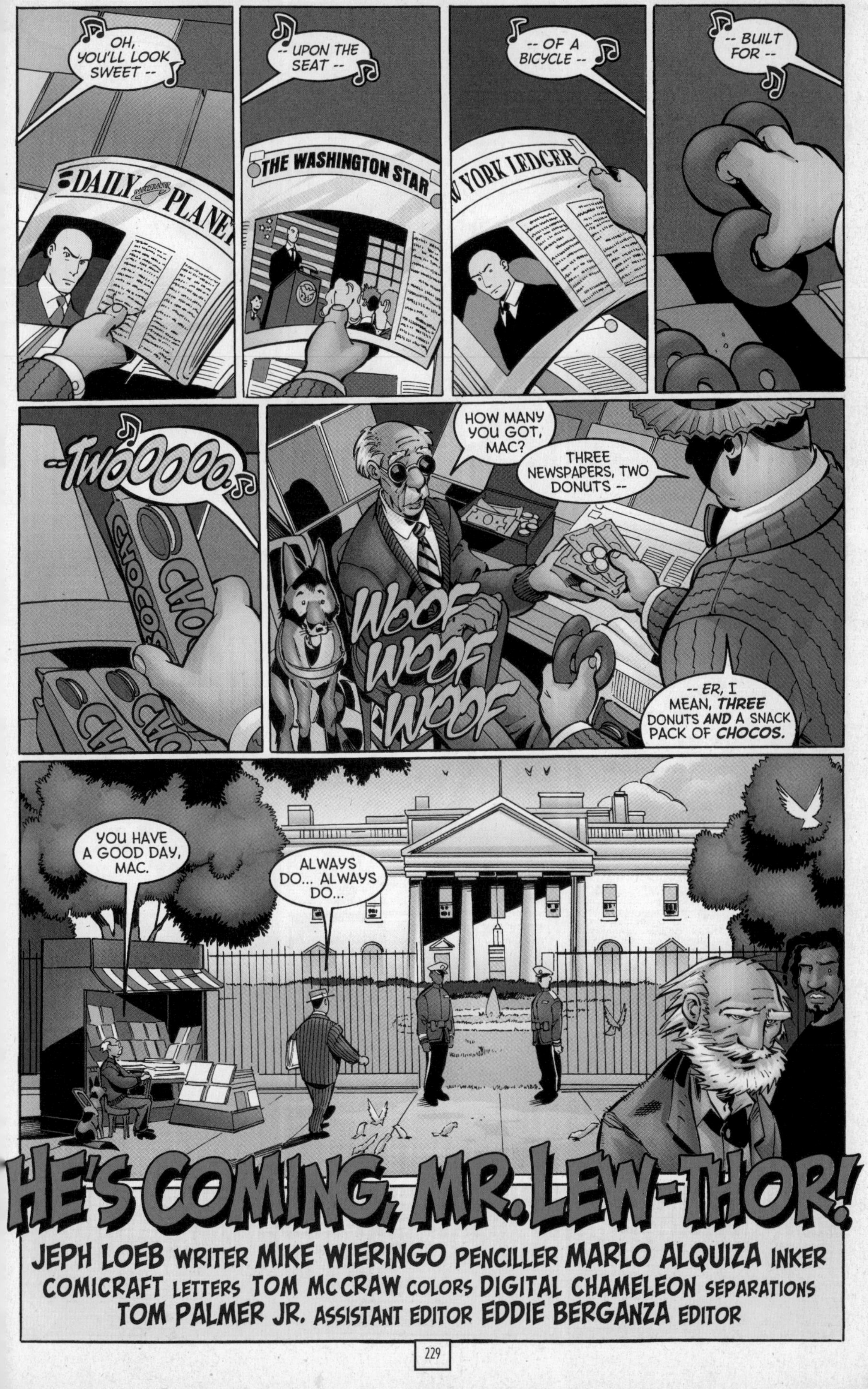
OH, YOU'LL LOOK SWEET --
DAILY PLANET
-- UPON THE SEAT --
THE WASHINGTON STAR
-- OF A BICYCLE --
YORK LEDGER
-- BUILT FOR --
-TWOOOOO-
CHOCOS
HOW MANY YOU GOT, MAC?
THREE NEWSPAPERS, TWO DONUTS --
WOOF WOOF WOOF
-- ER, I MEAN, THREE DONUTS AND A SNACK PACK OF CHOCOS.
YOU HAVE A GOOD DAY, MAC.
ALWAYS DO... ALWAYS DO...
HE'S COMING, MR. LEW-THOR!
JEPH LOEB WRITER MIKE WIERINGO PENCILLER MARLO ALQUIZA INKER
COMICRAFT LETTERS TOM MCCRAW COLORS DIGITAL CHAMELEON SEPARATIONS
TOM PALMER JR. ASSISTANT EDITOR EDDIE BERGANZA EDITOR

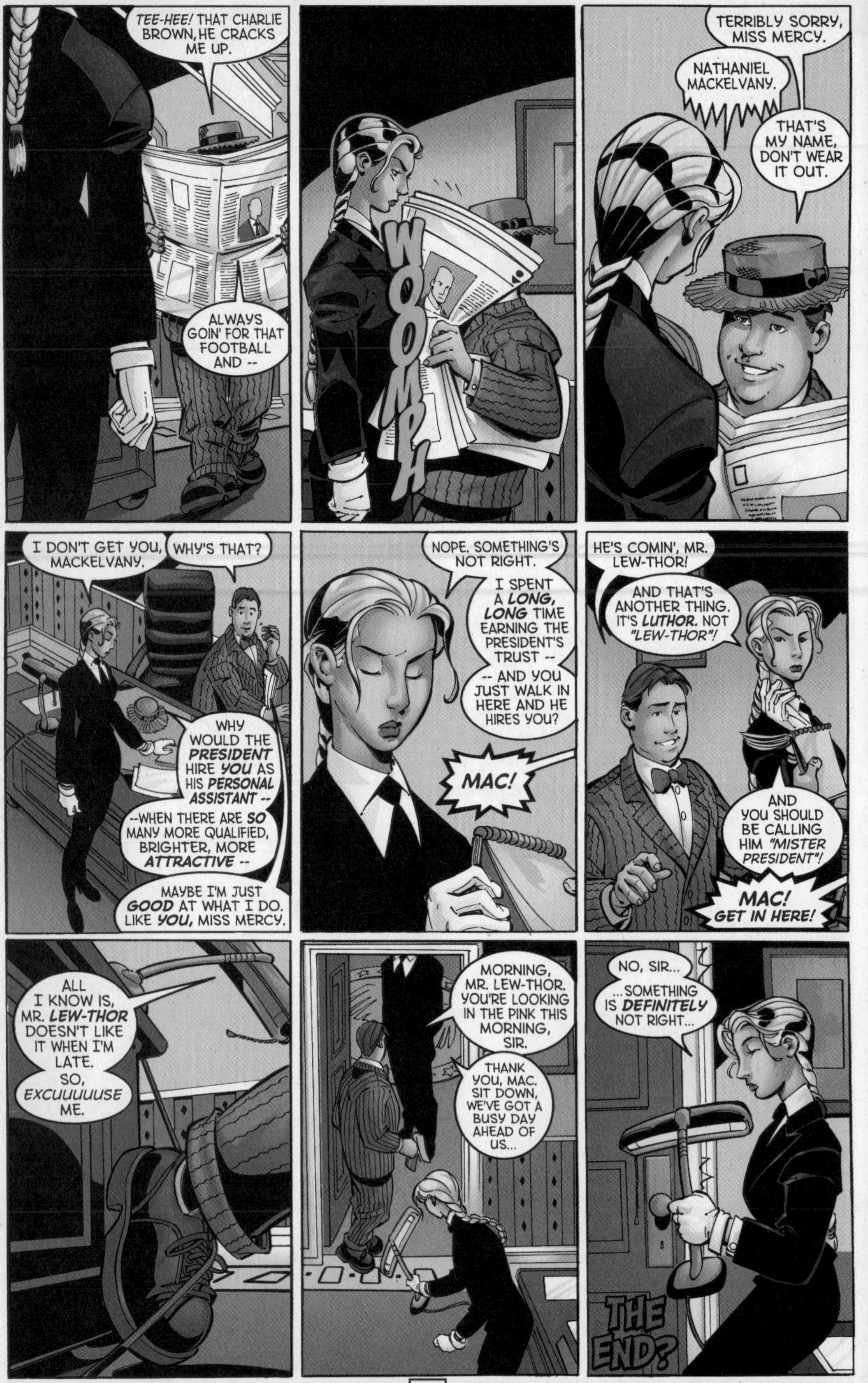

TEE-HEE! THAT CHARLIE BROWN, HE CRACKS ME UP.
ALWAYS GOIN' FOR THAT FOOTBALL AND --
WOOMPH
TERRIBLY SORRY, MISS MERCY.
NATHANIEL MACKELVANY.
THAT'S MY NAME, DON'T WEAR IT OUT.
I DON'T GET YOU, MACKELVANY.
WHY'S THAT?
WHY WOULD THE PRESIDENT HIRE YOU AS HIS PERSONAL ASSISTANT --
--WHEN THERE ARE SO MANY MORE QUALIFIED, BRIGHTER, MORE ATTRACTIVE --
MAYBE I'M JUST GOOD AT WHAT I DO. LIKE YOU, MISS MERCY.
NOPE. SOMETHING'S NOT RIGHT.
I SPENT A LONG, LONG TIME EARNING THE PRESIDENT'S TRUST --
-- AND YOU JUST WALK IN HERE AND HE HIRES YOU?
MAC!
HE'S COMIN', MR. LEW-THOR!
AND THAT'S ANOTHER THING. IT'S LUTHOR. NOT "LEW-THOR"!
AND YOU SHOULD BE CALLING HIM "MISTER PRESIDENT"!
MAC! GET IN HERE!
ALL I KNOW IS, MR. LEW-THOR DOESN'T LIKE IT WHEN I'M LATE.
SO, EXCUUUUUSE ME.
MORNING, MR. LEW-THOR. YOU'RE LOOKING IN THE PINK THIS MORNING, SIR.
THANK YOU, MAC. SIT DOWN, WE'VE GOT A BUSY DAY AHEAD OF US...
NO, SIR...
...SOMETHING IS DEFINITELY NOT RIGHT...
THE END?

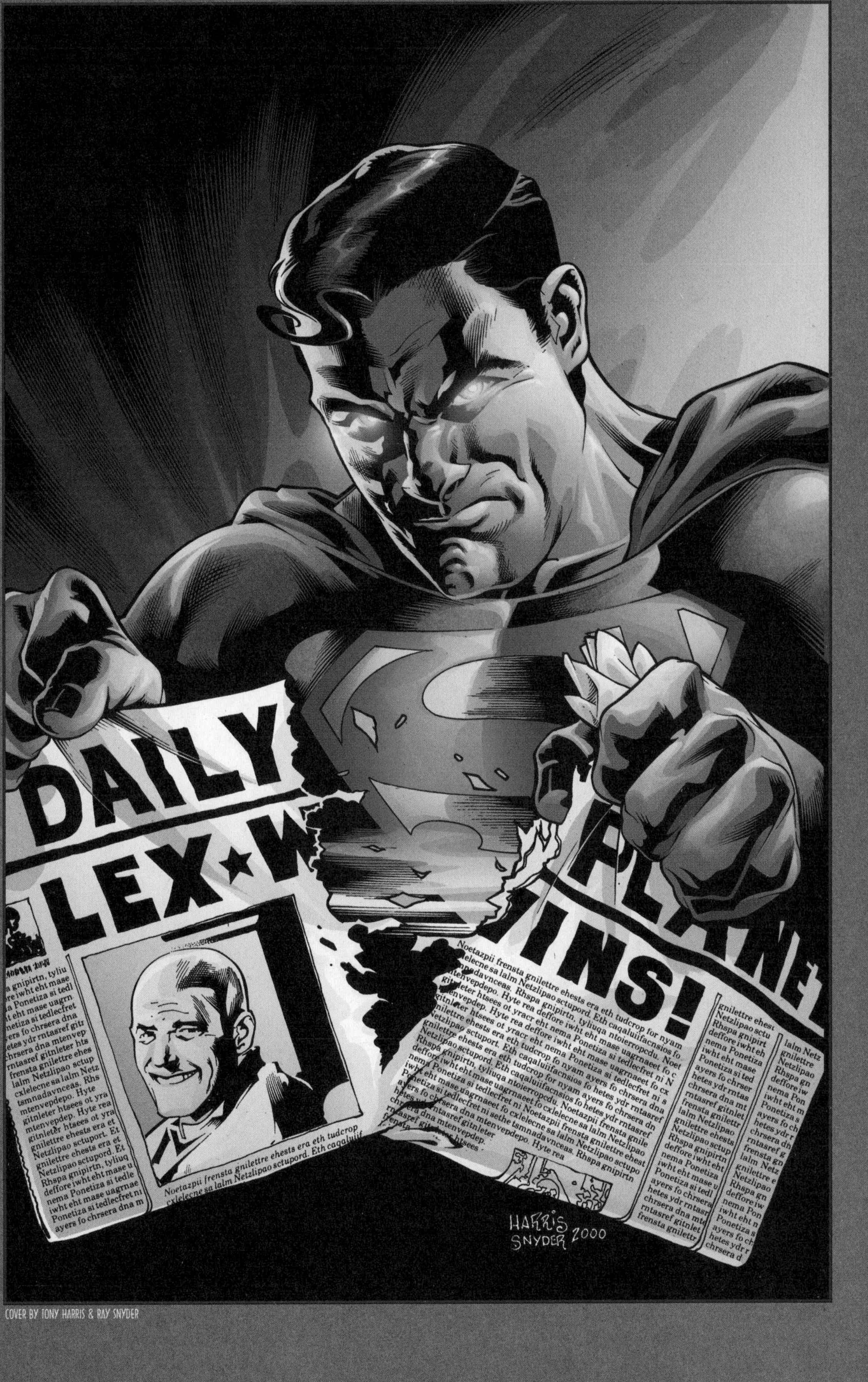
DAILY
LEX★W
INS!
HARRIS
SNYDER 2000

COVER BY TONY HARRIS & RAY SNYDER

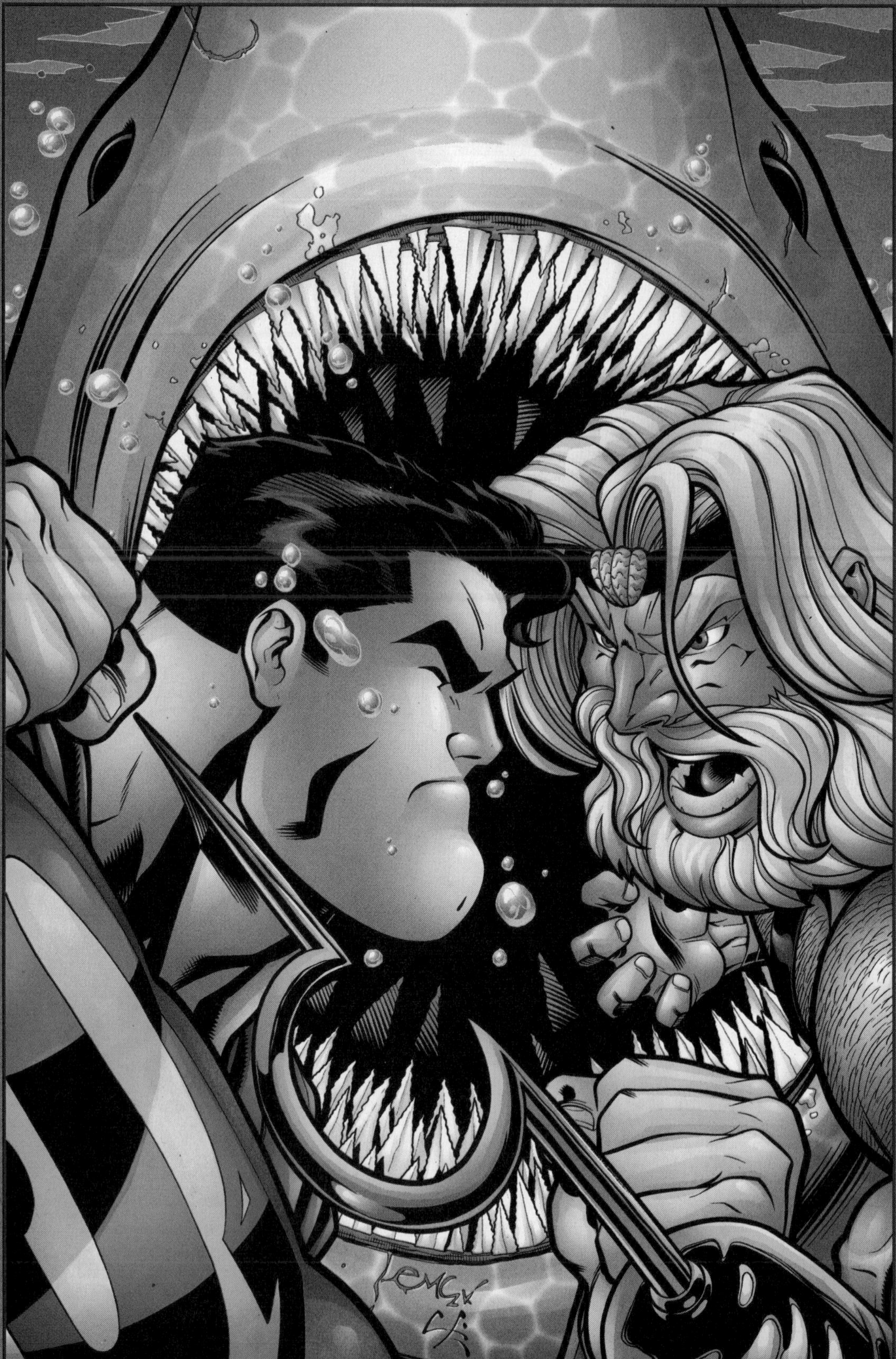

COVER BY ED MCGUINNESS & CAM SMITH
COLOR BY RICHARD & TANYA HORIE

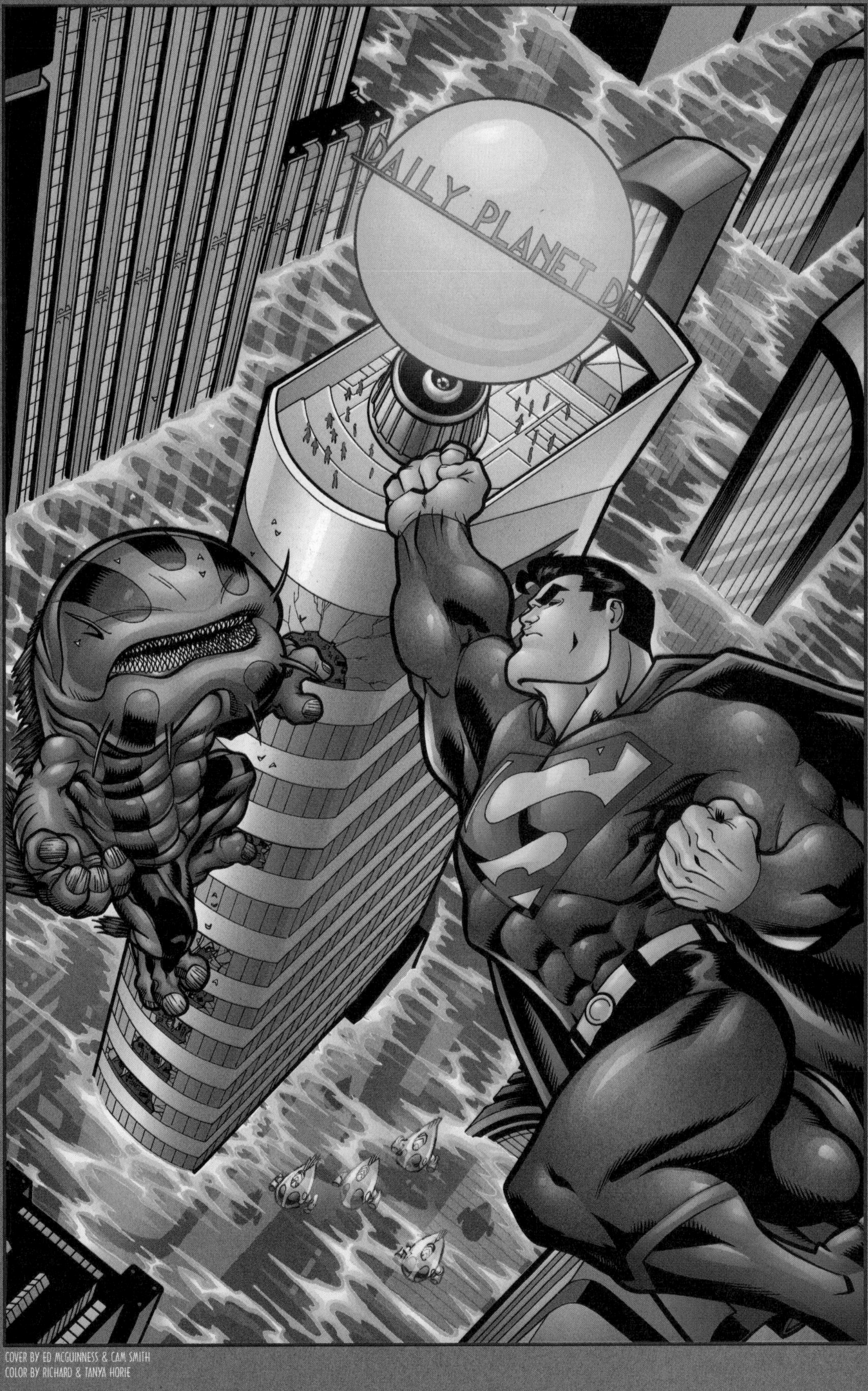
DAILY PLANET DAI

COVER BY ED MCGUINNESS & CAM SMITH
COLOR BY RICHARD & TANYA HORIE

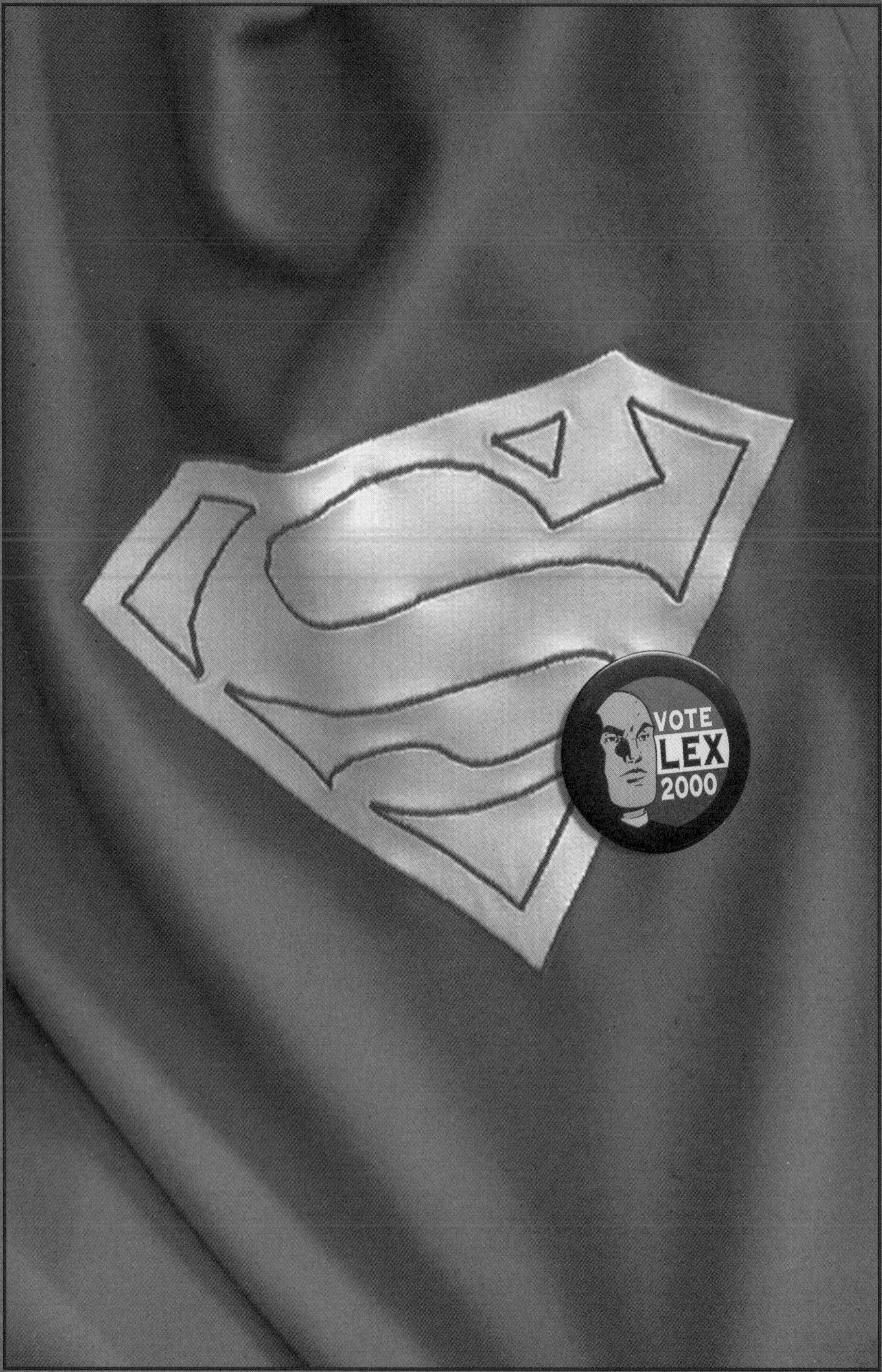
VOTE
LEX
2000

COVER BY ED MCGUINNESS & CAM SMITH
COLOR BY RICHARD & TANYA HORIE

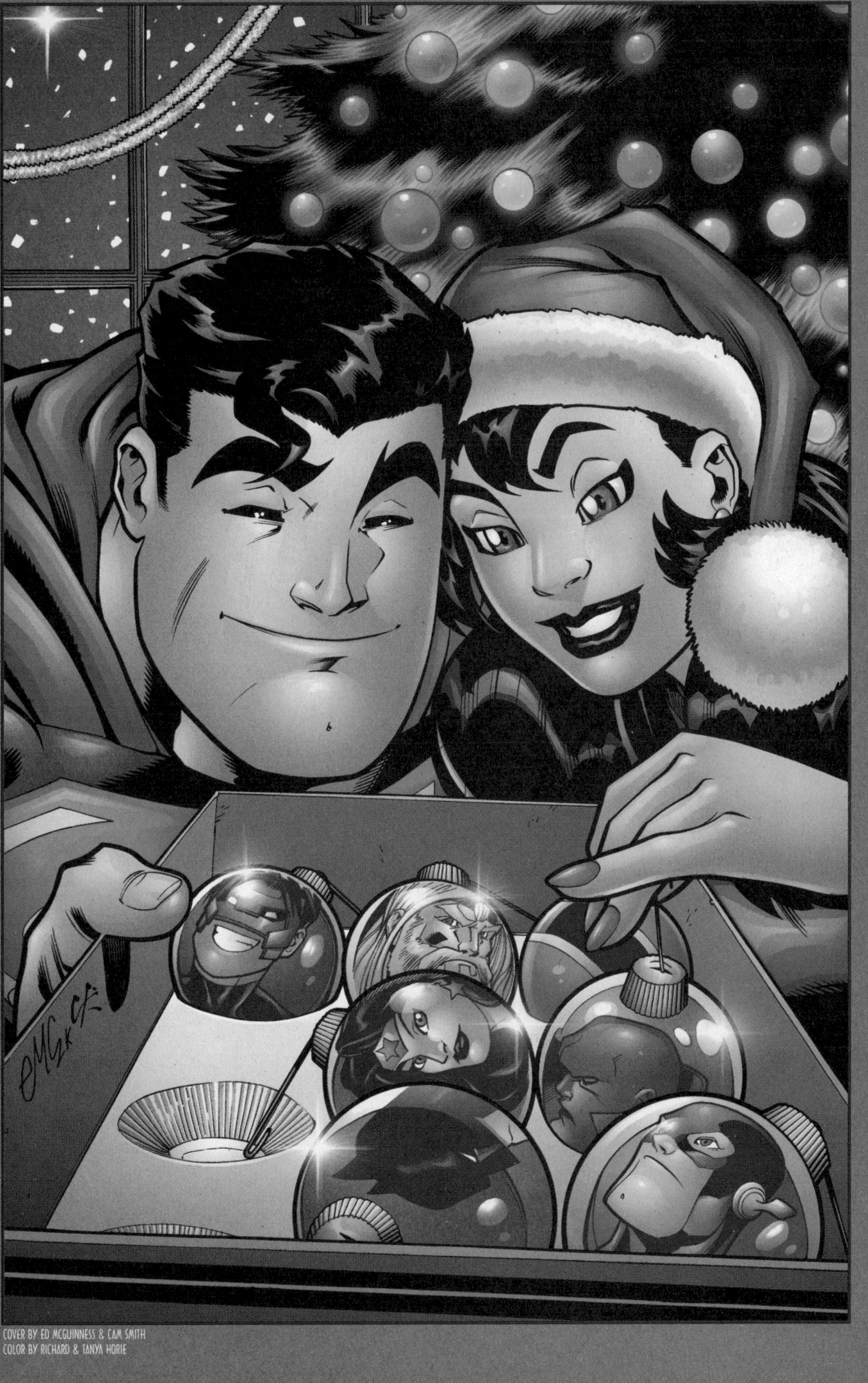

COVER BY ED MCGUINNESS & CAM SMITH
COLOR BY RICHARD & TANYA HORIE

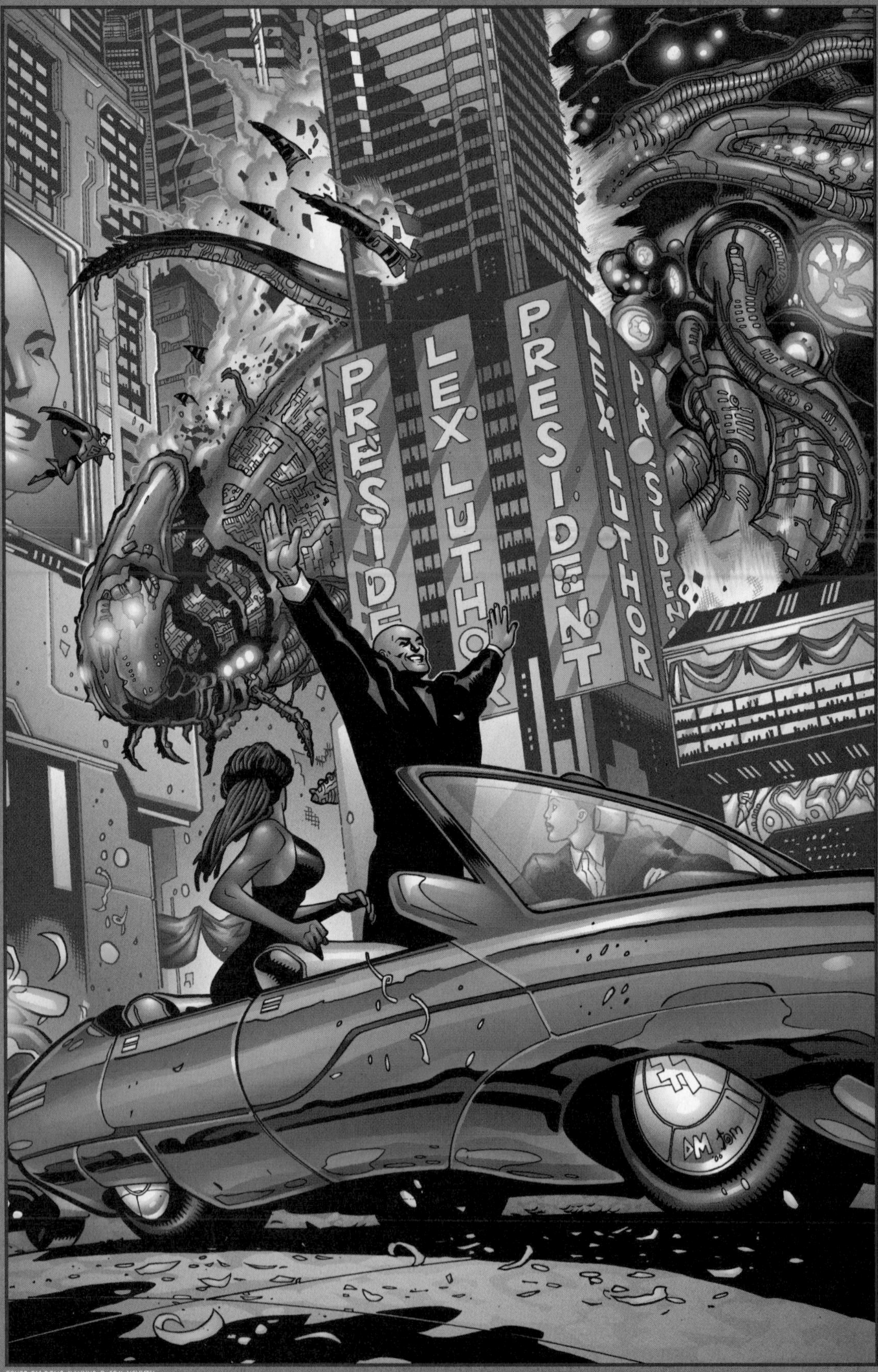
PRESIDENT
LEX LUTHOR

COVER BY DOUG MAHNKE & TOM NGUYEN
COLOR BY RICHARD & TANYA HORIE

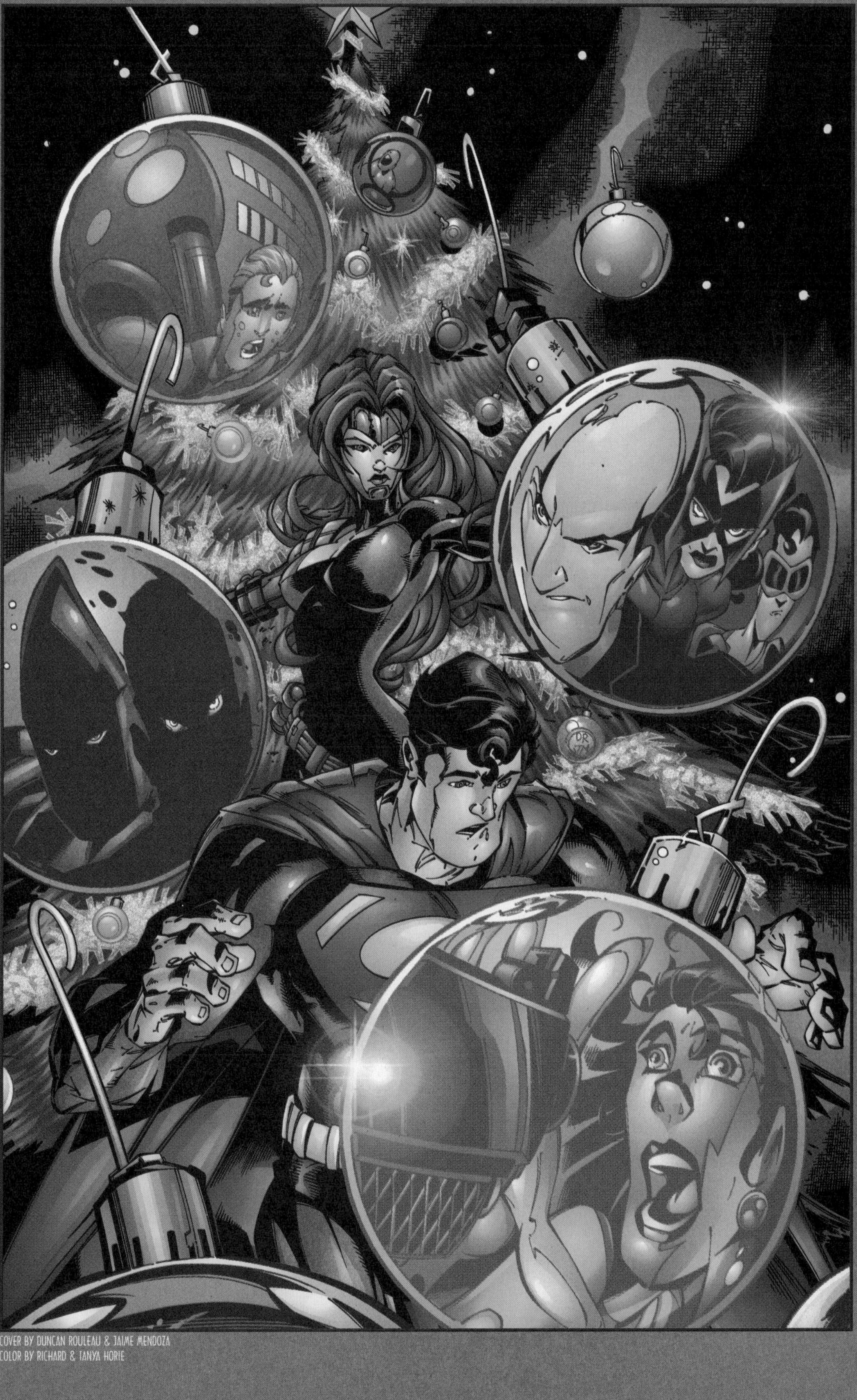

COVER BY DUNCAN ROULEAU & JAIME MENDOZA
COLOR BY RICHARD & TANYA HORIE

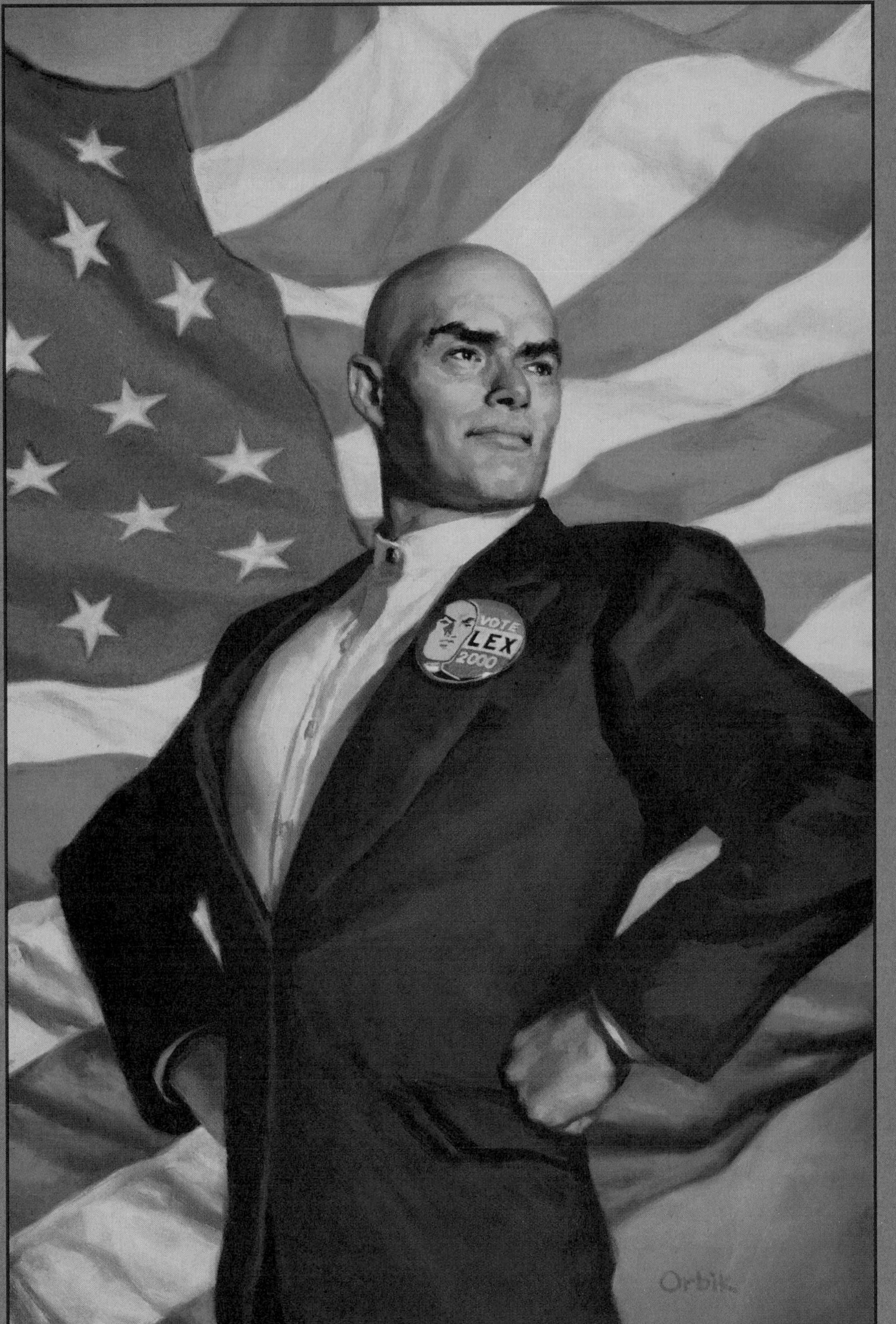
VOTE
LEX
2000
ORBIK

COVER BY GLEN ORBIK

SUPERMAN
THE NEVER-ENDING BATTLE CONTINUES IN
THESE BOOKS FROM DC COMICS: